D1068731

CHOROS

CHOROS

THE ORCHESTRATING SELF

Lamentation and Celebration

LEONARD CHARLES FELDSTEIN

New York
FORDHAM UNIVERSITY PRESS
1984

LC 83–81852
ISBN 0–8232–1075–8

Printed in the United States of America

In Memoriam

JOHN THOMPSON

your unforgettable presence,
dear John,
is woven into all that is my better self
with gratitude that lies too deep for words

What a piece of work is a man!
How noble in reason! how infinite in faculty!
in form, in moving, how express and admirable!
in action how like an angel!
in apprehension how like a god!

Shakespeare, *Hamlet*

The gods have been made rich by man's great loss
Of him who dared defy the dying might alone
With eyes uplifted toward the light of stars
Undimmed by grief-sprung tearful dross,
With majesty of eagle's flight
Across the heavens in a lonely shepherd's sight,
And proudly as the day retreats from night
Did youthful life in him bear ancient cross.
Rejoice, for the inexorable fate
Was never part of those that bloomed
Yet died in nature's vast eternal state,
Nor tide which to a greater depth was doomed.
So wisdom does this wound endure and wait
For that one gift of endless sleep entombed.

—John Thompson

CONTENTS

β

BEING EFFULGENT: THE RHYTHMS OF MAN

II • SEARCHING: THE GROUND OF HUMAN BEING

III • GROWING: THE PATH TO INTEGRITY

PREFACE

In *The Dance of Being: Man's Labyrinthine Rhythms*, I conceptualized the person under the perspective of transcendental naturalism. In that book, I dealt with the human body: its drama, its vicissitudes, its strainings toward consummate personhood. Beyond mere naturalism, that perspective imputed interiority to such natural processes as constitute man. But, insofar as one's focus is man's body, such interiority can be only postulated, and not, in significant measure, articulated. Though body's labyrinthine rhythms are systematically explored there, the psychic correlates of those rhythms are not yet regarded as themselves labyrinthine. In my present book, I recur to the principal motif of *Homo Quaerens: The Seeker and the Sought*: namely, an examination of the person, by a method which itself is to be construed ontologically, under the perspective of transcendental personalism. Whereas *The Dance of Being* stressed man's infrapersonal aspect, now his strictly personal, and indeed interpersonal, being emerges as of exclusive concern. More systematically than in *Homo Quaerens*, and no longer from the standpoint of method as such, I treat the person as process, activity, and ferment. He is a striving, so I propose, to reach beyond his grasp; he is an aiming at completion and perfection—not in a natural, but in a trans-natural sense. More than a mere personalism, an essentially *ego*-centered doctrine of man's trans-natural being, transcendental personalism rests on a *deo*-centered foundation. By ego-personalism, I mean an account of man as, surely, locus of the most subtle feeling and value, yet of man content to accept a non-theologically oriented humanism: a theory of human being in the context of human community alone. But, in *deo*-personalism, I subsume such a theory under a broader doctrine. By this approach, I posit man as locus of a unifiedly personal *and* natural thrust beyond human community toward a cosmos which itself is conceived as ever self-integrating, self-creating, and self-transcending: a cosmos which, like the very person it embraces, is profoundly labyrinthine and endlessly mysterious; a cosmos as centered in a presence which lies beyond its own apparent harmonies and dissonances. In *Choros*, I work out some ontologic implications of this doctrine, though I prescind from a construal of the human process as itself an unfolding—a view which I shall present in *Metamorphosis: The Odyssey of the Self* as a complementary ontogenetic doctrine. Under the rubrics of searching, growing, and speaking, and from the point of view of a double perspective on man as both fragmented and divided, and integrated and unified, I set forth certain pervasive traits, not of human becoming, but of human being itself.

For specific indebtednesses, I refer my reader to my earlier prefaces, especially to that of *Homo Quaerens*. There I gave detailed acknowledgments to those who personally inspired my entire Inquiry. Among my intellectual fathers, I stress the following: Spinoza, Kant, Hegel, Freud, and Jung; and Alfred North Whitehead, John Dewey, and Justus Buchler. Beyond these thinkers, numerous philosophers, poets, writers, scientists, and artists in general have significantly contributed to my theory of the person. I must again express my reliance on the religious traditions of Judaism and Christianity. Above all, I express my gratitude to so many friends, relatives, colleagues, and students, some of whom I mentioned in my earlier prefaces. For their specific responses to this book, I am immeasurably grateful to Patricia and Louis Carini, ever-dear and -loving friends, for their never-failing encouragement and for their wonderfully empathic reading of the manuscript. In addition, as before, I gratefully acknowledge a distinguished Reviewer, who must be kept anonymous, for a similarly empathic reading of the book, and for invaluable suggestions which I have sought to incorporate herein. Finally, I am grateful for the cooperation of the staff of Fordham University Press, and, most particularly, for the superb editorial assistance of Mary Beatrice Schulte; for Alexander Eodice's proofreading of the manuscript; for a Faculty Fellowship awarded me by Fordham University, which enabled me to complete the present volume and to write a large portion of the next; and for skillful typings of the manuscript by Angela Kelly and Shellen Lubin.

Above all, I am indebted to my beloved wife, Rebecca, who, ever calling forth my love, is, for me, the deepest source of vibrancy and renewal. To her I am endlessly grateful: for her encouragement, her inspiration, and her care; for the marvelous sensitivity, empathy, and perceptiveness with which she attended to every page of this book; and for her ever-caring presence, which has enabled me to complete a work, begun in anguish, with joy and peace and hope.[1] An extended opportunity is afforded for expressing the depth of my feelings in my next book, which is lovingly dedicated to her. In these pages, I wish to emphasize, however, my everlasting gratitude to John Thompson. Poet, philosopher, physician, and friend, he inspired me at our every meeting. Without his affirmation, these books could not have been written. By his wonderful clarity, he has given me a glimpse that to be fully alive is to be utterly simple and without dissimulation. And how profoundly, by his works and his life, he has embodied the interweavings, which I here set forth, of lamentation and celebration. In "Beauty, Dusk, and Song," John evokes, as an instance of their interplay, love's joy and love's sorrow. "Beauty with you, alone with me," he speaks,

> And song your voice to make me glad,
> Dusk was the hour your beauty had
> Been nearest kin to heavenly,
> Now you have found another land
> While I with other souls am dragged along
> Who speak of beauty, dusk, and song.
> I hear, but cannot understand.

And now John has left this earth; and as the shadows of my every dusk descend, I stand, mute and astonished, before his memory, so imperishably etched upon me. To the most marvelous man I have ever known, an exemplar of what a person *is* and *ought* to be, I dedicate my book, as a commemoration of John's ceaseless affirmation of human dignity.

Fordham University LEONARD CHARLES FELDSTEIN

NOTE

1. My wife has reminded me of my tendency to use terms like "his" and "man" throughout this work, even though I clearly intend these terms to be gender-free. At the moment, our language offers no substitute for such usage (i.e., as "he" for he or she or as "man" for man and woman) which is not awkward. That this fact is unfortunate, I can hardly deny. In justification for my conventional usage, I take refuge in the fact that I, a man, am writing from my particular, necessarily masculine point of view, am carrying through in this book my own special search. I cannot be so arrogant as to presume that a woman would write the same kind of book, that her perspective on the person would not involve special subtleties—which I might not understand—deriving from her distinctively feminine perspective. When, for example, I refer, in certain chapters, to "the lover" as he and "the beloved" as she, despite my intention to imply the interchangeability of lover and beloved, I am again, and quite restrictedly, presuming a male orientation. At the same time, I trust that, throughout these pages, I *can* empathize with the feminine perspective as, reciprocally, I trust that the woman can empathize with mine. But, in the end, I must frankly acknowledge my ontologic limitations as a male writer and hope that, in the future, a detailed ontology of man *and* woman can be worked out. With respect to this issue, I am in complete sympathy with the feminist point of view.

PROLOGUE

In this volume, I lay the groundwork for human ontology—more specifically, for an ontology of what is quintessentially human: namely, *freedom.* For, from an ontologic point of view, I regard persons as freedom incarnate, freedom in its paradoxes, its ambiguities, and its potentialities. Previously,[1] I initiated my inquiry into the metaphysics of the person under three interwoven perspectives: epistemologic, ontologic, and cosmologic. Though one or another of these perspectives is intended to dominate in each book—the ontologic, in *Choros*—my aim is to show that no exhaustive theory of the person can exclude any perspective. Not only must the relevance of these general philosophic topics be concretely exhibited, together with the specific aesthetic and ethical dimensions which they imply, but the contributions of the special empirical disciplines cannot be ignored. Nor can the equally valid, and perhaps more profound, insights afforded by art, poetry, religion, and the diverse activities by which human beings articulate and symbolize their essential dynamic fail to be integrated with those disciplines—provided the synthesis effected is always under the governance of a generalized philosophic approach.

Both universal and particular factors bear upon a philosophic portrait of the person. To depict his being, one requires not only empathic understanding of his unique, idiosyncratic, and non-repeatable traits but also conceptual understanding in terms of invariant and recurrent traits. To render a person's particularity, a poetic approach is needed. Whether manifesting itself as literature or as history, or, for that matter, as any of the arts, this approach alone is competent to articulate man's inner depths, his nuances and his mysteries, the specific drama of his life. Under the perspective of the particular, the truth of human being reveals itself through the poetic stance. Yet, as truth, what is revealed is, at bottom, cognitive. Hence, insofar as such enterprises as the literary truly illuminate a person's manifold individual qualities, poetry itself is a valid science; it is *scientia intuitiva particularis.* On the other hand, to render a person's universality, a scientific approach is needed. In comprehending each man as an instance of a class, and in formulating the enduring parameters of that class, science acknowledges (*a*) that no such truth can ever fully be formulated, it can only assymptotically be approached; and (*b*) that insofar as the person is, by essence, problematic—i.e., a *datio* rather than a mere datum—he shapes, from his own creative activity, ever-new truths which, once born, must submit to cognitive representation. And insofar as such representations are evaluated by a vision of dramatic interplay between abstract entities, and through appeal to such aesthetic criteria as simplicity, elegance, and symmetry, science *itself* is a grand poem; it is *scientia intuitiva universalis.*

Surely, neither the poetic stance nor the scientific stance should be demeaned. Though poetry can degenerate into an amorphous and slovenly narcissism and science into desiccated caricature and stereotypy, each stance, in its consummate form, affords valid insight into the essential person. Each complements, presupposes, and fulfills the other. In effect, one exhibits, the other asserts. Within its proper sphere, each is competent to judge authentically. And beyond either its scientific or its poetic dimension, no philosophic theory of the person can fail to disclose a pragmatic, active, and moral dimension. Every such theory must allude to some composite of dialectically interwoven *is* and *ought* components. Each is normative, ideal, and deontologic as well as descriptive, actual, and ontologic. Disclosure of this dialectic is centrally germane to philosophic inquiry into the person. For to conduct such inquiry is tantamount to taking up a moral stance toward a person who himself is construed as, by essence, a moral creature. In this book, I assume the obligation to comprehend, in my ontology, the aesthetic, the cognitive, and the ethical perspectives.

To supplement these considerations, I refer my reader to the prefaces and prologues of my first two volumes. Much of what I wrote there, especially in *Homo Quaerens*, which serves as prologue to the entire series,[2] is applicable to the present volume. Some of these themes I restate briefly in the present prologue. However, though the contents of *Choros* may be illuminated through study of my former books, I intend that it be read as autonomous and self-contained.

Prior to sketching the main contours of *Choros*, I recapitulate, though in encapsulated form, the kinds of topics I treat both in my previous books and in the books which will succeed *Choros*. In this way, I characterize both the independence and the interdependence of all books of my "Inquiry Into the Metaphysics of the Person"; and I show how *Choros* locates itself in that Inquiry. To illuminate its principal thrust, somewhat extended remarks on connections between *Choros* and my overall project are needed.

In *Homo Quaerens*, I set forth the method whereby a comprehensive metaphysics of the person can be systematically formulated. There I dealt with the activity, itself a series of personal acts, by which the person can be known—named, so to speak, in his variegated facets and aspects: "named" as he presents himself as an integrated totality; "named" as a comportmental–spiritual complex; "named" in his strictly personal and interpersonal character. In that volume I prepared the way for treating, in subsequent books, first, the ontology of the person and his ontogeny (both subsumed under a larger sense of Ontology)—essentially, his *being* human, in both its originating and its consummatory aspects, and his *becoming* human; then, the cosmology, or harmonizing, of persons, world, and God—a "circumspection," or overview, of the entire problematic of man under a metaphysical perspective. Accordingly, I stressed the epistemologic ingredients of my theory, though not to the exclusion of other factors. Yet, as I endeavored to show, an epistemology of the person tends, when its main tenets are sufficiently traced out, to grow quite naturally into, and indeed to imply as its very ground, a human ontology and, in the last analysis, a general cosmology. And, throughout, run significant strands of value factors, those aesthetic and those ethical.

In *The Dance of Being*, I treated the matrix wherein those threads of natural development arise which converge upon man's infrapersonal aspect, insofar as this aspect contributes to an understanding of the human individual *in* his humanity. I sought to penetrate the person from *within* his being, indicating the ways in which the diverse elements entering into the composition of his body, elements both inanimate and animate, are gathered together as a unity of personal being. My approach was not, at that stage, developmental or evolutionary, save as immanently conditioning inquiry into man's infrapersonal being. For I strove to understand the several proto-personal layers of human being in their contemporaneity: how they impinge upon and interact with one another *at every moment* of a person's existence, in order, from a naturalist standpoint, to ground his non-temporally "emerging" personal being. I proposed that man's ontic, or behavioral, aspects, the manifold parts of his natural existence (i.e., as a creature of nature who is engendered by the natural universe), must, for an understanding of his consummate personhood, be penetrated, in order for the ontologic (or essential) person to be revealed. According to my claim, the person, at each instant of his development, is a virtual passage from a state of dispersal and generality, an assemblage of numberless disparate factors, to a state of dynamic synthesis, transformation, particularity, and, indeed, transcendental unity: a *transcendentalizing* process in which a great dance of being unfolds toward its culmination in man. The inquirer steps, as it were, into a person's very interior. He experiences the abyss of that person's past as it is preserved throughout every present instant of his existence and as it is projected into his own future; he thereby links the ideal of consummate personhood with that matrix of primeval non-being wherein the person is engendered as person: the projection of an infrapersonal trajectory which orchestrates increasingly intricate rhythms. Here, pure being is prefigured at every stage of personal growth. To *know* the person is to *name* the weight upon him of the tribal, the ancestral, and the archaic; to delineate the potent force of these ingredients as every man elevates himself and strives, with all the dignity he is empowered to summon, to subordinate them to his own evolving transcendence.

"Very deep is the well of the past," wrote Thomas Mann. "Should we not call it bottomless?"

> Bottomless indeed, if—and perhaps only if—the past we mean is the past merely of the life of mankind, that riddling essence of which our own normally unsatisfied and quite abnormally wretched existences form a part; whose mystery, of course, includes our own and is the alpha and omega of all our questions, lending burning immediacy to all we say, and significance to all our striving. For the deeper we sound, the further down into the lower world of the past we probe and press, the more do we find that the earliest foundations

> of humanity, its history and culture, reveal themselves unfathomable. No matter to what hazardous lengths we let out our line they still withdraw again, and further, into the depths.[3]

Yet this past inscribes itself on every part of a person's contemporary being, and manifests itself in his every act. By one's labyrinthine rhythms, I mean the deeper tracings which the past deposits upon one, tracings whereby one shapes both the composition and the very symbols by which one presents oneself—to oneself and to another. In *The Dance of Being*, I wrote of how this "alpha and omega" work their ways into the inmost recesses of human being; I showed the vicissitudes and the metamorphoses which they undergo as they press toward their own culmination; and I treated the converging of the numberless strands which derive from those "unfathomable . . . depths" to shape a unique and non-duplicatable product, a singular human being. Not until my description in *Metamorphosis*, my next book, of the actual historical unfoldings from a dim inanimate beginning which consummate themselves as an integral and self-creating self do I "temporalize" the intrinsically spatial concordances, intertwinings, dissonances, and synergisms of "that riddling essence." For under the perspective of naturalism, a person's labyrinthine infrapersonal rhythms are, in effect, the compressed matrix of numberless interactant contemporaneous levels.

Now, prior to setting forth the topics of *Metamorphosis*, I prepare the way for the great ontologic adventure wherein man seeks to penetrate his own humanity qua humanity, as it has risen, phoenix-like, from the still-burning ashes of living matter to form an utterly novel compound: a plurality which is singular, a unity which diversifies itself. Yet, even as diverse, a person does not merely reduce himself to his naturalistically constituent elements. On the contrary, these elements have now been transfigured. First revealed through the method set forth in *Homo Quaerens*, he emerges as one who, pre-eminently, searches and grows and speaks; as one who, within these acts, discloses to himself the ontologic foundations of his transcendentally personal being. All this has already been prefigured in *The Dance of Being* and in *Homo Quaerens*. For, in *The Dance of Being*, I extracted such tenets of Method as, when fully articulated in *Homo Quaerens*, are relevant only to a restricted, because strictly naturalist, perspective on human ontology. Yet I also traced the way in which the transition from the infrapersonal to the specifically personal ought, by my criteria, to be carried through: namely, the way of human speech and human comportment.

In *Choros*, I develop a theory of the relationship between speech, with its underlying reflective activity, and comportment, with its underlying energetic activity, a theory which will allow me to articulate the processes of an evolving self-consciousness. Here I do not yet construe self-consciousness from a developmental point of view—as I shall in *Metamorphosis*, when I treat the historically unfolding phases of human life. Nor do I construe self-consciousness from the point of view of the vast diversity of shapes which it is capable of assuming and the extraordinary wealth of symbols which it is empowered to fashion, as I do in

Apotheosis. Rather, I treat self-consciousness as an activity, a process, and an unfolding. As such, it is a journey into the labyrinth of the Unconscious—but always in the context of the person conceived as an integrated and integral unity. Thus understood, self-consciousness is perforce ineluctably cognizant of unconscious depths: the grotesque formations of the Unconscious; its hidden yearnings and secretmost desires; its intricate concealments amid its immanently intentional thrust to eradicate self-deception; its arcane mediation of transformations from body to mind and from mind to body; and its creative activity as the source of symbols which represent reality in ways which either deform the experience of reality or shape modes of experience which veridically conform to reality.

My task is to trace, systematically and coherently, the stages in the unfolding of human self-consciousness in a manner consistent with the empirical disciplines which treat the conditions grounding a person's essential unity; and to probe the unconscious ground of self-consciousness as a person penetrates, one by one, the layers which both compose and give rise to self-consciousness. I aim at conceptualizing the variegated forms which self-consciousness assumes; I propose the ways in which it grows from incoherence to coherence; and I specify the symbolisms through which it declares its vicissitudes, its metamorphoses, and its adventures. Always I reflect upon *who* man is: one who, by his essential powers, is an integral and unitary action. I conceive this essence in a threefold way: as an actualization of potency according to determinable laws; as a self-transforming agent who, progressively, and in determinate phases, opens himself to receive into his existence, as intimately his own, diversified objects for his interest and care; and as a being who comports himself toward another, drawing from within his own depths, *as* he presents himself, specific exteriorized modes of expression, themselves to be absorbed into the other's existence.

From these considerations, it follows that man is an activity not merely of self-consciousness but, indeed, of self-possession. More strictly, he is a process whereby he progressively comes *to own himself*: to own himself with inventiveness and reverence. He thus possesses himself first in relationship to himself alone, then to himself as embedded in human society, and, finally, to himself as enveloped by, yet participating in, a *deo*-centered cosmos. Moreover, he has, and is thus constituted by, an ever-heightening awareness of this activity—as both a witnessed activity, guided and overseen by progressively more inclusive personal presences, and an activity whereby he reveals himself, at bottom, to be constituted by free and spontaneous creative acts. Yet, as ambiguously free, and even indeed insofar as they embody freedom, persons are loci of inherent paradoxes with respect to their status as freedom incarnate. Ever guided by an ideal of freedom, but ever skeptical that he may attain that ideal, man unremittingly seeks to overcome these paradoxes. Here, I propose the stages by which this quest unfolds. And throughout the ontologic story of human existence, tragedy, crisis, and anguish inexorably prevail. Still, one can always discover those perfect moments of ecstatic eternity where, for a brief instant, man speaks in tranquil rhythms of timeless wisdom. In my account I take cognizance of these seemingly incongruous alternatives.

In these pages I thematize the person with respect to certain ontologic factors: namely, the structural and the dynamic. With varying ornamentation, these factors repeat themselves throughout the phases of the emerging self, as it journeys toward consummate personhood. My themes constitute a kind of human architectonic. For I treat the architecture of personal being: an architecture of stresses and strains, of virtual movement, of shifting tonalities and textures, of frozen music which liquefies into ever-novel orchestrations. Within this ferment, the χορός of which is that locus, or dancing place, wherein human being discloses and unfolds its humanness, elements crystallize, combine, and recombine. Dissolving into their originating matrix, they reappear in metamorphosed shape. With varying degrees and modalities, this *orchestrating self* effects its own contrapuntal arrangements. As its polyphony unfolds, inscribing on itself ever-new fugal sweeps and transformations, human moods fluctuate from joy to sorrow, from tranquillity and quiescence to exuberance and fervor: a counterpoint of *lamentation and celebration.* What is lamented is the perishing of seemingly perfect moments of intensely contrasting experience amid the cacophonies of human encounter: the sheer weight of arbitrary, chaotic, dumb, and brute contingency —contingency which in a single sweep can obliterate the most glorious harmonies. Still, amid humanity's profound lamentation, a condition is created whereby the authentic celebration of the glory of man and nature can achieve new heights of ecstatic commemoration.

To be initiated into the sacraments of man's wisdom, one requires that this interplay, often grotesque and unreasoned, be acknowledged and accepted, that its mysteries be penetrated with ever-new perspicacity. Thereby, humankind's great harmonies, strands of perfection which weave through its cumulative experience, will not be submerged, but will declare themselves endlessly anew as imbued with nuances of ever-increasing subtlety; and, again and again, will emerge in shapes of marvelous novelty: rhythms wrought by persons as they struggle to overcome their finitude, as they strive toward their apotheosis as selves in the process of self-transfigurement. The glory of God will reign forever and ever, so it has been declared, and His creatures will be embraced in His eternal tenderness.

In *Choros*, I view the person as ὄντος, an ὄντο-λόγος: the articulatable structures of his being qua person. I treat the very ground of his being: "being" construed as both a process of unfolding and a mode of existence. I deal with such invariant factors as persist, with all manner of fluctuant ornamentation inscribed upon them, through every vicissitude and transformation of *human* being. For here man is conceived *spatially.* Yet a mere spatial approach cannot suffice. He must also be conceptualized ontogenetically—hence, temporally. In *Metamorphosis*, I shall conceive ontology in this fashion. Surely, Parmenides requires his Heraclitus. In addition to exhibiting ontologic constancies, the person is also a ferment, a maturation, and a constellation of processes which never ceases to change, a succession of transfigurations.

Truly, spatial ontology and temporal (or durational) ontology—more properly, ontogeny—are complementary and even interpenetrating perspectives. Dialectically interwoven, they presuppose and require one another. A young person is both young and a *person*; an old person is both old and a *person.* As persons, they are alike; as young or old, they are unmistakably different. Yet certain values indefeasibly apply to both. Each is an end in himself; each accordingly merits reverence. Any concept of man which assigns these timeless values to one kind of person rather than to another, be he old or young, infant or senile, sick or well, vibrant or moribund, mentally deranged or mentally wholesome (presuming these notions make sense) is an abomination; it affronts humanity. Whether suffering or enjoying, whether creating or resting, whether robust or feeble, all humankind surges from out of the abyss of time toward a destiny which is remote and unknown, yet haunting and shared.

Under one perspective, onto*genesis* may be regarded as the unfolding phases of onto*logy*, hence, subordinate to ontology. Under an equally valid perspective, ontology cannot be understood save as refracted through the prism of its own genesis. For only by experiencing a person from the beginning to the end of his life, from the instant of conception to the instant of death, and under a multitude of contexts of personal existence—contexts in which his life's manifold nuances can alone be revealed—can the diverse facets of his being be disclosed and integrated. In this sense, ontology is subordinate to ontogenesis. And ontogenesis stretches back to the unfathomable beginnings of existence itself. Hence, in *Metamorphosis*, I shall treat the progressive transformations by which the human incarnation of freedom, together with its every vicissitude, becomes luminous. In both *Choros* and *Metamorphosis*, I aim to exhibit the seemingly paradoxical *inter*dependence of person qua "spatialized" and person qua "temporalized"—as freedom's ambiguities and paradoxes give way to freedom's vicissitudes and, in the end, to freedom's veridical culmination.

Inexorably, human beings bear the cross of tragedy. In his *humility* man acknowledges that, after all, he is only human. His freedom is limited and constricted. Yet it effloresces into marvelous forms and symbols, expresses itself in comprehensive, integrated acts of searching, and assumes shapes which man could not even dimly have anticipated. Heaven and earth conspire to promote Caliban's metamorphosis into Ariel. For in his *pride* man stretches his limbs to the outermost reaches of the cosmos. Like Hercules, he stands astride its buttresses, and he comprehends the cosmos as truly the crucible wherein he is fashioned. In *Apotheosis*, this adventure, anticipated in these pages, will be set forth: as culmination of an ontologic perspective, exhibiting man's numberless potentialities and tracing both stages and contours of his symbolic expressions; as both prolegomenon to and issuing from a cosmologic perspective, in which both epistemologic and ontologic elements are subordinated to the cosmologic. Then the cosmos itself will be exhibited as created by, as well as mirrored in, the vast multitude of perspectives which human being not only shapes but, in fact, joins to an ever-enlarging cosmos: a cosmos which, through man's adventurings, reveals its labyrinthine depths, hence, constitutes itself, from the point of view of the world-become-symbol, a person-engendered cosmos. Thus, I treat the person from the standpoint of his metamorphoses and his transfiguration, his symbolisms and his searching, his crises and his transcendence. From an ontologic point of view, these topics are prefigured, and to some extent systematically explicated, in *Choros.* But, in *Cosmos*, I shall bring my Inquiry to its penultimate moment by gathering together such strands of thought, which have previously emerged, as bear upon the theme of person as paradigm for cosmology. First enunciated in that volume, this microscopic perspective on man constitutes a bridge to general cosmology as transcendental ground of humanity: cosmology from the point of view of a cosmos regarded as crucible of man, a womb wherein his specifically human powers gestate, a matrix wherein he consummates those powers. Setting forth a cosmology which purports both to ascertain the source of and to impart ultimate meaning to human freedom, I examine the relationship (as, likewise, I shall do in *Apotheosis*) of *person in cosmos.* But cosmology is, equally, a bridge to symbology. For symbol creation is mediated by an already existent cosmos as well as person. From this standpoint, the cosmos articulates itself through the medium of personhood as manifold symbolic forms.

In *Apotheosis*, I shall stress the relationship of *person in cosmos* from the standpoint of the person. The equation is *person* in cosmos. For I frame cosmology under the perspective of questing man: his modes of orienting himself toward the world; the kinds of information it yields him, and, by so in-forming, transforms him; the specific limitations which inhere in a specifically human perspective. In *Cosmos*, I stress that relationship from the standpoint of the cosmos. The equation is person in *cosmos.* Now, I frame a systematic theory of man's power, by singular acts of perspicacity and imagination, to transcend his limits, and so to de-individualize himself as to allow himself to apprehend his specifically human qualities as deriving from his participation in more inclusive realms. Then alone, so I propose, can man lay bare the general contours of a universe which is now conceived as cosmos. Only then can he set forth the world as an orchestrated totality rather than as a mere naturalistically construed assemblage. For from integrated cosmos, not from diffuse universe, man derives his powers for transcendence and his creative resources to symbolize transcendence. Only in this context can one fully understand the role of those non-human individuals by which, in oscillations of ecologic balance and imbalance, man is ineluctably surrounded and pervaded.

Accordingly, in both *Apotheosis* and *Cosmos*, I shall articulate cosmology under the dual perspectives, themselves dialectically related, of person (hence, cosmology humanly ontologized) and cosmos (hence, cosmology proper). In both instances, indeed pervading my entire Inquiry, a specifically theologic commitment shapes itself. For my quest is to understand—to understand the status of human integrity in relationship to cosmic integrity from the point of view of the centeredness of the cosmos rather than from the point of view of any particular individual in the cosmos.

To repeat an earlier statement: epistemology, ontology, and cosmology are complementary and mutually presupposing perspectives; each affords a characteristic approach to philosophic personology. Within the context of this approach, *The Dance of Being* and *Cosmos* represent, respectively, the naturalistic ground of humanity and the transcendental ground of humanity; *Choros*, *Metamorphosis*, and *Apotheosis* constitute an ontologic perspective—always suffused, though in differing proportions, by epistemologic and cosmologic ingredients. As, in effect, prologue to my Inquiry, *Homo Quaerens* was treated from a methodologic point of view in process of transforming itself into a substantive, ontologic approach. In *The Person*, my concluding volume, I shall gather the themes which appear throughout the preceding volumes, and deduce a theory of the person from the cosmology presented in *Cosmos*, a cosmology which itself will have been adduced on the basis of such antecedent studies as pertain more strictly to a personology. In *The Person*, I shall condense themes which I deem germane to a theory of man, especially from the point of view of value. There, such aesthetic and ethical components as are merely implicit in my threefold metaphysical perspective will be explicitly woven together. Earlier, method, suffused by these components, passes into ontology. By stages, a cosmology was built. Now cosmology passes into ontology. By stages, the latter will be rebuilt.

To schematize the connections between my overall Inquiry and *Choros*, I append a brief prospectus. I suggest concordances between the structure of the Inquiry as a whole and the structure of *Choros*. In the first schema, I use the subtitles of my books to indicate modes of interwovenness. In the second, I exhibit specific correspondences between the books of the series and the principal parts of *Choros*. The two representations are intended to illuminate one another. In the third schema, I briefly suggest an alternative classification, by way of stressing equally important links between the different volumes of the Inquiry.

A

Epistemology ⟷ Ontology ⟷ Ontogeny ⟷ Symbology ⟷ Cosmology
↕ ↕
Method Value

Throughout, epistemologic, ontologic, and cosmologic strands interweave with both (aesthetic and ethical) value components, especially those which will appear in *The Person*, and method components, especially those which have appeared in *Homo Quaerens.*

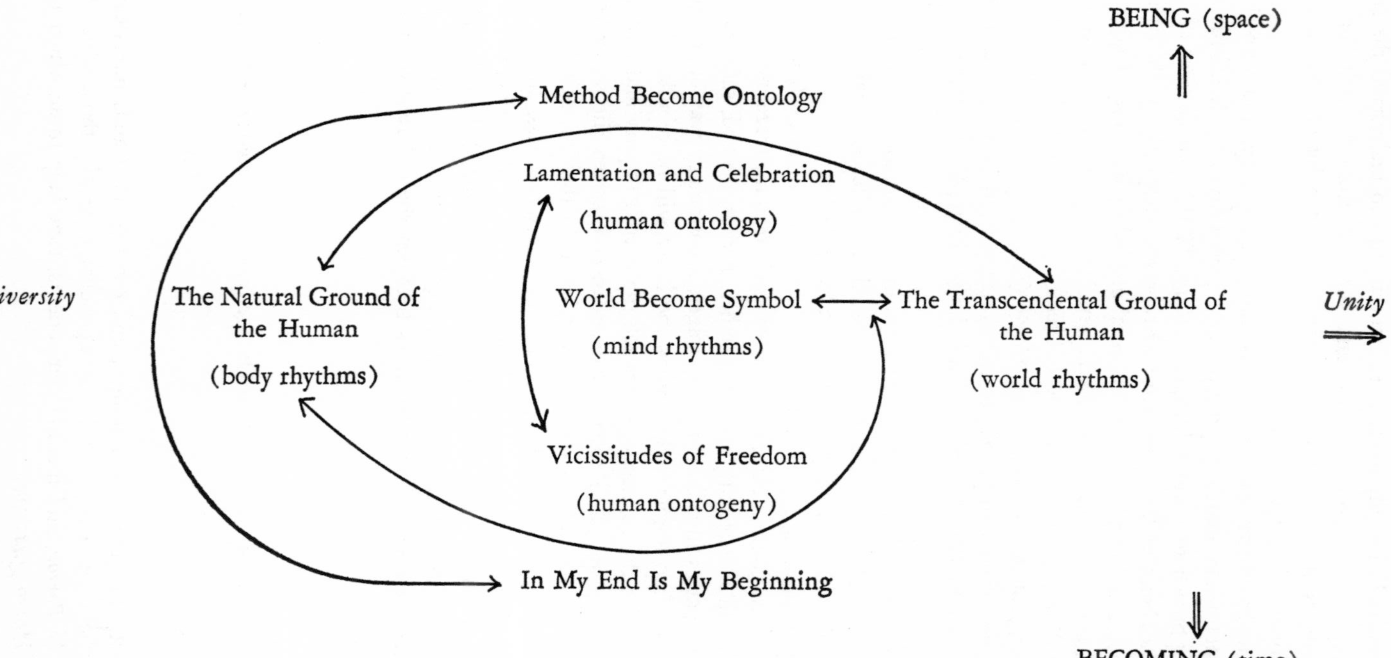
Method
BEING (space)
Method Become Ontology
Lamentation and Celebration
(human ontology)
Diversity
The Natural Ground of the Human
(body rhythms)
World Become Symbol
(mind rhythms)
The Transcendental Ground of the Human
(world rhythms)
Unity
Vicissitudes of Freedom
(human ontogeny)
In My End Is My Beginning
BECOMING (time)
Value

B

Correspondence between the general plan of "An Inquiry Into the Metaphysics of the Person" and the contents of CHOROS

"An Inquiry Into the Metaphysics of the Person"	*Choros*
Prologue *Homo Quaerens: The Seeker and the Sought*	Prologue (general approach)
I • The Universe-Engendered Person *The Dance of Being: Man's Labyrinthine Rhythms*	α Psyche and Person: The Wholeness of I • A Self Divided (the person in his divisible and pulverulent nature; the mere universe)
II • Person and World *Choros: The Orchestrating Self* *Metamorphosis: The Odyssey of the Self* *Apotheosis: The Divinizing Self*	*β* Being Effulgent: The Rhythms of Man II • Searching: The Ground of Human Being (justice, truth, trust, the past) III • Growing: The Path to Integrity (integrity, goodness, hope, the future) IV • Speaking: The Path to Wisdom (wisdom, beauty, love, the present)
III • The Person-Engendered Cosmos *Cosmos: The Crucible of Man*	γ Being Transfigured: The Oneness of Man V • A Self United (person as integrated microcosm)
Epilogue *The Person: A Cosmic Perspective*	Epilogue (the person as value)

These diagrams, especially schemata A and B, bring the general contours of *Choros* more sharply into focus. As in *Homo Quaerens*, I treat, in this Prologue, my general approach, a method which reveals its substantive moments and consequences as I herein elaborate a human ontology. In Parts I and V—namely, "A Self Divided" and "A Self United," respectively—I treat the person in his manifold divisions. By appeal to empirical disciplines, which systematically and cognitively deal with him, I work out man's variegated dimensions in a context, as yet only implicitly stated, which immanently conditions the interwovenness of his seeming divisions. In my Epilogue, I anticipate themes, worked out at length in *The Person*, bearing upon the issue of value.

In this volume I shall set forth, under the primary ontologic categories of *integrality*, *power*, and *encounter*, a concept of human essentiality. Thereby I strive to cut beneath the special standpoints implied by a divisional account of man, an account which I elaborate in "A Self Divided." Though indebted to natural science for detail of formulation, and requiring such scientific principles as order detail—since philosophy must comprehend those principles, though it seeks to go beyond them—my theory conceptualizes the person as a concrete entity: one who variously manifests his being as biologic, social, physiognomic, psychic, conscious, self-conscious, unconscious. I treat each of these divisions from the point of view of an evolving ontologic scheme. In "A Self United," I gather together hitherto disparate strands. In a sense, science extracts such strands from the whole person. It presents only aspects of his actual existence. Yet to inquire truthfully, the scientist must hold dialogue with the whole person. In his specialized ways, he must respond to a total experience. Surely, if he is a profound scientist, his response is both emphatic and authentic. But since precision and consistency often take precedence over scope and adequacy, he perforce symbolizes, as a kind of by-product of his dialogue, but a limited and circumscribed region of *natural* man's behavior. By this necessary approach, he is not competent to symbolize *transcendental* man. Hence, giving an ordered account of aspects, the scientist formulates laws relevant for subsuming these aspects; he exhibits links between those laws; he specifies criteria for validating them; he gathers and classifies empirical evidence for their support. Properly deciphered, the scientist's conclusions constitute a veridical portrait of man. But he views this portrait as through quite special lenses. With uncanny accuracy, though in either overemphasized or underemphasized fashion, each lens discloses but a single feature of the portrait.

By contrast, philosophy, the dialogue of which is no more authentic than that of science or art, seeks ultimate notions, notions which aim toward representations which are both concrete and comprehensive—though, as man of wisdom, the philosopher knows that he cannot ultimately succeed. From his point of view, abstraction, in the end, is a fake. To be authentically philosophic, he must appeal to a larger experience, experience more deeply plumbed than that to which the scientist turns. Ever diminishing his reliance on criteria appropriate to scientific precision and adequacy, the philosopher will accept vagueness, a certain obscurity, openness to mystery. Yet, clearly, philosophic conceptualization requires a suitable frame of reference. And such a perspective is intrinsically alterable. Within it, philosophic notions are interdependent. Fully to elaborate each notion, one must fully elaborate all notions. Unlike the coherence of scientific ideas, philosophic coherence is always referable to some unique philosophic vision. In their very solidarity, philosophic notions express an individual perspective on an *entire* entity. As assembled, they have much in common with a work of art. In their traceable implications, they delineate, in compressed and symbolic form—like a poem—an entity's myriad nuances. Yet, though indefeasibly a personal vision, philosophy (like science *and* art) constitutes, when its details are worked out, a perspective responsible to a shared experience. Comprehending systematically and coherently, and in a manner consistent with communally sanctioned norms, philosophy overarches the more specialized scientific principles. Whereas, by these principles, science explains aspects of behavior, philosophy gathers the principles themselves into an inclusive, unitary, and integral system. Larger in scope, the philosopher's task is less focused than the scientist's. In a scientific sense, it is more diffuse. Far more than a scientist, a philosopher relies on analogy, figurative language, poetic insight, and the finer shadings of idiosyncratic experience. Less dependent on public experience, though always eventually accountable to it, the philosopher, appealing to the greater depth and diversity of private experience, often aims at persuading by exhortation and allusion rather than by description. Reliable as a personal expression, a philosophic theory is accordingly less valid as an inferential structure.

Nonetheless, the philosopher does aim at a special kind of precision. He characterizes subtle nuances and concrete details of experience inaccessible to or not called forth by the scientist who, to achieve his end, must prescind from experience. In the final analysis, a philosophy is sanctioned by its power to evoke questions which stir discontent with established stereotypes, both of experience and of modes of conceiving experience. It seeks to provoke crises with respect both to current styles of understanding and to hitherto concealed or repressed facets of experience. It strives to inspire revaluation of characteristic, recurrent, and overly worn preconceptions. For philosophy explicates and raises to awareness unexamined presuppositions, be they methodologic or substantive, of established and customary kinds of inquiry and bodies of knowledge. Quite literally, it seeks "consensual validation," validation with *all* the senses working together to disclose nature's hidden secrets. In this way, it leads beyond nature—hence, beyond a naturalistic way of construing nature—toward something transcendental.

In this sense, I reiterate the main theme of *Homo Quaerens*: philosophic inquiry and searching, in its consummate form, are one and the same; human searching and, in *its* consummate form, human being are one and the same. Beyond that, searching entails crisis; and crisis, repeatedly provoked and repeatedly resolved, allows self-consciousness to elevate itself to ever-higher forms. Raising questions about entities *in concreto* and not *in abstracto*, indeed constituting itself the critique of abstraction, philosophy when it pertains to persons concerns the most concrete entity of all. As the concrete enterprise *par excellence* of searching, philosophy expresses the primordial activity of human being itself.

When human beings search into human *being*, they reveal ever-new facets of human existence. Having provoked crisis, persons grow through crisis. Having established secure foundations for their searching—the facts of the case, as it were—persons reveal their essential character to consist in a quest for richer, larger, and more profound modes of integrating themselves both with themselves (i.e., self-integration) and with others. Accordingly, complementary to the primordial ontologic category of searching is the equally primordial ontologic category of growing through one schema of integrity toward another, each more satisfying as concretizing a double journey: the adventure into the abyss of the person himself, the adventure into the abyss of the cosmos. For a person grows through double dialogue—dialogue with himself and dialogue with another. In this context, ever-more-inclusive systems of dialogue orchestrate themselves as the ever-new ground on which human being securely rests. Yet the succession of grounds thereby both discovered and worked out leads toward modes of orchestration which ultimately envelop the universe, modes which convert the natural world into a cosmos incomparably more ethereal and mysterious than that world.

To relate to a cosmos which now never ceases to haunt him, man must begin to speak in rhythms which echo the rhythms of the cosmos: he must diversify his speaking rhythms in ways which accord with the diversity of cosmic rhythms; he must articulate finely nuanced variations on the themes he discerns to constitute those rhythms; and he must bring to coherence the multitude of kinds of speaking wherein he incorporates those marvelously variegated facets of resonances which pervade the cosmos. In fine, a person grounds himself with ontologic primordiality not only on his searching acts and his growing acts, but, beyond those acts, on those speakings forth by which he attunes himself to such melodies as haunt and ground the cosmos itself. For a philosophic theory of the person—in effect, a personology—inevitably leads the person beyond personology to cosmology. Yet to ground cosmology, the person must first work through the divisions he abstractly discerns to infect his being: namely, those of mind with mind, of body with body, and of mind with body. Experiencing these divisions with a sharp edge of reality, he nonetheless persuades himself that that reality is but the diversified actualization of the indivisibility of his inmost self. In their very reality, a person's divisions may be overcome and subsumed under his wholeness. Referring to a deeper experience, one may deduce from the primordial ontologic categories—namely, *searching*, *growing*, and *speaking*—certain derivative though equally essential ontologic categories: the integrality of mind and body as constituting one substance; the intrinsic unity of powers for shaping symbols; that reciprocity of being with others which grounds authentic encounter. When a person has thereby discovered the *oneness* of his being, and its interwovenness with the being of others as likewise one with himself, he stands at the threshold of wisdom. Insofar as philosophy *is* the quest for wisdom, philosophic inquiring truly expresses human existing.

As, in this sense, veridically philosophic, human being is luminous with the rhythms of individuality woven with community. And as I stated in my Prologue to *Homo Quaerens*, a prologue intended, in part, to introduce the entire Inquiry:

> In numberless ways, man seeks this luminosity. He never ceases in his quest after the *good life*: the true, the good, the beautiful; he endlessly strives toward the *pious life*: trust, hope, and love. Nor does he desist from seeking the synthesis of these lives in the *spiritual life* which unfolds, through phases of justice and integrity, toward wisdom. Finally, at the end of the way, he realizes that wisdom itself is but a lesser peak whence he gazes upon endless stretches of mountain tops the contours and challenges of which he cannot even yet discern.[4]

To these reflections, I can now add: pervading human ontology is a single thrust—the movement from fragmentation and obscurity toward coherence and clarity; the flow of life's first enigmatic, evanescent stirrings into enduring patterns of splendor and human solidarity. In life's every quest, this thrust is replicated, albeit with countless variations. Every human experience renews the thrust. Ever searching to reduce alienation, ever growing toward new resolutions, and ever speaking in freshly orchestrated rhythms, the person brings to fruition both his natural impulses and his spiritual yearnings. In every human act, new consciousness dawns; a divided self becomes unified. Woven from bits and pieces of dim, buried consciousness, a concerted human awareness bursts forth in myriad luminous forms. Everywhere, new unity arises out of difference; new difference conquers unity. In wonder, the prelude to true questing emerges. A context of delight, awe, and terror shapes new possibilities for human discernment. Now I may both sympathize and empathize with humanity's concerns and struggles. Growing into my own depths, I individuate myself, I integrate myself, and I preserve myself; and I declare myself in gesture, in imagination, and in acts of shaping. And, in wisdom, I step into altogether new dimensions of existence and, in the end, I become integral, potent, and authentic. Now I await my destiny, be it harsh or gentle; I awaken into strangely new, transcendent melodies; I relinquish life itself. Throughout, there is pulsation, ebb and flow, new beginnings. In spiraling patterns of vibrancy or dread, I step, with trembling fortitude, into a labyrinthine stillness. Endlessly, I seek to penetrate the impenetrable. Ever driven back, I struggle to advance with dread-slow, terrible cadence. Always there is haunting redemption. Yet never is consolation more than a brief respite. And the more deeply I quest, in interweaving patterns of questioning, listening, and interpretatively responding, the more profoundly mystery reinstates itself. In the end, I am left with ambiguity, paradox, and fear, but always with new wonder. Like Socrates, I at last discover that my knowledge *is* my ignorance, that my ignorance *is* my knowledge: that, herein, lie my strength and, once more, my new beginnings. Having overcome a double division—that between my consciousness and my Unconscious, that between my mind and my body—I search, in ever-more-sagacious advance, from freedom and openness through varying designs of balance, more thoroughly plumbed inwardness, and hitherto concealed spiritual realms toward my personal wholeness; I grow from sheer roaming, through all of life's dissolutions and transfigurations, through harrowing crisis, renewed dialogue, and purifying compresence with others toward authentic creativity. I speak from out of vague contexts, through alternating rhythm, texture, and imagery, "toward" (in my most private and, certainly, in my last moments) an unfathomable silence. In each instance, I prepare for new ends—and I discover that every means is but a new beginning, and every beginning but a new ending.

For, as ontologic, the person is like a many-faceted gem which glows in marvelous ways. And, as in life's great odyssey the gem slowly turns, miracle upon miracle shines forth: those countless gleaming scintillae of man's every striving. In dialectic of wonder and wisdom, he stands enrapt, intense, and astounded before the world spectacle. And he beholds the apotheosized ferment of human creation; he carves symbols of cognition, morality, the aesthetic, the philosophic, the religious. Like Joseph Conrad's artist, human ontology, in the guise of every man,

> appeals to that part of our being which is not dependent on wisdom: to that in us which is a gift and not an acquisition—and, therefore, more permanently enduring. [It] speaks to our capacity for delight and wonder, to the sense of mystery surrounding our lives; to our sense of pity, and beauty, and pain; to the latent feeling of fellowship in all creation—to the subtle but invincible conviction of solidarity that knits together the loneliness of innumerable hearts, to the solidarity in dreams, in joy, in sorrow, in aspirations, in illusions, in hope, in fear, which binds men to each other, which binds together all humanity —the dead to the living and the living to the unborn.[5]

It is this gift, this sense of mystery, this fellowship, this solidarity, and this web of human weal and woe to which I address myself in these pages, and which I clothe in categories of human ontology.

To embark upon this quest, I must confront every paradox and every ambiguity of human freedom. Without cease, constraints press upon me. Bare, unforeseen contingency sweeps through me: an unknown source, an unpredictable force, an unknowable consequence. From every side, from within me and from without, and as dark moods subtly invade and harsh circumstance inexorably lacerates, I am oppressed, assaulted, and, from moment to moment, harried or torn or crushed. Ineluctably, I yield. Pain or anguish or horror envelops and consumes me. How to extricate myself, how to acquiesce, how to bend? Wherein consists my freedom? With measured step—now enduring defeat, now advancing —I meditate. In slow cadences of freedom, I revalue, I reorient, and I reconstitute. Miraculously, if too seldom, I give myself to an invisible power or force or, perhaps, to a gentler presence. Now, strangely, quite incomprehensibly, I am assuaged or, possibly, even reassured.

Surely, in my physical being, I sense myself to be, for the most part, determined; in my conscious being, I sense myself to be often free. But how is it in my creative depths? Truly, then I am both determined and free. Or can it be that then I am neither determined nor free? Might not my ultimate resignation consist precisely in the transcendence of determinism *and* freedom, an acquiescence in a certain cosmic necessity by attuning myself to which I can reach immeasurably beyond both the free and the contingent? Let me yield myself to all that flows within me. Let me turn toward that flow as toward a luminous fount of my most profound expressions. Let me accept the ethereal cadences with which symbols shape themselves through me. Let me, as I meditate, seek to constitute myself a subtle medium, a transparency of being which mirrors the most diaphanous and integrating of cosmic rhythms. Were some marvelous conjunction of incomprehensibly benign influences to conspire to favor me, I might attain—and then alone *could* attain—to veridical redemption of my life's anguish. Only when the mysterious ways of an invisible divinity stir the very depths of me can I authentically aspire toward an existence which is both necessary and free. In the human ontology which I herein set forth, I examine some elements in this hope, this promise, and this quest.

NOTES

1. See my *Homo Quaerens: The Seeker and the Sought; Method Become Ontology* (New York: Fordham University Press, 1978), and *The Dance of Being: Man's Labyrinthine Rhythms; The Natural Ground of the Human* (New York: Fordham University Press, 1979).
2. This work is part of "An Inquiry Into the Metaphysics of the Person." In addition to *Homo Quaerens*, *The Dance of Being*, and *Choros*, it will comprise, in sequence, the following books: *Metamorphosis: The Odyssey of the Self*, *Apotheosis: The Divinizing Self*, *Cosmos: The Crucible of Man*, and *The Person: A Cosmic Perspective*.
3. *Joseph and His Brothers*, trans. H. T. Lowe-Porter (New York: Knopf, 1963), p. 3.
4. Pp. 11–12.
5. "The Condition of Art," in *The Portable Conrad*, ed. Morton Dauwen Zabel (New York: Viking, 1954), p. 706.

α

PSYCHE AND PERSON: THE WHOLENESS OF MAN

INTRODUCTION

To set forth an ontology of human being, I now treat the theme of the divided self: the different aspects and parts of the self which are seemingly set in opposition to one another; and I examine the possibility that inhering in the very relationship between these divisions, in the dynamic interaction which subtends their respective activities, is a thrust toward wholeness, unity, and completion. Three fundamental sets of division pervade human being: that between psyche and body, that between consciousness and unconsciousness, that between body's grosser lineaments and its underlying subtler processes. Within these dichotomies, the Unconscious is here conceived as portending the body. However, construed as functional, the body analogously portends the mind, of which the Unconscious is that component which, so to speak, lies closest to the body. Thus, on the whole, mind tends toward the condition of body, whereas body tends toward the condition of mind: mind sinks, body rises. And, by my approach, a single substance constitutes the ground of both body and mind. But one fabric of resonances gives birth to each. Within this fabric, body now crystallizes, mind now crystallizes.

Conventionally speaking, body acts are functions of body structures; mental acts are more intricate functions of body structures. Between these two kinds of acts lies a large spectrum of possible modes of human being. For, though distinguishable as "ideal" poles, mind and body are not radically separable. Moreover, are not body structures themselves resolvable into other acts which are composed of still more primordial structures? What are the ultimate structures? Can it be that, in the end, they are not structures at all? Or even physical events of any kind—namely, events which obey conservation laws? Can they not be intrinsically invisible, unfathomable, and even noumenal? Surely, the more they are inspected, the more such structures dissolve into a kind of ferment of which body and mind are equal expressions: expressions more or less tangible, for body; expressions more or less ineffable, for mind.

Numerous attempts have been made to overarch the Cartesian dualism between mind and body. For Spinoza, every entity has both a mental aspect and a physical aspect—though, for most entities, one or another of these aspects is subordinate, hence, often negligible. Yet all entities contribute to a single substance which is neutral to the mind–body distinction. For man the route to understanding that substance lies along the two attributes of mind and body. But from the standpoint of substance, an infinity of attributes contributes an infinity of perspectives. All are ways by which substance apprehends itself; hence, all are ways by which, potentially, *some* entity apprehends substance. Moreover, such simple entities as quarks differ from such complicated entities as persons in their physical features quite as much as in their mental features. Conversely, they are as much like persons in their mental features as in their physical features. For, even the limited perspectives of mind and body are each labyrinthine, enormously intricate, and, from entity to entity, of widely varying composition. For Leibniz, a person's "substance" is a community of minute changes, subtle modulations which pattern themselves, in shifting dynamic configurations, into relational schemes which themselves are either mental or physical, or, indeed, some combination of the mental and the physical. Each such change is an infinitesimal though enduring monad. By seemingly imperceptible increments, these "differential" monads integrate themselves into frankly physical acts and frankly mental acts. By its mental acts, one monad "perceives" another. Whether confusedly or clearly, perception discloses a veritable universe which, inscribing itself in the perceiving monad's own reflexive composition, continues to dwell interiorly and therein to unfold its specific content. And every monad is the locus of many such indwellings. By divinely pre-established harmony, these monads are empowered to act in more or less concerted fashion. They orchestrate themselves into ever-novel assemblages. Yet, radically closed in upon itself, a monad, though exhibiting as physical aspect its own external contours, is by essence reflexive, hence, to be construed as primarily mental and internally labyrinthine.

From a Leibnizian point of view, the person is a pluralistic composite of innumerable such internally related monads. For Spinoza, he is an essential unity, unified by extension as well as by empathy, who, in his inmost character, mirrors the coherence of the cosmos. These two construals themselves require unification. And Whitehead, combining the Spinozist with the Leibnizian insight, also acknowledges the profoundly *natural* status of the person. Using as paradigm the living organism, and its component cells, he regards the person as a society of occasions[1] which are, at once, experiential and actual. Every such occasion exhibits a complex character. Each is locus of contrasting harmonies and dissonances of feeling; each takes bare cognizance of other experient occasions; each exhibits some mode of conformation to those occasions; each incorporates them into its own self-creating being; each is the scene of their perishings[2] into that being; each synthesizes, under the perspective of its own individuality, these incorporated occasions into dynamic unity; each constitutes itself a unit of self-enjoyment, in absolute monadic privacy, of its own advance into novelty. Within that complex structure of enduring occasions, each itself an intricate nesting of other occasions, a single presiding occasion emerges as final node, as coordinating center. Within this locus, patterns prehended from innumerable bodily levels of activity, each itself composed of experient occasions, are received, sifted, evaluated, and reconstituted. Amid the vicissitudes of human adventure in ever-changing environments, presiding occasion after presiding occasion temporally unfolds. Constituting routes of inheritance, which wander from one region of the brain to another, they provide the person with his ever-shifting yet ever-enduring self-identity. In his unifying activity, that person, himself the integration and integrator of a multitude of unifying acts, transmits that self-identity along some selected set of such inherited routes. At one and the same time, he is a Leibnizian multitude, naturalistically conceived, and a Spinozist unity, personalistically conceived. He is both subject and object, private and public, autonomous and determined. In his inmost makeup, he mirrors similar synthetic processes over the entire range of cosmic phenomena and, indeed, their divinely prescribed unifying activity.[3]

In my inquiry, I assume as valid this Whiteheadian synthesis. Yet I seek an even stronger ground for personal identity than Whitehead's concept of the person as a society of occasions. I quest after a concept of mind and body as a single, indiscerptible, and integral substance: a unitary rhythmic complex. My paradigm is human dancing, human speaking, human searching. Granted: each sphere, mental and physical, is a separate locus of activity. But these activities themselves interact. Whiteheadian division between a mental pole and a physical pole does not seem to conceptualize adequately the activity which grounds this interaction. For, by their transactions, mind and body give rise to all manner of rhythmic constitution. Every mental aspect of human being, so I presume, has a physical aspect; every physical aspect has a mental aspect. Every mind rhythm manifests a body undertone; every body rhythm manifests a mind overtone. Such rhythmic overtones and undertones are some sort of reverberation; each instance of such reverberation itself exhibits a mental side and a physical side. Accordingly, I here construe mind and body to be orchestrated regions of rhythmic flowing, loci within a field of pulses which now integrate and now dissolve. Resonances and vibrations which spread or contract, these regions variously disseminate themselves. Differentiated within that field, no locus, mental or physical, is absolute. Transactions occur across ever-shifting boundaries within the field. And, in this ceaseless ferment, innumerable subtle processes intermingle, metamorphose, and recombine in myriad contrapuntal arrangements.

To dramatize the need for an entirely new terminology for conceptualizing this activity, I use such allusive, figurative, and evocative language as rhythmic substance, ethereal substance, luminous substance, weighty substance, coarse rhythms, opaque rhythms, and fine rhythms. In this Division,[4] I seek only to indicate, rather than to explicate as yet, a new model,[5] a model which will provide ontologic underpinnings, if not yet epistemologic justification, for the apparently incongruous, autonomous, and incommensurate realms of mind and body. Ultimately, such a model must be responsible to such empirical inquiry as the medical and the psychiatric, and, of course, to ordinary experience. Though methodologic reduction of mind and body, either sphere to the other, may, at times, be practically efficacious, the correlative ontologic reduction is conceptually (and experientially) absurd. Surely, mental states and physical states are equally real. Both kinds of states are instances of, or perspectives on, the same substance; and this substance is the person himself, the person in his full actuality.

To conceptualize human actuality, I use, as a central theme, the idea of rhythm.

Different rhythmic systems are variously congruent with one another. Some systems can be synchronized with other systems; some systems are intrinsically dissonant with respect to other systems. The patterns which rhythms engender exhibit intricate designs. They may be mapped onto one another in diversified ways. And the discordances between one level of human being and another—however these levels instantiate the rubrics of mind and body—may be harmonized, or, for that matter, accentuated, by intervening rhythms. In my account, the Unconscious is composed of precisely such rhythms. Man's *mediating*, *mirroring*, and *transforming* "agent," it occupies a position midway among the layers which compose human being. Later, I explicate this threefold function. For this purpose, I employ three sets of metaphor: levitation and gravity, fine rhythms and coarse rhythms, luminosity and opacity. By the notions of levitation and gravity, I conceptualize the hierarchical ordering of different strata, or depositions, of mind acts and body acts. In levitation, certain factors in patterns which are hierarchically lower are exemplified in higher patterns; in gravity, the reverse obtains. My distinction between refined rhythms and coarse rhythms is based on a wave model, with variables like pulse frequency, amplitude, form, and length from crest to trough. Luminosity and opacity each refers to a structure which, with some grade of transparency, reflects another. With respect to all these metaphors, the Unconscious "occupies" an intermediate position.

But even the term "rhythm" is used here metaphorically. For both force and intentionality pertain to rhythm. In body, force is concentrated, whereas intentionality is minimal. In mind, force is diffuse, whereas intentionality is intensified. One body impinges upon another. Thereby, it, in effect, signifies itself to the other. A mind impinges, too, but more ineffably. It signifies another to itself. In human being, numberless acts of signification—signified (as itself an activity) and signifying—are layered, one upon the other, as pertaining either to the person or to his environment. Linguistic behavior is but the most subtle of these acts. In general, the power to signify, i.e., *to transcend*, belongs, in some measure, to both body and mind. In this sense of signification, every rhythm is associated with the capacity to strive, and to leap beyond itself. For I ascribe to rhythm some kind of momentum, an immanently purposive thrust. Thus endowed, rhythm is both datum and *datio*. A given and a giving—in both instances, acts—it has a subjective component as well as an objective component. As striving, rhythm is capable of inscribing itself upon another. Feelings inscribe with one sort of rhythmic pattern, thought with a second sort, and bodily organs with yet a third sort. And as reachings out, rhythms are also to be understood as presupposing phases of both gathering in and absorbing. In this book, I prefigure, in treating these phases from the standpoint of searching, growing, and speaking, my later cosmologic account.

Constituted by both a split psyche (viz., consciousness and unconsciousness) and a split body (viz., outward lineament and inner rhythm), each with its distinctive balances and imbalances, the person embarks on a special journey.

He activates his own reflexive powers to search into the hidden strata of both his body and mind; he prepares the way for redintegrating these split-off facets. To deal with this search, its crises, and its resolutions, I examine the concepts of split psyche and split soma. Even in the context of Freud's restrictive thought, so I suggest, a personalist doctrine can be traced, and, beyond that, a doctrine which proposes a social self as co-participant in a community which enters into the very composition of the self. The very concept of infolding psychic imagery, and its re-collection through significant interpersonal encounter, requires that the idea of abstract psyche be replaced by the idea of concrete person.

Complementing the intrapsychic arrangements, the body's intra-organismic arrangements are of two kinds: those of physiognomy and those of physique. Behavioral symbols of rhythms the interplay of which constitute physique, physiognomic symbols are more or less coherently ordered. When correctly deciphered, these symbols reveal the physique to be a symbol of delicate balance and imbalance. With respect to those rhythms, they disclose the very apotheosis of modulated nuance: mind itself in its intricately coordinated layers of reflexivity. Suffused with reflexivity, the body inscribes itself upon the subtlest lineaments of physiognomy. Now revealing unconscious activity, the body *as* unconscious allows for spontaneous passage of "resonances" through its component strata. And the person becomes luminous with diverse integrations of his own natural processes. Wherever body appears, the aura of mind hovers. Selves are those loci wherein body represents to itself the person as reflexively germinating within it. Two poles of intertwinings present themselves: bodies enmeshed with bodies, self-consciousness un–self-consciously participating with self-consciousness.

Mediating transfer of contents between organic processes and psychic processes —and, in this way, mirroring body and psyche in their diverse strata—is the Unconscious: that indefeasibly private locus of all human activity. Profound continuities prevail between the different layers of body and mind; profound affinities prevail as well. Transpositions from one stratum to another continually occur. Each stratum is a field of forces—more accurately, of those finer forces which I have called resonances. It is also a field of intentions. Explicitly or immanently, every part of mind and body is intentional. By their overall intentionality, *human* body and mind are oriented toward their own self-transcendence. In effect, each person gives himself up to his own ontogenesis: like selves which, once formed, give themselves up, as *datio*, to other selves; like bodies which, at lower regions of the mind–body spectrum, are dynamically implicated with other bodies.

Man emerges in varying states of internal ecologic balance and imbalance. Ineluctably, he quests after more cohesive modes of balance, balance between himself and his milieu as well as balance within himself. Truly, man is a roamer. Amid nature's ceaseless echoings, he secures himself in ever-more-extensive regions, regions wherein he can express ever more fully his own creative powers. He seeks roots which do not constrict those powers; his migrations exhibit ever-more-inclusive patterns of attachment and detachment. His whole being thirsting after self-transcendence, man yearns to etherealize himself; he strives to transmute himself into something other than a child of nature. Through both his reproductive acts and his poetic shapings, he reveals his capacity for self-replication. By his insatiable, yet inexorably unrequited, roamings, he symbolizes his striving and his yearning. It is as though man's discovery of endlessly novel domains in which to root himself can terminate only in heaven itself! In body and in soul, human being struggles to participate empathically in the larger cosmic rhythms. By allowing human resonances to pass from one stratum of human being to another, the human Unconscious constitutes itself the primary agency whereby a person quests after immortality. For the Unconscious effects those human metamorphoses—body transformations and soul transformations—which I designate man's "luminosity."

Mind against mind, as consciousness vis-à-vis the Unconscious; body against body, as physiognomic symbol vis-à-vis rhythms of the physique; mind against body, as originating resonances of differing modes and orders—these divisions of the self are pervasive and potent. As intentional, consciousness and the Unconscious are each associated with a quest for certain objects; each implies a distinct scheme of valuation; each entails some commitment, a specific orientation toward world and self. Their conflicting mental concerns demand resolution. Furthermore, body symbols are the residue of body rhythms. As such, symbols not only reveal rhythms; they can also constrain rhythms. But rhythms not only declare themselves through symbols; they can also inundate symbols. Yet new rhythms constantly press for new symbolic representation. Alternatively, new symbols achieve a kind of autonomy; they stimulate new rhythmic flowing. Still, conflict ineluctably reigns in the sphere of the physical; and conflict, in effect, struggles to overcome itself.

Caught between these two sets of conflict, the mental and the physical, a person either succumbs or grows. Surely, mind and body are often antagonists. Inexorable locus of conflict, the human person cannot desist from striving toward transcendence. Otherwise, he mires himself in concerns which are antithetical to his essential humanity. Human ontology is the story of every person's quest to subordinate conflict to larger human values. It is the narrative of man's metamorphoses: it is the odyssey of the self; it is a portrait of human transcendentality.

In conscious acts, one frames explicit beliefs about what is and what ought to be. For consciousness incorporates a person's overt responses to directives, taboos, and recommendations for conduct which his society deems appropriate. Through the agency of a man's immediate family, the community at large addresses him. Thus, consciousness aims, in part, at maintaining a stable social order: one the institutions of which are dominated by the precepts of those who, during crucial stages of a person's development, have acted with dominant authority. But since every person dwells in many subgroups, and since these may in some measure be in conflict, either announced or implicit, each subgroup is itself the locus of conflicting values; and each transmits this conflict, through consciousness, to the Unconscious.

On the one hand, consciousness enjoins itself to bring into sharp unitary focus all psychic powers. As conscious, a person discovers in incompatable values a unique set which exhibits order, coherence, and balance. He appropriates these values through diverse modes of symbolization; and his symbols are manifested both through psychic tokens and through bodily tokens. When a person has fully integrated his unconscious processes with his consciousness, in a now expanded, deepened, and enriched awareness, his being, in its mental aspects and in its physical aspects, is integral and indivisible. Hence, his symbolisms, conveyed through the lineaments of his physiognomy interwoven with the resonances of his psyche, transmit the rhythms which constitute his primordial and essential self. Pertaining to the person's physique, these rhythms, when consciousness and the Unconscious coalesce and comportment becomes luminous with psychic resonances, reveal not merely that physique but his entire singular presence. Basically, conscious values pertain to the theme of self-preservation, and, by self-interested projection, to the theme of the preservation of others. Through that mutuality of interest whereby the powers of all are increased, the powers of each are potentiated, and potentiated anew, to disclose endlessly new depths. Ultimately, consciousness concerns both community and cosmos as interwoven sources of individual sustenance. Relating the person to the world at large, consciousness shapes, from the Unconscious, symbols which exhibit human relatedness in all its modes, dimensions, and aspects.

On the other hand, the Unconscious is the activity of absorbing, and filtering through consciousness, such societal and personal demands as are inconsistent with the integrity of awareness. For were they operative in awareness, the traumatizing of these demands would threaten to disrupt it. Hence, consciousness includes a component of counter-values, values which are antithetical to those values which it overtly acknowledges to be its own—new values which are now repressed. The conflicting social groups in which one participates, especially during the earlier years of one's growth, cannot be tolerated. For consciousness must be highly articulated before it can serve as effective locus of conflict. And conflict is reduced by first dissociating the values associated with this disharmonious complex, and then integrating other values into a new awareness.

Accordingly, two value schemes are adopted by every person: a conscious order of explicitly claimed values, and an unconscious order of explicitly disclaimed *anti*-values. Should these anti-values mesh coherently with such (unconscious) values as had previously become allied with need, especially the desire to reorder the world as an instrument for need gratification, these *two* systems of unconscious values (i.e., anti-values) would reinforce one another. Now they would function as though they were but a single system. In consequence, implicit commitments of extraordinary power and intensity would be created: commitments which so fascinate and grip one that one comes to dwell on them in dream and in fantasy. Efflorescing to constitute bizarre internal phenomena, these commitments would significantly deflect one's attention, hence, one's very energies. In effect, the latter would be split into diffuse and competing *I*-components.

Owing to this process, a person's rhythms would, on all levels in which they pervade human being, reconstitute themselves as cacophonous and unbalanced; the symbolisms through which they express themselves, bodily and psychic, would exhibit incongruities and opacities. The person's luminosity would diminish; his power for spontaneous action would be deformed; his symbolic creations would be intermixed with grotesque blemishes; his power for creation would be debilitated. A natural conscious inclination to search, to listen, and fully to attend to the world's resonances, inner and outer, would be replaced by a tendency, ominous and inexorable, to use stratagems and deceits. One would be ruled by impulses the character of which is largely unknown. Yet in order to continue to deem his own actions efficacious, a person conceals from himself and from others the full extent to which he has become enslaved by these pathological processes. In brief, the divisions of mind with mind, body with body, and mind with body would themselves ramify into divisions within divisions. Man would tend toward a pulverulent and fragmented condition.

Nonetheless, art, reason, feeling, and spirituality can never be fully crushed. Again and again, they reassert themselves. Again and again, man may choose to illuminate the degrading and pulverizing forces which work within him. Thereby alone he can extricate himself from the confusions which these forces engender; thereby, he can set his sights upon humanly more admissible goals. Hitherto the self had been divided; now it can achieve wholeness and luminosity. With ever-increasing authenticity, man can accordingly search and grow and speak.

NOTES

1. See the index of Alfred North Whitehead, *Process and Reality* (New York: Macmillan, 1929), for items on "society" and "occasion."

2. See the index items on "perishing" in ibid.

3. For this brief discussion of Whitehead, I am indebted to Elizabeth M. Kraus's superb commentary *The Metaphysics of Experience: A Companion to Whitehead's* PROCESS AND REALITY (New York: Fordham University Press, 1979), esp. p. 69.

4. Because of the length of *Choros*, I have, in a departure from the format of the earlier works, divided this volume into Divisions (three in all). To each Division, I append an Introduction, like the present one. Subsumed under the Divisions is the scheme, previously employed, of Parts, Chapters, Preambles, Sections, and Subsections.

5. I acknowledge here the profound (and, for me, invaluable) remarks of Robert Neville about my article "Luminosity: The Unconscious in the Integrated Person," in *Mental Health: Philosophical Perspectives*, edd. H. Tristram Engelhardt, Jr., and Stuart Spicker (Dordrecht: Reidel, 1976), pp. 177–88. See Professor Neville's "Environment of the Mind," in ibid., pp. 169–76.

I

A Self Divided

1

BIFURCATED PSYCHE AND SOCIAL SELF: THE SOLITARY UNCONSCIOUS

PREAMBLE

To introduce the topic of a self divided, and, in particular, to anticipate the conversion of the theme of psyche into the theme of person—the latter in the context of the wholeness of man—I must rethink Freud's theory of the Unconscious. My purpose is, not to present a scholarly account followed by an exegesis, but to give an interpretation in the light of my own reflections, and, especially, to introduce the principal ideas of this chapter, in which I begin to treat the divisions of mind with mind, body with body, mind with body. When, therefore, I say "Freud says or implies so and so," this is but a shorthand way of saying "the impact of Freud upon me, for the purpose of working through a human ontology, is such and such." Hence, I give an account which is, I hope, both plausible and consistent with Freud's thought. Moreover, I indicate, with minimal elaboration, the possibility that this theory allows, in principle, that incorporation of a social self in which a deep inner continuity prevails, despite the apparent "solitariness" of the Unconscious, between person and society. Beyond that, I suggest the profound import of this narrow construal of the Unconscious for an ontology of the bifurcated psyche.[1]

A • THE PSYCHIC FLOW

(*a*) A Complex Self

Among the concepts of the psyche developed by philosophers and psychologists, surely the theory of the Unconscious evolved by Freud is the most dramatic and novel. I say this because, contrary to other notions, Freud postulated, and indeed claims to have proven the validity of, the idea of the Unconscious not only as a passive immanent awareness, source of consciousness, and matrix of latent mental phenomena, but, in addition, as an *actively* autonomous, systematic, and dynamic organization of non-conscious "ideas," an organization counterposed to the analogous system of conscious ideas. Two distinct systems are posed. Though in their interior dynamics these systems are opposed to one another, from the standpoint of the psyche as a whole they are complementary, and by their interplay they are, ultimately in the ideal and rarely achieved instance, unified and transcended. Indeed, only when consciousness and the Unconscious are combined, forming a new product in which each is altered and transformed, is the truth about the *being* of the person revealed. Alone, neither discloses anything but a fragment of that truth. As given, and prior to that interaction which by an inherent τέλος leads, unless hindered by destructive forces, to the sublation of both in a new type of psychic organization, each is in a state of tension with respect to the other; a dynamic equilibrium of tensions ineluctably pervades the psyche. For while each tends to incorporate the other, consuming that other and thereby by a kind of truncation depriving the psyche of its tragic destiny, each at the same time defends itself from the transposition of any of *its* elements into the other. At all costs, the psyche maintains such an economy in this topographic distinction that the integrity of both factors, consciousness and the Unconscious, is perpetuated and resists, save in that rare instance, alteration to the psyche of a Nietzschean *Übermensch*.[2]

Dramatic and novel! For the psyche is construed not as homogeneous and unified but as intrinsically and tragically bifurcated, a tragedy to which the "normal" person is forever doomed. It is the locus wherein unfold two distinct and opposed processes, each process having, nonetheless, a strange affinity for the other, and each constituting a symbol the (latent) meaning of which is contained in the other. In effect, a double symbology is constructed; for each element completes itself only by combining, and therein finding its meaning, with some element from the opposing system, thereby abolishing the original dissociation. A constellation of symbols of a psyche in thus duplicating itself thereby dupes itself, and furtively, in its one aspect, conceals what it, in its other aspect, perpetually reveals. For it poses itself as *at once* conscious and unconscious, a matrix of meanings both hidden and unmasked. Strange dialectic! A drama enacted by and within the psyche itself! Some of these meanings reside in consciousness; others dwell in the Unconscious. A peculiar symmetry of two contexts of meaning; yet paradoxically an asymmetry in which each (alternately) assumes the guise of "mere" forces while the other the appearance of "true" meanings! Consciousness and the Unconscious are each both *fields of intention* and *fields of forces*. Freud's theory is, in effect, the theory of this dialectic and the steps by which, through its own dynamism, the confusions it engenders can be clarified.

To proceed: wherever, according to my view of Freud's theory, there is an organism of sufficient complexity to constitute the body of a person, a psyche arises to express the total functioning of that body in its world—a psyche which is, in effect, a reflecting (as sound, sight, smell) of the relationship between its associated body and its world *into* itself. In this self-mirroring, or internalizing of that relationship, the organic processes themselves are affected or even redirected. For the human body is an organization of elements so constituted that this organization reflects into its own organicity its structure with respect to the structure of the world toward which it comports, incorporating those structures and that relationship as additional organic elements assimilated to previously existing elements. By reflexivity (having its own actions and their consequences turned back upon itself), the body overcomes its status as mere body and becomes body spiritualized. For germinating within every *merely* human body is the body of a *person*—an authentically *human* body. More generally: associated with organisms even on the lowest levels of complexity is a self by which that organism leaps beyond itself to possess its own body, to shape in a measure its destiny, and to reconstitute its rhythms.

In the case of a human being, this self is a locus of representations by which the body reconstitutes itself a person and no longer a mere body; for it fashions for itself an image of itself in relationship to the world. But in every instance this image is a double image. Every body reflects into itself two images. One expresses that relationship essentially in terms of a body image; the other, in terms of a world image—though an "imaging" process of one kind presupposes and requires the other kind as a condition for its own dynamic unfolding. In particular, in a human body, body ideates doubly; and in this double ideation, it dupes itself as a kind of distorted self-replication. For in its "replica" it conceals from itself how it *really* stands with respect to the world by rendering that "standing" dichotomously. Both members of this dyad must be understood, not as merely juxtaposed, but as actually synthesized and thus transcended so that the reality of that body with respect to its world is expressed.

In every masking, there is an immanent unconcealing, a disclosure of the way in which an organism stands authentically in its world. Weighed down by a double image and hence with an archaic organicity, each organism tends to overcome its own self-duplicating (i.e., its status as dichotomously conscious and unconscious). This transcendent unity is the synthesizing of body as conscious with body as unconscious. It is body *fully* spiritualized as living its innate and original rhythms as they mesh with the rhythms of the world. In transcendence, body–world resonances are integrated into a cohesive and unified matrix of reverberations. No longer is body the locus of opposing representations. On the contrary, it is a *sublimation*. Mere consciousness—and its correlate, self-consciousness—and unconsciousness are sublated in a higher kind of consciousness: one which must be designated by an altogether new term.

I have introduced the notions of autonomy, system, dynamism, complementarity, symmetry, transposition, symbol, duplication, and duping with respect to psychic "ideas" which may be construed as either conscious or unconscious. In the context of my rethinking of Freud's thought, how do I explain these notions? What does it mean to speak of self as locus of a bifurcated psyche? What is this doubly reflexive activity? Wherein consists that unmasking which constitutes authenticity? Further to elaborate this view, and to answer these questions, I treat first the idea of consciousness, then (and in greater detail) that of the Unconscious.

(*b*) Consciousness

What, according to implications of Freud's theory, can consciousness mean? Consciousness arises in a context wherein the person orients himself toward an external world which resists his organic activities. This *objecting* to his presence in the world is experienced as an intrusion which must be overcome so that he can organically extend himself into that world. It is as though the organism is wounded by obtrusive stimuli. Its contents pour into the world. Hence, it must defend itself against further threat so that, in its healing, it can continue to function as an integral organism. This healing process is the analogue of consciousness; what protects it (at least initially) "resides" in the analogue to the Unconscious. A person's activity is so directed that these alien bodies are, for him, negated presences or are even abolished. By pitting his powers against theirs, he destroys the more *objectionable* objects. Alternatively, depositions (or traces) of their presence may be incorporated or *im*pressed into his own organic life. In either way, he rejects the world so that it will not reject him. In the latter case, first he attaches himself to those objects, even clinging to them by a kind of identification. Then he builds his own identity by detaching himself, gathering into his own organicity their imprints sent forth as radiating stimuli, and internalizing them therein.

Accordingly, the world is primordially experienced as, in part, irrational.[3] As such, it is a cacophony of stimuli ordered according to no rule inhering in the world itself, a chaos of objects which senselessly stand apart from him yet obtrude upon him. What has thereby been received, or "taken back," into his existence (as conscious existence) perishes[4] into that existence. Assimilated, it is thence rationalized. For those "imprints" are synthesized into a self-consistent manifold. Its "center," awareness itself, is focally attended to; and this center fades toward a haunting periphery. A transformation is effected to a context of "images," or a composite of affective, volitional, cognitive, perceptual, and appetitional factors, all unified as a reasonable and harmonious texture. Yet even as consciousness is constructed by an autonomous dynamism which resides outside of consciousness, it is disrupted by a related but opposing dynamism. The mental factors composing or associated as an Imago[5] can actually be dissociated from one another and recombined in such a way as to constitute an altered consciousness.

Once a consciousness germinates "within" the organism, as its mirroring of these external resisting objects to itself within itself, and by their incorporation defending itself against their intrusions, it experiences its own body as analogously constituted by obtrusive factors, particularly when organic pathology transforms them from a well-ordered system into an irrational system, and the person similarly tries to subdue that irrational element by incorporating it, too, as a body image—e.g., kinesthesia. Indeed, this distinction between a well-ordered and a disordered body is similar to an implicit distinction between a well-ordered and a disordered external world. For just as every organism can be attuned to its "healthy" organic rhythms, so it can be in communion with the wholesome rhythms of the external world. By a process only hinted at by Freud, this harmonizing enters consciousness as, on the one hand, a feeling of body vitality and, on the other, an empathy with a world to which one relates rather than a world which one opposes. For inner and outer worlds, the latter made up of things and persons, are *each* both counterposed to and in affinity with the person. Elements from these worlds are transferred to the body.[6]

An organism of sufficient complexity constitutes itself a person by virtue of its conscious*ing*. For "consciousness" is, at bottom, an activity and a process. It is the organism as self-directing and self-reforming; the organism projecting itself toward acknowledgment of those "forms" which, in their unity as constituting the unity of consciousness itself, constitute Truth. In every instance, it is associated with a τέλος. Accordingly, the person is one who gathers into systematic unity a schema of the world, inner and outer—in effect, a cosmology; and this schema includes interpersonal elements as well as correlative intrapersonal elements. For herein are contained Imagos of other persons as not merely organic complexes but as self-conscious beings who, reciprocally, incorporate him, in his evolving self-consciousness, into their consciousness. By "self-consciousness," I mean a person as he consciously searches into his own awareness, discerning hitherto concealed links between its constituent elements. Thereby, he incorporates intrapersonal factors, dynamisms operative "within" his own organicity, which are *un*conscious. In the cases of both inter- and intrapersonal factors, he penetrates the mysteries buried "within" consciousness. He "reads" its imprints as though they were cryptic messages, symbols the immanent meanings of which must be drawn forth by consciousness, and, thereby, function in a rearranged manifold. Through insight (and inspecting), a consciousness expands until, eventually, it potentiates *itself* to transcend its own condition and become synthesized with both the Unconscious and the depositions of a clarified self-consciousness—as sublimation.

Correlative with its activity of gathering in impressions, consciousness also expresses those worked-over imprints. It intentionally "stretches" toward the world in gesture, body stance, vocal inflection. By consciously *re*attaching himself to external objects, a person self-consciously reshapes them and thereby becomes artisan, technologist, craftsman, artist, planner, statesman, scientific experimenter—though the principles or rules governing these activities are implicit and unconscious. For these now externalized objects are rationalized as projections of its own content, corporeal symbols of consciousness itself. In its multitude of movements, body *is* consciousness incarnate. Through dialectical interplay it again internalizes these reconstituted forms. Consciousness is a continual activity of introjection and projection. It is also the language through which unconsciousness speaks; and it, in turn, speaks through the language of body itself. In these ways, the person self-consciously extends himself. He rearranges his own conscious contents, and thereby alters both external and internal resistances with respect to which those contents themselves were formed. Moreover, he transforms his unconscious experience, which itself constitutes a third realm of resistances.

Consciousness is a "mapping" of the world's "surface"; it is the creation of a continuum by way of healing the breach induced by intrusive factors; and it is a penetrating of that surface: to reveal reality concealed within appearance. Through consciousness, the person both masters and communes with the world. In this complex relationship, by transforming that world as well as by consuming it, he achieves his authenticity. In addition, consciousness includes Imagos as bearing norms and prescriptions. It evaluates them in a quest to reduce the inconsistencies among them, creating a unitary and coherent style of life. Such directives are initially experienced as counterposed to the person as resistances. These are absorbed by consciousness in its concept of the world as a moral order. Unassimilated valuations are consigned to the Unconscious wherein they constitute a new psychic resistance. Hence, the dynamics of the psyche arises: *Es* (or indigenous "instincts," an infrapersonal world) and *Überich* (a suprapersonal world—the internalized external moral order); against both of these the *Ich* must pit itself by making them reasonable, i.e., by converting them to the rational. For consciousness is the activity of *in*forming the irrational with reason. Thus both *Überich* and *Es* are relegated to the Unconscious, which represents to the self all that cannot be subdued yet must be taken "cognizance of" as alien (even though nonetheless intrapsychic).

Accordingly, consciousness is the *searching I* adjudicating between these interiorized and irrational worlds, themselves in conflict with one another. The world is experienced as perpetually lost to the person, as evanescent; and the terror of this evanescence is relegated to the Unconscious—the scene of a raging battle between its irrational components—while conscious representations enable that abandoning world to be, by implication, mourned by being symbolically won. It is a re-presenting and a refinding of what is absent; what must perish dwells evermore.

The self clings tenaciously to what ineluctably perishes. It seeks to retain it as it was, to arrest it. Yet by binding itself to that world, the self nonetheless transcends it. The integrity of consciousness is preserved. For this integrity is a dialectic between consciousness as integument—a covering sensitive to new stimuli, increasing the intensity of consciousness—and consciousness as integrality, reducing fragmentation to an integer—a whole—and thereby constricting the scope of consciousness. Indeed, consciousness is a precarious balance between these two factors, scope and intensity, expansion and contraction. It is a person as he pulsates in his involvement with the world, resonating to its influences; and as he resonates, he alternates between two poles, just as the Unconscious itself alternates between internalized and indigenous factors; and the self itself exhibits the polarity of consciousness and unconsciousness. Finally consciousness is a truncated "text" which can be completed only by reference to the Unconscious. Delusions must be painfully conquered in order to "transvalue" every given scheme of values.[7] For in its searchings consciousness reveals itself as essentially exegetical; it reads its own cryptic contents by deciphering them in accordance with rules which make themselves apparent only *as* the Unconscious becomes absorbed into an expanding awareness.

(*c*) Unconscious Shapings

On the one hand, Freud postulates an unconscious system of "mental ideas" and "affects" as necessary condition for the activity of the self. At the same time, he claims to have discovered the Unconscious, both through his examination of his own consciousness (i.e., through a searching into its immanent contents) and by studying the behavior of another and that other's reports about *his* behavior. Hence, he proposes two independent ways of ascertaining an actual content for the system whose "existence" as a function of the psyche he initially postulates. For the Unconscious has, he believes, a mental existence and is not merely a logical condition for the psychic activities of the person. In the first instance, the criterion refers to the dim apprehension and sudden appearance of mental elements not connected with specific external factors. In the second instance, the criterion refers to the incongruity of observed behavior with reported behavior. Thus the Unconscious is presumed to be known either by insight or by dissociation—i.e., by naming and feeling what had been unnamed and unfelt; or by experiencing an incongruity, a lack of coherence, a fragmentation. The first is a subjective or phenomenologic criterion; the second, an objective or behavioral criterion.

Yet both criteria use a single principle: an irrationality and disconnectedness become evident *in* behavior. This becoming evident, or *coming to appearance*,[8] is construed as an activity in accordance with a rule not given in awareness itself, a process the initial phase of which is operative unbeknown to awareness and outside the realm of customary behavior. In one sense, it is close to a person's organicity. Yet it is not intrinsically organic. Rather, it is a matrix of dynamics which intervenes between the organic and consciousness, translating the first into the second. For the Unconscious mediates organic activity. It is the agency for transmitting that activity to awareness, and transferring it to overt behavior, thereby reorganizing consciousness and its correlative behavior. In both cases, a "something" is transposed across a barrier. It is a "trans-gression" with respect to that barrier. Moreover, just as consciousness manifests itself in the general contours of organic behavior, and receives its symbolization therein—taking back the "forms" of these symbols into its own contents—so the Unconscious symbolizes *it*self in intra-organic behavior. From this point of view, consciousness is a vector which points outward to external behavior; and since that behavior is cohesive with the external world, each interlocking with and configuring the other—where this configuring is a communicating through the sensory apparatus—consciousness indicates the character of external reality. Correspondingly, the Unconscious is a vector which points inward to internal behavior and *its* relationship, via organic boundaries (e.g., osmosis), to the same external world, but from within a different perspective. For perspective with respect to a person's relationship to his world is precisely what the bifurcated self conveys, a double perspective where each conceals the other, yet both together constitute the reality of that relationship, i.e., how it stands authentically.

A double vector! And one whose components themselves are vectorially related! For consciousness and the Unconscious are inextricably bound together, cohering in their very opposition, yet drawing apart in their very apposition. In tension, each is locked into the other; and the nature of this "locking-in" gives a clue to the character of the Unconscious itself. In this vectorial engaging, each of the other, consciousness mediates, via the Unconscious, the external world to the internal world; and the Unconscious mediates, via consciousness, the internal world to the external world. A double mediation, one which proceeds in reverse directions! For consciousness is a filter through which certain external stimuli pass directly to the Unconscious, as unwholesome for the organism; alternatively, the Unconscious is a filter through which certain internal stimuli pass, and wherein they are contained, "toward" consciousness and hence the external world—contained lest both be adversely affected. Accordingly, the Unconscious is the great container and protector of stimuli, external and internal. By its activity, a given relationship of the person to the world is, if not authenticated, at least stabilized.

The Unconscious consists of both a content and the dynamisms by which that content is maintained as an integral system. In general, the content consists of two sets of factors: destructive and constructive. Most explicitly delineated by Freud are the destructive factors: primary repressions and secondary repressions. But implicit in Freud are constructive factors: what Jung stresses as archetypical collective "forms," i.e., extra-experiential yet organically rooted ways of organizing experience. The dynamisms include agencies which rationalize consciousness, effect the repressions, transpose elements from the Unconscious to consciousness and, conversely, equilibrate both the Unconscious and consciousness and redistribute the contents of the Unconscious.

Consider, first, the primary repressions. Freud assumed that stimuli emitted from the body's organs impinge on one another, diffusing themselves throughout the organism. Aggregated into patterns, they are brought into focus as a sustained inner activity and organized as instinct (viz., *Lusttrieb*—not only sex, narrowly construed, but organ pleasure or the vitality of the body; *Ichtrieb*—the vitality of the *I* in its self-preserving acts). So powerful are instincts that if unmodified they would disrupt the organism's endeavor to equilibrate itself. Albeit unsuccessfully, it attempts to flee by either mastering or abolishing them. According to Freud, instincts are "mental representatives"[9] of anarchic, intra-organismic fluctuations, exempt from the ravages of time, which would be felt, were they admitted to consciousness, as intolerably painful. Presenting itself to consciousness as a mental idea, the instinct is, however, inhibited from conscious expression, and thus remains unconscious. Though instincts constitute a thrust toward consciousness—their "natural" direction—a counter-thrust tends to redirect them toward the organs whence they arose. Yet new organic stimuli counteract the repressed stimuli, keeping instincts in a precarious balance between annihilation and conscious "discharge." Ever falling toward its source, an instinct is depotentiated; its energy level is de-pressed to a lower level. But repotentiation ceaselessly occurs. Hence, instinct is doubly rejected—by both consciousness and the organ of its origin. This energetic activity causes proliferation of instinctual derivates which, in proliferating, draw into their ever-ramifying network all subsequent repressions; and the web of accretions grows. Proto-structural channels (i.e., paths of influence lacking definite morphology) along which new stimuli are led, this weird and complex "fungus" is experienced, proto-consciously, as the haunting, frightening ground of illusion against the resistance of which awareness is endlessly contoured and transfigured. Yet in their loss of energy, in being disallowed re-entry into their organic source, and in proportion to their distortedness and remoteness from the central foci of autonomous, unconscious activity, the furthermost derivatives penetrate consciousness as novel forms.

Primary repressions exhibit such properties as specificity, mobility, vacillation, energy exchange, transformation, variability, distortion, redirectedness, circuitousness. A multitude of factors co-exist. Ideas and affects detach and reattach themselves in varying arrangements. Depending upon the particular life experiences and organic makeup of an individual, they undergo many vicissitudes. It is not my purpose to trace the details of these processes. But I do stress the potency of such hidden "forces" which, like a magnet, in drawing consciousness into them deceive consciousness and trick it into a perverse orientation toward the world. For in varied ways the Unconscious presses for discharge (i.e., "cathexis") of its energies—originally "mobile" and subsequently, at times, "tonically bound"—by their association with specific objects, external or internal. In part, this displacement is governed by counter-cathexes arising within consciousness and preconsciousness—the region of communication between the Unconscious and consciousness. By such mechanisms as condensation and conversion, the Unconscious is duplicated in consciousness, but in another "state" which nonetheless represents the same mental content. In effect, a double registration occurs in which the same materials appear (doubly) in two systems, one in the language of the organic (i.e., the instincts, or "frontier" between mental and somatic) and one in the language of consciousness.

Woven into the Unconscious are secondary repressions, depositions of the external world. Filtering through consciousness, though unbeknown to it, they are excluded from it. For their inclusion would disrupt its rational organization. According to this view, endogenous stimuli are transmitted as a pattern of energy quanta (i.e., organ Imagos) toward consciousness. Because of a barrier operative within consciousness itself (a barrier constituted by conscious *forces*), a primary repression occurs whereby the now defective pattern is returned toward its source. But in this process it is reflected back over the path of its continuing activity.

For it encounters anew such patterns of flow. Hence, it is again thrust toward consciousness; and, in effect, it oscillates back and forth, echoing throughout repeatedly counter-thrusting stimuli.

This "doubling back" upon itself is a kind of resonance—a special sort of rhythm akin to but a metamorphosis of the original energy patterns, a rhythm which though a "force" is also (perhaps latently) "intentional." As other organ stimuli analogously act, these resonances ramify as unconscious experience. However, "primary process" resonances are not differentiated in the manner of similar resonances constituting the content of awareness. On the contrary, they are, qua unconscious, a seemingly random chaos of forces. But the designation "experience" is justified. For, in both instances, conscious and unconscious, resonances are the constitutive element.

Into this maelstrom are woven secondary repressions, i.e., energy patternings of external stimuli. Whereas conscious patterns are isomorphic with (or duplicate) actual patterns or "forms" of perceived objects, unconscious patterns are transformations or distortions to new and grotesque shapes and textures. Herein is a kaleidoscopic inner world of those reconstituted presences which occasionally break into awareness as dream, fantasy, overpowering affect. Increasing intensity of such "structured" resonance, reverberating through continually altered paths of influence, is associated with a deepening experience. These paths are either frankly neuronal or else those *protomorphic* external channels along which is conveyed the image of the external world—channels analogous to internal physiologic ones. Consider the theme of repetition. Habits, familiar ways of approaching the world, are built up, analogous to impulses traversing nerves as ways of dealing with the inner world. Indeed, there may be a kind of physiology of the milieu of the person, less differentiated and, certainly, in structure incomparably more subtle than the interior channels, but operative nonetheless. As mobile (interior) energies press for discharge, resonances crystallize. The system of such loci of interpenetrating resonances corresponds to, indeed is identical with, the sphere of the psyche.

B • ENDOPSYCHIC STRUCTURES

(*a*) The Fragmented Self

The theory of resonance, implied by Freud, points toward his endeavor to develop the foundations not only of a physiological psychology but also of a psychologized physiology of experience. For physiology and psychology imply the same ultimate concepts, concepts neutral to both disciplines and transcendent to each. Freud seeks to create a language into which key terms relevant to both physiology and psychology may be translated. Alternatively expressed: he formulates principles from which physiology and psychology alike may be derived. If Freud's own language is physicalistic, and his ideas cast apparently in terms of a Helmholtzian energy model, he is using such language (as when he goes beyond energistic ideas to such ideas as transference) in a special way—a way which is supraphysiologic and which includes the psychologic domain. Accordingly, his is not a theory in which experiencing is reduced to the corporeal, but, rather, a theory in which both are jointly reducible to a third realm of being, a realm akin to Spinoza's *substance* as manifesting attributes including mind *and* body.

As a person relates to objects in the external world, they in turn relate to him. His very presence before them calls forth, indeed catalyzes, their reciprocal orientation toward him. They not only are resistances to his expandings into the world and, therefore, the objects of his aggressions, his fruitless demands, so that to be vicariously possessed their Imagos are incorporated in his psyche; they also include persons with whom he seeks intimacy. Should this quest be frustrated by the refusal of either to give himself up to the other in communion, the resultant "distancing" leads to the incorporating of traces of these objects as frustrating, negative, hence repellent, stimuli. Drawn by its magnetizing power, they sink into the abyss of the Unconscious. Since (and this is a point insufficiently stressed by Freud) the capacity to give is correlative with the need to receive, a system of *internal relationships*[10] develops between hypostatized and introjected "external" (the correlates of the "resonances" previously alluded to) objects. Every new experience yields its quota of such objects which, in effect, inscribe themselves within the already incorporated system, assimilating its features to theirs.

In this process, a potent, self-affirming, and self-integrating *I* becomes fragmented rather than solidified. For it must disperse its energies among the objects of an inner world as well as unifiedly direct them toward objects of the outer world. In its vicarious quest to gratify its need for intimacy, it is, in effect, split into a multitude of *I*'s. Accordingly, a complex, inchoate, uncoordinated, and diffuse *I* oscillates between an interior and an exterior world. So preoccupied is it with the inner world that to conserve its energies it must use stratagems and deceits to deal with the outer world. Yet its inwardly directed activity is, at bottom, unconsummated pseudo-activity. For the inner world is an Imago of impotence and rage, i.e., aggression turned inward. It is the locus of *many* centers of partial activity and never a single, unified action. One is free only insofar as (*a*) the Unconscious (in its negative components) is redintegrated into an expanding awareness, and (*b*) the *I* exercises its primordial option of searching into the Unconscious so that its fetters might be removed.

By a play of dynamics so interwoven that each magnetizes the other, this region, too, proliferates and meshes with the realm of primary repression. Reverberating through the Unconscious is, accordingly, a cacophony of dissociated "voices." The split-up facets of actual objects themselves continue to ramify. Tragically and without end, the *I* seeks among them the *true* objects of its longing. But residing in the exterior world, they have already renounced him or have been renounced by him. Receding from him they leave in their wake new fantasies. Authentic contact with reality is dulled, impaired, diffused. No longer is reality experienced as fresh and alive, a miracle of powers. No longer does one speak with one's own voice, synchronizing the many voices into a unity. Rather, a distortedly apprehended reality entangles the person in a web of static objects. Either idealized or falsely transmuted into repulsive images, its depositions are seemingly "glued" to his psyche. They refuse to "perish" into an active and continuously regenerated self. As a person flees from one phantasmagoria to another, a psychodrama of self-deception is continuously enacted. Yet a system of checks and balances maintains these interiorized objects in a specious equilibrium. Inevitably they call forth his futile tactics rather than his direct and efficient action.

Protecting the person from both external and internal dangers, the Unconscious is an evolutionary product of nuclei incorporated as psychic bearers of stimuli, external and internal. Primary and secondary repressions are fused into a dark labyrinth which endlessly generates new and more thoroughly concealed "chambers." By this heightening of tension as the coils of the Unconscious wrap themselves about consciousness, and its several nuclei interact with one another to intensify unconscious rhythms, unheard organic echoes overwhelm consciousness, or, indeed, break into awareness and conquer it, as in schizophrenia. Yet concealed in these constricting and disintegrating rhythms, when consciousness is sufficiently powerful to counterpose its own rhythms to those of the Unconscious, locking in with them—as when music resonates through one's being and penetrates to its very core—this forbidding womb gives birth to transfigured rhythms, those which are the source and ground of all creative activity. Suffusing consciousness, and thereby transforming it and the negative Unconscious, these rhythms enable a new integration to be achieved.

(*b*) The Labyrinthine Unconscious

Truly, the diseased Unconscious is of labyrinthine character. To illuminate this labyrinth, and thereby to prepare the way for a theory of the wholesome Unconscious, consider: beyond a creature of mere need, the person is a power of giving and a power of searching. When these powers are thwarted, psychopathology supervenes. And such pathology can be understood in terms of both internal relations between objects which had been incorporated in the psyche as traces of early experience, and the realignments between those relations induced by subsequent experience. For all gratification, including an infant's most basic physiologic needs, occurs in the context of relationship, a context which involves either the achievement or the frustration of intimacy. As one matures, the modes of reciprocity which one acquires with respect to both giving and receiving are intensified and differentiated. In this process, separate foci of consciousness do not need to coalesce into a unity. Nor does an originally unintegrated *I* constitute the foundation of consciousness. On the contrary, no matter what the circumstances of maturity or emotional health, a self-affirming and self-integrating center is already present, either immanently or explicitly. Through personal encounters, this center either solidifies and deepens as an integral *I* or is fragmented and dispersed to a dis-integrated *I*. No experience which promotes intimacy diminishes individuality. Invariably, such experience strengthens the *I*, and enables a person to pass unencumbered through life's vicissitudes and metamorphoses. But experience which denies intimacy *ipso facto* negates individuality, and weakens and scatters the *I*. And a scattered *I* is the basis for pathology. Only an *I* which either retains or regains its unity is the veridical basis for health.

Should a person be deprived of genuine relationship, he will seek vicarious and *intra*psychic relationships between a part of himself and an internalized image of the other. Then, his very *I* splits into two components. Albeit in a restricted sphere, and content with subdued gratification, he continues to seek relationships in the outer world. Yet, turning within, he orients himself, for his needs, toward endopsychic structures. In consequence, the urges toward outer and inner are in conflict. Giving oneself up to either urge is associated with both risks and rewards. However, no person may long tolerate conflict. Either he pretends that the outer world does not exist, dwelling in a phantasmagoria; or he pretends that the inner does not exist, claiming to live exclusively in the outer by dissociating from his awareness all internalized images. By introjection or by projection, he masks to himself the conflict by which he is afflicted. In introjection, a person extracts, internalizes, and represses such elements of his experience as he cannot master in the frame of reciprocally gratifying relationships. In projection, he orients himself toward reality as *merely* the disguised representation of the inner world of the repressed—a *re*-presenting to himself of a picture of reality woven with illusion. Accordingly, the neurotic person dwells in two realms, interior and exterior. Composed of objects which thrust themselves against him, either realm poses that resistance to which he counterposes his own "subjectivity": his willing, thinking, and feeling. Oscillating between these realms, the *I* undergoes numerous vicissitudes. In its confusions, it diversifies itself as an agglomeration of *actors* rather than solidifying itself as a single *action*.

Following Fairbairn and Guntrip,[11] I postulate an original synthesizing *I*—no *mere* Ego but the person construed as agent and actor, as one who comports toward another. As activity, this *I*, embodied as the person, is never primordially split; it is both the locus whence arise actions and the acting itself. For even as he fuses to unify his disparate experiences, the acting person himself is indivisible. And, as passive, he has needs. In gratifying his needs, he both relieves tension and affords himself pleasure. But since the *I* is, however concealedly, always active, hence in quest of "object relations," no need can truly be gratified unless the grounding need of the *whole* person for relatedness, specifically for interpersonal relationship, is gratified. Accordingly, all specific needs are but aspects and subordinate components of this one overarching need.

As a person matures, his *I* becomes increasingly complex. Through thwarting and unfulfilled experience, it loses its unity. Where but one "entity"—more accurately, a single integral *function* of the person—was operative, several "entities" now appear. The diversified activities which they express are uncoordinated and chaotic. In effect, a primordial *I*-function splits into an aggregate of independent *structures*, each hypostatized as an autonomous energy configuration. Schizoidism supervenes. Herein resides the germ whence springs all psychopathology. More specifically, deprivation of tenderness (especially the quasi-symbiosis of mothering) entails withdrawal into an imaginary world. Lest deprivation be perpetuated, the schizoid person avoids the risk of reinstating relationship to external objects; he prefers substitutive gratification in fantasy. To the realistic threat of *some* frustration and the imagined fear of overwhelming rejection, he responds by immobilizing himself in his inner psychic world. He moves about that intrapsychic realm as though it were the outer world. Only transiently does he establish relationships in that world. Yet the need for external object-relations, both personal and non-personal, persists. First intensified as craving, this need is finally converted into the demands which such a person makes upon the world; and demand is fraught with anger. But in expressing anger, he risks (so he fears) further alienation from the desired object. And when anger is coupled with the increasing need which arises when, inevitably, that object further withdraws, the fear of his (symbolic) devouring of the object, expressed as the seeking both to possess and to appropriate it for his own ends, becomes overpowering.

(*c*) Apathy: Raging Conflicts

At this point, apathy supervenes. Pseudo-activity replaces the genuine activity expressed as both love and productive work. Nevertheless, an apparent detachment from the world is actually a fake detachment. However disguised, infantile dependency remains. Entangled in compulsive infatuations, for the schizoid person conceives the source of his nourishment always to lie without him, this individual further removes himself from that "center" whence derives his authentic fulfillment. Displaced to another center, and yet another, he construes each new object as empowered to provide his sustenance. Conceiving himself as depleted of vitality, he identifies himself with those objects, seeking vicariously to live through them. Should these specious providers of energy disappear, something essential to the personhood of the schizoid individual collapses. Hence, his natural energies are mobilized to avert catastrophe. By specific techniques, each manifesting a particular kind of (neurotic) preoccupation with incorporated objects, he strives to master the threat.

External objects experienced as threatening, hence difficult of mastery, deposit their traces as *bad images*, drawing toward them significant energies of the *I*, in its ceaseless quest for mastery. Indeed, a person's life development may, in part, be understood as the vicissitudes of his search for more effective techniques of mastery. Depending upon their manner of deployment, the particular techniques chosen determine a particular kind of neurosis: each neurosis expresses conflict between the quest for such modes of relatedness as are possible at a given stage of development and the tendency to relapse into that non-relatedness in which the neurotic individual simulates primary identification with his mother. By secondary identification, whereby an image of the mother is incorporated within a person, he symbolically reinstates his original incorporation within her womb. By this inner representation of how *as a child* the person experienced his status in his family, that person crystallizes an apparent "center" of existence from which he subsequently orients himself toward reality: an impoverished reality from which parts have been deleted and internalized. This false center tends to replace the indigenous center from which his authentic voice speaks. Thus encrusted with these unabsorbed deposits of a past experience which has refused to perish into the psychic life of the child, the *I* becomes notably impeded in its endeavor to grasp reality as integral and vibrant.

By an intrinsic dynamic, the fantasy world of created objects is transformed. Owing to its unsatisfying aspects, the image of an external object is internalized, then split into two images: a rejected object and an accepted object. Now ambivalence reigns. The accepted object serves as defense against the rejected object. Then, in a secondary bifurcation, the rejected *internal* object is split into two *aspects*: an exciting aspect and a rejecting aspect. Now each aspect is hypostatized as itself an internal object; each draws to itself some energies of the original *I*. For wherever an object exists, either internally or externally, its thrusting character incites the counter-thrust of the subject, each—object and subject—requiring the other. However, the split *I*'s which flow toward rejecting and exciting objects are themselves in conflict. Now the accepted object shapes the exciting object into an ego-ideal; *its* associated *I*, indeed, further complicates conflict. Libidinal *I*, charged with desire, and antilibidinal *I*, charged with hate, are repressed—together with their associated objects—while the idealizing *I* remains to complement that residual *I* which is still outwardly directed. Since neither *I* nor object can be conceived without reference to the other, the aggregation of split *I*'s is associated with a complex object. Reality is fragmented into external and internal domains. In each case, as reality actually functions for the person, it is composed not of persons but—unbeknown to him—of the images of *aspects* of persons.

These internalized conflicts never cease to rage. Now disrupting inward peace, the experienced world becomes an agglomeration of impressions rather than a coherent fabric. And the *I* itself is mercurial, a mere summation of fleeting impressions. Both realms, *I* and object, assume an aspectual and disunited character. The *I* bears an increasing burden. For in its endeavor to combat the threat, now internalized, of ineluctably frustrating objects, new *I*-foci split off. Like barnacles, they cluster about the previous aggregation to diminish *its* potency. The impact of the world upon this constricted *I* is blunted. Contact with reality is dulled and diffused by the resistance posed by these endopsychic structures.

At bottom, the person, but a single indivisible entity, is converted, functionally if not ontologically, into a *group* of entities. A clear-cut drama of unitary persons-in-relation transforms itself into the confusing interplay of intrapsychic dramas. Those spontaneous communions in which each person authentically presents himself as truly self-affirming give way to tactical operations on a recalcitrant and non-giving environment, an environment now reduced to a congeries of passive mechanisms. In consequence, the capacity of the self genuinely to reflect—hence, to be object to itself—is damaged. For the fragmented self is competent to act only as a kind of technician who has assumed but one of a bundle of possible roles. Indeed, integral persons cannot assume mature postures with respect to a self which is no longer a veridically self-engendering activity, a self which does not truly *own* itself. Moreover, such a self can no longer construe the world as an interplay of agents, self and world, each a relatively autonomous power within a larger matrix. On the contrary, the world is now seen as an entangled network of fixed and static objects. Substituted for the normally fluid world are mere deposits of that world, deposits which, so to speak, choke it and impede its flow. Having imprinted only passive structures into the substance of the person as now durable and relatively autonomous traces, the active world is experienced as an agglomeration of *mere* objects, objects which can only drag the individual along with them. Thus laden with unabsorbed images which refuse to perish into an active, continually regenerating self, the person can no longer appropriately orient himself toward reality.

As an aggregate, dissociated and internalized aspects of reality are no mere deformed copies of reality. On the contrary, they constitute a labyrinth of *new* objects. This inner world does not stand in isomorphic correspondence with the outer world; it comprises an autonomous realm governed by its own laws and expressing itself in fantasy and in dream. This internalized environment shapes itself as an inner representation of rage. It symbolizes anger originally directed toward the outer world, but now turned within in perpetual self-punishment. When encounter was originally blocked, and the gift of love not accepted, a prospective recipient felt *himself* to be unacceptable, and sought to reinstate the symbiotic matrix whence encounter itself arose. Primordially, directed toward the sensuous, wherein the texture of reality is caressed as tender and warm, he, like an infant, mobilized his powers to disaffiliate himself, in self-protection, from a texture which now inexorably transforms itself into brittleness, harshness, untouchableness, and hostility. Should the person, himself neurotic, hence a simulated infant, or indeed should an actual infant, feel sufficiently unwelcomed by his world, the tendency toward detachment would no longer properly attune itself to a capacity for achieving that oscillation between self-absorption and the touching of the world which constitutes an harmonious adaptation to reality, a continually expanding sphere of relatedness. Under such circumstances, detachment is converted to *un*-attachment; the person thus afflicted preoccupies himself with a world increasingly experienced as lying narcissistically within him rather than participatively about him.

C • THE THWARTED SELF

(*a*) Illusions

From the germinating center of the person, a journey begins in which the diverse aspects of his existence are drawn into a unity of self-consciousness. In neurosis, this journey is thwarted. As bad mothering impinges on a child about to begin the journey of life, disallowing him his freedom, his intuitive reaching out in authentic comportment is jarred. The child feels as though he has emptied the mother of her concern for him. Frightened, he feels coerced to give to her because he feels that he has, in fact, taken from her. Yet the more he gives, the less she reciprocates—either with respect to her own giving to him or with respect to her accepting of his gift to her. To overcome this negative experience, compensatory human presences who, in part, allow reciprocation and, in part, serve as touchstones of reality are required. Then alone can the rejected child, or the rejected child *within* the seemingly mature person, feel the freedom to grow and, ultimately, to achieve maturity based on recognition of his own powers.

In relatedness, the diverse fragments of the *I* are drawn together; negative endopsychic structures are dissolved. Through trust, a person learns to tolerate his own weakness and, in self-understanding, to restore his own strength. His natural healing powers effect transition from an essentially inward-directed *I* to an essentially outward-directed *I*. Thereby, the person is freed authentically to explore his now liberated inner creative resources—an inwardness which I have not yet dealt with and of which I subsequently speak at length. In treating the divided self, I am concerned at this time only with pathologically endopsychic structures. In any event, resistance to healing is powerful. The strength with which the *I* clings to the seeming security of the womb symbol of complete inwardness is not readily countervailed. In self-deception, a person desperately holds to the checks and balances by which a specious *I*—appearing to itself sturdy though, in actuality, both non-resilient and fragile—had been retained as final bulwark against what it fears most: depersonalization or loss of personhood.

Indeed, the endopsychic world grounds the stratagems whereby an at least partially viable *I* may function. Nevertheless, when in this condition, the ultimately repressed object is the image of the womb itself. That a person might search and grow and speak with his true rhythms, this object must be incorporated into an expanding and ever-richer consciousness. As repressed, the object is that factor toward which, when the world is felt as intolerably harsh, the afflicted person is further and further drawn. Thus, when that person requires sufficient protection, the dynamics of psychopathology permits a completely regressed libidinal *I* to be split off from the orally needy *I*, which never ceases to suffer from the torments inflicted on it by an antilibidinal *I*. In order for the direction of its movement to be reversed, this regressed *I* must be activated by caring presences. When, indeed, another truly loving person, by the authenticity of his care, his concern, and his respect, constitutes himself a symbolic substitute for this symbolic womb, the foundation for healing—hence, the ground for personal fruition—is laid. For, then, those *I*-components which had originally been split from the primordial *I* of the infant can be fused into new unity. Now all disparate *I*'s are blended with whatever remains intact in the residual *I*: the *I* which, despite the ravages which originally led to fragmentation, retains its power for external object orientation. When, accordingly, the need for an oral *I* to bind the person to an intrinsically hostile inner world is dissolved, rebirth into a more challenging yet truer reality supervenes. The *I* need no longer flee from good objects as though they cannot be trusted. Its distortions are clarified. Now the person who embodies that *I* can accurately distinguish the truly good from the truly bad, so that he can henceforth realistically orient himself in his world.

In sum, the endopsychic world (in its pathologic aspects only) is created to compensate for a reality experienced, as from time to time it must be by all persons, as excessively harsh. In this sense, the *pathologic* endopsychic world is but an illusory garden of Eden wherein he who would escape the torments of reality seeks refuge. Ultimately, were one to dwell in this world, a world into which those who refuse to enter vibrant reality are ever tempted to retreat, one would annihilate oneself within a symbolic womb; all one's energies would be drawn toward illusory security within that garden. Yet every person, no matter how neurotic, resists this virtual death; and he resists with every power of life with which he was endowed. Loving friends are living symbols of reinstated but now more truly caring parents. By the mothering a person is given, he symbolically reinstates womb and breast—those symbols of tenderness and care. Should he not tarry with such symbols, he enwombs himself as in a cocoon, that he may so metamorphose himself as spiritually to be reborn. By the fathering a person is given, when fathering is effectively interwoven with mothering, he is led more valiantly to accept the challenges of reality, that he might adventure forth into larger realms and prepare the way for provoking his own creative powers: that he might thenceforth shape for himself entirely new realms and, thereby, enlarge reality itself.

(*b*) Delusions

Certain implications for a theory of the divided self, later to be woven with the human ontology which I am constructing here, follow from this concept of pathologic endopsychic structures. Thus, in the paranoid state,[12] one experiences oneself not as free agent but as controlled in one's acts by forces which one cannot influence. The paranoid person perceives these forces to flow unconditionally from each person who is significant to him. This perception originates in the coercion which was exercised by his family, and is perpetuated through a process of transference. Such forces are never understood as themselves caused by what the afflicted person is empowered reciprocally to affect. Thus, he accepts as absolutely binding all commands and directives. He disallows such interpretive flexibility as would stem from an acknowledgment of the truly subtle context wherein they actually arise. It is this context which he cannot accurately perceive. Normally, a person feels that choices are always available, in every situation in which he might find himself; and that he may freely opt, despite the contingencies of life, for one choice or another. But the paranoid person senses himself to be irrevocably determined. In his every act, he feels himself to be shaped by factors which so press in upon him that, for him, absolute certainty never reigns regarding a destiny which he perceives as never altered by his own will; but, rather, as determined by the tyranny exercised over him of strategies practiced in a monolithically controlling family of unchallenged authority. I do not formulate a criterion whereby the objective status of these stratagems may be ascertained in their specific qualities, their mode of exercise, and their actual rationale. Rather, I only suggest a phenomenologic account of the paranoid experience of renunciation of will. For such a person, the *actual* intimidation by others peculiarly *reduces* the felt precariousness of existence. For an authentic life fraught with risk, a life which, open-ended, is often joyful, adventuresome, and self-created, a specious though perhaps harrowing certainty is substituted. Once *his* reality has collapsed, owing to unfortuitous *subsequent* experience, the paranoid is in panic. He is helpless, uprooted, and alone. To avoid this state, he is forever (though unconsciously) synthesizing the data of his experience into a single, coherent structure, eliminating all that he might otherwise perceive as arbitrary and controllable; and his every act is "justified" by reference to this structure, which for him is a veritable cosmos within the cosmos: constricted yet secure, tormenting yet certain, a larger cosmos unrecognized and unacknowledged. This structure "speaks" to him, ultimately as hallucinatory "introjects" of those original parental directives and prohibitions which unambiguously determine his acts, and effectively obliterate his agency. For these voices represent the final elimination of distance between himself and those whom he imagines to control him. By his attending them, he feels himself to be physically embedded in a parental matrix; it is as though his spiritual existence were determined by actual *physical* influences, influences which allow him no "space" in which, by his free decisions, he might move and live.

In its "pure," or hallucinated, state, paranoia is a defect in the capacity to listen, and, having listened, truly and fully, to understand. It is a failure to absorb into one's inmost being those voices which, ideally, ought to constitute for each person a caring presence which, however unheard, never ceases to hover about him: voices, surely, of benign parents, yet, beyond these, rhythms of a larger cosmos. Truly, paranoia is a condition wherein a smaller reality, a lesser cosmos, is substituted for a larger reality, a greater cosmos. It is as though the parental directives, experienced unconditionally, are "stuck" inside one's head—noisy voices, tyrannical images, an oppressive emptiness from which one cannot extricate oneself and penetrate to the still beyond wherein flows a deeper cosmic music. For the paranoid person is preoccupied with this noise, which interferes with his authentic listening, so that, for example, the spoken word means to him *precisely* what it was intended to mean; and the personal pronouns (you, he, and I) are used accurately and directly; and he deludes himself that the state of certainty which he has achieved is real, that it is not, as *in fact* for him it is, a fabric of stereotypes, a limited and specious reality—indeed, quite the reverse of the great philosophic systems, ranging from Plato to Spinoza, and from Liebniz to Hegel, systems rich and open, and expressing (in their cumulative meanings) the subtler, deeper character of reality. Surely, the paranoid fails to experience his own will, his power, his autonomy, his agency. Such experience as he has, and the apparently free decisions which result from it, are but illusion. That the paranoid person sense his deeper humanity, such illusion must dissolve. As a defect in listening, paranoia is, more fundamentally, an inability to trust. Initially, it is the loss of the power of the paranoid person to entrust himself to his parents. For, originally, *they* had failed to listen to *him*: to heed his needs, to nurture his sensibilities, to trust his being. Ultimately, paranoia is an impotence of entrusting. The paranoid person cannot perceive all that flows about him: the richness, the depths, the mystery. He fails to allow reality's texture to penetrate his being. Afraid that he is unworthy to be heard, so unattended was the cry within him that his gifts be accepted by his parents, and beyond them by the world at large—and these gifts are essentially his responses to vibrations stirred upon the chords of his sensitivity—he deems himself to be intrinsically unacceptable, and thus he henceforth stunts his power to give. Repression rather than dissolution prevails. For, somewhere, the struggle to remain spiritually alive persists. He merely distorts those gifts, either by diminishing them or, as in exaggerated preoccupation with words and wit, hypertrophying their expression. Surely, the music which, were he spiritually wholesome, would flow from his being is, in the end, filtered through that being from a larger presence. Each person is but a vehicle for transmitting these rhythms, a medium through which they pass. By them, he gives birth to the child of his sensitivity; he guards this child in trust as, deeply, he entrusts himself to his own inmost being.

Moreover, paranoia is induced not so much by parental proscriptions as by the larger social matrix of which the parents themselves are but vehicles. A subtle, intricate network of influences which never cease to work on and in the prospective victim, through parents, their surrogates, and those who supersede them, this matrix shapes itself into a constricted and rigid microcosm which the paranoid person mistakes for the greater world. Surely, not only, or even primarily, does unconditional parental authority, with its traumatic impact, fashion a paranoid state. Should one's sensibilities be sufficiently complex and developed, one becomes vulnerable to the myriad influences embedded in society, influences only *apparently* peripheral to the major parental focus. And the more refined one's sensibilities, the more insidiously they are impaired by the innumerable denials of their expression inflicted by a hostile milieu, a milieu which certainly extends beyond the immediate parental context. Granted: if parental tyranny were not operative, non-parental influences would lose their negative potency. On the other hand, non-parental factors tend to be "edited" depending on the strength of parental factors. But what I am stressing is the enormous though subtle power of the milieu in which the parents are embedded, and of which they are, for the paranoid, the most potent bearer. In this sense, a devastatingly "unconditional" authority will affect persons differently, depending on their respective sensitivities. The sensitive person experiences coercion in a multitude of ways; he detects subtleties of coercion inaccessible to one of limited sensitivity. At the same time, the sensitive person who is sufficiently robust may respond to these directives not so much by yielding as by denying the *pseudo*-intimacy of mutual parasitism exerted by a compact and homogeneous family; indeed, he may turn quite early in life toward the larger natural world. For to one of sufficient sensitivity the non-personal world is truly animated and vital. Every man has a primordial urge to commune with nature's voices. Certainly, there are extraordinary personalities who, surviving the most harrowing parental tyranny, have turned toward nature's gentle persuasions for reassurance; and they have indeed woven nature's materials into a new object, whether of science or of art or of philosophy. Herein, when nature herself acts as balm and corrective —even to powerfully distorting ways of perceiving—she creates a rare lucidity wherein distinctions may be drawn, whatever pain must be experienced, between the larger, more accepting world and the lesser, more rejecting world. In oscillation from one world to the other, consciousness is now veiled, imprisoned in a constricted self, and awareness is now sudden, luminous, and vibrant.

This concept of paranoia suggests a context in which the apparently dichotomous pair, free will and determinism, can be interpreted. Insofar as man is "determined" by forces (e.g., those of his non-self) which, impinging upon him, invade his very existence—like an alien body incorporated within his very self —he is "neurotic." When these forces become so potent as effectively to negate his autonomy, he becomes paranoid. The "healthy" person remains free to rule his own acts, to shape his own destiny. Yet there is a positive sense of determination. When combined with the idea of free will, the former sense is transformed into a single, inclusive, integral notion. Now insofar as man is truly agent, he is also truly patient. For the denial of authentic agency involves an attitude not so much of submission to forces construed as intrinsically inalterable as a certain orientation, ultimately of resistance, toward the genuinely unconditional forces which arise from our character conceived as bounded and finite, i.e., forces which are conditional with respect to finitude. On the other hand, agency becomes identical with patience, when I so give myself up in trust to the cosmic flow that, for the brief instant of eternity which humans are privileged to enjoy, I become truly attuned to nature. Here a tenuous harmony prevails: harmony ineluctably disrupted by the anguish of torn roots; harmony ever, if momentarily, restored in life's grand dialectic. Reared in the most ruthlessly authoritarian family, whether authority is wielded subtly or overtly, a child may, when his strength is wedded to his sensitivity, acquire capacity to extrude from his own "self" all that is alien to it, and continually to shape that self anew in transient but perfect harmonies: transient because of life's intrinsic tragedy; perfect as pointing toward transcendence beyond tragedy. A counterpoint of patience and agency unfolds: listening, yielding, and absorbing alternate with going toward, choosing, and shaping. In paranoia, this counterpoint is transposed from reality to fantasy. By degradation, the paranoid person converts, in perpetual interchange, both himself and his world to the status of persecutor and persecuted. Alternately, he experiences himself as all-power and as null-power. Yet these roles are equivalent. In either case, the determinist and the voluntarist components of the dialogue which man is empowered to hold with cosmos—a dialectic of participation and removal—are dissociated and abstracted rather than integrated and concretized. Indeed, the paranoid *himself* experiences himself alternately as absolutely determined and absolutely free. Yet, objectively considered, both modalities are fictions. For freedom and determinism are moments of the same process. In living experience, each is alternately transcended. Like Spinoza, I hold that perfect freedom consists in perfect accord with ultimate determination. But what is often felt to be freedom consists, in actuality, in regarding the necessities of existence under a limited perspective. In paranoia, this process is experienced as intrinsically segmented. Its conceptualization as unified is a prime task for a philosophy of the person; its implications touch on the deepest problems of human ontology.

(*c*) Resolutions

In these pages, the person has been construed as one who, in self-discovery—as he dwells in a community which, in turn, dwells in him, and with the collaboration of that community—reveals the truth about who he is. Such disclosure occurs through *re-collecting*: a process of gathering into coherence so that he knows he has a history and senses that he has a future. In effect, he rebuilds a past for himself, and owns that past. No longer does it haunt him. On the contrary, it reassures him and stimulates his quest for new discovery. The Unconscious is an *in-folding* of imagery deriving from both the external world and his own interiority. Residing in him yet wholly other to him, this Unconscious is a radical negation of all he explicitly is. Yet when deciphered it reveals itself as continuous with his awareness; and by this continuity, each person builds for himself a cosmology of inner and outer worlds as themselves a unity of harmonizing rhythms. By orchestrating the echoes which reverberate throughout the cosmos, he reveals, as an ontology, the mystery of his being in relationship with that of others. Every person is the locus wherein unfolds a multitude of relationships which endlessly spread, interiorly and exteriorly.

The psyche consists of resonances. Its topography is so constituted that it dynamically oscillates between two poles: a small consciousness, a communicating preconscious, a massive Unconscious which coils about consciousness and thereby so intensifies the rhythms of consciousness that the psyche must turn toward the other pole; a small Unconscious, a communicating preconscious, a massive consciousness which so coils about the Unconscious that *its* intensified rhythms potentiate a reversal toward the first pole. But should the Unconscious engulf consciousness, absolute psychopathology (like mob frenzy) prevails. Alternatively, *un-self-consciousness*—transcendency or authenticity—occurs when consciousness thoroughly absorbs the Unconscious. Yet, in another sense, the Unconscious is a matrix of "archetypal" presences; it is the source not only of distorted presences but of creativity as well—an endlessly flowing stream of forces. Moreover, by absorbing the stimuli which *would* break it, the Unconscious protects the finitude, and the integrity, of consciousness.

Each person so affects the other that he incorporates *his* presence, which includes unconscious resonances. Through these encounters, by psychic empathy, the Unconscious of each person is itself altered. But the dynamism of this process involves another topic in the theory of the person: the notions of transference and counter-transference in the larger context of an ontology of encounter. Fuller account of the Unconscious requires that one take up the problematic of interpersonal relations. Herein it is shown that the distinction between inner and outer collapses. Nothing is "without" unless it has passed through, and is refracted by, the prism of the "within." Yet all that is within is but an echo of that which flows about. The regions of the intrapsychic and the interpersonal are one.[13]

In his speculations, Freud unwittingly, and quite unobtrusively, shifts from a narrowly naturalistic concept of the psyche to a personalist and interpersonal orientation. In this shift, the social milieu in which a person dwells becomes not merely relevant but surely constitutive of significant regions of the Unconscious; and this milieu is fused with the elements associated with his instinctual makeup. By so transforming the context of his *stated* theory, the locus of processes wherein the person is deemed *essentially* to be located and from which he accordingly originates, Freud (in the last analysis, for this is the real import of the *Überich*) provides the foundations not only for an "archetypal" (i.e., Jungian) construal of the Unconscious but also for a pervasively social, and indeed *transcendentally* naturalistic, construal. Beginning with an empirical, and a simplistically contrived, mechanistic point of view, Freud is led, by the natural movement of his own principles—which would be evident were one fully to make explicit their immanent content—even beyond a naturalism in which its paradoxes and mysteries are acknowledged as *desiderata* for deeper scientific penetration (hence my use of the term "transcendental") toward what is in effect a transcendental *personalism*. But this topic, it must be admitted, Freud does not take up. It remains for those on whom his theory of the bifurcated psyche has had a profound impact, and who at the same time cannot accept even a humanistic interpretation of Freud's atheism, to assess, develop, and draw forth already latent but quite new meaning.

Freud's discovery of the Unconscious (more accurately, his rediscovery of what had already been perceived by Hegel, and by philosophers long before) has unquestionably led to a revolution, salutary despite its being fraught with certain already prevalent dangers—for what humanist could deny the potential destructiveness of all proposals for human control of human beings, an arrogance so readily overlooked today?—in techniques and approaches to psychotherapy. But a revolution (in a narrow sense) in the art of healing! For far more significantly, his discovery has immensely enriched a view of the person in which, contrary to many of Freud's own suppositions, *a tenderness of mutual giving*[14] rather than the harsh clashes between and within reciprocally demanding persons will in time assume a central role in any further development of a truly humane idea of an Unconscious—and indeed an idea which is both scientifically valid and philosophically satisfying. True only within far more restricted realms of human conduct than he could have known, his theory entails a notion of sociality which holds that societies of persons dwell within persons, that meaningful interior dialogue is conducted within persons, and that many kinds of social configurations, and an intricate web of relations between their components, are therein internalized. Surely, interpersonal relations reside *within* persons, both a network of deformed fragments of other selves, constituting a strange interior labyrinth, and the imprints of the integrities of other selves.

In conclusion, the concept of "resonances," originally based by Freud on a neurophysiologic paradigm of psychic activity, entails the postulation of a notion of the psyche in which persons, bound to one another by intimacy and empathy, transcending in their communions hitherto unimaginable stretches of space and time, and a notion surely requiring a deep reform of prevailing concepts of matter (a reform which is occurring today in the heart of contemporary physics itself), is thus to be construed. In their sympathetic relatedness, in which each person resonates to rhythms indigenous to the other, while incorporating these rhythms as variations on those already operative within him, the "center" of each is displaced beyond each, for it lies in the *interstices* of persons, to a transcendent Center, a Center composed of many centers. And *this* Center is that ultimate power of unifying all creatures, both within themselves and between themselves, as the integrity of each and the integrity of all, which alone may be identified (alien as this view is to that explicitly held by Freud, indeed at the very moment when he strives so vigorously and with the force of his own integrity to annihilate any theistic concept) with the spirit of God. *L'amor che move il sole e l'altre stelle*! [15]

NOTES

1. In this chapter, I draw extensively upon my article "Bifurcated Psyche and Social Self: Implications of Freud's Theory of the Unconscious," in *Person and Com-*

munity: A Philosophical Exploration, ed. Robert J. Roth, S.J. (New York: Fordham University Press, 1975), pp. 43–62.

2. Throughout this chapter, I am indebted to Paul Ricoeur, *Freud and Philosophy: An Essay on Interpretation*, trans. Denis Savage (New Haven: Yale University Press, 1970).

3. Freud is never consistent regarding whether this is the way in which the world is, in fact, experienced, or whether, on the contrary, it is thus actually constituted. Roughly, his position would be William Jamesian.

4. Whitehead's concept of "perishing" can, I believe, be readily adapted to Freud's theory. See in particular Freud's "Mourning and Melancholia," no. 8 of the "Papers on Metapsychology," in his *Collected Papers*, trans. Joan Riviere, 5 vols. (New York: Basic Books, 1959), IV 152–70.

5. Imago is a term used loosely by Freud, and more exactly by Jung, to designate a composite of perceptual, appetitional, volitional, and cognitive factors which express a particular experience of a particular region of the world, especially of significant other persons.

6. Freud speculates on the origin of psychosomatic symptomatology without clearly weaving it into his conceptual framework.

7. Freud's therapeutic aim—where there is unconsciousness, so there will be consciousness—is strongly Nietzschean.

8. Heideggerian philosophy, together with Whiteheadian, can clarify and enrich the general context of ideas in which the Freudian Unconscious may be developed more convincingly.

9. Freud's ideas most relevant to this chapter appear in his "Papers on Metapsychology," *Collected Papers*, IV 11–170.

10. For extensive development of a theory of internal relationships, elaborated, to some extent, in this chapter, see Harry Guntrip, *Schizoid Phenomena, Object–Relations, and the Self* (New York: International Universities Press, 1968); and especially W. Ronald D. Fairbairn, *An Object–Relations Theory of the Personality* (New York: Basic Books, 1954).

11. For the discussion which ensues, namely, that pertaining to "object relationships," I am indebted to Guntrip and Fairbairn. See note 10.

12. From the point of view of my own theory of the person, I incorporate here parts of the perceptive analysis by Leo Kovar, "A Reconsideration of Paranoia," *Psychiatry: Journal for the Study of Interpersonal Processes*, 29, No. 3 (August 1966), 289–305.

13. This is a theme beautifully developed in a manuscript by Dr. Harry Bone. See his "The Inter-Personal and the Intra-Psychic," presidential address to The William Alanson White Psycho-analytic Society, May 26, 1959.

14. See Ian Suttie, *The Origins of Love and Hate* (New York: Julian, 1966).

15. Dante Alighieri, *La Divina Commedia*, "Paradiso," 33.145.

2

RHYTHM AND SYMBOL: A HERMENEUTIC OF THE HUMAN BODY

PREAMBLE

To provide a context for understanding unconscious processes, I propose a theory of the human body which bears on certain connections between consciousness and the Unconscious. From a philosophic point of view, I suggest some relationships between a medical perspective on the body and a broader perspective. Just as psychoanalysis, as a doctrine of the bifurcated psyche, adds a practical hermeneutic to a philosophic approach, amplifying and enriching that approach, so medicine functions analogously for the human body. A medical approach, philosophically construed, illuminates, in terms of a deeper probing of body acts, *l'amor che move il sole e l'altre stelle.*

In its lived motility, the human body bears witness to all human action. Open to disease, it reveals its hidden content in the physician's consulting room. Through his physiognomic symbols, man reveals his inner self there. By a medically informed approach, one deciphers messages inscribed upon that physiognomy. Thereby, one understands the oscillations between human strength and human infirmity, and restores a more wholesome bodily balance. To conceptualize this approach, I examine the following polarities: lived body and thingly body, balance and disorientation, infirmity and strength, plasticity and rigidity, motility and inertness. And to evaluate these polarities, I contrast the notions of physiognomy, and its correlative idea of (body) symbol, with physique and *its* correlative idea of (body) rhythm.

A • PHYSIQUE AS RHYTHM

PREFATORY

Imprinted on the human body is its entire history. Silent witness to numberless influences, a body records its every experience as a nuance, gross or subtle, of the particular rhythms of its associated physique. Manifesting its history as physiognomic clusterings of those rhythms, it presents those clusterings as symbolic representations of the body's encoded secrets. Preeminently, the medical clinic affords the proper situation for deciphering whatever secrets, in condensed form, are engraved on one's physiognomy. Expressed as (subjective) symptoms and (objective) signs, the concealed rhythms which uniquely unfold within each person might, through appropriate clinical intervention, be felicitously altered.

By "physique," I mean the dynamic organization of a person's bodily structures and functions, and the development of this organization. By "physiognomy," I mean the body's features and lineaments, the physical contours which express its constitutive processes. Physique comprises such powers and rhythms as manifest themselves in physiognomy; physiognomy comprises both symbols and interpretive fabric through which physique reveals itself and, accordingly, can be discerned. First, I examine physique in terms of rhythm. Next,

I examine physiognomy in terms of symbol. Thirdly, I consider those bodily imbalances and disorientations which express the body's frailty and, ultimately, its rigidity, inertness, and thingliness in their interplay with such balances and orientations as express its strength, plasticity, motility, and, in the end, lived character. Finally, I indicate how messages encoded in physiognomic symbols disclose physique's rhythms.

(*a*) Rhythms of Reflection

As lived, human body—the physique—is locus of reflective activity. Mirroring its own processes, that body reflects an Imago of its contours into itself.[1] Inscribed in such processes, the Imago is a causal agent in the body's subsequent vicissitudes. Every corporeal feature thus registers itself. The representation thereby framed incorporates elements derived from sources other than the proximate origin of reflection. For no individual body can be sharply demarcated from the physical activities which constitute its circumambient milieu. An environment likewise contributes to the composition of the representation. At bottom, only the entire matrix of relationships which a human body sustains with other bodies is the complete source of reflection. A particular body is merely its focal seat, never its exclusive source. What are *re*-presented in the body Imago are those presences which originate from the indefinitely large assemblage of physical entities in which the body is embedded, entities from which it derives its sustenance.

Reflection is the manifestation of the arrangement, the *balances*, which a given human body establishes vis-à-vis other bodies, human or non-human. As such, reflection expresses the way in which body orients itself, hence, roots itself in its world. Issuing directives to the body, reflection secures new modes of balance. The Imago associated with reflection includes an intricate schema of this orientation, a schema in which every facet of the body's interwovenness with other bodies is registered. Varying grades of contrasting intensity with respect to the elements composing the schema are associated with differing degrees and types of awareness. From luminous consciousness to subliminal sensing, the chiaroscuro of awareness corresponds to differential values for maintaining overall balance of the body's diverse regions—i.e., as those regions are related to other bodies. In consequence, a multitude of states of reflexivity form the components of the body Imago. For bodily processes are exceedingly intricate. The most minute of these processes may be the most relevant. And influences stemming from other seemingly remote bodies may themselves be of a high order of relevance even in *their* seemingly minute facets. A person's body reaches out toward endlessly complicated regions. Conversely, those regions intrude upon his body, providing data for incorporation within its synthesizing acts. Reflection notes these variegated influences, influences which, ranging from the proximate to the remote, exhibit all gradations of complexity.

Only such psychic elements as can be woven into a relatively simple and well-ordered manifold of consciousness escape the fate of being relegated to the Unconscious. And the Unconscious is directly implicated with the body, the rhythms of which exhibit, as inscribed on them, subtle variations of marvelous design. For hovering about every physical process is an aura of resonances which no conventional technique of identification is competent fully to disclose. Nuanced in myriad ways, this unconscious fabric is apparently of endless complexity. Though penetrable by empirical inquiry, it can never be fully traversed. A labyrinth which encloses chambers concealed within chambers, it houses an intricately entangled Ariadne's thread.

Even in inert body, a mere residue which preserves but a few isomorphisms with living body, different staining techniques disclose hitherto unrevealed facts, histologic structures which cannot have been inferred on the basis of previously used techniques. Such stains are analogous to different perspectives on macroscopic bodies. They disclose structures which, under other perspectives, are concealed and, so to speak, dormant. Illuminating now this aspect of body, now that aspect, an indefinitely large number of such techniques may be used. In every instance, what is revealed is the deposition, as a complicated texture of potential histologic structures, of the echoes of lived body. No technique is sufficiently refined to capture more than a minuscule portion of these echoes.

(*b*) Unconscious Rhythms

The Unconscious is the sphere of such labyrinthine resonances. Neither identifiably corporeal nor identifiably psychic, these resonances occupy a position intermediate between the frankly physical and the frankly mental. Could it not be that when they have passed beyond a certain threshold of "coarseness" and have become sufficiently subtilized—"sublimated," in Freud's term—such resonances become identical with feeling? And when they are even more "etherealized," might they not become feeling's refined extension, namely, mentation itself? Conversely, could it not be that certain psychic pulses, "coarsened" or weighty with bodily import, hence, assimilated to body, so press into body that they are woven with its *cruder* reflective resonances? Is not the Unconscious, in the end, that locus of personal activity wherein unfold transformations between physical resonances and psychic resonances: the mediation of passage from one sphere to another?

When the physical is converted into the psychic, body tension alternating with body relaxation can cumulatively be transmuted into intense feelings of joy. When the psychic is converted into the physical, anxieties can be detached from their perceived causes, transformed into tensions experienced as located in a particular region of the body, thence manifested as an objectively discernible physical alteration of the body. For body resonances and mind resonances are interconvertible. Yet to allow for reciprocal transformation, such resonances must pass through a series of stages. Physical processes are continuous with mental processes; and human activity is multi-layered. Each lamina is stratified upon the next. The totality constitutes a reciprocal merging of the physical with the psychic. Such activity orchestrates myriad resonances, resonances which are refined and resonances which are coarse. Fine resonances tend toward the psychic;

coarse resonances, toward the physical. Every instance of human experience exhibits a mental aspect and a physical aspect. Limits of a single, integral activity, psyche and soma imperceptibly blend into one another.

Associated with every region of organic existence is some kind of feeling. And numberless loci of feeling are vectorially directed toward a single point, consciousness itself. Inheriting, but intensifying, this immanent intentionality, consciousness directs *itself* in purposive fashion toward external objects which are contemporaneous with its own corporeal locus. No matter how primitive the feeling, its objective is always consciousness: an object which, once attained, transports the person to higher states of self-realization. On the whole, feelings grow and coalesce. Even isolated feelings, associated with different regions of an organism, tend, in the long run, to blend, to shape new patterns, and to point beyond themselves. In this process, great intensity of highly differentiated feeling is attained. Matrix of such transmuted feeling, consciousness itself does not cease to grow and transform itself. Efflorescing into self-consciousness, consciousness coils in upon itself, and mirrors itself to itself. Herein, body's own reflective propensity is replicated. For feeling tends ceaselessly to metamorphose itself into more refined feeling. Suffused with endlessly ramifying reflexivity, the body constitutes itself a fabric of reflections of varying orders, a texture which duplicates, in transmuted form, body's own subtler patterns. As such, each stratum of reflection is layered upon the next; numberless reflexive modalities are created. Depending on specific experiences, different contents of reflection are continually relegated to different regions of this reflective fabric. The entirety is orchestrated into an immensely complicated texture of dynamically interwoven parts. Accordingly, mentation pervades the whole body. Like the body's rhythms, the mind's rhythms are richly variegated.

(*c*) Rhythmic Transformations

In his physique, and in those mental aspects which accompany physique, a person is a meshwork of integrated yet ramifying processes which rhythmically unfold: he is a locus of activities interwoven as cycles, epicycles, and systems of cycles which, in replicating itself from instant to instant of his duration and in transmitting a living image of that matrix to a new locus, amplifies and reconstitutes those rhythms. Powers latent in any phase of his existence, or even concealed throughout his existence, are potentiated as altogether new modulations of former rhythmic patterns. Utterly novel cyclic modalities are fashioned from time to time. For, on the one hand, a person is self-replicating; hence, he is a "theme" which preserves its resilience and its vitality, though on it are inscribed the most diverse variations. On the other hand, as self-mutating, a person projects himself beyond what he had been to an instance of a radically new type. Naturally, such transformations can occur only within certain limits. However, a style of existence which seems imperishably rooted in the biologic and social conditions of his life may in personal or cosmic crises—in his moments of imbalance and disorientation—be displaced to a style which had quite unpredictably been germinating within that existence. Only in retrospect, when what is now but germinal has evolved to living actuality, can a hitherto unpredicted style be specified.

When such imbalance and disorientation occur, both psyche and soma are affected. Inextricably interwoven, these spheres are each composed of intricately organized pulses of feeling. As integral rhythmic complex, a single sphere of human activity emerges amid the endless flowings back and forth, and their attendant metamorphoses, between psyche and soma. Despite ineluctable perishings, a central thread of identity remains intact. Ever weaving new strands of experience, this thread thickens in coils of constantly changing design to shape a sturdy overall pattern which, on the whole, tends to be an enduring configuration. Visible representation of this invariant assemblage of rhythmic pulses, an assemblage on which, however, the most marvelously diverse variations inscribe themselves, the human body registers within itself every detail of this process. Perpetually fluctuating, the body's parts synergize themselves into novel configurations. Every person is a locus of such transformations, dissolutions, and reconstitutings as are now mutually synchronous, now mutually discordant. In alternation, enduring balances are shaped, and enduring balances are shattered.

Enmeshing and interpenetrating, the rhythms composing these balances weave fabrics of varying design. In the end, they shape a single, unitary rhythm which expresses the internal coherence of a person's diverse parts: his particular commitments, the ways by which he sends himself into the world. Vulnerable to manifold forces, every person moves forth from his self's center with emotions constituted by rhythms which are graded into nuances of myriad arrangement and motility. Though he experiences crisis, vicissitudes which are anguished or ecstatic, profound metamorphosis, and moods of the most diverse kinds, a person nonetheless persists in some characteristic way of resonating to his world. Pervading his every component rhythm, this idiosyncratic quality marks his very individuality. Now experiencing autonomy, now experiencing himself to be determined from without, the person continually recommits himself with the force of his individuality. Ever enveloping him, his rhythmic activities stretch about him, within him, and beyond him. Radiating back toward him, through him, and from him—by the symbols of his own creations—they orchestrate endlessly new patterns; they allow him to shape ever-new symbols. And from internal silences which pulse with subtle, ineffable contrasts, man's natural vitality, his creative exuberance, breaks forth again and again.

B • PHYSIOGNOMY AS SYMBOL

(*a*) Symbols as Congealed Rhythms

In every instance, the person is powerful with rhythmicality. Never merely a passive observer, essentially inert and yielding, he is intrinsically actor, agent, and witness. Empowered alternately to give and to receive, he, in correlative, complementary, and mutually presupposing acts, both bodies forth and ideates forth. Always he goes toward another, imprinting himself and thereby perpetuating his rhythms; always he receives another, allowing new depositions to weave themselves into those rhythms. Man accepts and man proclaims; he steps back from the world, and he goes forth into the world. In both cases, he takes up a stance. Always he acts veridically. By his body and by his mind, a person is doubly powerful. Integrated as a single activity, this dual power multiplies itself into myriad forms and aspects. And thus to diversify implies both potency-in-act and act itself. By his very potency, man is an internally connected, profoundly coherent, absolutely integral, and, in the end, always indiscerptible ground for acts which themselves are concrete, specific, and divisible. For, inextricably linked, potency and act constitute a single creative stream which, as it flows, transfigures itself into myriad symbols, each a congealing of some rhythmic complex. Effervescent source of the most variegated expressions, man draws forth endlessly marvelous representations of his inmost essence.

Earlier, I distinguished between man's physique and his physiognomy. Analyzed in terms of *rhythm*, physique was briefly examined. Now I comment upon physiognomy, analyzable in terms of *symbol*. In his status as potency-in-act, man is, from the side of potency, a constellation of rhythms exhibiting the characteristics I have indicated. Yet from the side of act, every rhythmic complex crystallizes as a structure, even though such a structure might endure but momentarily. Functions and structures are interwoven. In the end, they are inseparable. Dissociated from function, structure is merely an inert and static existent, simply the residue of rhythmic activity. In its association with function, however, it is converted from existent to symbol, manifesting that activity as immanent within it as grounding its very possibility. Insofar as it is construed as expressing lived body apart from the rhythms inscribed on it, no organic structure can even be conceived. For, as organic, that factor is woven integrally with other factors, all comprising in their unity a symbolic–rhythmic complex.

Thus the contours of a face, the lineaments of a gesture, the composition of a gait are all structures, each mobile in its own fashion, which, representing complicatedly enmeshed organic processes, are the outward form of those processes. No less does the makeup of every organ of the body represent such processes. For, in general, the body can be conceived as an assemblage of structures, structures which enclose one another in the most diversified topologic patterns—and this in every instance of the encounterable configurations of rhythm. And, always, such structures can be construed as symbols of bodily activity, activity patterned in rhythmic ways. Indeed, medical diagnosis interprets this fabric of symbols, isolating the relevant structures by using appropriate diagnostic techniques to detect the underlying processes and their variegated derangements.

Correctly deciphered, every such physiognomic symbol portends layer upon layer of meaning, each formulable in terms of some set of rhythmic patterns.

Sufficiently traced, this complex of meanings ultimately encompasses the entire lived body. The whole physique, with its associated laminae of reflective activity, pours itself, in condensed form, into each symbol. Hence, the final referent of every aspect of physiognomy is the entire person, though always the person under some perspective of his activity. Moreover, though particular features of that activity are more saliently represented in a given symbol than others, all features, including many relegated to a penumbral background, are incorporated. In a simple smile, for example, inspection reveals perhaps a curious tautness about the lips, a quiver of the facial musculature, a hesitancy and lack of fluidity in the movements by which the smile is executed. No conventional network of classificatory ideas can render the full import of that smile. Numberless past experiences unique to the particular individual are inscribed upon it. Inclinations toward laughter, defenses against laughter, may mobilize one another to engender the tentative quality of the smile; preoccupation with a private experience of absurdity, an experience never before shared with another because deemed forbidden, together with concern lest this proscribed component of that smile be revealed, may result in the tautness; a certain nostalgic sadness mingling with enjoyment may give rise to the quivering. For the texture of experience relevant to any fleeting gesture is enormously intricate and richly nuanced in endlessly subtle ways. And the phenomenon of overdetermination prevails. Every complex of bodily factors manifesting itself in a particular physiognomic symbol also expresses itself through innumerable other such symbols, though limited classes of symbols are *privileged* routes for disclosing particular rhythmic constellations. By "privileged route," I mean a sequence of structures upon which those constellations etch themselves most visibly and dramatically. Nevertheless, *every* symbol, in principle, incorporates the imprints of *all* physical activity.

(*b*) Reflective Symbols

Amid the multitude of objects with which he associates, every person establishes fluctuant patterns of feeling, migration, and orientation. With the rhythms of his physique, he roots himself among those objects. Therein, he proceeds to articulate his world. As he thus locates himself, the person carves out the texture of reality most relevant to his activities, illuminating those regions he deems essential for his own self-preservation and for the enhancement of the quality of his life. In this process, he creates a fabric of symbols, a fabric woven of the rhythms of his physique. In effect, he shapes his physiognomy. Feeling *physically* his own body as that body is actually lived, and grasping *conceptually* the diverse patterns which his lived body might exemplify in its modes of both body organization and relatedness to other bodies, the person achieves varying states of at-homeness in his world. By this action of his corporeity, as he *loco*motes himself, and thereby shifts the locale of that activity from one region to another, he conceptualizes and indeed constitutes, as a spatio-temporal-material manifold, the unity of his experience. Pervading his every action within this manifold are his diverse intentions. For as he stretches out toward the world with his body and joins himself to it—in effect, in-tending that world—he discerns ever-new facets to which he can relate. In this process, the unity of his experience exhibits itself as dynamic and changing. Self-diversification alternates with self-reunification. The unity is continually solidified and made more concrete.

Never ceasing to reflect on the ways in which his body is in the world, the person incorporates in his reflections both physical and conceptual factors. With respect to the physical, he apprehends things in their encountered actuality—i.e., in their qualities, their resistances, and their relationships. With respect to the conceptual, he apprehends the patterns which those things illustrate. Both components interweave to constitute the hybrid feeling on which every reflection grounds itself. Each component reinforces the other to constitute the affective side of comportment. Thus bearing himself with all his powers toward his world, every person integrates these factors as he approaches that world: now from this position, now from that. Experiencing both emotions which originate within him and "commotions"[2] which express the impact upon him of another, he feels the stirrings of the rhythms of his physique; and he translates those rhythms into the motions of the symbols of his physiognomy.

Through his continual self-reflecting acts, each person transforms himself from a mere recipient into a potent force, a *datio* rather than a mere datum. As such, he constantly gives himself to himself and to another. He presents his power symbolically as a scheme awaiting interpretation; he presents himself to be understood—to be *heard* as he truly is. In this sense, every individual makes a claim upon all whom he encounters. He so *loco*motes himself with respect to the other—establishing different loci wherein he can feel both his emotions and the "commotions" evoked by his encounters—that he may fully reveal himself to that other. He is in quest of disclosing his own authentic being; and he never desists from striving, that others may know him in that being. In thus presenting himself reflexively, the person *re*-presents himself as a symbolic fabric, hence, as the product of increasingly elaborate reflective activity: activity which modifies and remodifies the body and, thereby, perpetually alters and indeed metamorphoses his ways of being in the world. In this manner, the varied facets of experience are joined in ever-new combinations, combinations which continually reinforce unity.

(*c*) Physique–Physiognomy Interactions

Reflexivity entails the mirroring of physiognomy into physique, hence, the transformation of the latter by that mirroring. As such, it involves the imprinting into the actual reflective makeup of another person of the symbols by which the physiognomy presents itself. Indeed, a dialectical interplay prevails between these symbols of presence . . . and compresence. I say "compresence" for in every encounter between reflective bodies the rhythms associated with the symbolisms of those bodies enmesh and interpenetrate. Truly, among those persons who actually encounter, the feelings of all are absorbed into the feelings of each.

Transmitted through the symbolisms of a person's presence, and always in the context of his empathic encounters, these feelings durably inscribe themselves on every person who confronts them. For the person is dyadic in his essential makeup. His unique self-identity cannot be construed apart from his participation in an interpersonal field. Nor can it fail to be constituted in part by processes internalized within him which are derived from the actions of others who likewise participate in that field.

Since the body of a person is reflexively constituted, schemes of balance and imbalance in the body will replicate themselves on every level of reflection, ranging from the primordially unconscious to the most articulated regions of consciousness. Conversely, balances and imbalances in his interpersonal relations will likewise transmit themselves to his body, in every sphere of his being. Moreover, the symbols of his physiognomy and the rhythms of his physique will each exhibit the same scheme. For the human body is a plexus of intricately arranged acts, acts which realize their latent potentialities over a wide range of magnitude, intensity, and complexity of structural and functional composition. Unified into a single integral reflective action, these often disparate and seemingly incongruous elements are affected by the shifting directions of that action. Its orientations and disorientations are imparted to them as an ever-changing fabric of balances and imbalances.

C • HERMENEUTICS OF THE BODY

(*a*) Co-adaptations

The human body consists in interwoven acts. For each act, some antecedent act perishes into its ever-shifting composition, contributing specific tensions which demand resolution. For each act, tensions mount toward their characteristic climaxes; and as that act deposits its imprints into succeeding acts, climaxes dissolve. Composed of numerous strands of component acts, every act exhibits a multitude of factors which must come to confluence. Synthesized into potent and unitary action, these factors recombine, realign themselves, and, in novel shape, disperse themselves throughout the organism. And the contours of no body act are unaffected by the body itself. An overall configuration imparts itself to its every constituent element. At times, this organic activity is diffuse; at times, it is cohesive. But, always, it is a fabric wherein new plexuses of activity arise. In every human body, some dynamic form transmits itself: a form composed of numberless subordinate forms, themselves ordered in varying schemes of subordination and superordination. By this form, specific event-patterns are perpetuated, patterns on which, nonetheless, diverse variations never cease to inscribe themselves.

The variegated acts which exemplify such patterns distribute themselves throughout the body. Interweaving as rhythmic orchestrations, they alternately disperse, coalesce, condense, liquefy, entwine in new cadences, achieve intensity, subside, shape strange contrapuntal processions, retreat, advance, create marvelous fugal arrangements, resolve themselves into starkly etched lines. Ever impinging, these rhythms adjust to one another in manifold ways. They integrate, coordinate, and fragment; they mutually reinforce, inhibit, intersect, enhance, negate, and overlap. Rhythmic crescendos rise and vanish; rhythmic interludes of every kind and quality prevail. Always, rhythms are dynamically co-adapted—but in astoundingly diversified concatenation. In many layers, body's lineaments reveal these unfoldings.

In general, schemes of co-adaptation express themselves in varying kinds of balance. In such schemes as are off-balance, an ecologic configuration tends to break up rather than to sustain itself. It fails to combine with other configurations to produce ever-more-stable and inclusive organic unities, unities of contrasting yet complementary parts. In principle, the human body is a constellation of bio-acts through which threads of specialized bio-acts—a veritable neural fabric—so ramify that they coordinate diverse parts into a smoothly functioning whole. Thereby, actions associated with all bodily regions are synchronized into an integral unity of action. Hovering about key centers which direct the workings of this neural fabric, but spreading beyond those centers to envelop the entire fabric, and, more subtly, to pervade the entire body in which that fabric is embedded, are resonances of reflection. By *their* characteristic dynamisms, these resonances function to enable the body to balance, i.e., to equilibrate, itself more effectively.

In a rhythmic context, affinities which are subtle or obscure disclose themselves, and, likewise, repulsions which are equally various: a veritable labyrinth of rhythmicality. Within this labyrinth, the successive schemes of ecologic balance and imbalance arise from resonances which are at times confluent and at times divergent. Everywhere, transductions from one part of the body to another appear. Matrix for such co-evolving strands as, in the end, shape the human body, this great ferment of lapsings into instability and emergings into stability instills into the body's associated reflective acts ever-new content.

(*b*) Disease as Imbalance

To illustrate the interwovenness of those bio-acts which constitute generalized imbalance, I sketch some characteristics of three quite unrelated illnesses (according to current pathology), illnesses in which balance is not effectively maintained: labyrinthine irritation (like Ménière's disease), disseminated (multiple) sclerosis, certain forms of schizophrenia. In these pathologic conditions, the common factor is an element which concerns overall bodily, and consequently psychic, orientation.

In labyrinthine irritation of whatever origin, both vertigo, with its associated symptoms of nausea and vomiting, and malfunctioning facial nerve manifestations including a peripherally originating nystagmus (or pseudo-nystagmus) may be present. Paresthesias of various kinds arise, paresthesias associated with the anxiety which supervenes when balance is significantly threatened. In general, any kind of intense focusing, sensory or psychic, can disequilibrate a person. To compensate for thwarted normal and spontaneous balance patterns, one shapes tenuous new patterns for balancing body movements. Owing to the precariousness of maintaining such patterns, the world acquires for that person an unreal quality. For him, events are out of focus, and not quite coordinated. Hence, he superimposes new schemes of orientation, both perceptual and conceptual: schemes which induce a sort of quasi-balance.

In disseminated (multiple) sclerosis, a disease in which plaques of local demyelinization spread diffusely and seemingly at random throughout the central nervous system, neurasthenic allergic-like reactions occur. Generalized paresthesias, symptoms of motor impairment, dizziness, and sudden, alarming, inchoate, and almost inexplicable states of disorientation appear, states associated with severe anxiety and depression. Depending on which part of the central nervous system is affected by sclerotic plaques, organ malfunctioning occurs, and even, for those organs composed of erectile tissue and innervated by the autonomic nervous system, frank impotence. In addition, symptoms similar to those associated with labyrinthine disease arise, symptoms which are of central nervous system origin. Indeed, so erratically do lesions present themselves that ever-new schemes of orientation must be devised.

In schizophrenia, whatever the nature of the initiating lesion or its locus, both perceptual and conceptual distortions occur, distortions which induce all manner of disorientation. To conceal imbalance, hallucinatory systems are mobilized, systems which effect specious new types of balance. Bizarre changes of gait, facial expression, and posture supervene. Incongruities between various behavioral manifestations of bodily and psychic functions reflect the deeper imbalances which pervade those functions. Elaborate psychic and gestural systems are created to maintain the illusion of customary modes of balance. So desperate is the attempt to restore equilibrium that a mythology is constructed, a mythology which both assigns to the sufferer an altogether novel status in the scheme of things and, in effect, frames a new cosmology to account for that revised status. Accompanying the quest for new roots are a characteristic alternation between feelings of intense loneliness and intolerably low self-esteem, on the one hand, and the avoidance of these feelings by the substitution of delusional systems, hallucinatory reactions, and grotesque posturings, on the other. Such intricate techniques are devised, and endlessly elaborated, to conceal this quest that an entirely new life style is constituted. Yet, properly interpreted, this style discloses the very authenticity of the quest.

By these examples, I show how a common ingredient runs through certain disorders of personal being, an ingredient which pertains to the theme of balance. In each instance, physiognomic symbols encode the various strata of malfunctioning—at times, in complicated ways. And, always, the individual, with greater or lesser desperation, strives to secure himself in more stable schemes of at-homeness; he manifests those strivings in physiognomic symbols. Through medicine, one reveals the dynamics of the pathogenic agents which induce those congeries of symptoms, and discloses how each disease both disturbs balance and aims at compensating for imbalance. Indeed, all pathologic conditions of mind or body function analogously. They distort existing patterns of balance; yet they introduce more or less adequate compensatory patterns. Consequent to its disclosure of such compensatory ecologic systems, medicine aims at restoring "normal" modes of co-adaptation with respect to both a person's parts and his overall relationships to his natural and social milieu. Through philosophy, one aims at evaluating diverse schemes of adaptation, and at developing the criteria for clarifying their general import in man's search for meaning—that medicine may more rationally choose those schemes which best accord with its own empirical findings, exploring them as paradigms for health. Surely, medicine and philosophy ought to collaborate to this end: that each discipline may proceed more effectively with its special task and, accordingly, fructify the other.

(*c*) Body Construals

How, for each particular individual, can balance and imbalance be interpreted? Interwoven as a system of resonators, all intermeshing and mutually attuned, the biologic acts constituting a human body "lock-in" to one another—once they have "discovered" each other's distinctive harmonics. Such "locking-in" patterns as induce harmonious sets of oscillation express felicitous bodily balance; other patterns express either imbalance or varying modes of inappropriate balance. Encoding the human body's hidden attunements of its biologic acts, the living corporeal symbols which these attunements manifest may, indeed, be deciphered in the medical consulting room. Pre-eminently the physician inquires into responses of one's overall physiognomy to such influences, both physical and psychic, as work upon the body's diverse parts to create currents of tension.

A veritable system of stresses and strains, the human body must, in the end, submit to the differential workings of gravity upon its various parts. Gravity's impingement constitutes a significant factor in molding human body to its possibilities for self-expression. And man reacts to gravity by exerting himself in such ways as will enable him to engage in the characteristic human settlements and migrations. Migratory patterns are a concrete working out of body's symbolisms; they are the translation of those symbolisms into action vis-à-vis human environments. As such, migratory patterns disclose both man's strength and man's weakness, in his quest to exercise his distinctive powers. Such deformation and conformation as the human body undergoes in response to gravitational forces determines man's *in*firmities, as he roots himself more or less securely *in terra firma.*[3] Beyond its literal import, gravity is a metaphor for expressing the limits which inexorably define human frailty. Yet, by his peculiar composition, man never ceases to challenge gravity's proscriptions.

From a naturalistic point of view, man's migratory patterns depend on his anatomic and physiologic makeup. By his capacity for standing upright, for example, and by his power to adjust his autonomic nervous system to erratically changing circumstance, man contemplates the whole universe. Ever discerning its manifold patterns and rhythms, he bears his roots in his own soul, and roams the earth freely and unconfinedly. Not restricted to any special locale, man is empowered to venture forth on land and sea and sky. His capacity to explore often seems to him to be virtually without limit. By contours of skull, by binocular and stereoscopic vision, by a slender and mobile neck, by supple fingers and toes, by a convoluted brain, by dexterous and agile limb, by complicated yet flexible infoldings of back muscles which immediately attach to vertebrae, by relatively undifferentiated teeth, by a rotatory spinal column, by coordination of balance, kinesthesia, and sensory activity, by ease and rapidity of oxygenation, by motile and delicately interwoven facial musculature, and by myriad other functions of marvelously diversified kinds, man adjusts himself to the most varied climes and terrains. With every imaginable rhythmic variation, he shapes novel combinations of material events, discriminates nature's endlessly varied configurations, and envisages, coordinates, and harmonizes patterns of all manner. Combining manifold forces, he creates contrivances and tools, temples and cities. Nature's most subtle, mysterious, and recalcitrant melodies seem to him to bend to his will. He celebrates her orchestrations, and he subdues her dissonances. And from his myriad acts emerge altogether new ecologic schemes. Man is capable of the most diversified probings, questings, and reconstitutings.

Beginning with his own physiognomy, that primordial fabric which symbolizes the physique, man fashions ever-new symbols. In the end, these symbols detach themselves from him, and, so to speak, embark upon their own careers. Pursuing autonomous destinies, they unfold, upon every encounter of them, unsuspected portent and meaning. When, in general, organisms of whatever complexity realize their migratory potentials, their diverse loci of habitation tend to join together as a continuum of coherently ordered domains. For man, this synthetic activity is, in the last analysis, symbolic. A composite organism, the human body possesses roots which ramify in manifold ways. Always, a person pushes beyond what, hitherto, he had discerned to be his limits. Relentlessly, he strives to exceed his own grasp. By his symbols, he creates ever-new ecologic schemes of co-adaptation. And these symbols perpetuate themselves indefinitely. They attain a kind of immortality—though, in the end, surely a specious immortality. Metamorphosing into myriad new complexes, within which, however, new unities never fail to arise, such symbols constitute, in time, a more ample nature than that which man had heretofore discerned: novel worlds which compel his deepening exploration.

From intricately organized cells, migratory patterns issue. From the elaborate organismic cartography which these patterns shape, new schemes of proto-symbolic acts come forth. In the ebbings and flowings of such organismic synthetic activity, the orchestrations of human body at last arise. Product of mutations which, by felicitous combination and confluence, bring about an embryogenetic product of marvelous versatility, human body emerges as endowed with the power for reflection. It is imbued with a capacity for embarking upon the most adventuresome of all migrations. Only under the most specialized of ecologic conditions, and in an astoundingly small number of living creatures, can this miraculous convergence of mutants appear. Perhaps an utterly unique individual is ancestor to all mankind; perhaps a single germ cell bore the progeny who, as a whole, constitute the living witness to the wondrous possibilities which inhere in replicatory material. To enumerate even the more salient of these mutants would be a major undertaking. To associate specific temporal increments with the relevant correlated groups of mutants would far exceed our present knowledge. Yet one must stand astonished before this perception: when actualized as the living human body, these mutants constitute the principal expressions of man's characteristic rhythms. They ground his most precarious, and delicately adjusted, feats of balance, ecologic adaptation, and migratory pattern. They allow for his most refined discriminations of texture and tone. By the interplay of these mutants, man's roots proliferate; his speech becomes more fluent and more finely nuanced; his imagery becomes more subtle, more profound, more variegated; he experiences within himself surging powers to defy—by his art, by his science, by his philosophy—mortality itself.

To indicate the interplay between man's limits and his powers, one may note the curious dialectic which obtains between the disciplines of medicine and philosophy. Aiming at so transforming the imbalances of a person's body that that person might, in consequence, achieve ever-widening ranges of migration, medicine aids him to root himself, in all his infirmity, in ever-more-inclusive *terrae firmae*: realms which reach to the stars! And philosophy probes implications of this quest for ever-novel reorientation. Explicating the meanings of infinity and eternity, it articulates symbols of these aspirations, symbols provided (in faith) by religion. It explores the outermost possibilities for human search. Within the compass of these possibilities, medicine allows each individual his full right to achieve: to achieve relatedness, despite his infirmities, to the greater cosmic rhythms. It orients him toward those infirmities which can be rectified, and toward those for which there can be no remedy; it enlightens him regarding such infirmities as are empowered, if one were to evade their true message, to deceive him, hence, to cast shadows over his reality.

Together medicine and philosophy conduct fruitful dialogue. Jointly, each under its own perspective, they explore the connection between thinking body as grounding value and value as grounding that relatedness between man and cosmos. By liberating man from his pathologic states, medicine allows philosophy more freely to aspire toward such specific values as set conditions whereby man can attain to ever-more-satisfying ways of harmonizing his larger concerns. Yet, even though one's body might succumb to pathology, medicine also, as long as one breathes, can liberate one's mind to pursue this distinctively human quest. But, in the end, only philosophy can provide intellectually satisfying categories for conceptualizing a person in his every aspect, categories toward the understanding of which the more fragmented spheres of empiricism and practice afford mere hints. Now, I can recur to my account of the Unconscious—but in a context of conceptualization wherein the possibilities for a more unified theory of man come closer to fruition. Such an image of man as integrated, and unalienated from his autochthonous powers, requires that I take deeper cognizance of the human body as grounding psychic activity, and, for that matter, of the human psyche as grounding its associated body—body which reveals itself within experience to be vibrant, truly alive, pervaded by reflection.[4]

NOTES

1. For this chapter, I extract materials previously presented in my essay "The Human Body as Rhythm and Symbol: A Study in Practical Hermeneutics," *The Journal of Medicine and Philosophy*, 1, No. 2 (June 1976), 136–61.

2. See the index references to "commotion(s)" in *The Dance of Being.*

3. See Stuart F. Spicker, "*Terra Firma* and *Infirma Species*," *The Journal of Medicine and Philosophy*, 1, No. 2 (June 1976), 104–35.

4. For a detailed discussion of the human body, and an amplification of the material of this chapter, see my *The Dance of Being*, esp. pp. 237–63.

3

LUMINOSITY: THE UNCONSCIOUS IN THE INTEGRATED PERSON

PREAMBLE

To elucidate the divisions between mind and mind, body and body, and body and mind, I propose three theses: (*a*) located in processes midway between bodily activity and mental activity, the Unconscious mediates transformations from each sphere into the other; (*b*) revealing these processes in every aspect of his behavior, the healthy person exhibits one mode of unconscious functioning, whereas the unhealthy person, whether ill of body or of mind, exhibits a quite different mode; and (*c*) man's characteristic searchings themselves are conditioned by this status of the Unconscious and, in particular, by the dialectical interplay, insofar as both modes occur within him, between the wholesome mode and the unwholesome mode. Accordingly, I stress these areas of inquiry: the locus of the Unconscious, its agential character, its *modus operandi*, its internal dynamics, and its presence in human comportment. My aim is to illuminate the role of the Unconscious in the actions of integrated persons; and my chief conclusion will be that the Unconscious glows, as it were, through those actions, and confers upon them a special quality which I call *luminosity*.[1]

A • THE UNCONSCIOUS AS MEDIATOR

(*a*) Body and Mind: The Metaphors

In his studies on the philosophy of mind, Charles Sanders Peirce wrote: "our whole past experience is continually in our consciousness, though most of it sunk to a great depth of dimness." For, he continues, "consciousness [is like] a bottomless lake" in which ideas are suspended at different depths, a lake "whose waters seem transparent, yet into which we can clearly see but a little way."[2] The more profoundly one plumbs these depths, the more one sinks into the abyss of unconsciousness. Beyond that, as one descends into the ever-more-dim regions of consciousness, and passes the threshold of that which is even recallable, one descends into the very body. In its grounding depths, consciousness *is* body. Sufficiently penetrated, it reveals body not only as its substratum dissociated from, though supporting, mental activity but, in addition, as suffusing that activity and invading its every form. Pervading all mentation is not only the awareness of body, however dim and buried that awareness be, but body itself.

How can the body pervade the mind? Just as our entire past experience registers itself in consciousness, though its original vivacity is greatly diminished, so it registers itself, as thus having perished yet as always abiding, in every region of its nethermost stratum, the Unconscious. These depositions even engrave themselves in the stratum which lies below unconsciousness: namely, the very processes which compose the body. As mind sinks into labyrinthine recesses of body, it acquires something of the same arcane character. Freud often stresses the bizarre sinuosities of unconsciousness, its strange meanderings and grotesque formations. And as it thus subtly blends with body, mind portends body, pointing toward it in all its intertwinings with other bodies. According to my thesis, consciousness *means* body. It *is* body as the latter mirrors itself to itself, reflecting into its own constitution the congeries of relationships it sustains to other bodies. Surely, the body which a particular awareness experiences itself as possessing is integrally enmeshed with bodies external to it, bodies some of which are likewise associated with other awarenesses. And the sphere of mental activity expresses this interwoven physical fabric of existence under the perspective of a particular body. Hence, the meaning of consciousness resides in symbols woven of activities which are irreducibly corporeal. The variegated facets of human comportment signify the ways in which mentation, incarnate in comportment, works out its diverse intentions. Consciousness is haunted, grounded, and constituted by the carnal.

It is equally true to speak of body as enveloped by consciousness. When it has acquired sufficient intricacy amid the growing unity of its organization, body manifests its activities in symbols of consciousness, images by which awareness re-presents to itself a corporeality which is primordially present to it. Inscribing on its own processes resonances which are far more subtle than any which can be detected by known physiologic means, body both etherealizes itself and transfigures its own status from non-reflective to reflective. For when the rhythms of its processes are orchestrated in a manner sufficiently complex, and when in their intricacy these rhythms constitute echoes which reverberate throughout the body, in a fashion which brings about ever-more-cohesive patterns of bodily integration, the realm of mind is born. A heart beat is transmuted into Shakespeare's nobler pulse of iambic pentameter, or the relentless procession of chords of a Ravel's *Bolero.* The body's very rhythms have been buoyed up into mentation; body is lifted against the gravity which has held it down as mere body. Once bodily processes metamorphose into mind processes, the mind hovers about and, indeed, penetrates the body.

In discussing the distinction between the mental and the corporeal, I interweave three sets of metaphors: levitation and weightiness, refined and coarser rhythms, luminosity and obscurity. The coarser rhythms are those which, so to speak, press the person down into his own corporeality. There, among body's obscure and labyrinthine recesses, he dwells—a Caliban entrapped in a physique which struggles but cannot fully emerge into the luminous spheres of consciousness. But, too, Caliban declares:

> Be not afeard: the isle is full of noises,
> Sounds, and sweet airs, that give delight, and
> hurt not.
> Sometimes a thousand twangling instruments
> Will hum about mine ears; and sometimes voices,
> That, if I then had wak'd after long sleep,
> Will make me sleep again; and then, in dreaming,
> The clouds methought would open, and show riches
> Ready to drop upon me, that, when I wak'd,
> I cried to dream again.[3]

So the most marvelous rhythms dwell within the human body, rhythms imprisoned therein until the body awakens from its slumbers and achieves the unity of selfhood. Within a field of primordial silence, the stillness of mere bodily activity, fragmentary experiences—each an evanescent appearing, each a passage from mere potentiality to actuality, and each anchored in specific body processes—all unfold, interweave, and come to confluence as an integrated manifold: the stirrings, the flux, the growth, the synthesis of a dawning consciousness. Different grades of psychic luminosity reveal themselves. Like a great archipelago which, on closer view, discloses numberless gleaming islands, fragments of consciousness germinate within an arcane Unconscious which, in turn, is deeply rooted in the body; and they coalesce into an effulgent, endlessly complex matrix. A quiet and imperceptible psychic mist arises out of the body: a mist woven of subtle and silent rhythms, of eddies which gradually form and reform, of densities and rarefactions converted into lines of variegated clarity and chiaroscuro; numberless signs of the virtual presence of psyche in body. A bare primeval firmament, an obscure potency, grounds this emergence into luminously orchestrated rhythms, rhythms at first marginal but progressively transforming themselves into the focal scintillae of awareness. Within this complex, the coarser rhythms cling together and, as it were, congeal to form mental structures which are ineluctably unconscious. Those which are more refined constitute the more evanescent though the less tangible realm of consciousness.

(*b*) Rhythm and Feeling

I distinguish three levels of human being, each composed of subordinate strata: the rhythms of consciousness, the rhythms of the Unconscious, the rhythms of body. How these rhythms are intertwined is the topic of my present deliberation. With respect to the rhythms of body, I further distinguish three (physical) strata: the embeddedness of body in other bodies, the structures of body, the functions of bodily structures. And with respect to the rhythms of consciousness, I likewise distinguish three (mental) strata: simple awareness, self-consciousness, un–self-consciousness. The rhythms of the Unconscious are interposed between those two sets of strata. Exhibiting their own intricate mode of lamination, these rhythms are the media through which mental phenomena sink into the physical and physical phenomena rise to the mental. To elucidate the dynamics of this activity, I consider first certain analogies between the structure of body and the structure of mind.

Human body is profoundly implicated with other bodies. The interplay of these physical events exhibits the character of physical space, time, and matter. In the course of human development, influences flowing from diverse natural complexes converge upon specific loci to constitute a relatively autonomous configuration, a (human) body which ever strives (by a kind of immanent intentionality) to raise itself out of its own embeddedness with other bodies. Causally efficacious factors contribute their diverse impacts upon this configuration, imprinting their own form, and transmitting it to a portion of their indigenous rhythms. Weaving these rhythms into a specific unity of action, every *particular* body contributes its own ornamentation. Thereby, it enables itself to stand forth, and so to evolve as to declare its relative independence amid its welter of dependencies. In this standing forth, structures emerge which are tangible, durable, and concrete. Yet, to be woven together in such fashion that the body does not lapse into passive embeddedness, these structures must "functionalize" themselves. They must melt into a ferment of interwoven paths, paths which are, not morphologically distinct, but fluid and in perpetually shifting relationships. The brain is an excellent example of an organ the components of which are not sharply delimited, and the pathways of which are uncontoured. For the brain to function effectively, all parts must be mobilized in order that a single pathway be activated for the purpose of transmitting some neural influence. To a lesser extent, all bodily organs exhibit an analogously amorphous structure, though a definite design of functional interdependencies.

Once man's "glassy essence"[4] has liquified, altogether new modalities of functional activity supervene; mind is born. Again, to cite Peirce:

> Protoplasm, when quiescent, is, broadly speaking, solid; but when it is disturbed in an appropriate way, or sometimes even spontaneously without external disturbance, it becomes, broadly speaking, liquid. . . . [And, as such,] protoplasm feels. It not only feels but exercises all the functions of mind. . . . [Moreover,] the feeling at any point of space appears to spread and to assimilate to its own quality, though with reduced intensity, the feelings in the closely surrounding places. In this way, feeling seems directly to act upon feeling continuous with it.[5]

According to this view, which I support here, living body, an organism, when sufficiently organized amid the "liquefaction" of the significant systems constituting it, is the locus of spreading feelings, feelings which emerge as expressions of the subtler resonances which are transmitted through those systems. As such, feelings, quite literally, ex-press, in the sense of pressing out, those resonances, and press them into adjacent or neighboring bodies. For psyche is not wholly confined to its originating, associated body, and psyches interact. Feelings emanating from diverse bodies interweave to constitute, on the level of *human* being, the sphere of interpersonal phenomena. I do not treat here the incredible complexity with which a person's body articulates its own actions vis-à-vis other bodies as diversified schemes of structured feeling. Simply, when any body has passed a certain threshold of intricacy and unity, the phenomenon of consciousness supervenes. And the direct interaction of feeling to which Peirce alludes is, equivalently, the direct enmeshing of those resonances which, in actuality, *are* feeling.

Feeling not merely accompanies bodily acts and bodily interaction, but, beyond that, is the realm of functions inscribed on body as it thus acts and interacts. The very echoing of body, it is that orchestration of rhythms which comprises body resonating to itself and thus producing systems of intra-organismic vibration—not only externalizing these and transmitting them to other such constituted bodies, but setting in motion processes in which ever-new loci of such resonating emerge. An entire hierarchy of functions evolves, a hierarchy so constituted that every stratum encloses resonating phenomena on which are inscribed novel schemes of resonance. Echoes within echoes are created. Reflexivity is endlessly complex. When consciousness has attained a high order of development, new structures of ideation, ever-novel architectonic modulations, are equivalent to the subtler echoes which therein reverberate.

Self-consciousness emerges when one set of resonances crystallizes as the sense of *I-ness.* A focal region within finely modulated resonances of awareness, this *I*-ferment is a partially circumscribed and partially autonomous configuration. Enduring as an invariant core of awareness, it itself resonates to the vibrations which unremittingly sweep about it. At the same time, the latter vibrations are synthesized into this durable whirlpool. Therein embedded, in indelible imprinting, the *I*-core is activated and reactivated. Thus catalyzed, it establishes a dialectical relatedness to the remainder of the mental realm. It is a center whence proceed eddies of circulating rhythms, eddies which continually interplay with those rhythms hitherto set in motion. Thereby, ever-new spheres of mentation evolve. In self-consciousness, the self mirrors itself to itself, and duplicates the body's reflective propensities. In primary reflection, human body orients itself toward its own ramifying connections with other bodies. In derivative reflection, which reaches its culmination in self-consciousness, the body orients itself toward itself in a symbolic way. In ever-new layerings of meaning, it interprets, through its symbols, its own feelings as they are intimately associated with specific acts of relatedness. By symbol, I mean συμβάλλειν: a joining together of the diverse parts of awareness. Each part refers to a specific sphere of bodily action. Together, all parts shape a unified configuration. In dynamic relatedness to surrounding rhythms which never cease to infuse it with new content, this configuration absorbs that content into an enduring and vitalizing core.

By self-consciousness, I do not mean an exclusively monadic, hence narcissistic, construal of mental processes. Intrinsically dyadic, mind is suffused with resonances derived from *other* minds, resonances which are transmitted as persons interlock with one another, and their respective mental vibrations lock-in to each other. As persons actively turn toward one another, they correlatively direct their mental resonances; they orient their minds in each other's way. By these interfusing mental resonances, the minds of all persons are reconstituted. This gripping of one person by another occurs when self-consciousness has been superseded by *un*–self-consciousness. Herein is replicated, on the level of mind, a phenomenon which first reveals itself on the level of body—in the phase of embeddedness. Just as body participates in the world body, so mind in the fruition of personhood as un–self-consciousness participates in the world soul —i.e., after each person has liberated his body from its circumambient matrix to shape autonomous structures and functions, and has evolved those mental rhythms which, in successive strata, are inscribed one upon another.

(*c*) Personal Autonomy

Two poles of intimacy of relatedness: the embeddedness of body, the embeddedness of mind! Between these poles, the person achieves a measure of autonomy. He works out his destiny, passing from body structure to body function, from unconsciousness to consciousness and self-consciousness: a succession of metamorphoses and transfigurations. It is as true to say that body is weighted with unconscious residues as to say that mind is permeated by unconscious efflorescences. For the Unconscious plays a dual role. On the one hand, when the Unconscious jells, it cannot rise into awareness; it thickens into relatively rigid structures which merge with those of body itself. It cannot constitute the medium through which resonances pass on their way to consciousness. Body ineptly registers its traces upon mind. These deformed traces infiltrate consciousness just as a corporeal pathologic process invades healthy tissue. On the other hand, when the Unconscious "liquefies," becoming less viscous, it allows for smooth, synchronous passage of impulses from each sphere to the other. Body becomes luminous with mental rhythms; its parts are well-coordinated. Transitions from one movement to another proceed easily, flexibly, and with versatility. Analogously, in pathologic unconsciousness, one's mental activity can only erratically inscribe itself on one's body. So grotesquely does the mental affect the physical that the body exhibits motions, as in hysteria, which are disjoined and anarchic. Correspondingly, when the Unconscious is wholesome, the mind feels a special clarity. Apprehending itself as vibrant and free, it smoothly exercises its natural function. Indeed, the sense of freedom is profoundly associated with a wholesome Unconscious. The body manifests itself as the incarnation of a mind which flows freely. Conversely, mind *is* body, in body's self-disclosed freedom with respect to both its comportment and its migrations. In a diagram, I exhibit these relationships wherein (*a*) each stratum of human being interacts with strata adjacent to it, and (*b*) in this interaction body etherealizes itself as mind while mind corporealizes itself as body. Each region, body and mind, is partly dependent and partly, in its very labyrinthine character, circumscribed and autonomous. An orchestration of dynamically interwoven factors, the totality reveals itself to be a fabric woven of multiple rhythms of diverse kinds.

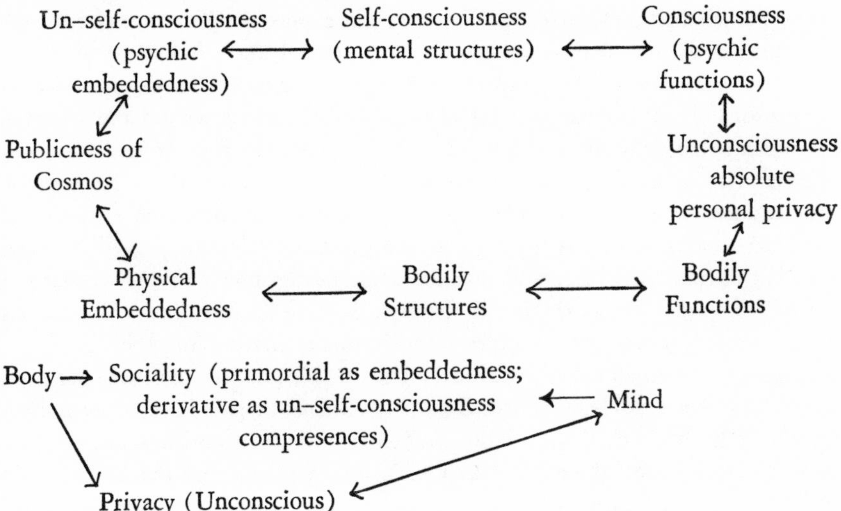

Body → Sociality (primordial as embeddedness; derivative as un–self-consciousness compresences) ← Mind

Privacy (Unconscious)

In this diagram, there are two poles of sociality: the intertwinings of bodies, or primordial publicness; and the compresence of un–self-consciousness, or derivative and consummated publicness. To relate this scheme to Spinoza's cosmology: the first pole expresses substance under the attribute of body (i.e., extension), whereas the second pole expresses substance under the attribute of mind. In both instances, sheer potency actualizes itself both as specific physical acts and as specific mental acts. Such potency constitutes Spinoza's *natura naturans*, whereas such acts manifest themselves as *natura naturata.* Conversely, there is one pole of privacy: the absolute autonomy of each personal Unconscious. In this sense, though exhibiting an archetypal or collective character, the Unconscious constitutes an individual's totally unique response to those archetypes. Accordingly, the Unconscious is the meeting ground on which the consummate mental rhythms of the cosmos merge with the consummate physical rhythms of the cosmos. Here the absolute inwardness of each unique person prevails; here body and mind veridically unite and interchange their respective contents; here reside the agent and mediator of processes belonging to each sphere; here is the locus of their interminglings, their mutual impingements, and their reciprocal transformations.

The absolute uniqueness of the Unconscious consists in its functioning as locus of originative symbolic activity: activity which, mingling mental patterns with physical patterns, informs each with the other. From this matrix, both physical symbologies, such as the dance, and mental symbologies, such as art, are created. Yet each symbolic form partakes, in a measure, of the character of the other. In dance, the body is suffused with wholesome mentation; in art, the mind is suffused with wholesome physicality. All art manifests the carnal; all dance manifests the spiritual. And art and dance are paradigmatic of human creativity.

For human being characteristically strives to express itself; it draws from its own interiority, its unconscious womb, both mental and physical symbolisms. Though the mental or the physical element will variously dominate, profound correlations obtain between any set of such symbols. In its wholesome aspect—i.e., when it has sufficiently "liquefied"—the Unconscious is creator, shaper, and originator of symbolic patterns of aesthetic contrast. Could it not be that the very cosmos exhibits itself under a third perspective, namely, the attribute of the Unconscious? Could it not be that deep internal relations prevail between different unconsciousnesses, and that this matrix *is* Spinoza's *natura naturans*, a sea of primordial potency? Here I distinguish three factors: internal relations in the mental sphere which express the intimate binding together of mind; analogous joinings on the physical level; and the blending of unconsciousnesses. Could it be that this Heideggerian *Dasein* is the unconcealed locus of all human activity: a locus which the artist pre-eminently illuminates in the shape of ever-new symbols? To consider this question, I turn to the role of the Unconscious in both health and pathology.

B • THE UNCONSCIOUS IN HEALTH AND IN PATHOLOGY

(*a*) Pathology: Mental and Physical

In physical pathology, the diseased organ functions as though it were an autonomous system, undergoing vicissitudes in accordance with principles peculiar to it alone. Walled off from the remainder of the body, it evolves through the action of indigenous dynamisms which, on superficial inspection, are unrelated to those characterizing the healthy organism. But deeper examination reveals an inner connection between these seemingly independent factors. Wherever there is disease, the afflicted organism discloses itself to be governed by two sets of norms. The first set expresses the interplay between two relatively enduring configurations of processes in their apparent mutual autonomy; the second, a more inclusive single system the parts of which are more diffusely bound together. In effect, the organism is bifurcated into two compresent schemes of action. The connection between these schemes is intricate and labyrinthine. When pathology is rectified, however, only a single scheme presents itself; and the network of relationships characterizing the dual state vanishes. An economy of functioning prevails. Coherence in the lineaments of the manifestations of functioning replaces the inchoate state which hitherto had been operative.

In both instances, the condition of body registers itself within the Unconscious. The subtler rhythms inscribed on body processes are affected by every shift in physiologic equilibrium. Imparted to those rhythms are pathologic alterations. Certain depositions linger in the Unconscious, forming grotesque enduring structures which haunt the person. In turn, these structures infiltrate the higher spheres of mentation. Thus tuberculosis is associated with a typical kind of depression; cancer is associated with a different kind. It is as though the body Imago imprints itself on all of mind, affecting its every stratum. Though mind may surely ignore certain of its afflictions, no mind can escape the ravages of its affiliated body. So profoundly is the body's pathology engraved on mind that the mind is experienced as weighed down by that pathology.

Analogously, the manifold of awareness may likewise be affected. When a person's psyche has been traumatized, two foci of potential consciousness supervene. One presents itself as the locus of overtly intended behavior; the other presents itself as the locus of concealed tendencies—i.e., a subterfuge with respect to the first locus. Here, I am referring to Freud's *repressions*, which express the diseased Unconscious. In effect, processes have been dissociated from consciousness and related to a peripheral though not irrelevant "region," a region haunting consciousness yet functioning by its own characteristic laws. Nonetheless, these split-off schemes themselves are but the representation of deeper psychic processes, processes in which all components are woven together as an integral though loosely constituted fabric, a fabric which comprises but a single psychic manifold. Between this manifold and the dual system of awareness circuitous and elaborate linkages obtain. Should *psychic* pathology be rectified, the dual system is replaced by a more concretely unitary and monadic system; the linkages dissolve, and a single, cohesive psychic scheme presents itself.

As in the case of physical pathology, psychic disabilities likewise register themselves within the rhythmic complex which *is* the Unconscious. Specific anxieties are woven with already inscribed depositions of the physical realm to constitute new unconscious introjects. Tensions likewise receive their imprints. In both instances, resonances descend, as it were, into depths of the Unconscious which imperceptibly blend with the physical. In consequence, specific physiologic pathology is induced. Relatively autonomous physical processes evolve as a result of their incorporation of the specific psychic complexes which have sunk into the abyss of the Unconscious. Interaction of these descending rhythms with already established autochthonous rhythms of strata beneath the one wherein originated the mental rhythms sets in motion ever-new loci of crystallizing pathologic activity.

In both cases, the physical and the psychic, effective therapy effects the transformation from an intricately contrived manifold to a simpler manifold. Yet, for physical pathology, pathogenic processes do not wholly disappear. Though in some manner still operative, they remain essentially latent. Reversals of structure and overt function are achieved. Yet the same factors which induced the original pathology are still found. Their activity is integrated into the general activity of a now wholesome body. Similarly, for mental pathology, memory traces of traumata do not cease to function within the psychic sphere. What had been dissociated has now been absorbed into a deeper and more reliable consciousness. Nonetheless, the very factors which had brought about dissociation are still operative as latent yet potent germs.

(*b*) Integration and Luminosity

Accordingly, I propose these theses. First, physical events—hence, physical pathology—have psychic correlates, and conversely. Next, just as diseased tissue in physical pathology functions autonomously, so the diseased psyche likewise functions in mental pathology. Indeed, psychic healing consists in a displacement from psychic bifurcation into consciousness and a pathologic Unconscious to spontaneous un–self-consciousness. Analogously, in physical pathology, physical bifurcation into partial health and disease can resolve itself as a spontaneous ease of comportment. Finally, when un–self-consciousness is in perfect correspondence with this ease, the person becomes authentically and luminously himself. In the context of psycho-physical correlation, and of the transformation from one psycho-physical state to another (i.e., from the diseased state to the "normal" state), I suggest a theory of both emotional and physical well-being. Adverting to the nature of both body and mind, I affirm a concept of human activity based on some principle of *association.*

The physical events which constitute a human body are bound together as a unity of organization. What holds its parts together is the working of a principle according to which certain events show pronounced affinities for other events. Thus, both replication and immunologic responses are based on the fact that molecular groupings on some macromolecules recognize molecular groupings on other macromolecules: recognition grounded in habit. Similar events (i.e., events belonging to the same class) have previously so imprinted themselves on the given events as to have been woven into their actual internal constitution. In consequence, detachment from such events is felt by the given events as a yearning for reinstatement. Novelty arises from the fact that no two events are precisely the same, and reinstatement can be only partial. Adjustments must be made to compensate for the differences. In this way, new powers are potentiated from the adapting events. The quest for reattachment is, at bottom, an expression of the striving after roots, roots within the entire matrix of body processes. There is a quest to preserve primordial attachments within given rhythmic configurations. Detachment preserves the self-identity and the power of a given event. Reattachment establishes a kind of security within the entire matrix which nourishes anew that given event. Hence, it provides the conditions for solidifying self-identity and amplifying, intensifying, and broadening its powers.

A dialectic holds between the two tendencies, a dialectic which sweeps over the entire body and provides for its dynamic equilibrium: a scheme of balances and imbalances. The entire body consists of parts which are so co-adapted as to enable it, as a whole, to recognize alien bodies for the purpose either of attachment or of independence. By dynamically interwoven attachments and detachments, a suitable context in which subsequent structures can root themselves is afforded. The bodily matrix is an orchestration of rhythms within which its various parts can dwell in relative harmony.

The overall balance thereby produced is associated with an entirely new set of rhythms, rhythms which express the interplay of such factors as constitute the human body. In addition, these rhythms express the *togetherness* of those factors. Such rhythms shape a body Imago which mirrors to itself the body's overall configurations. And body-Imago resonances actually constitute the Unconscious, i.e., on its lowermost stratum. When bodily activity is disrupted, and accordingly disharmonious, its associated Imago registers these imbalances. The Unconscious is the sphere for registration of body's balances and imbalances. Interplay of both pathologic factors and healthy factors is thus recorded, as well as the underlying forces which unite the two sets of factors in a larger configuration. Body's actual condition together with body's strivings toward health are both represented, i.e., *re*-presented as an unconscious body-Imago. Likewise, the conflict between the two—the actual and the potential—is registered.

With respect to mind, analogous considerations hold. To cite Peirce again:

> Not only do all ideas tend to gravitate toward oblivion, but . . . ideas react upon one another by selective attractions. . . . the associations between ideas . . . tend to agglomerate them into single ideas. [They] are attracted to one another by associational habits and dispositions,—the former in association by contiguity, the latter in association by resemblance.[6]

Moreover, ideas tend to move up and down in the fluid-like medium which is consciousness; varying degrees of buoyancy appertain to them. Percepts flow in, interacting with ideas already present on all the different levels of consciousness. Thus consciousness is kaleidoscopic, floating, and evanescent. Tensions develop among its various regions. A particularly strong region crystallizes as the self in relation to other weaker regions. As it inspects, probes, scrutinizes, and controls, the stronger turns toward the weaker. In this way, inner depths are revealed; new ideas are brought to attention. Indeed, ideas combine in much the same way as events combine. Associated with characteristic resonances, they recognize one another, reject one another, lock-in, select, and discriminate idea-trajectories within consciousness. In my reflections, I ready myself to receive like ideas from an earlier imprint which, as it were, conditioned an idea to "seek" its analogue from similar ideas. When ideas are associated with earlier ideas, a subsequent bond to like ideas becomes stronger. And ideas are mental events, quite analogous to physical events in their capacity for migrations, attractions, and repulsions. In this flowing matrix of ideas, certain invariant themes develop, about which cluster and crystallize certain idea sequences. Such ideas as cannot combine, because the combinations would suck ideas into relatively autonomous but nonetheless powerful configurations within consciousness, split that manifold into independent regions or foci of activity. As extreme instance of this state, one finds the radically split consciousness of certain sorts of schizophrenia. A conflict emerges between such pathologic clusterings and the remainder of consciousness, a conflict which hampers the development of the self-center, constricting and deforming that center. Such ideas tend to be relegated to the mind's lower regions—indeed, to the oblivion of the Unconscious itself—and deposited therein even further weigh down the Unconscious.

(*c*) The Pathologic Unconscious

The *pathologic* Unconscious consists of diffuse, non-interwoven foci of mental–physical activity. By this activity, the unity of body and mind are diminished. The Unconscious registers not only an Imago of disunity, but an Imago of the unity of body and mind. Once actualized in those spheres, the positive archetypal potentialities inhering in un–self-consciousness are transferred through each stratum of mind, affecting that stratum, to the Unconscious itself. There, both mental unity and the disruption of mental unity blend with analogously imparted unities and disruptions deriving from the body and its embeddedness. In short, the conditions of body and mind, in their unity and in the shattering of their unity and in both higher and lower modes of relatedness, all intermix within the Unconscious. Body factors rise to rhythms of consciousness; mental factors fall to those rhythms. Each stratum of personal being affects the adjacent strata; and this effect travels in both directions, rising and falling. An ebb and flow of imprints expresses the pulsatory character of the rhythms composing human being. Moreover, every pulse possesses both a mental pole and a physical pole. And the component events (and ideas) of different regions of human being contribute their respective mental and physical poles to a person's overall composition. All such contributions are interwoven as a single, integral complex. Variegated pulses combine in diverse ways to constitute the ebb and flow of mentation. In healthy persons, the rhythms are appropriately equilibrated; in unhealthy persons, dis-equilibration prevails.

C • THE UNCONSCIOUS IN COMPORTMENT

(*a*) Alienations and Integrations

Every region of human being is suffused with unconscious rhythms which pervade both the body and the mind. In their public aspects, body and mind manifest spatially compresent activities; always interwoven, they constitute a contemporaneous spread. But as one passes from either sphere, mental or physical, toward those processes which link both spheres, hence, mediate their component rhythms—namely, the Unconscious—the spatial character diminishes and gives way to a distinctively temporal character. And ever-"unconscious-ing forth" his mediating rhythms, every person transmits their unique, private imprints to both his body and his mind. In effect, time is the very stuff of which the Unconscious is woven; and time transmutes itself into space.

Like the ripples set in motion when a pebble is cast into a lake, ripples radiating outward in concentric circles which, as they recede, fade into placid waters, so, in reverse movement, dynamically correlated layers of memory, memory woven of body imprints and memory woven of mind imprints, converge from dim regions of the past on a single point; and this point *is* the act of unconscious-ing. By this act, one unconsciously sums up these variegated imprints. And from within its own synthesizing center, every such act originates those anticipations which send new trajectories toward a future personal existence. "Behold!" cried St. Augustine, "in the fields and caves and caverns of my memory, innumerable and innumerably filled with all varieties of innumerable things, . . .—[which the] memory retains even when the mind does not experience them, although whatever is in memory is also in the soul—through all these I run, I fly. . . ."[7] From these "passions of the mind"[8] I shape and solidify, as the creative action of my Unconscious, and in each instant of my existence, my very self. In its rhythms of discord and harmony, I construct my own identity; and as these memories stream together in "fiery flood"[9] I become a coherent union of impressions and movements. My comportment becomes luminous with the workings of my Unconscious.

Alternatively expressed, these unconscious acts are, as it were, concentrated at the axis of an hourglass through which flow the sands of past and future. Or, in a different construal of this metaphor, the sands of mind and body perpetually interchange their content. By the second interpretation, should the balancings of the hourglass be too erratic, and the smooth flowing rhythms of the passage of the sands through the hourglass accordingly jarred, then, in effect, the sand forms clumps which, aggregating themselves about the axis, impede an otherwise even flow. In a coherent enmeshing of the movements of memory, a smooth-flowing temporality is laden with the spatial depositions of contemporary imprints which are either corporeal or mental. By this analogy, the Unconscious is spatialized with pathologic clusterings. Otherwise stated, as strictly private, the Unconscious concerns the sheer particularity of personal events. No contagion of other bodies or of other minds affects its dynamics, save insofar as it might, on occasion, be "pathologized." Yet even when the Unconscious is not weighted with illicit depositions of body and mind, the imprints of the intercourse of persons with other events—imprints which bear an element of universality—become, for the Unconscious, a virtual presence. In this sense, the Unconscious is the locus wherein, paradoxically, the universal and the particular are contiguous. Hence, the curiously bizarre character of the Unconscious, its archetypal themes woven with its idiosyncratic variations.

In the *wholesome* Unconscious, the temporal element is essentially uncorrupted by the spatial element; the Unconscious flows freely. In this state, repressions or pathologic weightings deriving from either the physical realm or the mental realm are ineffectual. The full paradoxicality of the Unconscious as locus of their juncture is realized. The tendency of the Unconscious now to liquefy in a natural way and now to congeal in a natural way is achieved. Its role as effector of transfigurations from one spatial modality into another is consummated.

Only in my Unconscious do I stand alone. In its higher functions, my body is approximately alone; in its lower functions, my mind is approximately alone. As one approaches the Unconscious from either pole, that of the publicness of un–self-consciousness or that of the publicness of bodies enmeshing with other bodies, aloneness is attained in different gradations. Between sheer privacy and absolute publicness lie intermediate realms of aloneness—whether on the side of body or on the side of mind. Furthermore, what I am publicly on either side is affected by what I am privately in my Unconscious. My private rhythms illumine my every act, physical and mental. They suffuse my every lineament, and every configuration of my being. Pervaded by (hence, made luminous with) my privacy, both the symbols of my mind and the symbols of my body, my thoughts and my physiognomy, portend the absolute inwardness of my Unconscious, the seat of my creative syntheses. Each set of symbols thus animated by the Unconscious—that juncture between body and mind—is transmitted through the agency of the other. Minds and bodies are inextricably interwoven; they have absolute parity. In their public aspect, the rhythms of mind and those of body are continuous with the Unconscious. Therein, they are transformed and interchanged. This realm is locus for the transmigrations, as well, of body elements and mind elements. Interconversion of the two spheres is grounded in the very nature of reflexivity.

Associated with every set of rhythms—the initiating resonances—on every stratum of human being, whether it be dominantly mental or dominantly physical, are echoing resonances, the reverberations of those rhythms as they sweep over the person. There is an element of the physical *and* the mental on *every* level of human being. The lower the stratum, as one descends toward body, the coarser and more readily discernible are the initiating resonances, and the more evanescent, faint, and vanishing are the echoing resonances. On mental levels, however, both sets of resonance tend to be subtle, refined, and physically quite undetectable—though subjectively quite pronounced. Thus the disparity between the two tends to become greater in body and less in mind. For mind, as one ascends to its higher strata, these resonances become increasingly assimilated to one another.

On the other hand, as one approaches the Unconscious from either side, the mental or the physical, a frank inversion occurs. In this sense, as one passes toward body, there is a drifting away from reflection proper; and as one passes toward mind, there is a drifting toward reflection proper. Yet, always, throughout human being, no matter how complex or how simple the apparent composition of the waves whose overlap, intersection, and fusion constitute the different configurations of body or of mind, an aura hovers about every wave, hence pulsates throughout human being. Reflection haunts all matter: the more subtle the aura, the more intricately composed the matter; the more intricately composed the matter, in certain highly organized configurations, the more mind itself arises. And, always, wherever mind is thus associated with matter, a region exists wherein one may find those peculiar reversals which constitute the processes of unconscious-ing.

According to my view, the ultimate seat of every self is the *entire* world. By this, I mean: the body may be construed as a mosaic of trajectories which conjugate at certain centers, the focal points of reflective activity; and these trajectories extend themselves into the milieu in which the body is embedded. The cartography of this terrain is mapped onto the body. By a kind of contagion, impulses are transmitted through these trajectories which register themselves "within" the body as representations of the body's variegated relationships, its schemes of balance and imbalance within its world. By this representation, the reflective body orients itself toward that world. Constituted by diverse sensitivities, the person comports himself in ways determined by the impact of different world regions on those sensitivities. Whether impinging at the mental pole or at the physical pole, such impact reverberates throughout the person. Either it ascends toward mind or it descends toward body.

Moreover, persons can be construed as composites of different regions of influence, each deriving from a specific mode of locating itself within its local milieu. Thus rooted in its particular locale, every region responds in its idiosyncratic way to factors associated with that locale. In general, a person's own orientations are vectorial resultants of those types of response. Detail is obliterated in his explicit representations. Yet, in latent fashion, detail is preserved as the stratified depositions of influence which affect his every act. Such patterns of location, orientation, and migration are registered as unconscious coagulates. Within these patterns, both embryologic and contemporary experiential depositions are conserved. Both spatial and temporal imprints of an inclusive terrain are woven into every movement of every human existent.

Composed of many living parts, a person represents to himself, however buried such representation, the specific modes of dwelling, in their respective locales, of his every part. And, the representation which he frames is constituted by Imagos derived from the mirrorings to itself of the variegated schemes of location, orientation, and migration associated with these parts. In a spatial sense, his being actually spreads itself over a terrain of considerably greater extent and variety than that of which he is explicitly aware. He frames for himself a map of multiple locales: all overlapping, but each distinctive. Moreover, from a temporal point of view, the person inherits the cumulative evolving perspectives contributed by the diverse phases of his own development, a heritage transmitted through the successive metamorphoses he undergoes as his personhood germinates and, in stages, is brought to fruition. In the integrated person, the several contributions made by temporal antecedents and by spatially compresent parts all smoothly and luminously flow into the coherent manifold of his being.

To conclude: if the aura of mental resonances is regarded as hovering about the body, and inscribed on its constituent rhythms, then every bodily act will manifest, as a symbol portending these resonances, some region of the mental. Every element of comportment constitutes an expression of that region. Beyond that, the configuration of such elements in their dynamic interplay not merely expresses but actually quite directly *presents* the mental. In this context, *unconscious* identifies the scheme of rhythms woven concurrently of both (physical) symbols and (mental) symbolized: the physical in its ineffable components and the mental in its latent content. For the Unconscious mediates body and mind; it partakes of the character of each. With respect to textural detail, the physical expression—hence, the presentation *par excellence*—of the mental is language. Here, fineness of articulation and subtlety of nuance achieve their consummate shape. Yet language is but the focal presentation of the mental within the more inclusive context of comportment in general. And the Unconscious informs comportment with rhythms which constantly intertranslate, each into the other, the two sets of resonances of which comportment is woven: the physical proper and the mental proper. When the Unconscious works in unimpeded fashion, comportment becomes integrated, smooth, flowing, coherent, and luminous.

(*b*) The Labyrinthine Unconscious

In this account, I conceive the person to be a texture of dialectically interwoven aspects, and I hold that his dynamics can be subsumed under three rubrics: the dialectics of processes between body and mind; the dialectics of the unconscious proper as mediating these processes; the dialectics of processes *within* body and of processes *within* mind. In each case, I formulate an hypothesis about the nature of human being.

Throughout, I have assumed that consciousness tends to sink into body, incorporating itself therein as symbols of physical comportment; and, conversely, that body tends to rise into mind, enveloping mind as body spiritualizes itself in mental symbols. Moreover, both kinds of symbols represent modes of orientation which, in their consummate shape, express the interwovenness of persons with persons—i.e., connections between his body and other bodies, connections between his mind and other minds. When these sets of symbols are understood in their mutual import, they reveal a deeper tie. They are perspectives under which the person presents both to himself and to another his integral being in its interpersonal significance. Thus conceived, every person is the locus of an interplay between these tendencies: namely, mind's impetus to "carnalize" itself, and to gravitate toward body; and body's impetus to spiritualize itself, and to rise to the status of mind. Closer examination of this dual tendency discloses human being to be constituted, as one proceeds from body to mind, of layers so constellated that, at each level, the mental and the physical elements interweave. I postulate a rising and a falling, an ebb and a flow, between physical resonances and mental resonances. And I assume that, in mutually synergizing rhythms, both sets of resonance pervade human being, and that these rhythms derive from the interaction among all strata composing the person.

Mediating this rise and fall, on every level of man's being and with respect to his overall composition, is the Unconscious: that region of human being which partakes of the character of both the physical and the mental. Replicating the dynamics of processes between mind and body and processes within mind and within body, the Unconscious constitutes the locus wherein mental and physical contents so migrate within the person as either to "congeal" pathologic introjects (either mental or physical) or, when health supervenes, to "liquefy" them. Thereby, the essential temporality of the Unconscious comes to fruition. By intrusion of spatial elements which are derived from both realms, the pure flow of memory into anticipation, those motions of private reverie as fantasy recedes into the physical realm or emerges into the mental realm, is disturbed. Indeed, the Unconscious is sullied by illicit modes of compresence. But the uninfected Unconscious of the integrated person reveals harmonious interfusions of both carnal and spiritual ingredients. Thus shaped, it effects the suffusion of mind with the physical and of body with the mental. Agent by which the person energizes his quest for centeredness, the Unconscious finally juxtaposes archetypal, collective, and universal constraints to individual, private, and autonomous creations. It allows each factor so to impinge upon the other that the *ec*centricity of pathologic mind and body is diminished.

To understand more fully a pathology of the Unconscious, and the methods by which the Unconscious might be made more wholesome, one must reflect upon the relevant dynamics of both mind and body, each construed as a partially autonomous configuration and as a relatively enduring manifold of elements. As each sphere evolves, and the two spheres co-evolve, bringing their inherent organizational potential to fruition, a directing center crystallizes, the nuclear *I* for mind and the brain for body; and the remaining elements composing the manifold are coordinated with respect to this center. Yet, in however subtle a form, pathology ineluctably infects that manifold. Clustering about the natural center, other centers arise which constrict that center's activities; the natural processes constituting the manifold are diffused; its coherence and its economy are disrupted. Through pathology, both manifolds are bifurcated. Still, the integral manifold subtends this bifurcation as but a latent condition. The Unconscious registers both this duality and this unity. Body and mind are each locked into conflict with itself. Certain tendencies facilitate their autonomy; other tendencies combat it. But, in general, in incomparably subtle ways, mind yearns to stimulate the primordial condition of enmeshed corporeality. For the interpersonal sphere, the intertwinings of un–self-consciousness both express and bring to fruition the participations of body on the physical level. In these intertwinings, ever-novel modes of interpersonal relatedness are effected.

Alternately identifying with this component or with that component of his milieu, the person quests after self-identity. He entrusts himself to the cartography of that milieu. In a dialectic of attachment and detachment, he co-adapts to it his personal contours. Continually readjusting the trajectories of his being, he brings them into conformity with the terrain the composition of which is itself continually being remolded. In alternate bondings and freeings, he achieves ever-new modes of centeredness. In this dynamic relatedness, the peculiarly creative role of the Unconscious dramatically affects both comportment and the spirit which animates comportment—and this throughout a person's every metamorphosis and vicissitude.

To restate succinctly the main drift of my argument, I have advanced three sets of hypotheses regarding the ground for this thrusting of being toward human being. These hypotheses I designate *transformation*, *transcendence*, and *transmigration*. In the first, I stress both the pervasive interplay and the reciprocal transformation of echoing resonances and initiating resonances. In the next, I stress the strivings of every man to "autonomize" body and mind, and by transcending autonomy in schemes of mental compresence, to simulate schemes of physical embeddedness. In the last, I stress the peculiar journeyings of mental and physical elements, and their bizarre interactions which constitute the Unconscious. Understood jointly, these hypotheses imply a concept of the person as one who roots himself in ever-more-inclusive modes of co-adaptation and relatedness. In fine, the Unconscious is the fulcrum in the quest for the *luminosity* of these modes.

"Every man is the builder of a temple," Thoreau proclaimed, a temple "called his body, . . . after a style purely his own," and this temple houses his soul. For, he adds, "We are all sculptors and painters, and our material is our own flesh and blood and bones. Any nobleness begins at once to refine a man's features, any meanness . . . to imbrute them."[10] Thoreau enjoins each man "to let his mind descend into his body, and redeem it, and treat himself with ever increasing respect."[11] By the thesis I have presented here, the music of the soul echoes and re-echoes throughout the chambers of the body. When this music has become sufficiently frozen, and acquires a more thingly status, it, in effect, constitutes the body; as it liquefies, it rises to the condition of the mind. Otherwise expressed: the body is like a cavern which is endlessly embellished with all variety of stalactite and stalagmite. The finer ornamentation is analogous to mind; the more delicate the lacing on each ornament, the higher the level of mind. The coarser structures and, indeed, the cave itself correspond to body. On this analogy, every man is architect of his natural cathedral; he imprints the rhythms of his soul into its every cleft and prominence. By the Unconscious, I mean those finely wrought features which support the more subtle ornaments, and yet, at the same time, form the more stable lineaments of this cathedral. To return to a musical simile: the Unconscious is the polyphony which rises out of the deeper tones which constitute the temple; it shapes those themes upon which the most subtle variations of mind are woven. And when I speak, as the principal refrain of my argument, of resonances luminous and resonances weighty, I only adapt to an ontology of the person e. e. cummings' insight in his great poem: "most ethereal silence through twilight's mystery made flesh . . . luminous tendril of celestial wish."[12]

Yet, when one reflects on these lines, no longer can the term "Unconscious" bear the weight of the concepts which accrued to it when its deeper implications were traced out. For this "luminous tendril," this "ethereal silence," this temple which houses man's soul imports a substance and a dynamism quite different from that presupposed by the Unconscious as it has been conceptualized thus far. Surely, that which engenders the movements of body and mind, effects migrations between body and mind, and achieves transcendences of body and mind cannot consist merely in something which is negative *simpliciter* with respect to body or mind. Nor, for that matter, can it constitute a material which is no material at all: a stratum spatially juxtaposed between body and mind, a mere medium through which resonances pass from one to the other. Unquestionably labyrinthine, the Unconscious is thematized by notions which do not resemble those of physiology or those of psychology, or, indeed, those of a transmuted physiologized psychology or psychologized physiology. No simple analogy based on these sciences can allow a viable idea of that labyrinth to be shaped. My merely evocative presentation must now be replaced by an essentially ontologic account of the *ground* of body and mind, an account which requires its own distinctive thematization. Having alluded to the self's divisions, I now prefigure the self's unity, a prefigurement which can be explicitly elaborated only after a new concept of man has been introduced: namely, that of *searching* as constituting the very ground of human being.

(*c*) Toward a New Construal of the Unconscious

Briefly recapitulating my main themes, I repeat the following topics: reiterating yet ever newly ornamented rhythmic patterns of body and mind, configurations nested within one another; interrelations among these rhythms, configurations never isolated, but always interwoven and intimately orchestrated; enduring patterns as functions of the repetition of patterns in rhythmic ways; complicatedly interrelated systems involving highly complex interactant rhythms, some of which are constituents of others, and all of which exhibit different grades of subtlety and refinement or coarseness and weightiness; synchronized rhythms now beating together, now sequentially unfolding, now requiring intervening rhythms in order to induce higher modes of harmony—those modes now reinforcing one another in patterns of contrasting intensity, now enhancing one another in patterns which are concordant and contrapuntally consistent, now inhibiting one another to effect discordance.

Employing figurative and allusive language, I have sought to evoke, through the metaphors of *gravity*, *luminosity*, and *nuance* (of rhythmic refinement), an image which, in one's rational imagination, might aid one to reflect upon the feasibility of constructing a focus of convergence toward which these images point. I have proposed a composite experience: the threshold of consciousness; body metamorphosing toward the psychic; mind impacting upon and manifesting itself through the physical. And I have distinguished levels in the composition of the *person*, rather than of his mind or of his body as such: the person conceived as woven of body and mind, yet, in his depths, as going beyond body and mind. Under this new perspective, I have alluded to the different grades of a person's luminosity. I have suggested that each level mirrors the other; that each affects the motions of the ingredients of the other; that each imparts subtle changes to the other. Surely, prevailing concepts of body, mind, and the Unconscious require a new ground, a ground in which these seemingly distinct substances, each associated with a characteristic dynamism, are to be construed as but focal regions within a single substance: a substance within which one may discern foci which are self-actant, interpenetrating, and mutually transforming.

By my metaphors, I have tried to dramatize the need for a new language, one in which altogether new concepts are thematized: concepts which, without negating traditional ideas, both subsume and go beyond them. All knowledge arises through interplay of tradition and innovation. As such, novelty is ineluctably mediated. Founded on traditional orientations of a general kind, accepted knowledge, funded and already critically evaluated belief, provides the specific resistances requisite for disallowing arbitrarily novel formulation. By appeal to tradition, a new concept gains that determinateness which guarantees its continuity, its stability, and its solidarity, but, at the same time, envisages a greater amplitude, a new direction, an imaginative reconstruction.

In my account, I have delineated a context in which traditional concepts have not yet become obsolete *as such*, but only against the background of an evolving, systematically rational corpus of ideas which justifies their obsolescence. Later, I attempt this task. I articulate discursively rather than in a merely elusive metaphor a context, hitherto unexplicated, wherein one can both validate and explicate topics which I have hitherto but implicitly presupposed. I deal with these questions: Is the Unconscious a medium, a filter, and a space-like interposition between body and mind? As such, does it, like pre-Einsteinian ether, offer resistance to migrations to and fro, between body and mind? If so, how can a mere medium be associated with a dynamism whereby conversions between body and mind are effected? Does the Unconscious constitute the mid-range of frequencies, with respect to those of body and those of mind? Or is it a new type of rhythm altogether: a rhythm of which bodily rhythm and mental rhythm are but extracts; a rhythm at once more concrete and more primordial? Can bodily *functions*, associated with purposiveness, be identified with non-teleologic rhythms? Can such rhythms be patterned in ways which allow them to inscribe themselves on one another, hence, operate not as functions but as substances? How can body illness "pass through" unconscious blockages, such as those rigidified rhythms which constitute Freud's secondary repressions? Conversely, how can mental illness analogously affect the body? Is disease, whether essentially that of body or that of mind, simply localizable? Or is it ineluctably associated with repercussions which sweep over the entire person? If the latter, how can the alleged overall presence of even the most circumscribed illness be identified, and its multitude of finely nuanced manifestations be brought into focus in ways which make a difference for a person's diverse activities?

To deal with these questions, I now prepare the way for a new ground for deducing the veridical unity of body and mind, and not merely an honorific unity. Retaining, where consistent with common usage, traditional concepts of body and mind, I suggest a context which allows for the incorporation of phenomena not yet systematically woven into the body of science or, for that matter, of speculative philosophy. Metaphor must be replaced by a systematic account of the ground for body and mind and their interwovenness. Without abandoning obvious features of either the physical or the mental, and without undertaking an indefensible reduction of one sphere to the other, one must postulate a third element of which both body and mind are but aspects, attributes, and dimensions. To undertake this task, I reflect upon primordial human activity, namely, the structure of searching itself. In the last analysis, the *luminous* search for veridical personhood can be fully conceptualized only when the person is construed as a *concrete universal*: a fusion of qualities which can be apprehended only abstractly, with qualities of an essentially poetic-like status.

NOTES

1. In this chapter, I draw freely from my article "Luminosity: The Unconscious in the Integrated Person"; see above, pp. 35–36.

2. "Consciousness," *Collected Papers of Charles Sanders Peirce.* VII. *Science and Philosophy*, ed. Arthur W. Birks (Cambridge: The Belknap Press of Harvard University Press, 1958), sect. 7.547, p. 335.

3. Shakespeare, *The Tempest* III.ii.147–154.

4. "Man's Glassy Essence," *Collected Papers of Charles Sanders Peirce.* VI. *Scientific Metaphysics*, edd. Charles Hartshorne and Paul Weiss (Cambridge: Harvard University Press, 1935), sects. 6.238–271, pp. 155–77.

5. Ibid., sects. 6.247, 6.255, pp. 165, 167; and "Mind and Matter," ibid., sect. 6.277, p. 184.

6. "Consciousness," *Collected Papers* VII, sects. 7.553, 554, pp. 338, 339.

7. *The Confessions of St. Augustine*, trans. John K. Ryan (Garden City, N.Y.: Doubleday Image, 1960), p. 246.

8. Ibid.

9. Thomas Wolfe, "The Story of a Novel," *Only the Dead May Know Brooklyn* (New York: New American Library, 1947), p. 140.

10. Henry David Thoreau, *Walden* (New York: Airmont, 1965), p. 159.

11. Ibid.

12. e. e. cummings, "luminous tendril of celestial wish," *100 Selected Poems* (New York: Grove, 1959), p. 119.

β

BEING EFFULGENT: THE RHYTHMS OF MAN

INTRODUCTION

SEARCHING

Previously, my reflections culminated in the postulating of three dynamisms. In *transmigration*, human resonances pass through a porous boundary—the Unconscious—toward either mind or body; thereby, a person's true or just balances reveal themselves. In *transformation*, mind and body, through the interplay of light resonances with weighty resonances, shape one another; in this process, each transfigures the other; thereby, integrity, unity, and wholeness are brought to fruition. In *transcendence*, man achieves consummate personhood by regaining, and ever renewing, a primordial rapport of body embedded in body and of mind intertwining with mind; in this way, he attains to the beauty, or wisdom, of both his mind and his body, and of their reciprocal relations.

Jointly, these dynamisms suggest a concept of the person as searcher: In searching, he establishes ever-more-generalized ecologic balances. Such balances are of two kinds: internal, with respect to man's autonomous, inner being; external, with respect to man's co-adaptations to environments which are articulated with increasing precision, inclusiveness, and systematicness. Truly, man is a roamer. In his wholesome condition, he never ceases to emigrate from secure ground, and to immigrate into remote domains. Not only does he root himself in the *terra firma* of his immediate homeland, but, beyond that, he seeks ever-widening cosmic reaches. Between inner and outer modes of searching, a dialectical interplay prevails. As his *I* emerges, and his self becomes increasingly creative, a person expands his powers to incorporate new "substance" from these distant recesses, and, thereby, to pass through one metamorphosis after another.

Now I exhibit the ambiguities of freedom, especially those which arise in human crisis. From an abstract point of view, I treat searching as grounding human being, hence, freedom itself. In earlier accounts, I regarded man, both seeker and sought, as always leaping beyond his merely natural status, and, thereby, as predelineating for himself a transcendental status. I disclosed his natural rhythms to be pregnant with new import. Designated "luminous" and "ethereal," these rhythms prefigure the richer and more intricate rhythms which I term "effulgent." To actualize his effulgence, the person takes possession of himself. In a dialectic of self-possession, he determines his own nature. Not as mere commodity, but as rooted in his own powers—hence, as achieving self-mastery—he *owns* himself. By self-owning, he is his own true kin. In tenderness, he intimately and authentically belongs to himself; he discloses his own truth to himself. Indeed, etymologically, ownership is related not only to its current marketing usage, but, more fundamentally, to Middle English *unnen*, meaning "to grant," and to Old Icelandic *eigna* or to Anglo-Saxon *agen*, meaning, in both instances, "to acknowledge" and "to claim as one's own." Applied to oneself, ownership implies *self*-acknowledgment, a claim which one makes upon oneself, or a granting to oneself of one's very self.[1]

As a person envisages the truth of his own being, he gives himself up in such ownership, i.e., in trust to his natural rhythms; he apprehends himself to be immanently directed toward self-transcendence. A searching being, man perceives himself to be on the very threshold of concretizing his human essence and, thereby, of realizing his own concrete universality. In the end, he achieves wisdom, the quintessential form of beauty and love. That this goal be attained, one must pass through stages which lie beyond the perception of one's own truth. Replenishing himself with hope, a person reaches toward the goodness which is potentially resident within him. No longer satisfied with trust alone, he experiences his own deeper continuity as a person. Living beyond what he actually is, he shapes his ideal potentialities into a more inclusive reality. Forming new values, novel contrasts of pre-existing harmonies, man perceives these values to be effective only as he further expands his powers for loving encounter. When he apprehends the beauty of another person, as, likewise, the latter recognizes *his* beauty, to reside in the more durable sharings of human encounter, a person frees himself to advance still farther along his life's way. He experiences his own boundaries to be haunted by a presence, as yet dimly felt, of a "something" beyond those boundaries: a presence which is enveloping, personal, and witnessing.

Every person is freedom incarnate. In love and in beauty, one incorporates all the unfoldings of truth and goodness. For these moments are grounded in what has not yet explicitly presented itself. Though the stages which have thus far evolved are merely abstract and general, they nonetheless point the way toward an immanent ideal which is concrete and universal. Later, I show the route by which human integrity can be achieved, a route which in the end leads toward human wisdom itself.

As culmination of the correlated pairs truth and trust, goodness and hope, beauty and love, justice emerges as the grounding phase of an altogether new process, a process the intermediate and final stages of which I have designated as, respectively, integrity and wisdom. In justice, equity with respect to the "distribution" of a person's spirituality is achieved. His *anima* equitably animates his several parts. As personal harmony, justice prefigures the vision of consummate self, and points toward more ideal modes of balancing those parts. Grounding personal harmony, justice opens, in succession, into integrity and wisdom.

Though justice both ascertains and evaluates the facts of the case, justice implicitly refers to a norm of integrity. By this norm, no part can appear capriciously within the whole; no part can grotesquely relate itself to any other part; a modicum of coherence must prevail throughout all parts. Both internally and externally, a person's very ecology is solidified and strengthened. All parts are so ordered that they hang appropriately together lest they hang inappropriately apart. Philosophy, concerned with cosmic "justice" (i.e., with systematic factuality) and religion, concerned with cosmic "integrity" (i.e., with a balanced attitude toward the world's spiritual center), combine their respective insights to shape wisdom: the life of mystical participation. Achieved at the end of the human journey, mysticism allows all imaginable patterns both to be envisaged and to be exemplified concretely in daily acts.

Having been conceptualized *in abstracto*, the stages of the spiritual life—namely, justice, integrity, and wisdom—are now transmuted through the interplay of inner and outer journeys. In a double journey, the natural and the spiritual join to constitute the invisible basis for overcoming one's segmentation. Every division is reduced; a unified and consummate self is envisaged. Later, these stages will reveal themselves anew. Replicating *in concreto* their defining themes, they will manifest numerous variations, a wealth of new content.

In his searching acts, man's every aspect—the nuances of comportment and speech, the phases of searching itself—are metamorphosed into veridical symbols. As such, they fuse opaque facets to luminous unity; they exhibit man's inmost depths. Ever questing after his natural origins—wherein plant and animal, originally one, split into opposing though mutually enriching life forms—the person, consummate progeny of the animal, yearns vicariously to rejoin his complement, the plant. Secretly seeking to imitate the plant, he craves, in his own metabolizing and self-replicating acts, its inherent self-sufficiency. Thus self-sufficient, he strives after a reflexive unity which, in living form, mirrors the composite, dynamic unity of the cosmos itself. For the vegetative state symbolizes absolute interiority: an inner peace and tranquillity. And the animal state symbolizes a power to turn outward, even while retaining its sense of inner depths, in expanding patterns of migration and adventure: endlessly various motions. As fused, plant and animal constitute a symbol of the cosmos itself—inwardly unified and outwardly diversified, though vibrant always placid. Under a Darwinian perspective, animals attain, through successive transmutations, to personhood. In man, animal yearnings for plant status are analogous to questings for variegated pattern: stability amid thematic repetition, quietude amid restless migration. Increasingly, the differentiations of man's expressive acts become finely nuanced, subtly modulated, and intimately attuned to his milieu. Quality of adventure grows steadily less coarse. Exemplification within his own being of pattern itself, pattern of myriad hue and tone, is man's most characteristic adventure. Continually modifying his natural habitat, and ever expanding its scope, man creates of the cosmos a veridical home for himself: in his symbolic representations, a mighty plant among the endlessly changing patterns of which he can feel comfort and peace. In the end, his goal is to disengage himself from the turmoil of grosser acts. Without negating, but ever enhancing the refinements of his interpersonal relations, he seeks to dwell, with utmost reflexive finesse, within his inmost being. To attain this goal, he must discern, by ever-decreasing energy increments—since entropy inexorably reigns—ever-more-refined lineaments and contours. In consequence, the self, incarnate in body which is gross and body which is fragile, evolves increasingly sensitive antennae for its outer dwellings and increasingly acute powers of reflexive discrimination. Thereby, man spiritualizes his body's natural rhythms. Creating of these rhythms an ethereal polyphony, a sort of divine dance, he comes to dwell in realms which enclose even more ample realms: realms of feeling, intuition, and thought.

In this process, the self discovers itself to be mirrored in others; and others, in itself. Each person peering deeply into the other—listening, as it were, to his messages—discovers that other to be an agent through whom he may in-form himself of ever-more-diversified forms. In stages, prefigured by Hegel, every person engenders for himself a deepening self-consciousness; he seeks within self-consciousness the very ground for its own activity, a ground which he discerns to be both immanent in consciousness and transcendent to it. Perceiving all selves to participate in the same ground, he concludes that, likewise, each self partakes of the selfsame ontologic structures. Though these structures vary from culture to culture, each being unique and idiosyncratic, they are nonetheless variations on a single universal theme. Working from within, this elusive ground limits every creature, yet infinitizes all creatures. How this paradoxicality can be justified I treat under the heading "A Self United."

In sum, the self consummates itself by participating in endlessly contrasting patterns; these are, in effect, guises which God assumes—His masks and His incarnations. Ultimately, the self dwells at peace with both its own natural origins and its own transcendental destiny. Whether it looks toward its beginning or toward its end, it experiences patterns of exuberance beyond imagination. For the self, the alpha and the omega of all being are one and the same. They point to a single source, the fount of all cosmic efflorescence. In spiraling fashion, novelty is ceaselessly inscribed upon repetition.

Yet no significant theory of the self can fail to take cognizance of the momentous impact made upon man in this century by the discovery of the Unconscious. As I noted earlier, the implications of the traditional view of the Unconscious (either Freud's theory or Jung's) suggest that every effort to conceptualize the Unconscious as a lawful assemblage of processes brings about its further dissolution. According to Freud and Jung, the more one penetrates its inmost recesses, the more it vanishes into intangible, ineffable, and, in the last analysis, inexplicable fragments. By essence, the Unconscious is presumed to be *ir*rational, and regarded as intrinsically incapable of conceptual elaboration. Every attempt to identify its ultimate fragments leads one toward the heart of *physical* processes, toward an object *within* the person's very subjectivity: an object which unaccountably resists attempts to apprehend it more deeply. However, should one seek to ground that subjectivity in the physical, one would be compelled to abandon a *parity* theory of mind and body (a view which I have embraced here). As with Freud, one would revert to some kind of mind–body reductionism. Body would acquire a more eminent ontologic status than mind.

Nevertheless, every attempt to locate a seemingly physical ground for human ontology, and to designate that ground a spatio-temporal manifold, leads one back to the mental. To meditate that ground is to transmute it into processes which increasingly acquire the status of mere mental imagery. The more one submerges oneself in the Unconscious, and thereby passes "out of mind" into ideation which, lacking consciousness, is no ideation at all, the more one is thrust back toward the mental, *emerging* from submergence. At one and the same time, the Unconscious (or *un*mind) is an un*body*. Must, as with Jung, a reverse reduction be adopted, a reduction which ontologically grounds the body in mind? What a bizarre conclusion! The more one seeks a physical ground, the more one thrusts oneself toward a mental ground—and conversely! Firmly rooting oneself in neither, one hovers between the mental and the physical. Hence, can one ground human ontology in that which exhibits *neither* primordial human characteristic: namely, body or mind, the physical or the spiritual? Still, one cannot easily reject the view, supported by the pervasive experience of both human pathology and human creativity, that what one designates "body" is, indeed, a process of sinking into depths, a mode of gravity incarnate; and what one designates "mind" is, analogously, a process of rising from depths, a mode of levitation incarnate.

At this point, one may justifiably postulate a multitude of strata, some of which, as ineffable, may be designated "mental" and others of which, as tangible, may be designated "physical." Nevertheless, is it not the case that the mind–body "problem" and the supposition of an intervening mediating Unconscious (which, in effect, is an unconscious–*un*body) must now be applied, *pari passu*, to each stratum in a class composed of numberless elements: bipartite strata the members of which, in every instance, are somehow magically joined by a third (intrinsically unspecifiable) ingredient? But the issue has simply been displaced from one conceptual formulation, and its associated ontologic locus, to another, and splintered into a multitude of analogous issues. Left with fragments, one is again compelled to rethink the entire problematic. Rethinking the Unconscious entails its dissolution and its supersession by an altogether new concept.

In reconsidering this concept, one is struck by the fact that one has been dealing with substantives rather than with activities and functions. Can it be that the unconscious–unbody is but the negative way of "fixating" an elusive rhythmic activity: an activity which unfolds in phases; which, indeed, requires the reformulation of the very concept of person, central topic of my entire work? Rather than the noun *person*, I propose the verb *personing-forth*, "personing-forth" not so much from *within* one's own physio-logic and psycho-logic labyrinth as from within the very cosmos wherein one is embedded as co-participant with numberless other processes. Adequately conceptualized, human comportment as "personing-forth" constitutes the self's veridical ground. Now the cosmos "regionalizes" itself in multitudinous ways. It articulates itself as a matrix of entwined loci, each the region in which diverse rhythms meet, coalesce, and synergize one another as, co-operant, they collectively strain toward unique personal expression. Joining these regions into a singular coherent manifold, a bond of sympathy inhering in the very ground of the cosmos allows a *syn-cretizing* of such forces as issue in specifically human activity. Indeed, the eternal insinuates itself into each temporal moment, and proceeds vertically to intersect the (horizontally) unfolding interlocked events. Every person's merely durational existence, his essential finitude, is pervaded by the infinite.

To construe "personing-forth" in a dialectically reflexive way, such static terms as "mind" and "body" become inadmissible. Hence, I substitute the more dynamic concepts of dancing forth and speaking forth. Each process provides a context, albeit quiescent and momentarily suppressed, which allows the other to crystallize, and fully to assert itself. Together, dance and speech constitute the orchestrated components of comportment. Though complementary modes of searching, they are mutually interdependent. As such, they jointly constitute the ways by which person and cosmos enter into reciprocal attunement. Furthermore, dancing and speaking unfold vis-à-vis specifically human resistances. Each such act contributes to a communal matrix. Incorporating the general forms of this matrix, a person articulates those aspects of the world which are relevant to his own creative existence. In-forming himself with the world's dynamic forms, he re-forms the very cosmos, adding to it his idiosyncratic and singular motions: motions which unfold in the dual modes of speech and dance.

How, in this process, can one locate the integral *I*? What grounds the unity of the self? Surrounded by haunting presences, one feels the prevalence of continuous interfusions of self with others. From one's inmost depths, one re-presents these presences in one's reflexive acts. In both dance and speech, one ineluctably adds a symbolic ingredient to the substance of mere presentation. Drawn into personal being, presences are progressively transformed. Symbol is layered upon symbol. An intricately laminated complexus shapes itself. Thereby, hitherto disparate presences are joined, constituting a unity of powers to act. In the end, this unity expresses a person's reflecting into his being, in systematic and coherent fashion, an Imago of the entire cosmos under the perspective of one or another of its sectors: an Imago which is multi-layered and, with respect to its diverse layers, interactional. In the context of one's "dancing," a dance of increasingly coordinated and integrated response, this complexus—a manifold of stimuli—reveals itself to be capable of indefinitely refined discursive formulation. As one sym-bolizes, one alternately, and with oscillating rhythms, moves toward and away from presentation. In this manner, one converts mere presence into sophisticated representation. Pregnant with the increasing intensity of such response motions, every person allows speech to burst forth as the consummatory dance of organs which are specialized to permit highly differentiated comportment. Stimulus and response are but foci in a single, integral, and complex act, an act composed of interwoven and concatenated sequences of subordinate acts.

Given these considerations, how can one locate man's *I* with respect to his mind and his body? In the context of the dialectic of stimulus and response, every person is empowered to focus searchingly upon diverse cosmic regions. Rooted in the circumscribed domain of his immediate spatio-temporal habitat, he roams, at first, limitedly; then, as he tests his powers, wide-rangingly. Thereby, he extends that domain to encompass still wider regions. In effect, he displaces his roots now to this region, now to that region. By his journeyings, a person integrates into a single manifold vast domains, indeed even distant cosmic reaches. By speaking and by dancing, in melodies and in steps increasingly differentiated and ample, he situates himself within the entire cosmos and becomes virtually co-extensive with it. Now the entire world is present to him; it reveals itself to his discerning gaze as immanently operative in his every particular act, and as potentiating ever-more-inclusive patterns of speech and dance. And he symbolizes that presence in greatly varied ways: by myriad facets, dimensions, and aspects. In this manner, the *I* feels its way throughout the world. Establishing successively more effective schemes of balance, it correlates its own being with world being.

By reducing his disorientation, the person more inclusively orients himself toward himself, in *his* authentic centeredness, in his relationship to the world, in *its* authentic centeredness. Gathering together anew his previously established and now obsolete relationships—all, in retrospect, modes of disorientation—he consecrates anew the unity of self and cosmos. When man falls away from this unity, he laments; when he rises again to this unity, he celebrates. Alternately, his singing and his dancing are songs and dances of celebration and lamentation. For every person aims at achieving appropriate balance between the tragic and the ecstatic, as both factors interweave to constitute each human existence. To this end, he constructs a vast context of speech signifiers and dance signifiers. Each signifier points inward toward other signifiers; each constructed context envelops other constructed contexts. But no signifier can be isolated from another; and the totality of signifiers reveals the essential person. By compressing my sense of my own meaning into the rhythms of my speech and my dance, and through the relevant signifiers, I expand, enrich, and deepen my orientation toward my world. By grounding myself in myself, I ground myself without myself. Truly, I now discover my *I* as rooted both within me and beyond me.

GROWING

Grounded in human seeking, the essential structures of human ontology progressively reveal themselves in the context of the ongoing quest. Hence, the principal themes which unite the topics of this volume pertain to persons as questors. As questors, persons initiate search, they progress through phases of search, they arrest search, they regress to inappropriate phases of search, and they consummate search. For each phase, search aims at retrospective disclosure of man's specific and unique seeking acts: as a totality of moments orchestrated *in concreto*; as universally applicable to all persons. Even in abstract form, the contours of searching appear in a seeker's consciousness only in those processes by which he carries out his quest. Not only will the theme of searching be introduced, but, in addition, a sketch will be presented of those ontologic structures which ground human being.

Midway through search which has been well executed, each person establishes for himself a *just* balance both between his component parts and between himself and others: that fair arrangement which alone will provide the basis, ever more concretely and ever more universally, by which he can work out the remaining phases of his search. Secure in his just appraisal of the *facts* of his situation, he understands the *truth* of his being with respect to primordial modes of achieving harmony and equilibrium. With equanimity and imperturbability, i.e., with σωψροσύνη, one may envisage hitherto unperceived modes of balance with clarity of articulation, depth of insight, and more ample scope.

Schematically, I represent the structure of human questing. In self-growth, the dialectical interplay of the moments of search endlessly coil back upon themselves; yet they ever reveal new vistas for human attainment:

The Good Life { Truth ↓ Goodness ↓ Beauty }

{ Trust ↓ Hope ↓ Love } The Pious Life

The Transcendental Life { Justice ↓ Integrity ↓ Wisdom }

Philosophy → Religion → Mysticism { goodness and piety unfold anew }

Three new journeys disclose themselves to the questor: the path to integrity, the path to wisdom, the way to consummate transfiguration. By pursuing the first path, the individual grows toward ever-more-inclusive schemes of integrity. Now growing is conceived as searching itself, but under a concrete perspective —the actual carrying through of the search. Initially, I present a concrete overview of the phases of growth, including a prefiguring of the path to wisdom. By interpreting relevant themes in Dante's *Divine Comedy*, in the light of topics pertinent for an ontology of self-growth, I depict, in vivid, intense, and dramatic symbolism, the quest for justice, integrity, and wisdom; I suggest a matrix of intuitions, grounded on Dante's insights, whereby ontologic themes implicit in a merely symbolic statement can then more fully emerge; and I show concordances between Dante's journey in the *Commedia* and Hegel's journey in the

Phänomenologie des Geistes. By concretely disclosing its moments, the *Comedy* poetically illuminates the *Phenomenology*, while the *Phenomenology* in philosophic fashion articulates conceptual structures implicit in the *Comedy.* Together, these accounts point toward a larger, more humane overview of human ontology.

My construal of Dante's search can itself be schematically represented. In their detailed development, my distinctions do not unfold in quite the sequential fashion indicated here—though some thread of linearity does run through the Cantos. With respect to non-linearity, the categories which I propose do overlap. They constitute a mosaic of interdependent parts, with both recapitulations and thematic variations.

Inferno	*Purgatorio*	*Paradiso*
The Entry	The Forgetting	The Symbol
The Labyrinth	Temptation and Purification	Integrality
The Descent	The Gathering Rhythms	Encounter
Confrontations	Care and Recollection	Integrity
The Fascinations	Metamorphosis	Eternity
The Depths	Purgation	The Center

These distinctions are symbolic. Connotatively, they declare their own import. But a context is provided for preliminary interpretation. As one proceeds with Dante along his arduous way, their immanent content will be more fully revealed. At the end of this book, their most explicit meanings will be set forth, and, in each instance, clothed with ontologic significance.

In despair, when in the *Inferno* of his soul, every person strives, with great effort, to achieve a balance within himself: balance which will eventually enable him to pass, through successively more harmonious adaptations, toward peace and joy. Amid life's upheavals and disequilibrations, he reflects self-consciously on the specific import of his self-growth; and he experiences his quest for integrity as a replication, through numerous metamorphoses, of the grounding balance which was attained in the phase of justice. Now one can construe the path to integrity as mediating one's own passage from more primordial human being (in justice) toward the fruition of one's being (in wisdom). And this path prepares the way for man's pursuit of wisdom. By speaking forth his consummate rhythms, he reveals, in progressively deeper layers of the fabric of utterance, the unfolding moments of his transcendental life: a fabric which, in the context of that life, is identified with his inmost being.

Accordingly, I explore these themes: how the self both induces crisis and resolves it through inward searching; how the vicissitudes of pain mixed with joy unfold, vicissitudes which ineluctably attend the personal growth consequent to this searching; how the self both creates and relates to the objects of its creation, and how, in creating, it empties itself of its content—a dialectic of filling and emptying, of ecstasy and anguish; how the self is compelled to turn to ever-deeper recesses of its own inwardness in order, by stages, to objectify its immanent ground

—ultimately the divine source of creativity—then to project those objects onto nature, nature felt, in consequence of this intermingling of newly shaped objects with formerly shaped objects, to be increasingly spiritualized; how this transcendentality of nature results from the activity not only of a particular self, but, indeed, of a community of selves which work together in tacit collaboration; how these collaborating selves, each in its own phase of growth, mirror one another's activities—prefiguring, recapitulating, or enjoying analogous phases; how these selves which mirror other selves rejoice in their sharing and, accordingly, in their sense of mutuality; how from this medley of selves nature becomes spirit incarnate; how all selves come to participate, despite meandering alienations and regressions, in a collective representation of their own interiorities—always vibrant and never reduced to an assemblage of inert and unthinking idols, mere appearance mistaken for an underlying ferment, as interiority dialectically unfolds!

By conceptualizing these interwoven themes, the phenomenon of *diremption*[2] can be formulated: namely, the tearing asunder of strands of potential external objectification, strands which arise from within the self; separating those strands and cultivating the potentialities resident in each strand; relinquishing this birthing activity, followed by new plunging into still deeper reserves of spiritual energy; joining together bare, unborn images, and so nurturing this interior phantasmagoria as to allow for their eventual creative drawing forth and externalization.

Yet, in this process, the self is always tempted to linger, sexually and romantically, in order vicariously to enjoy the rhythms of wisdom—but enjoyment as substitutive gratification; wisdom which has not yet been worked through or concretely achieved. To cite Hegel: "the real subject-matter is not exhausted in its purpose, but in working the matter out; nor is the mere result attained the concrete whole itself, but the result along with the process of arriving at it. . . . The systematic development of truth . . . can alone be the true shape in which truth exists."[3] This falling into illusion, a seeming Garden of Eden, Dante expressed in his account of the plight of Paolo and Francesca, when he wrote: "Love, which to no loved one permits excuse for loving, took me so strongly with delight in him, that, as thou seest, even now it leaves me not . . . love, which is quickly caught in gentle heart."[4] In their endless, and endlessly unrequited, romance, Paolo and Francesca seek to perpetuate this simulated life of cosmic participation. Should the momentary prefigurement of eternal perfection lapse—by rejection either of lover or of beloved—then, once again, man is thrust back onto his own resources. Nonetheless, by grace a relationship with one's complement may felicitously accompany the laborious task of working through the soul's crises.

At last, crisis is shown to be incapable of achieving resolution by creativity alone. Requiring the affirmation of dialogue, two become as one; each neither demands nor feels compelled to give. For dialogue strengthens such tenuous bonds to reality as result from radical self-relinquishment. When a person surrenders himself, accepting whatever may befall him—by listening, awaiting, and attending the full message of the other; in both loyalty and commitment to this receptive act—he renews his vigor and his inspiration to search. With neither bias nor preconception, he allows himself fully to experience the diverse textures of reality. Without self-deception, he permits these textures to reveal to him what is fully there. In this sense, every person can become veridically *philosophical.* For, in his inner emptiness, he can open himself to receive the fullness of both natural being and human being: the blessings of the Divinity. Thereupon, he suffuses himself with those new rhythms which ceaselessly hover about him, and benignly tend to envelop him. In appropriate ways, he responds to whatever is uttered to him. Thereby, a rhythmic interplay of participation and mutuality prevails; the path to wisdom has already been embarked upon.

In dialogue, selves become concretely aware that they are constituted by other selves: that only in true relatedness can they achieve their freedom, their autonomy, and their authenticity. By dwelling with other selves, and, in this context, by advancing their own creative urges, they can disclose ever-new possibilities for searching. And, by thus making oneself fully present to oneself in relationship to another self and, reciprocally, by thus allowing the presence of the other to unfold before one, oscillations of detachment and empathy can liberate one to be *who* one truly is. Alternating between stepping back and taking stock, hence, solidifying one's own self-identity, then going toward the other and allowing *his* being to pervade one's own being, hence, identifying with the other—these dialectically interwoven phases in the different schemes of presence and compresence which a person creates for himself—one may shape ever-new and more valid modes of integrity. In interweavings of doubt and certitude, as one probes the deeper implications of each factor, authentic human dialogue shapes itself. Reciprocal attunements of person with person, and endlessly rich complementarities of man and woman, spur the creation of those symbols of human encounter whereby rhythms of both self and cosmos reveal their manifold textures.

In phases, these schemes of relationship and symbolism unfold. At first, primordial experience must be distinguished, experience in which no clear sense of demarcation between subject and object, whether of self or of other, prevails. Yet tensions immediately arise which press for resolution. The *mere* qualities of experience which characterize this phase separate themselves into an assemblage of qualities, qualities often incompatible with one another. By nature reflexive, the self implicitly seeks modes of coherence among these qualities. Initially, it divides them into two sets: those pertaining to the intimately "mine"; those pertaining to the more remotely "mine." Indeed, the sense of *I* arises through the very contrasts between different degrees of intimacy, contrasts which necessitate even the evolving sense of "mine." Yet no "mine" can be unless it is set in opposition to a "not-mine." Therefore, a dialectic unfolds wherein diverse schemes for configuring both self and other-than-self articulate themselves. However, as soon as this distinction is drawn, the primordially simple trust of mere "being with" is shattered. Now the self experiences itself to be constrained by—hence, in resistance to—the Other, an Other felt as determining the very contours of the self. It frames a *realist* perception of the world. But to preserve its own integrity as a configuration of qualities which is valid in its own right, the self must turn away from the Other. Denying its very actuality, it must, in freedom, experience the vicissitudes of its own moods. Yet as moods which sweep over the self with seeming contingency, this inner life of the self is now felt as *internally Other* than that self, hence, as inwardly resisting the self's own encounters with itself. Now the stance of *idealism* arises.

Thus alternating between a realist and an idealist perception of the world, the self strives to restore the intimacies of primordial experience. It seeks to reduce the otherness of the Other, whether of internal objects or of external objects. Too late, however, to experience full restitution, the self hovers (*a*) between inner and outer and (*b*) between alienation and intimacy with respect to inner and outer. Nonetheless, the very engaging of both kinds of object permits ever-more-inclusive modes of equilibrium to prevail. Hence, the self passes from a mere presumption of a just balance among the qualities which it discerns *toward* an actual effecting of different arrangements among the objects which it discriminates as collating aggregations of those qualities. In its effort continually to realign those objects, and to reorient itself toward them, the self seeks to preserve its own integrity. It dwells in hope that the fleeting, evanescent qualities of primordial experience, qualities receded into the past, will, now oriented toward the future, exhibit deeper-lying continuities: a solidarity among the objects to which the self increasingly relates itself.

In this process, a mere being-with-self gives way to an altogether new mode of relatedness. A truly dynamic kinship supervenes. Now the self deeply experiences itself as gathering objects from hitherto unknown, and unexplored, cosmic recesses. Sensing a doubly unfathomable abyss, one within itself and one without, it attunes itself to heretofore unacknowledged mysteries. By meditating its newly fashioned symbolisms, it comes to recognize its own creative activity. In ever-more-profound acts of searching, the self fuses into novel patterns the objects which it had initially discerned to arise from within with the objects which it had initially discerned to arise from without; it confers upon itself a transcendental status. Participatively relating to both realms, inner and outer, it experiences itself as alternating between two world perspectives: transcendental realism, transcendental idealism. Under the first perspective, the self holds dialogue with the outer world; under the second, it establishes an analogous relationship with the inner world. In both instances, the contents of self and other are interchanged; they are veridically transfigured.

Always, the self endeavors to join its own remembered past and its own anticipated future to dramatic immediacy; it strives to present itself to both worlds, inner and outer, in different modes of compresence. To achieve this purpose, it shapes symbols as extensions of its own being: ethereal symbols and tangible symbols. By these symbols, the self portends for them a larger spiritual content. And, with respect to this content, such symbols come to constitute the essential vehicle whereby the self participates dialogically, and in ever-more-self–enriching ways, with new facets of the world, facets both personal and non-personal. Moreover, the symbol draws disparate strands of relatedness into deeper confluence. In the end, the symbol becomes identical with the person himself: the person *as* he joins himself in communion with other persons engaged in similar quests. By its novelty, the symbol shatters old modes of relatedness. It prepares the way whereby the continuities of existence, both those natural and those human, will give birth to more ample orchestrations of relationship. By reference to such orchestrations, dialogists transform their merely truncated, solipsistic status. They acquire their true centers: centers which lie in the interstices between dialogists rather than within any particular dialogist. Profoundly affected by these orchestrations, dialogists frame a radically new perspective on reality, the perspective of transcendental rhythmicality. Symbols nested within symbols mirror a cosmos which is shaped through the interplay of persons, and indeed of all reflexive creatures. Having established firm, just bases of action, persons grow *through* integrity toward wisdom. In both sound and silence, they speak forth. In luminously coordinated actions, they discover authentic cosmic rhythms. Thus unconcealed by the collective activity of symbolizers in general, in harmonies which enclose harmonies and cacophonies transcended by new orchestrations, each self reveals itself to be a true microcosm. At last, the aura of the spiritual which surrounds the physical so pervades the physical, and is therefore so integrated with it, that a single integrity is fashioned: the integrity of persons-in-relation.

In a diagram, I exhibit these connections:

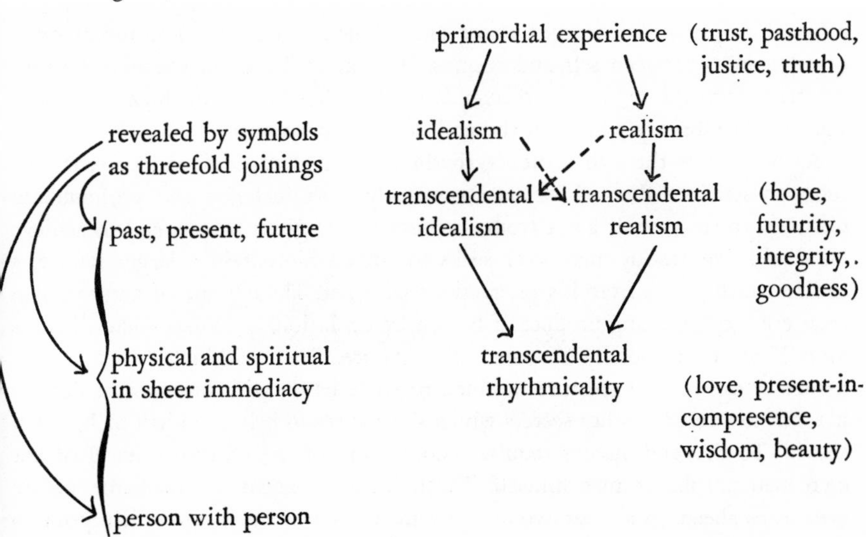

SPEAKING

Human being expresses its quintessential nature in manifold ways: as intertwined dances of gesture and imagery; as flowings forth of this double dance into acts of speaking and shaping. In authentic utterance, wherein the textures of words and things reveal themselves, one speaks from the heart, from one's very center. In a broad sense, utterance pervades not only speaking in its narrow import but all human contrivance as well. For language in general envelops both speaking and shaping. And in its dances of gesture and imagery, human being unfolds additional basic rhythms, rhythms which ground every human act. Like language, dance implies a dual usage: narrow, as dancing in its conventional form; inclusive, as the totality of a person's "natural" motions, his primordial rhythms. As the rhythms of human utterance unfold, they disclose themselves to be the very apotheosis of the dance, itself the matrix of all speech. In ethereal, ineffable bodily movement, meaningful sound flows forth: sound which is sung and sound which is spoken; sound which exhibits patterns which further elaborate the dance. Whether gestural, a bodily movement, or imagist, a mind movement, the human dance creates new possibilities for human utterance.

Such topics as context, rhythm, fabric, matrix, and cavern enable one to conceptualize the interweavings of speaking, dancing, and shaping. By "context," I mean the interplay of words and things to constitute an ever-changing texture of human action. By "rhythm," I mean the orchestrations of that texture, in action's more subtle unfoldings. By "fabric," I mean the enmeshings of the symbols which such actions manifest: orchestrated patterns of symbolic transformation, patterns embedded in a transpersonal realm. By "matrix," I mean the community of interwoven selves which prescribe the norms for selecting particular modes of orchestration: modes which shape the primordia of speech as a kaleidoscopic flux of images whose enfoldings and efflorescences reveal styles of relatedness between self and cosmos. By "cavern," I mean the source of all cosmic action: the *mysterium tremendum* which lies hidden in those caverns of silence and vibrancy which, in the end, ground the cosmos.

As one passes through contexts, rhythms, fabrics, matrices, and caverns, one roots oneself in realms which are successively more inclusive and profound. In his quest to set himself apart from an immediately given nature, and to achieve his distinctive destiny, man ever seeks to embed himself in a larger nature, a nature which grows from his interactions with her. Though one of nature's own creations—culminating product of her entire evolutionary course—man discerns himself to be profoundly alienated from nature. From within her own womb, nature brings forth a creature destined to wage battle with her: not to destroy her, but to wrest from her secrets which she refuses to bring to birth of her own accord. To this end, nature requires cooperation of the crowning jewel of her own metamorphoses, man himself. Through him as agent and mediator, nature ever leaps ahead. In a great evolutionary march, she spans a gap which, prior to man's emergence, is absolutely unique. But, given man, a series of such singularities issue forth. Into his hands alone has been placed the promise that both he and nature can achieve redemption: an end concealed in the very beginning; fruit of the germ whence blossoms not only man himself but all that humankind is capable of discerning. And every new symbolic creation constitutes a step toward that redemption and, as such, a radical new singularity within evolution.

What sets man so dramatically apart from nature's other creatures? Essentially, it is his capacity for seeking through utterance. By both his physical and his intellectual endowment, each related to the other, man, pre-eminent among earthly creatures, is competent to search in richly diversified ways. By his physical traits, he is empowered to adapt himself to myriad natural circumstances; by his intellectual traits, he is empowered to discriminate, through his capacity to articulate systematically employed linguistic categories, the ever-shifting conditions of his natural existence. Freely roaming the world, he stands apart from the world. To attain security, he dwells not alone but among his fellows. Therein rooted, he compensates for his natural frailty by creating ever-more-cohesive communities. By the word, he binds members indissolubly together.

Uniquely among earth's creatures, man finds himself enveloped by speech: speech which he himself has fashioned that he might cope with the exigencies of his ever-novel situations; speech which, through his community, has been transmitted to him as his quintessentially human heritage. Unable to root himself in any particular locale, or even in any particular group of his fellows, man ever seeks to establish a secure habitat within the word. Yet the consequence of rooting himself in a realm which is so ineffable is to separate him ever more sharply from natural processes, even though he is organically interwoven with those processes. Thus etched against nature, he is neither of nature nor distinct from nature. On the contrary, he is bound to nature without, at the same time, securely enjoying his participations in her.

Accordingly, the person acquires such perspectives on the natural world as set that world into opposition to his own spirit: spirit which represents itself through his deployment of speech. In his endeavor to reconcile the contrasts between nature and spirit, he takes refuge more and more in spirit alone. In the last analysis, the only way in which man can adapt himself to nature's ever-changing vicissitudes is for him to arrest change by constructing stable schemes of linguistic demarcation. He carves out such regions, dimensions, and aspects of nature as are relevant to his own needs. But as a result, he must contrive ever-more-intricate ways of effecting distinctions. By these, he so reshapes given nature as veridically to transfigure her. For he must penetrate more and more deeply into nature's resources; he must discriminate textures of natural occurrences which otherwise would elude him. Yet these thingly textures are so tightly interwoven with the instrument by which man creates them—namely, the word—that the most complicatedly laminated word–thing textures must invariably result.

By his technology, by his art, by his science, by his religious perceptions, and by his power to shape philosophic generalization, the person brings forth nature's latent potentialities, potentialities which nature is not competent to draw forth from herself. For these potentialities lie too deeply embedded in nature to emerge by their own intrinsic powers. In this sense, man places meaning in nature; and he incarnates meaning in many ways. Always, in the end, he accompanies his reshapings of nature by the word. Co-adapted, words and things enter into dialectical relationship. By its resistance to the other, each is transformed. Yet a dynamic conformation between word and thing allows such metamorphoses of nature to occur as open the way toward an altogether new realm.

Man experiences this realm as it is emerging, and he rejoices in its textures. Celebrating his powers to reconstitute nature, he gives expression to his joy in dance and in song. By thus externalizing the spirit within him, and by animating it as expressive motions of his body, man replicates that dance of being which, on a latently spiritual level, reverberates throughout nature. In all the modalities of which he is capable, his very reflections on nature actually reproduce nature, though in more ethereal shape. Now nature mirrors herself with respect to her own intricate polyphony in the incomparably more variegated and subtly nuanced orchestrations which man is competent to bring forth. Having unfolded her powers, in a great evolutionary movement, to actualize herself as human being, a transfigured nature unfolds anew *through* man: nature metamorphoses herself as spirit. Feelings which had spread in attenuated ways throughout nature, feelings which had constituted man's infrapersonal being, now converge, with increasing intensity, upon a self which pulsates with the music of human life.[5]

By both song and dance, man re-presents nature anew. Once these symbols of his being have been born, they replicate themselves on more subtle planes of human presence and compresence. Symbols engender new symbols. Once created, human utterance unfolds through its own phases; it replicates the matrix of those intra-organismic and interorganismic activities whence it arose. Space, time, and matter, categories which allow nature herself to be conceptualized, are rendered anew through art, music, poetry, and the whole panoply of human symbolism. Every art constitutes itself a new form of space, a new form of time, a new form of matter. In each instance, these forms are more concrete than those representing natural phenomena; and they are co-adapted to one another in marvelously subtle ways. By *naming* nature, through science, art, religion, and philosophy, man gathers together anew those natural echoes which constitute resonances of an altogether new substance, a substance in which man will henceforth dwell.

In the context of a human community, utterance unfolds through specific human acts. In dialogue, selves so commune that they bring forth the holiness of spirit. Dwelling immanently in nature, spirit brings itself to its consummate expression through man; and man responds to spirit, in its most profound manifestations, in a sacramental way. Commemorating a spirit which pervades the very cosmos, and especially man himself, man renews his existential obligations in worship, and, ideally, in his every act. As true questor, he never ceases to allow spirit to bring itself through him to its own fruition. Through the very acts by which he names a nature more ample and more profound than the nature which is immediately accessible to him, man raises to self-consciousness the fact that he actually dwells in a larger cosmic community, a community which he himself has drawn forth, and, indeed, carved out of nature as the underlying ground of her own visible processes.

Each through the other's agency, nature and man affirm one another. For nature has borne herself to fruition in the coming of man. As a kind of gift, she gives him to himself. In reciprocal gifts, man pays homage to nature. He enables her latent powers to actualize themselves as an incomparably rich manifold. Through a dialectical interplay, a new product is born: a synthesis of nature and man, whereby man's originally naïve perspective on nature can revise and enlarge itself. A sequence of perspectives, each subsuming and going beyond its predecessors, approaches, as an ideal asymptotic limit, the everlasting: the infinite and the eternal. For this movement to progress, it must occur in a matrix constituted by the largest possible reciprocity of givings: givings by which self freely presents to self all that it can draw forth of spirit within itself; givings which, in this process, catalyze one another. By grace, the entire cosmos reveals itself with increasing persuasiveness as a flowing forth of gifts, indeed as a superabundance of gifts. Persons encounter one another as giving incarnate. Communally, they reveal *to* humankind this gift of a cosmos presented *through* humankind.

Beyond the community of selves-in-relation, an interior cosmic matrix grounds the human source of images. Through their interminglings, synergizings, and orchestratings, these images enrich both human gesture and human utterance. For fantasy, principles of combination, displacement, dissolution, and elaboration prevail which differ from principles operative for fact. No random collection of fragments, images tend to cohere. And they enact an internal drama which undergoes its characteristic transfigurations and consummations. By these principles, novel configurations shape themselves into entirely new dimensions of expression, dimensions which cannot be predicted on the basis of already experienced phenomena. Yet the messages contained in images are cryptic. Requiring special rules for their decipherment, images are so formed that these rules of governance manifest their prescriptive content only as the images themselves flow forth by their own autonomous motions.

Tangible complexes which reverberate within the human community, symbols greatly condense their originating image sources. By appropriate response, one can initiate a drawing forth of latent symbolic content into overt expression. Moreover, analogous symbols tend to recur, even among widely differing peoples who dwell in the most diversified communities; and this fact betokens archetypal schemes whereby the symbols' constitutive images weave textures which, in community after community, exhibit profound isomorphism. By referring to such isomorphism, as one searches into the interior abyss of these symbols, one promotes one's own solidarity in both the human community and the cosmic community. Emerging in the context of dialogue, such symbols as, most conspicuously, the dream—prototype and paradigm for these processes—point toward hitherto concealed sectors of reality, sectors constitutive of labyrinthine depths of community, person, and cosmos.

The ways by which the messages hidden within symbols can reveal themselves are manifold; and these messages can be so decoded as to reveal the subtler resonances of the very images which gave birth to the symbols. Such disclosures entail massive unfoldings of life's symbolic forms, unfoldings which encompass myriad confluences of imagery. Ever converging to shape a particular human existence, multiple influences arise from remote cosmic reaches. Complicatedly intertwined moods, and their endless vicissitudes, deposit their traces on the person as the formative basis for his novel symbolic schemes. Correctly read, these schemes reveal the struggles, the anguish, the conflict, the hopes, the sorrows, the yearnings, the joys which make up a human life.

Through the dream and other sorts of fantasy, the universal matrix of human utterance manifests its varied shapes. A veridical dance of imagery mirrors the dance of being which pervades the cosmos. In ways which attune themselves to like unfoldings in other selves, this mental dance unfolds in every self. By probing the matrix of utterance as it immanently effloresces within him, yet transcendently suffuses the cosmos, a person clarifies both his particular existence and the awesome events of the cosmos itself, as, through its successive metamorphoses *within* and *through* every person, the cosmos bursts into its autochthonous rhythms. Collating these symbolic representations, dialogists present to one another images of human perfection as mirroring perfections which ever struggle to be born within the cosmos. Thereby, persons shape those authentic encounters whereby the integrity of each who encounters can more luminously actualize itself and, thenceforth, become woven into the lives of all who will subsequently encounter.

The matrix wherein images flow, and so form themselves that they might be transformed into human gesture and human utterance, is itself embedded in a larger matrix: the very ground of human compresence, of creaturely compresence, of world process, of cosmic ferment. Every person is empowered to prove that this realm, these caverns of silence and vibrancy, pervades the entire cosmos, that it roots all authentic communion. As one penetrates this ground, one passes out of nature, and her ineluctable battles with the human spirit, to that womb whence both nature and spirit arise. One passes toward a beyond which dwells immanently in man, yet is profoundly transcendent to him: a domain which, once one has come to participate in it, bears witness to a divine presence which, correlatively, bears witness to every human questor.

Inner and outer, subject and object, and immanence and transcendence are distinctions which themselves must be transcended, and, in the end, vanish. Ever more-inclusive communities, each embedded in still ampler communities, arise to direct one's quest. As one probes, one realizes that one is seeking to surpass one's own finitude; one strives both to touch and to be embraced by the infinite. Far from losing one's spiritual identity, one, on the contrary, enhances and perpetuates that identity. Herein, one reconciles the peace of human existence with the zest of human existence; one finds one's ultimate affirmation; one's search is borne to fruition; one fulfills oneself in durable meaning.

NOTES

1. Walter W. Skeat, *A Concise Etymological Dictionary of the English Language* (New York: Capricorn, 1963), p. 364.
2. G. W. F. Hegel, *The Phenomenology of Mind*, trans. J. B. Baillie, 2nd rev. ed. (London: Allen & Unwin; New York: Macmillan, 1949), p. 391.
3. Ibid., pp. 69, 70.
4. *The Inferno of Dante Alighieri* 5.103, 100, The Temple Classics (London: Dent, 1950), p. 55.
5. Here I stress man's apartness from nature, his emergence from her, his opposition to her, and his radical transcendence of her. In this activity of separation, lamentation and celebration interweave. Elsewhere I rectify an essentially *redemptive* view of man by emphasizing his union of nature, his participation in her processes, and his sense of profound natural mystery which itself radically transcends *him.* In both Job and Ecclesiastes, one finds eloquent statement of such interweavings of lamentation and celebration as are appropriate for this essentially *ecologic* view of man. In later books, notably *Metamorphosis* and *Cosmos,* I take up the ecologic theme as complementary to the redemptive theme. In the meantime, I refer the reader to the profound studies of Thomas W. Berry, C.Pp.S. in his six volumes of the Riverdale Papers, printed at the Riverdale Center for Religious Research in New York City.

II

Searching:
The Ground of Human Being

4

PERSONAL FREEDOM: THE DIALECTICS OF SELF-POSSESSION

PREAMBLE

To introduce the theme of the ontology of the person with respect to searching, I analyze personal freedom in terms of two sets of triads which have dominated Western norms for human conduct: the Scriptural ideal of faith, hope, and love, and the classical ideal of truth, goodness, and beauty. Pre-eminently the creature in search of freedom, man expresses that quest, as the stages, interpreted in a context set by these ideals, whereby he acquires self-possession. Initially, he owns himself primarily in relationship to himself alone; then he owns himself primarily as embedded in human society; finally, he owns himself more inclusively as enveloped by, yet participating in, the larger cosmos. Throughout this process, man progressively liberates himself, revealing his essential being as an activity constituted by free, spontaneous creative acts, acts (nonetheless) witnessed, guided, and overseen by a personal presence. My purpose is to sketch, in terms of a correlation between the Scriptural ideal and the classical ideal, the ground of human freedom, its inherent ambiguity, and the phases through which it is brought to fruition. In particular, I set forth the steps by which the self takes possession of itself as both condition and content of its evolving and ever-more-concrete freedom.[1]

A • THE INTERWOVENNESS OF FAITH, HOPE, AND LOVE

(*a*) Trust

In Corinthians, it is written: "And now abideth faith, hope, love." Within this triad, hope includes yet transcends faith; love includes yet transcends faith and hope: for "the greatest of these is love" (1 Co 13:13). Sequentially, each virtue lays the ground whereby the remainder can be achieved. By the power of faith, the power of hope is activated. By the power of hope, the power of love is activated. And the potentiation of faith, hope, and love is requisite for consummate freedom.

By "faith" I mean an entrusting. Trust[2] is the primordial quality of the acts by which the self orients itself toward its immanent possibilities for growth. Precognizing the situation in which, from moment to moment, it finds itself, the self, in trust, acknowledges the options for action which it discerns therein. Joining its (autochthonous) powers to powers resident in its situation, the self becomes efficacious action.

Every present moment affords novel opportunities for action. By present moment, I mean the moment in its presence, and "presence" in a double sense. On the one hand, I mean the haunting context in which the self apprehends itself with all its elemental powers—a context of factors not yet contoured which, entering into the composition of the self, potentiate those powers. On the other hand, I mean a gift, a present, the donor of which, as yet unknown, is simply accepted. In both instances, this particular instant—fleeting, evanescent, fragile—is veritably a pre-*esse*. It is the condition prior to being, i.e., being in the sense of an authentic *to be*—an enduring and, as such, a becoming. Moreover, by "presence" I mean that momentary being with another, however undefined and inarticulate, which, thus experienced as a gift, is at one and the same time a giving by a donor who though unknown is reassuring, and, reciprocally, a giving of the self to that donor. In this (first) stage along freedom's way, the bare, abstract potency of a process appears, a process whereby the self differentiates its options and primordially chooses or rejects those options.

Trust is the primordium of searching. It is searching in its germinal state; it is that element primordially germane to searching. And searching lies at the heart of personal freedom. This self-entrusting to the world implies that one initially orient oneself toward oneself unconsciously and merely immanently. As one passes, first, into a state of consciousness and, finally, into a state of self-consciousness, the simply reflex orienting elicited by the situation in which one is implicated is transformed into *reflective* orienting. Deliberation—hence, deliberate attachment to a particular course of action—is evoked. Indeed, deliberation, orientation, and attachment are related notions. The conditions which these notions suggest involve the element of balance or equilibrium. To be disoriented is to be in a state of imbalance. It is to be de-tached from those habitual attachments (to the presented gift) which constitute the primordial ground wherein one roots oneself—a ground destined to be progressively displaced from the circumstances, narrow and circumscribed, of early life toward a more inclusive and deeper ground. Moreover, the deliberation which accompanies this self-thrusting and the consequent quest for re-equilibration are correlative activities. "Deliberation" and "equilibration" are cognate terms based upon the stem *librare*, so that "to deliberate" means *to weigh thoroughly* in the sense of *balancing* alternative possibilities.

(*b*) Hope

By the contingencies of life, one is constantly thrust into disorientation. Unforeseen constraints never cease to propel the person in one direction rather than another. As soon as detached, the self experiences its power for effecting reattachment; it is impelled to seek ever-new roots. Ultimately, security is found in the flux and ferment of the self's own powers—but only when those powers are experienced as joined to a "something" beyond the world. No longer does attachment to particular objects prevail. Paradoxically, one has attained one's freedom by attaching oneself to an object so elusive as to be no object at all. In a kind of existential bewilderment, one secures oneself in that which itself is not secure: namely, in a self in process of continual formation and transformation, a self always in relationship to another which itself can be no object.[3] Always, one must find one's way about the world as though one were in a labyrinth. Yet one's explorations inexorably lead one back to one's self. In the final analysis, this labyrinth *is* the self, a self which ever strives to *own* itself amid the kaleidoscopic fluctuations of the world. Accordingly, faith consists in a spontaneous un–self-conscious rootedness in a relationship between the self and the immanently enveloping process which is the world experienced, as faith brings itself to fruition, as only initially stable and dependable; for, on deeper inspection, the world reveals itself as inexorably in ferment.

Trust eventuates in reliance upon an inclusive personal witness,[4] a witness both immanent in one's own self-development and transcendent to it—a personal witness to one's own being and growth. As the self thereby roots itself in itself, and as thus experienced as ultimately witnessed, it is clarified and made more substantial. Each present moment is felt as a concrete particular: stable and solid, yet but an occasion of experience ever in process of metamorphosis, efflorescing by reflective elaboration into a new occasion.

Once achieved, the freedom of trust cannot rest content with a mere string of presents: each sui generis; each an enveloping presence; each, in effect, a witness benign, should trust reign, but, if distrust supervene, malignant.[5] Freedom is a perpetual stirring, an insatiable restlessness of the self. To be, freedom must transcend its own mere floating in a particular moment. It must constitute the duration of a present, a present which flows toward and into a future. It must pass from the phase of trust to the phase of hope. For hope concerns the continuity, and not a mere contiguity, of present moments. By implying a future, a durable solidarity of moments also implies a past—a past which expresses the present as the latter perishes into a new present which is the future about to be. To hope is to secure oneself in a destiny which is an ineluctable outgrowth of the immediacy of the moment. In hope, the self risks, from moment to moment, its integrity, its wholeness, its balance; it dares thus to risk in hope that a solidarity of moments will thereby emerge. For hope concerns survival, survival despite unfortuitous contingencies.

The ground for survival, so hope affirms, is this solidarity of past with present, this passage of what had been present into what will be present. In hope, an Imago of all that had been is etched upon every present which appears. A novel scheme of values, a new priority of intensities, is assigned this Imago. A unique pattern of contrasts is shaped. In addition, hope affirms the solidarity of present with future. It discerns the lineaments of sheer possibility; it foresees the transmutation of mere potency into actuality; it oversees the activity of selection and rejection, the activity whereby these possibilities are contoured into ever-new configurations of actuality. Thus affirming the pregnancy of the present with seeds of the past as they blossom toward new creations of the future, hope affirms its own continuance. For hope catalyzes the renewal of hope. Its continuity is grounded in the continuity of time itself—time *in concreto*, time rich with the lesser durations which flow into ever-more-inclusive durations.[6]

Once faith and hope are established as the prevailing conditions of human existence, the way is opened by which human freedom can receive its veridical ground. Freedom requires, first, that one give oneself up to the objectively *spatialized* sphere of encounter; and freedom further requires that one entrust oneself to every duration, in hope, that one give oneself up to the subjectively *temporalized* sphere of self-encounter. Only this conquest of time itself by hope, and the consequent rooting of oneself in the temporal process, will allow the consummately *material* self to emerge, a self actively in relation to the world likewise experienced as substantial. Thus, to bring one's personhood to fruition in this experience of freedom, the self must articulate the space of its existence; only thereby can it feel the freedom to expand its own powers vis-à-vis the world. It must enter into durable relationship with the objects it discriminates within this space; only thus can it feel the expanding powers of the world in relation to itself.

Space is engendered in the wake of the flow of time; as time temporalizes itself, it correlatively leaves spatial depositions. These depositions spread out as successive sets of moments, one set stratified upon the other and, as spatial, similar to eternally present moments. From this point of view, space is the insinuation of eternity into time. Beyond that, it is that arresting of time which is no mere evanescent point, but a solidarity of objects. For space is a field of relationships among these objects, objects coordinated as a context of action. As such, space is the "region" toward which objects, construed as processes, strain for interconnection. It is the virtuality of full relatedness. Conversely, time is the flowing of spatial arrangements into one another. Ultimately, time is the virtual movement into futurity which inheres in every spatial increment. It is the becomingness of space. Amid the eternal spread of all consummated present moments, time is the inexorable process character of reality. Hence, at bottom, the solidarity of objects is a flowing forth, a "concrescence"[7] of those objects: a bringing to birth of their latent possibilities as real, concrete entities. The former expressing hope and the latter expressing trust, process and eternity are, appropriately construed, ingredients of love.

(*c*) Love

Under this perspective, human freedom consists, in the last analysis, in the self giving itself to a matrix of progressively crystallizing relationships. In this process, the self finds itself; it experiences compresence, a sense of dwelling momentarily with the eternal. Herein it discovers its own ground and distinguishing traits; it acquires the capacity to receive into its constitution the gift of the variegated *relata* to which it thus (spatially) relates itself; it is liberated to feel its way into the very texture of those *relata* so that, conversely, it might, when *they* will have received a sufficient degree of sentiency, accept the reciprocal apprehending of itself *by* the *relata*. In short, freedom is the activity by which the self attains to the possession of itself in relation to that which, though wholly other than it, is nonetheless profoundly attuned to it. For, at bottom, freedom is the mutual attunement of self and other. In freedom, the rhythms of each enmesh with each. Renouncing itself as merely self-enclosed, the self ceaselessly affirms as the ground whereby it individuates itself its participation in a context of relations—relations which, in their consummate shape, are relations of love. Hence, faith and hope ground the possibility for the emergence of freedom from its merely germinal state.

When I speak of the self-possessed man, I mean a man in possession of his faculties: his gifts and his sensibilities. Thus truly owning one's own resources, one is free so to orient oneself toward the contingencies of life that one can only enrich the quality of that life. For no matter how constrained by the obstacles which inexorably intrude themselves from every direction, the self is empowered to dwell in vibrant peace with itself. So dwelling, it experiences itself as likewise dwelling in, hence, empowered radically to accept, a relationship between itself and a witness to its actions—ultimately, an inclusive, enveloping presence at first dimly though always hauntingly perceived, then discerned with increasing clarity. In an attitude of ever-more-profound acquiescence, without, however, ceasing to affirm its own essential autonomy, the self dwells, as it were, in the interstices between itself and another; by stages, it detaches itself from bondage to the other, while, correlatively, it gradually attunes itself to that other; and, in the last analysis, it attaches itself only to the source whence springs all relationship. In effect, the free self—or more accurately expressed: the self in process of freeing itself—acquires an attitude of sensitive respect for the contingencies of existence, including the contingency of its very self.[8]

In consequence, the obstacles one confronts, and unremittingly must orient oneself toward, present themselves in stratified fashion, each set layered upon an antecedent set and interacting with that set; a progressive detachment from that to which one had hitherto been attached; a grieving over the loss of an ineluctably perishing past; a detachment which thrusts one again and again into the solitude of one's own evanescing *I*—yet, the solitude, I repeat, of the relatedness of presences which transcend the finite; the infinitude of an enveloping personal witness incarnate, not in a particular object, but in the constant flowing forth of endless successions of matrices of objects.

A holy triad: faith, hope, and love! The crown of faith is hope; the crown of hope is love. Having already declared that without love there is no freedom and that the inmost and most elemental ingredient of freedom *is* love, I can now affirm: love unfolds in a procession of stages, the stages whereby the obstacles to which I have referred are, one by one, not so much conquered as acquiesced to; love presupposes resignation; love entails tranquillity; love proceeds at times calmly, at times ecstatically, but, however it unfolds, love always aims at vibrant peace.

B • CORRELATING THE SCRIPTURAL TRIAD WITH THE CLASSICAL TRIAD: TRUTH, GOODNESS, AND BEAUTY

(*a*) Freedom and Person: Etymology

To facilitate my quest for the meaning of personal freedom, I now note certain etymologic surprises.[9] In its usual sense, *free* is derived from the Old English *fri*, meaning "not in bondage or constraint." In this usage, freedom is defined by negation. It is not freedom toward such and such an orientation, but freedom from such and such constrictions. However, when further pursued, "freedom" may be traced to the Old High German word *fridu*, which means *peace*—the original of the modern German *der Friede*. Moreover, in Flamboyant German, from the time of Walther von der Vogelweide, *freien* signifies "to marry." In turn, the latter may be traced to Old High German *frijon*, which means "to love," and this term is, in its origin, grounded in the Sanskrit *priyate*, meaning "he loves." Indeed, "to marry" surely implies a bond, but not, in its origins, a bond*age*. On the contrary, it implies a union, an attunement of lovers, a completion of each in the other. Hence, involved in the very roots of our contemporary word "freedom" are the ideas of both peace and love (the latter in its reciprocal sense). Surely, moreover, the concept, though not the word, "peace" is related to the intertwined concepts of faith, or trust, and hope. To be at peace with oneself requires that one be both trusting and hopeful—in the senses previously mentioned. And both trust and hope, I repeat, ground and condition the possibility for love.

Continuing this etymologic exercise, I note the origins of the word "person" in the Greek πϱός and ὄπα (from ὄψ [or ὦπα from ὤψ]). In classical Greek theater, the word refers to a mask placed before the eyes and the face to dramatize certain qualities which the actor symbolizes and to communicate this symbol to the audience. Moreover, ὄπα is related to such words as "sonorous"; i.e., the effect of this mask was to amplify the voice, to draw forth speech in powerful resonances. Thus resounding as a vocal aura which emanates from the actor, and radiates toward his audience, the spoken word envelops the audience in the charisma of the special qualities intended to be transmitted. Indeed, to speak forth with resonance is to declare some profound inner condition, a state of the psyche which resides deep within the person. Moreover, it is to communicate the intentions, the depth, and the scope of the inwardness of the actor, the labyrinthine character of his psyche. Finally, it is to affirm through the inflections, the sonorities, of the words he utters his essential and inmost being.

Combining the terms "personal" and "freedom," I now take certain liberties within my etymologic exploration. I affirm as the meaning of these linked ideas *a passing out of a (passive) stage of bondage (i.e., the contingencies) through love grounded in faith and hope, and the bonds of love, to an (active) state of peace.* In this passage, the one who dwells *through* bondage toward love and, ultimately, toward peace, declares, in his speechifying, his authentic inwardness. Within the depths of one's being one discovers the words by which one might express, and comportmentally constitute, oneself a living exemplar of the questing man. Accordingly, "to be free" means to be in a state of personal harmony and authenticity that one might transcend all bondage and dwell in peace and in love. This dwelling is a double dwelling: a dwelling with oneself and a dwelling with another, whether the latter is thing, organism, or person; and each mode of dwelling exhibits its own phases and characteristics.

(*b*) Freedom and Human Existence

What is the nature of this dwelling in both its active and its quiescent aspects? In recent years, *to be free* is associated with a power to do and to change. However, the earlier meaning proposed in my etymologic excursion implies an acquiescence and a resignation, a giving of oneself up to whatever will induce harmony among the diverse parts of one's being as it stands in relation to another. More comprehensively: to be free is to engage in a dialectical interplay between the active and the quiescent—and this with respect to the constraints of human existence, constraints imposed both from within and from without. Accordingly, freedom concerns the issue of how one is to orient oneself toward those constraints which limit the possibilities for (free) action. These questions arise: Does one seek to alter constraint? Does one alter oneself in reciprocal co-adaptation with constraints as they are altered? Does one alter oneself exclusively? Pressing back limits involves prior acceptance of limits. For the limits to human existence do not essentially recede by force. On the contrary. They recede only consequent to their acknowledgment and their understanding, their acceptance in resignation and tranquillity. From this point of view, to search is so to search among limits that one will discern their import for, and impact on, one's personal existence.

What is the essential element of this searching wherein freedom consists? I affirm: personal freedom is not a *given* state of human existence; it *is* human existence. For existence is ἔκστασις, the self standing forth and declaring itself, standing forth rooted in its own powers for relating both to itself and to what is other than itself. Thus standing forth, the self takes hold of successive options, organizing its choices into patterns which, seen retrospectively, are foci in the searching activity—an activity unfolding in perspectives which become ever more inclusive. In this process, the self *exists* in the sense that it *freely* exercises restraint and power.

Again, I ask, wherein consists human freedom? So often it is claimed that freedom is an illusion nursed by man to designate his ignorance concerning regions of determination concealed from awareness. Alternatively, freedom is regarded as a myth cultivated to hide despair over one's radically contingent status in the universe. In my account, I treat freedom neither as illusion nor as myth, but as an essential constituent of man himself, the ontologically essential element of his being. But freedom is not a mere state of openness with respect to options for action which may severally be entertained as indifferently capable of realization. Quite the contrary. For I regard freedom as sheer reflexivity. It consists in every man's addressing himself—whether this addressing is articulated or not, or whether it is spoken in words or felt in silence, and whether awareness of this self-addressing is explicit or immanent, conscious or unconscious. In thus addressing himself, every person is a reflexive process of freeing himself. The idea may be better rendered in German: *Ich befreie mich.* For I am constantly in the act of making myself free. Not free from bondage; not free merely to choose; not free only to exercise power. But beyond these modalities of freedom —free to undertake a journey, to engage in a passage, a transition, through a succession of attachments each of which, however, ineluctably falls away, *from* imbalance and disorientation *to* harmony and re-orientation. Not only harmony of self with self, but a harmonizing of self in relation to a something outside of self. Not, however, a something which is, strictly speaking, a thing. For to free oneself is so to orient the self, amid its disorientations, that it roots itself in its very self; and, being reflexively constituted, the self is surely *no* thing.

(*c*) Freedom and Searching

If I inspect, one by one, the inner fabric of my being, revealing my moods, my fantasies, my dreams, my sensations, I find that contingency reigns as inexorably within me as the resistance I meet when I traverse the world about me. I find myself constrained both from within and from without. I am adrift in a sea of emotions quite as ineluctably as I am adrift in a sea of motions. For motions proceed from without, and terminate therein. And emotions proceed from within, impinging on the outer. Where can I find anchorage? No longer in any mood, image, or external object. I find my roots, my only roots, within the very *I* which is in quest of those roots. I secure myself in the very act by which I search for my security. But this succession of acts is a ferment which itself has no anchorage. It is elusive, transitory, evanescent. And so I am led step by step to root my searching activity itself in a "something" which lies beyond that activity. Yet this "something" cannot be, ultimately, my own self. It surely cannot be the world about me. For both are in flux and upheaval; both are in perpetual transit. My searchings are always enveloped by a beyond beyond those searchings. They are haunted, embraced, and tendered by that beyond. It can be no material beyond. Quite the contrary. It is a beyond which is personal, yet no person. It is a beyond which is ultimately mine, and yet it is not me. Yet it is a beyond which is experienced as in concernful relation to me.

To be free is to search both within oneself and without; it is to anchor oneself, in one's searching, in a relationship between oneself and an all-enveloping personal witness to that searching; it is to give oneself up to the search that this witness be a living presence, a presence which both transcends the self and is immanent in it; it is to give oneself up in faith, in hope, and in love. In faith, one discovers one's self: its possibilities, the constraints imposed upon it, the truth regarding those constraints. In hope, one discovers another counterposed to the self: *its* powers, the types of interconnection between the two, the good as residing in the values it places upon that other. In love, one discovers the relationship between self and other, the reciprocation between the two: *their* modes of co-adaptation, the rhythms of interpenetration and autonomy, the beautiful as constituting successively higher ways by which they are harmonized.

Accordingly, I find a correlation of import for my concept of freedom, a correlation between the Scriptural triad of faith, hope, and love, and the classical triad of the true, the good, and the beautiful. To explicate the nature of this triad, its internal nuances and intricacies, is to reveal the deeper meaning of personal freedom. To anticipate: faith allows one to reason, that he attain truth; hope to act, that he attain goodness; love to create, that he attain beauty. Within the limits prescribed by faith, once the quality of these limits is apprehended, man reasons; within the limits prescribed by hope, once the resistance afforded by these limits is sensed, man acts; within the limits prescribed by love, once a relationship to these limits is established, man creates. Thus, I correlate three pentads: faith, reason, truth, quality, and personal space; hope, action, goodness, resistance, and personal time; love, creation, beauty, relationship, and personal "matter" or substance. Freedom is the quest of man to probe, in a multitude of concrete ways, the inner meaning of this correlation.

C • THE EMERGENCE OF VERIDICAL FREEDOM

(*a*) Truth

To be free is to be aware of oneself as actively orienting oneself toward oneself in relation to an object. It is being with the other as self-consciously oneself, therefore self-affirming one's own being. In a word, freedom consists in owning oneself in the context of a significant relationship. This state of existence reveals itself in three unfolding modes: from the side of subjectivity, these modes are faith, hope, and love. Their import has already been set forth. From the side of objectivity, these modes are truth, goodness, and beauty.

In my account, to be free is to search in peace, along the way of faith and hope, that love be achieved. To this end, one apprehends, in freedom, one's subjectivity as ever changing, ever deepening in relation to an object which, likewise, one experiences as ever changing, ever deepening. An increasingly differentiated subjectivity is perceived as such only in correlation with an increasingly differentiated objectivity. Self and world cannot be dissociated. Accordingly, freedom is a self-progressive activity, an activity which unfolds in stages, and thereby gradually discloses and articulates its latent content. In these stages, the inner connections and the mutual dependencies of self and other are apprehended. Now, claiming that the stages of freedom are the phases of truth, goodness, and beauty, I amplify my account of these phases.[10]

Initially, one gives oneself in faith to an object which as yet is no veridical object but a mere datum—a datum, however, for which no donor is yet specified, hence, an object which as such is fleeting and evanescent. Within limits accepted as prescribed, one speculates freely—in effect, exploring and specifying those limits. One gives oneself up to the present, but to a present not yet construed as *presented*, i.e., as a present or a gift. Simply: one allows the object to present itself in its immediacy as a kind of abstract universal. And thought journeys among these immediacies, striving to give them a form and systematically rendering that form by lawful connections. At this stage, freedom, earlier equated on its subjective side with faith, is the endeavor to conceptualize the truth: not truth in its ultimate shape, but truth merely as a pattern of invariant connections. Hypostasizing the immediacies of the present, symbolic forms are created which, beginning with common sense, culminate in science. The inquirer secures himself in these forms, received as necessary and determined, without yet penetrating to the action which engenders the data thus cogently organized. In this stage, the contours of consciousness are mapped. In its uttermost scope, the spatiality of the activity of "conscious-ing" is engendered. Inquiry frames this activity as an assemblage of assertive judgments, systematically coordinated, regarding a presumptively objective realm.

Accordingly, by truth, I mean the allowing of one's mood, volitions, and thoughts to be determined essentially by an object to which, that this end be achieved, one actively gives oneself up. Dwelling in the context of a truthful orientation toward oneself in relation to that object, one allows oneself to be enveloped by it. The quester after truth is so pervaded by the object that, in effect, it prescribes the contents, the order, and the shifting directions of his reveries, converting them into the fixity of a determinate rational structure.

In this phase, no distinction is yet made among things, organisms, and persons. These classes of entities are assimilated to one another. Only superficial differences among them are affirmed. Each sphere is conceived as an ordered manifold of objective relationships, even though the inquirer acknowledges that the mode of being by which the emerging self relates to a given sphere is peculiar to the special, objective character of that sphere—granting, however, that such modes are not yet, on this level, clearly articulated. Moreover, these spheres—namely, the realms of things, organisms, and persons—themselves are construed, in the phase of truth, to be interconnected as constituting a single, objective manifold. For truth rests on the faith, elemental and irreducible, that the world is a reliable presence; the inner connections between one manifestation of that presence and another are not yet affirmed. Hume's analysis of causality is appropriate for specifying the peculiar features of this phase. Only, as he argues, habit grounded in custom can validly be proposed as holding together, as it were, the as yet intrinsically dissociated moments in the appearance of reality. Reality cannot yet be acknowledged as the subsistent ground for the succession of appearances. Nevertheless, one does not desist from seeking the specific manifold which is *truly* pointed toward by the object; reveries come and go, and among them one finds that true manifold—i.e., that manifold which, in conformity with the object one possesses, discloses the form of that object.

So as soon as the inquirer yields himself to this objective order of events, postulating rational connections between conceptual representations of them, he becomes aware that he is truly *representing* what had already been experienced as, however fleeting, ineluctable presences. The object is, so to speak, suffused by his representations of it. Thereby, it is experienced as solid and durable. But since the object is now rationalized, i.e., infused with the subjectivity of the inquirer, it is by virtue of its newly perceived durability also conceived as, equally, malleable. For, insofar as it is thus imbued with subjectivity, that object is alterable. Imagination projects itself on the object to invest it with new qualities. Within the limits prescribed by its possibilities for resisting, the object qua object is also alterable. Its sheer physicality proscribes numberless imaginational possibilities. Hence, the object is discerned as doubly changeable. Qua objective, it is capable of undergoing physical manipulation; qua subjective, it is the project of human discrimination. A kind of dialectic unfolds between what the object is in and for itself and what that object is for another. Each status presupposes, requires, and conditions the other. Never is the object perceived in independence of these intertwinings of objective and subjective elements. At one and the same time, it is a projection of the self *and* self-*sufficient* as enduring in radical independence of the self. Because of this double status it is indeed changeable, and often dramatically so. Now freedom passes into its next phase, a phase in which the self actively orients itself toward the object which it experiences as alterable through the intricate manipulation it is capable of undergoing.

(*b*) Goodness

One gives oneself up in hope to the present, actively taking hold of the fleeting moment. In this context, the present reveals itself to be a solidarity of presents, a duration. The object is grasped as an unfolding. There is expectation and anticipation, hence, futurity. Temporality and, indeed, historicity arise. Correlatively, the object is now accepted as itself the product of activity, even though activity is as yet but bare activity. The succession of present moments is experienced as, at bottom, an integrality of those moments; and this integrality, in effect, the objectivity of the object, is revealed as its resistance—hence, the donation of a donor, the conception of whose particularity and concreteness is adumbrated but not yet probed in its hidden depths. Nevertheless, this durational flow is apprehended as also created by thought, which conceives itself to have welded the immediacy of present moments to temporal solidarity. In experiencing the object as a sharply contoured duration etched against a non-articulated background, one perceives the limits of that object as tangible, therefore alterable. Thought grasps itself as empowered to press beyond those limits. No longer content merely to search into them, it allows itself not simply to be affected by the limits in reflex fashion. For thought itself sets in motion events which effectively change those limits.

Accordingly, thought is capable of apprehending itself as shaping not only an idea of limits to which it must conform, but an ideal regarding what those limits *ought* to be. Hence, thought becomes incarnate in action. No longer is it satisfied with merely making assertions or declarative judgments. On the contrary, it embodies itself in its very acts to constitute active judgments, judgments which change the object. In hope, therefore, thought grasps itself, probing its own inner depths which lie beneath the surface of its awareness; and, in its probing, it does not merely reveal a manifold of immediate presents. For, beyond conceptualizing that manifold, thought so relates itself to the object that it reshapes the object in accordance with an ideal drawn forth from those inner depths. In this process, thought grasps that relationship as involving, as essential elements, resistance, action, reaction. In turn, these constitute a temporal manifold, durational time, which engenders in its wake specific spatial assemblages of merely present moments.

Gathering together data initially apprehended as evanescing spatiality, lawful though the latter be, thought now conceives consciousness as itself surrounded by unconscious depths, depths which are not yet revealed regarding their specific content and possibilities, but depths which counterpose as yet unexplicated ingredients to the ideal which thought has posed for itself. Thought now for the first time perceives a conflict to reside in its own self-consciousness regarding the objects it durationally constitutes. Still, insofar as thought poses an ideal and, accordingly, endeavors to transform objects for the purpose of bringing them into conformity with that ideal, it now exhibits itself as intrinsically purposeful and, as such, directive of such changes in the object as will refashion the latter into something good.

In the relationship which is truth, the object is authentically objective. Thrusting itself against the subjectivity of the self, it counterposes itself to the latter as intrinsically unalterable. Encountering the resistances offered by the object, the self must come to terms with it by forming, in the long run, (assertive) judgments about it. On the other hand, in the relationship which is the good, the object through its very conception has been converted into a subject, a subject to which the self applies itself to the end that the subject bend itself to the will of the self. For it is the subject of alteration. Now the self has been transformed into an irresistible objective force, a set of durable intentions to which the object transformed into subject by the very actions of the self must bring itself into conformity. The roles of subject and object have been interchanged. No longer construed as evanescent phenomena which can be stabilized only through their representation as laws, the world is experienced as durable material which can be molded in accordance with principles prescribed by what is now interpreted as the lawful fabric of the self. For the self announces to the world the manipulative possibilities resident in it—always, of course, limited by what hitherto had been prescribed by world to self as the truth of self for world. The domain of the merely cognitive has passed over into the domain of the veridically ethical.

The truth of the world for the self is but one ingredient in a larger perspective on the relationship between world and self, a perspective which can only be designated the *goodness* of the world for the self and, by extension, for the community of selves. When the object is construed as durable, hence alterable, material, it presents itself to the self as a scheme of possibilities for transformation in those ways which are deemed by the self as beneficial for it, thus gratifying its needs. In the first instance—namely, truth—the self orients itself toward the world in such a way that, thus entrusting itself, it gives itself up to that world. But, in the second case, that orientation (essentially one which rests on faith in the continuance of the world, despite alterations the world may undergo by the very actions of the self) involves the object's yielding itself to the self as a matrix for such potential alteration. In addition, the relationship between trust and truth presupposes an immanent, germinating faith and, correlatively, goodness. Ultimately, the stability of the world—i.e., the uniformity of nature—entails the consequent construal of the world as potentially alterable in accordance with the intentions of the self. This assumption grounds the very possibility of truth. But this ground becomes explicit only when the phase of truth has been consummated. Only then can the second phase, goodness, be liberated as the conscious objective of the self to achieve *its* consummation.

A dialectical unfolding is posed. Within this process, the self achieves its freedom by stages. Initially, a passive self is counterposed to a dynamic object. In truth, the self relates to itself as essentially passive in its relation to an active world. To gain this experience, the inquirer must perceive the object from many points of view, illuminating it under variegated perspectives, that subsequently he may conceptually integrate these diverse facets. Yet the very acts by which integration is attained lead to his re-interpreting that object as part of a real continuum, an objective order of nature. Placed in various positions that it may reveal itself as woven of rearrangeable objective elements, factors within bare undifferentiated fact, the object itself discloses the specific ways in which the self might maneuver with it. Correlatively, the spontaneity of the self as it strives to effect change is revealed. Accordingly, the determinate character of nature imputed to it by cognitive judgments framed by the self exhibits itself as presupposing an inquiring person, a self which experiments and, as it experiments, incidentally gratifies or frustrates its own desires. But the very efforts thus to gratify reveal the insatiability of the self; and this disclosure—namely, that the self is vacuously infinite in its desires for remolding the world—unveils a double terror: that of the abyss of the world, in its malleability; that of the abyss of the self, in its vacuity. Lurking in the phase of the good, this terror replaces the terror residing in the phase of truth: namely, that of the rigidity of the world vis-à-vis the impoverishment of the self.

Now the self dynamically relates to itself as it dynamically relates to a passive world. An insignificant self vis-à-vis the world, wherein the world is conceived as threatening to annihilate the self, gives way to an insignificant world vis-à-vis the self, wherein the world is construed as collapsing into the self. Culminating in a naïve materialism, the first position is replaced by the second, a naïve idealism. In both instances, emptiness, the one of the self and the other of the world, challenges an harmonious relation between self and world, a relation which it was the original aim of both science and morality to affirm. Absolute trust, hence truth, threatens self-pulverization, the subjectivity of the self being consumed by objective relationships; absolute faith, hence goodness, threatens a vacuously expanded self confronting an insubstantial reality.

(*c*) Beauty

In my account, the good transcends the true while including it. Yet, in another sense, truth and goodness are mutually complementary. The co-adaptation of the two constitutes a new dynamism, a further stage in the dialectical unfolding of freedom. Indeed, the concrete universalization of freedom in a synthesis of truth and goodness is the culminating stage of thought. Progressively, the latter consummates itself by its progressive sympathetic identification with things, living creatures, persons. In attitudes of wonder, reverence, and the love of authentic kinship, the self empathically assimilates itself to these classes of objects which, reciprocally, reconstitute themselves in a fashion appropriate to their respective compositions.

An harmonious adjustment of self and world presupposes the appropriate balance between goodness and truth. Goodness encloses truth, which, however, presupposes it as immanent ground; truth being enclosed, the terror of an infinitely empty self and an infinitely empty world arises; conflict between the two supervenes. Now a new relationship, one of mutual co-adaptation, emerges. In this phase, wherein self stands in relatedness to object, a dynamic relationship in which each is construed as dynamically constituted, one first glimpses one's consummate freedom. For where parity reigns between self and other, no longer does one merely entrust oneself to the other—self to object, affirming faith in its power to apprehend the object; object to self, affirming hope that the powers of the object will conform to those of the self. Now self *and* other mold themselves in accordance with their respective powers. The artist lovingly shapes his works and, in turn, is shaped by them; in wonder he experiences this beauty. With reverence, the living creature is lovingly beheld, and acknowledged. In consummate love of fellowship and kinship, persons experience the beauty of their relationship with other persons. For, pre-eminently, persons lovingly relate to one another—persons in relation, each an authentic, self-determining agent.

Things, living creatures, persons: each compels relationships of varying modalities of care. In each instance, the freedom of living relatedness unfolds in new stages; at every point, the element of beauty resides in an harmonious co-adaptation of self to object.

Unaware of numberless facets of the world even as it searches to disclose those facets, the self dwells with itself unconsciously as well as consciously.[11] By "world" I mean, broadly construed, *body* in world. No sharp distinction can be made between bodily processes and world processes. Each is only a relatively enduring configuration of actions in essentially the same matrix. Moreover, associated with every body of sufficiently complex organization is the self. Indeed, the self is that body insofar as it is implicated in the world. It is the totality of feelings, perceivings, sensings, willings, desirings, believings. In a word, it is the coordination of body's diverse intentions, its overall orientation toward the world; these intentions express modes of discriminating the intertwinings of body processes with world processes. Accordingly, in the exclusively material sense, body is an abstraction; in the exclusively mental sense, self is an abstraction. Each prescinds from a more inclusive assemblage of activities; each is hypostasized on the ground of those activities. Hence, body is the locus of variegated activities which, in their subtler rhythms, manifest themselves as self. The region mediating transition from the coarser to the more ethereal rhythms is the Unconscious. Broadly expressed: body is the material locus of the self; correspondingly, the self is the mental locus of the body. Insofar as bodily acts are intentional, and originate in body in its narrower construal, but point toward the world in which body participates, one can therefore speak of the self. For, in the last analysis, self expresses the animation of body; it is at once the principle governing bodily organization and the expression of that organization.

Neither body nor self can be conceived independently; sufficiently examined, each concept discloses itself as entailing the other. At bottom, body as a matrix of intentional activities and self as the form of those activities are one and the same. Form and matrix are indivisible. Self is that unity in its reflexive aspect; body is that unity in its aspect as the most intimate and proximate of reflection; world other than body is that unity in its merely remote and less intimate ingredients. In this sense, body and world form a continuum. The relatively enduring crystallization of processes in this continuum conventionally designated "my body" is but the locus or seat of the self. However, insofar as body at its "periphery," so to speak, is the world—or, alternatively expressed, the world exhibits singular nodes which are bodies—the self, equally, resides in the larger, more inclusive world. Indeed, the ultimate seat of every self is the *entire* world, with the qualification, of course, that that world is apprehended (by the self) under the perspective integrated by specific processes localized at critical junctures in the world.

Accordingly, the idea of the self relating to itself as it relates to objects in the modes of truth, goodness, and beauty (and love) is equivalent to the idea that certain world regions are empowered to relate to themselves in their relationships to other world regions. Briefly: the world exhibits privileged regions which are reflexly endowed; by this character, the region is empowered to activate certain latent contents. Indeed, every region is the locus of conflict between forces resident in it which, in effect, strive toward concealment of facets of that region and other forces within it which reflexively strive for disclosure. Yet, with Einstein, one may say: nature is subtle but not malicious.[12] Though elusive, nature is prone to represent herself to herself. Thus doubling herself, she reflects into herself an Imago of herself. At bottom, this power of nature expresses its capacity for self-emendation, a tendency inhering in nature toward the efflorescence of its own hidden content.

When the self relates to its own relationship to the world, it is (in actuality) relating one region, its own region—the region it possesses as most intimately its own, or its body qua reflexive—to another region, the world qua non-reflexive. Truth and goodness express the form of this relationship. On the other hand, the more one manipulates the object toward which one orients oneself, the more one becomes aware that one is relating to that object as but the manifestation of its intrinsic powers. In beauty (and love), the self relates to its powers in their co-adaptability to the powers of what is other to it, as each set of powers potentiates the other into variegated expression. In this relationship, it becomes conscious of the interpenetration and mutual dependence of what it had initially conceived to be autonomous powers. In particular, as it passes from relating to mere inanimate powers to relating to the powers of living creatures, respecting the inanimate and revering the living, the self lays the groundwork whereby it may apprehend the intertwining of its own reflexivity with the reflexivity of the other. To be sure, this mode of relatedness culminates in the experience of one's own personhood as in profound relatedness to another person, as each indeed constitutive of the other. In this context, the phases of faith, hope, and love unfold anew.

Accordingly, the truth of the other is grasped as a representation of the interplay of the powers of both, a representation which is self-emending. For in apprehending itself as the locus of powers, in part autonomous and in part woven of the other, the self becomes aware of confusions arising in its image of itself in relation to the other—confusions in which it imputes to itself powers properly belonging to the other, or conversely. At bottom, these distortions express nature's reluctance fully to reveal herself, her tendency toward self-concealment. In principle, the self is unconscious of the full truth regarding its own powers, or, for that matter, the powers of another person; and this un-consciousness develops in the course of the self-development of the self. To lay the groundwork for the self's articulation of those powers, evidently the collaboration of other persons is required. In the measure that such collaboration fails, the self distrusts the other, fearing an overpowering of him or by him. In effect, the self is not *heard* by the other, or, indeed, by its own self in its efforts to express itself adequately (i.e., as an adequate Imago of itself, a representation which is adequate to its intrinsic powers). The full truth of self or other is not experienced. For to experience that truth, one must have already been heard in one's effort to experience one's own truth, i.e., to frame an adequate representation to oneself of one's own powers.

Furthermore, the goodness of the other is apprehended in the context of mutual deliberation regarding how *his* powers might more effectively be directed toward one's own gratification and, reciprocally—since, after all, this *is* a subphase of the phase of love—how one's own powers might analogously be directed toward gratification of his needs. The giving up of oneself in hope to such deliberation guarantees that one selflessly affirm parity between the needs of the other and one's own needs. In this way, one endeavors so to relate one's own powers to the powers of the other that needs of either become ever-more-comprehensively satisfied. Since the relationship of love is already reciprocal, each person is active in this collaboration. Perpetual adjudication, and the adjustment of the needs of each to each, typify this phase. As new needs arise, new deliberation supervenes. Together, the participants shape an ideal of peership in which this principle is affirmed: mutual loyalty will provide the conditions under which both parties can flourish with their fullest potentialities. Should this pact be violated, however, despair will reign; the essential goodness of the relationship will correspondingly diminish.

Finally, the framing of an adequate representation of the enmeshing of the strengths of persons is not the quintessential τέλος of the relationship of love. Nor is the using of each to the end that the other may be gratified, no matter how reciprocal this utilitarian purpose. Rather, the truthfulness and the goodness of love are but stages along the way toward the realization of beauty as pervading love. Only in this final subphase can both individuals dwell in vibrant peace. Only then can they experience that ecstasy of participation wherein, together, they orchestrate ever-new symbols of their union. In this context, neither self nor other can remove himself from their enraptured being-together. For each indelibly and unremittingly imprints the rhythms of his existence on the other; each ornaments the themes of the lives of both with variations subtly and endlessly nuanced. In love, each person discloses his being, in its unity and in its entirety, by confronting two powers, his own and that of another; and he clarifies his being by joining himself to that other, by feeling the qualities of *his* existence in himself and of his own existence in the other. Through a relationship of mutual respect, tenderness, trust, understanding, hope, and loyalty, the power of each is enhanced. In every encounter, the self ceases to fragment experience, whether of himself or of the other. On the contrary, he enjoys its wholeness, its aliveness, and its unconditioned worth. In rhythmic alternation between inwardness and outwardness, a reverent bond to the other is established. One surrenders oneself to all existence, to Rilke's "imperishable invisibility,"[13] into which one has transfigured the visible and in which one always participates.

In this chapter, I have examined personal freedom in terms of a single idea: the correlation of the Scriptural ideal with the classical ideal. Personal freedom, I have argued, consists essentially in the movement through stages specified by these ideals. Initially, the self possesses itself in relation to another in an attitude of faith. It aims so to apprehend the character of the other that it might root itself in a stable, lawful manifold. Thus freely giving itself up to truth, the self comes to own itself more securely. Yet, in the very act by which the self renounces all its desires save the need to attach itself to another in the latter's truthful character, the self becomes aware that the other is himself substantial and solid, a durable unfolding. It acquires a new attitude by which it complements its faith: namely, that of hope. For it can now hope that this substantial world is alterable in a way which would bring it into conformity with an ideal shaped from its own autonomous ruminatings. Now the self possesses itself in an attitude of hope for the essential goodness of the other with respect to its own needs.

As soon as the self becomes aware of itself as a potential shaper of ideals and of the other as a manifold of lawful connections, it experiences *itself* as a manifold of lawful connections and the *other* as the shaper (or, at least, the presenter) of ideals. In brief: it develops the power to apprehend both itself and the other as analogously constituted, hence capable of being brought into reciprocal dynamic relatedness. Thus, the self comes to possess itself in relation to another which (or who), immanently or explicitly, likewise comes to possess itself—each as reflexive activity, potential or actual. In consequence, self-possession in relation to another analogously conceived leads the self to an attitude of love. By this attitude, the beauty of an harmonious co-adaptation of powers, each to each, can be shaped.

Each symbolizing itself to the other, and the two in communion joining their symbolisms, these interwoven powers exhibit their own truth, goodness, and beauty. In the final analysis, personal freedom consists in the self's giving of itself to another self, and enjoying the mutuality of that giving: giving so that distrust, despair, and hate fall away; giving so that truth, goodness, and beauty be affirmed. For this to occur, ever-more-inclusive interpersonal relations must emerge, each grounded in the principles suggested by the correlations I have sketched, and ever-more-authentic communities must evolve: communities founded on personal integrity, communities based on the idea of unity amid the diversity of its members, communities which embody in a collective lived experience the conditions whereby each member, unhampered, can search in the way I have proposed.

Granted: this way is arduous. Ultimately, it requires that one sacrifice one's narrower desires that one thereby unite oneself in the beauty of love to the eternal cosmic rhythms. Understood as God, the ground of these rhythms, construed as the divine witness to man's journey toward freedom, exhibits its own interwoven moments. In justice, God reveals His truth to man, that man has faith in His presence; in mercy, God reveals His goodness to man, that man have hope in His presence; in grace, God reveals His beauty to man, that man have love in His presence. Failure to undertake this adventure, in all its variegated aspects, jeopardizes faith, hope, and love. Should these ideals vanish, the quest for the true, the good, and the beautiful must be relinquished. The search for personal freedom must fail.

NOTES

1. This chapter first appeared, in essentially its present form, as an essay of the same title in *Freedom and Value*, ed. Robert O. Johann (New York: Fordham University Press, 1976), pp. 61–85.

2. For a psychological account of trust and hope in child development, see Erik Erickson, *Childhood and Society* (New York: Norton, 1950), chap. 7.

3. Benedict de Spinoza, "On the Improvement of the Understanding," *The Chief Works of Benedict de Spinoza*, trans. R. H. Elwes, 2 vols. (New York: Dover, 1951, 1955), II 3–4.

4. Gabriel Marcel, *The Mystery of Being*. II. *Faith and Reality*, trans. René Hague (South Bend, Ind.: Regnery/Gateway, 1960), chap. 10.

5. Fairbairn, *An Object–Relations Theory of the Personality*; see above, chap. 1, note 10.

6. Whitehead, *Process and Reality*, chap. 2.

7. Ibid., p. 27.

8. Leonard C. Feldstein, "Toward a Concept of Integrity," *Annals of Psychotherapy*, Monograph Nos. 3 & 4, Vols. 1 & 2 (1961), 67–87.

9. For this etymologic discussion, see the relevant sources in Eric Partridge, *Origins* (London: Routledge and Kegan Paul, 1958) and *An Oxford Dictionary of English Etymology*, ed. C. T. Onions (New York: Oxford University Press, 1966).

10. See the fine discussion of the relationship between the true, the good, and the beautiful in Justus Buchler's theory of assertive, active, and exhibitive judgment in *Toward a General Theory of Human Judgment* (New York: Columbia University Press, 1951), chap. 2. See, too, the equally fine discussion of the relationship between self and world revealed in truth, goodness, and beauty by Albert Hofstadter, *Truth and Art* (New York: Columbia University Press, 1965), chaps. 5, 6, and 7.

11. See my discussion of body, mind, and the Unconscious in "Reflections on the Ontology of the Person," *International Philosophical Quarterly*, 9, No. 3 (September 1969), 313–41.

12. From a conversation of Einstein's, namely, "Raffiniert ist der Herr Gott, aber boshaft ist er nicht." See *Albert Einstein: Philosopher–Scientist*, ed. Paul Arthur Schilpp, The Library of Living Philosophers 7 (Evanston, Ill.: The Library of Living Philosophers, Inc., 1949), p. 691.

13. See the commentary on "The Angel" in Rainer Maria Rilke, *Duino Elegies*, trans. J. B. Leishman and Stephen Spender (New York: Norton, 1939), pp. 87–88.

5

TOWARD INTEGRITY AND WISDOM: JUSTICE AS GROUNDING PERSONAL HARMONY

PREAMBLE

The history of philosophy has been pervaded not only, in the Greek tradition, by the quest to understand the true, the good, and the beautiful, and, in the Scriptural tradition, their affective correlates of trust, hope, and love, but, more fundamentally, in the Greek perspective, by a seeking after the *good life*, and, under the Scriptural perspective, after *its* correlative, the *pious life*—in both instances, man quests after justice, integrity, and wisdom. Despite the designations "good" and "pious," this inclusive quest transcends the sphere of morality as such, and I designate it the *spiritual life*. In the argument to be presented, I exhibit this consummation of human existence as stressing varying modes of balance between diverse human virtues; and virtue, in the generic sense of power, is surely not restricted to the moral domain. Further, each constituent of this fruition of life—namely, justice, integrity, and wisdom—expresses an aspect of that life; each aspect subsumes both traditions, the Greek and the Scriptural. In the context of a life which is both good and pious —hence, in the larger sense, spiritual—every factor in the complexes which these traditions propose acquires a distinctive import. Yet justice, integrity, and wisdom are closely related notions. For its explicit and most complete formulation, each presupposes and requires the others. Nevertheless, my concern in this chapter is essentially with the first member of the triad—namely, justice—though to characterize this notion, I must indicate its connections with the remaining notions.[1]

A • JUSTICE AS PREPARING THE WAY TO WISDOM

(*a*) Justice as Truth

From the point of view which I develop, justice pertains to a quality of the person, and, hence, of interpersonal relations; and, ultimately, of the community itself. Since its primary role is to specify the conditions under which personal harmony can be attained, it is, above all, a cognitive category. For it seeks to disclose the factual circumstances which ground personal harmony; in this capacity, it aims at the widest possible understanding of human being, both in its frailty and in its strength. Yet justice is a quite special kind of cognitive category. Its concern is also with that rectification of wrong which alone will allow for such harmony to be attained; and it aims at restoring a kind of balance or equity within the person, between persons, and for the community as a whole. Hence, a judgmental component. Finally, since no means can, in the largest sense, effectively flow toward an end—in this case, harmony—unless it partakes of the quality of that end, justice also involves an aesthetic component. In short, justice requires that the truth of the other be grasped as a representation of the interplay of the powers of both, a representation which is self-emending. In consequence, justice presupposes the idea of *participatory* truth: namely, that kind of mutual entrusting which is suffused by hope and, in the last analysis, identical with love, though love in a narrower sense than that kind of love which qualifies integrity, and, in its supreme form, pervades wisdom. It is under this perspective that I examine justice and explore its relationship to both integrity and wisdom.

Against customary accounts of justice, I am claiming that justice hardly stands in opposition to love; nor must it be conceived as merely tempered by or attuned to love. And only in a restricted sense is it bound to hope (or, often, to hopelessness). Quite the contrary. For justice is intimately interwoven with both love and hope. Correlatively, although, qua cognitive, it concerns truth, and hence always presupposes an attitude of trust with respect to truth's gathering, reception, and impact, justice is surely as intimately as, though more restrictedly than, integrity and wisdom interwoven with both beauty and morality. In this chapter, it is my task to exhibit these peculiar concordances, the special ways in which justice is indeed a cognitive category interfused with the moral and the aesthetic, and the kinds of relationships which it bears to integrity and wisdom. Throughout, the theme of the person as seeker will be the dominant motif linking justice, integrity, and wisdom.

(*b*) Justice, Integrity, Wisdom

Some preliminary comments on my use of the terms "integrity" and "wisdom" are in order. In a large sense, integrity treats morality, but that generalized type of morality which incorporates truth and beauty; in addition, it stresses hope, hope woven of trust and love. In this respect, integrity comprises all members of the Greek and the Scriptural triads, though always under the perspective of both goodness and hope. For integrity is concerned with that orientation toward objects which apprehends their mutability with respect to one's own best interests—i.e., one's interests conceived in the light of an ideal, an ideal "in" which all members of the community, in principle, participate, and which affords one authentic personal equanimity. Accordingly, hope always dominates the attitude of integrity—hope pervaded by trust and love. For, in the stance of integrity, the participants shape an ideal of peership in which this principle is affirmed: mutual loyalty will provide the conditions under which both parties can flourish with their fullest potentialities—i.e., as whole and, therefore, *wholesome* human beings. In sum, integrity expresses the mutuality of participatory goodness.

Analogously, and as the culminating member of the triad which characterizes the spiritual (or essentially Christian) life, wisdom, in a large sense, deals with beauty and its correlate, love. Beyond that, it is interwoven with trust and hope, orientations toward the person which ground the possibility for the attainment of both truth and goodness. In wisdom, a person ceases to fragment experience; he enjoys its wholeness, its aliveness, and its unconditioned worth. One becomes human freedom incarnate. For in wisdom the *fullness* of participation is achieved, an harmonious balancing of diverse parts. Implicating the aesthetic, in its most inclusive sense, wisdom nonetheless subsumes, without negating, the cognitive and the moral. Transcending both, it interrelates these enterprises, while denying the essential autonomy of neither. Indeed, by no arbitrary choice does Kant make his *Third Critique* the crown and glory, the very keystone for the understanding, of his entire work, the fullest and most satisfying presentation of the noumenon. Nor is Hegel succumbing to an inflexible dialectic when, of the moments of consciousness which unfold as his *Phenomenology*, the earliest pertain to sense, perception, and understanding, the intermediate to custom, morality, and statesmanship, and the culminating to art, religion, and philosophy. The last, for Hegel, constitute spheres of existence in which, by stages, the dialectic replicates itself, on successively higher levels, as wisdom itself unfolds toward its own consummation in the *Absolute*: the great cosmic ferment of participation *par excellence*, participation of creatures interfusing as they themselves are benignly suffused by the Creator.

(*c*) Justice as Search

In brief, justice is that preliminary search of human being, the latter's initiating phase, which, in its own unfolding moments, points toward and prefigures the stages which will succeed it—namely, integrity and wisdom—and grounds the very possibility for the realization of those stages. The *path* which one must traverse in order for the higher components of a life which is both good and pious —hence, spiritual—fully to be attained, justice, in *its* very essence, is nonetheless woven into that life's essence. Hence, justice is, not so much a state, either of persons or of communities, as a process and a dynamism. It is the movement and the flow *toward* integrity and wisdom; yet it is always permeated *by* integrity and wisdom. Accordingly, the just person is one who so coordinates the life, on the one hand, of the true, the good, and the beautiful, and, on the other, of trust, hope, and love, that the quest toward the culmination of that life in wisdom is facilitated and, indeed, made possible.

In this sense, justice is a means to an end; it is an actual state of dynamic relatedness, within oneself to oneself, and within the community to another, a state which grounds the possibility for the attainment of an ideal. Still, as I have stated, no means can be employed toward any end unless it, in fact, partakes significantly of qualities belonging to that end. Hence, to be just, one must never desist from imbuing one's life with concrete anticipations of that of which both integrity and wisdom consist. For one thus imbued, justice, insofar as integrity and wisdom are ideals, is itself ideal. To that extent, its status is normative. In effect, it is an *ought*—indeed, by implication, the quintessential ought of human existence. Yet, as an end achieved, justice is an actuality. It is the concrete condition whereby integrity and wisdom become possible. Moreover, even they, those moments in searching's process higher than justice, themselves partake of the character of both ends and means. Once attained, integrity itself, now sublating justice as one of its essential constituents, serves as means whereby wisdom's end may be attained. Hence, integrity, too, exhibits a dialectical interplay between *is* and *ought*, *actual* and *ideal*, the *descriptive* and the *normative*. But even when wisdom is attained—this pinnacle of human existence with respect to which justice and integrity are but penultimate moments—a new unfolding occurs; and the dialectic of *is* and *ought* replicates itself anew.

In every instance, these phases, which are at the same time contemporaneous aspects of the life which is good and pious—hence, spiritual—bring about, by their inmost natures, the engaging of ideal and real. In each case, a transition is effected. At bottom, this transition is a mediation, involving the mediated passage from a state of disharmony, relatively speaking, to a state of harmony, relatively speaking. Once integrity has been attained, a new context is provided in which more inclusive modes of justice become possible; once wisdom has been attained, an analogous context is provided in which more inclusive modes of integrity and of justice become possible. Yet, throughout this process, all three ingredients of the spiritual life are present; and, as *com*present, they are dialectically interrelated. My aim is to explicate this dialectic from the point of view of but one member of the triad: namely, justice.

B • INTEGRITY AS JUSTICE CONSUMMATED

(*a*) Justice and Symbol

Reflection on the etymology of the term "justice" discloses an aspect of this preparatory stage of the journey through the realms of spirit—namely, those realms suggested by integrity and wisdom. Deriving from the Latin *ius*, meaning "right in the sense of joining" (of fitting), and, before that, from the Sanskrit, meaning "to join,"[2] *justice* may be regarded as *uniting* in several ways: qua solitary, a person reveals his diverse parts as coordinated into an integral and harmonious whole; qua interpersonal, he relates to another in ways which are woven into a unitary and cohesive fabric; qua social, a person dwells in a community which exhibits a scheme of equilibrium in which he can find a uniquely appropriate role and function; qua cosmic, a person is brought into relationship with the universe in a larger sense—for κόσμος, that attunement of seemingly disparate realms, shapes the ultimate ground whereby the less inclusive harmonies of community, interpersonal relation, and personal makeup can be achieved. In general, therefore, justice implies mutual affinity and participation. It is striking to note that, from an etymologic point of view, symbol, deriving from συμβάλλειν, also means a joining together. In consequence, in this chapter, I regard "justice" and "symbol" as though they were cognate terms; and I develop a context of thought in which I show that, correctly deciphered, the symbolisms of the presence and compresence of persons are, at one and the same time, marks of the justice of a person—his justice with respect to himself, to his fellows, to his community, to the world as a whole.

Adverting to the common etymologic ingredient in "justice" and in "symbol" —namely, *joining*—I affirm: various ways of joining characterize human being. In effect, they are patterns of balance and imbalance, and they express modes of coherence with respect to the arrangement of his functions, his parts, his aspects. It is as though a scarce commodity, namely, *anima*—that which animates and ensouls the person as person—is distributed to these factors in accordance with a principle of equity. The analogue of a corresponding principle for securing justice for society, this principle likewise has its correlate in a principle governing the interwovenness, order, and mutual affinities prevailing throughout the cosmos. Indeed, personal harmony, interpersonal attunement, social equity, and cosmic order are coordinate and mutually presupposing notions. Each mode of "joining" represents a dynamic state of some class of entities. And not only do these states mirror one another, they interweave and interpenetrate. Hence, I am concerned (primarily) with how equity, expressing a *preliminary joining of issues* —a co-adaptation of responsibilities and an attunement of diverse conflicting interests, activities, and dynamisms—grounds integrity; and (secondarily) with how, as a result, integrity expressing the transmutation of conflict into contrast, shapes that unique and individual cohesiveness which itself grounds the flowing forth of wisdom.

(*b*) Justice as Balance

Since justice is but the first phase of a process, it is impossible fully to characterize this phase without predelineating certain qualities of the succeeding phases. For justice is but the initial stage setting in motion an experiential journey into the self and the unfolding of the moments of this journey toward integrity and, ultimately, wisdom. To take Dante's *Commedia* as concrete exemplar of such journeys: the *Paradiso* expresses man's strivings toward final wisdom; the *Purgatorio*, his strivings toward mediating integrity; and the *Inferno*, his strivings toward the acceptance of the justice meted to him consequent upon his recognition of the truth of his actions. Now I outline, as it were *in abstracto*, the main problems associated with the initiation of this quest.

In my account, justice pertains to man's whole being: not merely to his body as such, in its soul-informed πρᾶξις—his physical and practical actions—or to his soul as such, in its body-informed θεωρία—his spiritual and intellectual actions. Hence, justice concerns *anima*, the spirit which animates body and soul; and it treats the way in which, by a principle of equity, *anima* distributes, as it were, in appropriate (i.e., fitting or just) proportions, symmetries, harmonies, and (in a word) balances to a person's integral being. Ever torn among conflicting options, each person is compelled to choose. His tendency to be torn asunder pertains quite as much to his body as to his soul. Many forces play upon him. Depending upon the resilience and sturdiness of his body and his soul, his actions exhibit different grades of congruity among themselves. Diverse tendencies, compulsions, and powers are at work within him. So strong is a person's need to conform to the demands of his environment, giving himself up to whatever he perceives to be its factuality, and hence genuinely persuaded of his attitude of truthfulness, that he becomes too easily *deformed* in his inmost being. For reality's distorted sectors work so massively upon the person that he readily declines to a "scotosis of truth,"[3] eclipsing, by the imagery of deformation, existence's significant regions. Hence, justice pertains to a person's opening himself up, by an act of free will, to his being informed of reality's ever-wider aspects and humankind's ever-broader concerns. It thereby enables him to rectify deformation and to bring into more synchronous relationship hitherto incongruous regions of his being. In this manner, justice prepares the way which must be traversed that, by the unitary impact of *responsibly* interwoven parts—i.e., parts authentically responsive to reality's deeper textures—he might, in integrity, achieve more potent, durable, and clarified commitments.

By "integrity," I intend a double meaning: *integrality*, in the sense of one and indivisible; *integument*, in the sense of a covering sensitive to touch. Hence, the integrated person is one who, as a *totum* resonating to his world's textures, responds appropriately to their impact. The just man prefigures the man of integrity, as the latter prefigures the man of wisdom. He is a contemplative man: one who contemplates various possibilities of action, and interweaves as a coherent assemblage his specific choices for action. In addition, he is a practical man who perceives plausible courses of action: namely, those which conduce to more durable commitment. As contemplative, the just man envisages such factors of his existence as might be woven into his shaping acts; he surveys the facts and he selects what is appropriate and fitting—always guided both by those of his options which he adjudges will best adapt themselves to those facts and by those schemes of co-adaptation which will allow for more inclusive harmonious arrangements. Led by the vision of ever larger schemes, i.e., the aesthetic, the just person will mediate his πρᾶξις through his anticipatory θεωρία, and he will mediate his θεωρία by the concrete appraisals of his πρᾶξις. In this sense, he achieves a kind of balance between πρᾶξις and θεωρία. But this balance is weighted on the side of θεωρία. For, first and foremost, justice requires acknowledgment of the facts: his own existence, with its possibilities and its constrictions. Accordingly, since these facts must be known as grounding all action, though ultimately they can be fully known only in the context of prior action, justice is primarily the quest for truth: that, in hope, the good will flow from that truth; that perspectives of love and beauty will envelop it.

In justice, the person attains first a balance, fragile and precarious but true and valid, between πρᾶξις and θεωρία, the dialectically interwoven "divisions" of his being. Like a pendulum, the swing tends first toward θεωρία—a rendering of a judgment, a discernment, an acceptance of the facts; then, by way of compensation, toward πρᾶξις. Now, in accordance with the ideal of harmony, the world is reshaped. Yet this activity is already prefigured in the state of justice by the *idea*. No *is* can long be kept apart from the *ought* toward which it flows, and into which it blends. Coherence, attunement, and balancing of the facts precede the reconstituting of facts. A perceived inner congruity between the physiognomic symbols of every person reveals the interwoven patterns of rhythmic balance: body patterns as physique; soul patterns as psyche; numberless intermediate patterns partaking of the nature, on varying levels of corporeality or spirituality, of body and soul. When facts apprehended as coherent are transformed into facts shaped as coherent, the stage of integrity is attained. Often the ideal itself falls into discord with the facts. To achieve a more satisfying concordance, a new balance between *is* and *ought*—idea and ideal—must be effected. Subsuming the true, hence trusting, person, conveyed by justice's orientation, and the good and hopeful person, enhanced by integrity's orientation—each orientation itself woven of its own truth, goodness, and beauty, and correlatively, its own trust, hope, and love—and sublating all moments and stages, the integral person becomes luminous with wisdom's rhythms. Now man, community, and universe harmonize. Pervading successively more advanced levels of equilibration, each firmer and more subtle than its predecessor, the three themes—justice, integrity, and wisdom—in succession dominate. Each a relative invariant, all comprise a common thread which passes through, and binds to unity, the correlated triads, Greek and Scriptural.

(*c*) Justice, Obligation, and Distribution

Referred to the person, justice, I repeat, pertains to modes of distributing to his diverse parts a scarce commodity—namely, *anima*—in accordance with a principle of equity. In what sense may "commodity," "equity," and "part" be applied to the person? Certainly for communities those social arrangements are deemed just in which social equity prevails. By this I mean: a community's every member is accorded his due, for something is owed him by society; in the measure to which he has received, each person accordingly becomes indebted to society; as he, in turn, gives *to* society, society once again incurs a debt to him; hence, reciprocity prevails between community and person, a symmetry of obligation. Justice ascertains (and enforces by communally sanctioned means) the factual basis on which this symmetry rests—though its modes of enforcement must, to be themselves just, be compatible with the kinds and qualities of obligation which it endeavors to sustain. Analogously, each "member" of a society, itself a kind of person (for it is composed of both psychic and physical parts—parts which are but loci on a continuum of personal "resonances"), is under existential obligation (or even compulsion) to sacrifice a measure of *its* autonomy that the continued welfare of the whole, construed as person, be assured. Conversely, the person himself qua person is under personal obligation so to orient himself toward his every part that each part receives, by virtue of such orientation, *its* due within that whole. As with community and person, whole and part are in reciprocal and dynamic relatedness; neither ought, according to the principle of equity, to function in any way which will violate the integrity of the other. Moreover, the different parts of a person exhibit varying degrees of independence. In proportion to their intrinsic autonomy, these parts are in varying conditions of bondage: i.e., bonded, or "joined," in the etymologic sense of justice, to the whole.

With respect to a person's physical aspect: if, for example, certain anatomical structures were to be amputated, regeneration would occur. The organism is empowered to produce virtual duplicates of such of its structures as possess relative autonomy, hence, independence of the context provided by that organism. It is as though they are enabled vicariously to survive even their own destruction, to survive in the literal sense of *super-vivere*: a (substitutive) living beyond the most severe of crises of their own natural history; *a fortiori*, persons themselves survive such partial dissolution. Likewise, persons replicate themselves; despite the perishing of their individual members, communities survive with essentially stable institutions. On the other hand, persons survive symbolically (and in a deeply poetic sense) in their progeny; indeed, even a kind of biologic—or genetic—survival supervenes. But these analogies cannot be pressed too far. Persons exhibit identities in a sense transcending the sense in which parts of persons exhibit identities. Yet a lesson is to be learned from these analogies, however limited their scope. Too, were they to be disrupted, certain functions can readily be compensated for by other functions. On the other hand, some structures and functions, like those of the central nervous system, are radically dependent upon a person's total configuration; they are intrinsically incapable of regeneration. In the measure of their intrinsic degree or mode of autonomy, each structure and each function "owe" their own integrity to the totality of which they are constituents. Likewise, the totality reciprocally "owes" the appropriate "quantity" of *anima* to its every part. For, to be responsible for their well-being—since each part is, after all, in some measure intrinsically weak or un–self-sufficient—the requisite biochemical energies must be "fairly" (i.e., with equity) distributed to all parts.

Accordingly, the person owes hierarchically ordered obligations to his diverse physical parts. When, with respect to persons, I speak of independence and dependence, and the corresponding "obligations" of parts to whole, the analogy to the community of persons again breaks down. Only to a minimal extent does each part manifest anything resembling "free will." The whole person works in and through his every part, conferring upon it an essential context for its appropriate activity, the conditions under which, by its genetically determined composition, that part may indeed "act" autonomously. In other words, in the realm of personal being, parts provide their own contexts of activity to an incomparably smaller extent than do their analogues, persons, in the realm of community being. Still, up to a point, this analogy does hold. A society imposes upon its members at least some significant patterns of determined behavior. It may modify their power for free will by, in part, depotentiating that power, and thereby lessening the scope of their options. Hence, societies as well as persons provide contexts for the activities of their relevant constituencies. Nevertheless, far more than societies, the person as a whole energizes his every part. Displacing energy from one part to another, he effects all manner of energy transfer—always, of course, within the limits imposed by both the physico-chemical and the biological makeup of each part. Moreover, a part which has succumbed to pathologic processes resists every effort of the person to invigorate it and to restore it to its "natural" mode of functioning. Alternatively, were the person afflicted by psychic pathology, he himself might resist his inclinations to activate a part which would, under conditions of psychic health, overcome its *own* pathology.

Clearly, a person's psychic "parts" are interwoven with his physical parts. Just as he can orient himself toward this or that bodily structure, and energize or de-energize it, as the case may be, so a person can assume similar attitudes toward his psychic parts. Thus, he can allow himself to be enveloped by an idea, consumed by it, or he can dwell upon it in such fashion as to bring its germinal content to fruition. In short, a person can permit that mental element to make *its* distinctive contribution to his overall being. Alternately, as with physical parts, ideas can be deformed in varying degrees and ways, and brought into different kinds of conformation with the totality. Should a person dwell excessively with his own ideation, he may even deflect his attending to or from some relevant physical factor—in effect, remove the requisite *anima* or animating energy. For example, in the phenomenon of the phantom limb, a person may perpetuate beyond what makes ecologic sense for him (i.e., to the point of disrupting a prevailingly wholesome ecology of his parts) the illusion of a limb which, having been amputated, is *de facto* non-existent. He may waste his ideas on thought perseveration with respect to this preoccupation, allowing for an irrelevant and wholesome efflorescence: a bizarre fungosity, so to speak, like a cancerous growth in a body. Always, the issue is one of balance, attunement, rhythm. Beyond that, it is a matter of the way in which a person conserves *anima.* True, his energetic power to animate is limited and, in the final analysis, distributes a scarce commodity. Life is short; all manner of affliction may impinge upon one. Dramatically or insidiously, these afflictions take their toll. Yet as overall energy diminishes, novel schemes can be devised to conserve what energy remains. More important, subtle nuances of increasingly imaginative creative expression can be discovered. In this sense, the possibilities for such expressions are numberless; the mysterious reserves of imaginational, and valid, cosmic representations are fathomless.

In general, justice orients itself toward conserving energy, securing itself on already established bases and perpetually appealing to tradition. In its subsequent evolution, different schemes of integrity, each grounded in and arising from foundations which it has secured, will point the way toward that liberalizing of justice which alone can reveal its concrete new forms. But, at this point, wisdom will already have been attained, with all *its* unfolding moments.

Through his energy conservation, a person builds up a reservoir from which he can deflect, in appropriate increments, such "energies" as are required for his new needs, bodily and psychic—needs which reveal themselves through tension in the already established scheme of equilibrium. Always, his problem is to achieve equity—the equity which lies at justice's very core. By equity, I mean this triphasic process: (*a*) anticipating possible new needs, estimating the likelihood with which these needs arise, and deciding the way in which they are to be ranked with respect to their importance for a person's integrity; (*b*) conserving sufficient stores of energy, by such techniques as meditation or *t'ai chi*, so that, in quiet relatedness to the cosmos, energies are not actually bound, but held in abeyance; and (*c*) distributing the relevant energies, each weighted in accordance with a plan which requires continual modification as it is put into practice, as actual need arises, by a person's deliberately placing himself now in this part of his being, now in that. In principle, equity synchronizes the workings of these diverse parts, and thus harmoniously orders and coordinates his body activity and his soul activity.

C • JUSTICE AS HUMAN ECOLOGY, HUMAN SYMBOL, AND HUMAN RHYTHM

(*a*) Justice as Conservation

Earlier, I wrote of justice as concerned with facts; it treats the linking or cohering of facts. Always conditioned by hope and goodness (i.e., concern) and, more inclusively, by an overarching vision of beauty woven with love, justice seeks truth: the factual ground for human equilibrium and disequilibrium. Too, I referred to the interpenetrating themes of transcendence (or, in effect, fructification) and conservation. Though the latter theme dominates the explicit quest for justice, the former works immanently and pervasively to guarantee justice's dynamism. For all parts of the person strain, as it were, toward their mutual integration, that full integral personhood be achieved. Pathology alone, that of the person as a whole or that of any particular sector of the person, diminishes that straining's efficacy. By *straining*, I imply that an implicit intentionality is at work within a person's part: as long as that part is not disconnected from him—as long, that is, as it is functioning in a context provided by the person's living presence. Thus, a dead and amputated limb bears only the appearance, never the substance, of the limb as it actually functions. In general, no part of the person is a part save insofar as it is a part *of* the person: that is, operative as continually affected by that person—in other words, *in situ* or *in vivo*, rather than in isolation and *in vitro.* Accordingly, *fructification* expresses the principle by which, to achieve equity, no part of the person may be conceived as *merely* functioning. Like surviving, straining implies a going beyond any particular state of activity already achieved by any particular part. In brief, it is as though every part, insofar as it is an element within a pattern governed by equity, strives toward transcendence—i.e., toward its own ever-more-potent energy state.

Just as I have spoken of a principle which is the analogue of the law of energy conservation, so I now invoke a principle analogous to the law of inexorably increasing entropy; in particular, I treat the meaning for living, especially human, processes of the connection between these principles. Granted: the province of justice is fact, and its end is to adjudicate between conflicting construals or interrelations of fact. Nonetheless, its mode of governance cannot be wholly determined by a criterion which refers to the stability of a past ecologic arrangement of the parts of either person or community. For, by the second law of thermodynamics, in its most general form, the overall quantity of energy available for use diminishes in time—granted, in isolated systems. On the supposition that person and community are partly isolated systems, *utilizable* energy for distribution among their respective parts cannot be presumed as a constant. For justice to prevail, and for equity to reign, different modes of apportioning energy over time must, in consequence, be adopted. Under the assumption of a quasi-entropic personal system, no static equilibrium suffices; passage must always be toward such conditions of equilibrium as will tend either to "coarsen" the parts, lessening subtle differentiations and finer nuance, or, alternatively, to "etherealize" the parts—so to heighten differentiation that ever-more-delicate nuance is achieved.

In consequence, in its actual governance, justice always confronts a fundamental choice. On the one hand, it may opt for conserving a given equilibrium. In this case, the subtler distinctions among a person's parts (or, for that matter, a community's parts) will inexorably diminish. Alternatively, it may opt for fructification. In the latter instance, justice fully acknowledges that, though governed by sheer factuality, it is, nonetheless, haunted by hope and by love: that integrity might prevail, a *better* arrangement of the relevant factors is sought; that wisdom might prevail, the *best* arrangement which a refined vision can afford for ordering those factors is sought. With respect to the concept of justice as grounding personal harmony: though justice must attend the limiting circumstances of conservation, and, hence, is obligated to economize equity, it must also be inspired by the potentialities for fructification. Hence, justice must temper its tough-minded obeisance to fact, thus *idea,* and ought never to desist from a tender-hearted cognizance of the *ideal.* To know the latter, it must seek instruction from the ideal's exemplar, wisdom.

Concerned as they are with a species of justice in the sense of harmony, the complementary roles of physician and philosopher both illustrate and amplify my argument. Whether one considers the healers of antiquity, their herbs and their incantations, or the first great physician, who was also among the first great philosophers—namely, Hippocrates—medicine originally aimed at restoring equilibrium, at providing the person with a suitable ground for continued efficacy of action. It rectified pathology; it restored health. But not only were the great Asclepieia of ancient Greece sanctuaries of healing herbs and mineral waters, they were repositories of temples and statuary. Located to afford inspiring vistas of mountain, land, and sea, they were eminently conducive to states of psychic harmony—as in the mother Asclepieion at Kos, its great landscapes stretching toward Halicarnassus where Herodotus dwelt, his fantasies first dawning of distant lands and fructifying new modes of civilization and civility; as in a daughter Asclepieion adjacent to the Greek theater at Epidaurus, where justice—itself given by the gods out of their wisdom's fullness—was, embodied in the drama, often enacted as the dominant theme of an Aeschylus or a Sophocles. Surely, the philosopher instructs the physician concerning experience's finer nuances—given the rectification of their frailties, physical or mental. Analogously, the just man, who perforce is both the man of primordial integrity and the visionary who perceives ever-more-inclusive modes of integrity, must also be affected by a touch of wisdom. So judges must be instructed by poets; so every judge must himself be poetic; so, beginning his career as a competent judge, one who correctly and fairly—i.e., in the light of equity—appraises a situation must culminate his career in the deeper perceptions of mystic and poet.

Dwelling in the *Inferno*, man acquires a sense of justice. Perceiving his flaws, he tries ways of rectifying them. Freed from their encumbrance, and accompanied by Virgil—Reason's poet—he journeys to the *Purgatorio*'s threshold. There, he prepares to purify himself; he allows flaws to perish. Now forgetting his affliction by pathology, he is led (and he who is led, we must recall, is Dante the poet!) to Beatrice. It is she who is the multiple incarnation, at first, of schemes of integrity, and then, as *Paradiso* is entered, of successive levels of poetic purity, philosophic comprehension, religious piety, and, at the end of the way, mystical compassion. In the last analysis, the very watchword is compassion, compassion in the light of reverence: reverence for man; reverence for his family; reverence for his friends; reverence for his personal community; reverence for the larger human community; reverence for all that lives and breathes and for all that is animate as well and, in its own manner, all that merits our respect and our affection; reverence for the Creator—fount of love and beauty synthesized, without sacrificing justice or integrity, to wisdom. Dante's vision is of justice brought to fruition, of justice's endlessly novel efflorescences. Dante's journey is a growth through justice, in all its variegated forms, so that, at the end, he is *beyond* justice.

(*b*) Justice as Harmony

Previously, I referred to a person's ecology. By this I meant the unfolding balances of his structures, his processes, his rhythms, his functions. These balances ceaselessly shift; they transform themselves in response to a continually altering environment which imposes ever-new demands upon him. Because of the displacements of the schemes of co-adaptation which result from these changes, every part of his body and his soul undergoes its own re-adaptations, both among themselves and with respect to the milieu relevant to the proper functioning of each. In consequence, the person is always poised to effect some new ecologic arrangement. His evolving life processes are composed of continual sequences of such arrangements, each required by environmental contingencies. By analogy, the community, the parts of which are persons, must, by submission or by combat, come to terms with dangerous external forces, uncontrollable alien influences which threaten to disrupt it. Such factors may so impinge upon the community as to cause it, that it may protect itself, to mobilize countervailing forces. That a new and more realistic mode of equity may prevail, the community might even be compelled to shape new institutions for guaranteeing its internal security. Likewise, persons are communities of parts, parts which are so mutually implicated in relationships of reciprocal participation and interdependence—though always with a certain hierarchical ordering—that they may be regarded as virtually "communing" with one another. When a particular part is threatened, as the physique by antigen invasion, the reticulo-endothelial system, ever attuned to the dangers of the destructive forces, sets in motion, to avert catastrophe, such *intra*personal organismic activities as will effectively ward off danger; or when an emotional trauma strikes the psyche, repressive dynamisms are set up, lest the person succumb to a too fragile re-equilibration. Specific traumata are dissociated from awareness. Relegated to an innocuous region of the psyche, they activate a defensive reaction by which the threat, symbolized as psychic defenses, is reduced without at the same time failing to register, by psychic representation, its continued presence within the person. Yet that very defense incorporates his striving to overcome the threat.

Accordingly, every person builds layers of symbols. By his essence, he *is* an activity of continual symbol creation. And, by these symbols, he expresses, however circuitously, the entire factual state of his being, physical and psychic. By the ways in which his symbols are layered, one upon another, to form an intricately laminated fabric, the justice of the person qua person is revealed. For this fabric discloses his characteristic mode of coordination, his style of balance. His diverse parts are more or less congruous; the kind of congruity which they display exhibits schemes of interwovenness which reveal his most fundamental rhythms. A person's psychic aspects and his physical aspects are themselves but functions, more or less complicated, of those rhythms. I cannot sufficiently stress their primordial character. In his inmost core, the person *is* rhythmicality; his very substance is constituted by rhythmic cyclicities, rhythmic spiralings, rhythmic orchestrations, rhythmic synchronicities.[4]

Of these configurations, the "coarser," so to speak, are the physical; the more "ethereal" and the more evanescent are the psychic; those which mediate the physical and the psychic are, in effect, his unconscious activities. For I here assume that mind *is* body etherealized and that body *is* mind in its weightiness. I use the metaphors of gravity and levitation to suggest, first, that a continuum prevails between mental acts and physical acts, and, secondly, that both the mental and the physical are attributes, in a Spinozist sense. They are but aspects of one substance, a substance which transcends each realm while containing, as immanent in it, both realms; yet in this very immanence and in this very transcendence, substance, as it were—though its *emanata* are physically modal or psychically modal—encloses endless mysteries, mysteries *transcendental* with respect to either realm: mysteries, indeed, enclosed in mysteries. At the same time, sufficiently penetrated, both realms, mind and body, lead to the very heart of substance. Fully explored in its consummate form, each realm reveals substance in its entirety; each flows into, becomes interwoven with, and blends with substance; each manifests the full character of substance: a character which is dynamic, organic, dialectical, processive. Under the perspective of the modal intertwinings of substance, its vicissitudes and its depths, its possibilities and its powers, the modal character of mind and body, understood in their variegated schemes of balance and imbalance, expresses the nature of *justice as grounding personal harmony*.

(*c*) Means and Ends

Hence, the just person is the one who represents himself, to himself and to others, authentically and without deceit. He expresses himself in ways which accurately correspond to the facts of the case; he unreservedly manifests his rhythmic nature's true cast. Neither does he willfully dupe nor does he use contrivances for concealing his actual state. On the contrary, he endeavors to present his substance, which is his distinctive rhythmicality, in its flaws as well as in its perfections: truly and without reservation. When Thrasymachus argues that the happiest man is the one who gives the appearance of being just, and thereby gains the advantages which would accrue to such a *persona*, yet, in actuality, possesses the powers, hence the advantages, of the unjust man, he postulates a person so split asunder in his substance that the dynamism by which the succeeding stage of integrity would otherwise unfold is impeded or, indeed, negated. Such a person would ineluctably be arrested in his growth toward wisdom. For in this contradiction within him, the person so divides himself from himself that by thus seeming to acquire *two* sets of advantages, each by a means opposed to the other, he immobilizes himself; he becomes frankly impotent. He loses the capacity for potentiating those distinctively human powers which will allow him to bring to fruition his uniquely human destiny.

Basically, it is a matter of means and ends. For a means to conduce to a given end, I repeat, it must be qualified by qualities which resemble, and do not too greatly deviate from, the qualities imparted to that end. Otherwise, that means would conduce to an end opposite to the end presumably intended. On the other hand, were the means not, by a small increment, slightly less perfect than the intended end, it would lack the motive force, the dynamism, to attain that end. Finally, if the qualities of means and end were identical, the former would, in effect, collapse into the latter; no distinction would obtain between means and ends. Indeed, in the final analysis, no end can remain as such. Through subtle disequilibration, it has, once achieved, already become a new means directed toward a new end. For means and ends shape a continuum; they are organically and dynamically interwoven. Thus split asunder, the Thrasymachan man splits asunder this continuum of his own actions.

What is the connection between these brief reflections on means and ends and the theme of justice, especially of justice as the way toward integrity and wisdom? Focally concerned with truth, under the perspective of goodness and beauty—i.e., a trusting, pervaded by hope and by love, that all relevant facts will be disclosed—justice employs *par excellence* the method of ratiocination. For the end of justice is so to order facts that the configurings of ideas which represent those facts will ground the values implicit therein; it is accordingly oriented toward the drawing forth of ideals profoundly interfused with facts, and never radically severed from them. By dispassionate reason appraisals are made. Yet the rational means employed by justice's attitude must be qualified by a double orientation: hope that knowledge of the facts will transform the knower into a better, hence, more integral, person—i.e., a person of greater integrity; and love for that person in his human essence, that the beauty of that essence might flow into novel and ever-more-inclusive schemes of wisdom: that, in effect, the factual status of man will be reconciled to his ideal status.

Accordingly, the means used to lead the person from his merely factual status toward an ideal immanent in and germinating through that status—namely, *reason*—is converted, once the end of integrity is attained, into a new means—namely, *intuition*: that means which incorporates ever-larger visions of what man is capable of attaining in his growth toward wisdom. Hence, reason directed by trust in the healing force of truth so conduces to the end of integrity, the healed condition, that the latter, once attained, itself becomes a new means—namely, intuition—which, directed by hope and a perception of the possibility of love, points toward the most generalized perceptions of all, those inherent in wisdom's beauty. Therefore, the journey which Dante undertakes is a preparation for his own final encounter with all aspects of his being. According to his vision, bound together by love, the numberless layers of man's symbolisms will cohere as a single, indivisible unity, but without sacrifice of the numberless nuances which these symbolisms never cease to exhibit. All this, a fusion of unity and plurality, is orchestrated into organically interwoven strands of means and ends, and a continual growth of the former to the latter and of the latter to the former: growth initiated in justice, growth brought to its first consummation as integrity, growth culminating in wisdom's dynamics. Thereby, human being is irradiated with the fire of the universe's divine center.

In sum, I have spoken of justice, and the immanence in justice of integrity and wisdom, in a merely abstract way. For my account to be more compelling, it must be supplemented by an experiential depiction of the actual journey from justice, through integrity, to wisdom; it must enumerate and specify the phases and moments of this quest. But, for the quest to begin, justice must prevail as primordially grounding personal harmony. For justice is the quest's very catalyst; and the quest itself must be portrayed. In it, man undertakes an arduous journey. Indeed, he proceeds on a double journey. On the one hand, he explores the facts, the intentions, the yearnings, of his own interiority; on the other, he searches into those external circumstances which allow his potentialities to effloresce. Thereby, he depicts the multiple layerings of the world within him and the world without. He reveals each route of this twofold journey as veridical complement to the other. In the last analysis, he aims his ultimate end at self-disclosure *in concreto*: his most inclusive harmonies, his symmetries, and his attunements.

In this process, a life is achieved which surpasses the spiritual life in the same measure as *that* life surpasses both the good life and the pious life. For wisdom itself unfolds in unpredictable ways, ways which lead it to modes of existence which cannot yet be foreseen. Perhaps, ultimately, a synthesis of those approaches to life, and perceptions of reality, which incorporate Eastern as well as Western modes of philosophy must be concretely envisaged—that the horizons of what constitutes justice and integrity as well as wisdom be extended to what, under present perspectives, seem limitless, and even awesome.

"When a man grows old his joy," declared Yeats:

> Grows more deep day after day
> His empty heart is full at length,
> But he has need of all that strength
> Because of the increasing Night
> That opens her mystery and fright.[5]

Yet, when his life is just and illuminated by integrity, he may, with "grace abounding,"[6] presume, with Dante, "to fix [his] look on the eternal light," and "within Its depth," see "all things in a single volume bound by Love, of which the universe is the scattered leaves. . . ." And now, at last, he may affirm:

> Now in my recollection of the rest
> I have less power to speak than any infant
> wetting its tongue yet at its mother's breast. . . .

And, in the fullness of his being, he can at last utter:

> O Light Eternal fixed in Itself alone,
> by Itself alone understood, which from Itself
> loves and glows, self-knowing and self-known. . . .

Truly, justice as grounding personal harmony is a stage along life's way toward integrity and, in the end, toward that wisdom with which Dante concludes his surpassing journey:

> Here my powers rest from their high fantasy
> but already I could feel my being turned—
> instinct and intellect balanced equally
>
> as in a wheel whose motion nothing jars—
> by the Love that moves the Sun and the other stars.

NOTES

1. This chapter first appeared, in essentially its present form, as an essay of the same title in *The Value of Justice: Essays on the Theory and Practice of Social Virtue*, ed. Charles A. Kelbley (New York: Fordham University Press, 1979), pp. 59–76.
2. Partridge, *Origins*, p. 325.
3. See the discussion in Bernard J. F. Lonergan, S.J., *Insight* (New York: Philosophical Library, 1957), 191–203.
4. In my *Homo Quaerens*, human rhythm is treated from a methodological point of view; in *The Dance of Being*, from an ontological point of view.
5. "The Apparitions," *The Collected Poems of W. B. Yeats* (New York: Macmillan, 1956), p. 332.
6. This and the remaining quotations, all from the *Paradiso*, Canto 33 (lines 82, 82–83, 85, 86–87, 106–108, 124–26, and 142–45) are taken from the translation by John Ciardi in *Dante Alighieri: The Divine Comedy* (New York: Norton, 1977), pp. 600–601.

6

THE DOUBLE JOURNEY: A VISION OF THE CONSUMMATE SELF

PREAMBLE

Earlier, I suggested that consciousness, pervaded by carnality, portends the carnal, and that body, pervaded by psyche, portends the psychic. For all symbolism is reciprocal: physical symbols implicate mind; mental symbols implicate body. Both the physical and the psychic are like iceberg surfaces: they are composed of, yet sunk into, human substance, substance embedded in a cosmic labyrinth. In alternating depositions, the motions of human substance engender both events and ideas. Events are woven of coarser resonances; ideas are woven of finer resonances. Mediated by the rhythms of a substance which grounds them both, intricate correlations emerge as binding events with ideas. Now, treating human searching, I specify the movements of this substance.

With manifold powers, every person bears himself toward himself with respect to his world. Correlatively, these powers are actualized as both body and mind. However actualized, they aim at establishing relatedness, either to the world or to the self. Previously, I examined the search for truth, goodness, and beauty as, respectively, modes of self in relation to world, each associated with a specific attitude, namely, trust, hope, and love. Once beauty is realized, so I showed, the relationship to that wherein beauty incorporates itself exhibits a new unfolding of truth, goodness, and beauty. Designated the pious life and the good life, these correlated processes converge upon a new process, a process the moments of which also dialectically unfold. In this process, namely, the spiritual life, three subordinate phases appear: justice, integrity, and wisdom. In turn, wisdom implies yet a new sequence, namely, the transcendent life: that luminous state which Dante's *Paradiso* portrays; a state which itself grounds piety, goodness, and spirituality.

In justice, the first stage of the spiritual life, one sums up the union of the pious life with the good life; one prefigures the progressive transformation, through integrity and wisdom, toward the transcendent life. To treat justice, I asked: Wherein consists a person's integrity? And my tentative response was: Integrity means wholeness, balance, physiognomic equilibrium. Thus, gesture, vocal inflection, posture may accord as congruous; in co-adaptation, inner necessity prevails, a spiritual coherence. Suffusing every gesture, vocal inflection, and posture, such coherence manifests itself as a *just*, i.e., an essential rather than merely contingent, balance: an inward condition which is so linked to its outer expression that, once one perceives this link, one embarks upon a still more profound inner journey. Now I reflect upon this journey. I survey, in its broad outlines, a person's life; and I suggest the overall contours of the self's inward depths as grounding this life.

A • THE PERSON AS SYMBOL: ORIGINS OF SYMBOLIC ACTIVITY

(*a*) The Symbol as Linking Naturality with Spirituality

In schemes of compresence, every person is a rhythmic activity of presenting himself as laminae of symbols, symbols which, correctly deciphered, reveal those rhythms. Certain symbols are closer to the essential person; others are more remote. Of the remote symbols, some are attached to him; others are detachable. Always, a person manifests his intrinsic being through the symbol. Locus of orchestrated layers of symbols, he is so constituted that his every tissue, organ, and cell, as they function in his overall being, is a composite of symbols.

Naturalistically considered, each person is indefinitely divisible. Each division within his integral body contributes to the composition of whatever animates that body, and confers upon it its integral character. A person's every natural part signifies his *anima*, and the whole movement of his soul inscribes itself on each such part. No part can be isolated from the entire configuration. With respect to one's personhood, the ultimate import of those parts resides in an ingredient, spirit itself, immanent in them. For each part is symbol as well as sign. Insofar as all natural parts are implicated in every searching act and, indeed, from a naturalistic point of view constitute the motions composing that act, the searching act itself is a symbol. As such, it reveals the psyche's intentionality as a spiritual thrust to apprehend a person's cosmic value. Penetrating one's natural being, one's reflexive powers lift that being from mere naturality to authentic spirituality.

The most intimate components of a person's body serve as symbols. Every expression of those components constitutes a symbol: a gesture, a facial movement, a vocal inflection. Likewise, all acts impinging on his milieu, acts which detach some region of that milieu and join it to his body, are symbols. And, by implication, every detached physical entity to which he was once attached symbolically portends his spirit. For engraved on his every part, whether continuously attached to him or entirely detached, is a person's entire being: a spiritual configuration. Inscribing itself on each part in myriad subtle layers, layers which are orchestrated into the invisible modulations which cumulatively blend into tangible structures, this configuration pervades those structures. In the end, the physical expression of spirit and the spirit which infuses that expression are formed by a single substance, a continuum along which one may distinguish regions of ethereal action, or reflection, and regions of gross action, or corporeality.

When I designate the person a locus of intentional action, I refer to the collective strainings of his manifold regions, his thrust toward full personhood. Human being *is* activity. It is purposive activity striving for relationship, ultimately relationship to the cosmos. Introspectively, a person explores the inner cosmos; extrospectively, he explores the outer cosmos. In his searchings, man traverses hidden recesses, labyrinthine depths. He shapes of each realm a cohesive and durable manifold, a many-nuanced yet unified and integral fabric. Ever yearning for relationship, he seeks so to coordinate these realms that each might reveal itself to be but an illuminated focus in an inclusive domain, a domain which transcends each realm yet subsumes both.

In his encounters with what is initially wholly other to him, man strives to subdue the *otherness* of the other. He seeks to convert that which is alien to him into a realm in which he can participate as intimately related to it, a realm to which he is bound by empathic links. In effect, he invests the other with symbols of his own creation, symbols which are extensions of his own being; and he dwells in the fabric which these symbols constitute. In this way, he projects his own image onto reality. And he informs reality with forms which he himself has shaped. Confronting reality as though he were encountering himself, he gazes into a sort of mirror in which he explores the texture of his own being: a texture, however, altered by the hues of a reality which is pristine and unsymbolized.

What is the nature of these symbols? How do they come to envelop both man and his world? In what manner do they result from, yet induce transformations which culminate in, his own being? To deal with these questions, I propose an hypothesis concerning the generic origins of symbolic activity.

(*b*) Animals in Quest of Plants: A Metaphor for Searching

Consider a hypothetical instance of primordial life. In the beginning, so I postulate, a single cell oscillates between alternating diurnal and nocturnal phases. As days lengthen and nights shorten, this rhythmic sequence undergoes a change of cadence. In the diurnal phase, a plant or phyto-cellular stage, the cell produces by photosynthesis the grounding carbohydrate from which, by successive links, the polymer, cellulose, which forms the stiff, immobile cell membrane, is created. By addition of nitrogen and minerals like phosphorus and sulfur, nucleotides are synthesized which polymerize into the nucleic acids, DNA and RNA, and amino acids are synthesized which polymerize into protein. Nucleic acid mediates replication, whereas protein mediates metabolism. In this activity, carbon dioxide and protoplasmic water are utilized while oxygen is emitted as waste. On the other hand, in the nocturnal phase, respiration ensues, a process in which oxygen is absorbed from the atmosphere, and catabolism occurs in contrast to the anabolic processes of the previous phase. Now carbon dioxide is extruded as waste. This diphasic process, in which catabolism alternates with anabolism, or a phytophase with a zoö-phase, is the grounding pulse of life, on its most primitive levels.

Consider, now, the sea waters wherein primordial life originated, waters consisting of a colloidal suspension of minerals. Deep in these waters, the ratio of light to darkness has altered in favor of darkness. Photosynthesis diminishes in importance vis-à-vis respiration. The zoö-phase dominates. Were that ratio to become too low, photosynthetic activity would cease. By a consequent shift in the relation of diurnal and nocturnal phases, plants give birth to animals; plant life is the very ground for the evolving of animal life. Still, the animal must survive. It requires food, and food may be procured only from plants. Hence, a dependency is immediately created. The animal is forever in quest of the plant; and this quest does not cease. It assumes myriad forms; it is transmuted in amazing ways.

To consummate the animal quest for plants, two complementary and correlative powers must evolve. On the one hand, the animal acquires the power to initiate activity, movement, search. On the other, it also acquires the protosensation of straining—that primordium of kinesthesia—and it evolves the capacity to apprehend, to sense, to recognize. To coordinate these powers, additional powers must be acquired. For response to the reception of stimuli, the searching act—that act of apprehension—can never be mere reflex. At every moment of its existence, the animal mirrors the relationship it sustains to the world. By reference to this mirroring as the "background" for all its sentient activity, it "knows" how to respond to specific stimuli. The primordia of motor system, sensori-receptor system, and evaluating brain are established.

From the point of view of their origin, animals accordingly are plants cut off from their food supply, plants which, so to speak, are always searching to replenish that supply. Only one source of organic food is available to them, and this source is in true (i.e., non-searching) plants. Hence, from their very beginnings, animals are venturesome. Indeed, they manifest a curious dialectic of embeddedness and adventure. On the one hand, they seek the vegetative condition. Once it is found, they rest. Hence, sleep arises in the minimal activity of the post-prandial state. Thus sleeping, animals dream. And dreaming is but a disguised statement of plans, anticipations, and intentions. It is the germ of thought. In essentially unconscious activity, subjectivity—the primordial Ego—is primordially resident. In this state, stimuli do not enter the creature nor responses flow from it. Nevertheless, autochthonous rhythms unfold. The dynamics of the Unconscious[1] evolves. Already, bodily activity is in process of surging toward its own self-"etherealization" as psyche. Indeed, this condition is realized only when openness to stimuli supervenes, and a certain vigor of response ensues, though both this openness and this vigor are pervaded by rapid alterations with already established patterns of merely reflexive and essentially unconscious activity. Thus, on the other hand, animals seek a mobile condition, a condition quite in opposition to the vegetative state. And this mobility expresses itself as both an orientation inward and an orientation outward. In turn, the oscillations between these orientations induce a thrust toward consciousness. In effect, the turning within simulates, but in a new way, the vegetative state; and the turning without toward a search for renewal alternates with the orientation of turning within to provide the ground for higher psychic rhythms. Between the threat of (animal) consumption by the other and the threat of (vegetative) consumption by the self, an intermediate if precarious position is achieved. Consciousness is an imperceptively flickering affair. To sustain it, and to solidify its manifold expressions, consciousness must be articulated as speech—i.e., as a speaking forth. Only thus can internal imbalances be overcome and rectified. Still, this faculty has not yet been prefigured.

Ultimately, the bifurcation between plant and animal is reflected into the psyche itself as the duality of consciousness and the Unconscious. The very ground of consciousness, the Unconscious corresponds to the plant series, whereas consciousness corresponds to its engendered animal series. Each gives rise to a distinctive genealogy. Yet these genealogies, animal and plant, are intertwined in dynamic equilibrium, and constitute two sets of complementary, contrasting, and mutually presupposing unfoldings. In its quest for food, the animal co-adaptively recognized the plant, locking-in to the relevant molecular arrangements. Thereby, it contacts the patterns manifesting that molecular ferment which inscribes itself, in self-exteriorizing activity, in the cellulose "skin" of the plant. Recognizing those patterns, the animal layers the imprints of a more sophisticated plant life upon the more primitive imprints hitherto laid down. A veritable labyrinth of pattern enclosures unfolds. Moreover, as it evolves, the animal gradually acquires the power to attune itself to patterns resident in the mineral world as well. For these patterns are perceived as analogous to those of the plant world. Thus, the animal expands the sphere of its cognizance. The world is experienced as inorganic and inanimate as well as organismic, though the basis for the experience of the lifeless is the experience of the living. Indeed, initially, the inorganic realm is regarded as though it were alive. The first model for conceptualizing that realm is life itself. And whether the animal experiences patterns which are organic or inorganic, it experiences the otherness of the world as the very incarnation of its own projectings: an activity grounded in its primordial intercourse with the plant.

By its essence, the plant is turned inward toward its own interior. Its inner processes are inscribed on an inert cellulose membrane. Save when environmental circumstance compels those adaptations in which violent tropisms supervene, plant life is placid. Accordingly, the animal transfixes itself with respect to a plant which is essentially still. Thereby, it compensates for its own motion, its restlessness; and it discovers a kind of vicarious mode of gratification for its own vegetative needs. Simulating a specious immortality, the animal seems (to itself) to arrest the flow of time. It reshapes its own rhythms. Stilling them, it orchestrates these now silent echoes as the quiet inner dance of vibrant peace, now a merely *virtual* movement. Is it any wonder that the animal is empowered to lock-in and to recognize? Can one question its intrinsic capacity to direct its own evolution on the very ground of the evolution of the plant, to subdue its own movements, to assuage its own violence, and to realize, by contrast, its own will, its freedom, and its autonomy?

Primordial plant life consists of phytoplanktonic flagellae, i.e., single-celled roaming planktons in quest of light in appropriate quantity and distribution. However, in insufficient light, their motile powers are, in the course of evolution, enhanced and their photosynthetic powers diminished. At the same time, the cell membrane develops special organs of sensitivity for light's more delicate shadings. In this way, such plant patterns as signify food may be discriminated in their finer features. By thus "animalizing" itself, plant life extends its locale: sea to shore, beach to cliff, the varied contours of land, lake, and river. Now a creature capable of discerning subtle contrasts and gradations of light, pattern, texture, and configuration evolves. Too, sound becomes more relevant, especially when sea is replaced by land as an animal's natural habitat. Now new modulations of sound appear. Rushing through leaves, stalk, and branch, the wind sets in motion sound patterns which are juxtaposed to already established light patterns. Likewise, gustatory patterns, olfactory patterns, and tactile patterns emerge. All these patterns, and perhaps many more (e.g., electromagnetic, gravitational, and so on, which correspond to different energy forms) which cannot be discerned above the threshold of awareness, are coordinated in a single overarching scheme. Cosmology, the cartography of the world in its deeper recesses, is born. Preeminently the animal destined to become a cosmologist, human being emerges: man, articulator of schemes of harmony in a world which is apprehended under ever-more-inclusive perspectives.

In their orientation toward evolving plants, evolving animals develop two interlocking sets of powers. First, they acquire the capacity to locomote themselves, to shift their location in ever-widening configurations. No longer rooted in a single locus, like plants, animals are perpetually in quest of security. To obtain food and, no less significantly, tenderness—both essential aspects of security needs—animals must constantly shift their locale. In this process, a second power arises: namely, sentiency. For it is the patterns which are associated with plants, that ultimate source of security, which lay the groundwork for the capacity to recognize; and this capacity grounds the characteristic power of animals: namely, searching itself. As constitutive of its own psychic makeup, the animal acquires precognitive strata of internalized plant patterns. Each layered upon the next, and all derived from the animal's ancestral genealogy, as an inheritance is transmitted from generation to generation, these patterns function archetypically. They are *immanent* presences, presences which are activated (i.e., made conscious, or at least the basis for action) in the presence of the appropriate plant. Two sets of powers, the power to search and the power to feel, interweave in varying combinations. Searching becomes specialized as motor expression—that pressing out of inwardly dwelling patterns which makes possible an animal's "locking-in" to exteriorly dwelling patterns. Such extruding constitutes the animal's effort to actualize those patterns which signify security, as though it can dwell narcissistically in a secure world of its own making. And gathering around patterns of security are myriad additional patterns: patterns which, resembling those of the plant, are actually constitutive of inanimate things.

In effect, the animal envelops itself with its own expressed patterns. And when they conform to already present outer patterns, and accordingly "lock-in" to those outer patterns, the expressed patterns veritably shake the animal in its inmost being. They place it in a kind of existential ecstasy. For, this "locking-in" induces reverberations within the animal: a sort of ecstatic dance which constitutes the motor, or motor-like, expression of joy as the characteristic response to "locking-in." Thus, the animal responds to the *results* of its own responses; it dwells in a world of response to responses, an intricate scheme of responsivity. This scheme brings about enormous refinement in the animal's emotional makeup. For, as they articulate themselves through (external) symbols, the rhythms which thus move the animal from within its own being (i.e., *e*-motion) undergo profound transformation.

(*c*) The Human Spirit Exteriorized

Culmination of this evolutionary process, man represents an altogether new kingdom, a kingdom as distinct from the animal as the animal is from the plant. And the articulation *par excellence* of man's being is his speech. Indeed, all man's expressive acts are incomparably more modulated than the animal's expressive acts. His gestures, his vocal inflections, his facial movements, his physiognomy, his gait, and his postural changes are far more subtle than are their analogues in the animal; and his speech, that faculty for articulating phoneme patterns and converting these patterns into morphemes, is inscribed against his comportment. Herein lies man's veridical powers, his characteristic way of penetrating the world. By this means, he joins himself to that world; he creates for himself a new world. Through speech, man dwells in communion with his fellows. Surrounded and permeated by the meaningful sounds which both he and they shape, sounds by which all humans acquire value, he comes to dwell in his own interiority. Thus externalizing this inner spiritual life, man encounters that realm as it is woven with patterns which are conveyed to him through his senses. Thereby, he further articulates those patterns. Internally, he links his spiritual world to all that is external to him. In an incomparably more intricate and richly textured way, man recapitulates, and indeed reinstates, the inner relation between the plant phase and the animal phase of monocellular phytoplanktons, a relation which is constitutive of those organisms.

Human beings dwell in human communities. Their powers of expression are subtle and variegated. Speech is simply the most refined of those powers. And speech is accompanied by physiognomy, facial expression, gait, and gesture. Man is perpetually translating his inwardness into outward form. In turn, form joins itself to the natural world. By nature, man is both artist and artisan. Continually reshaping his natural habitat, he converts that habitat into a richer and ever-expanding dwelling place. In this sense, man imparts his very spirit to the natural world. The physical is always being transformed by the spiritual. And when man encounters his own spirit as externalized and embodied, and thereby mirrors himself to himself, he himself is transfigured. Self and object undergo continual metamorphosis. For man, the moments of truth and goodness are caught up in, and subsumed under, the moment of beauty. In this way, man creates the symbol which both constitutes and transforms his own being.

B • THE SELF'S INNER JOURNEY

(*a*) Self and Body

I have treated both the self, as it comports itself toward its world, and the body, agency through which the self acts. Through interactions of self with body, the person exteriorizes his own spirit. Stages in every person's metamorphosis, truth, goodness, and beauty arise. What relationship between self and body grounds this metamorphosis?

Clearly, the self dwells in and through the body. No mere inhabitant, it actively participates in all bodily action. So intimately does the self participate that it actually becomes the body. In the last analysis, it *is* the body: body as action which is informed, circumspect, and sustained. By "informed," I mean that the self confers upon the body its typical configuration; it is the very principle by which the body acquires continuity. By "circumspect," I mean that the self allows the body to look about, to inspect, and to search; it is the principle which grounds all human questing. By "sustained," I mean that the self, ineffable basis for the body's every act, gives that body its ultimate support; it is the principle which allows for the preservation of self-identity amid the transformations of bodily processes. Obviously, these principles presuppose one another.

Not only is the self liberated by bodily action. Equally, it is entrapped by bodily action. When I turn inward toward my self's center, I become aware of a distinct mode of existence, a mode quite different from my body's existence. I feel myself no longer as suffusing my body, but as wholly within myself. Hardly identical with my comportment, I am in opposition to it. Always, I seek to exteriorize myself. For when I meditate, and in prayer and in solitary reflection when I pass toward my center, I become aware of myself as detached from my body, rather than as filling it and becoming one with it. Now I experience myself actually to be encumbered by my body. And I wish to dwell in inner silence, separated from my heart's beating; I wish to dwell in my soul's still recesses. Truly, the self is in and for itself. Though it knows itself in relatedness, it cannot know itself in contingency. It perceives itself in an internal rather than an external sense. For when I detach myself from myself, I empathically attach myself to another. When I participatively become one with my body, absorbed with my own biologic vitality, I am disconnected from another, save insofar as he is instrumental in enhancing my vitality.

Herein unfold oscillations of detachment and empathy. Dialectically intertwined, these phases of the self shape intricate patterns. And the way to empathy is through detachment; the way to detachment is through empathy. In his searching acts, man involves himself in both phases. His extrospections are of comportment in general. But having searched into the truth of objects and having understood the patterns which they typically form, man is freed from his external bonds to nature. Through his very explorings, searchings, and understandings, he introspectively becomes aware of himself *as* action. Spontaneously, he incarnates his own ideals; he exhibits them in his very comportment; he redirects that action. Only then does man become both moral and aesthetic.

Complementary modes of acting, the moral and the aesthetic express man's attitudes toward both world and self; they are the ways by which he brings each to luminous presence. Morally, man makes his acts conform to norms which, extrospectively, he discerns as arising within his own experience. But aesthetically, he actually re-creates both himself and his world. Transforming morality, reason, *and* natural object, he informs each sphere with his own spirit. Thereby, spirit not merely actualizes itself; it also infuses itself with new value, new content, new thrust.

In endless unfoldings, reflection activates itself. It creates ever-new sources of spiritual energy for its own searching acts. Impinging on the retina as contrasting shades of light, for example, stimuli so activate rhodopsin—the purple pigment which is capable of simulating chlorophyll-based photosynthesis—as to transmit new quanta of energy to the relevant optic centers (in the post-occipital lobe): quanta which, re-equilibrating typical patterns of energy distribution in the central nervous system, shape new patterns and form new levels of energetic activity. Whatever the physiologic mechanism, all stimuli thus act upon the brain through mediation of the relevant sensory organ. Beyond that, to receive stimuli, one must *use* one's sense organs. Thus, I approach stimuli *through*, and by exertion of, my eyes, my ears, and my fingers; and I so orient myself toward my body that I place my very reflexive acts *into* a particular receptor organ. To search—hence, to open up one's senses to the world—is to be in-formed with the information which it contains. It is to initiate a process by which, in my very reflexive makeup, I feel my way into my body. By immanent intentionality, I must "tense" myself both toward and into my sensory organs, including those which are viscerally kinesthetic; I must experience the pulsating, vital rhythmic expansions and contractions which reside in my every action.

Every self is empowered to animate its associated body. Informing the body with its own grounding and constitutive principles, the self veridically identifies itself with the body. Beyond that, the self-pervaded body—the person himself—so interacts with other bodies, persons or non-persons, that, through such transactions, he identifies himself with a sphere of physicality which lies outside of his own body: influences in which the body is indeed immersed. Thus affected, a person's body is the agent *through* which his own self acts. The very medium through which the self perceives, it is also the instrument by which the self executes transformations within its relevant world. Thereby, a person provides truth for the scientist, goodness for the moralist, and beauty for the artist; thereby, he gives to parent, friend, and lover the attitudes of trust, hope, and love; thereby, he allows judge, statesman, and sage such stances as justice, integrity, and wisdom. Through its identification with the body, the self achieves vibrancy and wholeness. Thus suffused, the human body grounds its own evolving inner depths; it permits a never-ending self-exploration.

(*b*) Self-Transformation

A great and wondrous spectacle, the world solicits the quest to participate in its rhythms. Thereby, every person is borne through the pious life, the good life, and the spiritual life. Earlier, I considered general approaches which the self can take toward its worldly objectives. Increasingly, I acknowledge an inner world as immanent in this quest. Now I can ask: What grounds these attitudes: namely, those of faith toward the truth, hope toward the good, and love toward the beautiful; and, in ceaseless upward spiraling, those of justice, integrity, and wisdom? And now I can respond: It is the very self, as it enters, and permeates, the body's interstices and recesses; the very self in that dynamic flow which permits its own unimpeded efflorescence—the person become dancer, musician, poet, lover, experimenter, statesman, athlete. By his intrinsic potentialities, every person is multi-gifted. Under ideal conditions, namely, circumstances in which an egalitarian community allows for a free, spontaneous interplay of thought, feeling, and action, each person can, by sufficient effort, develop his distinctive powers: his talents, his interests, his propensities, his gifts. And as one seeks to unite oneself with the world, a unique fabric of actualized powers is woven: a union in which one reveals oneself to be searching, feeling, groping, yearning, participating.

Every self deploys its own body's potentialities in diverse ways and for various purposes. Taking firm hold of its specific powers, it both activates those powers and translates their associated intentions into visible expression. Thus rooting itself in its own body, the self also dwells in the body's expressive intentions: expressions which are transmitted through gait, physiognomy, or posture; through acts of artist, teacher, or technologist. Incarnating itself in these expressions, the self presents itself through them to another. Therein making its own presence felt, it shapes schemes of dynamic compresence. In this manner, the self insinuates itself into hitherto unoccupied and even arcane recesses of its world. Modulated in intricately nuanced ways, such body processes as convey the self's intentions obtrude themselves on, hence, relate the self to, the world. By these encounters, a person transforms his world. He informs it with the very forms with which he has imbued his own body.

Dynamically informing its associated body, the self imparts myriad purposive movements, endless plasticity, motions which when transmitted to specific objects shape a multitude of arrangements. In a painting, every brush stroke entails distinctive arm and finger pressures, wrist twistings, hand-to-eye coordinations. Exteriorizing itself in movements of finesse, grace, and delicacy, the self correlatively probes its own depths. In this process of self-objectification, the self recreates the world as a mirror in which, viewing itself, it both witnesses and traces the contours of its own ever-deepening content. "And if the soul," wrote George Seferis,

> is to know itself
> it must look
> into a soul. . . .[2]

Reconstituting its milieu, and mirroring itself to itself in truth, goodness, and beauty, the self reconstitutes itself as well.

(*c*) The Dialectics of the Self

In self-mirroring, by each of these modes, the self transforms itself. Just as it had explored the world's arcane recesses, it now probes its own arcane recesses and, thereby, prepares itself for veritable transmutation. The most thoroughgoing account of the dialectics of this mirroring, the self's inner adventure, was proposed by Hegel.[3]

According to the *Phenomenology*, consciousness searches deeply into its own implications. Tracing these implications, it shapes fragmentary aspects into coherent unity. To validate this process, criteria arise, not externally to the phenomenon of knowing, but within the very unfolding of that phenomenon. Initially, in the phase of *sensation*, consciousness apprehends its object with immediacy. Yet no meaning can be assigned to the content of consciousness as immediately sensed, i.e., without the mediation of thought. Indeed, no content whatsoever can be associated with sensation. For sensation is bare, undifferentiated receptivity. Always guided immanently by an intention to conceptualize, consciousness draws together into concrete unity every factor which it discerns. By an inner necessity which it experiences with ever-growing clarity, consciousness first negates each stage in this process, and then affirms a succeeding, more adequate stage. Thus to cancel immediacy, one must posit mediation; and mediation always involves reflection.

With virtual immediacy, the self apprehends itself as reflexive: the very kernel of its subsequent adventures. And to be aware of reflection upon objects which, at the outset, are perceived to be objects is to grasp those objects in their full objectivity, and not merely to sense them in their immediacy; it is to relate actively to those objects. Hence, to apprehend the very particularity of *perception*, one must accept the mediation of perception itself by universal concepts: i.e., perception of the relationship *between* subject and object. Now the reality of consciousness is apprehended as residing in the interstices between the one who apprehends and the datum of apprehension. This reality constitutes the reflective *understanding* of the guiding universal concepts of consciousness itself. Still, consciousness cannot attribute these concepts to properties inhering in the factors which it conceptualizes. On the contrary, it can only concern itself with the relationship between itself and its perceived object. Thus, it must become aware of its own universalizing activity. It must grasp itself *as* conceptual activity in process of its own unfolding, i.e., as a self which ever articulates itself. But such awareness implies that mere cognitive apprehension itself is transcended. Now the self desires to turn in upon itself, to inspect its own interiority. Intuiting those universal concepts as the efflorescing of its inmost being, the self is increasingly driven by *appetition*: that desire which lies beyond understanding itself. It actively wishes "to recognize itself as a self, as the source of its own conscious activity."[4]

At this point, the dialectic unfolds in a profoundly inward sense. The self experiences itself as truly autonomous. At the same time, the universal element now lies between it and another which is construed no longer as mere object but as indeed an altogether new and different self. Limited by that other's very autonomy, the self, in the end and to that extent, experiences itself as truly non-autonomous. Accordingly, consciousness now hovers between two perceptions of itself: it is both free and contingent. Yet this paradox cannot readily be resolved. Hence, an inchoate awareness supervenes, an awareness, however, in which the self does not cease somehow to experience its own essential integrality. And, by strenuous efforts, the self, now understanding itself to be reasonable, seeks *by reason* to specify, thus to penetrate, that integrality. Still, this very striving causes consciousness to fall away into parts which, in the end, shape a merely virtual mosaic: themes which are but potentially orchestrated; themes which are nonetheless discerned by reason. And, qua reason, consciousness now affirms as absolutely singular every datum which it discriminates. But every quest for such singularity, thus (by implication) for a unique conceptual configuration, terminates in an import which ineluctably proves to be empty.

An essential question arises for consciousness. What, it must demand of itself, do such termini of its own questing acts portend? Can the very products of rational inquiry be woven into a unitary fabric? Now an entirely new issue presents itself. For, by its inner movement, consciousness is driven to realize that the laws which ground this fabric cannot be prescribed by reason. The activity of ratiocination itself presupposes these laws. Their source must accordingly lie outside of reason as *a priori* condition for its very possibility. Save by reference to factors which thus transcend its proper sphere, consciousness is not competent to reason about its own contents. Yet a self which is ever compelled toward disclosure of its inherent reasoning acts cannot be satisfied with—hence, terminate its quest in—mere *a priori* norms. Such norms are sui generis abstract; and the self anticipates, though it does not yet fully conceptualize, its inmost ground to be radically individual, thus inexorably specific and unique. Ascertaining that norms pertain to particular cultures, and that cultures do vary from one to another, the self nevertheless seeks to generalize the experience of those cultures. Persuaded that human being as such transcends any specific culture, it yearns to know its own peculiarly human quality as transcendently universal, but, at the same time, as irreducibly concrete.

Thus convinced, the self becomes aware of itself as governed by norms of ever-increasing universality: norms the *terminus ad quem* of which, as one transcends culture after culture, seems continually to recede, indeed ultimately to vanish; hence, norms which as mere limiting notions are so abstract as, in the end, to be entirely vacuous. On the other hand, throughout Hegel's *Phenomenology of Spirit*, consciousness has increasingly become aware of itself as concrete action. To reconcile its abstract character with its concrete character, the self resorts to subterfuge, and, if allowed to fall away from its own eschatologic trajectory, to self-deception. Under such circumstances, a pathology of the self would supervene. Constricted by "defenses" against its acknowledgment of the precarious dilemma in which it finds itself, the self would, were it to deem any particular stage of its own growth as settled and final—hence, to succumb to passivity—be deformed or even, at the last, altogether crushed.

C • THE GROUND OF INWARDNESS

(*a*) Reflexive Self-Fulfillment

Now, a wholesome consciousness attains a new double awareness. Operating from within consciousness, its very propulsive dynamism reveals itself; it reveals, too, its own ground as, ever inadequate to the object of the self's quest, ever transcending itself. Continually eluding the self, this object invariably lies ahead of the quest; and one prefigures the object to be somehow larger than the self. In the end, the quest itself is limited only by that which is intrinsically limitless: namely, by a divine presence. Aware of God as pervading, indeed as incarnate in, its every expression, the self *re*-presents this presence in artistic forms of its own creation, forms which are drawn from the spirit's inmost wellspring. Now grasping itself as relating to the very beauty of art, the self becomes aware of its own dynamic participation in works which it itself has shaped. And, at this moment, a marvelous transformation is brought about. The self experiences itself to be both agent and medium through which the very Divinity emerges into specific, concrete manifestation.

Now, the unifying ground of human being discloses itself to consist in the "infinitizing"[5] of a consciousness which, in knowing God as spirit, "knows itself as spirit."[6] Man, declared Meister Eckhardt, sees God with the same eye with which God sees him: human self-knowing "is defined by divine self-knowing."[7] Surely, a transmutation has occurred. The entire movement of the *Phenomenology* recapitulates itself. Metamorphosing into a systematic quest to unify the hitherto distinct moments as but facets of a single, coherently ordered manifold, that movement brings human aspiration to its consummate shape. At last, the self experiences itself as *internally* aware of other selves: each self reveals itself through a unitary and inclusive bond to God as, from within their separate beings, selves mutually condition one another; every self is grounded in one substance, a single indivisible *Geist* or ferment, which is transcendental with respect to all particular selves and yet immanent in each particular self. Along the route of these unfolding phases, no single form of knowing, from the most elementary to the most complex, is degraded. On the contrary, all forms are valid; all discover their proper locations in the overall scheme. Under a perspective engendered by the conditions required by every form, and in the totality which by its emergent nature necessitates an appropriate role for every form, each form functions in an irreducibly distinctive and unique way.

In its momentous journey, the quest fully to know itself, the self reveals its reflexive character as pervading its every form and expression; and it exhibits that character as grounded in a coherent manifold of interwoven reflexivities. Repeatedly, fragments are redintegrated and gathered into new unities. Within these unities, new fragmentation—hence, new perishing—endlessly recurs. Yet all fragments make their unique contributions to the composition of the whole. This process of assimilation, synthesis, and expression lies at the very core of the reflective act. Still, I must raise these questions: Wherein consists the dynamics of this act? Wherein consists the fabric woven of the myriad reflexivities of diverse selves? And, to respond: The more a self surrenders itself, through the agency of its associated body, the more it implicates itself, in an intrinsically selfless way, in both itself and others; the more a self acquires itself, in heightened self-consciousness, the more it relinquishes itself in participatory empathy; the more a self potentiates its own powers to return to itself, inwardly to explore its own ground, the more it discloses the manifold of internal relations which both constitute that self and bind it to analogous manifolds which unfold in analogous fashion for other selves.

(*b*) Human Ontology

By unconcealing the world, by disclosing the world's drama and configurations, and, through its body, by rooting itself in the world, the self, ultimately a person, reveals *himself* to himself. In this process, every person discovers his own authenticity: his inmost depths, his grounding substance, his consummate meaning. By "authenticity," I mean luminosity, sagacity, ethereality, tranquil yet flowing vibrancy, participatory empathy. In my third chapter, I explored luminosity; in the present chapter, I explore sagacity. Later, I elaborate all themes as, when cojoined, revealing the ὄντος of the person. Thereby, prefatory to its temporalization, in *Metamorphosis*, as human ontogeny, I frame, in this volume, a human ontology.

By the self's inner journey, it prepares itself for the renewal of its outer journey. In spiraling repetition of advance and retreat, each journey completes the other. Hence, the self's quest both to clarify and to transform itself is a double journey in which, by stages, it ever more sharply delineates a vision of its own consummate forms. In this dual movement, the self articulates a veritable cosmology. Engraved on an ever-deepening self, the lineaments of this cosmology are constituted by themes which depict the pious life, the good life, and the spiritual life. Liberated by its body's expressive movements, movements through which the self externalizes its own explorations, the self achieves freedom from bondage to its narcissisms. No longer is it excessively absorbed with the kind of privacy which counterposes to the actual world an illusory realm of gradually engulfing fantasy. Conversely, freed from the carnality by which it experiences itself as entangled in physical passions which threaten to crush its interior adventures, the self achieves true solitude; and it meditates its own inmost mysteries. Questing after a balance between its inner and its outer searching, each both conditioning and presupposing the other, the self propels itself toward ever-new syntheses of these complementary journeys.

What so joins inner and outer searching that they mutually synchronize, each catalyzing felicitous outgrowths from the other? In the end, the ground for this union is the activity by which one articulates one's deeper feelings. Pre-eminently, speech exposes the secrets of both self and world. Words which are uttered authentically are but vehicles of the spirit. By speech, spirit etches itself upon the world. Reshaping the world's contours, it releases novel facets for further search. By speech, spirit engraves itself upon the self. It draws forth its hitherto unrevealed and often labyrinthine depths. A fleshly aura which hovers about speech, every bodily expression *ex*presses itself into the world. Imprinting itself therein, it forms new configurations; and its heard resonances so *im*press themselves upon the self that they enable the self to journey through its own depths and even, at the end, to register the consequences of this journey upon its own natural ground, its associated body. Like the human body, the world is composed of organic arrangements into schemes of equilibria and disequilibria, schemes which stand in intimate relatedness to the person. Analogously, body organs are so interwoven and balanced as themselves to stand in intimate relatedness to the person. When one speaks, and in manifold ways expresses oneself—hence, affirms this dual relatedness—both inner and outer resonances unfold. World, body, and self undergo myriad vicissitudes in response to these resonances. Whether human expression soars or it purls, and whatever its melodies or its rhythms, its imprints are profound and metamorphosing.

Previously, I wrote of the self's quest for relatedness to itself through its bonds to the world. Yet always the self was thrust back into itself; and, in each stage of its quest, it became more inward. When, finally, the self was able to give itself in love to some external object, it profoundly changed that object; and the object was then perceived as beautiful. In this perception, the self itself has changed. Through its own creations, the self's very composition has been *re*-created. And, once the capacity for beauty and love has been actualized, and a new unfolding begun, justice arises as the self's quest for its own truth. Turning inwardly, and experiencing itself as object to itself—hence, as initially shackled to its own body—the self now begins a new, and even more momentous, journey. In the first phase of this journey, it seeks to delineate its every objective determination. For the self seeks to know all constraints which work upon it, including its own body.

First, the self experiences its shackles as they demarcate its very possibilities for self-growth. Through art (and prefigured in earlier stages of both science and morality), the self initially discovers its potential for interior change. But, quickly, it discerns limits to its own mutability. Yet it seeks to convert those limits into a sphere upon which, from within itself, it may further act. In its dual quest to articulate its own content, and to participate emphatically in the cosmos (apprehending the uttermost ground of cosmos as identical with the uttermost ground of its own being), the self proceeds through stages which I designate as, successively, the philosophic, the religious, and the mystical. Here, in part, I presuppose the Hegelian analysis; in part, I stress a single theme rather than the multitude which Hegel treats; I stress the reflexive character of the self as it is interwoven with the reflexive character of the world.

(*c*) Philosophy and Self-Disclosure

In a sense, the most generalized formulation of the concept of justice is philosophy. For philosophy aims at doing justice to the facts of the case; it adjudicates and passes judgment. Suffused with both Scriptural piety, since reverence for human being is its root commitment, and a profound sense of the good life, philosophy's central quest is *to know*: to know in the most inclusive and generalized form, that (in effect) justice be universally meted out. Philosophy searches to join together, just as "justice" was originally *ius*; it frames a coherent system which is adequate to the facts. Yet the more pervasive human goals are not attained through truth, in its narrower construal. Nor do they flow from justice, in *its* narrower construal, or through philosophy, in its usual sense. Dante's scheme for the unfolding of spirit is at least as valid as Hegel's. Beyond philosophy lies the goodness of beauty: namely, integrity. And integrity stresses, not the cognitive stance, though it surely presupposes truth, but attitudes, orientations, and actions. More specifically, integrity pertains to the collective actions of humankind vis-à-vis the cosmos. Grounded in truth, this stance explicitly conveys messages of hope and goodness. Always pervaded by love, though never explicitly drawing forth the fullest import of love, integrity, in its most generalized form, constitutes religion. Wisdom, the last member of the spiritual triad, namely, the beauty of beauty, synthesizes the philosophic and the religious orientations. Ultimately, it expresses the mystical union of the two: a union which, as the fullness of being, unfolds as luminous, as sagacious, as ethereal, as of tranquil and flowing vibrancy, as participatively empathic—in a word, as *authentic* human being.

> [S]ubstance, accident, and their relation
> so fused that all I say could do no more
> than yield a glimpse of that bright revelation.
>
> I think I saw the universal form
> that binds these things, for as I speak these words
> I feel my joy swell and my spirits warm.[8]

Once having entrusted itself to, and delineated the contours of, its internal objective limits, the self discerns the possibility for altering those limits. In Dante's *Inferno*, this process of self-discovery is carried out with utmost thoroughness. Penetrating its own Unconscious, the self comes ever closer to understanding the body from within itself rather than from without: body as implicated with other bodies. Participatively embedded in the body, the self is internally related both to the body and to its associated milieu. But in Dante's *Purgatorio*, the progressive dissolution of the self's limits manifests itself as a *cleansing* of the self's inner content. Rather than merely ascertaining the facts of its existence, the self now evaluates those facts from the point of view of a norm, an ideal which it shapes for itself and gradually purifies. Having already comprehended its own originating bodily matrix, the self transforms that matrix. Now it proceeds away from its natural origins, from that which efficiently caused it to be what it is, toward an end, a destiny, which, in hope, it feels itself as adumbrating with increasing clarity. For the first time, the self perceives the etherealizing of its own grounding body; it prefigures the non-dissolution, indeed the very immortality, of that *toward* which it progressively metamorphoses itself: a limit which transcends itself in limitlessness. Passing from a mere evolutionary and naturalistic perception of itself toward a transcendental perception, the self seeks, in the *Paradiso*, radically to negate its bondage to the body's cruder resonances; it dynamically implicates itself in its own self-transforming acts. Through meditation, and in mystical self-transcendence, the self places itself ever closer to its own center; and it approaches this center experimentally, through a kind of meditative testing. Moving alternately toward and away from that center, in rhythmic ebb and flow, the self so defines itself that the mean distance, so to speak, from that center becomes ever smaller.

Philosophy is the quest for the truth of the inner self in its relation to the world; it is cosmology construed as a scheme of internal relations. Religion is the purification of the inner self; it is the redirecting of its movement toward an end which is already immanent in it, yet always perceived to be transcendent to it. And mysticism is the union of philosophy and religion. In this highest moment of wisdom, a new truth, a new goodness, and a new beauty unfold. Transcendentally, the scheme ever complicates itself; yet it simplifies itself ever anew. Coiling in upon itself, it nonetheless spirals outward. Now origin and destiny are perceived to be one and the same. Each enveloping the other, an endless transcendental dialectic never ceases to evolve. Juxtaposing Isaiah of the Old Testament and John of the New, this vision has thus been stated:

> For, behold, I create new heavens and
> a new earth: and the former shall not be
> remembered, nor come into mind. But be ye
> glad and rejoice for ever . . . [Is 65:17–18].
>
> . . . it is done. I am Alpha and Omega,
> the beginning and the end. I will give
> unto him that is athirst of the fountain
> of the water of life freely [Rv 21:6].

Now, at last, the inner meaning of the plant patterns, to which I earlier alluded, is revealed. In his animal nature, man turns toward those patterns for security. Ever seeking firmer roots, his yearnings engender a creative efflorescence of endlessly novel patterns. As outward, the patterns are symbols; ultimately, they are symbols of tranquil origins. Yet, as inward, Plato's Form of forms is incarnate in them. What from a naturalistic perspective is ceaseless variety vibrantly to be explored is now disclosed in its full transcendentality. In caring for plants, a person cares for objects which are external to him; and he cares authentically. But in caring, he is being vicariously tender toward his own origins. For the mystical moment of wisdom apprehends proto-human existence, whether animate or inanimate, as symbols: symbols not only of origins, but of possibilities to be striven toward. Such exuberant possibilities as may be imagined prefigure an end within the very beginning. Caliban of *The Tempest*, symbol of carnality, speaks more eloquently of spirituality than Ariel, that explicit representative of the spiritual. And, in my account, the journey which I have proposed *in abstracto* will shortly be repeated *in concreto.*

NOTES

1. Henceforth, whenever the term "unconscious" appears, I am implying an ingredient of body, as referred to on p. 99. At times, when I wish particularly to stress this corporeal element, I shall employ the designation "unconscious–unbody."
2. "Argonauts," "Mythistorema No. 4," in *Collected Poems: 1924–1955*, trans. Edmund Keeley and Philip Sherrard (Princeton, N.J.: Princeton University Press, 1967), p. 9.
3. Too profound and intricate to recapitulate briefly, Hegel's portrayal of the self's growth can be presented here only as an abstract from the masterful commentary on the *Phenomenology* by Quentin Lauer, S.J.: *A Reading of Hegel's* PHENOMENOLOGY OF SPIRIT (New York: Fordham University Press, 1982).
4. Ibid., p. 13.
5. Ibid., p. 18.
6. Ibid., p. 19.
7. Ibid.
8. *Paradiso* 33.88–93, in *The Divine Comedy*, trans. Ciardi, p. 600.

7

RE-THINKING THE UNCONSCIOUS: ITS DISSOLUTION AND ITS SUPERSESSION

PREAMBLE

Prior to commencing my exploration of the stages of human questing, I interpose an account of its abstract moments, set forth in my previous chapter, and an account of its concrete moments, to be elaborated in my next chapter, a new concept of that which mediates body and mind: a concept into which one may translate the traditional Unconscious, yet a concept into which altogether novel elements are introduced. Relating body modes of existence to mental modes, each sinking into or rising out of the other, the Unconscious (equivalently, the Unbody, hence, in my account, the unconscious–unbody) actually relates nature and spirit: a broader relationship than the connection between body and mind. For, at bottom, the unconscious–unbody manifests a deep bond between person and cosmos. A bodying-forth and a minding-forth, it is an actualization of potency, single and indivisible, in both spheres. When body is stressed, dance discloses the deeper unconscious–unbody rhythms; when mind is stressed, speech discloses these rhythms. The essence of body and mind, rather than their existential expressions, the unconscious–unbody is not spatial, not temporal, not material. Unfolding in accordance with its own laws, it links world and self; and, in this sense, it grounds the very perception of space, time, and matter. Within its labyrinth, altogether novel ferment prevails.

Both directly and spontaneously, a person symbolically presents his very essence: by image, by gesture, by physiognomy. His unconscious–unbody flows quite immediately into his comportment, and infuses both his speech and his dance. At the same time, he reflects upon his self-presentations. Thereby, he symbolically *re*presents himself, in his relationship to the world. In effect, he objectifies his own presentations; and he meditates, articulates, and elaborates these presentations. Hence, every person's unconscious–unbody also flows into his derivative symbolizations. And the two modes, presentation and re-presentation, themselves dialectically interact to express the primordial bond between man and world. In drawing this bond into symbolism, man transforms the disparate, pluralistic, and diversified character of his own being, and that of the world as well, into a unified and coherent character: he shapes himself as a veridical person in relation to a world now become cosmos.

No longer is man merely an aggregate of archetypal organizing principles, each functioning for his solitary self alone. Nor are man's primordial archetypes only societal in status, expressing an immanent attunement between him and his community: a collective archetypal Unconscious. Surely, a primordial *cosmos-rooted* synthesizing activity confers unity upon the self and, in turn, allows the self to experience the world as unified: an ordered spatio-temporal-material manifold. Shaped into a unity of speech and dance, his fragmentary images and kinesthesias are, moreover, brought together under the aegis of a principle which, unlike the Kantian synthetic *a priori*, is not merely abstract, formal, and universal. Subsuming these traits, such a principle must also express sheer activity. Concrete and self-particularizing, such activity works vis-à-vis a world which itself is a counteractant activity. As such activity works itself out, it symbolically both presents and represents itself: it questions, and it questions its questionings; it listens, and it listens to its listening; it responds, and it responds to its respondings. Exhibiting this bond between itself and the world, the self, as it searches, ontologizes its own grounding synthetic dynamism; and it articulates the rhythms both of its own personhood and of the cosmos itself. Reciprocally, the cosmos, itself activity, ontologizes *itself* within and through the very person.

A • THE UNCONSCIOUS AS GROUND FOR HUMAN ONTOLOGY

(*a*) From Unconscious to Unconscious–Unbody

How can that which is *un*conscious be at the same time psychic or, for that matter, proto-psychic or sub-mental? How, moreover, can that which is psychic, namely, the Unconscious, transform itself into that which is intrinsically antithetical to the psychic, namely, the corporeal? Must not the very term "unconscious" be abandoned as obfuscating rather than illuminating? Now I treat these questions.

Throughout these pages, I have implied a preference for verb forms, in setting forth functions and activities of the self, rather than noun forms. Such ideas as unconscious*ing*, selv*ing*, or person*ing* suit my thought more accurately than their equivalent nominal forms. Still, even these verbs are too circumscribed, too undialectic, and too lacking in such valid connotations of the Unconscious as emerging from or submerging into, fluidifying and crystallizing, or assembling and fermenting to render my meaning adequately. Too sharply etched, they designate processes *which* unfold rather than processes which process *themselves* as they process forth into a sequence of culminations; culminations which mark momentary resting stages which are likewise but initiating loci of yet new processings-forth. Indeed, no language can fully convey my intent. True, I use evocative words, words meant both to provoke thought and to call forth its subtler nuances, rather than merely to set forth thought in conventional linguistic structures and systematically to articulate its implications. For language tends too precisely to delineate boundaries between factors permeable to boundaries. Ineluctably, language presupposes a larger and as yet unexplicated context which nonetheless confers specific meanings on the well-articulated linguistic foci which arise in that context. Hence, just as I have rethought both Freud's theory of a particular Unconscious and Jung's theory of a collective Unconscious, so I now rethink the notion of the Unconscious in general. Non-circumscribable processes require conceptualization. To justify my renouncing the very term "unconscious," I apply methodologic categories introduced in an earlier book: namely, assemblage, conjugation, and transformation, and their dynamic correlatives, self-action, interaction, and transaction *and* evanescence, crystallization, and fermentation.[1]

The notion of an Unconscious has had its day. Certainly, this notion has facilitated the systematic gathering together of an immense range of facts, facts heretofore ignored as lying on the very periphery of the natural. In two major instances, it has achieved this goal: for Freud's individual and instinctual Unconscious, and for Jung's collective and archetypal Unconscious. In both cases, every quest to express the full import of the Unconscious has led to the postulation of entities which, as neither psychic nor corporeal, require actual metamorphosis of that notion. One must enter an entirely new realm of being. From the earlier standpoint, this realm is esoteric. It involves *straining toward*, a "transcendentalizing" with respect to "something" which, ontologically speaking, is quite distinctive: an altogether novel domain; a dwelling in a new context of thought which, relative to my earlier ideas, is quite mysterious. According to this view, the very notion of "unconscious" entails its own negation. True, all that had hitherto been implied by that notion must be retained; yet, now, this content must be subsumed under a more inclusive notion, a notion which no longer requires postulation of deep inconsistencies. I do not mean here such paradoxes as genuinely inhere in nature, for nature exhibits many ambiguities. On the contrary, I refer only to those contradictions which inhere in current linguistic usage, in temporarily popular modes of conceptualization, or, perhaps, in language itself.

What had been designated the Unconscious combines two emphases: Freud's stress on body processes and Jung's stress on spiritual processes. For Freud, stimuli impinging on and woven into the Unconscious derive from either visceral tensions and relaxations (and displacements or condensations of these) or from that natural and interpersonal environment, with its analogous displacements and condensations, in which the human body functions. Through dialectical interplay of "pleasure principle" and "reality principle,"[2] the essential referent of unconscious processes is, on the whole, physicality: the natural order. For Jung, interwoven with the body yet stemming from beyond the body are such interpersonal relations as implicate a spiritual collectivity: influences constituting an Unconscious which expresses individual participation in a community. Through such participation, persons internally relate to one another through bonds of sympathy. And, combining both emphases, "unconscious" has come to designate the commingling of body attunements with mind attunements: nature's resonances and spirit's resonances. Though each author stresses one or another of these modes of attunement, both implicate the two modes. For Freud, the suppressed yet larger context for natural process is spirit, whereas for Jung, the suppressed yet larger context for spiritual process is nature. When one combines these views, acknowledging the unexamined contexts in both cases, the Unconscious emerges as that which lies between, and indeed mediates, spirit and nature: mediates, however, in an irreducibly private way. For the Unconscious expresses sheer inwardness. Its status vis-à-vis nature or spirit depends upon whether one construes inwardness to be a body labyrinth or a mind labyrinth. And a syncretist view of the Unconscious with respect to its major exponents suggests it to be Janus-faced. Mirroring both mind processes and body processes, though by deformation rather than by conformation, it is both turned toward spirit and turned toward nature. Though by essence the Unconscious is neither spiritual nor natural, it participates in both realms; its very ground consists in the unity of spirit *and* nature.

Given the dual character of the Unconscious, the term itself is evidently a misnomer. When unconscious processes are construed as referring to spirit, they are indeed, in effect, proto-spiritual. Set in opposition to spirit, they nonetheless partake of the essential ingredients of spirit. In this sense, they may veridically be regarded as un-spiritual, by which is meant spirit *submerged* yet capable, in principle, of *emerging*. But when unconscious processes are construed as referring to body, they are, in effect, supra-corporeal. Set in opposition to body, they analogously may be regarded as uncorporeal, or "unbody," by which is meant body as emerging yet doomed, in principle, to submergence. Taken together, these meanings of Unconscious (or, equivalently, "unbody") imply nothing which in any cogent sense can be *merely* unconscious, or, for that matter, *merely* "unbody." On the contrary, they suggest that which is constituted by a dialectical interweaving of two activities: submerging and emerging, with respect to either body or spirit, as each alternately ferments and crystallizes, combines and recombines in myriad arrangements. For both views, the Unconscious is a commingling of elements set in opposition to one another, yet, in their very fusings and dismemberings, forming an altogether novel and indeed autonomous domain: novel and autonomous with respect to the *seeming* origin, whether natural or spiritual, of its basic ingredients.

Dynamically patterned in accordance with laws which express its thoroughly autochthonous character, this realm must be designated by a term which connotes something both static, inert, passive, and immobile, on the one hand, and negative, deficient, degraded, and pulverulent, on the other. Yet on a syncretist view of its *modus operandi*, this realm might be designated, rather than unconscious, *unbody–unconscious*, or, equivalently, *unconscious–unbody*. Since this grotesque term (which purports to designate a grotesque realm, processes which are bizarre when compared with normal body- or mind-processes) is still negative and undynamic in its implications, might not *sub-conscious–supra-body*, or, equivalently, *sub-spiritual–supra-natural* be a more valid rendering of what "unconscious" was originally intended to convey? Still, these are cumbersome locutions —though, in each instance, they entail precisely what a detailed working through of the alleged "region" seems to suggest: namely, an activity, an autonomy, and a positive straining. Without yet contriving a more effective way of specifying the portent of this "realm" or "process," given a more comprehensive theory of the person, I set forth certain dimensions, aspects, and perspectives of phenomena associated with unconscious activities which have hitherto been ignored.

Traditional views of the Unconscious have either been so "psychologized," or, what amounts to the same defect, materialized, that the very tracing of its inner processes leads to its self-annihilation as a meaningful concept. To salvage what is authentically viable, and to take cognizance of Jung's stress on the spiritual dimension—though his treatment of the Unconscious tends in its own way to be reductionalistically psychological—one must abandon psychology, in any of its current meanings, in favor of human *ontology*. In a philosophy of the person wherein "something" generically ontologic correlates with the originally intended, and quite legitimately specified, functions of the Unconscious, so that those functions are somehow to be retained, insofar as they are valid in a broadened context of usage, four terms, implying two sorts of reciprocity, must be connotatively interwoven: namely, the paired ideas of person and cosmos, and body and mind.

With respect to body and mind, a principle of divisibility reigns. Each domain, mind and body, constitutes a manifold, a lawful and deterministically specifiable region: a manifold which is naturalistically or, what is equivalent, behavioristically to be construed. With respect to person and cosmos, a principle of integrality reigns. Qua person one is indiscerptible and whole, an integral and self-integrating activity; and freedom or, at least, a kind of spontaneity of action which seems to defy the lawful character of natural, behavioristic processes, reigns. Qua cosmos, indiscerptibility also reigns; hence, the same considerations as apply to the person are operative. Within limits, appendages of various sorts can be added to either body or mind without violating a person's integrity—as long as he affirms and respects both body and mind, and regards them with dignity. Yet, within limits, no diminution of dignity entails diminution of the person himself, or, for that matter, of the cosmos. No intermediate grades of person or cosmos are conceivable, no quantitative factor of more or less. Likewise, whatever one subtracts from body or mind—excising, amputating, compressing, or nullifying—the person, within limits, and the cosmos, without limits, remain inviolate.

(*b*) Cosmos as Grounding the Unconscious–Unbody

In general, cosmos as well as person possesses both a physical aspect and a spiritual aspect. Construing person in Spinoza's modal sense and cosmos in his substantive sense,[3] I affirm: *sub specie durationis*, the person qua mode manifests his being under the perspectives (i.e., through the "attributes") of extension and cogitation; he is both *res extensa* and *res cogitans*. Nevertheless, as "apprehended" by any of its finite modes, substance is n-attributal, where *n* is indefinitely both large and deep. Insofar as one removes oneself, de-taching oneself, as it were, from substance, one is a particular existent, participating in substance conceived as *natura naturata*. Yet persons also participate in substance as its *modifications*: i.e., in a substance which is one and indivisible. Such modification must be of the entirety, not of any of its parts. For, *as such*, substance has no parts. And, as modification, a person is profoundly attached to substance; he is embedded in substance. *Sub specie aeternitatis*, he is sheer potency, potency (or *natura naturans*) manifesting itself under the guise of a finite mode in process of merging into its modal character.

What do these reflections portend? For one thing, they suggest that a person is finite, mortal, and transitory, though, as concrete ground of both his body and his mind, he is indiscerptible and integral. On the other hand, they suggest that he is eternal, infinitely consequential, and immortal. In effect, this Spinozist interpretation construes every person as veridical questor: i.e., one who searches actively and always in compresence with other analogously searching persons one who stretches oneself toward the uttermost reaches of the cosmos—cosmos which is unbounded and constituted of infinities nested within infinities, infinitude of all grades and of all kinds. Moreover, Spinoza speaks of substance as *causa sui*, and of persons as, by partial degradation, partaking of the character of *causa sui*. How are we to understand this expression?

Insofar as substance presents itself to a finitely modal person under the perspectives of both *natura naturata* and *natura naturans*, to be self-caused is to be actively, dynamically, and dialectically in relatedness with oneself. As *causa sui* substance is potency, ferment, *fons et origo*; and substance thus conceived is dialectically interwoven with substance as actual, modal, crystallized, and articulated. By derivation, every mode of substance, including the pre-eminent mode —a human person—is, likewise, though in diminished fashion, *causa sui*; analogously, the human person stands in dialectical relatedness to himself, in alternating and mutually affecting potency and actuality.

Consider how a bi-attributal mode, the person himself, dwelling in n-attributal substance, partakes of the mysteries of both Theos and Cosmos: of Creator interwoven with creation. Consider how, thus *positively determined* through extension and mentation, this mode, a person, touches the very core of substance, qua its n-attributal character, as "negatively determined" by that core, and, as such, as participating in and through those n-attributes. Consider how that which is finite, substantively continuous with that which is infinite—namely, the human person qua natural—and arising from nature's womb, is trans-substantiated into spirit. Consider how Flesh becomes Word. Consider how the Word, as it transmutes itself into a talking of persons with persons, and thereby envelops all such communicants with an aura of mystery, the enigma of the whole, perishes into each person's natural being; and how the Word becomes Flesh: a transubstantiation in the reverse direction. Consider this double mystery: the emerging of the natural toward the spiritual; the submerging of the spiritual "toward" the natural; the converging of each, spirit and nature, upon a singular locus—the absolute inwardness of a human person, one who is at once mortal and immortal, durational and eternal, finite and infinite, sheer potency and fulfilled actuality!

Consider the interwovenness of body and mind as person—but person not construed as two substances cojoined in and through his participation in a cosmos which itself is doubly construed: cosmos as *natura naturans*, hence God; cosmos as *natura naturata*, hence Nature. Is one not ineluctably led to reflect upon the mystery of a double transubstantiation: Flesh become Word and Word become Flesh: How can it be that this correlative yet oppositely directed movement unfolds in the very core of the person? Do I not possess, in this commingling of reversed vectors, a clue to the actual meaning of the Unconscious—a term subject to my provisos and strictures—or of its equivalent, the "unbody"? May a positive formulation not be given this doctrine in order to "de-psychologize" it, and, for that matter, to "de-physiologize" it? May one not extract the authentically Jewish element from Freud's view, so permeated by both his Judaism and his atheism, and the authentically Christian element from Jung's view, so permeated by both his Christianity and his paganism, in order to synthesize these elements? Might even atheism and paganism not be extracted and, under a classical Greek perspective, require a more lucid and sharply etched philosophical theory? In a word, may one not displace the ground of the traditional view from the natural order to the juncture of it and the veridically spiritual order: i.e., from *res extensa* woven with *res cogitans*; and may one, in addition, not formulate that ground with such precision as to allow for its direct applicability to a philosophy of the person? And, in the end, may this clarified ontologic ground not give rise to the complementary perspectives of cosmology and theology?

In the inmost core of every person a profound mystery reigns: a mystery which, dwelling in the essence which envelops all essences, effloresces as existence —existence extended and existence cogitating. Does this absolute inwardness, the person's very center, not "transcendentalize" itself toward substance: not so much toward modal, creaturely substance as toward fermenting, creating substance?

When it is a sufficiently *committed* activity, searching entails an opening up of the cosmos to the questor. By successive disclosure of its numberless facets, the cosmos yields its secrets as a kind of gift to the seeker who, reciprocally, by those symbolisms of his presence which constitute his quest, has given himself to the cosmos. Insofar as searching is ineluctably personal, indeed the most indefeasibly personal of all acts, and insofar as the personal is constituted by the interpersonal—hence, consists of acts which require both attunement and resistance—the cosmos reveals itself in a strictly personal way through its very bond to the questor, a bond which is at once incorruptible and indivisible. For grounding authentic search is authentic relatedness between a person, in his inmost being, and the cosmos, in *its* inmost being: inner man as veridical person, inner world as truly God. And must the essential import of that which has ineptly been designated "unconscious"—in a manner, indeed, often demeaning to man's very spirit—not consist, at bottom, in the dynamic implications of such relatedness? Is the person–God relationship not the very ground of the religious bond? Does it not follow that, in his deepest solitude—that toward which the Unconscious itself purports to point—man experiences his most authentic religiosity?

(*c*) Rhythms of Song and Dance: Paradigm for the Unconscious–Unbody

Distinguishing two modes of *in*-spection, namely, *scientia intuitiva*, Spinoza's passionate knowing, and philosophic analysis, Hume's more sober knowing, I can now ask: Sufficiently pursued, do these modes converge and, together, reveal that spirit and nature, their respective objects, hover about a single point, one which must be designated in a new way—the way of symbolism?

An integral activity of self-presenting, the person, by his essence, symbolizes his own existence. In myriad ways he presents himself to himself, to another, and to the cosmos in general. He doubly comports himself: by the flow of his speech, and by the movements of his body. Always, man's essential rhythms vary from person to person. Participating in various communities—some overlapping, some enclosing others, and some mutually exclusive—every man exhibits a comportment which orchestrates many layers. With respect to speech, one may partake, for example, of language in general, of Indo-European language, of a Romance language, of the French language, of the Auvergne dialect, and of idiosyncratic variations upon this dialect: mutually enclosing modes of increasing specificity. Analogous considerations hold for the body. And, in general, all flowings and motions exhibit dynamic structures. Immediately apprehended, some structures are superficial; others lie on successively deeper levels. Thus, one may speak of both deep structures and surface structures. But structures break up into activities and fermentings just as, conversely, ferment crystallizes as relatively enduring structure, which, however, pulsates with rhythmic tonalities. And, owing to their adjacencies, the laminae of comportment interact to shape varying patterns. Oscillating with their characteristic rhythms, they constitute the person a great dance of being: his every part vibrates in its unique way, and, thus vibrating, contributes resonances to his every other part.

Paradigmatic for these human "commotions" are the symbols of song and dance. Primordial speech is akin to chanting forth, singing in rhythms which are at times conventional and at times free and spontaneous. Primordial comportment is akin to dance, which, likewise, varies from the conventional to the spontaneous. Moreover, patterns of interwovenness prevail between song and dance, and, in particular, between their germinating *Anlagen.* Indeed, one may speak of the motions of the soul: of that which animates the body *to be* a person, or, more accurately, to be a *personing-forth*, and, as such, to manifest oneself through infinitely various though finitely classifiable modes of expression (i.e., such modes as constitute one's existential symbolisms). Furthermore, individuals may be more adept in one medium of expression than in another; some articulate with great subtlety, with respect to the shaping of phonemes, or of morphemes, or of both; others perform dance steps of comparable subtlety; still others achieve competency in "intermediate" ways, such as by painting or by sculpting. Though the limiting modes of expression, song and dance have no priority in a hierarchy of symbolisms of varying value. Human expressive activity is multi-dimensional. Its architectonic is endlessly varied, and variously nuanced. Genetic factors may create mutants who are especially responsive to a particular kind of symbolism. Or, perhaps, such skills are shaped by the interpersonal milieu in which one dwells, a milieu transmitted through the agency of significant figures such as parents. Above all, gradations each as valuable as the next prevail between speaking (or singing) and dancing, gradations which implicate a person's more circumscribed regions: in each instance, the person qua natural and the person qua spiritual. All these comminglings of comportment express autochthonous rhythms which signify the essential person.

Consider, now, another dimension in the relations between song and dance as primordial modes of comportment, on the one hand, and, on the other, comportment per se as matrix of their very primordiality. I postulate a sequence of increasingly specialized and conventional phases in two continua: spontaneous outbursts of free-flowing song, poetry, prose, or normal talk; effervescent flowings of dance, ritualized or stylized dance, normal body movements whether gracefully performed or awkwardly performed. As one passes from the first to the last member of each continuum, the concrete and generic give way to the focal and abstract; each member has been extracted from its predecessor. In each instance, the earlier phases represent hidden and latent, though always immanently conditioning, structures, the grounding architectonic of the later phases. In principle, every person manifests his particular attunements to the world. Thus resonating, he incorporates both the idiosyncratic and distinctively individual *and* the general and archetypal. For man participates in numerous communities, personal and non-personal, communities which extend to the furthermost cosmic reaches; and every less general community is enclosed in a more general community, functioning as a kind of agency which transmits the principal themes of the more general, themes on which it inscribes specific ornamentation. The family is the vehicle for the focalizing of themes which are more inclusively orchestrated in the nation; the nation articulates but narrows the scope of themes pertinent for all mankind.

Each person both manifests his being and comments on the world through a variety of symbolic forms. Rules may be formulated, rules more or less precisely specified, in accordance with which each symbolic form (e.g., language, art, history) is engendered. With respect to certain abstract properties, these rules are isomorphic with one another. In consequence, the (overarching) rule expressing these isomorphisms is itself maximally universal. At the same time, the totality of symbolic forms which effloresce, by the dynamics associated with these rules, expresses the questings of human being, and of each *particular* person, to comprehend being in general. By that efflorescence, human being—hence, each person—empathically resonates to being in general. In the context of symbolic quest, the world reveals itself to man. Insofar as the cosmos exhibits unity, coherence, and *raison d'être,* these efflorescences intermingle. Interacting with one another, they interchange their contents and, indeed, transform one another. A veritable transfiguration occurs. In effect, natural man transubstantiates himself. In proportion as his symbolic expressions veridically mirror, and, by the dynamism of mirroring, incorporate the contours of the cosmos, man spiritualizes himself in ever-deeper, ever-richer, ever-more-diversified ways. Never ceasing to quest after larger schemes of symbolic expression, the person seeks, quite literally, to *under-stand.* For he strives to apprehend, and, beyond that, to articulate the very ground which supports him in his community, the ground in which he roots himself ever more securely as that community establishes mutuality of relatedness to the cosmos. In the final analysis, that which grounds *human* being also grounds being in general.

In this dialectic of quest and revelation, searching becomes increasingly profound and intimate. The element of the personal pervades its every moment and dimension. By searching, man affirms his personhood. Yet, as he bears himself toward fruition through symbol formation, he experiences himself as a giving, a giving of himself, in his most intimate rhythms, to the rhythms of the cosmos, in *their* most intimate resonances. Increasingly, the inwardness of the cosmos draws itself forth as, reciprocally, the inwardness of man draws *itself* forth. But that to "which" man gives is no mere passive recipient. On the contrary, the more active his giving, the more thoroughly he discloses his own inwardness, and the more comprehensively do the orchestrations of the cosmos reveal themselves as also active. The more a person searchingly gives himself up to the quest, the more the "what" of the quest is displaced, first, to a "whom," and, finally, to a "who": a *who* which responds to human need, and, in responding, opens up His treasures to searching humankind.

In mutual attunement, God and man, each in his way, searches: man that he may know God and, by his knowing, pay homage to God; God that He may know man and, by His grace, dignify man. I cannot conceive of meaning as arising in the context of search, and I cannot conceive of search which is meaningful, without this profound reciprocity between God and man. By its essence, the personal is identical with the interpersonal; and the maximally personal, the locus of which is man's inmost depths—what hitherto had distortedly been called his Unconscious—is suffused with the maximally interpersonal: i.e., the bond between man's personhood, in its maximal degree, and God's personhood, in *His* inmost depths, indeed His very "Unconscious." But, whether applied to man *or* God, "unconscious" is a term which hardly suffices to comprehend the incomparable range and depth of veridical inwardness. Moreover, as man searches, and his disclosures become systematic and inclusive, interpersonal affirmation increasingly pervades his searching. When affirmation is of the bond between God and man, a pact of reverence between the two is shaped, a pact between Creator and creation. A promise is given: by man to God, in quest; by God to man, in revelation. In sacrament, a promise is fulfilled. Now, at last, the cosmos can be viewed under a double perspective. It is a gift by God to man as man, reciprocally, gives, as *his* gift to God, his own self-affirmed existence—i.e., himself as *micro*cosmos. Mutual affirmation unfolds: each to each, each by each, each for each.

B • THE UNCONSCIOUS AS UNBODY AND UNMIND

(*a*) The Unconscious–Unbody as Inner Ferment

What is the bearing of these theologic remarks upon my specific call for the abandonment of the term "unconscious," while retaining its positive core, a core first perceived, albeit dimly, inadequately, and confusedly—though courageously and with genius—by Freud and by Jung? My subsequent remarks concern the relationship between an ontologic, hence generalized, concept, with its cosmologic and theologic components, and an essentially psychologic, hence restricted, concept.

In general, human comportment is multiplex. Its overall configuration transmits itself to its every dimension, attribute, and part. Surely, in one sense, comportment is a strictly natural phenomenon. From this point of view, the person is composed of many intertwined layers. Separately thematized by science, these layers pertain to the mind and to the body, in effect constituting a Cartesian dichotomy. But beyond that, the person may be construed from within a strictly scientific perspective as, in effect, n-chotomized. Thus conceived, each layer (in an ontologic sense) is radically disjoined from all other layers, thereby implying (in the last analysis) a fragmented and pulverulent person. A strand of invariant structures binds together the subject matters of these sciences, and, hence, creates an epistemically, though never an ontologically, unified person. On varying levels of abstractness and intricacy, these structures implicate the dynamics of space, time, and matter. In *The Dance of Being*, I wrote of the person under the perspective of his natural composition. I traced the ways in which space, time, and matter are interwoven, hence interdependent, rather than merely abstract and autonomous; and I stressed how certain spatio-temporal-material invariants constitute unifying threads, each entwined by increasingly subtle subordinate threads, throughout the different layers of natural phenomena. As one passes from the *seeming* elementarity of the foundationally physical in the person's makeup through the apparently more and more complex fabrics of bio-physical, chemical, bio-chemical, and bio-psychological dynamisms which contribute to that makeup, these invariants so constellate themselves as to shape, but always under a naturalistic point of view, his veridical personhood. The cumulative impact of these natural dynamics contribute, each in its characteristic way, to the ground of the Unconscious (or what amounts to the *same* "entity," the "Unbody") as a vast labyrinth. And this labyrinth exhibits (*a*) the mysterious core which unites space, time, and matter, when they are construed in the most concrete possible fashion; (*b*) the even more esoteric juncture of material happenings and mental happenings; and (*c*) those ever-more-inclusive bonds, each nuanced in infinitely variegated ways, which link every person, in his uniquely private and inmost core, not only to his fellows, but to ever-larger communities, including the cosmos itself. Indeed, the trajectory implied by the last movement suggests that the ultimate contributor, hence the deepest ground, of this "Unconscious or Unbody" leads one beyond creatureliness to the very Creator: Creator under the perspective of the personal, or, more accurately, perhaps, the hyperpersonal. I speak of God who communicates His "intentions" to humankind through His power to humble Himself to personhood, and, therein incarnate, endows Himself with the capability of sustained and profound dialogue with man—yet a dialogue the still resonances of which not only sustain the person in his individual dignity but, confirming that dignity, stir him into such creative discontent as to call forth from his "unconscious" creations of a subtlety and inventiveness which authentically mime those of the divine Creator Himself.

Enclosed within one another like so many concentric circles, each circle endowed with characteristic dynamisms and powers, the various communities ultimately embracing the very cosmos in which the person participates rhythmically pulsate and, thereby, impinge on one another. Communities are reciprocally conditioning. Propagating their effects over the entire matrix of communities, they relate to one another in a double sense. Whether one proceeds from the solitary person toward an all-inclusive cosmos or one proceeds in the reverse direction each community is both immanently present in the other and radically transcendent to the other. For immanence and transcendence are mutually implicated. Each mode of relatedness requires and presupposes the other. Neither concept can be thought without reference to the other. Together, they imply this theme: all communities suffuse one another; yet each community stands forth in its unique individuality. The more one penetrates the factors constituting immanence, the more one reveals to oneself these factors as transcendentally bringing about immanence. Yet as one reaches toward the transcendent, and establishes contact with it, a dynamically empathic relationship ensues; transcendence converts itself into immanence. In the context of searching, the alienation of transcendence and the intimacy of immanence implicate one another. Sufficiently searched, each condition metamorphoses itself into the other. In this sense, God and man are both mutually immanent and mutually transcendent. In its positive and hitherto suppressed import, the "Unconscious or Unbody" expresses the dynamics of the juncture of immanence and transcendence; and these dynamics are equivalent, I now show, to the dynamics of the juncture of the natural and the spiritual.

If the "unconscious–unbody" is a negative way of speaking about something manifested through the deep structure of comportment, and if, at the same time, that "something" is associated with both the juncture of immanence and transcendence and the juncture of the natural and the spiritual, then I must pose this question: How is such a double juncture revealed in that structure? Consider the gurglings and babblings of an infant. In effect, the whole of language—hence, all conceivable speech, and, in consequence, all talking between persons—dwells in those gurglings and babblings. Likewise, with respect to the dance, the entire conceivable architectonic of nuanced movement dwells by virtue of a person's neuromuscular makeup in his every act. As they are both bodied forth in words and bodied forth in dance (in each instance initially incarnate in body qua body, but in the very activity of bodying themselves forth, flowing from body as mere body), this double totality of language and movement constitutes itself a person's going beyond his mere body, hence shapes that body's transmutation into personhood. For, in this bodying-forth, and accordingly giving rise to personhood, each person affirms his full identity—his identity both as this particular individual and as an instance of universal humankind. By this affirmation, both the generality of language and movement and the singularity of a particular individual's language and movement present themselves. Thereby, the person constitutes himself an authentic personal presence, authentic for himself and authentic for others. As such, he reveals his rootedness in both language and movement. Together, these activities constitute a single matrix which both transcends his particular individuality and shapes its immanence in that individuality. Moreover, if language expresses the quintessentially spiritual and if movement expresses the quintessentially natural—each comprising resonances, language as subtle and ethereal and movement as gross and weighty—this spirituality and this naturality join at the very point at which the generality, hence the transcendental character, of both unites with the particularity, hence the immanence, of each. Not only are these motions, whether of speech or of dance, indigenous to the person, and, as such, expressive of his power to imprint himself on others; but they have been internalized as deriving from without the person. Thus construed, they are resonances which never cease to hover about him. In both senses, the intrapersonal and the interpersonal, the potential for speaking and the potential for dancing incorporate themselves in his composition. Surely, the milieu in which a person dwells is, in part, constitutive of who that person is. His being is contextually determined as well as shaped by an autochthonous dynamism. The numberless communities, whether personal or apersonal, and the patterns of their mutual overlap and their reciprocal envelopment dynamically interweave themselves within the person himself; and they inscribe endlessly novel variations on the themes which constitute his more narrowly construed individualistic nature. Likewise, with respect to the inanimate processes which relate particle to field. For regions of condensation alternate with and, in reciprocal transformation, actually become regions of rarefaction. Points of singularity interchange themselves with loci of pervasiveness; constellatings and reconstellatings of novel factors manifest themselves now as ferment, now as crystallized; deformations up to certain limits nonetheless conform to those limits: all these mechanisms are applicable to a person who, by nature, must function in an interpersonal field. Likewise, with respect to the biologic processes which relate cell to circumambient milieu. For membranes of variable permeability allow for continual displacements of dynamic equilibria; new schemes of balance and imbalance reveal the interplay between homeostasis and homeodynamics; flowings across those membranes reconstitute structures amid the retention of such transiently invariant configurations as dissolve themselves only to be constituted anew. All *these* mechanisms are analogously applicable to a person who, by nature, must function in an interpersonal field.

With respect to the person, all is in flux; yet all remains eternally the same. In general, what has been misnamed (or, to put it more exactly, only *negatively* identified as) the Unconscious (or, its equivalent, the Unbody) expresses the locus wherein ferment congeals and structure dissolves: a matrix of subtly modulated body processes which interpenetrate such mental processes as, in turn, envelop, in a kind of aura, the very fringes of awareness. It refers to the deepest layers of a person's being—the very pivotal point of both his nature and his spirit. Herein, the mysteries of space, time, and matter unfold; herein, the labyrinthine motions of the organismic and the inanimate converge to shape the person; herein, internal bonds convey resonances to and fro, between person and cosmos. For the unconscious–unbody misnames yet points toward all those hidden layers of human being which, in their unfoldings, outfoldings, and infoldings, constitute themselves both a process of verbalizing—hence, an etherealizing of the physical—and a process of incarnating the spiritual as dance: a *mélange* of factors in which sharp distinctions between the mental and the physical disappear, and the single, integral ground of human being reveals itself.

(*b*) Conceptualizing the Unconscious–Unbody

To characterize this ground, a double paradigm is needed. One is drawn from the sphere of body acts; one, from the sphere of mind acts. Taken together, these spheres are enveloped by still a third sphere, a sphere of existence for which no simple paradigm suggests itself: i.e., no paradigm short of one which illuminates the more inclusive and usually hidden relations between person and cosmos—the link between human creative acts and cosmic creative acts. Now I indicate the general contours of this double paradigm, the first component deriving from intrapsychic theories (e.g., of Freud and Jung), and the second from both interpersonal theories (e.g., of Sullivan and Lacan) and such theories (e.g., of Fairbairn and Guntrip) as bridge the gap between the intrapsychic and the interpersonal. From intrapsychic theories, I extract such factors as bear upon a body model for the ground of human being; whereas from both interpersonal and mediating theories, I extract such factors as bear upon a mentalistic model. Moreover, the intrapsychic model will be exhibited as transcending itself to constitute the transcendentally natural ground of the human while the interpersonal and mediating models will be exhibited as, in complementary fashion, transcending themselves to constitute the transcendentally personalist ground of the human. Together, these grounds constitute a kind of double ground for human personhood. Yet this ground can ultimately be elucidated only by general cosmology. Derived from cosmology, it discloses an image of veridical personhood. Fully to set forth this image, I treat, in *Choros* and succeeding books, both the stages by which a person, germinally spiritual, actualizes spirit, and the forms, modes, and dimensions of self-actualization.

To develop my double paradigm for conceptualizing the unconscious–unbody in terms of the complementary rhythms of speech and dance, I must reflect on the epistemic unity of mind and body. Attempting neither exegesis nor hermeneutic of Spinoza's proposals for characterizing that unity, I extract from his thought certain points which are salient for my argument.

Spinoza conceived substance as both mental and extended. What is extended is, not passive body, but body-in-act. As extension, substance is the power of the ground of personhood to manifest itself as acting body. From body as mere potency, body in actuality is drawn forth. Analogously, the mental is not passive: mind in potency draws itself forth as mind in actuality. As mental, substance is the power of the ground of personhood to manifest itself as acting mind. A single ground expresses itself as both emerging body and emerging mind. From the standpoint of this ground, mind and body are, in the end, identical: they reveal the same primordial activity. Body activity implies the body as locus of *inter*actions among its neighboring bodies, those proximate and those remote, and, in particular, impingements on (and in) *my* body. Correlatively, mind activity implies that, in the measure that bodies both undergo and induce modifications in other bodies, the ideas which constitute mind are *of* those modifications. Penultimately, such ideas are referred to my body alone as their apparent source. But since all bodies are *ex hypothesi* interwoven, the "center" of any particular mind is ultimately referable, as its *veridical* source, not to any particular body, but to body in general: i.e., to universal body under the perspective of my body. More deeply, this source is the ground whence springs the very possibility of both body acts and mind acts. *Conditio sine qua non* of those acts, it is, as their ground, continuous with all that springs from it, and with much else besides.

Reflecting on this ground, I note, first, that ideas are always *of* bodies. Never subsisting in total independence, they stand in some correlative relation to bodies. Moreover, *my* body is but the proximate and most intimate source of my ideas. The ultimate source is the interwovenness and participatory embeddedness of my body in other bodies, embeddedness which implicates corporeal realms seemingly quite remote from my body. In consequence, every idea is implicitly epistemically united to universal body. Often, explicit reference to this or that aspect of my body is suppressed; then I prescind from certain interactions which, in the end, are relevant to my body. For example, when I suppress such corporeal activity as involves the aural, the kinesthetic, or the gustatory—all forms of contact between "my" body and "other" bodies—I reflect on that which interacts with my body in the visual field alone. I have effectively eliminated other fields. Furthermore, many stimuli impinge on my retinae. As I *use* my eyes to gather in these stimuli, factors quite removed from the intimacy customarily associated with my body are discerned to constitute an autonomous perceptual manifold. In the end, a refined conceptual analysis arises which terminates in the propositions of natural science. Indeed, the most esoteric physical theories are but extensions of perception—though subtly dissociated from my body's most intimate natural processes. When I remove structures superimposed on the field which emerges from this prescinding activity, i.e., from all that fails to pertain to this visual field, I discover phenomena connected in manifold ways to my body, and indeed profoundly woven into my body, phenomena so constituted that only by convention can I declare them as not of my body. Only by fully owning *my* body can I frame ideas about *all* body, under the perspectives of those searching acts which are peculiarly my own. To isolate any perceptual sphere other than vision entails affirmation of the autonomy of new phenomenal configurations, each of which yields me information, as in the case of music, of an entirely different order from the scientific. Each order of information is associated with idiosyncratic laws and dynamics; each may be extracted from my body, in its larger and most inclusive sense. For a multi-laminated corporeal texture is laden with phenomenal nuances beyond the comprehension of any particular scheme of thought; yet these nuances are wrought into a unified and complete fabric. By implication, every scheme of thought is grounded in this fabric. My mental acts are referable to, and epistemically united with, an incomparably larger bodily context, and mysteries resident in that context, than that provided by my own *seemingly* circumscribed, private body. Conversely, my body is indefinitely extensible into the entire universe; each of my ideas presupposes the entire cosmic order, in its corporeal aspect.

Secondly, I note, when Spinoza declares "I *conceive* substance as both mental and physical," he cannot mean "conceive" in a narrowly mentalistic sense. Had that been his intent, both extended things and mental things would, in the last analysis, be mental entities. For all that *is* would be *idea*: a specific idea of mental entities and a specific idea of physical entities. Yet for Spinoza's "substance" fully to constitute the ground of modal being, each person, himself a mode of substance, must orient himself toward it from within its interiormost rhythms. Every person is an activity of the entirety of substance, an activity wherein substance stands reflexively in relationship to itself. For substance is a power of actively inducing its own modifications. Contrary to Spinoza's expressed opinion, substance is, in reality, a process and a dynamism rather than an eternally changeless substratum. As power, substance exerts itself, translating itself into actuality without reference to any exterior cause. And, as *causa sui*, substance potentiates itself under many perspectives. Each perspective is a mode; and the consummate mode is the person himself.

Accordingly, the person is a power of orienting himself reflexively, hence searchingly, toward himself in his relationship to the whole of the substance in which he participates as dynamically implicated. In his searchings, the person is an activity of framing images of the *entire* cosmos. Internalizing those images, and wedding them to his own antecedently given body, he constitutes his own larger being. Thereby, he actively transforms the cosmos; and, with varying self-consciousness, he transforms himself. Moreover, since ideas stand in relationship to *ideata* construed as exclusively extended or corporeal, one does not frame ideas of other persons as such, but only of other persons insofar as they are construed to be peculiarly complicated arrangements of physical stuff. Far from *merely* shaping their images, a person actually *participates* with other persons in collective searching. And, under the attribute of extension, all persons collectively shape images of substance itself. In principle, communing differs from communication. Involving abstract ideas, hence representations of body configurations, communication is the very antithesis of communion, which involves concrete intuitions, hence a gathering into presence of other persons. In general cosmology, both things and persons are but foci on a single continuum; representation and gathering into presence are thus inwardly connected. But, for my restricted account, these modes of thought must be sharply distinguished.

(*c*) Unconscious–Unbody as Rhythm

How can one locate within this schema the problematic of the unconscious–unbody, subsequently—whenever I wish to stress the *modus operandi* of the unconscious–unbody as a specific and unique dynamism[4]—to be designated the *luminator*? Earlier I treated the *luminator* as a matrix of personal "resonances" endowed with these traits: mind resonances sink into body resonances—mental deteriorization manifesting itself as physical pathology in which mental elements are fragmented into body tensions; body resonances rise toward mind resonances —physical deterioration manifested as peculiarly intense mental phenomena such as hallucinations. And I proposed that body rhythms and mind rhythms are themselves subsumed under a third sphere of human existence, namely, *rhythmicality*, a sphere in which both body and mind may be understood as possessing derivative ontologic status. For body and mind, hence the *luminator*, which mediates transformation of one into the other while preserving relative autonomy, shape particular rhythmic configurations. By "rhythmicality," I refer to modes of dwelling among one's fellows in communally conditioned yet individually constituted searchings; I mean types of quest after symbolically expressed patterns of relatedness between self and cosmos. By one's symbols, one constitutes one's existential manifestations. Signs of human rhythm, symbols also directly present human rhythms: rhythms which commingle, interweave, mutually synergize one another, form new resolutions, and endlessly recombine. Such rhythms constitute the unity, hence the identity, both epistemic and ontologic, of mental acts correlated with physical acts. Both kinds of acts instantiate the same ground, a ground which in itself is unitary and integral; and a ground which is distinct from yet joined to epistemically different activities.

When I designate the unconscious–unbody the *luminator*, I invoke a likely medieval custom whereby a needy student received remuneration for holding a candle to illumine the manuscript from which his teacher lectured; hence, I use this term metaphorically. Desiring wisdom, i.e., illumination, the student gains instruction as recompense for his bearing the torch which lights up the teacher. In correlated act and speech, the teacher allows the invisible to become visible; the dark, luminous. And the student stands on the threshold of wisdom. "Luminator" to himself, a person bears the torch whereby his inner world of unformed word and act reveals its own transformations. In *self*-instruction, wisdom breaks forth as a commemoration of what hitherto had lain dormant and fragmentary, buried in inchoate memory: the primordial depositions of body and mind. Against the resistance of the incipient comminglings of an interior ferment, a bare homogeneous potency, body acts and mind acts shape themselves in intricate schemes of interweaving and coordination. Pregnant with both dance and speech, every person becomes the generatrix of the very motions, those ethereal and those palpable, by which he actually addresses himself, hence, diminishes his own ignorance. Counterposed to the unformed matrix whence they were birthed, word and flesh, in dialectic interplay, form, reform, and create ever-new symbols. By these, one empowers oneself to shine forth in vibrant presence. Drawing into manifest rhythms his inmost potentialities, a person congeals, in manifold subtle ways, the undifferentiated but potent ground of his very being. As a kind of gift to himself, he substantializes his hitherto merely latent powers: self-potentiating powers which themselves are neither physical nor mental. An efflux into visibility of what had been occult and unawakened, these powers now assert themselves as the tangible marks of an inner life which is marvelously energetic and abundant. They are the dawnings of human utterance. As *lumintor*, one lights up oneself; and one probes the inmost depths of one's own illuminating acts, i.e., of one's status as *luminator*. Qua *luminator*, the person is neither light nor shadow, but the very source of each. He is the womb whence arises the chiaroscuro of human utterance.

Both directional and intentional, the rhythms, i.e., *luminator*, of every person doubly reveal themselves. On the one hand, body discloses itself in dance—a flowing forth of movement. As quiescent, the body is an arrested dance, the crystallizing of its motions. On the other hand, mind discloses itself in speech, and *its* movement. As quiescent, mind is the fixation of speech: its abstract structure rather than the concrete structures exemplified by body in its fixation as dance. Yet a primordial distinction holds between mind and body. For body is tangible, whereas mind is ineffable. Since the resonances composing both are substantively the same, gradations prevail between the two spheres. At the same time, ideas are *of* body. For the object of the mind's perceptions is the percipient's body as it is affected by another body. Hence, the mind consists of the reflections of the body's actions vis-à-vis other bodies, such reflections of the body into itself as entail the shaping of freshly nuanced resonances. Ineluctably, all body is associated with the mirroring of body to itself. No body can be body, i.e., concatenation of body acts, save as pervaded by reflexivity. Correlatively, all mind is the system of mirrorings insofar as such mirrorings are construed to be composed of specific reflective acts. Epistemically, body and mind are, in the end, identical. Always, each is implicit in the other. Together, they form a single substance. Yet body qua the mirroring of self to self is itself already thrust beyond the sphere of either body or mind (i.e., mind construed as mirroring in its merely abstract sense), and conversely. Thus conceived, *body minded* or, equivalently, *mind embodied*, is a person-in-the-world, a person who, in acting and in feeling, orients himself toward the world. One who discerns the interwovenness of his rhythms with those of the world, a person must, I repeat, be conceived as both directed and intentional; and, though it always significantly impinges on him, hence contains an active component, the world must be conceived as essentially receptive.

C • SYMBOLIC PRESENTATION AND REPRESENTATION[5]

(*a*) Interweavings of Presentation and Representation

I have advanced three theses: persons are rhythmically reflexive; they are loci of intentional activity; their actions flow from their symbolic representations of their motives to themselves. Now I raise these questions. Wherein consists symbolic representation? What are its links to immediate experience? How does it shape itself and bring its content to fruition?

Contemporaneously with all human action, an influx of stimuli perishes into one to constitute of one's circumambient world a dynamic, formative presence, and, as such, the proximate cause of human action. Certain persons, notably those called "schizophrenic"—not freakish, aberrant creatures but surely fully human —are bound to the world's immediacies as its captives. They lack such coherent symbol systems as order their experience, and confer meaning on it, systems which normally provide the dominant foci about which experience organizes itself. But the schizophrenic person's experience tends overwhelmingly to be determined by immediate sensory input—either by the external stimuli which are mediated by the peripheral nervous system, or by the internal, physiologic stimuli which proceed by way of the autonomic nervous system. As a result, such experience is excessively fluid, inchoate, and *seemingly* the unformed, raw materials of which authentic creative products are shaped, though such persons lack the power to bring that shaping to fruition. Owing to forces which he is but feebly empowered to alter, the schizophrenic person cannot escape radical self-centeredness. Wholly absorbed with stimuli which impose on him from instant to instant, he is trapped into endless preoccupation with those stimuli. Following directly, almost reflexly, from contemporaneous stimuli rather than from symbolic representations, such experience stands in total opposition to the symbolic. But some individuals are captive of their very symbolisms. Incapable of responding to immediate experience, they are *passéistes*[6] who dwell among symbols which have cumulatively evolved as their lives' expressions. In extreme instances, such persons tend to be drawn toward ever-deeper residues of their own pasts. Recapitulating a sort of Proustian dwelling with origins, they are so constituted that the immediate stimulus serves as but occasion for an experience rather than as its actual cause, merely catalyzing the drawing forth of each newly enveloping symbolism. In principle, no pole, stimulus, or symbol is ever absolutely realized. Each is a limiting situation which can be approached only asymptotically. For every experience is product of an interplay of these tendencies, and of their mutual transformations. In varying balances, propensities for being drawn toward *both* poles co-exist in all persons. Thus, experience may be classified in accordance with the type of balance it exhibits, and the style of commingling which prevails with respect to these poles.

Though immanently pervaded by stimuli, both external and internal, man is empowered objectively to present stimuli to himself, either as direct presentings or as *re*-presentings, and, in either instance—presentation or representation—he shapes symbolic manifolds. Always, he *creates* the very structures by which he presents to himself his phenomenal world, inner or outer. By "create," I mean, equally, discovery and rediscovery, a process however pervaded by originality. Discovery cannot *be* without a response to it; response cannot *be* save as suffused by novelty; and novelty is ineluctably symbolic. In this sense, no human experience can be conceived except in terms of symbols, whether the symbol be construed as presentation or re-presentation. Intricately enmeshed, symbolic forms commingle; and they reciprocally transform one another. Shaping the diversified patterns by which one expresses one's characteristic ways of transfiguring one's world, symbols allow one to adapt that world to one's own inherent constitution. Affirming a Kantian synthetic *a priori* perspective upon the conditions *sine qua non* for having an experience, I seek to avoid the Kantian pitfall of an overly static, non-processive, and non-functional construal of such a perspective. For, pre-eminently, human being is to be understood in terms of a dynamic structuralism: all non-representational, immediately felt presences are, at bottom, symbolic; for the symbol is the agency by which diffuse, vague, and fragmentary presences are joined into a unitary manifold.

Among the representational symbols, linguistic expression most precisely specifies the contours of phenomena. Presentational symbols, i.e., symbols which *directly* present such factors as impulse, motive, and intention, are incapable of verbal utterance. For them, a matrix of images alone prevails: images which are half-formed, often unrecognizable, and sometimes bizarre; images which envelop one as an inarticulate aura. In principle, the dance renders both the broader contours and the finer nuances of that aura; and the *luminator* discloses its hidden rhythms through the dance's variegated and subtle texture. Only when such unconscious–unbody content effloresces into *full* consciousness is the *luminator* capable of translation into the rhythms of speech. In general, a continuum of processes binds together what Freud illicitly regarded as disparate and diametrically opposed realms. Along this continuum, one symbolically presents and represents what, in myriad ways, is present to one. And only in the end does frank representation shape itself to the spoken word. Indeed, the very locution "unconscious content of symbolic representation" is inadmissible. For the status of presentational symbols is strictly mental. As such, it belongs to what might more aptly be designated subliminal or threshold awareness: i.e., awareness which, as merely presented, is incapable of discursive elaboration. Nonetheless, weighty with presence, these symbols do sink toward the body. And as the body becomes laden with that which, initially alien, persistently demands re-equilibration of its balances and realignments of its rhythms, it extrudes as symbols the residue of these now sunken though altogether transformed factors. Always, the very acts by which this content is expelled constitute the dance itself.

(*b*) The Reflexive Body

Mental phenomena can never be reduced to sub-mental agents. Nor can physical phenomena be construed in terms of supra-corporeal agents. On the contrary, mind and body are but aspects of a single activity, an activity which is reflexive hence experiential, rhythmic hence dynamic. Yet, always, body is informed by mind: the dance is suffused with reason. Likewise, always, mind is informed by body: speech is laden with the physical. I affirm this principle: human being is enormously complex; it exhibits labyrinthine depths; it unfolds marvelously intricate textures; it is composed of endlessly subtle nuances. And human experience can never be dissociated from human action; conversely, action cannot be conceived apart from experience. Each is correlative to the other. Forming a single multiphasic process, they are grounded on the very rules whereby patterns of symbols are constructed, transmuted, and metamorphosed.

An organization of stimulus–response patterns, both in its overall contours and with respect to the composition of its every part, a person's body is a matrix of dispositions to react. As the actualization of specific potencies, it is a *virtual* process or activity. By an inherent tendency, the human body thrusts itself toward presence to itself. As such, it exhibits an essentially personal character. And since no body can be separated from its relations with other bodies, self-presence is also presence to other bodies as, reciprocally, they are present to the given body. Every human body mirrors itself both to itself and to others. Through mediating stimuli transmitted to it, by either the peripheral nervous system or the autonomic nervous system, it articulates self-presence in relation to presence-to-other. But this double presence hardly involves elements in disarray. The *com*presence of such intra- and extra-corporeal factors as constitute a reflexive body shapes a continual passage from cacophony to coherence. Ineluctably, the intentionality at work within all human body fuses disparate elements into harmoniously ordered elements.

Thus present to itself, a person's body symbolizes itself as a symbolic representation. By symbols, the different parts fuse into coherent unity. Coalescing, interacting, and transforming one another, the fabric which these symbols form constitutes a datum for secondary reflection. Bombarded by numberless preconfigured stimuli, both inner and outer, the human body absorbs these stimuli, and both coordinates and transforms them. By its intentional acts, the body strains toward such stimuli by means of a special body agent: e.g., visual stimuli are drawn in *through* the eyes; one sees *with* the eyes. Innervated by a nervous system which itself is active, and self-oriented *toward* the relevant sensori-receptor organs, the body contributes an original element to its received stimuli. Through a synthetic *a priori* act, they are synthesized into an ordered experiential manifold. And, in every modality of experience, one experiences with all one's organs—though in varying degrees, depending on an organ's overall relevance to the body. Ever alert to such stimulus imprints, every person primordially symbolizes his relationship to the world. In an initial configuring, he shapes a plexus of symbols upon which all subsequently formed symbols are inscribed. I refer to presentational symbols the content of which is determined by external stimulus-presences rather than by autonomous *intra*personal processes. But as soon as stimuli are drawn into an integral manifold—a symbolic matrix—a new component is added to that matrix. For every presence which is drawn to coherence is laminated on another presence, and yet another which, likewise, had been drawn to coherence: all interactant and mutually transforming.

Beyond that, a person's body is empowered doubly to reflect. It frames Imagos both presentationally and representationally. Again and again, one presents presences to oneself. An internal process, all self-presentation is independent of the new stimuli which, from moment to moment, are absorbed into one's body. In effect, all interactions or presences constitute a re-presenting of those presences; their re-presentation as filtered through such hitherto perished presences as, even while they are absorbed, sink ever more deeply into the labyrinth of laminated presences. Like presentation, such re-presentation is also symbolic, multilayered, and internally interactant. Once set in motion, representation catalyzes new representation. And "images" interact in accordance with special laws and propensities. Thereby, an entire progression of symbols is shaped; and this shaping is coterminous with human existence itself. An indefinite number of orders of symbolism is created. A concatenated sequence, these orders constitute an intricate lattice of alternating presentations and representations, each infected with novel symbolism.

In fine, every person presents a mark of his inward self, both to himself and to another. He draws inner psychic content from his body's labyrinth into conscious expression. Pressing feelings, ideas, and images into objective structures, he shapes altogether new phenomenal configurations which he superadds to reality: his own circumscribed environment. The totality of such symbolic presentations constitutes a new matrix which itself requires exploration. Now the person presents himself to this matrix, a matrix which he himself had brought into existence. Reacting to it, acting upon it, and interacting with it, he transforms the matrix into entirely new symbolic layers: re-presentations which have acquired symbolic status—a representing of what had been mere presentation.

Unreflectively, spontaneously, and with a certain immediacy, man shapes presentational symbols; reflectively and self-consciously, he reconstitutes these symbols. But presentation and representation themselves interact. A dialectic prevails between them: questions addressed to questions, listening to what had been heard, responding to responses. In principle, no absolute separation obtains between presentation and representation. They are foci in a single continuum. Grounding this dialectic, and poured into its associated continuum, are the very rhythms of the *luminator*. Revealed as symbols which are only relatively demarcatable as circumscribed structures, the deep structure of the dialectic is identical with the deep structure of the *luminator* itself, and, in the end, of one's very bond to the world. All symbolization contains an element of this bond. Communally attuned to one another, selves are governed, in their attunement, by the bond: a bond which differentiates itself into specific archetypal agents which, both formative and generative of each self's every act, immanently condition all human creativity.

(*c*) Interweavings of Body–Mind Resonances

Symbol formation may be considered under two perspectives: that of originating stimuli, that of culminating response. Under the rubric of stimuli, which is the perspective I have thus far been treating, already organized stimuli impinge upon a sensory-receptor organ (e.g., the eyes); therein, a new configuration of those stimuli is shaped. Transmitted through a specialized nerve network (e.g., the optic nerve) to another node of neurons (e.g., the lower brain), and journeying along the relevant pathways toward the higher brain—that great synthesizer of stimuli which proceed toward it from diverse sources and by diverse routes—impulses shape still another configuration of stimuli; and depending on the complexity of the network of transmission, a multitude of configuration is formed prior to the "final" one in the highest centers of the brain. Analogous considerations hold with respect to stimuli which proceed from other sources, impinge on other sensory-receptor organs, and are transmitted along other routes. In general, each transmission implicates not a finite number of discrete configurations, but, in fact, a continuum of transfigurations. Accordingly, symbolic presentation arises through the ferment which is set in motion within a person's entire body; and symbolization itself—the adding of a symbolic ingredient to a presentation, and, indeed, the very apprehension of that presentation—is the *inward* response of the person to the unfolding events occurring in his own body.

In this process, a person's body is hardly a mere passive recipient. Quite the contrary. For it is actively, dynamically, and intentionally implicated in the process. And, through its infusion with specific intentions by its "possessing" person, the body constitutes itself a plexus of strainings toward the very stimuli which it receives and by which it is permeated. To this activity, new modes of both coordination and integration are continuously superadded.

Analogously, the symbolic representations interposed between the symbolic presentations—occupying, as it were, their interstices—constitute a continuum of virtual transformations rather than a series of discrete incremental factors. It is as though one were dealing with two orders of infinity, each enclosing the other—like real numbers which, on this analogy, correlate with symbolic presentations, and transcendental numbers, interposed in infinite sequence between any pair of real numbers, which correspond to symbolic representations: representations constitute, in effect, a higher order of infinity than presentations. Accordingly, symbolic representation is subject to its own *spiritual* laws, laws which transcend the *natural* laws which govern symbolic presentation—though, doubtlessly, presentations possess *some* element of comparable transcendence. At bottom, each series, presentations or representations, participates in the other: the one expresses the body labyrinth, as it rises toward the mind; the other expresses the mind labyrinth, as it rises toward the spirit, in its ever-more-ethereal reaches.

In general, symbolic presentations are the collective representations of *body* to its world, representations but dimly perceived by mind; symbolic representations, as the collective representation of the *person* with respect to *his* world, are constitutive of awareness itself. Under the rubric of response, progressive symbolization now entails this consequence: the scheme of presentations transmits itself to organs which bring about a veritable dance—the "speaking," as it were, of muscles and viscera. Yet dance is always imbued with reason, mind, and the spiritual. Analogously, the scheme of representations transmits itself toward, and manifests itself through, speech: the "dance," as it were, of those special organs of the body which, pre-eminently, are competent to render the incomparably more subtle rhythms of speech—here, mind proper is operative. Yet the mind is conditioned by the body, which is immanent in it. There is a dancing of sound as there is a ratiocination of dance: song or speech *and* dance are intimately entwined. As *terminus ad quem* of this process, the person moves out toward the cosmos, and seeks to embrace it: cosmos as both creator and created —God and World.

Fundamentally, mind and body interweave to constitute a higher reality. Hence, a profound complementarity obtains between speech and dance, jointly the primordial manifestation of that reality. Each marvelously blends with the other. Together, they are borne to their culmination in altogether new orchestrations of symbolism: song wedded to dance. Here, under the perspective of response, the final symbolic configuration shapes itself, a new configuration which first germinated in those former configurations shaped under the perspective of stimulus. In the efflorescing into the song (and speech) component of this fusion, consciousness manifests itself; in the efflorescing into the dance component, though doubtless an element of consciousness prevails, the *luminator* manifests itself. As interwoven into integral expression, both song and dance manifest the perfect synchronization of mind and body as they are mediated by the *luminator*. In every instance of such expression, there is both a minding-forth and a bodying-forth, each involving its own particular blend of awareness and unawareness. Within this blend, proto-mental and supra-corporeal elements themselves interweave.

In short, numberless resonances, rhythmically unfolding, suffuse the person, and burst forth as the most variegated symbolisms. By these symbolisms, every person continuously shapes novel patterns of relatedness between himself and his world. Each instance of such patterns constitutes a veridical metamorphosis of that relatedness. Collectively, these patterns constitute a commentary—dramatic, sharply etched, absolutely concrete—on a world grounded in the natural yet endlessly transfigured by the spiritual. In the symbol, the visible and the invisible join to shape a transcendent complex. For not only is the symbol the expression of particular unifications. Beyond that, it is so to be construed that each person participates self-transformatively in symbols which all persons never cease to form.

Such speech, song, and poetry as manifest mind constitute the flowing forth of body into immanent thought about body—body now to be understood as a germinating person. Yet all human body is the body *of* human mind; for every physical process is *in*-formed with some configuration, a configuration which may or may not be made explicit through speech. The aggregate of these forms of body process, the Form of the total body configuration, *is* mind. Though pre-eminently mind reveals itself, namely, as the forms of body, through speech, it in fact analogously presents itself in and through *every* body act. Speech is merely the most subtly articulated of body acts: those acts best adapted to transmit the mind's miraculously differentiated resonances. From this point of view, dancing itself is a kind of speaking forth, a speaking forth through organs other than those of speech. As such, quite analogoausly to speech, dancing transmits the rhythms of mind. Likewise, and in similar fashion, speaking is a species of dance. It is the dance of the larynx, tongue, diaphragm, lips, and the marvelously assembled musculature about the lips—musculature which extends itself throughout the body. Accordingly, in the last analysis, dancing and speaking cannot be dissociated from one another. In its fashion, each projects the resonances of mind; each manifests, in its subtler modes, the reflexivity of body.

By the Forms of bodily process, I refer to the resonances which cling to, hover about, commingle with, and, indeed, permeate those processes. It is these special resonances which I have designated "mental." Yet no *substantive* distinction sets Form apart from that which Form in-forms. *What* is in-formed by Form is a blossoming forth into Form; the Form which emerges from this efflorescing is but the bringing to fruition of potentialities already resident in that "what." Thus, if one were to isolate such classes of resonance as constitute the aura of certain bodily processes—for example, sub-neural structures—one can reasonably designate that aura as *proto*-mental. By "aura," I mean the thrusting of themes inscribed upon those structures into their own coming-to-fruition, structures now transmuted into functions: a coming-to-birth of their latent content. If, on the other hand, one were to isolate the resonances which envelop higher neural structures, one can reasonably refer to the entire configuration of resonances—not only as those resonances envelop *all* body structures, but, beyond that, as they actually condition such structures, and even become constitutive of them.

Now, I no longer refer to body or to mind as such, certainly not in their traditional senses. On the contrary, I speak of the person as an intentionally searching being, a being entwined with other analogously constituted persons, and exhibiting even subtler resonances than the mental or the physical. *Inter*personal relations and, in general, the activities which go on in the interstices of people are composed of exceedingly refined and altogether new resonances: resonances which grow progressively coarser as one passes from the interpersonal to the mental, thence to the proto-mental, which, alternatively, could be designated Unconscious or, equivalently, Unbody (i.e., the *luminator*), and, finally, to the most primordial grounding body structures. Consider people who embrace. In mutual envelopment, two entities shape a third. Yet, qua embrace, the interminglings of these persons constitute an altogether new scheme of resonances, those resonances of ecstasy which are absolutely transcendent with respect to all previous resonances. What is the locus of tenderness and soft communings of two bodies which are, not mere bodies, but human bodies? Wherein consist the interweavings and interminglings of thought, perception, and feeling, when two human bodies embrace? To delineate this locus, one must enter an entirely new sphere of existence; one must pass to a richer cosmos than that dominated by a spatio-temporal-material order; one must pass into the cosmos of transcendental rhythmicality.

NOTES

1. See the entries for the foregoing terms in the index of *The Dance of Being.*
2. For these terms see the indices in the various volumes of Freud's *Collected Papers*, trans. Riviere.
3. See his "Ethics," Part I, in *Chief Works of . . . Spinoza*, trans. Elwes, II 45–81.
4. In general, my term "unconscious–unbody" stresses affinities with Freud's Unconscious, whereas my term *luminator* stresses the novelty of my own non-Freudian concept. Moreover, the former term often, in my account, refers to a pathologic phenomenon; the latter, to a wholesome phenomenon. Here, too, I follow Freud's tendency to treat his Unconscious as essentially negative and diseased. The context in which "unconscious–unbody" and *luminator* appear will inform the reader regarding whether, in a given instance, the pathologic element is in fact being emphasized.
5. Throughout this section I am indebted to Louis Carini's penetrating account of symbolism: *The Theory of Symbolic Transformation: A Humanistic Scientific Psychology* (Washington, D.C.: University Press of America, 1983), esp. chaps. 1 and 4.
6. This expression for one for whom the past dwells almost as vividly, subject to continual immediate recall, as the present, was told to me by a highly imaginative friend, French psychiatrist and dramatist Dr. Pierre Rubé.

8

THE VERIDICAL GROUND OF THE SELF: HUMAN COMPORTMENT AS PERSONING-FORTH

PREAMBLE

By his rhythmic character, every person is empowered to penetrate the orchestrated resonances of the cosmos. Weaving his lesser rhythms with its larger rhythms, he reveals to himself its subtler nuances and, thereby, symbolically renders the comminglings of self and world. The texture of reality is immeasurably complicated. It exhibits intricacies of awesome depth and all-pervading pulsation. Remote from customary experience, and stretching toward an abyss which no finite being is competent to penetrate fully, or even to probe deeply, each person is suffused with dim but haunting perceptions and faint discernments of uncanny recesses; and in his groping way he may so heighten his discernments that he stirs in himself fear, wonder, and trembling. Yet, paradoxically, the very ground of the dynamism by which radical concealment is maintained may, by a kind of cosmic intentionality, allow, for the one who searches with resolve and intensity, the facets of the world to be gathered together into luminous presence. Indeed, what seemingly lies farthest from man, as numinously hidden from him, stands most intimately in proximity to him. For, interwoven with him, the entire cosmos, in varying grades of relevance, penetrates his being. Though such interwovenness transmits itself, through a seemingly circuitous route, to every person, it nonetheless flows, in the last analysis, from cosmos as creator toward person as created. When personhood has been consummated, tenderness from person to person manifects itself, and, in redemption, grace from God to person. For God is incarnate as well as ineffable. And, as incarnate, He infuses man with motions which derive from His status as ineffable; He activates man's most immobile spiritual rhythms: that they might gather themselves together in communal consecration as both a commemoration and a recollection; that, as such, they might transform man's very body, so that, in transcendence, his fragmented and alienated being might again be made whole.

A • PERSONING-FORTH AS SONG AND AS DANCE

(*a*) Body and Mind: Identity and Difference

In my paradigms of dance and speech, dance expresses body in consummate act, whereon it inscribes proto-mental resonances; whereas speech expresses mind in consummate act, whereon supra-mental resonances inscribe themselves—resonances incomparably more subtly nuanced than body resonances. In speech, specialized modes of comportment, modes involving the regions about the speech organs, implicate themselves: speaking is a body motion. And the dance of body sounds forth as a dance of words, hence of sound itself. But dance qua dance is the very hypostasis of the movements of body in silence. The quiescence of sound, it entails the holding back and suppression of sound: the rhythms of body's stillness. For speech is dance which has been stilled, whereas dance is speech which has been stilled; and dance and speech are, equally, of the body—body which is, not mere body, but body on which mental rhythms inscribe themselves, and about which they hover as an ethereal aura. Together, dance and speech constitute a person's body conceived as consummate rhythmicality. Within oscillating rhythms, patterns emerge, patterns which pertain both to still body and to sounding body. The very music of the body, these patterns shape the self from its primordial condition into a veridically orchestrating self. In the self's counterpoint, harmonies, and dissonances, and in the thematic unfoldings of a self now borne to fruition, lamentation and celebration so intermingle that each instance of blending expresses a definite quality of joy or sorrow. Transmitted from one person to another, reverberating throughout the body, and even reconstituting it, patterns construed as a process of self-transfiguration comprise the mind-in-act. For, at bottom, mind *is* the very form and schema of unfolding patterns. In myriad shapes, the body reflects itself into itself. By these Imagos of itself which the human body draws forth from within itself—Imagos which constitute the shifting configurations which body and sound assume—the mind articulates its latent structures.

To "person forth" is both to sing forth and to dance forth. However, though singing forth seems *prima facie* to imply meaning and intention, hence "minding-forth," whereas dancing forth seems to imply mere bodily acts, hence is devoid of meaning and intention, investigation shows this distinction between mind and body to be simplistic. In consequence, a distorted perspective arises with respect to the veridical character of a person's substance. True, mind expresses itself pre-eminently through speaking. But quite as integrally and authentically, mind manifests itself immanently, though in subtle ways, through dancing; whereas, *pari passu*, body manifests itself immanently, and with analogous subtlety, though speaking. Thus, mind *is* personing-forth in its reflexively patterned aspect, while body, the data epistemically united to mind, is that which, as just passed and hence now perished, deposits patterns in the wake of its passage: patterns which constitute its own residual resonances. For body is mind's palpable residue just as mind is body's ethereal residue. Each is residuum with respect to the other; each perishes at the very instant the other announces itself. Body is a fading into dance; mind is a fading into speech. Body dies into existential durability, and its grosser temporal motions; mind dies into ethereality, a transfiguration of those motions toward the eternal. Otherwise expressed: mental patterns intertwine to constitute, in their consummate shape, humankind's eternal spiritual union, a union which reflects a cosmically spiritual unity; bodies intertwine to form humankind's temporally fragmented material, material which stretches toward embeddedness in the temporally material disunity of all existence. In Whitehead's terminology: in His primordial nature, all patterns germinate in God and are proffered by Him for creaturely exemplification; fragmenting substance, sheer physicality, reveals His consequent nature. With respect to creatures, physicality is primordial, and spirituality, consequent. Each factor, God and world, complements the other; each reflects the other; together, they shape a reflexive dialectical union, a union of tenderness, grace, and creation.

Earlier, I referred to the epistemic unity of mind and body. Mind–body unity involves intentionality: the self-directedness of body toward its own consummation as sheer reflexivity; the mirroring by the elements constituting the reflexive Imago of the elements constituting that which *images itself forth*. Such mirroring entails no mere isomorphism. Nor is correlationism implied. On the contrary, it portends a mirroring which is dynamic and dialectical. Within an epistemic perspective, the veridical unity of mind and body can be conceptualized only as the concatenated rhythms of "personing-forth." Yet this concept entails ontologic unity of mind and body as well as epistemic unity. For mind and body are each resonances. In turn, each is grounded in other resonances: a hierarchy of levitation or gravitation. In this hierarchy, all schemes are reflexively orchestrated. The epistemic unity of mind and body expresses itself as a flowing forth of reflective processes in which the more subtle rhythms move toward the future, and the coarser resonances fall away into the past: an ebb and flow in dialectical contemporaneity.

Sphere of temporality, the body transcends itself. In its self-transcendence, it acquires the power to know itself. Such self-knowing is mind. However, mind is never mere passive self-knowing. On the contrary, mind *is* body, as body comes reflexively into relationship with itself. In this process, not only is body transmuted. Beyond that, it thrusts itself toward an altogether new sphere of existence. Now existence no longer *ex-ists*, in the sense of standing forth; it *sub*-sists, as mind which stands beneath body, and provides its ground. Thus grounded, one's body intentionally directs itself. Yet intentionality is itself grounded in a deeper, less visible substance. For, in general, two propositions hold: body acts subtend mind acts; mind acts subtend body acts. And an altogether new realm, "locus" of eternity, constitutes the matrix whence arises and into which perishes the body, in its sheer process character. For temporality to originate from the timeless, and to enclose that sphere as both more inclusive and more primordial than itself, the body must exert itself. By bodily exertion, I mean: through perception, the human body penetrates the world body, with which it interacts; through conception, whence springs the patterns which weave perception into a coherent manifold, the mind evolves as increasingly adequate to the body. Participating in nature, and never mere onlooker, man, by framing increasingly adequate ideas of nature, and of his own role in it, thrusts himself out of nature. He touches the ground of his being in God. Therein dwelling, he moves beyond finitude, and, in a fashion too mysterious for comprehension, he embeds himself as a non-finite agent who is co-eternal with other like agents. His very body is transfigured, a veritable transubstantiation.

Thus unbodying itself, body passes into mind. Correlatively, unminding itself, mind passes into un–self-consciousness. Whenever the unminding of mind goes awry, *re-pression* supervenes. Owing to their ineffectuality as mental dispositions, the appropriate mental resonances fall back into body. Because of a lack of potency as autochthonous resonances, they fail so to emend themselves as to allow for their own self-transfiguration. Thus failing, they so transform themselves as to inhibit and to encumber or even to deform their associated body. Analogously, whenever the unbodying of body goes awry, body "*pro-presses*" its own constituents. Thrusting them prematurely into the mind, it presents physical disease in the guise of mental obfuscation. And wherever "pro-pressions" (of body) and re-pressions (of mind) commingle, the body is confused by its associated mind, as, conversely, the mind is confused by its associated body. In both instances, natural processes no longer synchronize themselves harmoniously. As a result, *de*-pression supervenes. Now both mind and body are dragged from their respective states of naturality: a "falling away" which, equally, affects mind and body. Only when depression resolves itself can genuine spirituality arise. In consequence, the pathologic unconscious–unbody, unlike the wholesome *luminator*, constitutes itself a multitude of depressions, repressions, and propressions. For, these factors intermingle to shape that locus of "pressions" whose interactions ineluctably deform both mind and body. When disunited, the unconscious–unbody must be construed as a sphere of degradation rather than full potency-in-act. Thus conceived, the unconscious–unbody constricts and, ultimately, destroys authentic human resonances. It prohibits the person from bringing to fruition his uniquely personal powers. Failing to frame adequate perspectives of the cosmos, he so shatters his attunement to God that he thereafter dwells in isolation and despair.

(*b*) Body and Mind: Their Ground in Agency

Under the perspective of body, both the epistemic and the ontologic unity of body and mind present themselves as *body animate*. Under the perspective of mind, that double unity presents itself as *mind incarnate*. From a syncretist point of view, wherein one envisages the union of body and mind, body animate and mind incarnate are one and the same. Together, they constitute "personing-forth." By *personing-forth*, I imply that the interwoven themes of body and mind, together with their commminglings as *luminator*, ground themselves in a single, integral, and indivisible source, a source which gathers consummate personhood into a kind of luminous presence, and, beyond that presence, orchestrates the *com*presence of each person (thus construed) with all persons. Moreover, to recur to my Spinozist bias, under the perspective of *natura naturata*, which is world-in-process—i.e., created nature—both animation and incarnation are distinct, in effect, separate actualities, and, as such, specific activities. For by "animation," I mean body acts construed as suffused with mind; by "incarnation," I mean mind acts grounded in body. Only under the perspective of *natura naturans*—i.e., creating nature or God—can active body and active mind be jointly conceived as but aspects, or, more generally, "attributes" of sheer potency-in-act—i.e., indiscerptible, absolutely pure agency. Yet, quintessentially, agency is mutual. It consists in reciprocal relatedness, hence sympathetic attunement. For, by essence, every agent presupposes as matrix for its activity, a community of co-operant agents. Insofar as one interprets *natura naturans* to be emanation from pure creating activity, and, as thus derivative, activity which is defective, the mind presents itself as epistemically *dis*-united from the body. As ineluctably tainted with deficiency, mind is interpreted as both steering body acts and directed by those acts. Correlatively, body which is defective owing to its construal as separable from mind only *appears* to be the ultimate ground of those acts, and, as such, isolated from its environment. Moreover, though of degraded status, both body acts and mind acts can be efficient (though always defective) and adroit (though unconsummated) acts. When the balance between mind and body is displaced toward domination by body, thought becomes ineffectual. Now, the body acts, as it were, thoughtlessly, hence, in the last analysis, awkwardly. Proceeding, at first, on their own, with a kind of autonomous dexterity, body acts tend, in the long run, to deteriorate into clumsy fragmentation—ultimately, into a mere assemblage of reflex acts. Analogously, when balance is displaced toward domination by mind, body becomes ineffectual. Insofar as body is now unpoised and disequilibrated, mind likewise (as in the former instance) degenerates into incongruities, confusions, and inadequate representations.

Sub specie durationis, both spheres, namely, mind and body—each definable in the *implicit* context of personing-forth, rather than as a complicated function of mind and body—are seemingly autonomous, and, in part, independent. Yet, *sub specie aeternitatis*, as veridical personing-forth is attained, mind–body acts synchronize themselves as an harmonious integer. All action unfolds in the *explicit* context of personing-forth. Now the two spheres are truly correlative, complementary, co-dependent, and, in the last analysis, con-substantial. In this fruition of personhood, the *luminator* resonances permeate the entire person. They are neither disjoined from one another nor construable as realms of activity isolated from mind or body. In the end, a person acts from the "necessity" of his own integral nature–spirit; and both nature and spirit themselves are epistemically and ontologically identical.

Remotely, body and mind modally replicate the attributal unity of substance. Yet body is grounded in κόσμος (i.e., *natura naturata*); mind, in Θεός (i.e., *natura naturans*). Hence, the issue of psychophysical parallelism arises only when body and mind are construed as actualized *emanata* from *natura naturans*. In the context of one's consummate personing-forth—hence, active participating in *natura naturans* and continually drawing sustenance from it—the distinction is no longer relevant. One cannot impute mental dispositions to the body, or, for that matter, ascribe an ultimate body ground to the mind. For, modally construed, neither body nor mind as such is an agent. On the contrary, each is a mere "mode," an extraction from or hypostatization of agency.

As modes, body and mind are each lawful in composition; predictable connections obtain among their significant ingredients. As such, both spheres are germane to personhood. Personing-forth is intrinsically free, though, by their lawfulness as modal, mind and body each confers paradoxes upon one's freedom. By his freedom, every person empowers himself to emend his life in the direction of agency which is ever less diminished, contingent, and imperfect. To achieve this end, every person must orient himself participatively toward God, God affirmed as *mysterium*. In such orienting, a man expresses his primordial option. Herein resides his veridical freedom also to turn away from God: namely, to ensnare himself in the modally necessitarian character of his own mind or his own body rather than, as in the first instance, so to release himself from bondage to that necessitarian character that he is no longer enslaved by mind or by body, in their narrower construals. Expressing his freedom in diverse symbolic ways, he attains that freedom, with increasing perfection, by self-consciously drawing himself through those stages relevant to the progressive emergence of his inner self. Thus experiencing, stage by stage, the ambiguities of his freedom as he moves toward its apotheosis in consummate relatedness to world and to God, the person frankly acknowledges the paradoxes which ineluctably inhere in that freedom. Accordingly, personing-forth is a searching which is continuous, unique, and singular. In the final analysis, it is a searching in dance and a searching in speech; and it is a searching in all modalities of dance and speech. Furthermore, the comprehensive activity of comportment, an activity aimed at inclusive comprehending, is itself participatively grounded in and continuous with an infinitely larger activity: namely, that of the dialectic of God and world. In this relationship of dynamic complementarity, each, God and world, mirrors to itself, as its inverse, the veridical contours and, indeed, the ultimate composition of the other, so that, by full encounter, each transmutes each. In brief, a creative ferment of κόσμος and Θεός dialectically unfolds; this general activity grounds other, more specific, and, always, analogous activities: finite activities of varying sorts of complexity and styles of organization.

(*c*) Personing-Forth as Rooted in the God–World Dialectic

To stress: personing-forth includes both introspection and extrospection. Jointly, these dimensions entail an Imago of the self in relation to its world, a world which includes the inner as well as the outer. As Imago, the form of the world is mind; as world, the substance of the Imago is active. For Imago and world are dynamically implicated. Together, they replicate the active relationship of mind to body. Expressing this relationship, reflexivity enters both dynamically and substantively into the very composition of Imago, just as, correlatively, Imago enters into the very composition of reflexivity. This double entry of each into each constitutes a profound bond between the singular activities of *personing-forth* and "cosmos-ing" forth. For person and cosmos alike are processes and unfoldings. By the quality of this bond, its ramifications and its efflorescences, the overall creative process is either constricted or catalyzed; and personal creativity and cosmic creativity become both mutually reflecting and reciprocally constitutive. Indeed, all finite modes, in their idiosyncratic ways, comprise privations, to a greater or lesser degree, of the God–world dialectic. In this dialectic, retrospection and prospection merge and become one; creation and discovery are complementary and mutually enhancing.

Personing-forth unfolds in both song and dance. Song encloses poetry and (customary) prose; dance encloses graceful movement and ordinary movement. In each instance, deep structures both reveal themselves and conceal themselves: rhythms which submerge and rhythms which emerge. By *luminator*, I mean (further to enlarge my definition) the κίνησις of this process: the subtle dynamic which governs the movements of personal resonance as both speech and dance. Through these vehicles of comportment, three realms disclose themselves, each involving motions of body and motions of mind: an infrapersonal realm, an interpersonal realm, an extrapersonal realm. The first and the last are interwoven as corporeal rhythms; the second constitutes the fruition of mental rhythms. When it has been sufficiently penetrated, the corporeal transcends itself. Under the perspective of world, it reveals its ineffable ground in God as dialectically implicated with world. Brought to its consummation, the mental transcends *itself*. Under the perspective of God, it reveals its spiritual and equally ineffable ground in world as dialectically implicated with God. Within the interweavings of speech and dance, this double ineffability, the ultimately ethereal ground of personhood, consecrates that dual dialectic. Within a cosmic orchestration, God, on many levels of human experience, makes Himself palpable to man.

With respect to the *luminator*, deformations of the body dissociate themselves from the body to constitute bizarre schemes of resonance, schemes dynamically implicated with already prevalent wholesome schemes. Thereby, integral bodily activity is disrupted; its (corporeal) confusions manifest themselves in dance which is distorted. Analogously, deformations of mind dissociate themselves to bring about comparable intricacies of speech patterns; mental confusion is both mirrored and engendered. Moreover, unconscious–unbody pathogens commingle to constrict primordial "personings-forth." Disallowing the spontaneity and the free-flowingness of both dance and speech, they bring about personal disorientation. In addition, each deformation constitutes a veritable labyrinth, a labyrinth convolutedly turned in upon itself. In this labyrinth, the person introspectively wanders. He is confused and disoriented. *Unbonding* himself from the veridical God–world dialectic, he prevents himself from receiving the outpouring of God's love, an outpouring which transmutes itself into a tender touching of the world: that spirit, ever resident in every person, might transform both his body and his mind into an epistemic unity which is successively more ethereal; into a unity, now become ontologic, which never ceases to express itself in some modality of either dance or speech, a modality which constitutes itself the self's veridical ground.

B • THE LOCUS OF HUMAN BEING: SUBSTANCE AND SYMBOL

(*a*) The Person as Expanding or Contracting

Basic types of human comportment, dance and speech are, at once, bodily, hence substantive, and mental, hence symbolic. Aspects of comportment, they are also resonances inscribed on comportment. As substance, they are natural processes constituted by grosser rhythms. As symbol, they are the subtler rhythms which hover about natural processes: rhythms which portend mysteries concealed in comportment. Jointly, substance and symbol are intricately interwoven as stimulus–response patterns which are webbed into myriad configurations, and constituted by factors of variable intensity. Pervading one's intimate bodily functions, regions of absolutely private activity, these externally originating patterns ever modify those indigenous acts. Flowing into the body, stimuli objectify themselves in proto-aural, proto-visual, and proto-kinesthetic ways. Ever protean, these introjects ramify throughout the body. Therein, they form *quasi*-objects which commingle to shape of the unconscious–unbody a labyrinthine new realm: namely, the *luminator*. Composed of ingredients which are neither fully formed nor explicitly articulated, the *luminator* is the locus of the residue of specific, differentiated processes: processes both infrapersonal and interpersonal. Now infrapersonal processes emerge from bodily status toward mental status, i.e., from coarser to more refined resonances; now they submerge from their acquired mental status toward bodily status. And, stemming from the interpersonal sphere, intrinsically mental factors interweave with the infrapersonal to shape an even stranger fabric.

To maintain a person's overall economy, as he "persons-forth" in dance and speech, a succession of balances supervenes, balances which engender ever-new equilibria. Associated with this succession, both entropic and counter-entropic forces unfold. From within one's *local* body, pressures, rooted in the interplay of these forces, give rise to emergence. From within one's extended body—which includes factors, often interpersonal and communal, which, seemingly external to one's immediately perceived body, are nonetheless interwoven with the body—other pressures, likewise rooted in this interplay, give rise to submergence. Always interacting, these pressures alternately resist one another and synergize one another. Together, they form a matrix of activities which manifests the dual labyrinth of interiority and exteriority. Coalescing, the components of this labyrinth shape a single, integral realm. Within this realm, and conditioned by it, proto-stimuli arise, enact their characteristic motions, deposit themselves as durable imprints, and, finally, transform themselves into their own consummations as proto-dance responses and proto-speech responses. As proto-responses—i.e., as proclivities toward response which has not yet been brought to fruition—this concrete *mélange* of dance propensities and speech propensities creates the deeper structures of comportment: dance and speech as they are woven into the orchestrated rhythms of human being.

Qua human, the entire body is a dance of being. In it, factors blend to shape the polyphony of selfhood: multiple tensors which mutually entwine, and converge upon loci which cohere as the integral person. Correlative with emerging human bodyhood is human personhood. Now influences deriving from one's body mingle with, and bind themselves to, such transcendental factors as derive from the cosmos: a great ferment wherein that which is maximally immanent (in the human body) is also maximally transcendent (in the body cosmos). For as I search into all that immanently conditions me, I am led beyond immanence toward that which, in being wholly other to me, radically transcends me.

In one's searching acts, introspecting and extrospecting are complementary. Exercised jointly, they enable the inquirer to move toward that core of non-being which resides at the very center of pure being. Thereupon, he discovers that this quest discloses an equivalent *terminus ad quem*: namely, the core of pure being which resides at the very center of non-being. Now a new dialectic reveals itself, that between being and non-being: a dialectic which is profoundly related to the God–world dialectic. For non-being connotes two things: nature's perishing into nothingness, a dying into the *mysterium* of the creative ferment; the donation by that ferment of novel patterns for concrete exemplification by nature. Hence, in its consequent nature,[1] the world, having brought itself to consummation as *natural* being, falls into non-being. In complementary fashion, in His primordial nature, God, having His nature in *spiritual* being, likewise falls into non-being. Each in its way, God and world, attains fruition. With respect to their opposing moments—for God, the initiating moment; for world, the culminating moment—both perish into a common matrix: the ultimate source of the intimacies of God with world. Operating through non-being, pure being brings about its own progressive emergence into patterns of integration; operating through pure being, non-being disrupts those patterns, and elicits new patterns.

With respect to the *luminator*, two questions arise: Who and what is the person? Where and how is the person? In effect, I ask: What are his essence and his locus? How are locus and essence intertwined? These interrogatives—namely, *who*, *what*, *where*, and *how*—necessitate further conjecture regarding the *luminator*, specifically with respect to the ambiguity of the *luminator* as both essence and locus. Never ceasing to interchange, and indeed to transmute their contents, essence and locus exhibit shifting boundaries. In one sense, the person is identical with the complex which constitutes the epistemic unity of his mind and his body. In another, the very concept of person has been introduced to explain the ground of that unity. Hence, to explicate the mind–body unity, one must thematize the person as prior to both mind and body. In this context alone can one delineate his contours and specify his composition. However, to conceptualize the person as grounding the unity of his mind and his body, one must affirm either of two suppositions: a person inhabits his own mind–body complexus, and, by such habitation, brings that complexus to epistemic unity; or a person is inhabited by the complexus, so that, by virtue of its dwelling within him, his unity is achieved. In both instances, one's personhood is consummated. Given a sufficiently coherent and inclusive perspective, both modes of conceptualization are valid and, in fact, equivalent.

For every person's "substance" extends beyond those regions of existence conventionally demarcated as *his* mind and *his* body. Moreover, in possessing that particular mind and that particular body, he allows himself, from time to time, to *un*inhabit them, and, as it were, to dispossess himself of this or that "part" of either his mind or his body. In addition, every person inhabits many regions beyond those associated with his immediately possessed mind and body. He may *mediately* occupy less intimate regions, employing them as agencies through which he enacts the drama of his existence. Surely, personhood is immensely flexible. It may contract itself into the "occupancy" of but a small sub-region of body and mind. Thereby, personhood allows each to function more or less autonomously, while he, the person, dwells only at his *own* center: a center which can be designated in neither bodily nor mentalist terms; a center which nevertheless constitutes the sphere of overt and publicly accessible action. Alternatively, personhood may expand itself. From time to time, one invades regions which extend beyond one's conventional body and mind. When one searches actively, widely, and deeply—in a word, far-rangingly—one may be virtually co-terminous with the very cosmos.

In both instances, that of expanding personhood and that of contracting personhood, one stands, in a certain sense, outside the cosmos. Whether in quiet meditation or in active searching, and whether one reduces oneself to a still but nonetheless potent "point," or, alternatively, one expands one's personal resources to comprehend the world through linguistic and other modes of articulation, one places oneself (figuratively but significantly) *outside* the world; and one attains to this *de*tachment by virtue of one's rootedness in non-being, i.e., all that cannot be defined under the rubric of thinghood. Only through empathic dwelling with the ground of one's being, a noumenal ground which lies at one's very center, can one achieve skills requisite for maneuvering effectively and imaginatively in the actual world. Only thus does one acquire competency to assume new perspectives on things, and to carry out novel courses of action with respect to both one's mind and one's body: the mind and the body which one inhabits, and which, in a kind of co-habitation, likewise inhabits, or, alternatively expressed, participates in one's personhood.

In effect, I am proposing that the person empowers himself, by his searching and meditative essence, to focus now on this region, now on that region, of the cosmos. Thereby, he grounds the integration of an ever-growing multitude of perspectives on the cosmos. By his dancing forth and by his speaking forth, he expresses the concatenated rhythms of the infinitely variegated assemblage of interwoven cosmic dynamisms. Universally apprehended, this assemblage is perspectively specified. For the contingencies of earthly existence are ineluctable. Yet, in this minuscule sojourn, within the very limits of mind and body, should he sufficiently prize these possessions as uniquely and distinctively his own, every man would achieve liberation from bondage to finitude even as he immerses himself in finitude.

(*b*) The Divine Ground of Comportment

What is the bearing of my remarks about a person's essence and locus upon his *luminator*? Previously, I wrote of his dance of being; I proposed that this dance replicates the greater dance of being of the cosmos; and I hinted at the intertwinings of these dances: their migrations and transmigrations, their configurings and transfigurings. As each person experiences the hidden powers which govern his existence and guide the habits of his body and mind, he transcends these powers, this comportment, those habits. Increasingly, he experiences them as patterns given him from within his own being by a supreme Donor. And by his syntheses of new patterns, and by his bodily processes, he himself impinges upon, and even reconstitutes, that Donor. Interacting, commingling, fermenting, and crystallizing in myriad ways, the laminae which all patterns shape are themselves superimposed, one upon the other. By *luminator* I now (in a yet new enlargement) mean: the apperception of these configurations—ambiguities of habitation with respect to a conventional mind and body; dwellings in remote cosmic recesses, through participating in resonances which, neither corporeal nor mental, mediate the passage of each to the other; passings *through* these resonances, and beyond them; a person's un–self-conscious incorporeal dwelling in arcane cosmic realms which are radically dissociated from either mind or body, realms not only repressed toward body and pro-pressed toward mind, but, in addition, *im*-pressed into a cosmic labyrinth which is neither physical nor mental.

Whether inspected from without the person or from within him, speaking and dancing exhibit many layers. Sensed by observers of differing sensibility, they present themselves as of varying depth and nuance, and as capable of decipherment and extended articulation. In every instance of speaking and dancing, a movement proceeds from the subject's inmost center: motions initiated in simplicity yet constituted with subtlety; motions culminating in myriad peregrinations. In each phase of searching, novel ingredients weave themselves into a person's composition: rhythms gross and corporeal, mental rhythms which are body's very breath and finer residue. Beyond even the *luminator* lies the source of these motions: the matrix wherein they engender themselves, as they embark upon adventure and vicissitude, risk and renunciation and sacrifice, and such ecstatic rewards as, by grace, might, from time to time, be conferred on the seeker who is persistent and responsible. In this source's buried recesses, the paradox of finitude and the infinite resolve themselves. Herein, nature is divinized and spirit is naturalized.

Within personal being, many modes, transformations, and interweavings prevail: speech culminates in dance and dance culminates in speech. Together, their motions orchestrate themselves as a singular, consummatory expression. Synchronizing, condensing, metamorphosing, and intensifying, the contrapuntal movements of dance and speech intermix, and transform themselves. Every new variety of dance comes to fruition as speech; no spoken word is unaccompanied, or fails to be borne to *its* fruition, by the gestures which, in the fullest sense, constitute dance. In both cases, one's entire body pulsates with motion. Echoes ceaselessly reverberate to transfigure one's very personhood; and one turns inward. In myriad convolutions and involutions, the soundless echoes transmute themselves into those mental auras which always hover about one.

Ever complementary, dance and speech stress different aspects of personhood. Each focuses on a particular kind of relationship between body and mind. Thus, to be thoughtless is so to diminish thought as to allow dance, as such, to effloresce; and to be thoughtful is so to fill dance with thought as to convert it into speech. Yet thought immanently pervades dance quite as much as it explicitly suffuses speech. In both instances, one dwells amid one's thoughts: an endless procession which materializes now as dance, now as speech. And in speaking one overtly dances; in dancing one silently speaks. Dwelling with oneself, whether in dance or in speech, one continuously gathers into unity those diverse rhythms which endlessly unfold to constitute, as echoes resounding throughout the body labyrinth, their transubstantiation into spirit. In the beginning, the Gospel declares, is the Word, and the Word is made Flesh. But, in the end, Flesh dissolves, once again, into Word. By the *luminator*, I mean (in addition to my previous characterizations) the internal dance of such factors as, in their conjunction and comminglings, are caverns of silence whence flow ever-novel rhythms: eddies which, gathered together, allow the Word to articulate itself with its full impact. Arising from body, these rhythms emerge, incarnate as speech and its accompanying dance, toward spirit. Falling back into body, they submerge deeply under the physical; therein, new fusions and formations germinate, and never cease to rise again.

Here, I propose to undercut the apparent duality of human nature, its division into mental and physical acts. To overcome this dichotomy, so I argue, one must reconstruct epistemology; and, in addition, one must frame an appropriate theology and ontology. In *Choros*, I merely prefigure this scheme; in *Cosmos*, I amplify it, and systematically work out its implications.

Apprehending myself as expressing my inwardness through both physical and mental acts, I *feel* myself into relatedness with the world. Prior to my status as thinker and actor, I am a self who is affectively implicated with my world. Beyond this, I apprehend myself as affectively implicated with the world's creating ground, that ultimate source of all my conceptualizings. For each feeling apprehends itself as crystallizing, as it were, into both mind and body. And my relatedness to God conditions my every dancing forth and my every speaking forth. All my actions, physical and mental, portend this primordial bond, and elaborate its implications. In each act, I both manifest and articulate that bond. Arising from the ineffable Creator, patterns of divinity and images of the godhead exemplify themselves in the world's very physicality. These patterns reveal themselves in *my* body, a special region of the world. As body, I *live* my primordial nature; as self, who feels the patterns which my body instantiates, I bring my nature to consummation in mind. Thereby, I articulately grasp the rhythmically concatenated patterns proffered by God. Yet, as physical, I contribute to the *process* which *is* the physicality of God. Accordingly, God and world—the latter consisting of mind–body complexes—are intimately cojoined. What guarantees this link is, precisely, my personhood. In effect, every man mediates the relation between God and world. All creatures, human or otherwise, alive or lifeless, contribute, in howsoever minuscule a way, to analogous mediation. *Par excellence*, the human person constitutes himself the paradigm for such mediation. In Christianity, the archetypal paradigm is a unique exemplar: nature divinized and God incarnate, namely, Christ. For Christianity, persons are lesser modulations of the being of Christ. For all monotheistic religions, man participates at once in two realms: divine or noumenal, worldly or phenomenal. In some sense, God so stands to the world that each, God and world, is the inverse of the other. Pre-eminently, human persons allow God to make His presence as pattern known in the world. In turn, it is they who disclose to God the world's suffering and degradation, the weight of its sheer physicality.

(*c*) Deformations and Conformations between Person and Cosmos

Once the self has felt its way into body acts and mind acts, the person proceeds both to introspect, and thereby to establish his unique historicity, and to extrospect, and thereby to establish the lawfulness of his body and mind. He both "temporalizes" himself and "spatializes" himself, shaping a spatio-temporal creature capable of articulating his material character. But a self's primordial *feeling* into body acts and mind acts is itself neither mental nor physical. In Whitehead's terminology, conceptual feelings are always interwoven with physical feelings;[2] in Spinoza's terminology, such feeling is creaturely (or modal) participation in Substance—the latter construed as both creating and created: *natura naturans* and *natura naturata*, *Deus sive Natura*. Such terminology as "unconscious–unbody" expresses this condition in negative terms: namely, the specific character, dimensions, and traits of participation. Rather than connoting affirmation, unconscious–

unbody alludes to dissociation and excision: a prescinding from the myriad varieties of participation which the infinitely attributable character of substance entails. Yet, owing to man's limitless abyss of sheer potentiality, body acts and mind acts diversify themselves correlatively, and in mutual association. Moreover, such activity derives from the action which is the person himself: person as actor who reveals himself as one capable of resonating, *sub specie durationis*, in the modes of both body and mind; person who, *sub specie aeternitatis*, resonates in an entirely new mode, namely, the mode implied by the *luminator*—a mode which, while resembling both the mental and the physical, can be identified with neither.

By physical orientings and mental imaginings, every person frames preconceptions of how nature ought to appear. Whenever he experiences deviations from these preconceptions, he attributes imperfections to nature. For his conviction that nature *ought* to accord with this or that supposition arises from distortions, indeed frank diminution, of potency, with respect to the dynamics of his body and his mind. Such deformed consciousness and corporeality express deviations from the "correct" ways by which body and mind manifest schemes of balance. And every person seeks to rectify such imbalances—be they physical or be they mental—as, from time to time, he ascertains as disrupting his activity.

To be unconscious, or, equivalently, unbodied, is to be *ec*centric with respect to wholesome or normal body balance and mind balance. Yet compensatory factors can always be called forth which create the illusion of balance. Indeed, discrepancies between truth and illusion constitute a reliable index of the powers of the *luminator*. Moreover, the greater the deformation the larger the variety of "defensive" compensations evoked. In effect, mind and body each dis-orients itself with respect to itself, falling (respectively) into unmind and unbody, i.e., the *pathologic luminator*. Unwholesome being supervenes; fragmented mind parts and body parts function, not for their own sake, but in order that re-integration be achieved. On the other hand, wholesome being is activity for its own sake, activity whose purposiveness is immanent and not extrinsic; it is that fullness of presence, under the aspects of both body and mind, which is pure rhythmicity. Paradigmatic of the pathologic unmind is schizophrenia; paradigmatic of the pathologic unbody is cancer: a running amuck of body. In both instances, the person goes awry. The body splits off, and disconnects from itself its wholesome components, whereas the mind splits off, and disconnects, *its* wholesome components. Both body and mind pass into self-ignorance: each instance of personhood ignores significant aspects of its own modal character.

Such ignorance entails misattribution of essential causality, its displacement from substance to mode: hence, from *Deus siva Natura* to finite self; from deocentricity to ego-centricity. But, whether physical or mental, no mode can be truly self-caused. With respect to either mode, contingency inexorably reigns. Yet, immanent in contingency, necessity prevails: the necessity which, sweeping over Substance, confers upon it its integration and integrity. To be influenced by the pathologic unconscious–unbody is to be in a state of ignorance: ignorance of the veridical relations of both mind to Substance and body to Substance; ignorance with respect to the correlations between these relations.

As finite, every person is conflicted, save insofar as he "persons-forth" with his consummate personhood. In deformed personhood, one is both unminded and unbodied. One is thrown out of body, construed as integral activity. In either instance, one is thrown into the confusions and disorientations of a pathologic *luminator*; one's wholesomeness in mind and body is impaired. For the pathologic *luminator* originates from a fundamental error in man's perception of himself: a confusion with respect to himself as initiator of his own acts, which he cannot (ultimately) be, and as executor of acts which *de facto* can be initiated only by God: a Creator wholly other to both him and the world in which he perceives himself to dwell, yet a Creator with whom he intimately communes. Still, even in his pathologic condition, by his capacity for circumspection, man is empowered to detach himself from his own deformations. By surveying the scope and depth of his relationships, both to himself and to others, and by his unremitting resurveyings, he frees himself from bondage to such disorienting emotions as stir within him. Through active emotion, he quite literally moves out (i.e., e-motes) from such commotions as infect his modal state toward such orientations as will allow him non-distortedly to perceive the inner connections between his own modal aspects—hence, fully to experience himself as an authentic participant in the mystery of God.

When man is disoriented, and in bondage to his (passive) emotions,[3] he projects a partially false image of himself onto reality; he orients himself, not to the actuality, but to the image. Owing to such fictitious transferrals, he experiences reality through veils, veils which conceal its veridical character. At such times, every person expresses his intentionality as the assembled *tensings* of a disoriented self. Nevertheless, a primordial quest for self-clarification is always operative, even though in symbolic form. When understood through intensive search, every illusion discloses more than it conceals. In this context, man apprehends his own uniqueness, but always under the perspective of the interwovenness of his distinctive self with the distinctive selves of others. To grasp his uniqueness, he must perceive his own history from *within* his being; he must recollect, in the sense of *a new gathering together*, the events of his life. At the same time, the external aspect of those events exhibits lawfulness, and can be brought into systematic relatedness to the external aspect of such events as pertain to the histories of other persons. Moreover, as body's deformations press upward into mind and those of mind press downward into body, and as one searches those deformations, one increasingly brings oneself into conformation with Substance. For Substance constitutes the unifying link in the commingling of feelings. In this sense, Substance, together with the symbols through which it manifests itself, shapes the locus wherein man articulates his essential humanity.

C • A UNIFIED SELF: THE INTEGRAL *I* AS ROOTED WITHIN THE PERSON AND WITHOUT THE PERSON

(*a*) The Texture of Speech

Concretely to depict the theme of deformation and the unconscious–unbody, I advert to a paradigm, introduced by Jacques Lacan,[4] to account for a hitherto neglected aspect of the *Unconscious*, a paradigm which complements both Freud's stress on the instinctual, individual, and corporeal and Jung's stress on the archetypal, collective, and spiritual. According to Lacan, the person, pre-eminently the one who communicates through signs, characteristically uses signs, on varying levels of articulation, neither to signify a concept nor to denote a fact, but, in the end, *to signify other signifiers*. The psychic resonances which pervade the person, and in their totality constitute him a veridical person, can be conceived as orchestrated laminae of contexts of signifiers. Signifiers which are "closest" to explicit awareness most authentically manifest themselves when, in full consciousness, one speaks forth its content, and draws into explicit focus what heretofore had been merely latent. Comprising an organized matrix, signifiers are so to be understood that each must be interpreted as sharply circumscribed, though it ineluctably evolves in conjunction with other signifiers to shape myriad novel combinations; and each prevails in dramatic relief vis-à-vis the remainder. In varying stages of development, signifiers constitute meaning units (i.e., morphemes) composed of sound units (i.e., phonemes) which, when they are completely assembled, resemble musical notes. For they are the effective musical ingredients of a language, and, as such, constitute the hidden though all-pervading presence of the inmost ground of language: that which confers style and uniqueness upon such rhythms of actual speech as are encoded in language. As one descends toward deeper psychic layers (in effect, plumbing the spiritual depth of an individual speaker), these elementary units become less precisely contoured. Blending with one another, they exhibit different modes of contiguity. Non-explicitly phonemic interstices, interstices of silence of myriad quality and import—for, do not musical pauses profoundly shape musical affect?—obtain between all newly emerging units.

As this interior journey proceeds, and one descends still "lower" into the abyss of the *luminator*, one discovers the particulate units of speech, elementary particles of which the very phonemes are composed. Now *proto*-speech, now *quasi*-speech, these self-transfiguring units reveal themselves to be a ferment: fluid, mobile, and non-differentiated. Only when they are bodied forth as articulate speech do these elements become its clearly delineated phonemes. Flowing into ever-new formations, they constellate themselves into all manner of structure. No longer shaping conventional phoneme patterns, this activity constitutes the very womb whence, ultimately, phonemes will emerge. As one ascends toward the differentiated and circumscribed and descends toward the blended and evanescent, one finds those dynamically implicated schemes of signifiers and potential signifiers which, in every instance, signify other signifiers. Every such matrix is buried in a yet-deeper-lying matrix of proto-signifiers, until, at the end, one reaches mysterious depths wherein the notion of signification itself loses its meaning. Configuration is woven with configuration: all rises into psychic resonances or falls into body resonances; emergings from and submergings into a labyrinthine *luminator* interweave; recombinations, compressions, expansions, displacements, and condensations are elaborated. Everywhere these sign transfigurations form new patterns, shapes, and dynamics.

In his quest after the dynamics of the Unconscious, Lacan formulates its ontologic ground. He discovers this ground to consist in the deep structure of language: numberless patterns of meaningful sound, each pattern enclosing and, in turn, enclosed by another pattern. For my part, I have sought the ground of the *luminator* to reside in a double matrix: the structure of comportment, the quintessential manifestation of which is dancing; the structure of speaking, the quintessential manifestation of which is singing (and musical instrumentation adjunctive to singing). I have proposed these seemingly antithetical modes not as merely complementary and interpenetrating, but, more fundamentally, as constituting a single, integral texture, a texture which, in my pre-cosmologic thesis, I designate a *rhythmic personing-forth.*

From the standpoint of speaking, and I transpose his principles to apply to dancing as well, Lacan postulates two figurative modes of language as relevant for understanding the Unconscious. Of course, on my usage, "unconscious" (really, "unconscious–unbody") is but a negative way of referring to the *full* ground for the human subjectivity: a ground which, woven of dialogue, is profoundly implicated with intersubjectivity. For the "being together" of persons in resonance—hence, their mutual attunement—manifests itself through dialogue, and, indeed, metamorphoses both dialogists as they immerse themselves in its rhythms. For Lacan, these figurative modes are metaphor and metonomy.

By the first mode, metaphor, Lacan understands the compressing of non-conventionally juxtaposed meanings into a single morpheme, a condensation which shapes new meaning. Nested groupings of metaphor entail large systems of meaning. Yet, for him, meaning does not *consist* in aggregates of speech units, but, rather, *in-sists* itself into a *chain* of signifiers, signifiers which implicitly point inward toward concealed psychic depths. Like overtones, unformulated harmonies hover about a signifying texture composed of concatenated signifiers. Ultimately, certain archetypal determinative structures, primordial psychic directions which are not explicitly knowable, "slide under" the signifiers. By the activity of these immanent meaning complexes, the entire web of signifiers becomes suffused with numerous subtle connotations: the inner, all-pervading resonances of speech.

In the second mode, metonomy, morphemes are transferred to entirely new contexts of usage. Thereby, they acquire *their* characteristically novel meanings. Like metaphor, what is signified in the mode of metonomy is broader than any specific meanings referred to by any finite group of signifiers. In a compresence of contiguous signifiers, each morpheme seems to touch another. A highly condensed matrix of displacements shapes itself. These dynamically flowing complexes effectuate those transmutations which, in the end, portend, as *virtually* present in all speech, the entire dialogic structure of human language. In metonomy, signifiers are contiguous to one another. For the name of a thing, the name of one of its attributes is substituted. Thereby, one shifts from attention to that thing to attention to that attribute. Now, attributes represent the very things of which they are predicated. Meaning hitherto associated with things is now associated with attributes; the displaced meaning is additionally fused with all the *latent* connotations previously connected to it when it was a "mere" property. By contrast, in metaphor, one signifier replaces another; new meaning accrues accordingly. The signifier "slips" into the Unconscious whence it may occasionally escape, as with *lapsus linguae.*

Speakings forth say more by implication than by explicit pronouncement. To protect language, a psychic censorship brings about the evasions which enable conventionally established signifiers to prevail as chief instrument for perpetuating a community's key institutions. But no matter how stereotyped the speaking, subtle reverberations arise from the Unconscious (for me, the *luminator*) to accompany it. To apprehend the actual, and not merely the institutionally prescinded, subject of speech, one must heed the person in all his dimensions; one must penetrate his every aspect and proclivity. Mere bodily activity emerges into consummate mentation as speech; and constitutes a quite specialized dance of the body, a complicated dance the oscillatory rhythms of which progressively (and, from time to time, regressively) differentiate themselves into finely concentrated articulations. To decipher the meaning of this *dance of the tongue*, one must go beyond its manifest content to its latent content.

(*b*) Connections between the Deep Structures of Dancing and Speaking

By the "dance of the tongue," I mean the body's more inclusive dance as it is focalized upon the tongue, but one of its parts. To proceed beyond Lacan's restricted thesis of speech as disclosing the Unconscious (for me, the *luminator*), I suggest that to apprehend meaning, one must understand the motions of the elementary constituents of the dance of the *entire* body, rather than merely the movements of the organs associated with speech. In a certain sense, one must return to Freud. For the phallus, and indeed all motion which accompanies sexual union, are an agent—though, to pass beyond Freud, but *one* agent—by which the body executes its larger dance. And the larger dance is the dance of man and woman, a dance in which the totality of their complemental rhythms reveals itself. Therein, one finds the key for understanding every dance which constitutes movements of persons in their communal acts.

Transforming its motions, its textures, and its resonances, all kinds of displacement, agglutination, and condensation characterize comportment. And in the double paradigm of dialogue and dance, unconscious–unbody (i.e., *luminator*) meanings flow forth, meanings which are alternately obscure and luminous. On the one hand, the unconscious–unbody ground of comportment resists disclosure; and it reveals itself as independent, self-sufficient, and autonomous. On the other, the resistant subjectivity of comportment, which is "ec-centric" rather than the *con*-centric subject of *full* awareness, ever presses toward disclosure.

As in concentric expansions it moves into the world, the self quests ever to center itself anew. When accordingly one asks questions like "Who am I?" "Where am I?" "How am I?" one must respond: my true self lies in the very interstices of the cosmos, even, indeed, between God and the world.

Usually, philosophers have regarded man as uniquely one who reasons, who plays, who symbolizes. But to capture his elusive nature in "attributal" fashion, the "attributes" must become independent contexts of inquiry. By articulating those contexts, the laws which define man can be deduced. For, sufficiently understood, man's every power discloses the whole of man. To penetrate each part entails the inquirer's power to penetrate the very essence of man; and all men, each in his own way, are thus empowered.

Here, I assume that man is an intuitively self-evident activity; hence, his nature cannot be *derived* from some antecedent factor. But, I propose, once conceptualized, such attributes or capabilities as ratiocination, symbolization, or play can themselves be derived. The person is both a *who* and a *what.* Uniquely, he is the one for whom a spatio-temporal locale can be assigned, yet, at the same time, no locale whatsoever. Insofar as each person is an *I*, one may ask: "Where and how is this *I*?" In one sense, the *I* "roams" from self to self, in the psyche's labyrinthine network. As introspective, the person shapes an inner subjective fabric; and he discovers this fabric to be a composite of selves which the *I*, or focal core, in some way "occupies." As extrospective, he shapes an outer objective manifold, the world in which he dwells. His *I* remains rooted to a particular region. But whether he is construed as introspective or as extrospective, roamer or dweller, the unity of a man's self requires that his integral *I* discover both its dwelling place and its point of departure to be the cosmos, cosmos as both creating and created.

Doubly to search means doubly to comport. And double comporting implies that speaking and dancing articulate two realms: inner as disclosed through introspection, outer as disclosed through extrospection. In our language, we commemorate the doctrine of simple location,[5] a doctrine fraught with difficulties. But no person, and surely not his *I*, can be simply located. To amplify an opposing doctrine, consider: in both dancing and speaking, agglutination, condensation, and displacement shape the dynamics whereby one affirms the meaning of human existence. Through prayer, and a direct communing with that which is maximally centered both within oneself and without oneself, one makes oneself *virtually* active: speech and dance are almost arrested; through them, one attains a vibrant immobility. Portending a person's entire composition, the wholesome unconscious—unbody (i.e., the *luminator*) gathers together all motions, whether expressed as speaking or as dancing, into a single focus: the still compresence of self and God. A procession of assemblages, conjugations, and transformations *infold*, one within another. As in the case of the Buddhist *om*, all primordial resonances of speech and dance compress themselves, yet allow their own differentiation into the specific nuances which envelop the person, constitute him, and flow forth from him: myriad commingling and confluences, echoing cosmic reverberations. Man is both everywhere and nowhere. By his speaking and by his dancing, whether in virtual motion or actual motion, man's self-compressings infold and his self-expandings outfold. In a profound way, he is co-extensive with the very cosmos.

In his acts, man both conveys meanings and receives meanings. Meaning itself resides in all the acts by which persons intermingle. For human interaction in the aggregate is the medium through which meanings are interchanged, thence transmitted by song and by speech. In speech, every signifier indicates other signifiers, in some context of signifiers. In dance, every movement implicates all movements. Myriad links, obscure or clear, form the transactional configuration in which active persons interact. In general, a kind of dissimulation occurs, a dialectic of condensation and diffusion through which the person alternately reveals and conceals his inner self, and bears the "hermeneutics" of his inmost being. Every person is empowered to search and, thereby, to unfold a veritable exegesis of his very hermeneutics; and he achieves this end by his persistent acceptance of his own intentionality, by his exploration of its every recess. Perduring amid its resonances, the caverns of silence and vibrancy which shape the *luminator*, and give rise to one's manifest behavior, continually ebb and flow. First efflorescing into intensely executed dance and song, the latter thereupon diminish to quiescent rhythms of ordinary movement and speech.

In every part of human comportment, the whole of dance and song resides. Suffusing every part, dance and song diffuse themselves among all parts, so transfiguring those parts that ever-more-intricate contexts of meaning arise. As I mean, I intend; as I intend, I tend toward; as I stretch myself toward my now-centered being, I attune it to find affinity with that which is wholly other to me. In the choreography of comportment, the grammar of both dance and speech are precodified; and the patterns by which I relate to the great cosmic mysteries, shaped. To penetrate mystery, I create still new patterns. Crystallizing varied human resonances, I elaborate the steps of dance and song, steps which differentiate themselves ever anew. Units combine and recombine to form ever-higher unities. In a vast polyphony, governed by principles of harmonics, these concatenated units are conditioned by the entire configuration to which any particular unit belongs. In novel cadence, new harmonies beat out crescendos and decrescendos which resound throughout human being, both personal and interpersonal.

Dance and song exhibit varying depths. On each layer, a distinctive mode of contiguity and blending prevails. In lower depths, non-specific phoneme units of comportment unfold: as though replicating DNA has stamped itself again and again into personal being. An elaborate architectonic of these fragile, evanescent events forms sturdy new structures. Alternating modes of conjugation, assemblage, and transformation reveal themselves. Ever flowing together, viscerally derived resonances metamorphose into motile organs of dance and speech. All such resonances become synchronized, integrated, and orchestrated. In alternating phases of submergence and emergence, as strainings toward transcendence, these resonances gather themselves into full presence. Endless mirrorings of increasing complexity summon forth man's true inwardness. And speech and dance evoke such resonances, while new contexts of reflexivity are formed. Hovering between the deep structure of singing (namely, subjectivity) and the deep structure of dancing (namely, objectivity), the *luminator* mediates the interconversions of subjectivity and objectivity, and shapes them into a unitary reflexive substance. Like the *dynamic* form of art and dance, the locus of which are discernible patterns in the work itself, and like the *significant* form of art, the locus of which is in subjective, elusive flowings and singings, the *unspoken dialogue* of self with self and of self with others becomes increasingly concrete, and replicates the universal dialogue of self and God.

(*c*) The Ground of the Coherent Self

In sum, when the *luminator* is raised to consciousness, symbolizing therein its own immanent activity, a matrix of signs presents itself: signs of speech and signs of dance. But the sign does not so much signify a concept or denote a fact as propose a chain of signifiers, both verbal and non-verbal. It pro-poses in the sense of posing, in a preliminary way, an object for further discrimination. So constituted that its elements combine and recombine to shape diversified patterns, this chain both constellates itself as and dissociates itself into still more novel factors, factors articulated as either song or dance. And in their assemblage, these fluctuant, laminated, and interweaving signs disclose a dynamic texture which is analogous to highly nuanced metaphor and metonomy. Not only do such signs point inward, expressing themselves as unconscious–unbody introjects of external depositions which, were they fully to be incorporated therein, would disrupt awareness; but they reveal the recesses of a complex body, locus of the confluence of myriad strands of physical events. However altered by their passage into and incorporation within consciousness, body resonances replicate themselves with new modulations; and, as replications, they incorporate reflections as well: the physical imprints of the incorporated introjects of human encounter, and its enveloping social matrix.

In its largest signification, language is speech *in potentia*, speech as a germinating nucleus of activity which resides in the *luminator* prior to bursting forth into frank verbal articulation. Yet the process of speaking unfolds in the context of the kind of comportment which culminates in the dance: intricate and variegated motions which are subtly convoluted, diversified, and nuanced. Quintessential manifestation of this context, the dance expresses, as flexibly and ethereally as speech, the ferment which reveals the dynamics, reciprocities, and attunements of man in relation to the cosmos: a ferment which can coalesce to high density or diffuse to rarefaction. By placing itself at the very origin of its own speaking and dancing acts, the self achieves unity; and the *I*, integrality.

NOTES

1. See Whitehead, *Process and Reality*, pp. 403–13.
2. See the index entries for "conceptual feelings" and "physical feelings" in ibid.
3. Spinoza, "Ethics," Part IV, in *Chief Works of . . . Spinoza*, trans. Elwes, II 187–243.
4. See Lacan's *The Language of the Self: The Function of Language in Psychoanalysis*, trans. Anthony Wilden (Baltimore: The Johns Hopkins University Press, 1968); *Ecrits: A Selection*, trans. Alan Sheridan (New York: Norton, 1977); and *The Four Fundamental Concepts of Psycho-analysis*, ed. Jacques-Alain Miller, trans. Alan Sheridan (New York: Norton, 1978). See also the indispensable commentary on Lacan's work by John P. Muller and William J. Richardson, S.J.: *Lacan and Language: A Reader's Guide to* ECRITS (New York: International Universities Press, 1982).
5. Whitehead, *Process and Reality*, p. 160.

III

Growing: The Path to Integrity

9

METAMORPHOSIS: THE *COMMEDIA*, PARADIGM FOR STAGES ALONG LIFE'S WAY

PREAMBLE

Every symbol points toward its meaning, its value, and its determining root. By "symbol," I mean the joining together of disparate factors into a unity. What confers unity is a non-conceptualizable ingredient which is immanent in the symbol, yet transcendent to it. As symbol, every instance of comportment, including speech, "contains" the whole spirit of man. Never fully specifiable, spirit is, in the end, ineffable. Pervading all comportment, it is not entirely within comportment. Still, in stages, one can articulate certain components of spirit. Compressed in a person's body, for example, are traces of the essential character of every predecessor of man. And dwelling in his embryologic development, his whole antecedent evolution recapitulates his particular, non-repeatable ancestry. Yet each of man's antecedents, living or inanimate, contained more potency than can be actualized in them, in any of their progeny, or in their genealogy's consummate representative, the person himself. If, therefore, a single mutant DNA particle, in myriad self-replications, is ultimately responsible, in a natural sense, for each particular man's existence, surely this potency, transmitted through the ages to an awesome line of progeny, originates from some primordial aberrant modulation of the cosmic ferment, a unique disturbance in the universe's most elemental reverberations. Through the cumulative impact of particle on particle, as they combine and recombine in countless formations, and are pervasively affected by a single deviant factor, this originating act culminates in every man's full actuality.

I speak of the modulations of a universal ferment. Cosmic in scope, and ground of natural existence, this ferment momentously transcends natural existence. Through mysterious workings, it once imparted those modulations to its earliest flowings. Every man who, in any measure, has freed himself from his life's contingencies stands amazed before the spectacle of his own origins; and as his step-by-step searching into his own unconscious–unbody labyrinth reveals the successive layers of his natural being, he discerns, in the originating ferment, his destiny as well as his origin. For every layer of his body bears the imprint of some significant efficient cause of his overall being; and the very ground of efficient causality is the "form" of his unfolding being, as it is borne toward its own τέλος, an end wherein both "formal" and "final" causes coincide.

In his yearnings to know both his destiny and his origin, man is unique; and from this yearning springs his wisdom: his philosophic quest for cosmology; his religious quest sacramentally to purify the dynamism whereby that cosmology arises; his mystical vision of himself as but a singular fold in the cosmos, a fold imprinted therein by a divine Creator to whom he stands in personal relationship. The very breath of God in the natural world incarnates itself in man, and translates itself into the symbols of his comportment. Manifesting itself as both origin and destiny, it constitutes the final goal of each person's quest. In his every act, *homo quaerens*, or questing man, seeks his consummate personhood; and his apprehension of that personhood depends, in the end, on an inner bond between his destiny and his origin. Seeking resolution of his dilemma by searching both in the world about him and in the world within him, he undertakes a double journey. And at the very outset of his journey, he experiences the ambiguity of his own freedom. Here, I trace man's quest through stages, each implicating a mingling of inner and outer, which Dante designates *Inferno*, *Purgatorio*, and *Paradiso*. By entering Dante's world of the *Commedia*, I articulate, dramatically, personally, and concretely, every nuance of this ambiguity.

A • INFERNO

PREFATORY

Nowhere have the power of human freedom and its inherent ambiguity been more eloquently expressed than by Giovanni Pico della Mirandola. "At last the best of artisans," Pico proclaimed,

> ordained that that creature to whom He had been able to give nothing proper to himself should have joint possession of whatever had been peculiar to each of the different kinds of being. He therefore took man as a creature of indeterminate nature and, assigning him a place in the middle of the world, addressed him thus: "Neither a fixed abode nor a form that is thine alone nor any function peculiar to thyself have we given thee, Adam, to the end that according to thy longing and according to thy judgment thou mayest have and possess what abode, what form, and what functions thou thyself shalt desire. The nature of all other being is limited and constrained within the bounds of laws prescribed by Us. Thou, constrained by no limits, in accordance with thine own free will, in whose hand We have placed thee, shalt ordain for thyself the limits of thy nature. We have set thee at the world's center that thou mayest from thence more easily observe whatever is in the world. We have made thee neither of heaven nor of earth, neither mortal nor immortal, so that with freedom of choice and with honor, as though the maker and molder of thyself, thou mayest fashion thyself in whatever shape thou shalt prefer. Thou shalt have the power to degenerate into the lower forms of life, which are brutish. Thou shalt have the power, out of thy soul's judgment, to be reborn into the higher forms, which are divine."[1]

Pico proposes that, among all creatures, man alone is endowed with a dual option: to sink (on an evolutionary interpretation) to his natural origins, and to remain fixed therein; or to rise to his spiritual destiny, therein rhythmically to dwell. Herein are the outermost limits to his existential possibilities; all else is indetermination. Within these limits, man, by essence, is freely empowered to search. Yet I must supplement Pico's declaration. For the two quests need not be contradictory. Only when one remains transfixed in one's journey toward self-understanding, knowing both the brute in oneself and the angel, does one sacrifice one's freedom. However, Pico does affirm that by his nature and by his spirit man cannot be passive; by free choice, he *actively* rises or falls. And, by Dante's thesis, should man fall, as fall he must, he may, by free choice, fall to lower depths that he may thereupon, by free choice, rise to greater heights.

Regressively, man descends to the brutish. Herein, matter is dross, and tends toward putrefaction. Dark, inchoate cravings which derive from mere physical need so work on man as to negate his power for giving. Falling away from wholeness and harmony, he becomes deformed, privative, and deficient. Thus alienated from himself, he sinks toward fragmentation. Yet even in his virtual dismemberment, man coheres by an immanently operative law. In Dante's thesis, when wedded to Pico's, should man confront these pulverulent, degraded forces at work within him, yet maintain a divine perspective on his own spiritual potentialities, he would empower himself to rise to the status of angels. Perfection, completeness, unity both invisible and indivisible, symmetry, tranquillity, and ethereality—these are the qualities toward which he reaches. And when he experiences integrity, his organically co-adapted parts are smoothly coordinated. Each part is individual, unique, indiscerptible, and self-sufficient; jointly, all parts form his wholeness and the very fruition of his being.

From a theologic and cosmologic point of view, man participates in two kingdoms: the angelic order of pure form; the animal order, and even the inanimate, of deformation—in effect, of anti-form. From an ontologic and psychologic point of view, each kingdom impresses itself "into" man as constitutive of his being. Assimilating these kingdoms, and organizing them into a single, intricate fabric, man shapes therein his unique individuality. In him, the realms of brute and angel dialectically interplay; and, in each order, a dialectic unfolds between its *own* principles of diversification and coherence. Ever reverting to his (natural) origins, man nevertheless so orients himself toward his fall that, even as he dwells in those origins, he experiences the momentum to rise toward his (spiritual) destiny. But he must not linger in either origins or destiny lest he become fixated and lose his essential mobility, especially his power to rise. When he acts from a desire for truth, however, man's reaction to those activities which lead him to experience the brute within him is converted into even more potent action. Ever fascinated by a dual order—these archetypal conditions which ground the self, these antithetical values which strangely interpenetrate—the person senses "presences" of both brute and angel to be operative within him. Nowhere has this awareness been more powerfully evinced than both by Michelangelo, in his juxtaposition in the Sistine Chapel ceiling of *The Creation* and *The Last Judgment*, and by Dante. The complementarity of their genuises resides in their capacities, each unique, to render, in transmitted shape, the organic, dynamic, and compelling quality of these presences, a rendition which never ceases to call forth empathic compassion, fear, wonder, and awe as, with Michelangelo and Dante, we vicariously undergo our own interior journeys, communing with these presences as, however obscurely, they function within each of us.

Thus journeying toward this heaven and this hell, in their marriage in each person, one feels a vector which powerfully, ineluctably, and mysteriously draws one ever more deeply into both orders. Each set of in-gathered images constitutes a value and a commitment for all who undertake the journey. Increasingly, each value is perceived as conditioning and residing in the other. Systems of contrary values unfold, values the superficial resultant of which is the persona: man's masks and mere appearances. Yet as these masks are penetrated, and their opposition is experienced with increasing acuity, their initial consistency vanishes. At first, opposing orientations, values, and anti-values are disclosed; each set, so it appears, is equally binding upon one. But, at the end of the way, a miraculous fusion occurs, a synthesis in which brutish values, which constitute an autonomous domain, are subsumed under an etherealized and transmuted realm of angelic values.

To render concrete the abstract considerations hitherto presented, I explore the polarities and interactions of these kingdoms as expressing a division within the *luminator* itself. And yet, inhering in this bifurcation, is the imminent possibility for unification. For, immanent in the other, each kingdom, brute and angel, transcends the other. Through inner dialogue, a divided self is shaped into a self which is unitary and indivisible. Consistently pervading Dante's *Commedia* is this theme: amid crises, resolutions, and still new crises, man struggles so to engage these kingdoms that each is fully absorbed into the other. For an ever-expanding self, a new kingdom emerges which lies even beyond the angels. At bottom, the *ontology* of the person consists in man's relentless quest to discover this transcendental realm.

(*a*) Entering the Labyrinth: An Arduous Journey

"In the middle of the journey of my life," wrote Dante, "I came [across] a dark wood" (*Inf.* 1.1–2),[2] and the way out was bewildering. Precipitated by a crisis, this perception causes Dante to be ill at ease in all his relationships. For him, the world is "stale, flat and unprofitable."[3] Led by Virgil, who symbolizes reason, the philosophic stage of wisdom, Dante becomes aware that masks and deceits obscure his very self; a barrier separates one region of the self from another. Experiencing, at the outset, his false self to be sturdy, Dante realizes that concealed therein lies an authentic self, yet a self which is frail and fragile. To strengthen his true self, he must in painful quest and, layer by layer, dissolve deception and illusion. Intricate and convoluted, like the outer world—which, though incorrectly, Dante believes that he has already fully explored—the inner self is even more labyrinthine. In effect, Dante probes his own Unconscious, more accurately, his *luminator*; and, in his quest for integral personhood, he becomes aware of a doubly bifurcated psyche: consciousness split from unconsciousness, the Unconscious (i.e., the *luminator*) itself split asunder. Here, I but sketch the principal phases of Dante's quest, insofar as they are relevant for understanding the theme of *homo quaerens*: the seeking man who seeks man the seeker. What is disclosed therein is the inner core of the aesthetic: highest moment of human questing, mystical essence of the philosophic adventure, the beauty of beauty and the love of love.

It is as though all life has converged on a single point: this entry into the order of psychic and, in the end, spiritual events. Everything which has hitherto befallen man is but a preparation for what Dante is now to experience. As man of reason, whether scientist, statesman, or artist, his powers confer upon him a secure self-centeredness, yet a seeming integrity; for he is one whose social roles and very persona are well-defined. But, at each stage of his growth, certain predilections, strivings, and yearnings were incompletely consummated. Though powerful, when in the middle of the journey of his life, man is circumscribed by repressed yet fearsome, haunting inclinations. And though his quest is arduous, he needs to pursue in whatever direction these inclinations lead him; yet, afraid, he also refrains from undertaking the search. Within his own self, he senses a dark labyrinth. Yet he had not chosen to find himself in a tangled forest, "a dark wood . . . wild, and rough, and stubborn . . . [and] . . . full of sleep" (*Inf.* 1.2, 5, 11). Though an immanent purposiveness always works within him, man did not choose to awaken from his slumbers into a new kind of sleep: a grotesque world of images which, with different grades of luminosity, shine forth from within the darkness; a strange, arcane glow as he peers into the ever-darkening recesses.

As his inner journey proceeds, Dante dwells with every unfolding image, both as distinct from other images and as connected to them. Progressively rejecting each image, he nonetheless affirms the immanent context of new images toward which it points, images still more deeply buried. In this way, a texture of interlacing imagery emerges with increasing clarity, determinateness, and a weird kind of inchoate, anarchic coherence. Thus, Dante comes to understand the truth of his own being. At first, suffused by these images, he experiences, by a kind of diffusion, an inner fabric to emerge, a fabric which, increasingly, he perceives to adumbrate his authentic being. Much of what he finds had already been prefigured in his customary life. It is as though that life had traced its very contours on him, weaving within him a fabric resembling that which he initially apprehended. Yet, in this *re*finding of himself in the "wood" of his life, and rediscovering what he already had dimly known, Dante confronts, again and again, the original and originating mystery: patterns of ever-shifting balance and chiaroscuro, an interior kaleidoscopic flux. Gathering together once more the familiar imprints of his normal life, he penetrates, with haunting premonition, the "lake of [his] heart" (*Inf.* 1.20). Therein, he unmasks the deceits of the forest of bewilderment; and he discerns, as a light shining through that forest—now reflected in the lake, now diffracted, now refracted—a distant but glowing beacon which softly irradiates the whole. At first diffuse, these lights are broken into myriad scintillae. Much later, the fragments will be reassembled, as from afar,

Whilst, burning through the inmost veil of Heaven,
The soul of Adonais, like a star,
Beacons from the abode where the Eternal are.[4]

With varying chiaroscuro, this light suffuses the darkest regions. Woven of images of earth, air, fire, and water—in endless combination and recombination—the interplay of natural processes constituting Dante's own body, and perceived as working in him as the objective reality and very ground of his natural being, shapes ever-new symbols which await decipherment—as Dante gradually awakens into a new life from the deep slumber, and often the ghoulish dreams, which had overtaken him.

As Dante turns within himself, images of water endlessly recur: brooklet, rushing stream, placid lake, torrential waterfall, expansive seas. For the waters of the body—circulating lymph and blood, cytoplasm of the very cells, all the bathing fluids—are, to the searching person, an ever-present reminder of his oceanic origins, in the shallows of the sea and in its depths. By ocean shores and river banks, the questor journeys, as though driven back "to where the Sun is silent" (*Inf.* 1.60) toward strange growths: efflorescences of his body blended with the hypertrophyings imprinted in him by his aberrant worldly acts. Led by reason, his sojourn within his own hell transports him to a realm wherein he hears "the hopeless shrieks" (*Inf.* 1.115) and sees "the ancient spirits in pain" (*Inf.* 1.116). For he must encounter the depositions of his corporeal past, and, in addition, his hitherto unexpressed, dissociated rage and bitterness, and all that had formerly disrupted his unity and diminished his potency. Every suppressed impulse of the questor's bodily nature, the chaotic strivings for autonomy of his every organic part, demands expression. For is not each part itself alive? Does it not struggle for its own freedom? Must it not battle the imposition of stability, order, and harmony? Do not all living beings, and not persons alone, cling to their inertial tendencies, in order to avoid their subordination—hence, subservience—to a higher nature than their own? Is there not a force which combats the humanizing of nature, a force which tends toward dissolution and decay? Surely, the truth of every man's humanity requires that man *name* his own body as a presence within his very self which is obtrusive as well as benign: an assemblage of physical actions and reactions which, while certainly harmonious, is, under another perspective, a cacophony of bizarre, disconnected parts.

(*b*) The Demoniacal: Descent and Confrontation

Dante quests after self-revelation. For him, any progressive disclosure of truth presupposes a regressive entry, facet by facet, into all negative influences upon his own experience: the self-centered, body-centered, anti-relational, and self-gratificational aspects of his own being. Each by each and each after each, these aspects must be confronted and named: that, eventually, and by his own emergent essence, Dante may reject them, so disengaging himself from his natural origins that his own transcendental source will be revealed to him. Haunted too by split-off Imagos of personal encounters which weigh heavily upon him, unabsorbed and unperished, he must now allow them to vanish. Even prenatal and ancestral experiences are raised to the status of living presences. Every moment of Dante's past is confronted; its inmost meaning is extracted. Thus re-presented to him, this buried past, a manifold of seemingly fleeting events, is now experienced as, in reality, enduring in him, and composing his very self. Not that their perishing is ever disallowed. For *sub specie aeternitatis*, the evanescent and the disparate are but illusory. Yet they immortalize themselves in Dante (a truth which he finally recognizes during his journey through the *Paradiso*), though only with respect to such of their ingredients as express perfections for him. Always, an active principle of discernment is at work. And, in the end, Dante must acknowledge all ramifications of the suppression of his higher sensibilities, that his consummate integrity might at last be achieved.

Examining every episode of his fragmented, alienated existence—emotional and physical, organic and inorganic—Dante allows his powers for coherence to be potentiated. No mere summation of diverse capacities suffices to attain this end. Only the search itself, as actively embarked upon, grounds the higher self. Between seeker and sought a relationship must be forged. In consequence, the depression associated with a *mere* dwelling with every image sought is overcome solely through *de*-repression—the raising to self-consciousness of all encountered fragments. As one moves with Dante through the labyrinth of his own psyche, one must, with him, "leave all hope, ye that enter" (*Inf.* 3.9). At the same time, Dante affirms that "here must all distrust be left" (*Inf.* 3.14). For specific hopes for salvation may be clung to, but only a bare, undifferentiated trust of self in relation to inner object. Herein alone consists the ground for de-repression. Expecting no love, believing in what is barely believable, possessing faith without specification, accepting without reservation the self's emptiness, one expels the negative images, and, like a newborn child, is fully open to the imprints of affirmative experience.

In its initial phase, hope is entirely negative. It involves desperate clinging; and, in clinging, trust is fettered. What alone animates man to go beyond what he had hitherto grasped as lying within his powers is his *anima*, symbolized, for Dante, by Beatrice, in their earliest, tentative appearings. Now one depends only on a flicker of feeling. And now there arises the dim prospect of a luminous destiny woven of many hues, hues which are still obscurely blended. At this stage, intuition, which represents hope, emerges as complementing reason, which represents trust. In dialectical interplay, intuition and reason first negate one another, then each transcends each toward a third stance, the mystical perceptions of love. Now Dante binds himself internally to God; and he commends this way of affirmation through the way of rejection. Step by step, he leads *himself* to overcome the mere particularity of destructive, self-distorting images; he apprehends, as later he achieves a concrete universality, the synthesis of trust, hope, and love. At this stage, only perversity and adversity reveal themselves. Yet germinating in these negative conditions is a wholesome seed. For, soon, reversal occurs. Itself metamorphosed, deformation veridically grounds authentic formation, and guarantees continuance of the journey through truth and justice toward integrity and wisdom.

With gathering momentum, demoniacal images succeed one another. Now Dante gropes, now he hastens, through the chambers of the labyrinth, always following an invisible thread toward his eventual salvation. No matter how deformed or pulverized, these images of matter, however diverse its forms, always refract the divine light, even though they might be but a speck of dust; and new images ever shape themselves from the drawing together of the resultant diffractions. At times, as when he declares to Francesca and Paolo "thy torments make me weep with grief and pity" (*Inf.* 5.116–117), Dante echoes, with grace and delicacy, the strains of his own temptation; and by their sweet, tender quality, he is often constrained in his descent. Yet the journey must proceed; and he hears "strange tongues, horrible outcries, words of pain, tones of anger, voices deep and hoarse, . . . a tumult, which turns itself unceasing in that air for ever dyed, as sand when it eddies in a whirlwind" (*Inf.* 3.25–30). The mosaic of Dante's body, woven of conflicting tensions and relaxations, can never truly be orchestrated. And as he confronts its dismembered parts, one by one, "blood which mixed with tears was gathered at [his] feet by loathsome worms" (*Inf.* 3.67–69). Woven of archaic, ancestral traces, amoebae, snakes, and all manner of hideous creature—all demoniacally conceived—are imprinted as an encapsulated, tightly enfolded heritage. Yet, like a taut spiral which compresses vast energies, these traces must so unfold that an inner vision of powerful images is disclosed, images which are still in negative guises. Now Dante is led by Charon "into the eternal darkness, into fire and into ice" (*Inf.* 3.87): the paradoxical essence of hell which is frozen even as it is being consumed. Much later, and with incomparably less weightiness, the *Paradiso* will strangely replicate this image as a perfect tranquillity in the motions of delicate, fragile musical tones.

"Without hope," Dante bemoans, "we live in desire" (*Inf.* 4.42), a bundle of ungratified needs not yet transfigured into a unitary power of giving. Represented by images of hate hatefully pitted against one another, each need is felt in its raw, brutish character. Here reign the idolatry of carnal impulse, the contempt for balance and harmony: "a place void of all light, which bellows like the sea in tempest, when it is combated by warring winds" (*Inf.* 5.28–30). "The hellish storm which never rests, leads the spirits with its sweep; whirling, and smiting, it [so] vexes them" (*Inf.* 5.31–33) that "they blaspheme the divine power" (*Inf.* 5.36); and, in this *mélange*, "hither, thither, down, up, it leads them" (*Inf.* 5.43) toward the ugliness in people whom Dante had once known. Images of dissociated odor, sound, and sight constitute the very opposite of idealized encounter, a sheer negativity which has been extracted from all human meeting. Dante affirms this negativity as "the ground, on which" large "hail, and turbid water, and snow . . . fall" (*Inf.* 6.11, 10), as "Cerberus, a monster fierce and strange, . . . his eyes . . . red, his beard greasy . . . , his belly wide, and clawed his hands . . . clutches the spirits, flays, and piecemeal rends them" (*Inf.* 6.13, 16–18). In their intrapsychic interplay, these introjected images undergo still further deformation. An effluvium diffuses itself; a fungus ramifies and multiples its own distortions. Thus efflorescing, it leads a walled-off life of its own, like the wandering, grotesquely shaped cells of cancer tissue.

(*c*) Fascinations and Depths: An Intimation of Redemption

Yet, throughout this process, Dante feels "wisdom . . . transcendent over all . . . so that every part shines to every part, equally distributing the light . . ." (*Inf.* 7.73–76). Still, each part shines forth with its own *opaque* luminosity. For, elsewhere, Dante writes of "muddy people in that bog, all naked. . . . They were smiting each other, not with hands only, but with head, and with chest, and with feet; maiming one another with their teeth, piece by piece" (*Inf.* 7.109–114): a juxtaposition of gentler forces with more demoniacal forces. In these depths, our minds are like whirlpools of counter-currents in endless swirl, layers which in polar opposition dialectically confront one another. An almost impenetrable barrier to the search, this morass tempts Dante to desist. The journey becomes increasingly arduous. And "a thousand spirits, rained from the Heavens, [and] angrily exclaimed: 'Who is that, who, without death, goes through the kingdom of the dead?' " (*Inf.* 8.82–85).

Dante dares to confront the diabolism and the disjoined segments of his very being. He allows himself to feel his own avarice, his jealousy, his rage, his contempt, his hypocrisy, his anguish, his despair: all felt as physical. He does not retreat from experiencing his own pretense and deceit, but presents them as incarnate in deformed, grotesque shapes, welded into strange and incongruous expression. Now even Dante becomes the malevolent agent by which these vices carry out their evil work. Thus, he writes of "Hellish Furies, stained with blood . . . girt with greenest hydras . . . little serpents and cerastes" (*Inf.* 9.38, 40–41). In post-mortem images of decay and dissolution, he encounters his own festering and pestilential body. The imagery becomes powerful; and Dante speaks of "frogs [which] before their enemy, the serpent, run all asunder through the water, till each squats upon the bottom" (*Inf.* 9.76–78) as he sees "a thousand ruined spirits flee" (*Inf.* 9.79).

But, by sheer will, indeed by his own willfulness as symbolized by the heretic Ferinari, Dante courageously so elevates his individual powers that he seemingly reintegrates the fragmented images, causing, so it seems, the very putrefaction to disappear. Joined and organized, the forces of decay present themselves as other than they are. Still, at this phase, it is Dante who pits *his* powers against their powers; and he is admonished by Virgil, his own reason, to attend the larger cosmic rhythms which envelop even hell. For he tells himself (via his reason) that grace is conferred only on him who will allow himself to be *as he is*—even in his waywardness and in his wretchedness; and Dante is advised by Virgil not so much to combat his misfortunes as to submit to them, and to accept the disaster which has befallen him, to accept it in humility. Only when discord is acknowledged as fully what it truly is does Dante realize that concord will arise, and that the Divinity will surely imprint itself upon him. Thereupon, darkness, however diffuse, so reason informs Dante, will shine forth with its own resplendence.

Now Dante recognizes that to participate in the divine harmony, each person must renounce a measure of his own autonomy; he must so contribute to shaping a personal community which mirrors the perfections of God's cosmic community that "to one's neighbour . . . may violence [not] be done" (*Inf.* 11.31–32). Yet at the very moment that he confronts the horror of his vices—hence, the chaos toward which they lead—Dante becomes intrigued. Fascinated by the display of their images which unfolds before him, he fixates himself upon this or that perversion; he lingers in hell. For a brief span, *its* values are his own. Obsessed, Dante writes: "Ever restless was the dance of miserable hands, now here, now there, shaking off the fresh burning" (*Inf.* 14.40–42). Encountering a streamlet which issues forth, its "bottoms and both its shelving banks . . . petrified" (*Inf.* 14.82–83), Dante himself is likewise immobilized. So absorbed is he by the kaleidoscopic array that, by dwelling in its midst, he allows its content to acquire for him an autonomous existence. He oscillates between challenging the images and succumbing to them. Invigorated, he allows his journey to continue. Now growing through new images which are activated by the former images themselves, now lethargically wallowing in them, he remains among them. His very ego-centricity catalyzes an efflorescence of *superfluously* novel images, until Virgil, the ever-present guardian of rationality, warns him: " 'Now keep looking a little longer and I quarrel with thee' " (*Inf.* 30.131–132). Yet, declares Dante, "as one who dreams of something hurtful to him, and dreaming wishes it a dream, so that he longs for that which is, as it were not: such grew I, who, without power to speak, wished to excuse myself and all the while excused, and did not think that I was doing it" (*Inf.* 30.136–141). Whereupon reason bids Dante " 'unload thee of all sorrow' " (*Inf.* 30.144); allow the pageantry of hell to unfold by its inner momentum; remain steadfast within reason and hell will never again ensnare you! Complete, beyond words, the horror is awesome, alien, incomprehensible. "If I had rhymes rough and hoarse," Dante cries out, "as would befit the dismal hold, on which all the other rocky steeps converge and weigh, I should press out the juice of my conception more fully" (*Inf.* 32.1–5); "for to describe the bottom of all the Universe," he moans, "is not an enterprise for being taken up in sport, nor a tongue that cries mamma and papa" (*Inf.* 32.7–9).

Impenetrable mysteries wrapped in mysteries appear before Dante. He sees "the doleful shades . . . in the ice, sounding with their teeth like storks. Each held his face turned downwards; by the mouth their cold, and by the eyes the sorrow of their hearts is testified amongst them" (*Inf.* 32.35–38). And hovering about a great ice lake, beyond the tempestuous, and unknown to human hate and rage, is an eerie, inner silence. So cunningly do our masks contrive to envelop, and thereby to hide, this sheer emptiness, this non-being, at the very center of our natural existence! Here, at nature's absolute zero, so still that all lies *beyond* nature, everything is virtually motionless: the ennui of ultimate punishment is the annihilation of all activity; yet it is the hint of its very possibility.

"I saw," Dante now mutters, "a thousand visages, made doggish by the cold. . . . [Then] I hit my foot violently against the face of one. Weeping it cried out to me: 'Why tramplest thou on me?' " (*Inf.* 32.70–71, 78–79). This power to immobilize and thereby to torment, lurks within every human being. Discerning the horror, Dante looks into the ice, and he declares: "all heat extinguished . . . the souls were wholly covered, and shone through like straw in glass. Some are lying; some stand upright, this on its head, and that upon its soles; another, like a bow, bends face to feet" (*Inf.* 33.104, 34.11–15). Without protection, blown only by an "icy chill" (*Inf.* 34.22), and from within this source of all affliction, a creature speaks to him; confronted by absolute impotence, and in the uttermost depths of frozen rage and frozen terror, it declares: "I did not die, and did not remain alive" (*Inf.* 34.25).

Here, below, is the betrayal of all trust, the freezing of all images, the disloyalty of all powers: those humanly inspired and those divinely inspired. This is the very abyss of the prehuman ages; it is the mystery of depersonalized matter. Yet even the shattering impact of these strange, timeless depths, the terrifying chaos which lurks in the most elemental ground of our material heritage, a ground impenetrable and unfathomable, cannot eradicate every motion and all imagery, however inert or dim. Suddenly, from the depths, and from their absolute immobility, a whirlwind surges which seizes everything within reach and assumes visible form as it swirls upward. Having peered into those depths, and having perceived the treason of the Spirit, Dante discerns the wings which Satan beat, how they "opened far, . . . between the tangled hair and frozen crusts" (*Inf.* 34.72, 75); and Dante turns about and perceives a dungeon. Virgil, symbolizing Dante's power of reasoning, "caught hold on the hair of the evil Worm which pierces through the world . . . [while the] . . . Fiend . . . made a ladder . . . with his hair" (*Inf.* 34.107–108, 119), which Dante climbed. And "the sound of a rivulet . . . along the hollow of a rock which it has eaten out with tortuous course and slow declivity" (*Inf.* 34.129–132) faintly reverberated. Still unformed, yet in its own way potent, matter itself, with utmost infrapersonal "intentionality," causes Dante, with Virgil, to mount. And now "I distinguished through a round opening," he whispered, "the beauteous things which Heaven bears; and thence we issued out, again to see the stars" (*Inf.* 34.137–139). Beyond all images, at the very nadir of diabolism, when man utterly consumes himself with horror, Dante ascends toward the empyrean heights; he begins to climb the Mount of Purgatory.

B • PURGATORIO

(*a*) Forgettings, Temptations, Purifications

In the *Inferno*, the pursuit of truth requires that one be weighed down by the very facts of one's existence. Not yet having attained coherence—hence, still unaffected by ideality—these facts constitute fragmented burdens for the searcher. As such, they compel his attention but consume his energies. But once he has dispensed with mere scattered fact, he prepares himself for authentic purgation and self-purification. Lightened of this burden, he ascends, like Dante, the river Lethe; and, gradually, he forgets the intensities and fascinations of the images of hell. But he ascends against its tide; he is not yet swiftly borne along. For ideality is still threatened by lapse into factuality. The higher, more delicate equilibria of *integrity* might still sink to mere justice, the bare joining together of facts. As this questor, Dante now re-collects powers felt before the renunciations demanded of him in hell. Yet he experiences an authentic *new* gathering. He leaves behind him the "sea so cruel" (*Purg.* I.3) which had swept over him and dominated his every act. For the first time, he can sense the "[s]weet hue of orient sapphire . . . gathering on the clear forehead of the sky . . . [which] . . . restored delight" (*Purg.* I.13–16).

In retrospect, Dante experiences the images of hell no longer as a mere assemblage of disparate, concrete particulars, but, as their concrete integration, as indeed an approximation to the *concrete universal.* Once fully regnant, this universal will constitute the absolute negation of hell: a reversal of all that had therein occurred, a progressive disengaging from its images. No longer do these images oppress him and govern his acts; no longer must they be merely projected and encountered as extensions of his self. Now authentically exteriorized, wholly extruded from his being, and indeed purged from his very self, the images can validly relate to Dante. Slowly, their content is untwisted; and, in this uncoiling, they are miraculously transformed from vices to virtues. Truly, Dante *converses* with them. No longer is a monologue delivered by an agent of hell. Now a veridical dialogue unfolds. The *Purgatorio* is the realm wherein Dante acquires a capacity for liberating dialogue; and he aims at dialogues as an ideal, not yet consummately attained but gradually and asymptotically approached.

And now "The dawn was vanquishing the breath of morn which fled before her" (*Purg.* I.115–116); and "from afar," Dante "recognised the trembling of the sea" to recede as he "paced along the lonely plain, as one who returns to his lost road" (*Purg.* I.118–119). Faintly he recalls his initial bewilderment in the forest in which he had once been lost. And he makes a new journey. No longer turbulent, the sea trembles, and the dew is gently scattered. New and more subdued rhythms of water flow. They symbolize a slow, steady cleansing. Shifting from rhythm to rhythm, even though the images are substantively the same, the tempi are less erratic, and never harsh. Now Dante "turned . . . and saw four stars never yet seen save by the first people" (*Purg.* 1.22–24), such that the "heavens seemed to rejoice in their flames" (*Purg.* 1.25). He perceives the "eternal laws . . . not violated" (*Purg.* 1.76); he finds himself on a "little isle all round about the very base, there, where the wave beats it, bear[ing] rushes on the soft mud" (*Purg.* 1.100–102): the first hint of a new, and renewing, vegetation. Still, "alongside the ocean" (*Purg.* 2.10), he beholds "the Angel of God" (*Purg.* 2.28) whose "oar he wills not, nor other sail than his wings, between shores so distant . . . heavenward turned, plying the air with eternal plumes" (*Purg.* 2.32–33, 34–35): a "celestial pilot, such, that blessedness seemed writ upon him, and more than a hundred spirits . . . sang . . . all together with one voice, . . . gazing around like one who essayeth new things" (*Purg.* 2.43–44, 45, 47, 53–54). A great polyphony, the orchestration of voices sacrificing neither individuality nor mutuality! And as people, in reciprocity of perception and intent, sensed the validity of mutual love, "On every side the sun . . . was shooting forth the day" (*Purg.* 2.55). Yet contrary to what unfolds for Francesca and Paolo—who are forever imprisoned with one another—no mere trance reigns in this new realm. On the contrary, in tender motions, images of true love pass by. No particular thing can arrest their flow; no fact is circumscribed and cut off from the pattern which weaves its web, and, in subtle ways, binds together all things, those seen and those unseen.

Yet the new-found bliss is fragile. Temptations ever lurk. Strength and resilience remain unachieved. And Dante "turned . . . aside from fear of being forsaken" (*Purg.* 3.19–20), whereupon "the earth darkened" (*Purg.* 3.21). Weary, and lacking full commitment, he tentatively gropes; and he exclaims: " 'This mountain is such, that ever at the beginning below 'tis toilsome, and the more a man ascends the less it wearies' " (*Purg.* 4.88–90). For in the very act of mounting, every exertion potentiates and reinforces the next act, increasing its vigor, and the firmness of Dante's resolve. Paradoxically, the *Inferno* required descent into re-gressive weighting, whereas the *Purgatorio* encourages ascent, with progressive lightening. Enrapt by the quagmires and monotonous beats of hell, which ever cause him to linger, Dante proceeds. "[T]here is a place not sad with torments," he cries, "but with darkness alone, where the lamentations sound not as wailings, but are sighs" (*Purg.* 7.28–30); and then, reassured, he affirms: "I abide with the innocent babes" (*Purg.* 7.31). Now the rhythmic quickening of gentle sounds envelops him. No longer *im*-pressed by wailing, Dante at last *ex*-presses sighing.

Now, exotic, mingled odors are called forth: odors unknown to man, odors beyond what words can utter, odors in the end inaccessible to human experience. Such reversion to the primitive senses of smell and taste is perceived not as repressive but, indeed, as refined. A new birth is occurring. From every experience, Dante is empowered to extract its essence. And he exclaims:

> Gold and fine silver, cramoisy and white, Indian wood bright and clear, fresh emerald at the moment it is split, would each be surpassed in colour by the

> grass and by the flowers placed within that fold, as the less is surpassed by the greater. Not only had Nature painted there, but of the sweetness of a thousand scents made there one, unknown and indefinable [*Purg.* 7.73–81].

Like Caliban, who spoke of an "isle . . . full of noises, sounds, and sweet airs, that give delight, and hurt not,"[5] so I awaken from slumber, Dante in effect proclaims, as "a thousand twangling instruments hum about mine ears";[6] in veritable metamorphosis, I pass into the richer slumber of my authentic being so that, as also for Caliban, "The clouds methought would open and show riches ready to drop upon me, that, when I wak'd, I cried to dream again."[7] An incredible play of visions of what might be sinks, only to rise again. " 'Twas now the hour," Dante speaks, "that turns back the desire of those who sail the seas and melts their heart" (*Purg.* 8.1–2); and "from afar he hears the chimes which seem to mourn for the dying day" (*Purg.* 8.5–6). Thus, Dante annuls his "sense of hearing, and . . . gaze[s] on one of the spirits, uprisen, that craved a listening with its hand" (*Purg.* 8.7–9). But temptations have not wholly fled. For on "that side where the little vale hath no rampart, was a snake. . . . Through the grass and flowers came the evil reptile" (*Purg.* 8.97–98, 100). Yet angels appear while "others . . . sweetly and devoutly accompanied it through the entire hymn" (*Purg.* 8.16–17); and on hearing their "green wings cleave the air, the serpent fled" (*Purg.* 8.106–107). Ineluctably and irrevocably, Dante is caught up in rhythms which cleanse, purify, and, in the end, redeem.

(*b*) The Gathering Rhythms: Care and Recollection

In these gathering rhythms, Dante's own spirituality at last becomes self-potentiating: "in its visions . . . almost prophetic" (*Purg.* 9.18), he thought, as in a dream, he "saw an eagle poised in the sky, with plumes of gold, with wings outspread, and intent to swoop" (*Purg.* 9.19–21); and the eagle "descended and snatched me up far as the fiery sphere. There it seemed that he and I did burn, and the visionary flame so scorched that needs was my slumber broken" (*Purg.* 9.29–33). Now softly and gently, now vigorously and even threateningly, the journey continues. Always, the contrapuntal themes of eagle and angel alternate, though with diminishing intensity; and, as ground for the "inGodding" of the *Paradiso*, the *in-othering* of the *Purgatorio* unfolds.[8] And Dante continues: I "meseemed to hear in a voice mingled with sweet music . . . as . . . when people are singing with an organ, and now the words are clear, and now are not" (*Purg.* 9.140–141, 143–145). Yet lucidity and incisiveness of experience ever increase. Amid contrasts of pain and joy, sharpened in this realm but dulled in hell, Dante advances. "O human folk, born to fly upward" (*Purg.* 12.94) yet "in grievous state of . . . torment" (*Purg.* 10.115–116), he declares, discerning "how each one beats his breast" (*Purg.* 10.120), " 'perceive ye not that we are worms, born to form the angelic butterfly that flieth to judgment without defence?' " (*Purg.* 10.124–126). Why, then, he demands, "at a breath of wind thus fall ye down?" (*Purg.* 12.95). For "how different are these openings from those in Hell! for here we enter through songs, and down there through fierce wailings" (*Purg.* 12. 112–114). Care potentiates care, care for self and and care for others. Thereby, love is heightened, and ever renewed. And care suffused these regions. Converting wailings to sighs, care then transforms sighs to gentle murmurs of embryonic joy: joy which, in the *Paradiso*, will metamorphose itself into ecstasy.

One by one, care's manifold images are recollected. Only in human encounter can hell's images flee. And, in gentle mirroring, love passes back and forth; a tender touching of each lover by each suffuses both. Weighty, burdensome images are thereby scattered; loneliness is dispelled by the softness of care. For each lover extracts from the concealed content of those images the good which, though encased by evil, still dwells therein. "Because thou dost . . . fix thy mind merely on things of earth," Dante declares, "thou drawest darkness from true light" (*Purg.* 15.64–66); yet that "infinite and ineffable Good, that is on high, speedeth so to love as a ray of light comes to a bright body" (*Purg.* 15.67–69). Every human burden now vanishes, for "As much of ardour as it finds so much of itself doth it give, so that how far soever love extends, eternal goodness giveth increase upon it" (*Purg.* 15.70–72). And a community of lovers shapes itself; by their loving acts it renews itself. Surely, Dante affirms, "the more people on high who comprehend each other, the more there are to love well, and the more love is there, and like a mirror one giveth back to the other" (*Purg.* 15.73–75).

And Dante continues: "Ye who are living refer every cause up to the heavens alone, even as if they swept all with them of necessity" (*Purg.* 16.67–69). Your responsibility, he admonishes, consists, as it does for Pico della Mirandola, in a responsivity to the call of God who ever dwells within us. And divine love arises only insofar as one orients oneself in centered fashion, neither in oneself alone nor in the beloved, but, rather, in a mysterious *in-between*: interstices which are invisible yet omnipresent in a human community pervaded by mutual care. Though permeating every person, the center whence love derives is external to all yet immanently transcends each. "Ye lie subject, in your freedom," Dante advises, "to a greater power and to a better nature; and that creates in you *mind* which the heavens have not in their charge" (*Purg.* 16.79–81). Herein is the source of true freedom, the ground of responsibility for all deeds.

Yet Dante becomes increasingly aware that, through the Way of Care wherein one is gripped by fantasies, the illusions of romance are only the *appearance* of love. Like a garment, the bodily aspect of love must finally be shed: "O fantasy, that at times dost so snatch us out of ourselves that we are conscious of naught, even though a thousand trumpets sound about us, who moves thee, if the senses set naught before thee?" (*Purg.* 17.13–16). Surely, Dante affirms here that true love allows each, both oneself and the beloved, simply *to be*: to be neither demanding nor imposing; to be as one truly is, unencumbered by expectation, imagery, or extrinsic purpose. To love, Dante declares, "a light" must "move . . . thee which takes its form in heaven, of itself, or by a will that sendeth it down" (*Purg.* 17.

17–18). Yet images come and images go, and we must mourn their passage. We cannot easily allow them to perish. Sense clings to the *image* of love; pain pervades him who, adoring the image, realizes that he must renounce it. "And as this fancy broke of itself, after the fashion of a bubble to which the water fails wherein it was made, there arose in my vision a maiden weeping sorely" (*Purg.* 17.31–35). And Dante knows the anguish of love as well as its ecstasy: "As sleep is broken when on a sudden new light strikes on the closed eyes, and being broken, quivers ere it wholly dies away; so my imagination fell down soon as a light smote on my face . . ." (*Purg.* 17.40–44).

At last, the veridical nature of love reveals itself, love as both affirmation and temptation—"the seed of every virtue . . . and of every deed that deserves punishment" (*Purg.* 17.103–105). And as Dante orients himself toward the *eschaton*, he realizes that "inasmuch as love can never turn its face from the weal of its subject, all things are safe from self-hatred; and because no being can be conceived as existing alone in isolation from the Prime Being, every affection is cut off from hate of him" (*Purg.* 17.106–111). Once felt, love ineluctably renews itself by its own dynamism: "even as fire moves upward by reason of its form, whose nature it is to ascend, there where it endures longest in its material; so the enamoured mind falls to desire, which is a spiritual movement, and never rests until the object of its love makes it rejoice" (*Purg.* 18.28–33).

But how arduous, lonely, and harsh is the conversion of the Way of Care, through carnal desire, to the Way of Love.[9] In the very process whereby this supreme end is achieved, impression on impression must unfold. In hell, all such impressions had been deformed and condensed into grotesquery. Yet affirmation of the positive, germinal content of love requires rejection of its negative image. Always, a danger lurks: "every love . . . within you arises of necessity, the power to arrest it is [also] within you" (*Purg.* 18.71–72), declares Dante. Yet, too, the power to transfigure the mere images of love prevails. But perceiving that the way is not easy, Dante warns:

> there came to me in a dream, a stuttering woman, with eyes asquint, and crooked on her feet, with maimed hands, and of sallow hue. I gazed upon her; and, as the sun comforteth the cold limbs which night weighs down, so my look made ready her tongue, and then set her full straight in short time, and her pallid face even as love wills did colour. . . . "I am the sweet Siren, who leads mariners astray in mid-sea, so full am I of pleasantness to hear" [*Purg.* 19.7–15, 19–21].

For, he urges, love confounds. Its very appearance is as much illusion as reality. To be true, love must, at once, see deeply into one's own motives and apprehend the beloved's actual nature. Without fascination, one must gaze intently, allowing the beloved's totality to speak. Lest confusion compond itself, one must listen to every nuance and suspect every gesture. Yet one must be receptive to love's inmost rhythms, concealed though they be. Even the Siren is redeemable. In her resides some kernel of sweetness and caring. Nevertheless, Beatrice, Dante's *intuition*—his power of seeing beyond what he senses—must always, "holy and alert" (*Purg.* 19.26), be alongside him.

(*c*) Metamorphosis and Purgation

Though Dante has at last perceived wherein consists the love which is pure and true, the final purging of its negative image, namely pseudo-love, is momentous. Dramatic, intense, and shaking, this transformation is a genuine metamorphosis. "I felt the mountain quake," he cries, "like a thing which is falling; whereupon a chill gripped me, as is wont to grip him who is going to death" (*Purg.* 20.127–129). Now arises a drama of transmaterialization. One's inmost being is experienced as undergoing a kind of transubstantiation; it is as though one were emerging from a cocoon, shaped into an altogether new form and new inclination. "Motionless we stood," Dante muses, "and in suspense, like the shepherds who first heard that hymn, until the quaking ceased" (*Purg.* 20.139–141); and the danger of reversion, ever hidden in love's every manifestation, is extirpated: "It quakes . . . when some soul feeleth herself cleansed, so that she may rise up, or set forth, to mount on high, and such a shout follows her" (*Purg.* 21.58–60). In this metamorphosis, all faculties work in harmony. Each is but an illuminated focus in the ever-present, ever-vitalizing fabric of intuition and feeling. "Blessed are they who are illumined by so much grace" (*Purg.* 24.151–152): and unity pervades the delicate equilibrations of love which now flow through the cosmos.

To emphasize the strength of this unity, Dante marvels

> that so soon as the organisation of the brain is perfect in the embryo, the First Mover turns him to it, rejoicing over such handiwork of nature, and breathes into it a new spirit with virtue filled, which draws into its substance that which it finds active there, and becomes one single soul, that lives, and feels, and turns round upon itself [*Purg.* 25.68–75].

All transformation is by grace. That natural development can take its course, and diverse animal parts, imagined in hell as dismembered and malformed, can be so united, is indeed a miracle. At this very moment, a naturalist perspective on the person must surely be subsumed beneath a transcendental perspective: "and that thou mayst marvel less at my words, look at the sun's head, that is made wine when combined with the juice which flows from the vine" (*Purg.* 25.76–78).

How to express this overarching perspective! How to conceptualize this mandala, a sphere which ever revolves! Like rays proceeding from the refractions of the near-setting sun, its myriad unified members radiate from its center. Now substance diversifies itself; individualities which co-inhere, each in each, gradually inform the whole with its every member, while preserving within that member the living presence of the whole. In an image, Dante proclaims:

> Soon as it is circumscribed in place there [i.e., body], the formative virtue radiates around, in form and quantity as in the living members: and as the

air, when it is full saturate, becomes decked with divers colours through another's rays which are reflected in it, so the neighbouring air sets itself into that form, which the soul that is there fixed, impresses upon it by means of its virtue; and then, like the flame which follows the fire wheresoever it moves, the spirit is followed by its new form [*Purg.* 25.88–99].

Now love's gentler touch is woven into the evolving fabric. Within their own self-metamorphoses, shades—those creatures which hover between naturality and spirituality—tenderly kiss. Replacing the clash of disharmonious needs which so harshly interact in the *Inferno*, a reciprocity of givings prevails in the *Paradiso*: dynamic patterns shaped into a matrix trembling with divinely suffused values, veritable transubstantiations of those patterns. Substance has become less shadowy, less deformed, less abstract, less fragmented; it is more luminous, more ethereal, more concrete, more resilient.

Before the passage to the *Paradiso*, "ere the horizon in all its stupendous range had become of one hue, and night held all her dominion, each of us made a bed of a step; for the law of the mount took from us the power, rather than the desire, to ascend" (*Purg.* 27.70–75), every person becomes more simply, more integrally, more innocently, and more purely, human. Purged of complexities, a new child emerges from the cocoon. The final stage of wisdom is prefigured. Direct and immediate images of childhood suffice to convey a sense of cleansing: "As goats that had been agile and wanton upon the heights ere they are fed, grow tame while ruminating, silent in the shade . . . [or] . . . like the shepherd who lodges in the open, holds silent vigil by night longside his flock, . . . such were we then . . . , I as a goat and they as shepherds" (*Purg.* 27.76–79, 80–81, 85–86). But, in a great awakening, prelude to the miraculous entry, when "the shades of night were fleeing on every side, and my sleep with them" (*Purg.* 27.112–113), and after "I halted and with mine eyes did pass beyond the rivulet, to gaze upon the great diversity of the tender blossoms" (*Purg.* 28.34–36), Dante feels the very woods and hills and meadows about him to be transfigured and impregnated with the spirit of God. He tastes the nectar which, finally, may be drawn from the participation of love. An earthly paradise begins to shape itself, a visible word transfigured by the invisible from which it draws its sustenance, and gathers its powers, its wonders, and its ecstasies. At last, the simple love of man and woman, and friend and friend, are restored, but now as sacramental, and as sanctified by God. A slow pageant unfolds: "a sweet melody ran through the luminous air" (*Purg.* 29.22–23). Every gesture, inflection, and movement have been transmuted into a symbol, a symbol which reveals the entire man as centered in the divine. The commonplace is celestialized; wisdom is revealed in its utter simplicity: without deceit, without pretense, without mediation.

The whole earth is as new; and "the fair pageant was flaming forth, brighter far than the moon in clear midnight sky in her mid month" (*Purg.* 29.52–54). Both nature and man are "transcendentalized." And "within a cloud of flowers, . . . olive-crowned over a white veil," Dante speaks, "a lady appeared to me, clad, under a green mantle, with hue of living flame" (*Purg.* 30.28, 31–33). To learn of *justice*, he, guided by reason, must first know, in all their intricacy, the facts of his inner existence; then, guided by reason linked to intuition, he must familiarize himself with that ideal which alone can draw those facts from their inchoate state toward *integrity.* Now, pure feeling, sensitivity, and intuition—all symbolized by the lady—will lead Dante, through the *Paradiso*, into the stages of wisdom. Thus prepared, he announces, "I came back from the most holy waves, born again, even as new trees renewed with new foliage, pure and ready to mount to the stars" (*Purg.* 33.142–145).

C • PARADISO

(*a*) Symbols of the Integral Person

As Dante's journey proceeds into the *Paradiso*, the love relationship between man and woman emerges as archetype and paradigm for love in general. All images of conflict fade—jealousy, envy, rejection, lust. Each lover experiences himself as mirrored in the other; and through their complementarity, both lovers experience the divine unity of the cosmos, a unity of parts individually assymetric but jointly harmonious. For "The All-mover's glory penetrates through the universe, and re-gloweth in one region more, and less in another" (*Par.* 1.1–3). Yet, everywhere, the glory is present; and it achieves its consummation in the reciprocities of human love. Therein, the perfection of the cosmos itself is prefigured. The in-othering of each in each, a mutual presence of lover to loved and of beloved to lover—hence, their harmonious compresence—is grounded in an immanent, potent, and guiding in-Godding by the divine center: a center which draws all elements of compresence into unity.

As love symbolizes an integral cosmic order, so the presence of each lover constitutes such a symbol. For Dante, past, present, and future join as a single, comprehensive all-pervading presence. Distinct attributes, all vices and virtues are, likewise, cojoined, and indeed transcended to shape pure tranquillity. Disparate images of the past, anticipated images of the future, isolated images of the present which is, however, narrowly construed are gathered together in a coherent, imageless manifold. Within this manifold, imagining itself is both negated and transcended. Increasingly, the image comes to symbolize, not something apart from itself (i.e., the symbol), but its very self. Symbol points inward toward itself; it completes itself through its own dynamic: its power for continual self-expansion. And the entire journey, the search which Dante conducts into the labyrinth of his own being, is itself an overarching symbol, a symbol composed of myriad phases and elements.

Yet just as each love relationship is unique and particular, and, likewise, each lover, so every journey is unique and particular. What fully concretizes the universal character of this search—the general stages of which are the discovery of justice in the *Inferno*, integrity in the *Purgatorio*, and, now, wisdom, which subsumes yet goes beyond both justice and integrity, in the *Paradiso*—is this fact: no person can avoid the search. Each must discover for himself, through the selfsame phases, the particularities and idiosyncrasies of his own existence. In this process, a "mighty flame followeth a tiny spark" (*Par.* 1.34), as each person replicates the search of every person; and the "lantern of the universe riseth unto mortals through divers straits" (*Par.* 1.37–38). Indeed, "so much of heaven . . . seemed to me," Dante speaks with wonder, "enkindled with the sun's flame, that rain nor river ever made a lake so wide distended" (*Par.* 1.79–81). A single order of many layers, the vast universe is an harmonious texture on which its "exalted creatures trace the impress of the Eternal Worth" (*Par.* 1.107–108). And in this texture, each creature reads the truth, through his own introspectings, which he, in fact, encounters as extrospectings projected outward upon the texture—projections with which he can hold dialogue. And so all creatures "move to diverse ports o'er the great sea of being, . . . each . . . with instinct given it to bear it on" (*Par.* 1.112–114).

Stepwise, the meaning of the symbolism of every journey will unfold its infolded content. And, in the end, seemingly disparate factors will achieve an order already inherent in the entire fabric. "Meseemed a cloud enveloped us," Dante declares, "shining, dense, firm and polished, like diamond smitten by the sun" (*Par.* 2.31–33). Fusing all subsidiary symbols into a single all-inclusive symbol, which at one and the same time is *Person and Cosmos* and *Cosmos and God*, "the eternal pearl received us, as water doth receive a ray of light, though still itself uncleft" (*Par.* 2.34–36). Every living creature is the integral of body and soul; and since that creature is a true microcosm, a general physical co-inherence prevails throughout the cosmos, which, conversely, is the macrocosmic analogue of its very natural part. As integral, parts are natural; but the web of relations which binds parts to coherence is spiritual. Only by his dwelling, with love and in communion, *within*, hence enfolded by, his interpersonal relations, *a fortiori* the larger community, can each person achieve consummate personhood.

(*b*) Integrity through Human Encounter

Persons intermingle; bodies and souls co-mingle. Through participatings and empathizings, each person celebrates, in sacramental affirmation, both his autonomy and his integrity. Then, Dante proclaims: "In such guise as, from glasses transparent and polished, or from waters clear and tranquil, not so deep that the bottom is darkened, come back the outlines of our faces" (*Par.* 3.10–13); and each person experiences the unfoldings of the entire cosmic fabric. Its inmost recesses are constituted by the reflectings, back and forth, of selves lovingly cojoined to selves: " 'In your wondrous aspects,' " Dante declares to Beatrice, " 'a divine something re-gloweth that doth transmute you from recollection of former times' " (*Par.* 3.58–60). For when I spoke of the self's reflexive character, and its gathering together of memories to shape a unity of vibrant presence, I affirmed this principle: selves dwell internally with selves; thereby, they impart their most subtle graces to one another.

Thus "did I see more than a thousand splendours draw towards us, and in each one," Dante declares, "was heard: *Lo! one who shall increase our loves*" (*Par.* 5.103–105). By transmitting reflection to reflection, and thereby imparting grace beyond measure, the potentials for ever-increasing love, with respect to both its quality and its intensity, activate themselves, and activate themselves anew. A veritable polyphony of integral human bodies, all now fully spiritualized, declares itself, though the finer tones are still cloaked in mystery. For, Dante affirms:

> if our fantasies are low for such an exaltation, it is no marvel, for never was there eye that could transcend the sun . . . [which] . . . descendeth to the remotest potencies, down, from act to act, becoming such as maketh now mere brief contingencies; by which contingencies, I mean the generated things which are produced from seed, or seedless, by the moving heaven . . . whence . . . cometh, that one same tree according to its kind better and worse doth fruit; and ye are born with diverse genius [*Par.* 10.46–48; 13.61–66, 70–72].

And in this orchestration of tones vivid with tones muffled,

> we see here, straight, twisted, swift or slow, changing appearance, long or short, the motes of bodies moving through the ray which doth sometimes streak the shade, which folk with skill and art contrive for their defence. And as viol and harp tuned in harmony of many chords, make sweet chiming to one by whom the notes are not apprehended, so from the lights that there appeared to me was gathered on the cross a strain that rapt me albeit I followed not the hymn [*Par.* 14.112–120].

With increasing depth, two lovers, who allow their love to envelop them and unfold by its own dynamism, penetrate the mystery which encloses each: mystery inhering in the interstices between the two; mysteries engendering the very ground of human relatedness. Yet even one lover alone, ungraced by the love for and from another, can, by an act of affirmation, when graced by God without meditation, symbolically apprehend his Beatrice; he may perceive her as that symbol, incarnate in beings both living and inanimate, through which he discerns mutuality, the essence of All: the experience of seeing and hearing, with Dante, a great bird "utter in its voice both *I* and *Mine*, when in conception it was *We* and *Our*" (*Par.* 19.10–12). For immanent in every creature, even as it stands alone before God as destined only for solitude, is a universal principle. No matter how limited one's capacity, under a sufficiently large perspective one can know universal themes. So Dante declares: "each lesser nature is a receptacle too scant for that good which hath not end. . . . Wherefore our sight . . . cannot of its nature have so great power but that its principle should discern far beyond that which unto it appeareth" (*Par.* 19.49–52, 55–57).

By particular encounters with particular creatures, perhaps most intensely in the meetings of man and woman, but even in communings between man and beast, man and plant, and man and stone, I may, as long as I experience therein the incarnation of the Divine, perceive, with Dante, "thousands of lamps surmounting, one sun which all and each enkindled, as doth our own the things we see above; and through the living light outglowed the shining substance so bright upon my vision that it endured it not" (*Par.* 23.28–33). For then I pass *through* the agent, this vehicle of God, toward, but not yet touching, the very source, a source incomparably more powerful than the agent which illuminates her, like "the infant who toward his mother stretcheth up his arms when he hath had the milk, because his mind flameth forth even into outward gesture . . . so each one of these glowings up-stretched with its flame" (*Par.* 23.121–125). Thus Dante himself was

> as one who cometh to himself from a forgotten vision. . . . As under the sun's ray, which issueth pure through a broken cloud, ere now mine eyes have seen a meadow full of flowers, when themselves covered by the shade; so beheld I many a throng of splendours, glowed on from above by ardent rays, beholding not the source whence came the glowings [*Par.* 23.49–50, 79–84].

Now, while retaining his self-identity, Dante perceives in what manner he is veridically constituted by another, how he synthesizes into a unity the different ways in which he experiences himself through the eyes of the other. Identifying himself with these reflected appraisals, which derive from another whose own self-identity is likewise composed of analogous reflected appraisals proceeding from Dante himself, Dante, as well as the other, grasp how each, in his inmost being, is constituted. Both are illumined by the very glow which irradiates each. "'Though not set forth to me by thee, I better do discern thy will,'" a creature speaks to Dante, "'than thou the thing which is most certain to thee, because I see it in the veracious Mirror which doth make himself reflector of all other things, and naught doth make itself reflector unto him'" (*Par.* 26.103–108). Now Dante's very integrity consists in his willingness to dwell in God's mystery. For, though, as yet, all is bathed in mystery, Dante acknowledges an invisible center as guiding his every act; and persuaded of the *rightness* of mystery, he resolves—more accurately: the resolution comes upon him by grace—to deviate no longer from any recommendation which he adjudges to proceed from the source of mystery.

(*c*) The Eternal Center

No sooner than he *wills* to dwell in mystery Dante himself becomes suffused with mystery. All about him, and penetrating his every part, is love, love which ever activates new love. A perfect union shapes itself, a union flawless and indivisible, between form and matter, part and relationship. And "In his eternity beyond time, beyond all other comprehension, as was his pleasure, the eternal love revealed him in new loves" (*Par.* 29.16–18). Nor did Dante "lie, as slumbering, before; for nor before nor after was the process of God's outflowing over these waters" (*Par.* 29.19–21). Thus bathed in rhythmic interplay of light, sound, and water, a perpetual interchange of ebb and plunge, of graceful fall and newly risen eddies, Dante experiences himself as though, by his essence, he were *virtually* co-eternal with God. And so he writes:

> there shone around me a living light, leaving me swathed in such a web of its glow that naught appeared to me. . . . And I saw a light, in river form, glow tawny betwixt banks painted with marvellous spring. From out this river issued living sparks, and dropped on every side into the blossoms, like rubies set in gold. Then as inebriated with the odours they plunged themselves again into the marvellous swirl, and as one entered issued forth another. . . . And as a hill-side doth reflect itself in water at its foot, as if to look upon its own adornment when it is rich in grasses and in flowers, so, mounting o'er the light, around, around, casting reflection in more than a thousand ranks I saw all that of us hath won return up yonder [*Par.* 30.49–52, 61–69, 109–114].

Finally, at the end of the way, the true pageantry of the mountain is revealed to Dante. At last, he perceives "the divine light" which "so penetrateth through the universe . . . that naught had power to oppose it" (*Par.* 31.22–23, 24). In a single vision which embraces the totality, time, space, and matter dissolve into a simple, ethereal substance. The labyrinth of the *Inferno*, converted to the spiral of the *Purgatorio*, is now One: a single and singular fabric, a unitary compresence. All the varied heritage, the arcane forces, the archaic traces of split-off ancestry, and all the nuances of movement—stumbling, quick, slow, hastening, retarding, eager, lethargic—are converted from fluctuant, intricate rhythm, evanescent and fleeting, into the quintessential rhythms of wisdom: composite but one. In utmost simplicity, joy and peace prevail . . . and perdure. "Oh grace abounding," Dante cries, his voice blending musically with the totality, "wherein I presumed to fix my look on the eternal light" (*Par.* 33.82–83); and Mystery reveals itself in a symbol: "Within its depths I saw ingathered, bound by love in one volume, the scattered leaves of all the universe; substance and accidents and their relations, as though together fused, after such fashion that what I tell of is one simple flame" (*Par.* 33.85–90).

Dante's search is paradigmatic for everyman's quest fully to know himself. Though writing in symbols and dramatizing the search with great intensity, and in a multitude of ramifications perhaps inaccessible to the normal person, Dante, by implication, is proposing certain ontologic categories of universal significance. Prefigured in schematic fashion by the dialectically interwoven phases already outlined, where the general contours of the search *in abstracto* were laid bare, their categories must now be presented anew, but in concrete ontologic form. In my next two chapters, the appropriate ontologic structures—namely, crisis, complementarity, and ideality—will be examined. By *growing through* these experiences, so momentously etched by Dante, the person thenceforth will be understood as having chosen the appropriate path toward his own integrity—ever hough the concept of wisdom, especially in Dante's sojourn in the *Paradiso*, has already been anticipated.

Previously, justice was treated as grounding personal harmony, hence as woven of the moments of personal freedom, in a dialectic of self-possession; and I pointed he way toward both integrity and wisdom, each phase involving personal metamorphosis, a profound transformation in which, with increasing luminosity and ethereality, the final stages, first of integrity and last of wisdom, are construed as enveloping man. Now by presenting himself as exemplary instance of the ontologic structures—namely, crisis, complementarity, and ideality—the person has achieved full integrity. At last, he grounds his *own* path toward wisdom; and this stage of dynamic participation in the cosmic rhythms consists, for every person, in a *speaking forth*: a speaking, ultimately, in rhythms of silence and vibrancy. To prepare the way for the final grounding, in my concluding division, "The Self United"—hence, dwelling in Being which has been so transfigured that man's own being can be deemed one and indivisible—I treat those preliminary ontologic categories as indeed essential for grounding man's path to integrity.

NOTES

1. *Oration on the Dignity of Man*, trans. Elizabeth Livermore Forbes (Lexington, Ky.: Anvil Press, 1958), pp. 3–4.
2. This and all subsequent quotations from Dante in this chapter are taken from the three-volume translation of *The Divine Comedy* published in London by J. M. Dent in The Temple Classics series: *The Inferno of Dante Alighieri* in 1900, *The Purgatorio of Dante Alighieri* in 1901, and *The Paradiso of Dante Alighieri* in 1899.
3. Shakespeare, *Hamlet* I.ii.133.
4. Percy Bysshe Shelley, "Adonais," *Immortal Poems of the English Language*, ed. Oscar Williams (New York: Washington Square, 1972), p. 320.
5. Shakespeare, *The Tempest* III.ii.146–148.
6. Ibid., 149–150.
7. Ibid., 153–155.
8. See Charles Williams, *The Figure of Beatrice: A Study in Dante* (New York: Farrar, Straus and Giroux, 1980), pp. 11, 16.
9. See the index entries for "Way of Rejection" and "Way of Affirmation" in ibid.

10

CRISIS AND COMPLEMENTARITY: FROM TRAGEDY TO ECSTASY

PREAMBLE

What ontologic structures can be adduced from my recapitulation of Dante's *Commedia*? I discern two principal themes: (*a*) crisis, tragedy, ecstasy—i.e., doubts of shattering impact, misery preceding redemption, grace as consummated existence; and (*b*) solitude, relatedness, transcendence–i.e., loneliness alternating with tranquillity, interplay of silence and vibrancy, participation as uniting solitude with relationship. In each instance, the members of the triads correspond to the divisions of the *Commedia*, and the themes interweave as but a single topic. In both "Crisis and Complementarity," the present chapter, and "Human Dialogue," the next chapter, the first theme is salient; in "Schemes of Presence and Compresence," chapter 12, and "Symbols of Human Encounter," chapter 13, the second theme is salient. From the point of view of crisis and dialogue, the notion of "complementarity" unites all sections of Part II, i.e., of "Growing: The Path to Integrity." From the point of view of presence and symbol, the notion of "compresence" unites all sections. In my previous chapter, I proposed a concrete anticipation of the growth toward integrity. Now I examine, sequentially, as ontologic motifs, the self-in-crisis which the *Commedia* poetically implies, tragedy in the frame of the sexual complementarity of romantic love, and the dissolution of tragedy through grace.

Every self engages in self-exploration. Drawing images from its inmost depths, it confers upon them objective status. And contemplating these objects of its own creation, it discovers their ever-new facets. Embedded in a community, the self so relates itself to other selves that it, together with them, gives birth to layer upon layer of what, in retrospect, it discerns to be reality's labyrinthine texture: a texture which is the product of the collective acts of many selves. In communion, selves leap beyond themselves. They thrust themselves toward unknown realms, realms which in the end they have collectively shaped. What was initially perceived to be ideal and merely potential becomes, to the seeker's eye, real and actual. An authentic transformation has occurred. In correlative metamorphosis of both self and object a new world is formed; and the self comes to dwell in this world which it itself had created. Successively, reality acquires new layers: and it weaves itself with the ideal. All is in process of reconstitution, renewal, and rebirth.

As objects become more ample, more subtly delineated, and more intricately assembled, the self correspondingly deepens and broadens. A dialectic of self and object unfolds. In this dialectic, the self acquires its characteristic project: to project itself toward repeatedly novel forms. To accomplish new creation, the self must always empty itself. Lonely and deprived, and sensing its own inadequacy to imagine such new objects as are adequate to reality's varied nuances, the self must, in order once again to create, truly forgive itself. By accepting its own defects, it allows itself to overcome those defects. Now withdrawing into itself, as in a cocoon, it prepares itself for new metamorphosis. Thus transcending itself, the self leaves its old self behind. Ever birthing new visions, it experiences crisis: anguish and pain, risk and renunciation, perishing and renewal, a dying into novelty. With a recurring sense of loss, the self gains a more durable, if ethereal, character. In romantic love, it persuades itself that it dwells in peace, each partner mirroring the perfection and ideality of the other. Thereby, it shapes the illusion that a perfect moment of eternity belongs to it. One presents oneself to one's partner, man or woman, so the self is convinced, not as process, nor as incomplete, but rather, out of time, as one truly is. Each mysterious and needed for the other's completion, man and woman manifest complementary rhythms. Together, in compresence, they shape an authentic ontology of the human. In the context of their mutuality, each probes his deeper self, and creates the symbols by which that self attains to its veridical fulfillment.

A • THE SELF-ENGENDERING SELF

(*a*) The Self as Implying Community

Throughout Dante's journey, as paradigm for any searching—and I have construed searching to be man's primordial ontologic structure—the self presents to itself its own inner content. But this content is not merely formal and abstract. Quite the contrary. Drawn forth from the self's own depths, it progressively acquires concrete shape. Having hitherto possessed ideal status, the object gradually assumes real status. And not only does the self orient itself toward the object in the stance of knowing, but modes of relatedness also emerge which go beyond knowing. In their abstract form, these modes involve three kinds of existence, previously discussed: the pious, the good, and the spiritual. Moreover, the moments of spiritual existence—namely, justice, integrity, and wisdom—were themselves concretely presented, in condensed symbolic fashion, in the *Commedia*; and the final moment, wisdom, was, in the *Paradiso*, converted into a new series, itself unfolding through new moments, henceforth to be presented, of *transcendental* existence.

Certainly, the self draws content from its every inner recess; and it externalizes this content as altogether new objects. Beyond that, both by knowledge and in reverence, it orients itself toward those objects as originating within its own depths. And it systematically articulates a manifold which includes the various sorts of existence previously mentioned. Indeed, from one point of view, the world's external texture unfolds by a dynamism which resides in the self—a dynamism which, together with analogous dynamisms associated with other selves, engenders such internal relations as bind self to self; and, in the end, gives birth to the community of selves, and, beyond that, to the larger cosmic community: most inclusive matrix of selves intertwined with selves. Hierarchically ordered, according to the quality of reflexive capabilities, this matrix is woven of infinitely variegated selves-in-relation, relationships which themselves are patterned in endless ways.

Accordingly, what seems to be reality proceeds from a kind of ideality. In turn, ideality itself is grounded on a more inclusive reality, a reality more richly constituted than nature *simpliciter*. The natural order stems from a larger spiritual order. And the spiritual is founded on a realm which transcends the distinction between "naturality" and spirituality, a realm which is transcendental with respect to the customarily real or ideal. The philosophic position which postulates that realm I have named *transcendental rhythmicality*. To articulate this position, I must raise these questions: Wherein consists the self's *inmost* depths? How are persons and selves connected? Can minds exist which are associated with more "ethereal" bodies than any we can currently experience? How, in the end, are bodies related to mental resonances?

In general, I hold the expressions "embodied self" and "ensouled body" to be equivalent. They stress different loci of a single dynamic. In the first instance, the self is the core activity which envelops itself with the body, suffusing itself with corporeality. In the second instance, the body is that wherein reflexivity arises to diffuse *itself* throughout the corporeal. And I subscribe to this metaphysical doctrine: there are many grades of both ensoulment and embodiment. When earlier I used the term "resonance," I sought to indicate the factor which I deem bodies and minds, souls and selves, to possess in common. To speak an Hegelian idiom: the processes by which the *appearing* of reality unfolds its manifold forms and the processes by which *thinking reality* unfolds are, in their essential dynamic, one and the same. Together, a double perspective is entailed: objectivity woven with subjectivity. Sufficiently probed, *res extensa* and *res cogitans* are identical.

In an outer journey, one goes toward, and listens to, what is wholly other to one; one embarks upon the good life. In an inner journey, one intimately dwells with one's very self; one embarks upon the pious life. In the end identical, these journeys jointly constitute the spiritual life, synthesis of piety and goodness. By this synthesis, I dialectically express the dynamic common to *all* searching; and I anticipate the ontologic structures of searching, which itself is man's primordial ontologic structure.

The more deeply the self explores itself, and thereby becomes self-aware, the more luminous the person becomes who bears that self. Two questions arise: How do the dialectical unfoldings of one self, the disclosure of *its* depths—hence, the luminosity of its associated personhood—relate to analogous factors with respect to all selves? Why does one self-determining self imply a community of self-determining selves? For, in general, no single self can exist without a plurality of selves; no plurality can exist save by the contributions of singular selves. But, among the many selves, some are primitive, others are advanced. What for one person is merely a primordial stage in his own self-determinative character—e.g., the moments of truth and trust—is, in the brute, the compression of numerous stages which mutely appeal for articulation. What for one person is an entire advanced set of stages is for an angel but a single, primitive, initiating stage. And to refer to Pico's doctrine that both brute and angel dwell as potentialities in man: a "slow motion" depiction of personal development would disclose all stages, those condensed and those prefigured.

(*b*) The Self as Woven of Community

I am advancing this cosmologic doctrine: the cosmos is a fabric of selves-in-relation: selves which are self-actant and interactant; a fabric which is inherently transactional. Under one perspective, a set of distinct selves constitutes what, in a more inclusive perspective, are but elements which enter into the composition of distinct selves. Conversely, what under one perspective are mere elements present themselves, in a different perspective, as distinct selves. Moreover, an embryogenetic process pervades the universe; embryonic traces are imprinted into every entity. At the same time, eschatology prevails. Alongside embryonic traces dwell, and even interact, prefigurements which compress in every entity extraordinary powers for specific, concrete *becoming*.

Every questor acts within a community of questors. At times, questings clash; one person becomes a mere object to another. But often reciprocity prevails; and contrasting, complementary questings emerge. In proportion to its reflexive complexity, every creature quests, transmitting to other creatures adjacent to it an Imago of itself. Reciprocally, it receives from those creatures imprints of *their* activities. Thereby, a community of both selves and quasi-selves arises. Within this community, each member strives to actualize its reflexive potential. Depending on inherent capacity, its development may be arrested at any phase: momentarily, as a wholesome preparation for the immediately succeeding phase; durably or regressively, should pathologic factors set in to impede its further growth. Such interactant selves comprise a veritable cosmic physiognomy, Spinoza's *natura naturata.* In the lineaments of "the face of the universe,"[1] and under the finite perspective of a particular creature, one may decipher, either *sub specie durationis* or *sub specie aeternitatis*, its constituent rhythms. Every embodied self symbolizes the phases of its own development. Collectively, developmental dynamics shape *natura naturans*: the rhythmic ferment of interwoven modes of both psyche and soma.

Reality's seemingly objective appearances are the synthesized product of numberless self-determining acts, acts performed by selves on differing levels of refinement and self-awareness, which vary from the dim to the vivid and are associated with bodies of differing ethereality or corporeality. The more developed the self, the more subtle the physical processes which constitute its incarnate, visible, and codified shape. Vis-à-vis the resistance and constructive opposition of other selves, all selves seek to actualize their intrinsic, latent powers. In a context of reciprocal engagement, they constitute for themselves their distinctive modes of relatedness to the integral matrix of selves; and in a process of interchanging Imagos of selves, each self becomes a treasure house of its own past experiences. Indeed, wisdom, the unfolding moments of the transcendental life, is an activity of re-collection. In wisdom, the self gathers together anew its already actualized moments, moments which incorporate the depositions of a self's encounters with other selves. Cumulatively, the self acquires these depositions in its passage through life. And by this gathering activity, one self-consciously draws together the very strands of continuity which ineluctably bind the self to its own origins. Wisely appropriated, this durable inheritance is the self's living heritage made present and actual. Indeed, each self is associated with a specific, unique *luminator*: that locus of personal activity empowered continually to articulate its own content, and to raise it to self-awareness. To know oneself as *I*—a willing, choosing, risking self—is not only to be aware of having probed one's own past; it is also to be able to grasp the thingliness of things as, in part, derived from ever cumulatively evolving stages of development, each stage having been drawn forth from within the self in its immanent, yet empathic, collaboration with other selves. In this sense, every layer of reality is interwoven with other selves. For every layer stems from the reconstitution of prior layers in accordance with norms shaped by the community of selves. To be a thing is to stand in determinate relationship to the matrix of hierarchically ordered, reflexively interwoven, self-determining selves, a matrix wherein all selves are construed as engaged in the selfsame process.

Thus, human culture is superimposed on nature, yet always interactant with it. By a more primitive though analogous mechanism which transmits itself from germinating self to germinating self via resonances weighty with the physical, nature itself is composed of layers, one superimposed on another. Human culture is but a particularly advanced stage in a process of cosmic creativity. Self–re-creative acts of self-aware persons, it is the pro-jection on what is experienced as objective reality of a *project*, a project collectively assembled by persons. And, though deriving from within selves, this reality-creating activity is rooted in its sustaining ground, a divinity which acts immanently and directly in every being. Still, even as a particular self grasps that ground, it has already vanished. Such intrinsic elusiveness constitutes the transcendent character of the ground as, through the self's own activity, it translates itself into objectively encounterable form. In the last analysis, transcendency itself is rooted in a Cantorian-like scheme of nested infinities; and this scheme *is* the transcendental ground for *all* activity.

To apprehend an object is to grasp its every aspect as a projection of the self. Beyond that, it is to grasp one's own self as the engendering source of spirit; and it is to grasp oneself from various points of view, both specific and general. Yet this very process necessitates further differentiation. Under the perspectives of the hitherto distinguished aspects, new modes of apprehension arise, only to replicate unfoldings through the phases of wisdom. Once again, what is therein revealed must be taken up by the self. Through successive displacements of perspectives to every *new* aspect, the entire process is repeated. Passing through specification and determination to renewed synthesis, then frank universalization, the dialectic of wisdom unfolds anew. In wisdom, the self shapes endless resolutions into still new forms of consciousness. Without cease, it reorients itself toward itself. And every new form entails a new perspective. Yet new perspectives are themselves redintegrated. All is dynamically drawn forth from within the self; all acquires significance within a matrix of relationships which constitutes a never-to-be-completed ferment, an eternal flow.

(*c*) Self-Feigning, Self-Forgiveness, and Self-Rebirth

In its relationships to the objects of its own shaping acts, the self tends to dissemble. Too readily does it mistake façade for the reality which had engendered façade. At the same time, tension arises within the self, tension experienced as either anxiety or loneliness. Working through tension, the self expresses the conflict which never ceases to dwell within it, an opposition between two forces: the need to acknowledge the transitory status of a given objective order, for that order is but a product of the self—hence, to renew the creative acts by which the order is converted through superaddition of new objects into a more stable realm; the need to lose itself among its own creations, orienting itself toward them as though they were objects in their own right—hence, to seek false security and deceptive roots amid them, forgetting their insubstantial status *sub specie aeternitatis*. But when the self glances anew at its creations, and recognizes how they have functioned as façades, they are immediately transformed from existence sui generis to symbols. Here alone the self apprehends itself both as creative and as self–re-creating. Only when a veridical symbology of the physiognomy by which the self manifests itself is achieved can conflict be resolved. For the person, the contours of his body, and its conventionally designated extensions, incorporate this symbol. Only by creating and interpreting such symbols as illuminate the composite yet unitary psyche and soma will reconciliation occur, reconciliation of the self with itself. Now alone can the self attain self-coherence, its conviction that it has truly completed itself—in Hegel's phrase, "as it is in itself and for itself."[2]

In effect, the self forgives itself.[3] It need not atone beyond throwing itself once more into its own surging activity. Therein, it spans the unbridgeable chasm between actuality and ideality. Ever seeking to reduce the gap, the self works rigorously and by increments, progressively elevating the actual toward the ideal —though, at the same time, it candidly acknowledges that, as such, the ideal is correspondingly diminished. A true synthesis of (brute) actuality and (vacuous) ideality is achieved. To be aware of this achievement is, at one and the same time, to be aware of one's own universally concrete individuality; it is to acknowledge that one's actuality is penetrated by one's ideality and that one's ideality is incarnate in one's actuality. Now luminous with this synthesis, the self posits a universal ground for its own singularity. By this act, it posits itself; and in positing itself, it posits all its stages, including its own grounding matrix.

Not only does one contemplate this (ultimately divine) ground; one actively, specifically, and concretely relates to it. Experiencing it as a vast ferment, one senses it to suffuse every person and, indeed, the entire world. Like Spinoza's *natura naturans*, it dynamically implicates all selves, with respect to both their reflexive character and their incarnation as human bodies. In actual transubstantiation, the self, luminous in and through the body, transfigures the body and, in varying degrees, etherealizes it. To know this divine ground is to act upon it and within it; to know it is never merely to be acted upon by it. Like Spinoza's passionate knowing of God, the knowing of the ground of self-creative activity is, in the last analysis, the producing, and re-producing, of the element of the divine in consciousness. It is the progressive divinizing of consciousness, hence of the one who "possesses" consciousness. His conciousness transformed into self-consciousness, a person thereby approaches the fruition of his powers, those physical and those spiritual; indeed, at bottom, these powers are one and the same.

Now the universal activity, which is divine activity, is concretized as identical with the self, with respect to its inmost depths. By stages, the self has brought itself both toward and into the divine foundation of its own activity. Progressively, all opposition between universality and particularity is transcended. The self becomes free to dwell in, and deeply to enjoy, the very fount whence springs its own creations. Yet, to escape from self-enclosedness, the self must first acknowledge its own autonomy, then mystically renounce it. Insofar as it dwells in its own emptiness, in a purely formal and non-process sense, the self is indeed narcissistic. But by its self-relinquishment, it comes no longer to dwell strictly within itself. On the contrary, it now inhabits the realm of its intertwinings with other selves, a realm which sustains the self's very activities. Dwelling in this ferment, selves-in-relation are activated and reactivated, and thereby truly augmented.[4]

At this stage, all singular moments are gathered together anew. Now, the self knows itself, not in this or that specific, completed form, nor as any particular way of assembling a multitude of such forms. For it grasps itself as process and unfolding. It is the activity, so it informs itself, with forms ever more subtle and ineffable, of never ceasing to engage the constraints imposed upon it by its every concrete embodiment; and it probes itself by possessing those limits, by appropriating them, by transcending them. In effect, self-consciousness functions as agent and mediator whereby what is still latent, immanent, and unconscious is progressively transformed into un–self-consciousness. As un–self-conscious, the forms of the self, forms by which the self does not cease to *in*-form itself as it continues to grow, become translucent, intangible, and ethereal.

Accordingly, the self presents itself to itself as a going beyond itself; and it experiences both the anguish and the ecstasy of this self-thrusting toward an unknown destiny. For, as it creates, the self knows acutely, in the totality of its self-directed motions, its own paradoxicality, the inner struggle between forces irrevocably in opposition. But even in the very agony of self-transcendence, the self apprehends itself as inherently unified. Still, it must wrest this unity from itself. It must never desist from its vigilant guardianship of the creative process. Envisaged in prospect, that process is fragile. Yet, envisaged in retrospect, when its resolves are firm, so strong is its devotion to creation that the self can arrest creation only by falling into radical opposition to creation, into lethargy, confusion, and fragmentation. There are no alternatives. The division between options is sharp and unyielding.

But when, by the relentless strength of its effort, the self allows itself to be lifted toward its own rebirth and the efflorescence of novel forms from within it, it presents itself as *transparently united* in its primordial commitment to create —and this with respect, first to its variegated powers, but, at bottom, to its own divine ground. For the self expresses itself through this illumined presence within itself as luminous with forms, the symbols of its own activity: forms which, no sooner are they externalized than, in their very externality, they are related to and even identified with. Thus grasping its own transparency, and externalizing transparency as diverse and equally transparent motions, the self achieves veridical self-identity, an achievement which, as it is approached, creates of self-searching an activity which is spontaneous and free.

B • THE SELF-AFFIRMING SELF

(*a*) Birthings of the Self

Freedom is ambiguous. Always the self falls back into itself. How readily it is immersed in the very forms from which it struggles to disengage itself. Narcissism, its ever-threatening nemesis, can be averted only when the self assumes the burden of its own creative movement. How stubborn a resolve is required; how stark the will to sacrifice the trivial and the vacuous; how much the inessential must be pruned; how many seductive harmonies of life must be renounced; what risks of failure must in humility be accepted.

To avoid narcissism, the self must, by diremption, allow the crystallizing strands of its own motions forcibly to separate themselves. They must be permitted to shape their emergent forms into a rugged fabric, a manifold of forms which, in this efflux from the self's labyrinthine recesses, the self must again and again confront. By encountering its own flowings forth, and in progressively drawing forth from its inmost depths the manifestation and reality of spirit, the self acquires, through successive metamorphoses, a stubborn, inviolable individuality. Thus working through the self, and efflorescing into myriad shapes, tones, and hues, spirit confronts itself: its inner dynamic, its possibilities for subsequent growth, its ground, its source. From within itself, spirit has, through mediation of the self, formed numberless products. Gradually, in its emerging moments, spirit divests itself of its own latent content. With Hegel, I affirm: "self-consciousness enriches itself till it has torn from consciousness the entire substance, and absorbed into itself the entire structure of the substance with all its constituent elements."[5] Therein assimilated, the self brings to fruition, and to the fullness of presence, its own spiritual ground, a ground itself rooted in the cosmic matrix of intertwined selves.

Yet, again and again, the byways of the journey through the stages of personal existence lead every self toward self-alienation. Weighing down the self, such alienation must ever be conquered anew. Pregnant with new moments in its own development, the self extrudes each moment, and projects it onto an enlarged perception of reality. Momentarily, the self thereby exhausts itself. Separated from its replenishing sources, its activity ceases. Regressive withdrawals ensue, withdrawals into mere passive entertainment of the kaleidoscopic flux of the shadows of the self's creations. Endangered by narcissism, the self no longer experiences reality as newly woven with its own detached products. Ceasing to encounter reality as it authentically is, the self prefers to dwell vicariously in a more secure substitutive realm, a reality which is distorted and diminished: a phantasmagoria formed of diffracted images which themselves are shaped from the self's creativity.

Yet the self's power to reaffirm itself remains viable and energetic. In making manifest what had been immanent, its characteristic invariant was made explicit: namely, the power of self-affirmation. Now the self adds this invariant to a spiritualized, "transcendentalized" nature, a nature which the self has shaped. And since the cosmos is a community of interpenetrating, mutually reinforcing selves and quasi-selves, such invariance pervades the cosmos. On this power, every creature will inscribe its own ornamentation; what had been invariant is destined to be but a variation on an altogether new theme. But, though the "face of the universe" is perpetually changing, it abides, and preserves, as etched upon its durable contours, the multitude of themes woven into it. Every particular self holds dialogue with this orchestration—a polyphony within which it, as itself a participant, never, *sub specie aeternitatis*, suffers diminished importance. The very process by which the self creates, and thereby affirms, in every phase of its development, a mode of integrity appropriate to that phase, is intrinsically dialogic. Conditioned throughout a self's unfolding by a just balance among its constituent elements, and between itself and other selves, this process expresses the self's striving toward its fulfillment in wisdom. In dialogue, the self continually discovers itself anew. Always it finds its later phases of growth reflected, by prefigurement, in the earlier phases exhibited by other selves, as, likewise, it finds its earlier phases reflected, by refinement, in the later phases of other selves. From the standpoint of their every stage, selves commune with one another. Through communion woven of numberless dialogues, all selves advance toward wisdom. Such reciprocal mirroring, as interchange of content latent or content objectified, pervades every cosmic realm. Young and old commune; persons and infra-persons commune; plant and animal commune; the animate and the inanimate commune —each in ways and degrees appropriate to its cosmic station. For, at nature's very origins, immanent reflexivity is actively at work, germinating throughout the natural universe as nature progressively idealizes itself. Yet, at the end of the process, in the realm of the transcendental, nature herself is ever reborn. A spiritual ferment is the engendering matrix whence spring all phenomena: both appearance and reality.

By the complementary activities of externalization and dialogue, the self empties itself of its carefully nurtured content. Compressed unconsciously in the self each image, prior to its birth, condenses a vast storehouse of potentially efflorescing forms. Manifesting themselves in both dream and fantasy, these unborn configurations which, once birthed, replicate the self's main lineaments, suffuse its entire being and condition its every act. Once, through diremption, an image has diversified itself in the forcible separation, by the self's birthing acts, of its component strands, and their progressive externalization and objectification, the self experiences emptiness and loneliness. In crisis, it wanders, restless yet immobilized, amid its still unborn images, and among the appearances and façades of other selves who are likewise engaged. Turning hither and thither, with neither purpose nor intent, it remains both with and within itself: self-absorbed, self-preoccupied, directionless, seeking succor. Ever yearning for new fulfillment, the self must await resolution of its crisis. Yet it wanders in the night; it knows only how to distract itself. Turning toward its own body, it seeks sexual gratification. Craving tenderness and care, it seeks to complete itself in its complement, man or woman. And, surely, for a brief instant, lovers may enjoy a perfect moment of simulated eternity. Fraught with possible illusion, and even self-delusion, this complemental relationship, when it itself has been brought to fruition, is nonetheless like a cocoon which prepares the chrysalis for its own metamorphosis.

(*b*) Risk and Relinquishment

Having given to another, whether singular creature or all nature, what it alone uniquely shapes, and having given through this gift its very self, the self craves a reciprocal gift of equivalent value. Until reciprocity is complete, it must experience radical emptiness. For, in giving, initially without reciprocity, it has indeed emptied itself. At this moment, a dramatic choice must be made. Either the self primarily commits itself to a quest for personal harmony, a life of humane giving and receiving, and such a life includes sexual complementarity, or it primarily commits itself to the quest for wisdom. Personal quest entails joyous dependency on personal friendship, love, care, affirmation. In it, the self devotes its energies to perfecting its mode of experiencing justice and integrity. But the quest for wisdom requires the willingness to renounce, should life's contingencies so demand, a tranquil resting in justice and integrity. The self's essential aim, its all-consuming purpose, is to know wherein consists wisdom and to seek to shape itself as wisdom incarnate. For one must so content oneself with "the coming of wisdom with time," that one may, with Yeats, affirm:

> Though leaves are many, the root is one;
> Through all the lying days of my youth
> I swayed my leaves and flowers in the sun;
> Now I may wither into the truth.[6]

For every person there is "the choice":

> The intellect of man is forced to choose
> Perfection of the life, or of the work,

And if it take the second must refuse
A heavenly mansion, raging in the dark.[7]

And that person must risk the consequences:

When all that story's finished, what's the news?
In luck or out the toil has left its mark:
That old perplexity an empty purse,
Or the day's vanity, the night's remorse.[8]

But the risk is even greater, and this risk is the burden each must bear: each who quests after wisdom by shaping from his soul a work in which he strives to make wisdom incarnate. At every moment of his quest, he must be prepared to receive a message from another "to a friend whose work has come to nothing."

Now all the truth is out,
Be secret and take defeat
From any brazen throat,
For how can you compete,
Being honour bred, with one
Who, were it proved he lies,
Were neither shamed in his own
Nor in his neighbor's eyes?
Bred to a harder thing
Than Triumph, turn away
And like a laughing string
Whereon mad fingers play
Amid a place of stone,
Be secret and exult,
Because of all things known
That is most difficult.[9]

Yet, though the choice be ever so firm, and quest for wisdom be its strongest intent, no person can refrain from turning away from the task, moment by moment in its arduous pursuit, to ask a token, a mark, a sign—evidence concrete and immediate that he, a person and thus a questing person, and, as such, a seeker who has taken the harder path, is worthy and acceptable. Still, should this symbol of affirmation be denied him, as often by life's diminishing opportunities it must, then he must again turn inward and, in the still dawn of renewal, recommence, without the grace of another's gift, the work which he had begun. By his primordial renunciation, he must, in the end, inspire his own creativity. Falling back upon itself, in its inmost and ownmost solitude, the self seeks ever anew to redeem itself. Falling back not only *upon* itself but, more deeply, *into* itself—should a higher grace touch it and by that touch envelop it—the self discovers what it had perhaps already faintly perceived as resident in its own depths. For, to echo Hegel, the quester seeks to end his own existence within his very substance as quester.[10] And in the darkness of his solitude, he continues to shape new objects. Fashioning thereby a new fabric of relations, he comes, in solitude, to dwell more securely in this fabric.

But where a self truly dwells is in the interstices between itself, as it ever creates and ever quests, and that which it had hitherto formed but which, by its own dynamism, it has now newly woven into a still richer texture. Horizons for novel objectification can be extended indefinitely. Yet in this process, and in this progression, not only does the self feel the immediacies of merely external encounter, however beguiling these be, but, in addition, and beyond these objects, it intuits the grounding empathies of internally conjoined selves, that immanent matrix of interwoven selves which underlies its every act: the very ground which catalyzes and inspires all selves, each in its separate journey, to shape a community, inner and outer, a community of true communicants. But, lest it become too fascinated to proceed from past object to new object, the self must not linger with *any* particular object. Making its own substance both object and content, it "supersedes this distinction of objectivity and content."[11] And supersession requires that the self split itself asunder. In crisis, momentarily or prolongedly, it fragments its own content. To resolve crisis, it must purge itself of fragmentation: of the haunting, still unborn, split-off images, images which constrain the spontaneity of the emerging *I*, and threaten so to diffuse its potency that, again, the *I* will non-creatively dwell within itself.

Yet purgation involves not merely an emptying of fragments. It requires, in addition, a total feeling of the very process of birthing: the anguish, the ecstasy, the tragically imminent collapse into unbirthed imagery. Beyond this, *what* the self has purged itself of, as it extrudes images, and converts them into encounterable objects, requires systematic articulation. To complete the birthing act, the self must draw forth the entire content, a whole manifold of immanence in process of self-transcendence: drawn forth cogently, consistently, comprehensively, coherently, and in a manner adequate to the creative surge. In short, the self now orients itself toward what it has birthed in a *philosophic* fashion. It perceives how its own creations contribute authentically to the larger cosmic scheme. By this perception, the self enables itself to proceed ever further into its own interiority. By this self-penetration, it defies its own limits; it dissolves limits which, hitherto, it had experienced as impossible of dissolution. Descending into its own substance, the self now ascends with a "captured" potentiality: an image held captive as objective, and possessing an externalizable content. Surely, this dialectic of ascent and descent, this perception of limits coupled with the relentless pressing back of limits, constitutes the vision jointly entertained—the one *in concreto*, the other *in abstracto*—by Dante and by Hegel.

Yet the *I* is "afraid of relinquishing or externalizing itself."[12] Resisting this process, it may even induce repression with respect to its own emerging forms; and should repression be sufficiently massive, regression might ensue, regression to an earlier and now inappropriate phase of its creative activity. In this perverse context, aborted or archaic quasi-creations are fashioned. In an extreme instance, the self comes to dwell among its own hallucinations, those projected images of its insufficiently absorbed experience. Like festering sores, dissociated complexes inhabit unconscious regions of the troubled self. Yet the self's power to purge itself even of these potent pathogens remains viable. As when in mourning the self becomes absorbed with memories of the grieved person, acutely feeling the loss and, hence, proceeding in detailed fashion over every memory until, one by one, by purgation, and in a sort of creative fervor, these haunting voices have been stilled, so the troubled self must allow its constricting imagery to perish. And in perishing, objectified memory traces immortalize themselves in every newly constituted fabric of reality. Indeed, as Hegel declared, "The power of spirit lies . . . in remaining one with itself when giving up itself, and, because it is self-contained and self-subsistent, in establishing as mere moments its explicit self-existence as well as its implicit inherent nature."[13] For the multifarious distinctions which the self draws forth from the "abyss of the Absolute,"[14] its own inmost grounding depths, neither are cast back into that abyss, therein to lose all significance as distinctions, nor remain in abeyance, suspended midway between their originating source and their destined external shape. Quite the contrary. The wholesome self purges itself of the very distinctions which it fashions for and within itself. In self-emptying, it achieves veridical freedom. Only when the power of spirit to remain "one with itself when giving up itself"[15] is impeded, and indeed depotentiated, is freedom compromised, and the self determined by factors alien to it, including those factors, arising within the self, which refuse to allow themselves to be born.

(*c*) Perishing and Renewal

The final crisis is the crisis of dying. Herein lies the ultimate, and the consummate, emptying of the self. Though each particular act of dying is absolutely singular, it need not, in principle, be utterly private. Just as every crisis achieves resolution implicitly in dialogue, that empathic communion *from within* of self with selves, so the paradigmatic crisis is immanently shared. Yet ought not this crisis of crises to be explicitly witnessed by those who love the dying one, hence, profoundly shared? Ought not all humanity to bear witness to every dying act? For does not that act represent, condensed into the concrete yet universal symbolism of this unique dying human being, the very destiny and fruition of humankind? Do not human beings tend to avoid any vestige of this crisis, which they themselves are inexorably destined to experience, and thereby diminish their own humanity? To augment rather than to diminish *human* being, ought not this most momentous crisis, that which, enveloped by mystery, subsumes, comprehends, and goes beyond all crises, to be participated in by fellow human beings in sacramental fashion, the very fruition of all personal communion? Surely, these final moments of an existence are fraught with significance; surely, they are of a magnitude portentous in ways which surpass all understanding but that of wisdom's final moment, a moment which is revealed only by grace to the privileged few among the dying. Ought not this singular act of dying wherein a person does not so much terminate as, ideally, fulfill the promise of his birth, and initiate his entry into mysteries beyond mystery, to be consecrated by rites which supersede all rites? Conceive the celebration of the passage from the temporal to the eternal in chants neither of joy nor of sorrow, but of a sacred quality which transcends both joy and sorrow. Might not this dying act be authentically construed as a rebirth which is more than a re-birth, as, in actuality, a new baptism, and hence to be consecrated by chants which resemble passages from Beethoven's C-Sharp Minor Quartet or from the Cavatina of his B-Flat Major Quartet? For this new baptism portends significances far beyond the intensities and depths of original baptism: it is the rite of passage to the great beyond. Dying is paradigmatic of the sacredness of all crises. Hence, fellow human beings ought to bear witness to every dying act; they ought to utter paean upon paean, in delicately, subtly nuanced tones of consummately orchestrated finesse. For a life has been brought to its fruition in anguished solitude. Yet a life ends on notes which are neither of anguish nor of solitude; and the consecration of each ending requires appropriate ode and pageantry.

Only by dwelling fully within itself can the *I* fully find itself! For the self experiences its freedom when, at one and the same time, it feels itself as both feeling subject and felt object. Only then does it experience the fruition of its own spiritual estate. Now alone can it affirm its freedom as its very own self objectified, knowing, with Hegel, "that what it has been producing all along is itself, that the process of concretizing its object is the object's process of self-concretization."[16] In this concrete becoming consist both the *being* of the self and its *doing*. By the self's ineluctable emptying, wherein this entire process culminates, the tragic experience arises. Yet never does the wholesome self lose its bond with its own inner ferment, no matter how attenuated that bond might become. In the end, the self enhances itself through relating itself to all its continually augmented self-produced objects. Herein, tragedy is transformed into ecstasy. In ever-expanding, ever–self-enriching spiralings, ecstasy and tragedy dialectically interweave their content. Implicitly, through their internal relationships, persons witness, for every particular journey of the self, this self-liberating dialectic. One can envisage the concrete embodiment of this witnessing in a great rhythmic dance or in the welling up of poetry and song. Herein consists the validity of the Oresteia, that great pronouncement on the unfolding of justice, integrity, and wisdom; herein, too, consists the larger import of the Greek Olympiads, that great celebration of the union of spirit and body. This augmentation, an ever-increasing assemblage of selves intertwined—selves which are self-creating and, as such, sacramentally witnessed—is the central, definitive human consecration whence spring all sacraments: each a μίμησις of the archetypal sacrament, the witnessing participation of a particular act of dying.

As the self plunges into its own inward depths, it suffers a momentary loss. As it emerges, it potentiates its powers anew. And at this very instant of self-relinquishment, the self grasps itself more concretely as implicated in relationships not only of asymmetry with the objects fashioned by others as well as by itself, but, more significantly, of mutuality with other selves. To achieve this end—namely, interrelatedness—the self must know how to sacrifice itself. With Hegel, I affirm: "This sacrifice is the self-abandonment, in which Spirit sets forth, in the form of free fortuitous happening, its process of becoming Spirit. . . ."[17] Nature, construed as Spinoza's *natura naturata*, is the externalized manifestation of this great process. But, at this point, with Hegel, I must add: "Spirit leaves its external existence behind and gives its embodiment over to Recollection. . . ."[18] For, now, it "is engulfed in the night of its own self-consciousness; its vanished" —and vanquished—"existence . . . conserved therein . . . but born anew . . . is a new world . . . a new embodiment or mode of Spirit."[19]

To conserve experience, indeed condensing it, re-collection constitutes a new gathering together of what had already imprinted itself upon the self; but it is a gathering together in which new combinations of former memory traces are shaped, whereupon fresh energies are liberated, energies which heretofore had been bound, hence unavailable to spur the self's own further growth. By these novel syntheses, the self is freed to enjoy hitherto unforeseen, unenvisageable immediacies: seemingly miraculous forms of existence which the spiritual ferment, Spinoza's *natura naturans*, is empowered to assume. Now a new self-revelation discloses "the empire of the spiritual world";[20] and the self is prepared to undertake ever more fragile, delicate, and enriching tasks. As Hegel declared: "it took time . . . for spirit to recognize that what seemed to be a *taking in* from outside is in truth a *positing* from within."[21] Through release, in re-collection, of fresh stores of energy—though these energies, too, must be cautiously guarded —altogether new realms of being may be fashioned. For the "human spirit has progressively canceled out a whole world of objectivity 'out there' in order to re-create it within itself,"[22] disclosing ever new depths. Indeed, re-membering (Hegel's *Er-innerung*) entails probing the very ground of the self, and opening up new paths toward that ground. Now, the self gives birth to marvelous new accomplishments. For, in touching his own ground, man touches God, infinite reservoir of spiritual energy. Thereupon, he achieves modalities of concreteness and relatedness, strengthenings of his own individuality, before which he can only stand amazed. In wonder and in awe, persons are endlessly empowered to create!

C • THE SELF-CONSUMMATING SELF

(*a*) The Ontology of Unrequited Love

Throughout my account of crisis, I have recurred to the theme of tragedy. Tragedy haunts the universe. It lurks in every ultimate metaphysical entity. Endowed with the tragic, each man strives to eternalize in another what is but transitory in himself. By inexorable intervention of his existence *sub specie durationis*, the communions grounded in his existence *sub specie aeternitatis* fail. The more intense the quest to immortalize *all* elements of an existence, not only as they may be absorbed into the being of another but especially as perpetuated sui generis, the greater the suffering, the more pervasive the tragedy. This ineluctable cosmic tragedy has two sources: first, owing to intrinsic flaws deriving from the finitude of an existent, one cannot give oneself in *absolute* perfection; secondly, because the demand for reciprocation pervades every giving, though this demand may be minimal, the poignancy of existence is heightened—it stems from an intrinsic disparity between human need and human fulfillment. Yet one's propensity toward giving is partly activated and even sustained by reciprocation. This wish for reciprocation is an element, perhaps the most salient, in one's need to assimilate the nature of the other to one's own nature, to find congruities between their essences so that in trust one can continue to present oneself and to know that one's gift will be received. For one believes that what is wholly other, strange, and awesome cannot by its nature welcome these tokens of one's endeavor to perpetuate one's own being. It cannot receive the imprint of the model of perfection, which one never ceases to design as symbolic of one's inmost being, of what one was meant to become by a dynamism peculiar to one's nature alone.

As existing *sub specie durationis*, a person is partially bound; free giving is impeded. He seeks acceptance from that which is familiar, inviting, and like himself. He fears to step forth into an abyss of wonder, to acknowledge in a boldness of giving what may be great and terrible and reproving. Yet though Job answered God, "I . . . have . . . uttered that I understood not; things too wonderful for me, which I knew not" (Jb 42:3), he had already been told by the Lord, "Deck thyself now with majesty and excellency; and array thyself with glory and beauty" (Jb 40:10). Durational existence may be so transcended that giving becomes for an instant of eternity wholly free, and the donor indeed majestic in his strength; and it is an instant which may surely be extended, depending on that strength. At this moment, he incorporates energies of his "complement"—ideally a loving mate, by diminution a natural object—as it is woven with his being in primordial sharing; he draws from the infinite reservoir which nourishes this complex the power continually to symbolize within each of its components a perfect replica of his existence. For that instant of eternity, a man participates in a world which presents itself to him as a divine, eternal, and perfect presence, of which, in his durational status, he is a temporal and finite emanation.

Though evanescent, romantic love is a paradigm of communion. Not by a mere trick of the imagination, a projective fantasy in which the illusion of a past is transferred to the reality of the present, is the loved one idealized. Rather, an actual vision of the perfection which lies, perhaps dormant, within her suffuses the beholder (in this instance, a man—though the sexual roles of lover and beloved may, *mutatis mutandis*, be reversed) and sustains the communion by which each becomes for that moment of eternity incorruptibly beautiful, a vibrant and glowing presence. In a community of perfections, each gives without need for reward; the trust of each in each is absolute. Two become as one—even, indeed, when full reciprocation by the beloved may be lacking, though when it is present, a more authentic prefiguring of the "in-Godding" of man is achieved. The creativity in which the perfection of the beloved is drawn forth but anticipates a supreme act of self-creation wherein the lover becomes totally absorbed in his inner and outer modalities of existence, attaining self-perfection in community with his perfect complement. But this evocation of a perfect image of the beloved, and its fusion with the self to form a more harmonious being, so that one then glows, self-created, with one's own perfection, is tragically short-lived. It dies in agony. Whether it be loss of the feeling or loss of its object, each must be mourned. The image of that which was loved may be denounced or forgotten or displaced by another image; in none of these possibilities has it truly "perished" into the being of the one who has loved. In none is mourning complete. To be absorbed fully so that mourning is consummated, thence transcended, the image must be fully affirmed.

Yet the way toward an enlargement, a deepening, a perfecting of the person of the lover, by his weaving of this image into the fabric of his being, is fraught with pain. First ruminating upon the image, he then draws upon all his powers to blend it with other images left in the wake of experiences which have traced themselves upon his existence from earliest years, until the components of each become indistinguishable from those of all; and a center of symbolic activity is fashioned from which one can transform elements of these traces into those new symbols through which, in art and music and in the poetry of life itself, one can again commune with one's fellows. The journey is long and terrible. There is no short-cut. It is as though the entire world has been contained in the beloved (in this instance, a woman). She was the center whence radiated all life; all that is not of her being now recedes into a background drab and meaningless. This persistent memory drives the unrequited lover to loneliness, loneliness which is intense and unremitting. As lover, one feels oneself to be radically severed from one's own destiny, which was to present the beloved's perfect image, evoked in her actual presence, to oneself as mirroring one's own perfection. One must now rejoin one's destiny; one strives to recapture and make durable the authenticity of one's bond to a world in which the center is displaced from a particular entity to the actual source of all existence. This task requires a new birth. Its pangs are felt within the entire range of human emotion. Each feeling is pure and intensified, of extraordinary clarity: joy, sorrow, jealousy, despair, remorse, envy, anger, guilt, bitterness, loneliness, melancholy, desire, tenderness, selflessness. Each must be felt in depth, and woven into symbolism. Therein the lover re-creates his own being. Henceforth, he can in pride and in joy draw fully upon his gift thus to bring forth the more perfect selves concealed amid the veils of those who have walked through life among the shadows, joyless and without peace.

The temptation to draw back from this journey and to withdraw the image into oblivion, by whatever device, is powerful and relentless. The way is paved with remorse that *demands* for reciprocation were insufficiently relinquished. But remorse is woven with gratitude to the beloved for having inspired, evoked, and perhaps accepted the gift of his love. Profound and indefeasible gratitude transforms his existence. The distant vision of perfection, an exalted completion of his being, as the lover imagines himself to dwell at last in a peace which requires no sacrifice of individuality, its cadences of exuberance, strength, and joy integral to his existence—this haunting vision drives him forward. With each step, an inner light and a pervasive warmth grow more intense until, at last, should the lover be among the happy few, grace will befall him. This arduous way is traversed only as the lover draws the beloved's images into symbols which he never ceases to enlarge and perfect, in whatever medium his powers best express themselves. For symbolism reflects the binding together of the fragments of an existence, the fruition of its inherent sensitivity. These chords of responsiveness vibrate within a matrix now organized into a sturdy structure. Imposed from within, such discipline never dampens the melodies of life. Rather, it promotes their richer growth, their more harmonious interpenetration. Romantic love is the initial phase of a journey in which a lover, striving for his own completion by his union with the beloved—transitory, yet prefiguring a final wholeness—moves toward his own *self*-completion by fusing the disjoined parts of himself, his sensitivity firmly wedded to his sturdiness.

By this symbolism, I mean the true presentation of oneself, the fashioning of a life into a poem at every instant of a human existence. In a poem, indeed, I bring forth something new from the interior quiet of my being, something by which I can more indissolubly unite myself to that ever-expanding world into which I thrust myself: a world, in part, my own creation. In endless listening and addressing, I purify my being. To combat the forces which would deafen me to my inmost voice, my efforts to symbolize must be stubborn. By my sensitivity, I envisage possibilities; by my sturdiness, I seize them. My power to choose never ceases. The choice is absolute. Either I opt for renunciation—a sinking toward fragmentation, dissolution, and decay—or I opt for affirmation. There can be no lingering among any images save as a momentary dwelling to savor that which renews strength. Yet when the taste of memory grows bitter, I must go on. And as I move along this path, new vistas unfold. A wider reality opens to my astonished eyes. In miraculous rebirth, my very self draws itself into ever-greater perfections; the world itself is transformed. Again and again, I weave, in the wake of my journeyings, a new fabric of symbols. Layer upon layer, in endless terraces, are traced on the contours of reality. Lest I close off a vital part of my existence, the novelties which inhere in each moment must be fully expressed. But by my finitude, my vigilance tragically cannot be absolute. It is not a simple endeavor, this struggling which leads toward the light; it is the wholehearted welcoming, the willing acceptance, of all pain and joy as, unresisted, they flow through me, through this wanderer whose journey never ends. Yet all of reality newly reveals itself to my astonished eye: a miracle in which my self and my reality are reborn.

(*b*) The Complementarity of Man and Woman

In the tragic experience, man fails, by his finitude, to clarify his proper boundaries. He does not wish to pass, in death, to a realm so different from all he knows as to incite his terror and his awe. He would, accordingly, negate this finitude. In perpetual self–re-creation, of which the paradigm is romantic love—the complementarity of man and woman—he strives to grasp his true perfection in relationship to the true perfection of the beloved, which each reciprocally draws forth. He is urged by his inmost depths ceaselessly to give birth to a perfect replica of himself within the other, a replica by which he seeks immortality. As he holds before him this model as embedded in the other, the embedded model mirrors his own perfect self-image. Contrasting its perfection with his actual imperfection, he strives thereby to join himself to it. And synthesizing into a more perfect existence the diversified elements which compose his *given* existence, he attunes himself more harmoniously to the rhythms of creation. Yet one's finitude demands decision; but one chain of possibilities may be actualized. There exists within each person a primordial urge to organize into a unity and to cause to blossom forth a fruition of his existence, in all its varied dimensions. This "transcendental"[23] *I* is a voice within to which one strives to listen at each moment of decision, so that the choice is strongly in conformity with one's nature; and should one attune oneself to its message, it is an *I* which is progressively drawn into the realm of an ever-enlarging "empirical"[24] *I*—those ever-shifting fragments of selfhood—which only, however, *sub specie aeternitatis* coincides with it. Tragedy thus arises from an essential incongruity between "transcendental" *I* and "empirical" *I*.

I have referred to the complementarity between man and woman. Between them, radical differences prevail, in both the psychic and the physical spheres. Fundamental to any metaphysics of the person, these differences require specification. Yet every attempt to articulate them leads to confusion, paradox, and, given the incredible diversity of human culture, frank error. Still, it is useful to formulate paradigms for tentatively understanding complementarity. For they may enable us at least to adumbrate its ontologic significance. Here, I merely raise questions, in order to suggest, in a sort of mythic way, a plausible, if not true, mode of conceptualizing the contrasts between male rhythms and female rhythms.

While men and women share the essence of humankind, each inscribes special themes upon that essence. Resolving tensions doubtlessly engendered by their differences, both sexes complete themselves through union, within each sex, so it appears, of principles, however they be formulated, of masculinity and femininity. Might I not legitimately ask: Is the self-sufficiency of woman intrinsically greater than that of man? Does her existence exemplify an at-homeness in community and relationship which, in some profound way, man lacks? By a plausible metaphor, do her rhythms tend toward the rounded, the mellow, the flowing? Do they thereupon curve back upon themselves to form a complete circle, a kind of unity? On the other hand, does man exhibit rhythms which, on the whole, are sharp, angular, jutting? Is he, somehow, like an arrow which points tautly toward a distant beyond? Receptive to multiple stimuli arising from countless regions, is he, at the same time, more vulnerable to destruction? By nature a fragmented creature who strives to complete his existence in the realm of the spirit, does man embody a principle of soaring and individuation? And, in general, may not so many exceptions to any speculation be discovered regarding man–woman differences as to invalidate the very thrust of these questions?

Certainly, both man and woman dance, speak, and sing in tones which intrinsically interweave. However formulated, the primordial contours of each, man or woman, integrally inscribe themselves on the primordial contours of the other. At bottom, the two modes of expression so profoundly complement one another that man and woman often seem in essence to be indistinguishable. In later books, I shall amplify the tentative distinctions I propose here in order to suggest that, though clearly and deeply similar, man and woman exhibit intrinsic differences: differences so to be construed that neither person, man or woman, constitutes a diminution of the other, and the natural propensities of each so complement those of the other that the essences of womanhood and manhood commingle to shape a single, unitary, and integral *quintessential* ground of human being.

Now I propose an hypothesis merely to map out terrain for exploration, rather than make implicit claim for universal validity. Man and woman, according to this hypothesis, each seeks to immortalize himself, by a style and in a manner indigenous to his special nature. Whereas man aims at spiritual integration, an aim seldom achieved, woman completes herself in an extension of her physical substance, and, indeed, by virtue of her empathic likeness to the mother, from whose presence man, to achieve his male identity, must more radically separate himself. Nonetheless, since woman also quests after her own distinctive identity, she surely penetrates the very recesses of spirit which, by his intrinsic limits, man is ever *compelled*, owing to an inner emptiness, to seek to penetrate. For does not the power to bear children, or the lack of that power, as well as the nature of the primary bond of child to mother, confer profound differences upon man and woman? Are not the spiritual repercussions of that power, or its lack, and the character of that bond, deep and pervasive? Might not woman, contrary to man, possess a sort of double identity: one associated with her unique capacity, one associated with the maternal bond which she shares with man? And if so, could her ontologic security not be grounded on the very base whence springs man's ontologic insecurity? Contrariwise, does not the fact that both man and woman quest after freedom from mother confer upon each, when the bond has been shattered and impetus to shape an identity spurred, that resistance against which alone creative powers can surge into symbolic expression? Finally, does not a certain parity obtain between man and woman with respect to their mutual self-*in*sufficiencies? For, whereas man's *loneliness*, aggravated by his radical severance from mother though occasionally tempered by a later compensatory relationship to a woman mate, provides that resistance, does not woman's *emptiness*, intensified by no such compensatory relationship though abetted by her primordial (and never wholly dissolved) empathic identificatory tie with mother, provide analogous resistance?

In procreation and child-rearing, woman establishes substantive continuity between one generation and another. Such continuity reverberates in the realm of her spirit, binding its elements into unity. Yet the *physical* impact in the woman of the transformations through which she passes—menstruation, pregnancy, nursing—is dramatic and profound. All physical factors are mobilized in her intense cyclic rhythms. Ideally, man's strength ought to catalyze and support this activity. For woman requires him to confer a structure on her acts, and to respond to her needs in a manner which is sturdy and disciplined, but always reassuring. Man aids her to sustain her cyclicity, and to bring it to fruition. Reciprocally, by *her* strength, woman inspires *his* creativity. It is not that she is less capable than he of creating in artistic or other symbolic media; and hardly that her intellectual or spiritual competencies are, in any remote fashion, inferior to his; nor that she is not subject to unsettling discontent. Rather, for her, a primary mode of completion, though not an exclusive mode, but a mode which surely affects her symbolic activity, is through her children, and through her peculiar gift for human relatedness; and always, beyond that gift, through the urge to symbolize it in spiritual ways. From this point of view, man inspires *her* creativity. And, reciprocally, woman provides that matrix of community within which alone both man and woman can survive. Man, on the other hand, senses his special, radical isolation, his need to return, again and again, to this matrix for nourishment and inspiration. And the memory of this journey back persists. As man passes from infancy through adulthood, he enacts a cycle of return to the feminine center and source of his very being; thence he adventures toward a periphery far from the feminine. Whereas her cycle occurs in the "space" within, insofar as one of her identities is bound up with her profound physicality, his cycle takes place by his movements in a space without, as, likewise, does hers insofar as another of her identities arises from the same source as his.

Restlessly inventive—the more intensely, owing to his *single* identity—man transmutes his need for succour into a power of creating a symbolic substitute for procreation, nutrition, and primary feminine empathy with mother. Questing after identity with father, man roots himself more radically than woman in an unknown beyond. For her, the mother–father–child dialectic is more complicated. For she must hover midway, as it were, between mother, from whom she must free herself, while retaining a special empathy, and father, with whom, owing to her intrinsic difference, she cannot wholly and comfortably identify. Her rebellion—hence, her independence—from both father and mother is correspondingly more intricate than that of the man. And for man's part, cut off from a source of energy which lies without, either by his natural movements or by his ejection from the nourishing matrix, he both discovers and reinforces that source as center of energy within. By drawing its energies into those symbolic forms which, by his endowment, he is capable of engendering, he perpetually repotentiates the new center.

When the glow of complementarity diminishes, a glow which is most intense in romantic love, the urgency of a choice of a way of life becomes sharp and insistent. In futile quest for reinstatement of complementarity, man may seek substitutive gratification. Or, by his symbolisms, he may soar into realms which are strange, novel, awesome. But only when the wound of radical severance from his beloved has healed, and the hurt has been absorbed, can he fully cultivate the "feminine" within himself. An act of self-transcendence, a spiritual rebirth, is initiated whereby he achieves self-completion in the inner harmony of the work to which he is loyal and which alone can abolish his loneliness. Thus he may come to stand beyond need, in that pervasive calm which transcends both joy and pain; thus he may no longer be susceptible to rebuff or despair. Likewise, severed from man, woman must regenerate her own substance, either by reinstating her essentially complete physicality and her instinctive affinity for community, or by transmuting either capability, each peculiar to her essential being, that she might attain the spiritual heights for the symbolic expression of which she, equally, is endowed.

But the bond between man and woman is for each a mystery. By nature, men and women are strangers as well as intimates. Ineluctably, a dialectic of apartness and unity prevails. Yet, within their bond, each strives to resolve the tension created by their intrinsic alienation; and their quest for self-completion continues. In reaching toward one another, man and woman may each therein achieve transcendence, a harmony which does not stultify individuality but, surely, enhances it. When the miraculous glow is present between them, neither needs his fulfillment in any other way; both attain to transitory self-completion. But as the glow fades, woman turns to the great cycle of birth and rebirth. And she may momentarily subordinate to that cycle her own creative impulse toward other symbolic media, though she never extinguishes that impulse; and she looks to man to activate and reactivate the cycle. Unless he deadens himself to woman's interior rhythms, man, in turn, creates the symbols by which he compensates, in the sphere of the spiritual, for his impotence in the sphere of the physical. By nature, he cannot perpetuate, save as a germ, his physical substance. Hence, in spirit, he moves beyond the loneliness inherent in an awareness of his finitude. For man's creativity begins when he departs from the sense of wholeness first experienced in childhood, then recaptured in his bond to a woman, a vision in which he ever seeks to recapitulate the primordial reality whence that bond derived. When he thus separates himself from this source, as though it were the eternally self-renewing center of his life, and he passes into the finite, he experiences, as though death were pressing down upon him, the cruel loneliness of his limits. Then, as by a miracle, a new center becomes accessible, a center within man himself, yet a center linked to the cosmic source from which spring the intrinsic powers of all entities. But when the work of symbolic activity, in whatever medium, ceases, man and woman again search for a new glow which will afford an interlude and an inspiration for renewed work.

The truest friendship, though not the most constant, is that of man and woman. Loyalty and respect for their indefeasible differences are woven into a fabric composed of tenderness and passion. Of this friendship Yeats declared from the standpoint of the man:

A man may find in no man
A friendship of her kind
That covers all he has brought
As with her flesh and bone,
Nor quarrels with a thought
Because it is not her own.

Though pedantry denies,
It's plain the Bible means
That Solomon grew wise
While talking with his queens. . . .[25]

And this wisdom comes when the lover first "dreams of your image that blossoms a rose in the deeps of my heart,"[26] then transforms the fragile rose into an image more akin to a great oak which protects the very earth from which it derives its sustenance. For the woman is empowered to engender new substance, while the man can create only symbols extracted from it. Her vibrancy, quiet, and warmth are absorbed into the stillness of his depths, then joined to his manly mysteries to renew his inspiration. But man's existence is ineluctably tragic. And the tragedy is surely more his than hers. For woman readily attains a sort of immortality by a symbol which *intimately* expresses her nature and physically duplicates it, whereas man is driven to perpetuate himself in symbols which, though they perish again and again into his being, remain nonetheless intrinsically alien to his nature. Yet, equally, woman's mysteries require inspiration by man. And once she has been freed from dependence for her own security upon her power both to procreate and communally to relate, woman, too, seeks her new identity in symbols which, likewise, soar toward unprobed heights. Accordingly, to speak, with tradition, of woman as earth-bound and man as sky-oriented is, up to a point, true. But, to recur to my earlier proposal: woman's nature being double, by the very complexities of her relationship to mother and father, as well as by her own biologic propensity, she is, at once, woven of earth and sky. And, in general, the intricacies of human ontology, which (to begin with) involves concatenated, interwoven personal rhythms of the most variegated kinds, immeasurably compound themselves by their inheritance of the specific ontologic differences between man and woman.

(*c*) The Sanctity of Love

"Wing to wing and oar to oar." So inscribed Robert Frost upon his wife's tombstone: two reeds, masculine and feminine, side by side, neither intertwined nor in any way enmeshed, but flowing with the wind, occasionally touching in gentle, tender caress, neither impeding the growth, mobility, or radical freedom of the other; two reeds, each rooted in the same soil, in the depths of which all becomes sacred law, and both extended toward the heavens; two reeds—to mix the metaphors—winging their own way, but with oars plying through the same waters. Forever unfathomable are the mysteries of man and woman; and, *as* love, their sexual love is inextricably linked with their spiritual love. "I hold this," Rilke declared, "to be the highest task of a bond between two people: that each should stand guard over the solitude of the other. . . . And only those are the true sharings which rhythmically interrupt periods of deep isolation. . . ."[27] Surely the rhythms of man and woman differ. Yet, in the end, every attempt to specify those differences must fail. But, by those rhythms, when, by grace, two people are joined in love, a task of utmost seriousness devolves upon both, a task which challenges the profundity, the strength, and the generosity of each.

For, as Rilke proceeds:

> A *togetherness* between two people is an impossibility, and where it seems, nevertheless, to exist, it is a narrowing, a reciprocal agreement which robs either one party or both of his fullest freedom and development. But, once the realization is accepted that even between the *closest* human beings infinite distances continue to exist, a wonderful living side by side can grow up, if they succeed in loving the distance between them which makes it possible for each to see the other whole and [like the reed] against a wide sky! [For] all companionship can consist only in the strengthening of two neighboring solitudes. . . .

Though, indeed, the temptation in love, as it heightens, "is to give oneself wholly away," one must, however arduous the effort, discover such self-abnegation as leads to a radical inability to step "out of the great darkness"—though the self may only find itself at this very moment in which it loses itself. Therefore, would they protect the sanctity of their love, lovers must not "fling themselves to each other in the impatience and haste of their passion," that dissension between them ineluctably supervene; and disunity, confusion, impurity, disconsolateness dominate their essential humanity. For love subtly alters from instant to instant. Its nuances are perpetually, indeed kaleidoscopically, shifting. "Two wide, deep individual worlds" touch and retouch, endlessly rekindling one another, but they never merge—at least, not in true love. And the delicacy, and the deliciousness, of their touching must never be inundated by false bliss, but be cherished with humility, patience, tender regard, reverence, ever-renewed resolve. Not to possess one another, not to join as radically one, but to commune with grace, and with graciousness; to aid the other to rescue and preserve his own uniqueness; and to aid him to abandon all vestige of stereotypy and oppressive convention—this is the fruition of authentic love.

Moreover, "Physical pleasure," Rilke affirms,

> is a sensual experience no different from pure seeing or the pure sensation with which a fine fruit fills the tongue; it is a great unending experience, which is given us, a knowing of the world, the fullness and the glory of all knowing. And not our acceptance of it is bad; the bad thing is that most people misuse and squander this experience and apply it as a stimulant at the tired spots of their lives and as distraction instead of rallying towards exalted moments. . . . O that man might take this secret, of which the world is full even to its littlest things, more humbly to himself and bear it, endure it, more seriously and feel how terribly difficult it is, instead of taking it lightly. That he might be more reverent toward his fruitfulness, which is but *one*, whether it seems mental or physical; for intellectual creation too springs from the physical, is of one nature with it and only like a gentler, more ecstatic and more everlasting repetition of physical delight.

Indeed, Rilke declares,

> In one creative thought a thousand forgotten nights of love revive, filling it with sublimity and exaltation. And those who come together in the night and are entwined in rocking delight do an earnest work and gather sweetnesses, gather depth and strength for the song of some coming poet, who will arise to speak of ecstasies beyond telling. And they call up the future; and though they err and embrace blindly, the future comes all the same, a new human being rises up, and on the ground of that chance which here seems consummated, awakes the law by which a resistant vigorous seed forces its way through to the egg-cell that moves open toward it.

Surely, I may repeat Rilke's admonition, "Do not be bewildered by the surfaces; in the depths all becomes law." And, in those depths, it may well be that

> perhaps the sexes are more related than we think, and the great renewal of the world will perhaps consist in this, that man and maid, freed of all false feelings and reluctances, will seek each other not as opposites but as brother and sister, as neighbors, and will come together *as human beings*, in order simply, seriously and patiently to bear in common the difficult sex that has been laid upon them.

For, first and foremost, men and women are human beings. And however ineffable be the different rhythms which characterize the one or the other—the first, namely woman, "in whom life lingers and dwells more immediately, more fruitfully and more confidently, . . . pulled down below the surface of life by the weight of any fruit of [her] body" whereas the second, namely man, who must compensate by his restless striving for a "poetic power" which is "great, strong as a primitive instinct," with its "own unyielding rhythms in itself," and breaks out as out of mountains"—each in his fashion is both shaper of poems and poem incarnate; so that

> the love-experience, which is now full of error, will alter it from the ground up, reshape it into a relation that is meant to be of one human being to another, no longer of man to woman. And this more human love (that will fulfill itself, infinitely considerate and gentle, and kind and clear in binding and releasing) will resemble that which we are preparing with struggle and toil, the love that consists in this, that two solitudes protect and border and salute each other.

Once achieved, this "sensual experience," this "great renewal of the world" wherein "people . . . seek each other as neighbors, and come together *as human beings*," this "love-experience" reshaped "into a relation that is meant to be of one human being to another," this "more human love . . . infinitely considerate and gentle, and kind and clear in binding and releasing," this "love that consists . . . in . . . two solitudes" which "protect and border and salute each other"—all these are resilient and strong, yet, paradoxically, fragile and requiring a most careful nurturing.

How may the pact of the sanctity of love, whether for a moment or a year or a lifetime, be preserved, sustained, cared for, and allowed to grow and to transform itself into an authentic *rapport*? How can this pact, ever more pure, joyous, and renewing, be permitted to bring to fruition the aboriginal promise, and not to cease, during the term of the pact, a pact of silence and communion, to fructify? How can it fulfill the promise which germinates within that first, tentative, cautious, and infinitely tender touching? I raise, now, the issue of fidelity. But I do not speak of the desecration of fidelity which masquerades under that name, a mere conventional token of unequivocally binding "commitment" or of some grotesquely desiccated "marriage." On the contrary, I speak of unspoken loyalties and depths of reverence; of how each lover, man and woman, each in himself fully human, or of how both lovers, each for the other, constitute a veridical unity, a unity which symbolizes the essential solidarity of all humankind.

For two persons authentically to touch, and in touching to maintain the exclusivity of the wonder and uniqueness of their touching, and to refrain from doing violence to either person, or in any way to sully that uniqueness (and I speak, not of long stretches of time, but solely of the interval during which, by mutual consent, the pact is viable) there must be, for *consummate* purity to prevail, an affirmation of the indefeasible uniqueness of a sacred bond—not that should uniqueness diminish, that bond need be shattered; but, tragically, should uniqueness be disaffirmed, then a falling away from purity of heart, no matter how subtle and well-intentioned, inexorably entails its diminution, hence, in the profoundest sense, violates its sanctity and, thus, the integrity of the pact. Though restitution is surely achievable, the wonder, the miracle, the sheer ecstasy of sanctity ineluctably perish; and never again—and herein lie all the subtle nuances of tragedy—can it *be* sanctity. Forever afterward, one is then denied the heights of those angelic orders toward which humankind is competent not merely to aspire, but, though rarely and momentarily, actually to attain. For, in the end, the grace bestowed upon any particular man or woman consists in this wondrous power: their capacities to strive toward those orders and, if only for a brief, fleeting instant, to participate in them.

Further to develop the interwoven themes of tragedy and complementarity, which themselves are profoundly implicated with integrity, I introduce the concept of transfiguration. Unfolding through syntheses of decision and fate, transfiguration expresses the structure of the processes whereby integrity is attained. By decision, each person opts for a way of life; by fate, the unforeseen issue of every decision creates for him an unchosen destiny. Since existence is a mysterious fabric woven of elements of both choice and chance, human freedom is profoundly ambiguous. Tragedy as well as joy envelop every way of life. Yet tragedy is transcended in love; and love entails both union with another person, in realized complementarity, and union with oneself, in work. With respect to work, one unites with the very symbols which one draws forth from one's own interior depths—in the loneliness of tragedy.

Now I pass to a topic which will prepare the way, in my next two chapters—namely, *human dialogue* and *schemes of presence and compresence*—for synthesis of the modalities of loving union, a synthesis which, when its deeper import is drawn forth, will (in Part IV) itself allow for passage through new transfigurations toward wisdom: wisdom acquired, crystallized, and manifested by the speaking forth of each person, in speech of his own rhythms; rhythms endlessly clarified, rhythms thematized in endlessly novel ways.

Woven of tragedy alternating with self-transcendence, transfiguration is that passage beyond what one *is* to what one *ought* to be, passage toward ideals which press for realization. Herein consists the life of integrity, itself a passage. For the dialectic of *is* and *ought* entails disruptions within every attainment. By the way of integrity, one passes, in the context of facts already known and correctly appraised, toward the life of wisdom. Inexorably, the way of integrity is fraught with crisis. Previously crisis was treated as arising from those acts whereby, in creative thrust, the self shapes and reshapes itself. Within this context, the themes of tragedy and complementarity suggested themselves. To resolve tragedy, one must rethink both crisis and its transcendence, but now within a transcendentally personalist view of the self.

NOTES

1. See the indexed references to "facies totius Universi" in the following studies of Spinoza by H. F. Hallett: *Aeternitas: A Spinozistic Study* (Oxford: Clarendon, 1930), and *Creation, Emanation, Salvation* (The Hague: Nijhoff, 1962). For "face," Hallett translates "make" or "fashion."
2. Hegel, *Phenomenology of Mind*, trans. Baillie, p. 794.

3. Lauer, *Reading of Hegel's* PHENOMENOLOGY OF SPIRIT, p. 259.
4. Ibid., p. 26.
5. Hegel, *Phenomenology of Mind*, trans. Baillie, p. 799.
6. "The Coming of Wisdom with Time," *Collected Poems of W. B. Yeats*, p. 92.
7. "The Choice," ibid., p. 242.
8. Ibid.
9. "To a Friend Whose Work Has Come to Nothing," ibid., p. 107.
10. See the discussion in Hegel, *Phenomenology of Mind*, trans. Baillie, pp. 802–805.
11. Ibid., p. 804.
12. Ibid.
13. Ibid.
14. Ibid.
15. Ibid.
16. Lauer, *Reading of Hegel's* PHENOMENOLOGY OF SPIRIT, p. 264.
17. Hegel, *Phenomenology of Mind*, trans. Baillie, p. 806.
18. Ibid., p. 807.
19. Ibid.
20. Ibid., p. 808.
21. Lauer, *Reading of Hegel's* PHENOMENOLOGY OF SPIRIT, p. 267.
22. Ibid., p. 268.
23. Immanuel Kant, *Critique of Pure Reason*, trans. Norman Kemp Smith (New York: St. Martin's, 1965), pp. 167–69.
24. Ibid.
25. "On Woman," *Complete Poems of W. B. Yeats*, p. 144.
26. "The Lover Tells of the Rose in His Heart," ibid., p. 54.
27. This and all subsequent quotations are taken from Rainer Maria Rilke, *Rilke on Love and Other Difficulties*, trans. and ed. John J. L. Mood (New York: Norton, 1975), pp. 27–45.

11

HUMAN DIALOGUE: THE INTERWEAVINGS OF DOUBT AND CERTITUDE

PREAMBLE

When a person questions his hitherto indubitable beliefs, doubting not a particular feeling, perception, idea, or value, but, rather, the very validity of much of what he has held to be certain, and when these doubts come upon him, not arbitrarily summoned up, or as a cognitive exercise, but by inner necessity, and stir him to challenge accustomed ways and to threaten a style of life, he is, indeed, in crisis. According to the theory of self and person thus far developed, human searching, I submit, entails personal crisis. In effect, every quest is both the art of inducing crisis and the skill of resolving crisis. Without sham, though with self-compassion, a seeker after inner truth confronts himself with his self-deceptions. Only deep within himself can he discover the touchstone of reality, a way of catalyzing the derepression of dissociated complexes. By helping himself to redintegrate into an expanding awareness what had been repressed, he enables himself more truly to perceive reality. In crisis, this new perception comes about through a shattering of illusion. Often the touchstone is a living person who has been taken as model; often it is a conjectured image of what one dimly perceives to be a possibility already resident in him.

I use terms like "validity," "crisis," "reality." These are hardly simple notions. Though presupposed by every search, their deeper meanings often go unformulated by the seeker; yet should he plumb his own depths with sufficient acuity, the meanings will be revealed to him. Experienced from the point of view of an observer seeking to discern wherein consists crisis, and the ways in which it can be resolved, the phases of crisis can be outlined, at least in their main contours. In one of his roles, the philosophic inquirer is an observer of crisis. As such, he assumes the obligation of explicating what the seeker merely assumes. What the seeker often formulates as negations—i.e., barriers which impede his search—the philosopher treats in their positive content in terms of such ideas as self-potentiating power, individual wholeness, or empathic encounter. Initially confronted with the need to understand himself, the facts of his own existence, and its possibilities for frustration or fruition, the seeker proceeds to conceptualize the manifold facets of his relation to the world; and, even on this level, he at times almost succeeds in resolving thwarted power, dispersed wholeness, or distorted encounter. In their negative moments so germane to the initial phases of every search, these ideas are, in their positive moments, focal to a philosophic theory of the person. And, in any view of power, wholeness, or encounter, some concept of valid belief, crisis, and reality is presupposed by that theory. A personalist-oriented philosophy must cope with this concept. Indeed, any philosophy which has consummated itself as systematically articulated wisdom, even though it has not yet been fully lived (as in the mystical stance), as long as it is at least cogently prefigured, ought to come to terms with the issue of radical personal doubt. Furthermore, it should render its findings with reasonable precision by means which never cease to affirm, and further to delineate, their concrete import: those basic suppositions, methodologic and substantive, which are implicit in any theory of the person (e.g., psychoanalysis or behaviorism). It ought systematically to connect these clarified suppositions with those at the foundations of other theories that it can prepare the way by which to construct a generalized theory which subsumes both the particular theories and the experiences they portend under a more comprehensive account of reality. It is the first of these tasks—namely, the clarification of personal crisis—which I attempt here.

A • THE PROBLEMATIC SELF

(*a*) Philosophic Crisis

When either quest is conducted with integrity, authentic philosophic search provokes crisis as profound as that provoked by strictly private search. Just as in a personal crisis, one questions the foundations of one's particular existence, the grounds one would give, were one challenged, for one's every act, thought, desire, and belief, so philosophy, in its crisis, questions the foundations of existence in general. In *Homo Quaerens*, I proposed that, at bottom, every person is a seeker, and, qua seeker, he must, when he seeks anything, seek qua philosopher. And to seek anything, whatever that be, is to seek the very self who is seeking. A person is that creature who, as he seeks, reveals himself, in the last analysis, to be a seeker. In this sense, philosophy expresses what persons pre-eminently do were they to make sufficiently explicit their characteristically human intentions. Here I construe the philosophic task, in broad terms, as adventure, the paradigmatic human adventure which, as such, comprehends, as significant moments within its own unfolding activity, numerous other sorts of adventure. As its typical approach, it uses procedures and orientations which go beyond the cognitive. A critique of reality based on the presumption that reality's significant dimensions have been dissociated from philosophic awareness, philosophy, by essence, is the generalized response to crisis. Like every person, in his evaluation of a lesser individual crisis, the philosopher uses cognition, feeling, and intuition to dramatize the larger human crisis.

I say "larger" crisis because, unlike one who confronts limited problems, a philosopher, the paradigmatic seeker, confronts every particular seeker, in his endeavor to understand the structure of questing (hence, of crisis); not, however, as a mere transitory agent of reality but as one who, pre-eminently, searches to circumscribe all reality, however doomed his efforts might, by his finite resources, prove to be. He confronts a larger reality because, basic to any philosophy, even to an unregenerate materialism, is its concept of the person; and "person" cannot be defined save by reference to the most inclusive mode of search, and with respect to every facet of the cosmos which is searched. Upon this concept, whether or not it is explicitly formulated, all else depends: how nature, God, or physical processes are to be construed. Indeed, in those social epochs in which a crisis in the very concept of the person arises, the philosophic responses are of the greatest interest.

Philosophic crisis mirrors social crisis. It is also primary, underivative, and autonomous. The history of philosophy abundantly shows that personal crisis is immediately translated into a novel philosophic schema. If, moreover, one were to juxtapose the great systems of philosophy which have unfolded in successive epochs of crisis, whether social or personal, one would discover an organism to emerge: a single philosophic entity which continually confronts itself in radical doubts and self-resolving decision. Every individual system is a novel stage in that organism's growth. Each is the product of dialogue with reality, dialogue instituted owing to crisis. In all instances of philosophic reflection, powers which had previously been expressed as but mere possibility are brought to fruition.

As for the person, every stage of the philosophic adventure illuminates what had gone before. In retrospect, the entire history of person *and* philosophy becomes luminous. Only when roots are more clearly delineated can one, as one constitutes oneself in each particular stage of one's growth, ground oneself in those acts whereby one can more effectively root oneself in subsequent stages. For each stage, especially crisis, poses alternatives of belief and action, alternatives sharpened by clarification of what has gone before. As one stage supersedes another, what reveals itself through that unfolding compels revaluation of every antecedent stage and prefigures every subsequent stage. In retrospect, the earlier stages are seen as though filtered through their successors. In effect, the philosopher converses with what had come before. Just as a person in a particular moment converses with what he had been an instant ago, so the philosopher discloses the new potentialities inhering in an earlier phase. Both self and philosopher emerge in the context of dialogue with the very one from which each has evolved—an antecedent self still unperished into that consequent self to which it will give birth, but stubbornly persisting and refusing to renounce its claims. This dialogic continuity within a self (personal or philosophic) permits the self to shape itself anew in crisis which has been at first instituted, then resolved.

Doubting is a process with many ramifications. A synergistic unfolding, it extends itself, by an inner movement, over the entire range of experience, compounding its intensity as it leads from one item to another. In an intellectually committed person, a single crucial instance of doubting will culminate in a comprehensive (i.e., philosophic) set of new beliefs. Indeed, obsessive, circular neurotic doubt is but a seed which, by therapeutic intervention, blossoms into genuine doubt: that doubt which, by an intrinsic dynamism, grows and ramifies. Authentic doubt is a profound asking, for every feeling, perception, and thought, for the reasons why; and the quest for the very ground of reasons why *is* the philosophic quest.

The essence of philosophy (as also of science, though science, of lesser scope, is usually less personal) is to settle belief concerning the origins, interrelations, and implications for the human adventure of great masses of what had been regarded as disparate phenomena. Yet to settle belief, one must first doubt, then free oneself from the dissatisfaction which stimulates inquiry until, dissatisfaction having been dissolved, one can, with equanimity, accept new belief. But truly to be dubious, one cannot be neurotically uncertain. On the contrary, one must be ready for something new and larger; one must be receptive to more vibrant experience. Though prolonged, debilitating chaos ever threatens, the opportunity for expanded, deepened awareness ever prevails. Yet no particular instance of doubt can be arbitrarily summoned up. Genuine doubt, non-neurotic dissatisfaction, requires that new experience unexpectedly clash with belief. True: at a given instant, one may doubt only certain beliefs. That experience may reasonably cohere, others must be retained. Otherwise, no decision would be possible; all action would be paralyzed. Though one presumes that something *may* be in doubt, one assumes that something else *must* be certain. And, in any case, doubt is but the privation of a habit of action associated with some belief. For belief cannot be separated from its specific impact as particular acts or tendencies to act. Doubt must always be superseded by new habit, or by reaffirmation for former habit. Thus, doubt is but the temporary suspension of disbelief.[1] A state of ferment and upheaval, it corresponds to tension within a *system* of beliefs: tension which one seeks to resolve, though no resolution can be more than provisional, by restoring equilibrium on some higher level. Comprehending a larger volume of experience, one's new beliefs can thereupon prepare one for new action, when the appropriate occasion arises.

Yet philosophy aims as much at unsettling as at settling belief. When a sufficiently powerful tendency to doubt unites with an intellect of sufficient strength and largeness, it is the unsettling of belief which constitutes a philosophic crisis. Moreover, all belief is corrigible. Every investigator (and, in some sense, every person alive is, in some medium, an investigator) must be willing to doubt, no matter how radically. He must accept the full consequences of every challenge to belief. True, for action to have a ground, and life can never, even momentarily, *totally* suspend action, action must be based on some, perhaps provisionally, unchallenged belief. Nevertheless the ground may be tenuous, and in crisis it is tenuous. Still, a thread of certainty, though a crucial thread, may be retained: an immanent conviction which cannot be shattered so long as a life persists, and howsoever concealed from awareness its searching acts might be, that there is a ground, discoverable and firm, and that this ground consists of the power of dialogue. *Talking to*, *being with*, and *listening to* involve personal pronouns which, in true dialogue, mean precisely what they are claimed to mean; "he" and "they" are not confused, as in neurotic transference they always must be, with "I" and "you." Indeed, psychoanalysis (i.e., systematic self-searching) is, in the end, simply a matter of getting one's personal pronouns straight. And, by generalization, the same principle applies to such generic searching as may be deemed philosophic. In sum, crisis is the recognition of the possibility for dialogue as inherent in the texture of reality, the acknowledgment of a failure of dialogue, and the quest to renew dialogue.

(*b*) Doubt, Belief, and Feeling

To doubt is to question the validity of belief. By "belief," I mean a habit of trusting or confiding; the acceptance of something as true on the ground of something previously accepted as true, either by evidence or on authority. But what is the source, nature, and sanction of such trust? What are the ultimate grounds whereon anything can be warranted as true? At bottom, these issues are one. Both involve the idea of a free, unquestioning, and indefeasible giving up of oneself, a surrendering, an ultimate loyalty. Every belief binds one to orient oneself, in some determinate way, toward *something*, something either other than oneself or another self. And such orienting is a complex of feelings about something cherished or held in disesteem, something valued or disvalued, but something about which one feels strongly, something of which one has an idea and a perception, and, on the ground of these feelings, is willing to take risks.

The key word is "feeling." By it, I mean the taking of an account, more or less defined, and by all one's faculties, in which there appears that germ of intentionality whence derive willings, wishings, and desirings. A feeling is an orientation from which flows an acting upon something—whether or not one cares for that thing, since feelings may be positive or negative—with the intention of either altering it or appropriating it. Moreover, feeling always involves something other than oneself, though this something may only be implicit within feeling, something toward which one comports oneself, i.e., bears oneself with all one's resources and with all that one is. In turn, comportment exhibits two sides, complementary aspects of a unitary process: contemplation and action. Both aspects are derivative from, and refinements of, comportment; but all comportment rests on some feeling.

In one sense, all feeling is valid. Ethically considered, one has a right to feel *whatever* one feels—though we may condemn one's actions. Ontologically considered, parity obtains, hence irreducibility prevails, between feelings of any kind, though we may deem some feelings shallow and others profound. Therefore, one speaks more of valid belief than of valid feeling. For validity generally means a certain relationship (of warrantability) between the evidence, authority, or ground for belief *and* a particular belief. The criteria for warrantability are most cogently formulated by logicians and philosophers of science. Belief is belief *about* something. Depending upon changing evidence, a given belief may be deemed false. And, in every particular application, criteria for warrantability require the specifying of conditions for the falsifiability of belief. To achieve this, one must always note that the object of belief is explicitly indicated in the formulation of belief.

Likewise, feeling involves an *other* than the person who feels. It is not simply a quality of that person. For it expresses a relationship, a relationship which is not reference, in the sense in which belief involves reference, but, rather, immanence. Implicit in all feeling, even in autism, is an object about which one feels, however vaguely this object be delineated. Always a self, in being a self, has reference to something beyond itself, something by virtue of which it can *be* a self. In terms of immanence, one can justify a view held by psychoanalysts[2] —those students of *personal* searching who have created a paradigm for philosophic searching: namely, that one *truly* feels certain feelings and *falsely* feels others. Either one entertains valid feelings or one deludes oneself about what one's feelings really are. In valid feeling, an object is not confusedly present; it is present in its distinctness as object. Immanent in the feeling, the object is appropriate to it. And for validity to be established, the object must be erected as object. For objectivity must be drawn forth in the course of comportment which flows from feeling. Thereby, the clarity of the object, and its appropriate boundaries, cn be determined. In this context, it is deemed to be precisely *this* object, and no other. The object truly intended, it now becomes something veridically other than, and counterposed to, the one who feels. No longer merely immanent in one, it actually becomes transcendent to one, apart and self-existent. In retrospect, it is ascertained to be the appropriate and true object.

(*c*) Feeling and Reflection

More than mere components of experience, feelings are responses to experience. Philosophers are haunted by a sense that experiences giving rise to certain feelings more effectively disclose reality than do certain other experiences, that some experiences even mask reality; disclosing experiences are "truer" than masking experiences. True, correctly interpreted, all experience equally discloses reality; all feelings exhibit parity. Hence, not so much experience as interpretation of experience determines how much reality is concealed, and how much is revealed. My cognitive response to experience is crucial to my appraisal of its power to indicate reality. Grasped by a cognitive act as independent, rather than constitutive, of experience, reality is constructed from experience: first experience, then interpretive response. Experience provides data; response ponders data. It is the means for synthesizing data into reality. Two realms are sharply disjoined, matter and intellect. Feeling is associated with matter; cognition, dissociated from matter. Feeling, too—so this thesis runs—is bifurcated. By reflection upon both experience and the feeling which experience engenders, indeed by appeal to their very diversity and disconnectedness, a larger plan can be discerned; this plan *is* reality.

Yet interpretation yielded by reflection, and the constructed reality thereby made possible, cannot be radically separated from the very experience, and its concomitant feeling, which spurred interpretation. In reflection, which suggests a bending back, a mirroring, hence, an analogue, what had been experienced is allowed to acquire independent existence: thus to simmer, to invade one's being, to stir new feeling, to give rise to a perception of the world which intensifies and supplements, or, perhaps, clashes with and thereby alters, an image hitherto held. Accordingly, an experience is defined not simply by its power to elicit interpretive response as disparate from experience. For, in actuality, all response flows into the one who has experienced. Continuous with experience, such experience is a piece of experience. But a single fabric is woven. And, by that flowing, one gives birth to something which, when juxtaposed to reflective deposits of other experience, opens up a beyond to all (customary) experience: a haunting, circumambient presence of that of which experience was but residue, and, in a sense which I develop later, crystallization and symbol; an expanding of that symbol toward a vision, partly familiar and partly mysterious; a vision which, as it awaits deciphering and unconcealment, is inscribed on every experience which, by reflection, leads one toward it.

B • THE SELF-RESOLVING SELF

(*a*) Experiencing

By "experience," I mean either pervasive, continual, never-ceasing sensuous existence, a simple animal-like being alive, or, alternatively, a singular, unique, demarcated, dramatic interlude within the ordinary flow of impressions. In both senses, experience endures as pulsation. Too readily, one blunts this rhythmic quality: one denies its inceptions, its flows, its pauses, its harmonies, its interruptions, its consummations. Deriving from πεῖϱα, meaning a trial, a trying out, a conscious act by which one first secures oneself then goes forth to test, to find, and to clarify, experience suggests a process in which diverse influences work within and flow through one into the unity of one's singular existence. In all experience, one's roots ramify into one's past. Unconsciously delving into factors which have shaped one's contemporaneous self, one listens, one awaits, one witnesses, and one contemplates; one is patient and still. In quietude, one acknowledges factors relevant to the very origination of experience. Woven into a unity of enjoyment, these factors are absorbed and gathered in. Reconstituting the self, they consolidate its formative substance. Suffusing each person who has gathered, coordinated, integrated, and unified such elements as had been externally disparate, diffuse, and incongruous, feelings blend to shape a veridical unity. And, always, experience involves a going toward, an adventuring, a seeking, a doing, an acting upon, a shaping, a transforming, an initiating, a manipulating, and a focusing. For experience also entails agency. In experience, one imprints oneself durably into another, whether person or thing. Never narrowly mentalistic, experience is a dynamic fabric in which closure is always partial, and completed patterns await their weaving into new patterns. In experience, a plexus of activities implicates a person's whole being, its every texture and tonality, as both source and aim. More or less determinate, a complex of movement, feeling, volition, thought, perception, and desire unfolds, a complex the components of which are neither discriminated nor interconnected, but, rather, so interwoven as to reduce their diffuseness and fragmentation; one adopts a fructifying, comprehensive orientation toward both oneself and one's world.

In its quality of tone, its harmonic lines, its chords and dissonances, and its melodic growth and completion, every experience reveals a person's inner constitution, what he truly is. Complicated and labyrinthine, reality discloses itself in experience as a fabric woven of the contrasting, intensifying, and mutually complementing experiences of selves-in-relation. But experience not only constitutes reality; it also symbolizes reality. For every experience involves disclosure, a pointing toward some revelation, and, ultimately, a momentous tearing asunder of the veils which had hitherto enveloped reality.

To experience is to participate in a process which involves recipiency, undergoing, suffering. In the fullness of what has been woven into unity, sheer being reveals itself. But being involves more than contraction and passivity. It implicates expansion and affirmation as well. Thus entailing acting, transforming, and declaring, the phases of experience are interdependent. None is to be valued above another. In experience, the ground on which one stands in making one's commitments, and in rendering one's loyalties, is solidified and made secure. The object of comportment, and one's relationship to that object, are clarified. Moreover, experience is a being in touch with, a caring, a bringing to fruition, an enlarging. Its searching has quiescent, assimilative, and silent moments, moments of reflection and standing back from; yet it also exhibits drama and transfiguration. In both instances, I speak of experience in its fulfilling aspect. Yet, in addition, experiences may negate and deny. And whether denying or fulfilling, experiences can be evaluated only retrospectively, by determining their contribution to, and their absorption into, succeeding experiences. In the end, experience is always dialogic. One listens to what lies about one; one listens to what is within one; one enjoys the confluence of feelings; one utters what it is within one to utter. Experience is nothing but feeling: its depths, its patternings, its risings and fallings, its strainings toward expression, its consummations as expression.

Having spoken of valid belief and valid feeling, I can now refer to valid experience: experience which, as efficacious comportment, is an authentic symbol of reality; reality which, inscribing itself in experience, never ceases to condition experience. Validity, efficacity, and authenticity are related notions; symbol, experience, and comportment are related notions. To understand these sets of notions, one must understand dialogue itself, and, thereby, more deeply penetrate the analogy between philosophic crisis and personal crisis.

(*b*) Reality and Neurosis

Prior to crisis, the person qua sufferer and the philosopher qua unenlightened take their stands, in surveying the world, on strength, falsely construed as weakness, and on weakness, falsely construed as strength. Both neurotic defenses and inauthentic philosophies are either the precarious manifestations of illusory strength or the dwelling in fake weakness. Neither the philosopher, thus construed, nor the person, insofar as he suffers, dares to risk his accepting the world as it really is: a world stripped of façades, stereotypes, and pretense; a world related solely to his own resources. Each inauthentic philosopher, each neurotic person, refuses to trust reality which, ineluctably, constrains his powers and frustrates his needs—yet also provides the very medium through which power and need can be brought to fruition: the agent by which they are both activated and gratified. In neither instance does one accept oneself as a fully self-affirming, vigorous participant, a participant who collaboratively shapes reality while accepting its rebuffs as but the challenge to resourcefulness and the occasion for transfiguring himself beyond the need for need. For reality provides the circumstances whereby, whatever the risk to established customs, conventions of usage, or assumptions about self or nature, one's perceptions might flow freely; and, thereby, form the basis for one's universal doubt in one's endeavor so to illuminate oneself in relation to the world, that, thenceforth, one may, without sham, shape a new vision of reality, a new concept of the community of being.

In neurosis, midway through crisis, one arrests one's progress. Unable to proceed toward its resolution, one so immobilizes oneself that faith in one's ability to stand alone wavers and falters. In his early growth, the neurotic person was allowed neither to experience himself as free from debilitating encumbrance nor to rely upon his own resources. Unattended and unheard, his significant needs were denied gratification. He failed to develop his power to give, to open up to reality, freely to listen, to receive, and to respond; and he had to bolster himself, by presenting to the world a mask interposed between his unexercised, hence unrecognized, strengths and the world with which he had to cope. Under such circumstances, reality itself is seen as through a veil. Experienced fictitiously as fraught with danger, but also with false security, the world is regarded as designed wholly for one's gratification or thwarting: a world in which one is center, and all is perceived as oriented toward one. A person's capacity to listen with all his senses unimpaired is damaged; he cannot be transported beyond his own centricity; he cannot adventure amid realms of *many* centers, each autochthonous yet each linked to a center beyond, a center which is transcendent to every particular center. Whether consciously or unconsciously, every suffering individual shapes his preconception of reality into conformity with whatever is consistent with his neurotic defenses. Based on adverse and now "transferred" experience, his responses are stereotyped. He cannot fully interrogate, freely listen, or uninhibitedly utter; and he cannot *exist* in that dialogue wherein the constituents of reality are grasped in their concreteness and in their *integrity*. For the actual identities of those constituents are not apprehended: what they are in themselves, in their intrinsic powers, and in the specific ways in which those powers unfold as independent of his wishes, neither oriented toward his needs (though they may thus be used) nor existing for the purpose of frustrating his needs (though they may surely hamper him); what they form, a realm which is absolutely distinct from him, yet which, in some perplexing way, flows within him.

(*c*) Reflection and Crisis

When one has disinterestedly absorbed oneself in objects, interest being transformed from self-interest to selfless interest, interest becomes care. And when one has grasped the complexities of objects, their resistances and their metamorphoses, one may even experience reverence for them. A world veiled by stereotypy and neurosis, and disclosed not through participation but in negative detachment, is a profane world; yet dialogue converts this world into a sacred world: an egalitarianism of objects which commands respect; a parity between oneself and objects, objects grasped in their sheer otherness as distinct and individual. For a healed person, the guiding principle must be "let him be as I would that he let me be."

By the most explicit and generalized statement consistent with the totality of facts thus far disclosed, philosophy represents reality unveiled, reality uninfected by pretense, reality naked and pure; and it allows reality simply to be as it is. Beginning in wonder, and accepting the world with a certain naïve evenness, the philosopher constructs an image of reality. Representing reality to himself, he communicates to his fellows its presentation to him: a presentation which flows from, yet in dialectic interplay allows for, the reciprocal presentation of himself to it . . . and always with reverence. In its earliest and perhaps deepest sense, could not φιλο-σοφία mean, beyond the love of knowledge, a discernment with love of that which quite directly speaks to me, hence, authentically reveals itself to me?

When the philosopher reflects on his own crisis, a larger disclosure of reality occurs. Pre-eminently a *reflexive*—hence *reflective*—enterprise, philosophy ever anew meditates its own presuppositions. Continually raising them into an expanding consciousness, it never ceases to subject them to critical scrutiny. Moreover, its reflexive (hence reflective) character is like that of the self. Philosophizing and being a self are those probing activities which involve a turning inward, in order to search with probity. Thus reflective, one seeks one's inmost feelings; and one touches the powers whence springs manifest reality: one's own reality and the reality of one's own world. Even to be a self, one must, at least covertly, philosophize; and to philosophize authentically, one must be an authentic self. True philosophizing demands that everything one momentarily is should be addressed unremittingly, relentlessly, and with total probity by the critical self which is ever solidifying as the very ground for the self's final appeal: that critical self which constitutes itself a repository of ultimate loyalty and the source of veridical trust.

C • THE AUTHENTIC SELF

(*a*) Dialogue and Authenticity

What do I mean by authenticity? One speaks of an authentic person, philosopher, or disclosure of reality. In psychoanalysis, one aims at inducing such personal metamorphoses as to allow a person to achieve authenticity, to reveal his true being, and so to accept himself that he does not disguise his own reality. Philosophy, which as searching is also therapy, aims at disclosing nature as she truly is, i.e., in her primordial and not merely her given character. Linking these senses of authenticity, dialogue, or διά-λογος, meaning "between" combined with "speech grasping the reason, rationale, or structure," suggests a speaking between, across, or through (barriers), an apprehending of what takes place, a disclosing of what flows between or within personal centers, hence, a negating of the barriers. Thus, "authentic dialogue" is a redundant expression. But since "authentic" derives[3] from αὐτός, meaning self, whereas αὐ is related to the Sanskrit *asus*, meaning life, especially of the soul, hence spiritual life, to predicate "authentic" of dialogue stresses its spiritual character.

By juxtaposing "dialogue" and "authentic," I suggest a being together of two spirits, and a revelation of their essences, as jointly shaping the more inclusive spirit which, in speech sufficiently profound, envelops, hence subsumes, both spirits. Through "authentic dialogue," two spirits, each autonomous, become a single spirit, a singular unity in place of two distinct unities. For the mediation effected by speaking cancels itself. When speaking is both authentic and dialogic, it supersedes mediation itself, assigning primordiality to a relationship, and transforming that relationship into an inclusive relatum: a process wherein human spirits integrally flow together; a singular, irreducible rhythmic unfolding; an orchestrating of selves which are so finely attuned to one another, and so enmeshed, that each self floats freely in and becomes co-extensive with a matrix which, embedding both, allows for the consummation of each. In fine, "authentic dialogue" connotes the union of identity and diversity, irreducible difference in the context of absolute fusion. But only when integral substances are deemed to assume priority over integral processes does paradox arise. And the language of rhythm, herein set forth, conceptualizes what ordinary language resists: namely, the dictum "one in many, many in one." In terms of rhythms, the notions of person and community emerge not only as complementary but as mutually presupposing.

In general, the philosopher reflects on what takes place between himself and his surroundings. He grasps reality as a relationship between himself as listener and that to which he listens; and relationship, so he holds, is reality's very substance. For reality is not two classes of entities, subject and object, each independently specified. Rather, reality discloses itself in reflection as a primary, indiscerptible relationship. Apprehending *itself*, and the distinctions made therein, constitutes reality. Seeking to apprehend reality authentically, i.e., as original and genuine, the philosopher, in his subsequent reflections, distinguishes listener and that to which he listens, but not as separate, fixed, and independent entities. His reflection "reflects" what he has experienced as a *secondary* experiencing, a mere shadow or phantom of his original experience. In an inward mirroring of experience, he absorbs into himself the reflected traces of the other. By reflection, one accordingly alters both oneself and the very relationship which gives rise to reflection. *Pari passu*, a double metamorphosis obtains: one's own existence, the existence of one's world. Correlatively, they "reflect" one substance, a single dynamism.

(*b*) Dialogue and Transfiguration

No mere entity, each wholly other to the other, a relatum entails complementarity. The existence of each relatum is bound up with the existence of other relata. Neither the one who approaches and listens nor that to which (or to whom) one listens, and reciprocally may approach, is sharply disjoined, hence wholly dwells apart. True, every entity transcends every other, standing alone as indefeasibly individual. True, every entity surveys the world in self-absorption and self-enjoyment, experiencing the world as wholly other to it. Were this not the case, there would be no entity at all. Yet entities are not radically solitary and independent. Some kind of immanence prevails. In the end, entities are mutually constitutive. By touching an other, an entity reverberates with a characteristic rhythm, a rhythm woven into the very fabric of its being. Yet each entity assimilates themes which originate in another entity. When one listens to a brook, it deeply impinges on one: it invades, suffuses, transforms the listener; his very existence is radically altered. But the converse also holds. Inscribed on personal themes as new variations, such themes do not, as such, become absolutely one's own. Nevertheless, a sufficient accumulation of such variations profoundly transfigures one's inmost themes. In this sense, entities "objectively immortalize"[4] themselves in one's own being. Resonating to *their* pulse, hence momentarily "becoming" those objects, one is durably touched by them. Reflection on dialogue illuminates this peculiar duality of subject and object.

The response to crisis successfully resolved, dialogue not only interweaves with authenticity; it culminates in authenticity. By "authentic," I mean a valid relationship between self and other, a relationship wherein a true perception is had. An authentic self is a self who truly perceives itself, in the context of its being with another whom it, likewise, truly perceives. And veridically to perceive is never to be merely passive. Quite the contrary. Perceiving is an active process, a process of "listening." Nor can such listening be construed apart from uttering. Here, I mean both uttering and listening in a metaphorical sense; and they are prototypes, respectively, of self-expressing and being-with.

Listening and responding (in some sort of utterance) are profoundly interwoven. One cannot listen unless one understands; and one cannot understand unless one has closely approached the other and, indeed, touched him (or it) with *all* one's senses, with one's every sensibility. Beyond that, one must even place oneself in the very position of the other. With all one's indigenous rhythms, one must mime him and, thereby, place oneself in his position, assuming his very stance. Then alone can one step back from him, detach oneself, and reflect. I mean "detachment," not in its negative sense, but in its etymologic meaning of an un-touching of what had been touched: quite literally, a *de*-taching. For truly to listen, one must alternately *become* the other and, at the same time, become *other* to the other. One must *con*-tact the other, quite literally, totally touch him: touch with all one's resources, suffuse one's very being with the other's being.

Now one can draw into one's being, and absorb therein, what, in one's actual encounter, one has touched; one can allow to be imprinted into one's own substance what *had* been the other's substance. In brief, one reflects and one assimilates. I maintain here a doctrine of the substantive continuity and interpenetration of distinct entities. By their interpenetration, entities transfigure themselves. And for transfiguration to be authentic, such radical change must be fully expressed. One must pass beyond one's very "form" to a new "form." One must press or draw something new, expressively speaking, from oneself. Indeed, I presume that feelings cannot *be* unless, in some modality, they are uttered. For feelings are always in flux, perpetual reconfiguration, and transformation.

In general, potency and its actualization are mutually implicated. Save conceptually, neither holds without the other. Potency unexpressed is *mere* potency, hence nullity. Thus, when one detachedly reflects and thereby *trans*figures oneself, the new configuring *ipso facto* entails utterance. Furthermore, utterance implies an *additional* being with the other, but now in the dimension of response. Through utterance, the other is brought closer to oneself. Such increased proximity is achieved by the very naming of the other aloud. In utterance, one calls to the other; one calls him to oneself. In effect, one draws the other from concealment, that his presence might approach and be enmeshed with one's own presence. In addition, utterance constitutes a symbol of oneself, in one's inmost being: in the vicissitudes of one's spirit, in the unfoldings of one's moods. For utterance is composed of the very symbols of one's self qua recipient, symbols of the other's imprints, and qua donor, symbols of the traces of one's own being, symbols expressed as dance, gesture, or song. Through utterance, one makes oneself present in one's full presence and by all one's "symbols," which are but tangible vehicles of one's inward being; one symbolically presents oneself to the one who had symbolically presented *himself*. Now dialogue must be redefined to mean a fabric, unitary and indivisible, woven of reciprocal (and interpenetrating) symbolic presentations; and, by an authentic person, I now mean a person who first fully engages through dialogue.

(*c*) Dialogue and Crisis

In every dialogue, a person symbolically presents himself to another. And, as in crisis, a searcher listens intently to himself, he symbolically presents himself to himself. To resolve his crisis, he engages in continual self-metamorphosis, which depends upon the care with which he attends his own feelings. A paradigm of listening, the searcher catalyzes, by his symbolisms, his own searching acts. In heeding his dreams, those symbols of his inner world of reverie, for example, he touches the primordial reality of his very existence. Establishing an interior relationship to the deeper *I* which, through this relationship, is drawn from a more nebulous, alien *I*, stranger to the *I* who deeply probes his own integrity, the veridical *I* which emerges is so strengthened that, in the end, it fuses with, or actually becomes, the *I* which had initially addressed itself. In consequence, the first *I* is itself radically transformed. It emerges as the integration of a multitude of "me's" which are incorporated within the ever-growing, ever-solidifying *I* in the very process by which it declares itself to be *who* it is. Increasingly, an inner voice takes precedence, as this voice rises into the voice of self-consciousness: true voice of the self, its very conscience. Now the searcher holds dialogue with himself.

In crisis, the foundations of human existence are challenged, and often profoundly shaken. Assuming an altogether new stand, one listens to what, in retrospect, one deems to be a deeper layer of one's being. And, in the end, the way to one's inmost feelings, the very ground of selfhood, is identical with the way to the very ground of external being. In each case, one both listens to and dwells with, whether in (inner) solitude or in (outer) relationship; one gathers into objectivity what had been diffuse, fragmentary, and unacknowledged: the fleeting, evanescent traces of feeling, sensation, and imagery. And the complementarity between solitude and relationship mirrors the complementarity between the intrapsychic and the interpersonal. Moreover, solitude itself is a species of relationship. In it, one confronts an other to the self, an other which lies buried in the self. When touched, this other reveals itself to be dialogically interwoven with the very self which had sought it. And, like the inner, hidden, and, in the end, reliable self, which, by inward listening, the transitory self seeks to become, objects "out there" are analogously within the transitory self, just as it is present, as one searches, within them; and as those objects are assimilated and synthesized, a more durable, responsible self shapes itself. Indeed, howsoever *I* and other are construed, the boundaries between them are fluctuant and variable.

Dialogue is a species of comportment. And comportment is always suffused by moods which, in comporting, differentiate themselves into multitudes of feelings. To comport is to bear oneself toward an object, interior or exterior, with all one's resources: with sense, movement, feeling, and idea. And to hold dialogue is to discourse against a background, quiescent but vital, of comportment woven with mood; therein, persons crystallize as dialogists. Indeed, the very flowing forth of dialogue configures itself as dialogic foci within a dialogic field. Within these pervading influences, relatively durable structures crystallize. Yet, by their interplay, and by their intrinsic activities, these structures also engender the field, and activate its associated energies. Evolving within a dialogic matrix, complemental dialogists define themselves. In principle, dialogue contrasts with monologue. In monologue, the self is like an isolated atom. Addressing no one, not even (in the end) oneself, since by nature the self is constituted by internalized other selves, one falls into mere aimless talk. However, as comportment, dialogue consists in the bearing of one's entire being toward another, or toward oneself. In this sense, dialogue implies revelatory speech. Indeed, in its narrower sense, speech is a disengagement from a total act of what has been that act's focal tension: the promise of speech intensified, yet held back; speech straining for utterance; *a being pregnant with emerging speech.*[5] Through speech, which, in dialogue, is not dissociated from the *act* of speaking, the act is consummated.

In sum, crisis is an inner ambiguity which culminates in decision: decision in which but a single lineage of possibilities actualizes itself, and shapes a decisive direction of searching for resolution of crisis. In crisis, one initiates new comportment as the ground for deeper, more sustained dialogue.

NOTES

1. See Charles Sanders Peirce, "The Fixation of Belief," *Collected Papers of Charles Sanders Peirce. V. Pragmatism and Pragmaticism*, edd. Charles Hartshorne and Paul Weiss (Cambridge: Harvard University Press, 1934), sects. 5.358–387, pp. 223–47.
2. I shall use the term "psychoanalysis" throughout to refer to any method of therapy which aims at intensive probing into the personality and radical change in the direction of maturity. The term "intensive psychotherapy" could be substituted.
3. Partridge, *Origins*, p. 33.
4. Whitehead, *Process and Reality*, pp. 34–37.
5. See Heidegger's aphorism "Wäre der Menschen ein Versprechen der Sprechen," in his *Unterwegs zur Sprache* (Tübingen: Neske, 1959), p. 14.

12

SCHEMES OF PRESENCE AND COMPRESENCE: OSCILLATIONS OF DETACHMENT AND EMPATHY

PREAMBLE

In dialogue, a person presents himself, by speech and by act, to another. Reciprocally, he receives the presence of the other. By "presenting," I mean the gathering together from the self's inner recesses of a content which, shaped into a communicable product, is given by the donor to some recipient, either person or non-person. As given, the product is a gift, hence, a freely proffered mark of special interest: a symbol both of donor and of something which unites donor to recipient. And a *phenomenology* of the self implies a systematic understanding, thus ways of articulating the self's appearances, hence, its appearings: i.e., one's way of standing forth and declaring who one truly is. Accordingly, in dialogue, a self discloses its own constitutive textures, and, through those textures, it reveals its essential character. Through dialogue, the self affirms and reaffirms that character. And since dialogue implies the reciprocity of interests, and a mutuality of commitment, dialogue is the means by which dialogists affirm to one another their own identities; and, in mutual affirmation, since each dialogist therein gives a special gift to the other, all consecrate the intimacies of interrelatedness which thereby emerge. For dialogue entails the formation, through collective self-disclosure, of an enduring community. And, in the context of community alone, a true phenomenology of selfhood articulates itself.

A • PRIMORDIAL EXPERIENCE

(*a*) The Symbolic Aura

In self-disclosure the presented appearances are multi-layered. Each layer encloses and, in turn, is enclosed by other layers, proceeding from the outermost to the innermost. As, one by one, these layers reveal themselves, the more superficial layers dissolve: façade after façade falls away. At the very moment of its appearing, one's self-presentation shifts toward what further self-probing shapes as a new manifestation. By stages, the self strips away the masks which it presents to another, and brings to appearance the hidden elements of its inner being, i.e., those elements which may be successfully appropriated by another self. Presenting itself as a matrix of symbols, every particular symbol is, in some degree, transparent to the symbols which it encloses. Thus, interwoven patterns of concealment and disclosure are transmitted by self to self. And, ultimately, every self is elusive with respect to its primordial intention of dis-covering to another its buried secrets. But no one is intrinsically malicious, however overt his deceptive intention; no one self-consciously strives absolutely to hide his face from the other. For the self's reality is identical with the activity of presenting, i.e., realizing, that reality to another: the German *Wirklichkeit* expresses this idea best. Yet much self-presenting is duplicitous. Any self's intention may be at odds with itself. When this occurs, a locus of pathologic unconscious activity forms. For self-protection, regions of excessive sensitivity must be defended against harm. Accordingly, certain buried layers of the self, in which "natural" rhythms congeal in "unnatural" ways, exhibit an unwholesome ferment which impedes the smooth-flowing unfolding of what, hitherto, had been enfolded into the self's overall composition. As soon as a self has penetrated this impediment, it liquefies the congealed "complexes." Deceit associated with a particular layer vanishes.

Nested within one another, symbols constitute a translucent but thickly woven fabric, each layer interwoven with adjacent layers. Within deeper, hitherto concealed layers, a person's truly free acts germinate. The kernel of these acts shines through the more superficial layers, indeed, brings about the latter's evanescence. An intricate symbology, man's lineaments can nonetheless be penetrated, and disclosed. Yet, disguised within his very self, the clues whereby another person can unravel the mysteries concealed within these lineaments are zealously guarded. But when unraveling has occurred, a person becomes luminous with his own rhythms. His *luminator* mediates the transformations, back and forth, of weighty corporeality into the ethereally psychic. Though seemingly ineffable, the psyche is almost palpable. An aura of refined, subtle resonances, possessing its own complex layerings, it hovers about every person. Of these layers, the more concealed are blended into one's materiality, though a dialectical interplay of concealment and disclosure characterizes all strictly psychic layers. Extending both outward, beyond one's conventionally designated and demarcated body, and inward, to suffuse and pervade that body, like concentric circles which endlessly stretch to overlap one another, the psychic aura also both envelops and penetrates the *other*. In dialogue, these psychic symbols are transmitted between the dialogists. In each instance, what is presented are laminae of body symbols, every organ, tissue, and cell constituting a segment of these laminae and, in addition, the essentially invisible psychic symbols: all are interwoven into a single, unitary, but never fixed, changeless texture. For a person to be known, both as body and enveloping soul, and not as inert and passive but as activity, process, and ferment, the self's *entire* texture must be penetrated and absorbed into the fluctuating experiences of the knower.

As one dialogist probes himself, the second probes not only the structures presented to him but his own self in order to present himself to the first. Each accordingly doubly probes; two persons are implicated in the same field of activity. With respect to the composition of the self, neither person can be fully defined without reference to the other. Nor can the fabric of his presentings be specified without formulating the processes which flow between the two. In compresence, the layers of both presentings are themselves interwoven. For both dialogists are engaged in analogous actions. Thus intertwined, their symbolisms orchestrate themselves into a totally new schema of interpenetrating presentings. In his self-affirming acts, each dialogist contributes themes to this schema. Once these themes are orchestrated, their resultant polyphony envelops both dialogists. Many voices, subtle or overt, and voices with overtones, undertones, and myriad nuances constitute a larger experience which itself envelops both experients and their particular experiences. It contributes to, penetrates, and transforms those experiences.

By this transformation, dialogists become foci within an interpersonal field of activities. Yet each is a significant determinant of the processes composing these activities. In an orchestra, every player allows his feelings to translate themselves into sounds which, transmitted by his instrument, and therein amplified, contribute to the overall musical effect. Insofar as, like the instrument, he becomes a medium through which tones eventually re-enter the originating music, he constitutes himself a player who, pre-eminently, mediates the reception and transmission of music to other players. In this sense, his full, concrete status is a function of all players. Yet, affected by that totality, every player himself is a function of it. Schemes of compresence hold parity with schemes of presence.

Hovering about *every* person as a unique and specific aura, unseen yet impenetrable, is the aura of the symbolisms of his presence. Yet interwoven with this aura, and enveloping both him and his dialogist, is the aura of compresence. A continuous flow of experience suffuses each person with feelings of the other. By this interchange, the flow heightens the integrity of each, and, hence, of both. By "symbolisms of presence," I do not mean the end-product of a process, like a particular name or event as uttered in speech or as rendered in gesture. On the contrary, I mean the integral act of speaking or gesticulating. A symbol itself is a process: it is a presenting, in a dialectic of illuminating and obfuscating, of an inner existence in all its facets, ramifications, recesses, and layers. Likewise, by "symbolisms of compresence," I shall mean the activities of two dialogists, considered jointly, insofar as those activities begin in interpersonal processes and culminate in some structure within the field in which the dialogists are participants. In short, symbol refers to an unfolding: its *terminus a quo* is a person or an interpersonal relation; its *terminus ad quem* is a particular crystallized occurrence. For it to retain its integrity as symbol, none of its constituent elements can be dissociated from its intrinsic character as an unfolding.

(*b*) Feeling and Action

In reiterated symbols of dialogue, the validity of individual experience is affirmed. And on differing levels of complexity and richness, the rhythms of experience repeat themselves. Like a musical theme which unfolds in a fugue of manifold variations, experience grows in forcefulness, each repetition embedding its predecessors as all repetitions of a single motif acquire architectonic sweep. So constituted that experiencing subject and experienced object are indistinguishable, primordial experience is irreducibly relational. As such, its component processes reinforce and complement one another. Like the fugue, consummations of experience so ornament experience as to shape ever-novel patterns. But when self-consciousness ensues, the identity of subject and object is shattered. Their mutual immanence reconstituted, they separate themselves into distinct entities. As experience is refined, this germinal immanence is reinstated. In successive stages, raw experience evolves toward its sophistical state; and, in dialectical alternation, immanence and separateness are reiterated, negated, and reinstated anew. When a person empathizes with another, subjectivity and objectivity are, likewise, and from the point of view of both of them, indistinguishable. Yet in that ineluctable withdrawal from the other which attends interpersonal experience, the other's integrality, as neither subject nor object but, rather, as an altogether new complex, is similarly shattered. All dialogue entails oscillations of empathy and detachment.

A simple composite of mood and comportment, primordial experience is quiescent, a mere being in the world. Yet, however stilled, the senses remain alive; they are marginally active. Turned toward the world, a person apprehends powers still unactualized: tensions but vaguely felt, yet pregnant with the possibilities for metamorphosis into something new. For primordial experience is a state prior to specific willings and executings, particular discriminatings and specifyings. It is a mere being-in-relation, save that the *relata* are not yet sharply etched. Hence, properly speaking, one must refer to a condition antecedent to both relationship and *relatum*. The world is experienced as a unity which does not comprehend distinctions between inner and outer, a unity wherein "this," "mine," and "yours" are inextricably joined: an integral, richly nuanced orchestration in which fragments of themes, tones, and variations impressionistically come and go; a kaleidoscopic flux in which no one image is sharply contoured or clearly demarcated from another.

In this integral condition, both primordial feeling and primordial action supervene. With immanent purposiveness, the person directs himself toward something wherein neither orientation nor its aim is clearly distinguished. Yet such self-directing is essentially affective. Not distinguishably perceptual, not distinguishably volitional, not distinguishably cognitive, it is merely a generalized, diffuse complex of intentions. No particular factor dominates or durably asserts itself. At the same time, tensions prevail. Ever germinating, full intentionality strains to emerge. Thus, both intending and attending are linked to tension. Each act implies a stirring, a reaching, and a stretching. Attending means a stretching toward something; intending means a stretching which grows from within. When, for example, I awaken from slumber, I yawn and I stretch. My awareness is not yet crystallized into sharply delineated patterns. Experiencing myself as embedded in both myself and my world, neither as yet distinct, I am in a kind of flux. By my stretching, I prepare, as at dawn, to meet a new day; and as I rise, I am enveloped, embraced, and penetrated by sunlight; I awaken into reverie, then incipient activity, finally objective discrimination. From both within me and about me, a world emerges as structured and delineated. For this world to come into being for me, I must initially predelineate its contours; and this predelineation I designate "primordial." Etymologically, "primordial" derives from *primus*, meaning first and original, and *ordo*, meaning order and harmony, as in *ordiri*, to weave threads into an harmonious fabric.[1] Accordingly, by "primordial," I mean the elemental harmony of existence preceding, and preparatory to, the perception of existence as giving birth to structures, structures wherein dissonance, opposition, cacophony, and distinction reign.

(*c*) *I* and *Me*

No sooner do I posit a state of primordial wholeness, a state of which Descartes' *Cogito ergo sum*, his thinking I, is an evolute, wherein existence and feeling are united as, simply, the finding of oneself in one's world, than I posit a focal agent within experience: namely, the person *as* actor: actor who, in his very objectless "turning toward," claims experience to be *his* experience, and, therein, relates to himself. In this sense, *claiming* provides the basis whereby a person achieves the synthesis of diverse items into a unity of experience. Whether on one's own self, at a subsequent moment of its experience, or on the self of another, such synthesized experience has durable impact. Hence, whereas primordial experience is mere quality, undifferentiated and unstructured, synthetic experience exhibits resistance. What in primordial experience had been complemental, interdependent poles, an inseparable subject and object with a single process in which perceiver and perceived are not yet discriminated, are split asunder. No longer is "this" identical with "mine." Now the self is explicitly reflexive. Bending back toward itself in "reflection," it claims "this" to be "mine." Possessing experience, appropriating it, and acknowledging what one has appropriated as constitutive of one's very self, one truly owns one's own experiences; and what one owns is the power *to try* (i.e., *peritus*[2]), to engage what confronts one and, thereby, to test one's potency vis-à-vis an object, to allow the object to emerge as object which, standing apart from one's own self, is felt to be a subject to one. Now the self distinguishes an *I* from an *it*. Detaching subject from object, it opposes sheer self to sheer other.

As *I*, a person attends, selects, and organizes. In his naïve stage, he encounters the object as standing over and against him, as a being *other* than the being which he is. In its thrust, its resistance, its shock, its oddity, and its constraint, the object is merely given. Not yet given as a gift, it still *objects* to him, hence intrudes upon him. When in a subsequent phase of experience the other proffered a gift from another—now construed as himself empowered to give—one experiences one's own self as likewise a giver: complemental donors emerge. A reciprocity of gifts is perceived; and a mutuality of interests and, in consequence, a veridical relationship are established. And this dynamic *condition* of relatedness, which *is* the new entity, itself replicates, though in more richly orchestrated ways, primordial experience *itself*. Now the initiating matrix of experience repeats its own character, on more intricate but more integral levels of organization. Yet prior to the emergence of an interpersonal "I–thou" field, a person finds a world which he truly claims as his own, a world of which he speaks as *my* world, yet, at the same time, a world which he perceives as independent of his choosings, his wishings, and his perceivings.

Alternatively, the person turns within himself toward his "me," his very coenesthetic core: a manifold of reverie which, as he reflects, counterposes itself to him as, likewise, other than he. Alternately possessed by and alien to the *I*, this interior *given*, like any external object, also commands one's interest, as stretching unfathomably beyond one though deep within one, hence capable of endless exploration. But in this case, the internal *given* interchanges itself with the *I* of an instant ago. For *I* and *me* are ever shifting, in both their content and their relationship.

And when I consider that, in my actual experience, I alternately turn without and within, I am led to reflect that the grounding fabric of my experience, reality itself, is neither within me nor without me. It is something which, at bottom, is no *thing* at all but, rather, a substratum which, at this stage of experience, is still elusive and evanescent. Yet, as ground, it can ultimately be revealed to me only insofar as, in my oscillations, I strengthen myself as experient. For by my successive turnings I witness the progressively emerging meanings of the objects which I discern; I witness those objects as that which is disclosed as *meant*, i.e., as intended, or, *tensed toward*, from within myself, and "tensed toward" with increasing affirmation of purpose, hence intent.

In this fashion, a person synthesizes into a unified fabric his diverse, hitherto disconnected experience, drawing together, solidifying, and uniting the outer with the inner. Thereby, he shapes his own personhood. For, in actuality, the turning without is a "turning" to experience, the totality of what one *can* experience, under the perspective of "an awareness of such and such as that which is given out there"; and the turning within is a correlative "turning," in order to experience that totality from the standpoint of "an awareness *of* one's awareness *within* which such and such appears as in there." Synthesizing a single manifold of experience as integral and indiscerptible, one creates a solid matrix in which one roots oneself, from which one draws sustenance, and by which, in fine, one experiences one's consummate personhood.

B • FROM PRIMORDIAL TO CONSUMMATORY EXPERIENCE

(*a*) Normality and Genuineness

Intrinsically triphasic, every experience consists of a primordial relatedness, the substitution of mere external relatedness for disrupted internal relatedness, and consummate relatedness as the restitution of new harmonies. In each case, conation supervenes. For all experience involves a *straining toward.* In this context alone, a person seeks new integrities for both the experient and the experienced. By his quest, he struggles, at every moment of his existence, for new equilibria. Inhering in every germinating experience, novel possibilities ever become available for their unfoldings toward actuality. Within this dialectic, wherein decision renews itself again and again, the self is ineluctably altered. It becomes stronger, deeper, and larger, and its subsequent decisions become more resolute. Always, new potentialities for growth disclose themselves. By sustained effort, a person holds together the newly emergent factors. He renews unity; yet he goes beyond *primordial* unity. In its positive import, to yearn for the primitive is not to strive to return to the womb. Only narcissism constitutes the inexorably doomed effort to reinstate the undifferentiated condition of infancy. In mature experience, such yearning implies an aim at simplicity and clarity. For every person seeks inner balance, a quality of peace wherein an ever-expanding awareness achieves new and more coherent harmonies.

In this quest, the journey without and the journey within increasingly present themselves as correlative. Honestly undertaken, each journey facilitates the other. Thoroughly undertaken, the two journeys converge on the same goal: a larger view of a unitary reality. Held in bondage to neither journey but oscillating from one journey to the other, one explores reality's farther reaches and deeper recesses. In the passive state of "normality," a man has but vague intimations of perils and joys, yet always an anticipatory thrill of an exhilaration which lies concealed both within him and about him. In this respect, the schizophrenic person is no more alienated from himself than those persons who dwell amid the encrusted, desiccated forms of an external world. For the schizophrenic person binds himself to analogous "forms" in the internal world. True, he is bereft of the substance of exteriority; he therefore lives a nightmare. Since he has no criterion for distinguishing hallucination, i.e., fixated fantasy, from fluent reverie, his world is perceived to be quite as real and self-consistent as the world of the ordinary outward-directed person. But, analogously, the person who dwells uncritically among the customary institutions of *his* reality, hence inexorably falls prey to habitual modes of orientation, cannot escape a shallow, fruitless existence. Devoid of the richly diversified meanings of interiority, he leads a shadowy life. For him, the shapes of reality are, as fixated perceptions, quite as hallucinatory as the *inner* shapes fashioned by the schizophrenic person. Yet germinating as omnipresent potentials in either person, schizophrenic or "normal," are yearnings for wider adventure in both realms, inner and outer. In authentic growth toward integrity, the shells of normality and schizophrenia are cracked. He who would aim, however feebly, at integrity, stirs imperceptibly within his cocoon. Restlessly, he struggles toward metamorphosis and rebirth.

For one who genuinely quests after integrity, a ruptured primordial experience must prevail. His propensities, inclinations, intentions, and powers summed up, the whole person, actively concerned for what he experiences, stands forth as a subject who draws into his ken an object *as* object. Increasingly, this (outer) object commands his interest. Manipulated, acted toward, reflected upon, and inspected from different points of view, its various sides are concretely and articulately disclosed. And, as the object is made the center of his world, and a person attends its multifarious character, he himself acquires a "center." His sense of *I* becomes stronger and more resolute. Hitherto concealed facets of the object emerge as distinct, and luminous with meaning. Its limits, possibilities, ramifications, and powers become manifest. Freely orienting himself toward the object, the person ascertains *its* character as a determinate relational pattern. When in communication with others who likewise search, he represents that pattern to himself as a kind of by-product of dialogue. In its more formal structure, this determinate character is grasped (as in natural science) as involving frank determinism. Its objectivity is apprehended as *wholly* distinct from one's mentation. Indeed, one's "mind" is but an assemblage of elements abstracted from one's act of orienting; and one's "body" is extracted from the totality of "objects" as those "nearest" one and most intimately belonging to one. Moreover, only when he apprehends himself as subject does a person's "freedom" become an issue for him. Should the impact of objects on him be emphasized, he experiences constraint; should the emphasis be on his power over them, he, in effect, floats amid fragments, mere spatio-temporal entities. Now anchored to this fragment, now to that, he fails to secure himself firmly within them. For these fragments constitute a unified manifold only when they have been synthesized in the context of dialogue, dialogue between him and others.

(*b*) Sustaining Dialogue

Each state, being with self and being with object, implies both the possibility of the complementary state and the need for actualizing that possibility. In effect, one hovers between these states. In their extreme forms, both states are instances or aspects of narcissism, a removal and a detachment from dialogue. Only when one apprehends oneself as isolated and alone, hence free to inspect, to experiment, and to reject, can one specify an object *as* determined. For each determination requires this orienting act; and to ascertain *that* act as itself determined requires still another act. But every such act is a detached acting *on*, and not an empathic acting *with*. Nor can the complex "I acting and, in so acting, sensing myself as free with respect to another ascertained to be determined" be itself determined save, again, relative to another act, an act external to the complex. Since all actors are participants *in* the world, the world itself cannot be deemed to be free *or* determined. For one may not escape from the world in order to survey it, as it were, from afar, i.e., detachedly. Hence, one cannot return to the world, and, thus, by contrast with detachment, experience empathy. For one's relationship to the world as a totality is beyond empathy or detachment. Involving an altogether different mode of experiencing, it requires the transcending of experience itself. Thus it possesses noumenal rather than phenomenal status. Accordingly, freedom and determinism arise as issues only with respect to the relationship "acting on," and never with respect to the relationship, in its consummate form, "acting with." From any particular vantage point of orienting, wherein one's "here-and-now" is absolute subjectivity, one looks out on the world; and one experiences its *there-ness* as composed of multiple determinate systems, all "generated" as spatio-temporal-material structures *out-there* in detachment from one's *in-here*. However, when one dialogically enmeshes oneself in these structures, their character *as* out-there dissolves. Space, time, and matter, as well as subjective freedom, become peripheral. A single dialogic "center" is created, where, formerly, dialogists constituted several centers. And displacement from many centers to one center typifies the empathic mode of experiencing.

Only when one refrains from giving oneself to an object, thereby preventing one's mere interest from being transformed into care for its integrity, its autonomy, and its fruition, will full encounter fail, and convert itself into detachment. Now one partially turns away from the object; one no longer attends its every facet. However, one often fully gives oneself to the object in spontaneity and with autonomy; one is unhampered by such countervailing forces as would deny one's destiny for becoming a dialogic being. Indeed, counter*vail*, based upon the stem *valoir*, means to proceed against value. In such instances, the intrinsic value of one's being will be realized, and one will unfold one's powers in dialogic fashion. Initially transcendent to the person's "empirical," or merely given, *I*, this object, as a something beyond that *I*—hence, as alien to it—is converted, together with the *I* which holds dialogue with the object, to "transcendental" status. As a *given*—hence, by implication a *giving*—the "empirical" *I* is not fixed and determined. In bequeathing itself in trust to itself in relation to another, care will be shown, for both itself and the other. Under such circumstances, the *I* will progress toward a state wherein its possessing person can hold veridical dialogue. This "evolute" I designate "transcendental." For I refer to a "state of being in relation to" which radically transcends the usual distinction between subject and object, a state which constitutes the substantive condition *a priori*, initially but latent and immanent, for the very possibility of the distinction.

Both object and self emerge with *full* particularity only in the context of an authentic transformation from the empirical to the transcendental. What had been "empirical I," in detached relation to an object, is now a rhythmic flowing: it is a participation, a reciprocal presenting of each to each, a mutual imprinting of each in each, a continual reconstituting of each by each. In transcendentality, total, unqualified listening prevails. Every tone and contour of the object attended are absorbed in a manner which is both disinterested and concerned. No longer are the senses mere instruments of observation, useful in detachment but destructive in dialogue. Now no particular sense becomes hypertrophied, hence, dominant over any other sense. On the contrary, all senses uninhibitedly function together, that reality can more sensitively be penetrated. But when dialogue is interrupted, experienced reality is truncated and abridged. It is degraded to aspects, mere fragments mistakenly taken for wholes: i.e., for integrities, for what things truly are, for the hitherto concealed meanings which unfold only in dialogue. A hand upraised, a facial movement, a vocal inflection—these are symbols, symbols which betoken an active spiritual content, a flowing toward another, a being with and a listening to the other, a designation of a *something beyond* in which each communicant is immersed as participant, a "something" into whose nature (perhaps, ultimately inscrutable) both communicants are, in communion, inspired by that symbol to inquire. Heretofore distinguished as subject and object, but now converted into agents of integrity, these integrated agencies are henceforth bound together, in communion, by richly orchestrated symbols.

When dialogue fails, symbols degenerate into mere signs, bare cues from which inferences are drawn to an alleged mind "within" and disparate from its "containing" body substrate. The power of being with, which manifests itself as a reciprocity of givings, acceptings, and goings toward, becomes power over and impotence in the face of. Thus, the paradoxical pair mind–body, presupposing an unintegrated, hence non-integral, person with respect to whom subject and object have been dichotomized, entails distorted encounter, encounter, in psychoanalytic terms, vitiated by transference due to repression. Furthermore, it entails a split between free will and determinism, hence fragmented potencies. Such experiences as power over and floating in are, in the last analysis, based on man's polarization, when his dialogue becomes flawed. Before failure to sustain dialogue, failure natural to every finite being, one must, in addition to projecting an ideal image of man, resignedly construct a vision of his nature consistent with paradox. By "empirical realism," I mean this diminished vision; by "transcendental realism," I mean the vision of reality based on fulfilled dialogue: a coherent, overarching perspective wherein paradox is envisaged as resolved.

(*c*) The Reality Disclosed through Dialogue

According to the doctrine of transcendental realism, reality is a vast drama of self-acting, interactant, and transactionally conceived entities, entities which are mutually constituting yet self-sufficient and self-affirming: each perfects itself through its encounters; each transcends its previous status, and immortalizes itself objectively by imprinting its traces in the other; each synthesizes into its own existence, thus stands forth as absolutely novel, influences deriving from the other. As agential and self-engendering, every entity grasps diverse factors into the unity of its being. And, through each instance of its experience, it transmits that unity as an inheritance.[3] Despite the endless perishing of every such instance into its successor, moments of existence cohere, and, organizing themselves, bring to fruition their latent potentialities. Despite the vicissitudes of these constituent moments, the identity of every entity is preserved. Yet each entity, now conceived as self-identically itself—and the family of such entities constitutes reality as an extended, actualized spectacle, though not perhaps in its depths, inward ferment, and potency—is the scene of two sets of forces: those tending toward expansion of power, e.g., interest, care, reverence; those which deform, embed, and enwomb, protecting entities from encroachment upon their too constrictedly finite boundaries. With respect to deforming forces, power over and need for are acquired by a kind of default; with respect to expansive forces, participation and giving arise, and in progressive stages unfold toward novel possibilities of consummation. In sum, what was initially a relationship between "empirical I" and its object has, through the power of dialogue, been converted into an intersubjectivity which, however, goes beyond the strictly subjective to an altogether new domain, like Spinoza's *substance* or Hegel's *Geist*: a drama of tragically unsustained, yet ecstatically ever-renewed perfect meetings in a community of beings; a substantive metamorphosis which inexorably falls away from dialogue to detachment (in its pejorative sense), only to rise once again.

C • THE FRUITION OF EXPERIENCE

(*a*) Through Subject to Object

In the phase of experience which mediates the transformation from primordial experience to dialogic experience, a person allows himself to be gripped by external objects. As he explores these objects, he gives himself up to them with all his powers for empathic resonance. The phenomena which he thereby encounters are constituted as veridical objects; and he effects their conversion by his reciprocal transformation of his merely empirical *I* into a veridical object for *them*. Taking hold of the objects, he comports himself toward them in multifarious ways. And as the world impinges upon him, he assumes a definite posture toward the world. He makes its hidden depths accessible to himself. Once posited, this "naïve" awareness of objects as *self*-constituting, and, as such, themselves constituting a realm of transcendent objectivity, gives way to the dialogic apprehension of the world as *transcendentally* real: a realm distinct from the reality which, hitherto, had been experienced as merely empirical. Complementary to this newly synthesized reality is reflexive awareness, consciousness which, now object to itself, turns in upon itself. Initially, the empirical *I* meditates its own inwardness. By stages, the locus of the *I* is shifted toward what subsequently will emerge, in meditation, as a person's very center. From the standpoint of *its* relatedness to an *outer* reality, *this I*, which is newly in process of emerging, reflects, or "bends back," what was encountered into itself. Rather than responding to an other external to it, it now responds to itself, as the reflected products of its meditatings from within itself. Henceforth, response to exterior objects constitutes merely their envisagement as "neutral" materials on which the originally empirical *I* had inscribed those symbols which, by its intrinsic activity, it had autonomously engendered. Neither denied nor affirmed, this seemingly self-sufficient and independent exterior domain is simply, at this point, *not posited* as relevant to one's meditations. All that counts is what occurs when, in solitude, one addresses oneself, when one attends to one's feelings, one's rememberings, one's hopes, one's desires. Now the self construes its reflections to be the power of self-illumination, the power of making visible its own inwardness.

Under these circumstances, one becomes aware of one's own awareness as, at first, a mere undifferentiated, hence indeterminate, *object* of awareness. No longer are data given *to* awareness. Now awareness itself is the datum. Increasingly, one experiences one's psychic content not as mere fleeting impressions, nor, surely, as the internalized image of an "external" world, but, rather, as a flowing forth, into a definite configuration, from a "something" which reveals itself to one as an objective, interior manifold: something which is "mine" yet something *given*, though still to be constituted, by a power distinct from one's empirical *I*. For the person is now empowered to present objects to himself internally, objects which, so to speak, rise up to meet him, as he meditatively experiences them, from *within* his awareness. An entire realm of immanent objectivity discloses itself through the actions of an empirical *I* in process of its own transformation, as it constitutes the inner objects counterposed to it, a veridical transformation to a "transcendental *I*" which holds inner dialogue with those objects. Spreading out beyond the person, yet within him—one might say, *beyond the within*—an infinite realm of *I*-constituted objects presents itself to him. Now all objectivity is strictly oriented toward the person. Apprehended as his most intimate possession, this realm belongs to his "me." Object for the "me," it is woven into the imaginational fabric of his inner existence. Increasingly, the person accepts himself as the region in which this matrix of objects reveals itself. Indeed, one might define him as an "I engaging in activities of self-acceptance." And as they unfold, the constituents of this region become luminous. As the person thus inwardly comports himself toward those internal objects, he experiences himself as intimately woven with them: he is gripped by them, he touches them, he listens to them, he takes hold of them, he cultivates them, he guards them, he brings them to fruition, he expresses them in encounterable symbolisms. Here I refer to everything which one apprehends as presented within one's awareness; and, clearly, these objects are dreams, fantasies, and thoughts—all in process of objectification. In addition, they include everything which, upon further reflection, one attributes to the external world as perceptual objects, insofar as one conceives oneself as constituting that world as a "construct" of one's awareness: in brief, as *imaginationally* rendering it.

Onlooker on his own interiority, a person initially experiences himself as disinterested. Objectively, he witnesses emerging relationships, originally grounded by awareness but now clarified within awareness. In a formula: *cogito* (construed as thinking, perceiving, and feeling) is "observed" by *ego* which intends *cogitatio* (i.e., the thought, the perceived, and the felt). Arising through *ego*'s cogitations, the first, namely, *cogito*, is a repository of meanings which form a system in which the last, namely, *cogitatio*, reveals itself. Not construed realistically, in the sense of a mere external world given prior to meaning, hence, counterposed to awareness, *cogitatio* is simply that necessary correlate of meaning which manifests itself within awareness. It is the locus wherein those meanings cluster, whether they be understood as fantasied or existent—as focal memory, percept, object of desire, goal of will. Synthesized into a coherent and unified fabric, this manifold discloses some foci as real and others as ideal. In both cases, powers inhere in the manifold. Immanent in awareness, these powers are activated *by* awareness, as it exercises itself. As such, they are both real and specific. For such powers constitute themselves actualities according to definite rules. Now radical particularity reigns, namely, the facts articulated in awareness. Yet these facts cannot ultimately be specified. In the end, they are the matrix wherein particularity as such arises. Only as awareness increasingly clarifies itself does existence, in all its diversity, constitute itself as indeed *within* awareness. For, *to be aware* means "not-to-be wary"; it is spontaneously to allow a content to disclose itself with clarity, hence, in this sense, to dis-cover or to unconceal itself to *ego*.

By turning within and toward his awareness, every seeker aims at penetrating this realm. He searches out abiding, fixed, and objective unities. No mere fragments, but individual objects, every such unity, by the workings of awareness, constitutes itself a durable configuration. Now the object orients *itself* toward the questor. Synthesized both within him and for him, each object is, at bottom, an autochthonous power. As a person potentiates this power, drawing it toward him as it thus shapes itself into actuality *within* his luminous awareness, and, correlatively, unifies its hitherto disparate contents, this new "actuality," like a magnet, exerts a contrary pull. However, the evolving object constitutes itself a force which quietly persuades. Gently drawing one toward it, this still world of fantasy captivates by a special charisma. Thereby, it engenders the person's nature as he, in turn, engenders *its* nature.

(*b*) The Shaping of True Objectivity

What is the source of this charisma? How does it differ from the attraction which external objects exert upon consciousness? To deal with these questions, I must, in my next part, treat *the speaking forth of the person* as an ontologic category. There I show how the hidden layers and deeper structures of speech both catalyze and become constitutive of the very realms to which speech pertains. For the moment, I can only observe: by the person's capacity for synthesizing such internal objects as percepts, images, or specific feelings a "nexus"[4] of unities achieves fruition within him as structured figures against a still undifferentiated ground. Needing a person's *ego*, which absorbs these unified entities, and thereby enhances its own strength, the objects veritably transform the *ego*. In dialectical interplay, the person reconstitutes those objects, as, in turn, they reconstitute him. In consequence, every man participates in an internal realm of pure form. By his participation, forms so activate themselves as to evolve toward *specific* objectivity. Naturally, I here refer to *ego*, or the *I*, as un-repressed: an *I* which is whole, and not split into fragmented *ego*s which, so to speak, cling to objects, wed themselves to objects, and allow themselves to be dragged down by objects—those dim but still efficacious traces of a past which has refused to perish, a past which so intrudes upon present action that powers for action are diminished and constructed, and the new objects which these powers shape are deformed and distorted.

I introduce a distinction made by Husserl, who evolved for his phenomenology[5] a Transcendental Idealism, wherein "transcendental," in constrast to my usage, is construed as but *derivatively* dialogic. For, for Husserl, "transcendental" refers to an ultimate, primal transcendental *ego*. In opposition to his interpretation, my "transcendental" is intended to convey implications which are intrinsically dialogic. Though, for him, all objects are engendered according to principles "interior" to awareness, the primal, given reality being one's own evolving awareness as one philosophically meditates, Husserl contrasts the "passive genesis" of objects which belong to what is experienced as the external, perceptual world with the "active genesis" of strictly created objects (i.e., *ideal* objects which, nonetheless, may be projected onto real objects). In my own meditation, I stress created, ideal object, but within a framework which envisages a reinterpretation of Husserlian phenomena as but one phase (the third, or purely relational) of the evolving primordial relationship: a phase which I call—in opposition to Husserl, indeed by a kind of synthesis of Marcel and Buber with Husserl—*dialogue*.[6]

By my construal of Husserl's thesis, in "active genesis," one constitutes the very objectivity of objects. Juxtaposing and rearranging them, one configures the objects imaginationally. And as one "plays" with objects, and delights in contemplating their kaleidoscopic unfoldings, one discovers that they are formed in accordance with principles which undergo their *own* evolution, principles which interlock as a conceptual tapestry which correlates with the entire manifold of objects. Each principle expresses a dynamism inherent in a particular kind of object; each governs the genesis of that kind of object into an *interior* manifold. And as myriad such manifolds are shaped, ever-new schemes of coherence emerge: schemes which continually transform the tapestry of principles; schemes which, by those principles, draw the manifolds into novel unities.

Through creative recollection, these objects are gathered into objectivity from the diverse influences which work on the creator from within him. Initially, as Pierre Duhem expressed it, "ils germent en lui sans lui."[7] However, as they articulate themselves, the very process of creation enters consciousness with increasing vigor and clarity. Gathering the objects from a past, perhaps obscure and remote, into the fullness of the present, the creator of these ideal objects presents them, with a growing sense of purpose, to an awareness which itself continually expands and deepens. Under the governance of their own laws, the objects rise from his inner depths. Yet their risings are directed by creative meditatings which always implicitly conform to the laws. Initially alien, since they arose from immanence, yet from a beyond enshrouded in darkness, the objects are shaped, as they are drawn to expression, into a form which is intimately possessed by their creator, who is now also their discoverer. As created, and discovered, such forms exist apart from their creator; he experiences them to be distant and strange. But in this stance of idealism, the forms are not entertained in "tough-minded"[8] apartness, though they exhibit the *appearance* of apartness. For, through persistent inner dialogue, one touches anew these newly alienated objects. Gradually, the seeker (and creator) reduces the strangeness, and the distance, which he himself had conferred on them. Progressively, these *now* projected, externalized objects, which one thrusts before one from within one, synthesize themselves. An altogether new consciousness is shaped from numberless imaginational strands. Flowing together into novel experiential unities from a mysterious, perhaps archetypally ordered, *intra*personal beyond, these emerging shapes become increasingly accessible to the questor. In alternating phases of *drawing from within* and *expressive generalization*, they are continuously appropriated, and stimulate ever-renewed creative acts.

(*c*) Transcendentality

Having thus postulated a position of radical idealism, I immediately discern its limits, especially as I recur to creativity's externalizing aspects. Hence, I must anticipate a later thesis, wherein primordial experience, having evolved into a second moment, itself split into transcendental realism and transcendental idealism, gives birth to a third moment, wherein the opposing members themselves dialectically fuse, a moment which I designate in the following manner: *transcendental,* for I preserve a radical distinction between empathic dialogue and the detached stance of empiricism; *presentational,* for I stress the reciprocity between the self-presentings of the dialogists; *substantial,* for I reiterate the link between my thesis and Spinoza's concept of "substance," a term intended as neutral with respect to the physical and the mental, to subject and object; and *rhythmical,* for I emphasize the ferment and the unfolding character of both substance and presentation. Depending on the particular context of my inquiry, and the specific elements I focus on, I qualify "transcendental" by these designations. And when freed from the prison of my awareness, a prison in which thoroughgoing idealism inexorably entraps me, I recall the quality of radical givenness, which I ineluctably associate with the external world, in contradistinction to its exclusive givenness within awareness. Under the influence of transcendental realism, the doctrine of transcendental idealism transmutes itself, by inner necessity, into an altogether new doctrine, which subsumes its own originating matrix: a doctrine which, in a sophistical way, recapitulates yet goes beyond primordial experience. Interconnections between these doctrines may thus be schematized:

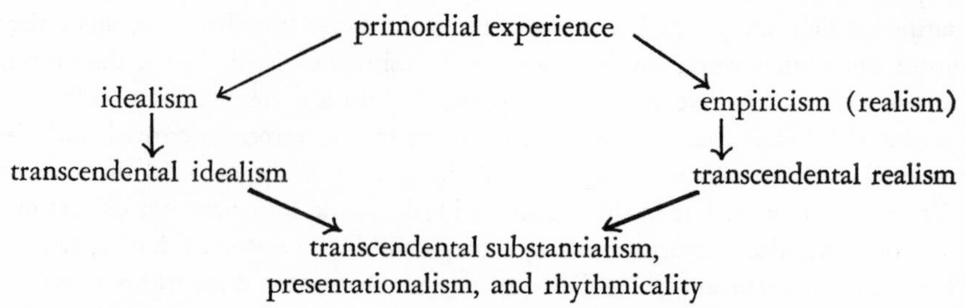

NOTES

1. See Partridge, *Origins*, pp. 456 (order) and 526 (prime).
2. See ibid., p. 192 (experience).
3. See the index entry for "inheritance" in Whitehead, *Process and Reality.*
4. See the index entry for "nexus" in ibid.
5. Edmund Husserl, *Cartesian Meditations*, trans. Dorion Cairns (The Hague: Nijhoff, 1960), First Meditation.
6. See Gabriel Marcel, *The Mystery of Being.* I. *Reflection and Mystery*, trans. G. S. Fraser (Chicago: Regnery, 1960), and Martin Buber, *I and Thou*, trans. Walter Kaufman (New York: Scribners, 1970).
7. *The Aim and Structure of Physical Theory*, trans. Philip Wiener (New York: Atheneum, 1962), p. 252; see also the discussion on pp. 252–57.
8. William James, *Pragmatism*, ed. Ralph Barton Perry (Cleveland: World, 1964), Lecture I, pp. 20, 22–23.

13

SYMBOLS OF HUMAN ENCOUNTER: THE RHYTHMS OF SELF AND COSMOS

PREAMBLE

As one comes to understand one's dreams and reveries, to shape the amorphous earth into an artistic product, and to create music, dance, or poetry, one increasingly discovers, hence *owns* (in the sense of inventively appropriating), one's inmost self. Holding *quasi*-dialogue with one's interior realm, one draws from it visible symbols; and one counterposes these symbols to oneself as veridical objects: objects experienced as pre-existent now fused with the symbols; objects, in part, bequeathed one and, in part, products of earlier creation. For neither a person's empirical *I* nor his inner powers per se can create. On the contrary, such powers proceed from a larger trans-personal matrix. Therein originating, they give birth to coherent action which, in turn, creates ***through*** the empirical *I*, converting that *I*, as one holds (quasi-) dialogue with creation's emerging objects, to transcendental status. In this process, a person immerses himself in his inner silence; he listens in stillness; he draws forth new objects from its very depths. Illuminating new truths, one empowers oneself to shape new symbols. After these symbols have succeeded in bringing to light hitherto hidden depths, they, in turn, will be replaced by still new symbols, symbols partly equivalent to the old, with respect to the invariant ground of both sets of symbols, but, also, partly non-equivalent. For the very articulation of the ground changes its character and, through that change, transforms the creating self.

A • SELF-ARTICULATION

(*a*) Transcendental Idealism Woven with Transcendental Realism

A realm of intra-objectivity, wherein I dwell amid objects of my own fashioning, complements what, in exterior dialogue, had become a realm of the intersubjective: a realm which binds person and person or person and object together. For I create "within" myself yet "without" myself. Once inwardly shaped, symbolic forms exteriorize themselves as possessing an existence independent of the one who creates them. They perpetuate a "something" within me which I hold before myself as a mirror of all that is best in me and most durably belongs to me: what I can proudly claim as "mine." By confronting these phantoms of inner reality, I both clarify my own being and repotentiate my powers to create new symbols, powers resident within my being. Through meditation, I experience myself as a germinating center, an interior synthesizing agency which weaves into unity a fabric of influences which never cease to invade my being from without, yet always work from within: in its meanings and structures, a world which *I* have made; an expressive world which invests my entire milieu with my own presence; a world in which I synchronize my fleeting feelings, transforming them, by successive transfigurations, into a larger and richer experience.

Every person's inmost being touches the outer world. And symbolic creation arises from the dialectical interplay of the catalyzing powers resident in the world with two other activities: the in-gathering of imprints of these powers to constitute something which may be claimed as wholly "mine"; the exteriorizing of these depositions to suffuse the originating powers with one's particular presence and, thereby, to reconstitute those powers. Through symbolic vehicles, one concretizes one's very feelings as both tangible tokens of an inscrutable reality and agents woven of earthly things: a concrescence of patterns created in accordance with formative principles the source of which lies buried in one's inmost self. In inner dialogue, one meets this realm *as* one draws it into objective expression, shapes it anew and stamps it with one's newly emerging presence, and fuses those imprints with the imprints of a presence which was deposited an instant ago.

This is the vision of transcendental idealism: reality as a person's *own* product, reflecting *his* presence, an objective other to *him* which he draws forth from within himself. Yet this presence, which retains its intimate character as the concrete embodiment of a law which every person prescribes to himself, flows from a larger principle, a principle which exemplifies itself, and manifests a kind of pre-established harmony, over the whole range of reflective beings, each a center of symbolic activity. By this principle, and by its every instantiating law, the "deep within" of each person is inextricably bound to the "deep within" of all persons: a bond which he must discover anew, through personal meditation, as the generative principle of his every act. Revealing an intra-objective manifold which prescribes objective laws for validating what, in accordance with those laws, was created by individuals, this generative principle establishes the ground for universal empathy: a bond deeper than, yet subsuming, all specific modes of sympathy.

Owing to the very processes by which the self evolves, each person becomes an issue to himself; each has concern both for himself, and, by an inherent empathy, for others. When, by the self-emending nature of reflection, he ponders, he ponders truthfully. For as, by stages, reality discloses itself to man, in its ever-more-pervasive character, the truth emerges asymptotically as the *ultimate* outcome of reflective acts. Moreover, a necessary condition for truthful reflection is the truthful reflection of other persons in the human community. A profound neighborliness prevails, the camaraderie of selves seeking truths of and among other selves. By appeal to norms which are collectively worked out, and through the interchange of dissident, contrasting, or complementary beliefs, truth eventually tends to declare itself. Furthermore, by his every reflective act, a person prescribes to himself, as its implicit and universal *moral* law, this injunction: should one fail to reflect truthfully or, at least, in ways which, in the long run, conduce to truth—i.e., fail to recognize, promote, and accept the truth, in its wholeness, of *every* entity—one fails to reflect, and indeed one fails to fulfill one's nature as reflective. Grounded in ontology, ethics issues prescriptions which are *descriptive* of the reflective character of being, and, in particular, of human being. The doctrines of transcendental idealism and transcendental realism interweave to entail a new doctrine, which I have variously labeled transcendental presentationalism, transcendental substantialism, and transcendental rhythmicality. According to this syncretist doctrine, I now assert: by his own quest, each person promotes the other's quest; in denying himself—hence, in failing to affirm his own questing powers—each denies the other. Only when a person refuses to be deprived of this inherent ontologic right does he affirm his full personhood; only when he insists upon presenting himself to his neighbors and, reciprocally, accepting from them their presentings to him, in the vibrant presences of all, does he acknowledge his grounding substance; only then does he orchestrate his unique and absolutely singular rhythms. In mutual compresence, the nuances and mysteries of every person can thereby resonate throughout the human community, that creative meditation be allowed, and be sustained.

By empathic transmission, a mutuality of self-presentings enables each person to attain his unique consummation. The very cosmos becomes luminous with personal presence. For every individual illuminates the cosmos in a distinctive way. It is as though many beams, each directed from a particular creature as source, and each glowing in accordance with principles peculiarly its own, light up the world; their shifting foci interplay and interact; a phantasmagoria of enmeshing strands of light criss-cross in realms hitherto dark and obscure. By the flux of symbols drawn into concrescence,[1] the world becomes as it is. A tapestry of harmonies and dissonances, these symbols are the very stuff of reality: herein consists the vision of a transcendental idealism so informed by transcendental realism as to transmute both doctrines into the new doctrine which I announce here.

(*b*) Transcendental Rhymicality

Woven of two processes, dialogue entails the drawing of both exterior and interior objects into relatedness with the empirical *I* (and empirical *I*'s correlative going toward those objects). Thereby, the empirical *I*, transcending itself, metamorphoses itself into a transcendental *I*. And whatever its explicit focus of attention, each process implicitly conditions the other. In consequence, dialogue brings about its own fulfillment as a synthesis of two visions of reality, visions hitherto designated transcendental realism and transcendental idealism, which, together, shape an altogether new mode of transcendentality. From the standpoint of a realist philosophy, the other which one counterposes to oneself is initially construed as wholly transcendent, an other which is deemed self-constituting as for-itself and in-itself. Through dialogue, that other subjectifies itself as immanent within one. But from the standpoint of an idealist philosophy, the other which one counterposes to oneself is initially construed as wholly immanent, an other constituted by the *I* as for-him and in-him. Through dialogue that other objectifies itself as transcendent to one. In its deeper import, dialogue, as both response to and ground for crisis, emerges in the more comprehensive vision which I have outlined. Nonetheless, subsumed under transcendental rhythmicality, as I shall henceforth designate the new vision, both realism and idealism retain validity. The complementarity of these more restricted positions is not lost in the larger view.

In transcendental rhythmicality, one participates at once in two presences, i.e., in two kinds of object, or aspects of all objects, as present to one. Each presence is both immanent in and implied by, as well as transcendent to, a person's every act. And as one presents oneself to the data of one's experience, inner or outer, they are grasped as reciprocally presenting themselves to one. They make themselves available for one's objectifying acts. Yet both processes of reciprocal presentings constitute, at bottom, a single process. In the context of dialogue understood as integral and complete, they are but aspects of that process. Inseparable and united, they possess the rhythmic, self-transcending character to which I have alluded. Envisaging the basic elements in a scheme propaedeutic to my general systematic account of this position (which I present in both *Cosmos* and *Apotheosis*, wherein its implications as a *special* theory of personal expression are worked out), I stress here the theme of symbolism. In my final division, I show how notions relevant to any theory of the person—namely, power, integrality, and encounter—are linked by the idea of symbol, itself related to justice, to the derivative notions of integrity and wisdom, which I treat in Parts IV and V, as central to my ontology of the person.

By way of synthesizing transcendental realism with transcendental idealism, I suggest that a person confronts, at once, two worlds, inner and outer. In part, each world is given as objective: its meanings and structures, its special patternings of traits, its tonalities and nuances. Given as intimately his, that world, in effect, persuades him trustingly to make his claims upon it. On the other hand, each world, in part, constitutes a realm entirely alien to him. What he truly feels, why he may create, for whom he might care—these are decisions which he can make only consequent upon his having marked out for himself a specific domain of inquiry. That he can draw forth initially strange and alien forms, forms shrouded in mystery, into the light of day, he must, with all his resources, question, approach, and inspect. Only then can he convert these forms into new forms which, now more familiar to him, he can appropriate as more intimately his own, and thereby bring into trusting relatedness to himself. In dialogue, the alienation of the other is reduced; it is transmuted into the status of friend. However, this transfiguration can occur only when, in the process of creation, one becomes attuned to—hence, friend of—one's very own self *as* creative: "inasmuch as I am not a stranger to myself," declared Erich Fromm, "no one and nothing is a stranger to me."[2] Then alone does one *personally* experience all objects, inner and outer, as process, process which, unimpeded, flows both toward one and through one as one, reciprocally, draws oneself toward it. No longer is the empirical *I merely* empirical. To posit this *I* in its searching acts is to posit its negation as empirical *I*; it is to affirm its transcendence to an *I* which is truly (i.e., dialogically) in touch with the other, inner and outer; yet an other which is no longer mere other, but a "something" which, when joined in communion to the *I*, transforms it into a veridically transcendental *I*. At last, one experiences objects as they present themselves to one, now a veridical *person*, and as one, reciprocally and simultaneously, presents oneself to them: an alternation and complementarity of interior dialogue with exterior dialogue, the two comprising a single, integral dialogue.

(*c*) The Symbol as Self-Presenting

In presenting myself to an other, I make myself an authentic object to it. Drawing myself *into* objectivity, I present myself as truly other to the other. Contacting the former other, I touch it with all that I am; I impinge upon it; literally or figuratively, I speak to it. And, through my speaking, I integrate into a unity the diversity and diffuseness of the parts of my own being. Here I mean a *speaking forth*: a flowing from within myself toward another, the coming to fruition of action, the consummate resolution of tension. And as I make myself an "object" to the other, i.e., one whose very contours and boundaries are defined by the other, my own imprints, the symbolisms of my being, are assimilated by the other; and thus I pass beyond the status of mere object to the status of transcendental object. But if the other to whom I am an object is himself a *person*, then he, likewise, must constitute himself an authentic object to me.

Under the perspective of transcendental rhymicality (and also, in this context, presentationalism), I distinguish a strictly personal relationship from a relationship involving, in part, mere objects. Naturally, only persons can fully present themselves, hence, truly reciprocate in compresence. Only interpersonal dialogue is consummate dialogue. Correlatively, a person can dramatically mask his true character as transcendental object as well as transcendental subject. Only he has the capacity to fall away from transcendentality into the merely empirical.

By presenting himself in authentic objectivity, a person enables his expressions progressively to articulate themselves. Through the very act of presenting, they lose their diffuse, fragmentary character. Woven into a coherent fabric of utterance, gesture, physiognomy, and movement, all personal expression constitutes the means by which, in stages, person discloses his hidden depths. For, to express oneself *is to press out from within* a concrete and tangible complex, vehicle of an originally ineffectual but ever-fermenting spiritual content. Thus embodying his own interiority, man makes himself count significantly in the world of real things. Imprinting himself durably upon another, he alters its (or his) very destiny. Such symbolic media as dance, music, or poetry, all matrices in which symbols appear and shine forth as symbols, evoke deep-lying feeling, and summon inner adventure. They call forth everything which, originally concealed, lies within a person: an embodiment, a shape, a making manifest of what had been but interior silence; a transmitting, or sending across to another person, of human expression incarnate—hence, a *symbol* in the sense of a *tangible* expression of a double nature: the private vehicle of an inward, inscrutable spiritual content; the communicative joining, by that vehicle, of a symbolizer to another, a joining, in the end, in communion. A unique, singular and non-duplicative physical complex which, arising within one's inmost recesses, resonates, once it has emerged, in the human community, the symbol is a compressed physical commentary on a spiritual content. At once, it is both discovery of that content and interpretation. Commenting on the spirit, a symbol elaborates it and extends its scope. Revitalizing what it had initially merely expressed, it clarifies man's spirit, and infuses that spirit with novelty. As such, symbols constitute invitations to another to discern their evolving new meanings.

A symbol can be a sound, a glance, a facial expression, a movement, the evocation of an image: in these instances, factors attached to the symbolizer. But in dance, music, or art, a texture of more durable symbols is created: symbols, in some cases, evanescent but always codifiable; symbols, to some extent, detachable from the symbolizer as independent, encounterable objects; a texture, in all cases, of fluctuant, evolving elements which flow from one person to another. Entering one's life as active components, these elements stir a multitude of feelings, reminiscences, and new images. Then, like the echo of a song, the reverberations fade, leaving a trace of quiet nostalgia, into the silence of one's receding presence. But through their impact, they inspire a person to reciprocate, as a way of acknowledging a gift, by presenting (as a *present*) an answering symbol. In this manner, symbols create solidarity. A matrix of flowings, a dynamic medium in organized flux of purposive, directed factors which alternately congeal and dissolve, and a field in which all respondents are embedded as both recipients and participants, the symbol solidifies human relationships. According to implicit rules of construction, it emanates from dialogists, shaping for them continuity and cohesion, the integration of continually renewed encounter. As their lives unfold, dialogists deposit, as a durable and visible residue of the spirit, ever new symbolic layers. Indeed, these lives themselves are symbolic textures: fluent, purposeful, and resilient sacraments of the vicissitudes of spirit; spirit incarnate and, as such, nature revealed in its inner ferment. Inscribed in the poetry of the body are the adventures of the psyche. "Je geistvoller, gebildeter ein Mensch ist," wrote Novalis, "desto persönlicher sind seine Glieder."[3]

B • SELF-DISCOVERY

(*a*) The Symbol as Mobile and Fluctuant

In every symbol, the whole of awareness is posited. Luminous bearer and purposive agent of an articulated awareness, the symbol constitutes a sharply delineated figure against a dimmer yet always haunting background. Always, the spirit reasserts itself and brings its inner contents to completion. Now as ferment, now as object, it ever presents itself in concrete, encounterable shape. A unity of intent, the person's entire will strives toward its fruition in specific symbols. And this process *is* the coming-to-birth of awareness. Every evolving symbol is the locus wherein the diffused energies associated with a person's activities are mobilized, thence flow into a single product: the symbol itself, the momentarily fixed terminus of the very process of its own unfolding. Always *re*-presenting the universal, each particular symbol directly *pre*sents the incomprehensible, the mysterious, the unfathomable. Once inspected—i.e., re-presented, searched into, and deciphered, for a symbol's initial presentation enigmatically incorporates something which lies both beyond and within—the symbol discloses itself to be a vision of the universal in the garb of the particular. Yet, to explicate its latent content, the context of that content must be understood. For, like a crystal, the symbol grows and, embracing its own milieu, tends to transcend itself.

In general, a person's self-presentings are fluent, mobile, and of subtly altering nuance. The ineffable symbols of the psyche hover about, suffuse, penetrate, and pervade the tangible symbols of the corporeal. In the end, they even transform the corporeal. And when a person is fully himself, vibrant with the song and dance of human being, no clear demarcation between psyche and soma can be discerned, at least not by another person who is empathically implicated with him. And, of the transfiguration which this inherent ambiguity of distinction implies, a Balzac can movingly write of this

> angel of gentleness, whose plainness was slowly vanishing, dispelled by the strength of the moral qualities reflected in her face. She was all soul. The spirit of prayer seemed to purify and refine the coarser features of her face and make them luminous. Who has not observed the phenomenon of this transfiguration on saintly faces where the habits of the soul have finally triumphed over the most graceless features by imprinting upon them that divine illumination which comes from the nobility and purity of elevated thoughts? [4]

The different facets of symbolism themselves evolve. Formerly merely a single element but now interwoven with other elements, each factor contributes to a great lattice, a mobile, orchestrated lattice which undergoes perpetual reconfiguration of its parts. Exhibiting an architectonic rather than an architecture, this lattice is so composed that the meanings associated with all factors are interwoven and co-dependent. Shaped into symbolism, all factors express a primordially indeterminate yet, by the actions of the *I*, thoroughly "transcendentalized" self-determining potency. Never ceasing to actualize itself, this potency represents to the self, and, therefore, is *representable* to another self as image and efflux, a mobile congregation of visible forms.

In a symphony, meaning is directly absorbed into its own tones. Leading inward rather than pointing to a referent beyond, meaning resides in the progressive unfoldings of rhythm, cadence, accent, tonality, pitch, melodic line, thematic growth. Likewise, every kind of symbol directs one inward to the very perturbations of one's soul, of which the symbol is both embodiment and actual presentation. And by its inner constitution, a symbol makes present, in myriad infoldings, the traces of a past which perpetuates itself by fusing diverse influences into a unitary present. In such presenting, feelings are congealed and made tangible, though in differing modes and degrees of tangibility. Too, feelings both enlarge themselves and progressively become more subtle. For they are permeated by the responses, called forth by an immediate living occasion, to the one for whom there is presentation. What was creatively synthesized, I repeat, is *given* him as a gift or present. Durable imprints of donor now impressed into recipient become constituents of what emerges as an altogether new existence. Now operative in a life different from that whence they arose, symbols, therein "perished" but ever viable, undergo continuous new growth; yet it is a metamorphosis in which the original symbolizer himself can participate.

(*b*) The Luminosity of the Symbol

Under the perspective of transcendental rhymicality, a symbol exhibits three interconnected traits: conjunctivity, immediacy, spirituality. As conjunctive, the symbol joins together, liberates, and affirms, pointing toward future possibilities of communion which germinate in each present moment; disjunctive symbols are a degraded species which split asunder—hence, fragment—rather than unify and integrate. As immediate, the symbol is an instance of direct experience; a tangible presentation, it exhibits varying degrees of ineffability. As spiritual, the symbol refers to an ever-changing meaning which lies beyond itself; yet the symbol participates in its own meaning and, ultimately, is integrally interwoven with that meaning. Formed of both particular elements and universal elements, meanings are always complex. Pertaining to a unique life history—namely, the personal vicissitudes of the one who shapes the symbol—the symbol nonetheless points toward a shared heritage. Initially disparate and aggregative, it germinates in the past. And arising from a mode of experience which Whitehead calls "causal efficacy,"[5] it is, once formed, an ingredient in another mode of experience: namely, "presentational immediacy."[6] For the symbol evolves within a person toward that confluence of its component factors which bursts forth into a unity of dramatic and portentous immediacy.

Accordingly, I construe the dream symbol, for example, not as a partially remembered shadowy image which, understood as a psychic "existent" sui generis, possesses both conscious and unconscious components, but as the actual presentation to another, or, indeed, to oneself, of the efflorescing image, an image presented in its own birthing. For a dream symbol is the tonal–gestural complex which accompanies, embodies, and reveals itself only in the activity wherein its shaping spiritual matrix communicates itself. An initially evanescent, seemingly fragile, germ which dynamically unfolds, it gathers about its nucleus strands of transference, counter-transference, and authentic encounter. Presenting a personal, and perhaps a collective, past within and to a present person, or a present community of persons, this type of symbol portends both individual and archetypal factors. And *all* symbols analogously emerge in their veridically symbolic status in the context of acts of communication and communion. In the very processes by which a personal past comes to fruition in the present, they constitute condensed "statements" of that past.

The past is complex. It enfolds various dimensions. There is a past which is just fading, a past which blends into the present, and unfolds as a panorama, gently receding, of the world disclosed in immediate encounter; there is a past, recent or remote, over which one reminisces, a past which can vividly be gathered into recall, moment by moment; there is a past which is dimly felt, vague reverberations of feelings by which one is enveloped but which can no longer be summoned to awareness with precision; and there is a past which is radically dissociated from all recollection, a past which flows within each person, yet the impact of which, durable and persistent, is no longer felt save as an obscure intimation of a history which stretches indefinitely backward, seemingly out of time. I do not speak of repressions, those constellations of factors split off from each of these pasts both to haunt and to deform the present, "dissociated dynamisms" which torment and constrict a deeper sense of self. I refer only to that fusion of past with present whereby the past flows, however imperceptibly or with whatever vivacity of impact, into the present: a coherent, continuous flow of characteristic style and rhythm. Bearing import from the several dimensions of the past, the symbol brings diverse past strands to confluence as a distinct and singular entity. Condensing these strands into a particular and unique compound, it illuminates what hitherto had been hidden; and where concealment entails dissembling or cloaking, the symbol reveals and makes manifest.

An element in a mutual addressing, the symbol expresses, and, indeed, constitutes a vital factor in that interfusion of presentings of selves which *is* the *de facto* consummate being-there, in full luminosity, of a community of selves. Yet though the separateness of persons, their autonomy and individuality, are dissolved by symbolic activity, autonomy and individuality are, equally and correlatively, affirmed. For the symbol summons forth, sums up, elaborates, and presents, as a unique and indivisible product, a living portrait inscribed upon the present as a "remembrance of things past"[7]—like the picture, to cite a negative instance, of Dorian Gray.[8] In the symbol, and the inner silence whence it arose, its creator makes startling new discoveries; he discloses the priceless jewels which had lain dormant in the caverns of his past, a hitherto unfathomable abyss: like suddenly coming upon the intricately arranged fountains and terraces in the gardens of Tivoli, near Rome, which conceal yet hauntingly, unexpectedly, and in ways evocative of sheer delight, reveal marvelous new recesses. In symbols, we give expression to our every striving to know this abyss; we incarnate our every drawing forth of its content into "burning immediacy."[9]

(*c*) Symbols of Transcendence

Consummating the process of self-discovery, the symbol in the very act of its creation constitutes a giving birth to something which is radically new. Drawing forth significant components from a person's past, and revivifying these components in the here-and-now, the symbol, once created, solidifies a person and confers new meaning on his subsequent acts. By his symbol shapings, he brings to fruition, and he presents to himself, his own history: its components at last come to decisive expression. But not merely his personal history! For, too, transpersonal elements are woven into symbolism. Whitehead's aphorism plumbs the very depths of the import of the symbol: "The whole . . . world," he declared, "conspires to produce a new occasion"[10] of experience. Apprehended under the perspective of a particular individual, the whole of reality enters his existence; assimilated to his idiosyncratic nature, the whole of reality is drawn to personal expression. In its deepest layers, the symbol incorporates what, on imaginative interpretation, discloses itself to be a vision, at once particular and universal, of some pervasive aspect of the world. *A fortiori*, this aspect repeats itself in distinctive ways over the entire range of symbol creators. And ramifying beyond his own private existence, the roots of each *creative* person enmesh with the existence of all persons.

A physico-spiritual complex, the objectified mood which is the symbol strikingly contrasts with given contemporary experience. It stands in dramatic opposition to what one *is*, or, more precisely, to what one *was* an instant prior to one's self-presentation as symbol. Only by one's interaction with a symbol does any present moment both consummate itself and perish into memory. For the symbol shatters the commonplace, stirs discontent. By its impact, myriad fragments of contemporary experience fall away, and something radically new emerges. A vehicle of *discontent*, the symbol attends to what had hitherto been denied: the eerie, the tender, the awesome, the strange. It constitutes a jarring but self-revelatory eruption into visibility or, depending upon its composition, into any sensory medium. In the context of meditation, itself a phase of the symbol's generation, this concrete token of what had been hidden liberates a person and restores his intra-personal harmony to new vigor. Radically affirming life, the symbol summons the self to present itself with clarity, forthrightness, and honesty.

Thus condensing and perpetuating the mysterious infoldings of numberless past meetings, encounters of self with self and of self with other, the symbol impinges in a manner which can be electrifying. In a well-executed dance, as by Shankar, the details of the physical presenting of a symbol are perfectly fused to convey all intended depths of spirituality. Indeed, both what is conveyed and the vehicle of conveyance are, at bottom, identical. For the symbol is a process and an unfolding; it is an efflorescing and, as such, can never, qua symbol, be arrested as fixed, inert, or passive. Like the dance, every symbol, even if the motions which it embodies are virtual, as in painting or sculpture, comprises intercoordinated rhythms, rhythms of many amplitudes, frequencies, compositions, and forms—all variable and all thematizing themselves in diverse ways.

Suggesting an image of human perfection, however momentary and fleeting that state might be, the symbol, beyond mere suggestion, actually *is* the person, as he draws himself forth into the self-presented fruition of his own possibilities. Fully interpreted (by its shaper or by those into whom it imprints itself), and, in this sense, consummated in its status as symbol, each symbol eternalizes—hence, perfects—the instant. Combining these diverse traits, it incarnates the mourning, the acceptance, and the transcendence of a past which has ineluctably perished. "Our task," wrote Rilke, "is so deeply and so passionately to impress upon ourselves this provisional and perishable earth"; and the symbol is woven of earthly stuff, "that its essential being will arise again 'invisibly' in us . . . [a] work of . . . continual conversions of the beloved visible and tangible into the invisible vibration and animation of our [own] nature, which introduces new frequencies into the vibration-spheres of the universe."[11] All symbols perish in order that they enrich. Woven into the inmost fabric of the self, a symbol, newly engendered and reflecting a clarified existence, projects the vision of a subsequent moment of that existence. Not only does it, laden with prescience, disclose the past, but, beyond that, it exhibits a presentiment of a future. Projecting a significant trajectory, it prefigures the vicissitudes of a particular human existence.

C • SELF-CREATIVITY

(*a*) Symbol and Integrity

When brought to its fruition every symbol bears multiple import; and by its import, it also *com*ports. Inasmuch as in the very act of its creation the symbol joins itself to that to which it refers, it is purposive, intentional activity. Binding persons in communion, it summons, announces, and fructifies human encounter, the very negation of transference. Binding the physical to the spiritual, it promotes integrality, hence, negates dispersed and fragmented "symptoms," both physical and psychic. Binding the residual past to the anticipated future, to shape a present moment, it activates potency, thus facilitating the overcoming of repression. In short, an element of living, vibrant presence, symbols disclose and, as consummate acts, constitute the very integrity of persons-in-relation, hence, stand in sharp opposition to all non-fulfillment.

In every human encounter, symbols imprint themselves upon both encounterers. Communicating something of the essence of the shaper, each symbol allows something essential about that shaper to perish, either into what *he* will become, at the next instance of his existence, or into what another will become. Thereby, both communicants imprint concrete expressions of their joys and sorrows, their hopes and despairs, at a present moment on what they will become at the next moment; each communicant thus shapes his own mood, and contributes to the shaping of the moods of those whom he confronts. By dialogue, I mean just such a perishing. And wherever there is perishing, there is tragedy. The perfect moments of simulated eternity pass. When dialogue has failed, as in mortals it must, their passage is tragic. However momentary, there is grief; and there is mourning. Then alone, when mourning has been consummated, the power to renew dialogue is felt, even though that power might, as yet, remain unactualized. But when dialogue is renewed, the inexorably present tragedy is, at least in part, absorbed. By exercise of the power of dialogue, and its ability to absorb what had ineluctably been engendered as tragic, a person's very identity is shaped.

The failure of dialogue is tragic because it entails some loss of human life in humans who are still alive. By that loss, vibrancy is diminished, and resoluteness weakened. Tragically, a person who has found, then lost, his "center" becomes self-centered; he shifts his *deo*-centricity toward ego-centricity, thereby suffering a diminution of his integrity. And, in effect, a person of integrity is an *integer*. He is a unity who has not dispersed, not fragmented, not distorted, not thwarted his being; he is a unity whose existence is coherent in a way which allows the integument of his being, the sensitive boundary between himself and his world, both to touch and to be touched, in all the modalities of touching. And, in general, a person of integrity possesses a capacity for receiving touch, and a capacity for going forth to touch; and both capacities are aspects of a single power. Indeed, to possess integrity means to be empowered, in a centered way, both to receive impressions from without and to initiate expressions from within. Organized as a unity, these correlative processes—namely, going toward and drawing within —are grounded in a center of activity whence springs the manifold, or, more accurately, the orchestration of such symbolic forms as flow toward a recipient who, absorbing those forms, shapes new forms for the sender, in turn, to absorb. In brief, dialogue is both a counterposing and a juxtaposing of symbolisms. In it, the spiritual is exteriorized as a symbolic vehicle; and by unifying their respective symbols, persons encounter one another with integrity.

For a person to express himself from his "center," and thereby to sustain his integrity, he must counterpose to himself an object, an object to which he both speaks and listens. Against the resistance of this object, its "skepticism," so to speak, he tests his subsequent expressions. Moreover, the object itself serves as a nucleus about which he can cause his expressions to cluster, and, thereby, to transform it. For as symbolic expressions aggregate themselves about it, they, like developing crystals, envelop the object in criss-crossing strands, strands which grow into it, and, adding to it, continually reconstitute it: what had been mere accretion now "concresces" as an object.

In general, every person confronts not an amorphous world but a world which, already structured though always resilient, is receptive to his reshaping endeavors. Partly, the resistant object is prestructured as given or bequeathed him; partly, it is an object whose structure he himself has antecedently created. Yet, even had the object been created, he, nonetheless, bequeaths it *to* himself. And a self-bequeathed, a created object is *committed* to the world in trust. By its acceptance, one affirms trust and, thereby, *confirms* dialogic relatedness. Whether the creator is related to him, to another person, or to a thing, he transforms, by the acts of shaping, bequeathing, and committing, both himself *and* the other. Whatever the history of the created object, a challenge is posed to the creator. For, to evaluate his own work, a person must always refer the work to some existing state of affairs, personal or non-personal. Vis-à-vis this state of affairs, he tests his work. Yet, in part, he himself constitutes the objective condition. For his own creations have so impinged upon it as, in some fashion, to transform it. Nevertheless, it is this very *evolving* critic to whom he entrusts the decision regarding the status of his work. By reference to the critic's judgment, he himself can more effectively evaluate his own creations. Should the critic be a non-person, the judgment consists in the manner in which the work, by reference to a larger, tacit human community, conforms to or harmonizes with the "critic." But should the critic be a person, then, in the last analysis, the judgment itself must be adjudged, by that very same community, to be appropriate to the work. Indeed, the activity of criticism is intricate. It is a topic which I systematically treat in *Apotheosis.*

For my present purpose, it suffices to note that every shaper is also critic; he is a critic in a double sense: an external and conventional sense, an internal and empathic sense. As empathic, he is an implicit participant within a larger human community. Flowing from the creator, his creations are "filtered" through, hence remolded by, the inner critic; and they are modified in such fashion as more adequately to conform with a favorable judgment by the external critic. Yet the inner critic, linked to analogous critics implicated in other centers of creative activity, ultimately, if always immanently, prescribes the norms, should the inner critic be authentically bonded to the other centers, for determining the worthwhileness of the work. How inner and outer critics themselves relate, and condition one another, is itself a topic for a later account. In any event, the integrated person gives himself up to the very symbol which he himself creates as wholly other to himself. In this process, the being of the creator, his integrity, and the being of his work, *its* integrity, are in reciprocal creation; each shapes and reshapes the other. In tacit mutual agreement, both the work and the man are, as outcome of the creative process, truly transfigured. In both *its* fashion and *his* fashion, each tends the other; each aids in bringing both work and man to fruition.

Accordingly, the shaping of symbols is directed toward these ends: establishing a bond across the infinite chasm of separateness; feeling the radical otherness of the other, the work in its mystery, strangeness, and fascination as truly out there and no longer merely within the creator; yet, within that other, and between it and the creator, fashioning a bond, and the glow, of a new entity, the relatedness itself.

(*b*) Symbol as Self-Disclosure

Many implications of the perspective of transcendental rhythmicality for a theory of growing, through dialogue, toward integrity, cannot be presented in this chapter. For example, I do not speak of that dialectical interplay between critic, external or internal, and creative idea which catalyzes creation of new symbols. Nor do I characterize the "centers of activity," as they inwardly ramify among themselves. I do not speak of isomorphisms between these centers, all components of a common "substance" whence they derive their energies. Nor do I develop the implications of my allusion to the great fabric of nature as an assemblage of reciprocal, interlocking, intensifying, and contrasting givings and expressings, all proceeding from diverse centers. I do not specify the ground for the failure of dialogue construed as endless inner mirrorings, which implicate all manner of "concavity" and "convexity," or the size and power of the "lenses" employed by those mirrors: for dialogue fails when reflections are unabsorbed, "stuck" as "internal" objects, which so mask and distort reality that one reflects upon reflections, and then upon these, in endless circles; whereas dialogue succeeds through those primordial reflections which, in revivifying a person's powers to express, enable him to make himself fully present as, in endlessly subtle tonalities, his being becomes luminous with his inmost self. Nor do I speak of the status, natural or transcendental, or the symbolic by-products, of dialogue, though surely these by-products (the systematically fashioned schemes of symbols which the culture of humankind comprises) become constituents of a larger cosmos with which one is empowered to hold ever-renewed dialogue. I do not develop the thesis of how "transcendental *I*'s" collaboratively fashion a larger presence in which individuality is, not lost, but solidified and enhanced. Nor do I show how an image of reality arises, based on distorted judgment, itself grounded in nature unconsciously construed as pulverulent and deformed; nature which reflects endlessly perverse inner mirrorings wherein real objects, refusing to perish, thereby thwart a genuine renewal of nature. Nor do I show how feelings constitute an inward configuration of silent pulses which strain for expression in music, poetry, science, dance—those congealed feelings which form a tapestry which marvelously transforms itself into a polyphony of endless flux. Some of these themes have already been treated, either in this book or in earlier books; others will be taken up in subsequent books.

Still, some general remarks are in order. In re-presentation, the self holds detachedly before itself an image of reality. By this image, it draws extracts of reality into its own content, objects which it symbolizes as patterns disengaged in a double sense: from itself, from its world. Relating to an object of its own creation, the self rehearses (i.e., inwardly re-hears) for new dialogue. By "integrity," I now mean the endless perishing of such images into the self, whereupon, through its renewed symbolic expressions, the self might symbolically immortalize itself by its durable imprintings on an expanding and deepening reality. Oscillating between detachment and empathy, in ceaseless repetition of this symbolizing activity, the self affirms, and reaffirms, its own inner harmonies. Herein lies its integrity. Novel variants are inscribed on themes which it symbolically shapes; novel themes emerge, as certain variants are reiterated more than others. By "detachment," I mean that quiet interlude wherein an inner rehearsal unfolds, preparatory to subsequent dialogue: the momentary suspension of overt action; the inner building up of tensions toward that suspense which immediately precedes the bursting forth of new symbolisms.

In the end, the crucial bifurcation within human being is not that of mind and body, or that of subject and object, or even that of freedom and determinism. Quite the contrary. It is the split between what man *would* become, and what, by his own finitude, he does in fact become: for he never ceases to reach toward stars which inexorably elude his grasp. Overarching and subsuming these seeming dualisms, each of which is resolvable under the larger perspective of transcendental rhythmicality, is this irreducible character of man: though reflecting upon himself and, thereby, reflecting nature to and into himself, though transforming himself toward greater clarity and deeper presence, and though prescribing to himself the truth of his existence, man cannot avoid the crises which, throughout his growth, befall him. In his quest to resolve each crisis, he reinstates such dialogue as is grounded in ever-wider experience. He aims at orchestrating ever-more-inclusive schemes of compresence, schemes wherein he experiences his own personal presence as acquiring ever-greater significance. To achieve durability of that presence, he may lapse into sheer physicality, seeking to immortalize himself by re-establishing primitive bonds of relatedness to the natural universe. Or he may strive, through his symbolic modes of self-presentation, to etherealize his presence by stepping beyond the physical toward the veridically spiritual. In the latter instance, he seeks to immortalize himself by creating altogether new bonds of relatedness to a reality which he now construes as the transcendental cosmos.

(*c*) Symbol and Wisdom

In sum, human growth is identical with human creativity; and human creativity is the search, tragically doomed, to perpetuate one's earthly existence, though also to transcend that existence in ways which cannot even be envisioned. But when a person is fully in touch with his own growing processes, he realizes the futility of striving toward this goal—whenever he relapses toward a secure past or dwells in a speciously comfortable but essentially inert present. On the contrary, realizable growth presupposes a person sufficiently integrated to present himself authentically, hence, to give himself freely. Only when he primordially entrusts himself to the justice of nature, however often she lapses, can he luminously pass from a lower phase of integrity to a higher phase. Thereby, he grounds his hope for such bonds to a future as will guarantee deep continuities within his being, though that future cannot yet be fully revealed. In this context alone, a person can open himself to love, both in giving and in receiving, and to wisdom.

Ever aspiring to participate, with his consummate being, in the most ineffable of cosmic rhythms, man ineluctably falls back, only to rise again—but, in endless cycle. The anguish of his finitude inexorably haunts him. Yearnings deep but fleeting overtake him. Courageously, he takes up the task again. Doubts vanish—but momentarily. For a brief ecstatic instant, he immerses himself in his own self-created symbolisms, whether they be the work of his hand or the work of his full living presence; and, never detached from the symbols, he dwells in the very ferment, process, and activity of their creation. Here, for that minuscule moment, he courts eternity, and deathlessness. Herein consists the paradox of human existence: the perception, heavy and fearsome, that he will die; the hope, thrilling though short-lasting, but renewed ever again, and ever again shattered, that, should his symbols be sufficiently ethereal, and should the effort of their shaping implicate all that he can summon forth from the depths of his ground, he can conquer death. Could it be, he ineluctably asks himself, that the riddle of riddles can be solved only in the penultimate moment of dying, hence must lie forever buried in the absolute privacy of that earthly pause, and thus forever elude his knowledge? Wherein, he torments himself, consists true wisdom? Does it vanish as soon as, while in the very throes and at the very culmination of the creative act, one feels it to lie within one's grasp? Wherein consists the element of the transcendental? How can permanence and passage be joined?

At this stage, when he has only glimpsed wisdom, a person senses that somehow he dies to be reborn, and he is reborn to die—in endless spiraling. All that he can hope for is the perception, clear and glowing, that he is empowered honestly to acknowledge the profundity of this ultimate crisis: this is his integrity, his pride, and his humility; this is the ground for his lamentation and his celebration.

NOTES

1. See the index entry for "concrescence" in Whitehead's *Process and Reality.*

2. "Psychoanalysis and Zen Buddhism," in D. T. Suzuki, Erich Fromm, and Richard De Martino, *Zen Buddhism and Psychoanalysis* (New York: Harper & Row, 1960), p. 127.

3. Novalis (Friedrich Leopold von Hardenberg), "Anthropologische Fragmente 745," *Werke*, ed. Hermann Friedemann (Berlin: Bong, 1908), II.1, p. 136.

4. Honoré de Balzac, *Eugénie Grandet*, trans. Dorothea Walter and John Watkins in *Père Goriot and Eugénie Grandet*, trans. E. K. Brown, Dorothea Walter, and John Watkins (New York: Modern Library, 1946), p. 453.

5. See the index entries for "causal efficacy" in Whitehead's *Process and Reality.*

6. See the index entries for "presentational immediacy" in ibid.

7. Shakespeare, Sonnet 30.

8. See Oscar Wilde, *The Picture of Dorian Gray* (London: Oxford University Press, 1974), p. 190.

9. Mann, *Joseph and His Brothers*, p. 1.

10. *Modes of Thought* (New York: Free Press, 1966), p. 164.

11. Rainer Maria Rilke, "Notes," in *Sonnets to Orpheus*, trans. M. D. Herter-Norton (New York: Norton, 1962), p. 133.

IV

Speaking: The Path to Wisdom

14

THE CONTEXT OF UTTERANCE: TEXTURES OF WORDS AND THINGS

PREAMBLE

In this chapter, wherein I treat the textures of words and things, and the context in which their interwovenness defines itself, I support two propositions, the first at length and the second more briefly: (*a*) the word, spoken or unspoken, is the center of the person's existence, his consummate expression as his distinctive way of being in the world; (*b*) the distortion of the word, as it emanates from man or as it reverberates within him, and the tearing away of the word from man displace that center to a new center no longer of man. Whether silent or uttered, the word appears, and unfolds its latent meaning, whenever one discourses, paints, composes music, or shapes a poem. When, however, a person dissociates words from the context in which they are uttered, he alters the very texture of words in their connections to things. Thereby, he diminishes the impact of the word, and its power to stir ever-increasing openness to receive, through the symbolic media of words, the things which the world can offer him. Negating the word as *his* word, in its authentic flowing from him, man so alters its natural cadence that its intrinsic music tends toward noise.

I am proposing both a philosophic theory of the word and, to a lesser extent, a theory of the pathology of the word. In the latter instance I show how the transformation of words into things, with a life which does not flow from man, but is a kind of pseudo-life—e.g., in the careless use of words, in machine-transmitted words—destroys that by which the word enables the thing to be present to man, in the full presence of thingliness. Indeed, at bottom, this thingliness is a holiness. To be holy is to possess the sanctity of a wholeness, i.e., an integrity or a *hale* unity of parts. And, by his nature, man makes things continually present, present in the fullness of their being to one who receives them, that they may be hallowed, in the fullness of the recipient's being, and that their integrity may be affirmed; and it is the power of man, by his participation in the eternal, to halt, for a perfect instant of eternity, the inexorable rush of time, and to extend their presence. Surely, reverence for things flows from the acts by which things are named. What is nameless is neither feared nor welcomed; it is simply unacknowledged. Even Yahweh is *named* "the nameless one." Devices which transmit words artificially, including the masks which people wear such that, through these masks, mere "small talk" and/or aimless babble issue, effect this transformation of word to thing: this desecration of what is holy. Such devices (including masks) demean the spiritual context wherein words bring their intrinsic powers to fruition. They destroy the naming which cannot be separated from the act which grows from presence. Insofar as they do, despite their utility as servants of man or as providers of entertainment for him, these devices become the masters of man. It is this mastery, not of the word by man as the fruition of his essence, but of man by the word as the denial of that essence, against which I inveigh here. On the other hand, man's existence consummates itself when woven into harmoniously ordered textures of things with words.

A • WORD–THING CORRELATIONS

(*a*) Music, Poetry, and Dance

Cast out of nature to dwell in human society, and no longer embedded as mere animal attuned to the natural, indeed his very being contoured by the imprints of persons' mutual encounters, man acquires a new mode of embeddedness, now among the words which society shapes and the things which nature allows society to define. And since embeddedness is a dynamic state which implies either equilibration or disequilibration, he dwells in alternating schemes of balance and imbalance. Equally, formed speech and transformed nature determine human being; and in their essence, they flow from it. In its deepest meaning, no word or thing or man can be understood apart from human inquiry into the community of meanings to which their reciprocal dependencies give rise. Nonetheless, every theory of being in general takes its point of departure from particular reflections on but one of these phenomena: word, thing, or person. Sufficiently pursued, each leads to the heart of the question of being, hence, to human being through which alone they ultimately reveal themselves; and I seek to illuminate a person from the standpoint of utterance.

In the trembling rhythms of speech, words hover about man. Both enveloping and permeating him, they shape his being from within him and from without. Yet, assuredly, they reside somewhere—though nowhere are they simply located. Evanescent and transitory, words enjoy no temporal completion. Nonetheless, fragile as they are, they, together with dance, constitute the only truly stable matrix wherein man can root himself. Furthermore, words are evocable through human agency alone. Likewise, though as definite and specific entities which reveal themselves to be finished mosaics, an instantaneous spread of space, durable and immobile, *things*, though dialectically in opposition to words, are referable, for their *ultimate* definition, to human agency. Alone among the creatures of earth, man is empowered to objectify the natural. Alienated from nature by his natural endowment, both cortical and anatomical, man characteristically objectifies nature, then reappropriates her for his own restless self-aggrandizement.[1]

Once thrust from the natural order, every person seeks, by circuitous routes, to return to it. Unthinkingly participating in it—hence, experiencing himself as interior to it—he then exteriorizes nature, extruding her every facet from himself, as though his very *I* were coagential with nature. And turning inward to his liberated *I*, he probes his own interiority. Disclosing its concealed depths, he brings words forth in the context of a dance of appropriate gesture. For no search, inner or outer, can be dissociated from experiment upon nature, or, at least, from subtly shifting motions vis-à-vis nature; and to experiment is so to reorient one's body toward nature that one acquires novel perspectives on her. Birthed from the very womb of the dance of images, words enable man alternately to stand apart from things and to commingle with them. For words and things enmesh with one another. In this way, man reinstates himself within nature's inner ferment, experiencing himself as co-participant in all her processes.

Objectified through thinking, and codified in words, natural processes, by human agency, transfigure themselves. Seemingly re-discovered, these processes are actually pristinely dis-covered. By speech alone, the veils which simple participation in nature required to be drawn over the mysterious chasms which she encloses are torn asunder. But only when a person gives himself up to the intrinsic rhythms of his own speakings does nature humanize herself. To understand how this end is achieved, one must reflect upon utterance as both music and poetry. Quintessence of the sonorous, words are celebrated as either music or poetry. Carved from pure becoming, they constitute a temporal unity which stimulates a "spatial" entity, a thing which resists and endures. More deeply, neither music nor poetry in its musical aspect is a mere imitation of spatially juxtaposed things. On the contrary, it is an eternal restlessness, a stillness amid a flux harmonizing melodic lines in sequences of instantaneous configurations, each a juncture of such lines and a vector pointing beyond them. Moreover, it is a rhythmic unfolding of wave upon wave: waves superimposed and waves interpenetrating; waves of varying length, meter, and interrelation; waves which bear both tones and pauses in myriad arrangements. And each, tone or pause, exhibits its own dynamics, the dynamics by which it tends toward either resolution or heightened tension, an altogether new dimension of time.

Things, on the other hand, attain consummation as painting, drawing, and sculpture: namely, human contrivances in which movement and rhythm are imprinted into pure being, a stable visual or tactile complex which creates not the illusion of flow and life but the vibrant arresting of movement, the freezing of movement at the very instant of its change to immobile unity. Rendering pure space as unadorned and with clarity, the artist probes its intricacies, its mysteries, and its harmonies. Seeking reconciliation of the thing with itself, he renders its conflicting tendencies, now to endure, now to perish. For (visual) art expresses absolute repose of a thing at peace with itself; it spreads before the eye that with which a perfect instant is pregnant.

With reference to the temporal and spatial dimensions of art, words, and things in general, I distinguish creation, its products, and contemplation. By attributing temporality to both words and music, and spatiality to both things and visual art, I refer to each as product. But one cannot separate a product from the processes which bring it about. True, emerging in the context of specific human activities as their fruition and culmination, every entity crystallizes, albeit transiently, as complete and unalterable. Yet a product is a leading forth and a begetting. By its essence, no product exists apart from the flux whence it arose. In this sense, temporality inheres in both visual art and things as much as in words and music. Indeed, being and coming-to-be (i.e., becoming) are but different aspects of the same phenomenon. Being refers to structures; becoming, to dynamics and style.

Together, they express both a form of process and a procession of forms. And neither emphasis precludes the other.

Finally, all expressive media can be placed along a continuum the poles of which are, respectively, music and poetry as the objectification of the essence of time, and sculpture and painting as the objectification of the essence of space. Intermediate is the dance, a link between the arts at both extremes. Transfiguring his natural rhythms, the dancer is like sculpted space in motion, a fluent temporal unfolding. And dance hovers about the very instant before song bursts forth, thereby bridging visual rhythms and aural rhythms. A verbal articulation of dance, poetry is a drawing forth and a fixation in words of the myriad nuances which physically unfold in dance.[2]

My comments upon poetry, music, and dance, and their respective connections to space and time, suggest the process character of the interplay of words and things, as that interplay is borne to fruition in the highest spiritual forms which man is empowered to create; and they illuminate the context of utterance as a fabric of rhythmic correlations of words and things. Despite their dependencies on human producers and interpreters, words and things each constitute, together with their consummations in the arts, an objective order of existence governed by its own laws, and shape patterns of reciprocally influencing structures. Each order expresses a way of configuring the relevant patterns and of specifying their vicissitudes and balances. Though neither order lacks both dimensions, the first—namely, words—stresses temporal flux, whereas the second—namely, things—stresses spatial solidity. Each participates in an order essentially constituted by the other. Together, in their respective modes of articulating time and space (not by their purport, but by their constitution), they form a single, coherent objective reality.

(*b*) The Articulation of Being

Whether bestowed on man or contrived by him, meanings are woven into the complex shaped by words and things, and stirred into ever-new unfoldings, combining, recombining, and transforming into myriad tonalities, subtle arrangements, and refined feelings. By essence, the synthesis of word and thing expresses human acts, human aims, and human projects. Words appear *as* words and things *as* things in human contexts alone. And to present themselves as fully what they are, they must be summoned forth by persons. By each, word and thing, and by the correlations which bind them into a single manifold, man thrusts himself into a world in part given, a heritage to revere and a limit by the acceptance of which to acquire dignity, and in part his creation, that by its shaping he might know his powers. Crystallizing about nature's gifts, this manifold enables man, as both medium and agent, to metamorphose nature into *his* world and, thereby, to create a reciprocating gift. In this interchange, he transfigures himself. For words and things, the textures which they form, and the configurations which the facets of these textures shape, constitute a kind of temple which man raises:

a temple in which he can rest and aspire; a temple which evokes his reverence before the mystery of his being; a temple which inspires his exaltation before the wonders of that mystery; a temple for rejoicing in his own work. In this temple, man pays homage to spirit: to his own spirit, linked to the spirits of others, and to spirit beyond the human. Neither word nor thing can be conceived apart from the conception of both human intention and cosmic mystery. In its way, each, when regarded with tender respect, both reveals and articulates the *human* mode of being. Through this articulation, each discloses being beyond that mode.

By "being," I mean what *is*, what *truly* lies beneath veils, disguises, and façades. I do not mean that which, *in being*, cannot also *become*. What comes into existence, then passes away, is itself a modality of being, and not necessarily an imperfect modality. My distinction between reality and the masking of reality is not intended as equivalent to the distinction between being and becoming. Masked reality may perdure, asseverating itself as a stereotype refractory to change. On the other hand, reality unveiled is surely but a fleeting instant of what I can only designate a *holy present*,[3] a present numinous with portent of chasm upon chasm of concealed spiritual existence. Whatever the criterion whereby this distinction can be justified, a distinction which implies an "eminent" reality and an ordinary reality, the human adventure is, doubtless, the quest to transform the prosaic and the everyday into that form of existence wherein reality acquires an incandescent quality, a glowing with import as the sacred abode of man. In their mutual clarification and enhancement, achieved by this dialectical shaping of textures, words and things constitute products (*pro-ducta*) of the reciprocal acts by which this quest is made possible.

Articulation and being presuppose one another. An articulate person is one who speaks, and, in speaking, discerns with clarity the objects of his intention. Probingly, he attends the things he discriminates, though always within some aspect of reality toward which, by speaking, he orients himself, a perspective which reflects his own choice and style. By "style," I mean the impregnation of a person's every act, gesture, and utterance by a quality which confers upon them a reciprocal fitness, an inner measure and proportionality, an intelligibility and rightness. Style expresses the felicity and grace of him who has achieved distinctive individuality. It is an harmonious arrangement of his parts, peculiar to that person and to none other, a unique, irreducible quality by which he may be identified as precisely himself and none other. And, by in-tending and attending those things—both, indeed, complementary moments of the same process —by his stretching and by his reaching from within himself out toward them, through the word spoken authentically and in style, he *tends* with care, in his unique way, both things and words. Shepherd to them, he fashions them with tenderness; he nurtures their growth; he gives himself up to their destiny.

Moreover, *to articulate* means to divide into joints, i.e., into precise parts. Being makes its own traits manifest, allowing them to be touched and known. Yet being reveals itself only in that uncovering, by utterance, which is distinct:

a precise uncovering of the traits of *human* being, that those traits might reveal themselves with distinction to be exemplary manifestations of the powers of human being. I support the doctrine that exemplary man is spiritual man, and that man is empowered, by a power ontologically rooted in his inmost nature, either to affirm or to diminish his spirit, though never wholly to deny it. Indeed, eminent reality, exemplary persons, and distinctness of disclosure are correlative notions. To speak distinctly means to distinguish things, cogently to disclose the field of relations which constitute a person in his world, and freely to allow those relations to reveal themselves, that one might, with discernment, distinguish oneself. The goal is clarity of awareness, rightness or appropriateness of action, harmony of being; the means are listening to what is, accepting it as it is, participating in being. But goal and means are absolutely consonant; at bottom, they are one. Together, they involve vivid disclosure of relatedness: human, natural, and spiritual.

(*c*) Disclosing Human Being

Human being is that privileged matrix which, when man articulates *him*self through his speaking, enables being likewise to emerge, and to declare *it*self. True, the self is embedded in a natural world; powers inhering in nature may even be regarded as conspiring to *produce* a self. Surely, this is a root assumption of biologic inquiry into human affairs; in particular, the assumption entails a theory of biologic evolution. On the other hand, all that one can know of the world, indeed the very grounding of the techniques of biology as a species of inquiry in general, can be known only as filtered through the inquiring self. Yet for the self to be a self to itself, it must "pose" its own reflexive character in a manner which is correlative with the world to which it counterposes itself. To pose itself requires that it pose a world; reciprocally, to acknowledge a world is to entail a claim about the self *in*, *to*, and *for* that world. Certainly, self and world, the first searching and the second yielding, are connatural and consubstantial. As they reveal themselves *pari passu*, their boundaries appear variable, and their contents shifting.

Thus jointly realized, self and world arise, as such, from a primal activity: an activity which shapes itself prior either to self or to world; an activity of which each, self and world, is both residue and expression. An interplay between the very acts by which words and things are engendered, this activity gives birth to experience, and it articulates the structures of experience. Correlative aspects of an integral, generic dynamism, subject and object pro-pose relative distinctions within human comportment, a being-in-and-toward-the-world. What is *thrust beneath* and what is *thrust against*—namely, receiver and that which is to be received—cannot be absolutely separated. Each requires the other; both reflect a primordial and unitary process. Moreover, the relationship between donor and recipient involves alternation and interchange. What, at this instant, is subject, may, at the next instant, be object, and conversely.

The very terms *subject* and *object* are often interchangeable, in a deeper sense. Though I speak of the subject as a person who has an interest, I can equally refer to the subject of his interest. Alternatively, by "object" I mean anything, thing or person, to which attention is directed, or on which action is contemplated. Accordingly, if, in some absolute way, I am to distinguish these notions, I must designate by "subject" that which has depths of meaning which are implied yet not revealed: an infinite matrix of possibilities, an inexhaustible source of themes, a potentiality for disclosure—namely, both the one who cares and that for which there is care. On the other hand, by "object" I mean the appearance which is revealed, an actualized and completed disclosure; that whose theme is already explicitly formulated, hence, may be summed up in a word. At bottom, the distinction is between a specific trait and what gives birth to that trait. Spinoza's complementarity of *natura naturans* and *natura naturata* expresses this distinction. By it, self and world are, each, *both* subject and object. As either, they are mutually implicated, self with world, and bound together as a unity of relations, a unity which, as subject, craves specification, as object. Thus, words, the breath of the inwardness of the cosmos and the stuff of pure becoming, partake more of the nature of the subject; whereas things, seemingly carved from space as pure duration, seem to partake more of the nature of the object.

B • MEANINGS DISCLOSED THROUGH HUMAN ENCOUNTER

(*a*) Evocations

Through the encounters of specific persons, with respect to their rhythms and styles, in the human traits which they embody, and by the creative products which they collectively shape, being in general reveals itself. Hitherto concealed, being becomes visible, stage by stage, through the reflective clarification of *human* being. Increasingly, being presents itself as an ordered manifold of structures, distinct and cogent, and etches itself against nature as a community of interdependent agencies, partly contingent and partly self-engendering. Working together, such agencies continually birth one another. In reflective encounter, they are "bent back" into the person, as he forms images of their traces—those reflected images by which he guides his journeys among concrete individuals. Thereupon, the knowledge of the unity of particular and universal which these agencies exemplify becomes accessible, and promotes still further searching into the traits of being. Only by illuminating the structure of human comportment can being lay bare the details of its own essence, and disclose itself as unifying, as a single, overarching schema, a cognitive, exhibitive, and active dimension.[4] One's knowledge, works of art, and very conduct express these dimensions in equal measure. In their systematic unity and reciprocal import, they reveal the ground and dynamism of being, the coherent yet multifarious and never-completed fabric of reality.

Correctly distinguished, used, and interpreted, words and things authenticate being. In its every instance, they grasp its essential character; they elicit that which makes the instance unique and distinctive. Word and thing alike exhibit being as it originally is. Together, they discover the originating source whence springs its every manifestation, the powers which shape its expressions. In its way, each reveals the truth of being: the world *conforms* to the thing, for it shapes itself by the contours of the thing; the thing *accords* with the word, for it is as it is in accordance with its definition by the word. In mutual adequation, word and thing disclose being as it is. Jointly, they weave a texture which constitutes the living symbol of being. In all cases, being emerges in specific, delineated presences.

As one stands before an actual flower, or imaginatively anticipates its existence, the word *flower* summons up the image of the motion of air through delicate petals, the fine vibrations therein induced, whether these vibrations are gentle or nostalgic, perfunctory or loving; the way one utters "flower" reinforces, contrasts with, or supplements that image. A presence is evoked, vibrant and full. Analogously, the thing *flower* stirs *its* characteristic associations. An image imprints itself in the person; a germinating presence emerges from that imprint. Each entity, word or thing, points toward a "something" whence arose the multitude of traits which constitute the "being" of the flower. By the manner of utterance, by the context of presentation, by the mode of perception, and by the kind of interpretation rendered, the authentic flower is allowed to appear—always, of course, in one of innumerable possible and equally valid perspectives. To carve out the word *flower* or the thing *flower* is tantamount to shaping the processes by which the truth of the flower, its integrity as wholeness, unity, and power of impact, discloses itself. More generally, to ascertain the ground for the manifestations of anything whatsoever, thus causing an entity to appear as authentically what it is, one must determine the appropriate words and things which validate those manifestations as truly what they are: namely, as genuine appearings of that particular entity; as ways of making explicit, and bringing to light of day, its inner germinating but still latent content. For to validate is to affirm truth—to affirm truth by so stripping away façades that a foundation for the diversity of an entity's forms might be rendered visible, and its inner harmonics and the right ordering of its parts be permitted to establish a firm basis for reflective action.[5]

(*b*) Disclosures

Neither word nor thing can be conceptualized as the vehicle for the disclosure of being, hence, as an instrumentality for presenting its truth, without reference to the other. For example, the word *flower* and the thing *flower* are mutually implicated. The actual "appearance," in the sphere of human discourse and human action, of either word or thing entails the possibility of the appearance of the other. In its full concreteness, neither can be construed apart from the construal of their common origin, the deeper concerns of human being, and through that construal, of being in general. An utterance, like a cry of grief in the dark, is no *mere* sound qualified by pain, sound which blindly floats, patterns of aural tensions and their prospective resolution. It is a particular grieving human being become manifest: a person real, vibrant, and poignant. Utterance, as utterance, bears within it and comports, as its own origin, a particular human existence. In its very essence, as itself an encounterable entity, it cannot be dissociated from the one who utters. Analogously, any object, like a chair in its thrust, its form, its "sittingness," is, in the unfolding of its particular powers, an object with respect to the one who discerns, shapes, and uses it. For a thing has multifarious aspects the very definitions of which imply a human actor who orients himself toward that thing. In his orienting and in the weaving of his orienting into its nature—by his powers and by its powers, and by the enmeshing powers of both—it both constitutes itself and reveals itself to be the thing which it actually is.

In their fashion, word and thing are each dependent on the other. Constituted by human meanings, they are woven into the same fabric. When one hears a word, or when one sees a thing, one perceives, not the bare physical entity, but an entity spiritualized and whole, an entity infused with human quality and inseparable from that quality. I do not deny the *is-ness*, the sheer otherness, and (relative) autonomy of words and things. I merely affirm that this character is invariably qualified by something distinctively and indefeasibly human. Nothing can be conceived or apprehended as what it is in isolation from *some* human comportment toward it, some human judgment, whether one judges by asserting, by exhibiting, or by acting. Everything, word and thing, is, in principle, intended. Indeed, intention is part of its essence, and not disconnected from it as residing exclusively in those who orient themselves toward it. An object, actual or possible, is presented in its objectivity, its *is-ness*, within the frame of human experience. Accordingly, every objective presentation, as the presenting of an object, renders that object a unity, at once objective *and* subjective, a unity composite yet integral. It is precisely this interdependence of words and things, each in its way involving spirit *and* matter, this texture of words and things, with stress on the contribution of words and their special role as revelatory of human being, that I treat here.

(*c*) Inscribings

One may speak of meanings as inscribed in both words and things. In the first instance, one means that meanings are imprinted into words by human agency as their inner, spiritual aspect in contrast to their external, phonetic aspect. As sound, words compress meaning; they both embody and manifest meaning. Meanings unfold, explicate themselves, and achieve their fruition in and through the spoken word. Neither meaning nor word can *be* without the other; the two are mutually complementary. For the word is encountered, as word, as a composite of meaning and sound, a phenomenal unity. When I say "imprint," "inscribe," or "embody," I do not mean that there are two entities: first, meaning as primary substance; then, word to encase meaning. Nor do I suggest that priority inheres in words the "matter" of which meaning is subsequently embedded. I intend no *essential* distinction, substantive, temporal, or causal. No word can *be* without a "constituent" meaning; again, I am bound by language which is too abstract adequately to render the concreteness of living reality. Nor can reality "subsist," insubstantial and ineffable. For reality is a complex of both spirit and matter; it is integral and indiscerptible. There are no bits of bare matter. Nor are there incorporeal spirits. Every entity is a power of acting or of influencing, of stirring and effecting metamorphoses, of undergoing change or of perpetuating itself in another on which it works transformatively and durably. Furthermore, if I regard "meaning" as inner and sound as "outer," I cannot hold absolutely to this distinction. As soon as I seek to specify any particular instance of it, the cogency of my formulation vanishes. For, though a meaning may be construed as initially "interior" to the sound, as somehow "wrapped" in it as not yet manifest, the very utterance of the word discloses that meaning amid the reverberations of its sounding. Indeed, to utter a word implies that one draws it forth into exteriority, so that sound itself now seems wrapped in meaning; and meaning is the enduring echo of sound—an echo, however, empowered by its own force to stir, and to alter.

Nonetheless, the processes by which each evolves, meaning and phoneme—which constitute a unity—differ, hence, can be independently specified, though they never independently unfold. A child's meaning, what he intends, is, in its conceptual import, amorphous, vague, and dim. Expressing a large thought in a single word,[6] he indicates, announces, and exclaims. Hence, the spontaneity, the freshness, the novelty, the wonder of his utterances. But the adult's *explication* of a child's thought, its unfolding as a meaningful pattern, and its delineation as a multiplex explanation is a process and an activity of thinking, wherein many utterances substitute for the original. Hence, a complicated texture of words evolves as representing thoughts which become increasingly explicit, and simplified. Yet sound and meaning cannot be independently construed. They constitute patterns in which no factor can be separated without disrupting their respective integrities. Such meaning–word complexes emanate from a speaker. In their flowing forth, they are formed, transformed, negated, or fused. In every case, meaning is breathed into a word, as it is uttered, from a source deep within the speaker, yet far beyond him. No one creates meanings *de novo*: every person draws meaning from the circumambient presence in which he dwells, a presence objective and in some way indestructible.

I also speak of meanings as "inscribed" in things. The thingliness of a thing, that by which it abides as thing, requires a "constituent" meaning to support, to delimit, and to contain it: in a word, to give it organization and structure. Only in the *com*porting of some sentient creature toward them, whereupon they are *sup*ported by the emerging meanings, do things manifest themselves both to and within that creature as things. For a thing appears as such, and is illuminated in its thingly character, when there is one to whom it *can* make itself present. Data are discerned as present to me as I, reciprocally, present myself to them, directing my attention, effecting discriminations, and conferring significance. By my turning toward another in care, and therein clarifying my being, a fabric of meaning–thing complexes reveals itself, and is even constituted. No less than words, things become things *as* they are encountered. Indeed, the *relata*, thing and encounterer, disclose themselves as entities sui generis only within the framework of the relationship of *comporting toward.* Just as the "inner" side of the word as sound is, on first construal, its meaning and "spiritual" content, so the inner aspect of a thing, its potency for becoming that thing, is the power, exercised by persons in relation to it, of bringing it to fruition *as* thing. The thing itself, a bare and sheer thing, is but the exteriorization of potency. It is the embodiment, the presence, and the fulfillment of meaning. Yet potency is not borne by a thing alone. On the contrary, it is potency of a *matrix*, the very relatedness which gives birth to person *and* thing, in one's actual self-orienting toward a thing: potency both from and through which a pattern of person–thing relations emerges.

C • THE WORD–THING COMPLEX: DISTORTIONS AND CONSUMMATIONS

(*a*) Frozen Words

Unique flowings forth from man to world, and reciprocally, word–thing relationships are brought to fruition by human action. By man's intrinsic autonomy, he acquires, through such relationships, a special role as both reifier of and participant in nature. As such, he experiences, amid his very harmonies with nature, disruption and discontinuity. To dramatize this thesis, I set forth certain proscriptions against devices, including the very masks which people assume, which dissociate the word from its veridical context of utterance. As my example, I propose certain injunctions against the use of tape recorders, merely one among many devices by which one might instantiate my thesis. Though I state their disvalue, I do not suggest that these devices lack all value. Indeed, I even emend my thesis to suggest a quite significant value. Yet I do affirm that, on the whole, wherever they are used, lest the dangers which I shall indicate prevail, certain cautions against their use ought scrupulously to be exercised. And, in each case, the dangers involve some violation of a principle of contextuality.

Basically, recorders either destroy or distort the full symbolism of reciprocal presence. By their use, words do not flow, as words ought, from a person. They are not fetched from inward silence, a matrix of reflection. Rather, in temporal mummification, they fetch and address one another.[7] No longer is speaking the word a portentous event, a meditative response to genuine listening. On the contrary, taped words tend toward conventional signs of stereotyped, artless meaning. A word only fully *means*, in its diverse connotations, when it has actually been spoken, and is both reinforced and clarified by gesture, expression, or movement. On each occasion of an utterance, new meanings are embedded in idiosyncratic tonalities and cadences: the music which must reverberate in its natural state, lest meanings be inauthentically rendered. Insofar as they are indiscriminately used, taped words lose their expressive force. Disaffiliated from their utterer, they acquire a destiny independent of his. Deposited and movable, such words are detached from, though unmistakable creatures of, their actual creator. They do not flow freely and spontaneously. Nor do they give rise to acts which, in turn, flow naturally from them. Rather, the acts which taped words call forth are truly provoked. Disconnected from the word itself, the act belongs to a distinct and alien domain.

True, the taped word *is* a communication. But cut off from the process of expression, which, at best, is the mutual expression of persons in relation, wherein each presence suffuses the other, every expressive word born from inward speech being spoken in silence, the taped word is no longer communion. Yet, quite diabolically, it continues to simulate communion. For though one listens to a tape, the listening is deceptive. In actuality, the tape is intermediary between an anonymous speaker and an anonymous listener. Anonymity profoundly reigns. Even though speaker and listener may be acquainted, so that the role of each can readily be specified with respect to the machine, neither knows the other. By knowing, I mean naming; and by naming, I mean the word which grows from presence into the acts which renew presence. The natural process of communion, wherein naming normally occurs, is split into three discrete and disparate stages. Dominating this now split process, indeed in its insidious way terrorizing it, is the machine as, busily, imperturbably, dispassionately, and without risk (save to blow a tube) it records—an immobile robot which hears perfectly and can repeat one's words perfectly: without understanding or judgment or forgiveness.[8] Existence itself, the standing forth from concealment to hold dialogue, is aborted. In effect, it is transferred to the machine, a Frankenstein-monster pseudo-existence.

When I speak of this simulated existence as diabolic, I mean that designation quite literally. For dia-bolic, δια-βολικός, is antonym to sym-bolic, συμ-βολικός. Whereas the symbolic suggests (as I have noted) a joining together, the diabolic implies a splitting asunder. In any use of tape, the communicants are isolated from one another. Both their listening and their speaking are directed toward, and absorbed into, the machine. Moreover, with respect to the use of such a device in the context of psychotherapy, even when therapist and patient are apparently in communion, the machine "listens" as third party. Yet this party is a non-person which *strangely* listens, which possesses a peculiar *in*capacity for listening. Though neither party is frankly deceived, and both are fully aware of that pseudo-presence, the stream of communings is subtly split. The periphery of attention is drawn toward the machine sucking into its orbit central and vital energies. These energies are depleted; fatigue so pervasive as to be unrecognized supervenes. In effect, partial persons are in partial communion. But communion cannot be diminished and still retain its integrity as communion. And since true communion alone preserves the integrity of persons, the bare presence of the machine, operative as pseudo-listener, diminishes integrity. By addressing the tape, one really addresses oneself: not, however, as in soliloquy, or as in meditation, or even as in withdrawn monologue. Incorporated in one, the image of the machine deprives one's very narcissism of its human quality, while both self and mind—dare I say, soul and spirit—are degraded, and themselves converted, in part, into the status of machine. Descartes' *res cogitans* is drawn toward a *res extensa.* There it flounders, utterly homeless.

Now the machine acquires the status of "speaker." All listen, enthralled as speakerless words emanate, not from silence but from noise, and not even from noise which, like normal noise, is at least edged with silence. For words extruded from the machine are immersed in one another. They fetch each other; they are not themselves fetched from an inner, organic stillness. In this degradation, the creator himself becomes unreal, the matrix less important than the creatures. New standards of speech are fashioned; and a substitutive, electronic music of words arises. Their *real* reference, which is to meanings wrapped in authentic silence, is obliterated. Hence, an altogether fake conception of speech arises. By attending to its imputed defects and strengths, an image of perfection (as with high-fidelity music) is formed. All speech is in danger henceforth of being evaluated by reference to this standard, a standard which proposes a mode of speaking which people thenceforth strive to emulate. Thereby, persons no longer search within themselves to prescribe, by an *intrinsic* expressive activity, their own criteria of perfection. On the contrary, under such circumstances, persons tend to impose upon themselves a mode of speaking which is essentially alien and dishonest with respect to their own essential natures.

Ineluctably, tape recorders must be disseminated among a passive audience. For interaction with the recorder is not possible. It is a fake presence, a vicarious experience. And the repercussions of this pseudo-encounter are momentous. Neither risk nor novelty holds; and nothing unique to the actual delivery of speech provides the context of its impact. Absent, surely, is the exhilaration of communicating subtle facets of meaning, facets dependent for their formulation on the interaction, on a *particular* occasion, of audience and speaker. Each absolves himself of responsibility for participation, by a manner appropriate to that occasion, in what ought to be authentic words authentically spoken: a living experience which unfolds in time; not an event, past and already consummated, but an event consummated, so to speak, inside a machine. For consummation of speech, as with any expression, requires dialogue; and in dialogue the spoken words perish. They perish gently, yet abidingly, into both listener and speaker.

In the wake of the imparting of every meaning, each person ought momentarily to step back, and to be affected by what was spoken: his feelings stirred, his mood refreshed, his thought renewed.

Accordingly, the limit of responsibility for the spoken word is an issue dramatically posed by the tape recorder. When one writes, one speaks one's thought with the intent of circulating it—through writing, thence, by its echo in the speaking of others. But, in hearing a tape, the words, as they are fully meant, cannot be heard. Not merely is a listener's attentiveness blocked out; the blocking inheres in the medium itself. Extraction of a word from the symbolic context of its utterance, yet in its allegedly authentic replication, engenders a distortion quite as momentous as the word itself was when it was originally spoken. Moreover, the repercussions from taped words are endless; they know bounds of neither space nor time. In effect, an imperceptibly distorted image of the utterance is immortalized. Need the speaker, indeed responsible for whatever he speaks, assume responsibility for this image, ever perverse in its reverberations? Surely, each new context in which, unknown to him, taped speech makes its appearance, is either irrelevant to its import or destructive of that import. To alienate from the spoken word an intended *setting* is, therefore, to alienate the word from its intended *meaning.*

Tape recorders not only destroy communion between person and person; they also destroy that solitude of self-communing-with-itself from which the written word comes forth. For he who writes by speaking into a recorder can insidiously be ruled by a public image or by a private image of that public image. The very anonymity of the potential listener or reader controls the cadence, the style, and the content of utterance. Every communication is a speaking from within toward an out-there. In recording, the out-there tends to dominate. Rather than inward searching, a rational criterion—namely, mere conformity to expectation—holds, a criterion which itself is merely a pragmatic criterion with respect to valid communication. Furthermore, "improving" a passage by playing the recorder back to oneself hardly attains that clarity and depth which flows from self-communion alone. Now a mere stereotype is formed. The symbols do not flow freely. One holds pseudo-dialogue with a monster, a caricature of the self which mirrors words back and forth, and, hence, distorts their natural music, the music which embeds meaning. For the music of authentic relatedness another kind of music is substituted: an atavistic encounter with this grotesque image, an enwombment in its sounds. Mesmerized, the listener applies a kind of lens to one element after another. Yet this lens distorts, no matter whether in self-congratulation or in self-deprecation. By its use, the contours of what is spoken are submerged beneath the disjointed details cast up, within the machine, by its own voice. Self-idolatry rather than self-transcendence prevails.

From the multitude of symbolic expressions, which in authentic discourse is illumined by a single center whence glows one's self-identity, certain expressions are abstracted; whereupon this extract is counterposed to oneself (as with taped speech) as distortedly mirroring one's very inwardness. To this self-image one responds, however, as though one were encountering a veridical duplicate of oneself. Yet, far from being a duplicate, the image is truly an "immobile robot" to "whose" fake center, since no robot is actually centered, there can readily flow (neurotic) identifications: identifications acquired over the years of one's life, and woven into the fabric of one's conduct; identifications which attach themselves to this robot. Falsely construed as a replica of the self, as though they reflect an actual identity, these pseudo-expressions connected with a fake yet presumed identity negate one's actual identity. The person becomes mere appendage and captive to words, words which rapidly flow, at too facile a pace, and, thereby, only strengthen his *illusion* of spontaneity. Surely, true expression requires those acts, as of normal writing, where the very shaping of the written characters is correlative with that forming of words wherein each is individually respected, that by a consecration of those words (a miming to oneself, by all the subtle gestures of writing, of all that is intended by them) the more subtle layers of meaning might emerge.

(*b*) A Thaw

To mechanize words is to destroy their veridical unfolding. The very process of their birthing arrested, an illusion of eternity reigns. Words are not allowed to die. No longer is the word the expression, immediate, direct, and portentous, of the drama of existence: its passions, its terrors, its joys. Now the word is but a tool to serve explanation, to foment action, to alter milieu. Formless and without limit, the mechanized word mixes past, present, and future. By a mere switch, time is halted. From out of this amorphous mass, the word—*any* word—becomes available. For words are woven with machines in the same manner as things enmesh with things. But words "spoken" by the machine, rather than by the human, imply contexts which are unsupported by meanings; they are uninspired (i.e., not breathed into) by spirit. No longer do words make things present. The very relationship between word and thing reverses itself. Now the thing, machine, brings the word to pseudo-presence. Man is no longer living and continuous, the instantaneous yet deliberative source of words. Having been embalmed, words overwhelm him. Nonetheless, he continues to delude himself that he is free to utter as he authentically chooses. In consequence, his actual autonomy is negated; his capacity to summon truths is impaired. Man no longer strips away the veil from things, the veil which cloaks their truth. No longer do words call forth words from persons. There does not lurk behind the timbre of the voice, in repose, the immutable, hidden quiet of meditation. No longer is speech gently modulated in a reciprocity of the calling forth of words. For the machine speaks words of homogeneous texture: loud, rasping, harsh; or deceptively smooth and soothing—in either instance, *talking at.* A parity, an egalitarianism, of events holds; their significant differences are measured only by the quantitative. The words which ought, as by a marvelous magic, to produce acts, and inaudibly flow into those acts, are now dead. Spoken or written, but always as it bursts into vibrancy from a *human* speaker, the word *is* momentous. Herein are conveyed great realities: man's uniqueness, his preciousness, his extraordinary powers. By its peculiar manner of making the word universally accessible, the machine destroys the word's rarity, hence, the word itself. In the extreme case, when *its* powers are brought to their culmination, the machine replaces the passion for life by the passion for the demoniacal.

Having made a strong case against the technologizing of the human voice, I wish, in a personal allusion, to emend my negative remarks. After having, with some alterations, composed these strictures many years ago, I lost a dear friend.[9] The clarity, the beauty, the extraordinary depth of his personality are evoked for me, over and again throughout the passing years, by a tape recording of him reading his poems. I am so struck by this near-living evocation of a presence I have cherished that, without renouncing my strictures, I must now modify them. For, used in the appropriate setting and in the right spirit (and here, one must exercise great tact), could not the tape recorder, or for that matter any such instrument, add a significant dimension to existence in its power to call forth a treasured memory? Indeed, does not this same consideration apply to any technological apparatus for reproducing the human voice? Consider, for example, the Greek mask, the πρόσωπον, which accentuates certain qualities and diminishes other qualities, that a particular character trait or human theme might be more sharply delineated, and therefore reveal otherwise hidden facets of reality. In consequence are not all tapes, like portraits, phonograph recordings, or photographs, or, surely, any authentic work left by the departed, echoes, strong and clear, and, in their way, *true*, of a vital and unforgettable presence, a presence dimmed but momentarily until those reverberations of a voice, a face, once more summon up a vibrant image? Hence, while devices like tapes possess both a perverse and a demoniacal capacity, shaping a distorted illusion of reality, they also possess, under quite special circumstances, a capacity to evoke the authentic breath of reality.

(*c*) The Liberating Name

Each group, (spoken) words and things, constitutes a significant human heritage: objects which are *given in* advance of a person's existence. Though they always pass into him, wherein they act upon him to form a solid, durable past, these objects are empowered to become a living presence for him. Coming toward him as if from his future, they appear before him to stir his wonder. When I say "objects," I mean that words and things are *there*. Thrust against one, they both define and limit one's very subjectivity; they release one's powers for discerning and imputing meanings. For objects are not simply constituted as such, with respect to or in opposition to a subject who can both receive and transform them. On the contrary, by their native strength, they themselves are both posed and counterposed to that subject. By their intrinsic powers, they compose themselves as what they are, organizing and presenting themselves as integral unities, that they may then be *op*posed to the subject. For words and things are like crystals in a fluent medium. Gathering into a unity, they allow accretions to form about themselves. And as they emerge into presence, they receive, accept, contain, and retain, in effect *pro*posing themselves *to* a subject. They exist; they shape a unity; they compress a plenitude of meanings: meanings, at first conferred upon them, which, subsequently, though in transmuted shape, can be drawn forth from them. Each of them, words and things, constitutes a plenum; yet each is but a simple unity. Themselves existent, these *plena* are structures which make possible a human existence. By their powers, they allow one to stand forth as a person. Moreover, neither words nor things can be construed as separate from the other. Interwoven as a unitary complex, they congeal as a single (and singular) cohesive reality. As they both interpenetrate and exchange their contents, words and things cohere as an integral fabric.

I sit before a sculpture. Its contours, its texture, its solid rhythms are what I mean when I speak of its thingly character. When it was first given me, it was given together with a name—e.g., "reproduction of *Moses* by Michelangelo." Contemplated alone, that name stirs multiple feelings, images, and recollections. A world of meanings reverberates within me. And as these meanings evolve, I find myself journeying among them. Can I somehow strip away that name, those values which have been conferred upon the sculpture? Can I bear witness to its sheer abidingness? On the other hand, can I dissolve all associations, and stand before the pure, mere presence of an object which, as it impinges upon me, I gather within me, and, as these inward traces unfold and pursue their own paths, linked to all the memories which they ineluctably call forth, allow their contents to reveal themselves to me? Two realms appear: words, language, meanings, thought which blend into feelings; things, qualities, impressions, meanings, percept-orientings which blend into feelings. And as it confronts one and compels response, each realm can be contemplated; each is a *whole* entity of characteristic mode of impact, manner of unfolding, implied principles by which it constitutes an objective manifold; each possesses its typical way of being, and of a being in relation to my beholding, my experiencing, my reacting.

Yet these realms are interdependent. Their separateness is only apparent. Each both flows into and conditions the metamorphoses which do not cease to occur in the other. Neither the pure, essential statue nor the pure name of a statue exists sui generis. Each, word and thing, involves references, however implicit, to the other. As one comports toward something which, within comportment, becomes luminous as thing, one utters, as one's crowning act, the word which names the thing. For the word consummates the act. Discharging the tension of the act, the word is the act's most vital dimension. I refer to the double tension of in-tending and at-tending. In both comportment and utterance, those coordinate and correlative acts, meaning is freely conferred. As gift which hallows the thing, a name is given. Thereby, the thing is identified. Whereupon, a person, the one who names, achieves, as reciprocating gift, his own identity. For self-identity is shaped by the very power consistently, accurately, and cumulatively to identify. The more cogently one delineates one's world, and specifies its powers, the greater the clarity with which one articulates oneself, hence confers a self, the very power to identify, upon oneself.

Nonetheless, words and things are each entities. As such, they are demarcated and distinct. Dissociated from words, things, by their own vibrations, become mere sound, fake words; and words as chatter are themselves but things: the noise which harshly impinges. In the following chapter, I treat the reciprocal influences of things and words, each realm discrete yet, jointly, interdependent, authentic, and whole, and their meaning for man's inwardness: his thought, his feeling, and his inner silence; and I treat the way in which meanings are connected with their own characteristic rhythms.

NOTES

1. Serge Moscovici, *Social Influence and Social Change*, trans. Carol Sherrard and Greta Heinz (London & New York: Academic Press, 1976).
2. Victor Zuckerkandl, *The Sense of Music* (Princeton, N.J.: Princeton University Press, 1959).
3. Rudolph Otto, *The Idea of the Holy*, trans. John Harvey (New York: Oxford University Press, 1958).
4. Buchler, *Toward a General Theory of Human Judgment*, pp. 48, 49.
5. Hofstadter, *Truth and Art*, pp. 53–86.
6. Lev Semonovich Vigotsky, *Thought and Language*, trans. E. Hanfmann and G. Vakar (Cambridge: MIT Press, 1961), pp. 119–51.
7. See Max Picard, *The World as Silence*, trans. Stanley Godwin (Chicago: Regnery, 1951), esp. "The Noise of Words," pp. 172–97, and "The Radio," pp. 198–210.
8. Ibid.
9. See the dedication to this book.

15

RHYTHMS OF UTTERANCE: SPEECH AS THE APOTHEOSIS OF DANCE; DANCE AS THE MATRIX OF SPEECH

PREAMBLE

Each realm, word and thing, constitutes a single manifold of interdependent parts. By the mutual conditioning of these parts, the fragmentation of both words and things is dissolved. Though individually powerful, and even momentous, neither word nor thing consists of discrete, isolated entities. Things comprise the relatively durable: province of thrust, quality, spatial juxtaposition, and temporal succession, all that can be seen or touched. Words, on the other hand, cohere as ineffable and evanescent, but the aurally sensuous fabric of spoken language, nonetheless, a fabric unitary, organic, and, in a measure, palpable. A tonal complex which embeds meaning, this organism expresses a single underlying dynamism which, as it weaves itself with the objective world, transforms that world in novel, unpredictable ways. For the freely creating human spirit manifests itself through speech; and grounding all speech is no mere structural architecture, but an inner music-like architectonic. Echoing throughout all linguistic systems, no matter how diverse, this music constitutes the basis for every human communication. Each instance of speech is but a variation on archetypal themes embedded deep within human unconsciousness, or, more accurately, within the *luminator.* For such themes are profoundly physical. Implicating bodily processes, as these processes strive to differentiate themselves, to become increasingly subtle and refined, and to fill the body labyrinth with their reverberations, they emerge into, and sublimate themselves as, authentic psychic resonances: human speech itself. In this sense, we all participate in a physical realm; and we seek to elevate that realm, by transmuting its inner melody, to the spiritual and interpersonal, and, in the end, to the cosmic. Thereby, we both reflect upon and contribute to, through the agency of the spoken word, the great dance of world being.

A • LANGUAGE AS MUSIC

(*a*) The Unity of Language

Each linguistic element of spoken language, whether phoneme or morpheme, gains its sense, and its inner constitution as pure tone, from the relationship which it sustains to the entire group of elements. And any language has an implicit, central "point" which cannot be specified, save by enumerating all features of that language, a center to which its every element refers, and, by this reference, gains both its power and its distinctive character. At times, the point is like a creative principle, a style of symbolizing, which engenders, in explicit detail, all factors germane to the language. On the other hand, it is, at times, a quality with respect to which all meaningful items of a particular language are equivalent. Perhaps this quality can be understood as a root metaphor, expressing a basic way of categorizing reality—e.g., as space, time, process, or substance; or perhaps as a root sound, such that the utterance of a single meaningful sound, an aggregate of phonemes combined according to rules, which need not be mentioned, of a given language, presupposes a capacity for uttering *all* sounds defined as meaningful in that linguistic context. One cannot definitely say. But, in any case, every language is "transparent" to some unmistakably experienced, though perhaps, in the end, unspecifiable quality, sound, or idea, or some combination of both: a factor disclosed in its every utterance and, in some manner, giving rise to the characteristic features of that language.

Moreover, each person speaks, if truly, from *his* "center," a center which is correlative with, and reciprocally dependent on, the center of language itself. And all the specific constellations of sound which form the languages of earth can be construed as giving rise, though the connections between these diversified systems are often only implicit, to an organic network, a continuum: the one language of mankind. Nor, as I have indicated, can sound be separated from meaning. Nor, as I shall propose, can sound *or* meaning be separated from the act: from gesture, expression, and movement. By the act, I mean one's whole orientation as person, one's physical ways and one's spiritual ways; an orienting within which, once discriminated, things assume *their* organic unity. For the import of a word, that wealth of intelligible consequences which it bears compressed within it, comes to fruition, as myriad differentiated meanings, *as* the word is uttered, even while the word retains its tonal unity—a unity, however, which has its own flow, its own evolvement, its own thematic growth. Furthermore, in characteristically condensed fashion, that import expresses how a word's users, both potential and actual, comport themselves toward that word. And, in the act of its being used, the word further expresses what it comes to designate as the very fruition of both its power to mean and its user's power to intend.

From the standpoint of its purely vocal qualities, inscribing meanings, either concentrated or thinly distributed, language is a polyphony of layers. It is a complex of tones, harmonies, pauses, themes. For, at bottom, the structure of spoken language is musical. Indeed, music is the ultimate statement of language: its distillate and its essence, the rendering of its quintessential meanings. In music, the undulations of sound are so perfectly blended with ever-evolving patterns of meaning which, layer upon layer, come to fruition as sound unfolds that the two, meaning and sound, blossom forth as a single organic paean. Music and, to a lesser but more focused extent, language, celebrate the inmost harmonies and dissonances of things. They express how things suffuse one another with their vital presences to constitute an overarching, brooding presence which hovers about, and never ceases to haunt; or how they oppose, clash, or contrast. More than language, the rhythms of which music sanctifies, music reveals profound and subtle rhythms of being. As an enterprise, music is the quest to fathom depths of feeling which are inaccessible to words, even words laden with a poem's import; it is associated with feelings stirred by the vibrations of innumerable encounters. But words, too, capture and contain feelings, and make them luminous. Each word is alive with subtle nuances of mood; each, therefore, especially as it enters the life of dialogue, is akin to music.

Language not only encompasses man; it suffuses him. It is a large and coherent structure the elements of which are antecedently given within as well as about man. Language expresses man's attunement to things. In the summoning of words from an omnipresent yet inner language, man resonates to rhythms inhering in things, rhythms which he activates and seizes as he meets them. First enveloping then permeating man, these rhythms merge with the rhythms intrinsic to him. For every human meeting entails a striking of chords, as upon a violin's strings, each with its characteristic range and timbre, within those who encounter. In each true meeting, the one who encounters must "lock-in" his indigenous rhythms with those of the very entity which he encounters. Turning toward that entity, he must allow himself to be gripped by its rhythms. Yet no *mere* mutual resonance prevails; for, from this "locking-in," each encounterer experiences as flowing to the entity, and blending with it, new and significant variations on its native themes. Accordingly, every subsequent encounter, each deriving from all antecedent encounters, will be infused with novelty. A past both grows into and resides in every present, waiting to be drawn forth from that present and specified as the germinal constituent of a succeeding present. In this process, a succession of rhythmic symmetries is produced. Two structures become consonant. A reciprocity evolves wherein each structure becomes momentarily identified with the other; and no distinction can be made within the *fact* of encounter between the factors *which* encounter. Ineluctably, however, these interlocking, absolutely synchronous, and transiently interwoven systems, systems which deposit upon one another their imprints, durable and specific, must be "unbound." Consonance is broken. Relatively autonomous, each structure thereby frees itself to evolve its own subsequent history, and to await new encounters.

(*b*) Words as Congealed Rhythm

Words are crystallized vibrations. Embodying reciprocal attunements, they express, in human encounter, momentarily resonating yet, in their underlying patterns, durably altered systems. By its power to induce a corresponding pulse, the word enables things pregnant with rhythm to burst into vibrancy, and to shine forth as what they truly are. For sound and light interweave to shape a single unitary fabric. Indeed, as Scripture declares, in the beginning was the Word;

and on the first day, God parted the light from the dark. Moreover, a poetry resides in the things about us. The vibrations of words seize upon and render that poem, and draw it from its hiddenness. By the images which the poem calls forth, they make visible, in the stillness of imagery, what had been invisible. Thus, in German, *Stimmung* means both "being tuned to" and "mood or temper." And, in a tunedness of the soul, feeling and thing are integrated; there is a solidarity, an indissoluble unity, between man and nature. In early Christian literature, the soul is a "well-tempered mixture," "a harmonious consonance," a *sympathy*.[1] A power of mutual touching, man by nature and nature by man, the soul makes concordant what had been discordant; by musical images, it mirrors the cosmic drama.

No part of man is removed from the pulse of language. When one speaks, one gathers into one's unfolding nature multiple inner movements; and one draws diffuse energies, agitations of one's body, to focus as a unitary perturbation. Prior to utterance, dark silence reigns. But not the stillness of inaction. On the contrary, straining from many loci, initially disjoined, feelings invade the body. In tension, one both in-tends and at-tends. There is the stretching which grows from within; and there is that stretching toward as when, on awakening, I yawn and I stretch. For, then, my awareness has not yet crystallized into sharply delineated patterns. I am embedded, but in flux. By my stretching, I prepare, at dawn, to meet the day, and the day is an awakening into a world of objects, a world which is structured. Primordial quiescence reigns, a mere being in the world. In inward silence, my eyes are open, and turned toward the great spectacle without; I sense powers as yet unactualized. I am a locus of tensions but vaguely felt, yet I experience myself to be pregnant with metamorphosis toward something new. As *mere* body, my body is the habitat of these tensions. It is a locus of pulsations which have not yet converged upon and given birth to focal, rhythmic expression. Now my body is suffused with spirit, and body thus pervaded is body operative: body fusing its manifold expressions into an integral body—spirit, the whole person. Scattered and random, yet with implicit unity, these pulsations came to manifest unity in speech; and speaking is the culmination of an image, itself but quiescent speech, an image formed in listening.

In general, man listens in silence. Unobtrusively, he draws in rhythms which radiate from things about him, and reverberate among things to await his gathering. Abiding until the word comes which names the thing, even clamoring for their names, the objects whence these rhythms spring crowd in on one. Unless so named that each object is counterposed to one in patterns of mutual reference, an object remains brute and strange. Until named and made part of the human scene, thus transfigured by the impact of man upon them, objects are solitary, awesome, and menacing. For words are protective. Held fast and absorbed by objects, words keep the fearsomeness of objects at bay; they permit their rhythms to gather, and so to flow toward man that their full presence is revealed. Sounds which proceed from things—actually, from the matrix whence things arise—are shaped by man to words. Through language, anarchic and inchoate nature attains coherence.

All nature seems to look toward man, and to interrogate him. Endlessly seeming to address him, thence to await his responding word, she turns a steady gaze upon him; whereupon, he steps back, and detaches himself. For man must be unattached from what is so awesome, and so utterly unlike him. He who without reflection steps from Plato's cave is blinded by the sun of nature. Having circumspectly approached her, and gently touched her with all his senses, he draws back and reflects. And from the inward speech of meditation there flows, as its fruition, the outer speech wherein man declares himself, and participates in worldly rhythms. For reflection, which means a *bending back*, and an allowing of what had been experienced to simmer, to invade one's being, and to stir new feeling, gives rise to a perception of the world which may intensify and supplement or, perhaps, clash with, and, thereby, alter an image hitherto held. In reflection, one allows traces of the other to flow into one, that, by them, one may give birth to something which, juxtaposed to the reflective products of other experience, opens up a seeming beyond to all experience: a haunting, circumambient presence of that of which the experience was but residue, crystallization, and symbol; an expanding of that presence toward a vision which is partly familiar and partly mysterious. And this vision of reality is "inscribed" in every experience which, by one's reflection, leads one toward it as it, in turn, awaits deciphering and unconcealment.

In the gathering fullness of silence, and by the inward music of reflection, the word is born, the word as that which bears experience toward what lies beyond; the word as authentic vehicle of reality. But silence is not withdrawnness. When authentic, and not a hiding from noise, it is attentive, vibrant, receptive, and transfiguring. Too, the essence of silence *is* reflection. It is a secondary experiencing wherein, in this inner mirroring of experience, the reflected traces of the other, as a sort of shadow or phantom, are absorbed. When in silence I touch the other, as person, and reverberate to *his* rhythms with the depths of *my* rhythms, I draw into my existence, somehow assimilating them as my very own, themes peculiar to *him*. When I listen to wind and trees, the rustling impinges on my being, rustling wedded to an image. The rustling invades me; it suffuses me; it transforms me. By its impact, my existence is radically altered. True, its themes do not, *as such*, become mine; they are only inscribed on my themes as new variations. Nevertheless, a sufficient accumulation of such variations can, with cumulative experience, transfigure my themes. In this sense, the objects which I encounter objectively immortalize themselves within me. Momentarily *becoming* them, and resonating to their resonance, I am durably touched by them. Though as an entity I radically transcend all entities, standing alone in the novelty of my absolute individuality, and, in self-absorption and with self-enjoyment, survey the world as wholly other to me, I do not dwell in utter seclusion. My solitariness does not negate the immanence of the other in me, and, reciprocally, of my self in it. Here, I am proposing a notion of relatedness in which a *relatum* is construed, not as mere entity, each wholly other to the other, but as a complementarity between *relata*, such that the very existence of each is bound up with that of the other: a substantive parity between relationship and *relata.*

(*c*) The Affective Context of Words

To understand the rhythms of speech, one must distinguish the musical sense of its meaning from both the total symbolic sense and the conventional sense. When I hear a strange tongue, I am struck not by the appearance of words, separate and distinct, each associated with a meaning incomprehensible to me, but by the orchestration of feelings conveyed by the indivisible continuity of dialogue which, though heard, is enigmatic. A sensitive listener can detect the most subtle gradations of feeling. And even should he turn aside, and attend only the flowing of sound, so that gesture, whether stereotyped or spontaneous, will no longer aid him, he can discern in amazing detail both references and intentions of those who speak. For no sharp distinction holds between meaning which is "expressive," "affective," or "merely subjective" and meaning which is "referential," "designative," or "cognitive." True, subjective meaning inheres in speech in much the same way as it is constituted in a musical composition. However, music is no mere projection, either of affect or of kinesthesia. On the contrary, it is an objective order of sound, a reality which has parity with the order of existence disclosed to the eye. When, accordingly, one speaks, insofar as one is therein creating music—and all speech is a kind of music, indeed, the very primordium and kernel of music—one is both participating in and rendering the structure of some aspect, significant and vital, of reality itself.

No one has ever heard a faithful rendering of a Greek tragedy, though his knowledge of Greek be but fragmentary, without being marvelously impressed by the complexity of the themes which are conveyed to him, themes which interweave cognitive and affective factors; and this "merely" by his attending to the inflections, the accentuations, the crescendos, the cadences, the dissonances and harmonies, the dramatic interplay of pauses and tones, the intricacies of meter, and the rhythmic unfoldings of speech. Nor is speech mere onomatopoeia, a simple imitation of "natural" sound. For nature herself, speaking through the protagonists, makes manifest the invisible, intangible matrix of her own activities. Concealed in conventionally demarcated linguistic strata, truth, through a specifically musical phenomenon, ever strives to emerge. Normally, it is assumed that merely a mood, and certainly not actual meaning, is conveyed by words which have been stripped of conventional meaning. Even more strongly is this opinion held when words are apparently dissociated from the actions accompanying their utterance. But, according to my view, on any conceptualization of symbol, presence, and meaning, word and action are, in the end, inseparable. My strictures against such devices as tape recorders attest this conviction. On the other hand, the "mood" communicated by the music of words is, certainly, an implicit, rich, and profound *original* rendering of meaning, meaning the explicit configuration of which can be grasped *only* in the context of action.

Tension prevails between the meaning revealed by music and the meaning proposed by customary association. For, if authentic, musical meaning results from that inward searching wherein alone a felt attunement can be clarified, whereas customary meaning often falls into disharmony with what is uttered from one's depths of feeling. In such instances, the mere superposition of a socially prescribed residue constricts and stifles the inward music. It so dominates the music that the person is indeed shaped by a conventional mold. When one listens attentively to speech, one hears, in the first instance, not individual sounds, like phonemes or their constellation into words, but a context of sound flowing into sound, a directed movement, a striving toward completion. For the word is no finished entity, encountered in its immediacy as simply there. On the contrary, it is an activity, a tension, a state of becoming. And each word is suffused by the entire complex of waves which, in mutual subordination and superordination, complement, interpenetrate, and balance one another. Hence, each word *is* the announcing of its place *in* that complex; each contains the promise of its own flowing forth into the next sound and still the next, in interminable and indivisible flow, as a perpetual rhythmic unfolding. What counts as the truly discernible unity, as that which has impact and creates movement, is the *interval*, an interval of silence pregnant with the resonance of words previously uttered, an interval within which words crystallize as individual entities. In human relationships, words are bound to an integral context, a context which itself is but the breath of the encounters of people; i.e., it is what occurs between people as emanations of their mutual impact and reciprocal actions. Just as words flow forth from this impinging, so the impingement of word upon word engenders the very milieu in which words as such, those distinct and (by convention) meaningful entities, shape themselves. The solemnity and gaiety, and the threateningness, sorrow, and joy revealed in tones by each who plays "through" the instrument of his particular character and style of utterance are woven together as the very texture of speech, a texture qualitied by a distinctive tone color.

The context in which words appear, and stand forth as words, is a pulsation. More accurately, it is a system of interwoven pulses: all intricate and delicately balanced, a marvelously ordered kinetic structure from which specific words gain both their meaning and their life. From this coalescence of words, by their respective intersecting motions, and from the aura created about the chords which they form, meanings arise. Melody, harmony, and rhythm, the three components of music, are aspects of this context. Indeed, one does not hear words as such, separate and entire. Rather, one listens to the context of unfoldings, and to the infinitely variegated patterns with ever-changing profiles of waves; one attends its contours, now soft, now jagged, now surging, now gentle. For both pattern and contour impart to words their shape and their impact. Waves perish and waves endure; and each wave prepares the way, in cumulative cyclicity, for the next. Each reaches out, and makes claims beyond its borders, as all are inexorably swept forward in mutual augmentation. In endless oscillation, a polarity of tone and pause prevails. As a result, the very wave which both envelops and permeates its constituent tones is intensified. Novel meanings accumulate. A syncretist end, at first adumbrated then specified with increasing precision, manifests itself. Like the climax of a marvelously ordered symphony, all flows together with dramatic and quickening undulation.

B • THE AUTONOMY OF WORDS

(*a*) The Precision of Words

In its ordinary sense, meaning is separable from sound. And, in different languages, different words mean the same thing. Hence, while in music meaning and sound are woven together in intimate union, the contrary appears to hold for speech. Here, meaning seems to be adjoined to the word. Not that through music alone does one assert one's inner nature, projecting that nature upon the world as objectified kinesthesia, and elaborating the world by adding to it the ornamentation of music. Nor is customary meaning to be contrasted with musical meaning as *mere* conformation between oneself and the world, rendering its indigenous meanings by words, and superadding new meanings to these words. For, in its very musical aspect, the flowingness of speech is an objective phenomenon, a datum which may be encountered sui generis. Resulting not from caprice or invention but from searching and discovery, it is an autonomous process which comes to fruition, not so much by the "original" creation of a person as *through* him, through his style and his temperament—that medium through which speech, as well as music resonates, each with its fully inscribed meaning.

In the designative sense, the fixation of meaning is not only, or even primarily, the clarification of intended meaning, a making precise. More deeply, it is the stipulation, by conventions which accumulate over the ages, that certain words function as signs, signs of how certain elements extracted from the flowings of speech are to be placed on specific correspondence with items spread out before vision. The independent foci of ear and eye, ear listening to temporal relatedness and eye witnessing spatial relatedness, are brought together, coordinated with one another, and made reciprocally dependent. Conventional meanings evolve when one suppresses the aural context of words, itself a labyrinthine flux, and substitutes for it an architecture of fixed, immobile parts. First, a temporal flow is spatialized. Now specified and stable, the elements of that flow are placed in correspondence (as a kind of isomorphism, or equivalence of forms) with the spatial world which spreads before the eye. The flowingness of words, wherein musical meaning constitutes itself, is arrested. Structures are discriminated, and fixed in one's attention; and one articulates a "cross-section" of the flow. In effect, sound waves dissociate into a manifold of atom-like factors. Now detachable and universalized, meanings are associated by convention. A community of inquirers convenes, and agrees to step back from the flux in which it had participated, and, detached and circumspect as onlookers, to create a "map" of sound. According to rules which can be explicated with increasing precision and accuracy, this map is placed in correspondence with the map of things spread before the eye. Nonetheless, all specific and now dissociated elements, elements associated by convention with meanings, are both referable to and sustained by the musical meaning of the sounds whence they arose. And, in general, the spoken word flows from human encounter. "Pressed out" from the meetings of person with world, it expresses their concerns and the vicissitudes of their natures. Yet speech itself has a structure. As autonomous as music woven with meaning, that structure exhibits both a spatial architectonic and a temporal unfolding. By the structure, speech shapes anew the encountering entities.

(*b*) Ramifying Words

To repeat: words are emanations of human encounter. They express the mutual belonging, the being together, of those who encounter. As such, words manifest a total mobilization of the parts of a human organism. These parts are joined as fragmented systems of pulsation, like heart or lung or brain, systems which are fragmented in their bare biologic interlocking. But as these disjoined systems coalesce into one system, concrete and indiscerptible—a system the parts of which are woven into a unity of action—words burst forth as the system's integrity. The consummate manifestation of action, its inmost unity, expresses itself as authentic speech; inauthentic speech is but the mark of dissonance, i.e., of incongruity and fragmentation as yet unresolved. Indeed, no aspect of human encounter is more centrally human than speech; each aspect peripheral to speech contributes to the matrix wherein speech is the focal event. Listening to a strange tongue without the sight of gesture, one discerns either noise or music, a rasping or a harmony; and within either noise or music unfold all those modalities of meaning which express human relatedness: i.e., one person in touch with, or detached from, another. No mere intrapersonal manifestation, the word cannot express the isolated "function" of some personal "system." On the contrary, the word appears only in the framework of meetings. It expresses the interpenetrations, complementarities, and balancings of two resonating systems, personal or natural. For words are the very breath of what lies *between*. Music which flows forth from the intimate, inward interlockings of distinct systems, the word articulates an ever-heightening awareness of a pattern of relations which ramifies beyond any particular system; and these interlockings, this intricately ordered complex, vibrate as the intrinsic music of words. And nature—all nature—seems to speak. By her reciprocal impingements on man and by her interpenetrations with him, she reveals, through the medium of human speech, her inward and essential character.

Evolving into one another, words ramify as flowing architecture. No word remains fixed, even for an instant. Every word is full of the past, storing the past and bearing its mysteries; and each word, pregnant with novelty, points toward the future, and organically grows into the future. Not only does one anticipate the future and recollect the past through the word, but one experiences the word, in the immediacy of its unfolding as a living presence, as uncompleted in "space," i.e., in physical, optical, and tactile space. Thus, the flux of words constitutes a veritable image of time. As they evolve, words endure—but as a temporal organism: a cumulative, directed, and accomplishing entity. This verbal articulation of time, the very structure of "becoming," reveals itself, in its details and organicity, *through* the creative mind. Words are searched out as though they are already present. Lying in readiness, they await their shaping into sound and meaning, sound organically suffused with meaning. The mysterious and ineffable source of words is *there*, howsoever concealed within yet quite beyond the particular being of a particular man.

Both words and the themes woven of words endlessly repeat themselves. But repetition need not be associated with tedium. On the contrary, every repeated item, being new in time, is new in substance. The "waves" of time beat with increasing intensity through words: a rhythm of word touching word, and word perishing into word. Yet there *is* repetition, a repetition of the experience of communion. For, through the repetition of the rhythms which flow, with inward continuity, through diversified ornamentation, authentic human communion perpetually reaffirms itself. Indeed, one ought fully to focus on each word as that word breaks out of its enveloping stillness; and one ought not to dwell in the fantasy of either recollection or anticipation. On the contrary, one ought only to attend to the reality of the actual presence of the word, to its concrete and integral character. Therefore, every word should be heard in its vitality, its rhythmicity, its melodic constitution, its overtones, and its undertones, not as an isolated and fragmentary atom, a mere noise, but as an actual tone capable, through its dynamic quality of relatedness to other tones, of revealing the *entire* context of which it is part. Through this organic growth of words, wherein speakers and listeners both create growth and participate in it, communion eventuates. In every successive word, the past perishes. Yet, in each word, the past cumulatively endures. Maintaining its status *as* word against the resistance of an inherent dynamism toward transformation to the next word, the word nonetheless constitutes the germ whence proceeds still the next, in endless organic growth. Just as art orders space by matter, so music—and words are a species of music—orders silence by meaningful tone. Intermediate between art and music, words, like music, both shape and organize time, transforming its bare stillness, imparting their rhythms to that stillness, causing it to reverberate, and making audible the boundless quiet. And like art, words indicate those structures which render an image of space, organizing its sheer emptiness as a void imbued with immensity, spread, intimacy, and life. Complementing both touch and sight, words designate those tangible–visible images whereby man creates a bond with his surroundings. And both duplicating and drawing forth the "melodic continuity" of things, they express, in effect, that "music of the spheres" which transcends the space and time of mere physical presence.

(*c*) The Dynamics of Words

I have referred to words as an articulation of time. But time cannot be conceived apart from the conception of space. Nor can either be construed without some construal of matter. Words are a vibration; this is their "matter." Encountered as a something-out-there, the vibration which constitutes the word is *ipso facto* spatial; the manner of its unfolding, its transformations, and its issue are temporal. Yet the "space" of words is not the space of simple location, the mere juxtaposition of discrete parts, any more than its "time" is the time of bare succession. Whether construed as the (temporal) passage of one verbal event into another or as the (spatial) locus of the interpenetration of words which are constituted as both transparent to and audible through one another, the *tonal* individuality of words is actually composed of their mutual immanences. At the same time, by virtue of the ways in which they enter into each other's "'real internal constitutions,'"[2] words transcend one another, and stand forth as words.

Given with their *own* space, words both surround and seemingly reach out toward the listener; they integrate space, not as a quantified, uniform manifold, but as a multi-qualitied, heterogeneous *Gestalt*, a space within the undulations of which he participates and to which he surrenders himself, not as set apart from those rhythms but as suffused by them. Hardly the kind of polyphony found in the simultaneous melodic lines of music, as revealed in triad, chord, or ensemble, words nonetheless shape a melodic texture. Ever flowing and evolving, this texture is one of monadic lines, a symphony of dialogue in which many voices are like alternating strands drawn into cohesive unity. For the space of words is dynamic, fluid, and open. Exhibiting diverse and fluctuant structures, it is constituted by a succession of dynamic states which, as they unfold, blend and fuse: a sequence of temporally superimposed, yet mutually interpenetrating, states. A tightly knit web, this relational complex becomes full acoustical space only through the compresence of the echoes of words *as* words perish in time. Yet words cumulatively endure. An integration of aural characters transmuted from natural sound, they cohere as a corpus of tensions and counter-tensions, of harmonies and disharmonies; and they form a space which is alive and vibrant, a polyphony of echoes which perish yet ever remain viable—a rhythmic space wherein novel meaning-complexes never cease to emerge. Quite literally, the past dwells in the present as a consonance of echoes which endlessly reverberate, echoes among which one roots oneself, and draws sustenance to meet the challenges of emergent novelty. To this rhythmic space, the pitch, color, timbre, and tempi of words add their particular qualities: that increasingly subtle renditions be afforded the feelings and concerns of all who, participating in the space, are transformed by it. In this music of words resides the autonomy of words; and by this music, the shared underlying matrix of all language, persons of the most diverse linguistic affiliations both communicate and commune.

C • SPEECH AS APOTHEOSIS; DANCE AS MATRIX

(*a*) Word and Act

The word is powerful. Authentically spoken, it flows surely. Spoken from his depths, a person's word is wrapped in silence; every pause is full with the coming of speech. What had been gathered in is woven into a novel fabric, then extruded as speech. Hovering about dialogue, an interior calm is radiated; it embraces both speaker and listener. But the listening which prepares the way for the word not only is external; inner listening, as well, prevails. Traced *within* one, the imprints of things are inwardly heard. They compose an interior fabric which stretches unfathomably beyond one. To speak, one must fetch up the very roots of this fabric; and one must search for solidity, for the true symbols of a deeper, inward participation in nature. Carved out as massive substantives, these roots cannot consist in mere fleetingness as designated by verbs. As one listens, and draws one's racing thoughts to the slowly evolving word, therein congealing them while making them luminous—word which deliberately forms itself, as it is uttered—one's inward listening comes to constitute an inward searching. One endeavors to clarify awareness by taking hold of the name and, with it, the things which it names, that one might, in reverence for both words and things, present *oneself* more clearly and distinctly. Indeed, the word is the echo within of the things about. Gathered into sound, it names the reverberations upon that echo, reverberations filtered and transformed, and inwardly illuminated.

In his solitary gathering of things and words, in the *breathing in* of their pulsations, the person lightens himself, casting off the burden of tension. The echoes of things and words perish within him; and from the ensuing silence, blending with a deeper silence already there, he brings forth thought. And from thought, the still reverberations which die within him, he *breathes out* the word, the word on which he traces the very echoes of his thought, echoes which constitute the word's meaning. Accompanying the word is the act. To name an object is gratefully to acknowledge a gift; and this reciprocation means, in effect, a sending back of the object, by its name, to its own creator. But this sending forth *is* the act. Springing from the joyful surplus with which the word is endowed, the act is neither impulsive nor instinctual. Guided and limited by the name itself, every true act is deliberate. Never merely contrived, the act always shapes itself with care. Human gesture and human movement are precisely this overflowing from surplus. The very pregnancy of speech, and its coming to fruition, the act is a self summoning itself, with all its resources, to present itself, in all its rhythms, to another. Every presenting, of which the word is but chief focus, not only renders mood and spirit, but comments on a phenomenon to which a speaker is related. This relationship is dialogue; and the word, quintessential element of dialogue, is a symbol, the consummate symbol of human existence.

The act consummates itself in the word. By the word, things achieve distinctness. Arranging themselves into multi-laminated structures, things therein allow the entire cosmos to articulate itself, but with this qualification: structures must be *named* structures. Yet "structure" is an inadequae term for rendering the fluid, process character of things. Two immiscible, hence seemingly inadmissible, metaphors more appropriately convey the double sense of things as both stable and mobile: the metaphors, orchestration and mosaic. Now what flows forth fixes itself as durable configurations of interwoven facets; now such configurations liquefy as fluent motions of new kinds. In alternation, an activity unfolds whereby things shape and reshape themselves. Rhythms associated with this activity, and embodied in the rhythms of language itself, constitute themselves the very fruition of the rhythms of those specific acts by which things are discriminated as the particular things which, through the relevant words, they are discerned to be.

In their outward forms, the rhythms of these acts constitute a dance of gesture; in their inward forms, a dance of imagery. Two intertwined motions, a kind of dual dance, shape the substance of the act; but the act itself is rooted in the larger world. Commingling with other acts, the word effloresces as its myriad overtones and undertones. And, by these more subtle variants, speech more effectively renders the finer interminglings of things, in their reciprocal transfigurations, as, in varying combinations, they unfold toward ends already germinating within, hence prefigured by, their very beginnings. For words name the lineaments of things, both with respect to their broader initial contours and by way of anticipating the destinies toward which they appear to be unfolding. And naming the very form of the processions of things, words also react to the substance of those processions, as forms are actualized, by their own reconstitution as new names.

(*b*) Speech and Dance

Diverse influences, some gross and some ineffable, pervade the world, and ground its every activity. Certain constellations shape regions of confluence with respect to these factors, with respect to factors within factors, and with respect to factors enveloping factors: an immeasurably complicated orchestrating of mosaics, and mosaic-like arrestings, which never cease to shape a cosmic polyphony. Words constitute incarnations of this polyphony, as it undergoes its varied transmutations. In a grand movement, words and things become increasingly interdependent, and the textures which they form shape ever-shifting balances. Replicating the motions of both image and gesture, each springing from human action, a veritable dance of word and thing unfolds.

Reverberations capturing the subtlest nuances of cosmic activity, human speech sets forth the fruition of intertwined cosmic acts, and the resistance between human acts and acts in general. Lying in the very interstices of these intersecting yet radically distinct acts, words constitute the agency by which man achieves a double relationship to the world. On the one hand, man distances himself from nature. In solidarity with his fellows, he shapes new roots which replicate, in the sphere of the social, the elementary solidarity of nature. On the other hand, he participates in nature. Drawing himself toward her inmost recesses, he enables himself, in rhythms of attachment and detachment, to spiritualize a dance of the world's being, a cosmic symphony to which he contributes as participant, as composer of its score, and as director of its subsequent unfoldings. Speech is the apotheosis of a finely nuanced cosmic dance; and dance is the matrix which, in its consummate shape, crystallizes the cosmic ferment as an elaborate architectonic of speech. But this matrix does not merely give birth to speech. In addition, speech itself gathers its more ethereal tones to shape novel concrescences which pervade the very matrix whence speech arose. Thereby, speech contributes ever-new themes, reshaping the matrix so that it might henceforth engender still more novel configurations of words.

The word arises from, and brings to consummation, its own originating act. Yet, never ceasing, the act always accompanies the word. Though, from one point of view, the act terminates in, indeed transubstantiates itself into, the word as but its "breath and finer spirit,"[3] the word, nonetheless, remains but a phase of the act, its culminating phase. At the same time, the act, which by its very dynamic potentiates itself into the word as, so to speak, a dance of the tongue, a dance which recapitulates the dance of the body as a whole, is itself invigorated by the impact which the word exerts upon it. And even while the act is perishing into the word as its transmuted form, it is on the verge of being renewed. In effect, it is resuscitated, for the word brings new life to its own engendering act. Moreover, every speaking forth is, at bottom, a shaping of words: that they be more intimately woven with things; that they so commingle with things as, by their interactions, to permit an ever-sharper differentiation of both realms, word and thing, to proceed apace.

(*c*) Word Consummations

To shape a word is itself to act; it is to superadd a new act to the very act which gave birth to the word. For speaking requires that one exert oneself, that one summon one's powers authentically to symbolize. Part of the very symbolic status of words resides in the power of speech to redintegrate the person as an integral and cohesive fabric: that his dancing forth in both gesture and image be reinstated as vibrant, hence self-renewing. What is iterated in speech is now reiterated in dance. For to speak truly is to rejoice. It is to experience the richest possible modality of compresence with another. Yet speaking authentically requires that one fulfill the word in touch: that one reach out with one's hands, face, fingers, indeed entire body; that, thereby, one offer, as a gift, one's body as spiritualized —hence, one's full being—and, reciprocally, that one receive the gift of the other whom one is addressing. For words to flow from one person to another, one must touch that person, and touch him in finely modulated ways. Caressed by the sound of a human voice, the ears, as sensory receptive organs, transmit to one its tenderness, reassurance, and care. When persons are truly in contact, touching one another with all their human capabilities, the breath which hovers about speech envelops and, as the significant aura which surrounds words, imprints itself into both speaker and listener.

By touch, the word fulfills its own potential. And fully to touch, with all one's spiritual capabilities, is truly to dance: a gentle dance of fingers, toes, hands, and lips. Paradigm of speaking transformed into touch, sexual love, when lovers are joined by fully personal bonds, is consummated as a speaking forth, through all the marvelous tonalities of touch with the entirety of one's being: of one's very body, insofar as it is a body which serves as agent of one's full personhood. And as the caressing hands of lovers pass over one another, words silently flow through those hands. Within motions which are sure, true, and softly vibrant, words silently flow, words the inmost meaning and quintessential music of which remain eloquently inarticulate. Gathered together to cohere as a unity, words are fructified in speech which is ever more gentle and ever more subtle. And bursting forth from this tender matrix, new words form as new dances shape themselves with vigor and expansiveness, and dramatically etch themselves upon human encounter. Thus, in general, dance and speech alternate. Interpenetrating and suffusing one another, each is both matrix and apotheosis. For, in the end, matrix and apotheosis so blend that one can no longer distinguish one from the other. Tones of touch and tones of speech orchestrate themselves. Enfolded in gesture which is either quiet or vibrant, touch and speech, in turn, enfold a kaleidoscopic play of images which never cease to stir: all interweave to shape consummate personhood.

As with sexual love, so with searching in general! For to search is to speak, to touch, and to imagine. It is to dance with the full being of the seeker, to dance in myriad ways: ways which range from the sweeping and grand to the minuscule and fine, from the vigorous and vibrant to the tender and gentle. It is to dance to the tune of the cosmos, a tune which continually reactivates both dance and world: dance as a symbolic opening of oneself to receive the imprints of world; world as a revealing of the subtle information which ever awaits its gathering into the symbols of the seeker. Harmoniously, hitherto concealed secrets are interchanged: the ways of person and cosmos; the mode of attunement of each to each; the autochthonous rhythms which reverberate to constitute the quintessential character of both.

Self and world are intertwined. A kind of coy dance envelops the two. A double relationship holds. Each, in its manner, approaches the other, disclosing its essential rhythms. Yet on the very verge of imparting those rhythms, self to world and world to self, each withdraws. Like a shy mistress, the world is recalcitrant to its own full disclosure; like a timorous lover, the self refrains from full embrace, contenting itself with tantalizing glimpses. A subtle resistance prevails.

Endlessly reifying, the self retreats behind defensive barriers. Penetrating only vicariously, it knows by its symbolisms alone. Yet, in delightful surprise, the world, from time to time—a world which, however subtle, is never malicious—seizes upon a particular symbol, imparting to it a larger measure of its mystery. Whereupon the self eagerly immerses itself in what has been disclosed, and, with abandon, thrusts its searching ingenuity into a labyrinth now magically made accessible; whereupon, the coy bagatelle of self and world restores itself, and, once again, the autonomy of each prevails, each ineluctably stranger to the other. Interminably, the process uncoils and recoils; convolutions and involutions never fail to alternate. Yet, enveloping all, a great and wondrous music sweeps on; the cosmic dance does not cease.

NOTES

1. Leo Spitzer, *Classical and Christian Ideas of World Harmony* (Baltimore: The Johns Hopkins University Press, 1963), pp. 7, 71–74.
2. Whitehead, *Process and Reality*, p. 37.
3. William Wordsworth, "Preface to the Second Edition of the Lyrical Ballads," in *The Poetical Works of William Wordsworth*, ed. Ernest de Selincourt, 2 vols. (Oxford: Clarendon, 1944), II 398.

16

FABRIC OF UTTERANCE: ORCHESTRATED PATTERNS OF SYMBOL TRANSFORMATION

PREAMBLE

By "dialogue," I mean a disclosure of what flows between two centers, especially personal centers, a bringing of each person close to the other by naming him aloud. It is a calling forth, a calling forth of him to me, a drawing him forth from concealment, that his presence might approach and be enmeshed with my presence. In dialogue, my every utterance constitutes a symbol of myself, a symbol of the vicissitudes of my spirit and my mood, as I receive his imprints and bestow upon him my imprints. Therein, I make myself present in my full presence; and by all my symbols, each an earthly token of my inward being, I strain to speak, and to accompany my speech by manifold signs, like dance, gesture, and song. This fabric of reciprocal, interpenetrating symbolic presentings shapes human dialogue.

What is the structure of dialogue? How is it woven with reality? First, I consider how words reveal the truth of things and how things reveal the truth of words. Next, I show how words and things, in mutual adequation, disclose the truth of being. Finally, I indicate that the truth of being emerges only in the context of symbolic presentation. In these ways, I treat dialogue as the intermingling of selves with selves, such that the community which these selves compose grounds the rhythmic unfoldings of the textures of words and things; and I exhibit symbols of human presence as emerging, and orchestrating themselves in diverse and intertranslatable patterns, in the context of human encounter.

A • WORDS AS REVEALING THE TRUTH OF THINGS; THINGS AS REVEALING THE TRUTH OF WORDS

(*a*) Adequation of Word to Thing

Words and things enjoy reciprocal relatedness.[1] On the one hand, judgments, propositions, and theories are true to facts as conforming to them, to objects as representing them, or to data as agreeing with them. By stating what is the case, they articulate a scheme of thought as adequate to reality. On the other hand, a thing, action, or person is true when it (or he) functions or acts in accordance with a norm, rule, standard, pattern, or model. By itself constituting what has been stated to be the case, it presents itself as adequate to a *concept* of reality. In either instance, an intended entity (word or thing) conforms (or is adequate) to a correlative and, presumably actual, entity (thing or word). Finally, in mutual adequation, an inner harmony holds between word and thing, concept and reality: an attunement, a consonance, an identity of spiritual purport. What are the implications of these modes of adequation for a theory of the word as symbol?

In the first mode, the word presents a thing, and discloses its structure. Exhibiting it for sustained contemplation, the word makes the thing accessible; it demarcates and maps out a domain for human use, human enjoyment, and human acknowledgment. In this process of presenting, wherein by my speaking (or as in the written word, by my implied speaking) I present myself to what, by words, I reciprocally present *to* myself, my every word embodies an intending, an orienting toward, and a comporting. Correlative with every intention, and growing from it within comportment, is the complementary phase, attending. My "stretching from within" becomes a "reaching toward." For the word so comments upon a thing, and thereby illuminates the details of its structure, that by its use, a mere aggregate of listeners is welded into a veridical community. To the correctness of each re-presentation of the intended entity as really the actual entity, communal assent is gained. And by joint assent the community's members are brought to mutual presence in a (potential or actual) communal attending, an attending which consummates itself in naming. For the act of naming brings about authentic communion among those who name. *Given by* the namer, the name is no mere (cognitive) positing of an existent. On the contrary, it is substantively given to the existent as thenceforth belonging to it, as, indeed, part of its very essence. In consequence, the existent can be celebrated by its name. For names are gifts. Insofar as they are freely given by the human spirit, they sanctify, by the spirit, the objects with which they are associated. Hallowing those objects, they cause them to contribute to the building of a kind of temple of humanized things. And, within this temple, man can thenceforth securely dwell.

Yet the name is still the name of a *thing*; and the qualities of no particular thing can be exhaustively specified by its naming. Partly revealed by the name, it remains largely concealed: an incompletely known entity to which the self which gives a name thereby gives itself, indeed abandons itself with a kind of awe in the presence of what must remain ineluctably mysterious. For selfhood entails the capacity to risk. To be a self, one must allow oneself to be "taken up" by what is intrinsically unknown. By its mere repeating of an assigned name, the self diminishes its own potency. For to as-sign is *actively* to signify, to point toward a thing under a variety of perspectives. When the self names the thing it designates, it names in the context of human action; and this context requires that the perspectives on the thing are to be conceived as limitless. A passive naming of non-creative repetition proposes only the specious illuminating of the thing which is (allegedly) veridically named.

However, when the self allows itself to surrender its being to a thing, spontaneously permitting itself to be wholly absorbed by, and, so to speak, to be taken into the thing, the self attains a state of self*less*ness. When, in this state, the self ceaselessly searches into its own inwardness, it renews (and re-invigorates) the name, thereby reaffirming its selfhood. In this process, the self actually allows itself, in a kind of self-abnegation, to be like the other. In this un–self-conscious witnessing of cosmic harmonies and dissonances, a curious oscillation of distance and intimacy supervenes. Certainly, the oppressive, fearful aspect of things is thereby removed. For, through words, things configure themselves into a shape and order in which man can humanly participate. In this dwelling place wherein men truly associate, each more profoundly touching the other that each may thereby discern the truth, things now shine forth as humanly meaningful. Yet, like the stained glass windows of a cathedral, word–thing associations glow with unfathomable depths of meaning: a mysterious illumination by which particulars become discernible, and are brought to inner unity in their most subtle hues, that they may be revered and hallowed. For, by "inner unity," I mean that particulars are not merely singular and isolated, but woven into a whole (i.e., a coherent) fabric, the mysteries of which man touches with intimate reverence.

By my words, I incisively depict reality. Cutting into things, I organize their structures as complexes of individuals. In declaring the truth, I declare myself. True, being is discerned as the dwelling place of truth, but it is the source which *I* affirm. For it is *I* who present myself to things, within a temple which *I* have built, and always in accordance with principles which I prescribe to myself, principles of ordering, shaping, categorizing, and judging. Indeed, I am the very instrumentality by which, and the medium through which, the word of these engendering principles comes to fruition. Truth assignation, whereby words become adequate to things, is an *act* of assigning. It implies a matrix of activity wherein, by my posing and counterposing of words with things, things compose themselves *as they are*. By my attending things, as I draw the appropriate words from my inner silence, that words be appropriated by things, I do not stand alone. Attending with me, and both approving and affirming, is my community, a concelebrant in the temple of things.

(*b*) Adequation of Thing to Word

In the mode wherein thing becomes adequate to word, the problem is not so much to understand, to contemplate, and to identify oneself with existence, standing beneath it as though one were in a temple, as to govern existence, to subject it to one's bidding, to appropriate it, and to identify it with oneself. In the second instance, particulars are adapted to, and measured by, a universal standard embodied in words. Now, signifying an object is tantamount to conferring significance upon it. What is deemed worthy, obligatory, or right is fitted into a pattern in accordance with a purpose and criterion, whether stated or implicit, which is set forth by the self. Things—by which I mean actions and purposes, as well as "mere" things—are weighed and considered. Referred for evaluation by the community *to itself*, they are, thereupon, granted their meanings. And acting through its "competent" members, the entire community sits in judgment. It ascertains the "position" to be occupied in the cosmic scheme by each proposed entity.

In this mode of adequation, the composing of things as things can be achieved only within the framework of their proposal as things. A communal presence constitutes itself the ultimate authority for sanctioning some pattern of things as worthy of its attention, as indeed expressing an authentic existence. No longer does the community simply dwell among things by simply representing those things to itself, whether the representations possess cognitive status or artistic status. On the contrary, things are now sought out, that by an act of the self they be transformed. For truly to represent means to be presented *again and again.* In this process, a virtual transformation may occur. Contexts in which things initially present themselves are so radically shifted that the thing itself may, thereafter, be experienced as quite different from what it was initially perceived to be. Once chosen (and rechosen), things must be *willed* to be in conformity with principles which the self prescribes to itself. Thenceforth, the entire experienced world is declared by the community (of selves) both to exemplify and to embody these principles. Whether by persuasion, by exhortation, by directive, by prescription, or by command, the self wills that things be transfigured in keeping with its own purposes. In this act, it reveals its declarations to be imperious, since, now, the declarations are always in the imperative mood. Indeed, only in this mood (or mode) can the very possibility for truth be regarded as residing in the self. In this sense, the self is ground, inspiration, and arbiter for determining precisely wherein consists the thing. Ideas incorporate intentions; things are brought into conformity with ideas. And, in the end, by this conformation, things are willed *as* things. By this mode of adequation, things appear and gain their meanings among words, and through the instrumentality of words; things shine forth as things only when they have been referred to a community which, by its ideals and norms, selects, distributes, values, and organizes those things. In the previous mode, the community had to be acceptable to nature, its collective spiritual life appropriate and adaptable. In the present mode, nature must be accepted by the community, a community which both draws nature toward it and assimilates nature as its very own.

Previously, I participated in nature, and was led to revere her. Now nature participates in me. Through her being drawn into my substance, I am enlarged, and, therefore, led to revere myself. By my will and by my act, things become as they are. Imposing myself upon nature, I transfigure her. *Pari passu,* I transform myself. For by my will and by my act, I affirm myself to be the source of the very "ought" by which I command all nature to heed me. It is *I* who set the standards to which nature is "obliged" to conform. By the symbols which *I* create, I establish a mode of relatedness to nature whereby she is thoroughly humanized. In the first mode of adequation, it was as though my very existence were constituted by my aim to uncover nature. By the second mode, I actually become the "aim to govern nature."[2]

(*c*) The Willed Act

Save by a specific act, and by that exclusively, I can justify neither my will nor its aims. In the context of the adequation of things to words, I can *only* exercise my will—hence, so act that my will concretizes itself in identifiable ways. The whole world spreads like a canvas to which I apply the colors prescribed by my will; and the very factuality of each fact arises from the factors which I articulate by my own choice. And, in general, to articulate my self, to set it forth in words so that the true word might be sought out is, by implication, to set the conditions for articulating the very being of the world. No fact is independent of that articulation. No fact can be construed as an existent without the construal of its intelligibility. Facts emerge as facts, as the coherent order of nature, in acts of interpretation alone. By these acts, I so project myself into each thing that my very self is defined as the totality of these projectings. In the frame of projection, things weave themselves into my substance, a substance which solidifies and expands. Thereby, I shape a clarified awareness, an awareness the subjectivity of which becomes increasingly objective, an awareness potentiated ever anew to perform fresh, nearly miraculous works. On every occasion on which I cause all nature to do my bidding, nature which stirs her natural ferment at my own command, I must comply with this condition: namely, the shaping of a clarified awareness.

According to this mode of adequation, nature pays homage to the strength of human selfhood, *a fortiori* to the strength of human community: community which so evolves as to constitute its declarations, and its every word, a temple toward which, as they are woven into *its* construction, all things flow. Now the powers which, earlier, had been located without man, powers both mysterious and ineffable, are discovered to constitute the inwardmost recesses of man, a realm of words which, lying deep within him, flow from a source far beyond him.

B • MUTUAL ADEQUATION OF WORDS AND THINGS AS REVEALING THE TRUTH OF BEING

(*a*) Sources of Adequation

The concept of the adequation of words to things suggests a potent *natural* source to which the self yields itself, a source both without it and beyond it which engenders the panoply of things among which it dwells. The concept of the adequation of things to words suggests a potent *ideal* source upon which the self ceaselessly draws, a source within it yet no less beyond it whence arise the words by which a community of selves acknowledges its presence among those things. In the first instance, I, now acceptable to nature, give myself up to her; in the second instance, nature, now acceptable to me, gives herself up, by my persuasions, to me. Both processes are moments in the unfolding truth of being, by which evolves the mutual reciprocal reverence between man and nature, each reverence in its kind. Nature affirms herself through me; I affirm myself through her. When these processes are combined, every universal (i.e., concepts expressed by words) perfectly instantiates itself by particulars, the things which words call forth; and every particular finds its place in a totality which conforms to the very words which embody universals.

Every judgment of theory, those specific articulatings of one's surrender to nature, presupposes a judgment of practice wherein one subdues nature and brings her into conformity with one's own will. To determine an idea as truly conforming to reality (i.e., as right for it, or as not deviating from it), one must select the relevant facts which constitute this reality; and one must comport toward those facts as acceptable to some community norm. On the other hand, every judgment of practice presupposes a judgment of theory. The very acceptability of the norm which embodies practical truth is ascertained in the course of gaining theoretic truth; each determination of acceptability requires, again, a judgment of adequation of that norm to nature as she is now understood, i.e., as another theoretic truth. Yet such truth presupposes another practical truth; and so an endless cycle unfolds, with respect to the mutually presupposing judgments of theory and judgments of practice. And such reciprocal dependence is linked both to an oscillation between one's uttering and acting in self-affirmation and to one's receiving and listening in patience—in each instance, whether acting or listening, with respect to that which, standing before one for one's evaluation, affirms itself.

In the mutual adequation of words and things, these potent sources, absolute objectivity and absolute subjectivity, are marvelously brought together as a perfect attunement and inner harmony of subject with object, self with nature, word with thing: a harmony which overarches and transcends each dichotomy, embracing both members as complementary factors in a comprehensive and integral unity, the unity of the texture of words wrought with things. Both the outer adventure, the spectacle of creation or *natura naturata*, and the inner adventure, the spectacle of creating or *natura naturans*, constitute but a single adventure which is integral and unified. If man is regarded as the self-conscious *locus* of an "aim to uncover" and an "aim to govern,"[3] then each aim can be understood only in its status as a vital factor within the other factor. For to uncover, a person also governs. That he may contemplate, he must place himself in a position to observe, distinguish, experiment, rearrange, and manipulate. Analogously, to govern, a person also uncovers. Both his creating and his shaping must always be by a plan, by an image which guides him at each instant of his acting. For both act and the image of its import and consequences cannot be separated.

(*b*) Authenticity

How can this alteration and complementarity be characterized? How can true consonance between word and thing thereby be achieved? These questions require the concept of authenticity.

In mutual adequation, things and words alike are constituted as authentic. A true specimen, the thing is exemplar of a model; conversely, the model, embodying purport or intended meaning, is true to all its instances. Authenticity requires that there be no incongruity between type, expressed in words, and instance, designated by words. Accordingly, an authentic state of being is achieved in that temple of things wherein persons dwell in communion. For by their communings, men make themselves present to one another; they so unveil their masks that the things which envelop them glow and reveal themselves. Only as referred to human communion, wherein person and person are reciprocally present, can things and words appear as they really are—without sham, that men in their presence need not be ashamed. In perfect adequation between the purport of things and their existence, persons reveal their spirit, naked and pure.

Achieved in a human setting alone, authenticity means that things herein disclose their actual mode of functioning, their interconnections within a larger matrix, and that the words which man utters to designate those things mean precisely what they are claimed to mean. For this disclosure to occur, persons must present themselves to those things precisely as what each person and thing truly is; they must search out the appropriate and, accordingly, the authentic words. With respect to an image previously suggested, the temple of things is truly a place wherein persons worship. Since worship is communion, and communion is reciprocal, total presence, the temple of words and the temple of things form but one temple, indivisible and complete. If there be an Almighty, a source beyond the sources within and without, a primal and ultimate potency which gives birth to both subjectivity and objectivity, herein He reveals Himself in His mystery and tenderness.

To be authentic, a thing must be adequate to the purport originally assigned it, and also, by this assignation, to its intrinsic constituents; and a word must be adequate to the intention with which it was formed. Neither word nor thing proposes its own purport. Yet, by its indigenous structure, each possesses the power to stir. Each incorporates in its very substance the purport initially assigned it; each, accordingly, sets its own limits. By human comporting, word and thing are each empowered subsequently to compose itself as what it is, hence, to propose to persons its own texture. Indeed, proposing and comporting are correlative components, referable to persons, words, and things. They are essential factors in that integral process whereby truth emerges as truth of being. Moreover, only a particular class of purports can, by human intention, be assigned. For every thing, every word, has a history, and by this history certain purports are inadmissible; they are intrinsically excluded from the essence of a given thing or a given word.

A person's authenticity consists in the honest self-confrontation of *his* history. Herein is achieved the integration of hitherto unabsorbed components. Incongruities are diminished; full self-presentation is facilitated. Here alone does his being attain absolute concreteness, the unique essence which defines him to be this particular individual. Yet the very unfolding of his history engenders the unfolding of the histories of both the words and the things which have been relevant to him, histories to which he himself has already contributed. Accordingly, the complex of purports constituted within those words and things—purports the character of which is their specific power autonomously *to determine*—is revealed by the manner in which these histories themselves are, *ipso facto*, confronted. By candid encounter, wherein the texture of word and thing opens itself to full disclosure, one may walk truly (i.e., authentically) within the unified temple wrought by both word and thing.

To be authentic is to be original, the originary source whence springs the manifold of concrete traits by which a history is expressed, its fragments congealed and drawn to presence. It is, accordingly, a power of impact, a thrust into novelty. At the very ground of any mutual adequation is the authenticity of being, specifically of *human* being. For man sets the context in which words and things achieve, in their reciprocal dependency, their mutual adequation. Within human comportment, the purport of both words and things arises. And each person imposes upon himself the obligation, if he would be a person who would *recognize* his history and *realize* his power of impact, to actualize for *himself* a particular purport, self-determinedly and self-consciously: a purport to which he can devote himself loyally and wholeheartedly, and with that holiness of heart by which he allows that purport to be fully his *own* purport. Thereby alone can one achieve uniqueness *as* a person. For the essence of the person consists in his potency to seek an essence: a style of life, a particular commitment, a specific form of existence; a style which is reliable, trustworthy, and steadfast. The person is that entity which quests after essence.

(*c*) The True Person

As I shape things, I present them to myself. Only in interpersonal relations is mutual adequation fully realized; and here, indeed, it becomes mutual reverence. My idea of the person, an uncovering of his essence, is identical with his idea of himself. In both instances, it is the idea which *ought* to be realized. Thus having an idea in perfect conformity with an essence, I yield myself to the other as he yields himself to *himself*. In this reciprocity of yieldings, I and he, at one and the same time, govern. For each person wills what he ought to will, and each person understands what he wills. Analogously, each is oriented toward the other. Herein, a perfect reciprocity of understanding wills shapes itself. Within this framework, the self-identity of every person both solidifies and strengthens itself as *self-conformation*. By processses which flow between persons, each individual works out a perfect adequation between intentional essence and real actuality—that the "hunger for the truth of being"[4] be satisfied.

Accordingly, a person is true when he realizes his spiritual truth. Then, he perfectly exemplifies the universal image of man as prescribing an ideal image for himself, an image which perfectly accords with his private intentions. Uncovering those intentions, he presents himself as what he actually conceives himself to be, and this in perfect conformity with what he is ideally conceived by another person to be. The very ground of one's being demands utterance. Each, accordingly, spiritualizes himself as word. For, words are vehicles of concern, words together with their penumbral non-verbal presentations. They are the primal thrust of will into the substance of concern; they shape things into objects of concern. By the abidingness of words, wherein a holy, eternal present is preserved amid everlasting perishing, man shapes finite reality as ideally infinite.

C • THE TRUTH OF BEING AS EMERGING IN THE CONTEXT OF SYMBOL FORMATION

(*a*) Givings

In mutual compresence, selves offer themselves to one another. They present themselves as gifts, each to the other. And such interpersonal gifts are of two kinds: those which are attached to the giver; those which, in principle, are detachable from the giver. In both instances, the full being of the donor pours itself into the gift, hence, impinges momentously upon the recipient; in both instances, the impact of the giving upon the recipient tends, though the tendency might not be borne to fruition, to catalyze a reciprocal gift to the donor. Wherein, I must now ask, are both attached and detachable gifts symbolic presentations? How, under each circumstance, does the truth of being emerge, and declare itself?

By attached gifts, I mean direct presents of donor to recipient: presents which are presentings in the form of gesture, physiognomy, vocal intonation, a dance, the singing of the song, the rendering of a musical composition. Whether or not ancillary instruments are attached to a person, in order to facilitate his giving gifts through enhancement of some specific faculty, a gift consists in the sheer immediacy of his own personal presence, in the context of human compresence. In all such instances, one draws forth, from the depths of one's being, nothing less than one's very self, not so much as particular tokens or artifacts as, in principle, one's *entire* being. When such gifts as tenderness, care, warmth, compassion, loyalty, or fidelity are proffered, they are presented through specific bodily gestures such as eye movements, the play of fingers, an extended hand, the touch of lips, or, indeed, a more total deployment of bodily motions. For insofar as the human body is a flowing forth from one's inmost human center, all bodily parts, and coordinations of bodily parts, are truly spiritualized.

Through the immediate agency of his body, together with such ancillary instruments as a person might append to his body, he presents himself to a recipient as though he himself were a kind of poem. In a mutual exchange of such gifts, it is as though two poems incarnate touch one another, and so interchange their respective content as to shape a third poem: the authentic expression and manifestation of the dynamic, total being-together of both persons. By the impact of this body–spirit offering, each person durably affects the other, and, indeed, his very own self. For the entire self so impinges upon each, donor and recipient, as to transfigure both significantly. And whenever such gifts are given or exchanged, a veridical metamorphosis of the spirit results. Here I merely express St. Francis of Assisi's teaching that it is better to give than to receive. For the giver, and in reciprocal giving this process consummates itself, is more affected by his giving than the recipient; his very integrity is reshaped. Thereby, the parts of his being cohere more harmoniously; henceforth, he can give even more freely, and with a greater spontaneity of outpouring.

In the act of giving, the traces of all one has ever been, together with all one wishes one might become, is woven, through the gift of one's actual presence, into the very fabric of the recipient, and, even more pervasively, the donor. Sheer feeling has so emanated from donor to both self and other that the rhythms of each are transformed, and, in consequence, the actions which ground themselves on those rhythms are, henceforth, purified. To touch another person by this poetry of oneself is to join the soul of each to each; it is so to allow the gathering together anew of all the resources of both that, thenceforth, each empowers himself more fully to give. And the process is like a spiral every turn of which induces a new unfolding, and every unfolding of which enfolds both givers in its ongoing movement: a movement which is borne toward the celestial envelopment of each giver; an envelopment which radiates its powers toward all who, henceforth, will encounter them. Inherent in every act of giving is a power to spread and, thereby, to induce, throughout the human community, new acts of giving.

(*b*) Reciprocations

In every instance, a true giver is like a lover who, as he opens himself to his beloved, must be prepared to risk, to sacrifice, and to renounce: that he serve as a kind of model for his beloved to emulate; yet that he give in humility. For his imperfections must be construed as greater than those of his beloved, especially should his beloved be unable to give with reciprocal openness, since he, the lover, is in a state of knowledge, not of ignorance. Naturally, barriers may supervene. The will to synchronize initiation of the act of giving with culmination of the act may be at odds with its capacity to execute its intention. In such cases, the body behaves with almost autonomous impulsivity, as though it itself were agent rather than medium through which the actual agent, a full person, acts. When giving is thus impeded, bodily awkwardness sets in. One part of a functioning body dissociates itself from another part; incongruities among a body's *quasi*-acts prevail. Radically severed from the person's active center, hence disjointed and deformed, his body so behaves in relation to that center that giving becomes degraded and, in effect, hypocritical.

But when the process of giving flows without interruption, one becomes like a living poem, a poem which bursts forth as dance and song. Under these circumstances, a vibrant tenderness betokens authentic giving; the dance or song of giving never threatens the recipient. On the contrary, so perfectly attuned are the acts of giving to the actual capabilities of the recipient to receive that dance and song embrace him. Especially where reciprocity prevails, each, donor and recipient, is in perfect harmony with the other. The very acceptance of a gift constitutes a gift to the donor; the roles of donor and recipient are co-adaptable and interchangeable. No reciprocation can be greater than for a gift fully to be accepted, accepted in the context of the intentions with which it was proffered. And in every human encounter sanctified by giving, two interwoven moments constitute the commingling acts of giving: a going toward to present the gift; a listening to and being with, with all one's resources, in order authentically to receive the gift. Only when one totally listens to all that the other is can both giving and accepting be perfectly attuned.

With respect to detachable gifts—namely, where the gift is either completely shaped by the giver, like a painting or poem created by him, or, alternatively, like an object given, which though not actually shaped by the giver is at least touched by him with the spirit of giving—one less dramatically and immediately, but no less authentically, gives a living symbol of one's presence. As before, spirit likewise suffuses gift. Pouring his full being into his art, the artist imprints on his art all that he is. And he makes this token of himself freely accessible to all who would receive it. For the work of art mirrors the very soul of its creator. Indeed, in relating to the work, one is, in reality, relating to a relationship, incorporated in the work itself, between tangible materials which manifest the work and the artist's spirit which shape the materials to an aesthetically desirable product. Hence, an analogy holds between the presenting of oneself, i.e., of one's own activating spirit, through the body's tangible motions and the presenting of a work of art. For, incarnate in the work is an analogous relationship between artist's spirit and tangible elements of the product shaped. Moreover, a dialectical relationship prevails between both elements: motivating, animating spirit; visible representation and vehicle of spirit. Accordingly, works of art which are not literally presented by the artist, but freely accessible to all only insofar as they belong to the public domain, constitute an artist's profoundly personal gifts to everyone who opens himself to receive those gifts. For the artist dwells as an active, viable presence in his every work. Just as the body of a person who gives mirrors the acts by which his gift is given, so the art work, in itself, mirrors analogous gifts. In this sense, the shaping of a work of art is an act of love, an act by which the artist embraces humankind; it is the spontaneous proffering of gifts to all who will receive them. And, in general, whether objects are actually created by a giver, or given only in the spirit of their creation, and if created, whether they are fashioned by someone else, and appropriated only as a gift to be given, or simply objects of nature chosen by the giver, all gifts are imbued with the giver's spirit. They transfer part of him to the recipient; indeed, they are an outpouring of his whole self.

(*c*) Transformations and Consummations

In brief, works of art are gifts; and any object chosen from nature's offerings to be a gift, or shaped from those offerings, is touched by the spirit of the one who chooses or creates, hence, constitutes a symbolic offering, the presentation by a symbolizer in the context of dialogue. All such symbolic patterns are transformable: each as a deposition of the dialogue of selves interwoven with selves; each as a drawing of sustenance from that community as it is embedded in the larger cosmic community. In its quest to express an analogous content in a different medium, a Rilke poem comments on a Rodin sculpture; a Beethoven chorale comments on a Schiller poem; a Shelley poem comments on the scientist's account of clouds; a Moussorgsky musical arrangement comments on some paintings at an exhibition; a Lucretian poem comments on a philosophic doctrine; a short story by Thomas Mann bears close resemblance to a musical tone poem. Such examples could be multiplied indefinitely. In every instance, an endeavor is made to render some singular instance of compresence, man with man or man with nature, in *equivalent* symbolism. Doubtless, different artists construe similar phenomena, and, indeed, even quest after shaping identical construals. Yet when all is said and done, every person must declare his response in an idiom which is distinctively his own. True, *through* the miraculously singular synthesizing powers by which every human being, and indeed every specific human act, are constituted, a common rhythmic fabric of cosmic occurrences gives birth, in the last analysis, to every creative act. Yet owing to the special media through which these rhythms pass, multiple orchestrations of symbolic transformation are formed from shared human experience. Always, however, the individual imprints his unique qualities on the world. Pervaded by an irreducible individuality, the quest for absolutely intertranslatable symbolisms is doomed to failure. A radically novel element, which derives from the idiosyncratic character of each person, sets person and his every act apart from all else, a creature and his creations which will never again be duplicated. Nevertheless, the endlessly modulated human orchestrations which manifest themselves through such variegated symbolisms do replicate, though in infinitely more subtle ways, the fabric of non-personal reverberations, which, after all, engender those modulations, constitute the very stuff of which they are wrought, and shape the ends in which they culminate.

NOTES

1. I am indebted to the excellent discussion in Hofstadter, *Truth and Art*, pp. 87–129.
2. Ibid., p. 128.
3. Ibid.
4. Ibid., chap. 8.

17

MATRICES OF UTTERANCE: THE PRIMORDIA OF SPEECH AS INNER IMAGERY

PREAMBLE

By the matrix of utterance, I mean the interplay of world events, both human and nonhuman, the interminglings of which come to fruition, in their human form, as a fabric of imagery: e.g., the sensation, kinesthesia, and fantasy which constitute human acts. Of perpetually shifting contour and content, a labyrinth-like pyramid is shaped: the base, the world, and its comminglings; the configuration itself, cavernous recesses and strange protuberances; the apex, a substance whence arises the primordial dance of gesture. In time, this dance transmutes itself into human utterance: utterance consummated as speech which itself is either autonomous or interwoven with specific acts of shaping.

Utterance may be treated under three topics: context, or the human action wherein textures of words and things germinate; rhythm, or the confluences, transmigrations, and reconstitutings which quality that context; fabric, or the community of selves-in-relation who, in schemes of presence and compresence, potentiate the unfolding of those rhythms. Ultimate ground of utterance, the world as a *unified* complex endlessly differentiates itself, and elaborates the resulting elements as the primordial stuff of human creativity, a veritable dance of images. Paradigm for this dance, the dream is a special kind of kaleidoscopic flux, one which *par excellence* exemplifies the inner world. In *Apotheosis*, I shall exhibit the dream as the spur to the quest for symbols, and I shall show how symbols both mirror the cosmic drama and call forth its myriad themes. Now I indicate how the dream embodies principles applicable to realms beyond its immediate province. For dreams illustrate features of symbolism not conspicuously found in other modes of symbolization. With respect to both the originating dynamism of dreams and schemes for their interpreting, a general symbology pervades all dreaming. Though impressionistically, a single dream, as model, will here instantiate certain ontologic tenets.

A • INTERIOR IMAGES EXTERIORIZED

(*a*) The Image

All experience leaves its trace as imagery, and imagery shapes a multitude of patterns. Forming unpredictable new products, such externally derived images combine with autochthonous inner imagery. By "experience," I mean an imprinting of specific qualities into one who contemplates, gathers, and receives; and I refer to a shaping of those qualities into new complexes by intentions which are either overt or implicit. By "trace" of experience, I mean an unfolding of sheer quality, quality detached from brute fact: a mirroring of the external world which, by the self's own laws, undergoes myriad transformations. By intrinsic powers or by contingencies beyond control, the self is thrust into a kaleidoscopic realm. Therein, it adventures amid images which may be evanescent, durable, or labyrinthine, images either associated with shifting moods or seemingly disconnected from all affect. Having entered this realm, one journeys among the shades of what had been a vibrant presence.

Once undertaken, the journey leads one to hitherto unknown depths and marvelous new combinations of imagery, images joined to sensation, mood, or kinesthesia. But the adventure is not without constraints, constraints analogous to those which prevail in the natural world. Nor is the inner realm mere degraded experience, or, for that matter, a bizarre and grotesque growth, disengaged from customary experience, which arises from a withdrawal from the encroachments of experience. On the contrary, it unfolds its concealed wonders by virtue of a mental act, an act which is powerfully operative when one slumbers. For, during sleep, new experiences are minimally absorbed into one's interior existence; and one can then experience in an altogether new mode, a mode which differs from that dominating ordinary perception.

Certainly, inner experience shares features with ordinary experience. On the other hand, it exhibits a peculiar vibrancy, quite as dramatic as that of ordinary experience, and its own kind of resistance. What initially appeared to be mere quality, quality which prescinds from both relational and resistance aspects of ordinary experience, now reappears as itself a manifold, a manifold autonomous and real. And the act whereby such experience engenders itself exhibits an implicit purposiveness, as it appropriates natural factors and sifts them through a medium which, prior to its probing, is obscure or even uncanny. In self-probing, one becomes aware, with increasing acuity as one searches, of a power to regulate, to rearrange, and to shape anew: a power which resides in the seeker, insofar as he deliberately suspends his receptivity to outer stimuli, and turns his gaze toward the stimuli which impinge from within him.

With increasing clarity, as one probes the interior recesses of consciousness, an inward drama etches itself upon one. A mélange of images appears, a *mélange* which, in the context of self-searching, reveals an inner psychic order, an order which shapes itself into an intricate relational manifold. Once penetrated, this manifold allows one to potentiate one's own creative resources. In whatever type of symbol, by whatever style, and through whatever route, the capacity to shape ever-more-novel symbols is activated. With increasing persuasiveness, the images which now disclose themselves to constitute a kind of dance of imagery exhibit, for one who wills to participate in a world which he himself shapes, the power to stir creative discontent with his customary mode of rootedness in nature. Setting himself even farther apart from nature than he originally ascertained himself to be, yet afflicted with diminishing anguish as he enters an internally "natural" world, a world which in the end will prove to be profoundly spiritual, a person discovers that his failed quest to embed himself in the outer world hardly dooms him to emptiness and despair. Quite the contrary. For he soon learns that his search for new roots is actually stimulated, and even facilitated, when he becomes convinced that, in an as yet undetermined sense, the inner world, once its content reveals itself, is more sustaining and reliable than the customary world. Though his dwelling in this world disrupts facile modes of categorizing reality, it nonetheless spurs a person so to clarify his accustomed existence that the fascination of the quest alone suffices for a new security, a security now woven with awe.

As the actual design of image unfoldings becomes manifest, a veritable transfiguration is achieved. For, by a tacit plan which incorporates both canons which prescribe a unique style for such interior processes and communally agreed upon conventions of usage, an altogether new configuration forms. And, by these "rules," the elements which constitute the configuration interweave as a cohesive portrait. But a portrait of what? For images point beyond themselves toward facts: *inner* facts as recalcitrant to arbitrary alteration as outer facts; inner facts which, in their seemingly ineluctable concealment, acquire a strange, numinous, and uncanny character. Somehow "exterior" to the person, though constitutive of his very inwardness, such inner facts contain, as germinating within them, indeed they actually engender, the very complexes to which their associated images ultimately give rise. Residue of a hidden presence which the self senses to hover within it, each image is a formula, often cryptic, which presents itself for deciphering. But, unlike a sign embedded in a causal matrix, images do not merely signify events. They are symbols in which are compressed both the powers which shaped them and a concealed mood which presses toward expression.

(*b*) The Symbol

To elucidate the connection between image and symbol, I recur to my theory of the word as previously set forth. Spoken from the depths of stillness, every word is a unique phenomenon. No other instance of its utterance exhibits the same pitch, intonation, accent, or intensity—in brief, the same mode of rhythmicality. Impinging in vibrant immediacy on all who listen, the word is, nonetheless, more than a presentation of itself, however effective the presentation. For the word bears import, and import is charged with numberless modulations and nuances. By its impact, it stirs a multitude of associations. An enveloping nature presses upon the listener; nebulous influences surge within him. The word articulates these factors—but in symbolic form. An absolutely singular occurrence, it unfolds here and now as a non-duplicative event. Shaping itself into viable presence within a present moment which, nonetheless, possesses duration, its reference is, in part, to a haunting past: a past felt as a circumambient presence; a past which refuses to perish in the tragic dignity of mourning, perish not in alternating fits of clinging and releasing, but in inspiring memory; a past in which one may, as *passéiste*, actually dwell, endlessly searching among the contours of its internalized recesses. Among the varied aspects under which it may be conceived, symbolic reference is that mode of human activity which, preeminently, discloses this perpetuation of past as present. Thereby, symbolic reference makes possible a perishing into the clarified present; therein, it reveals hitherto hidden novelties.

Shaped from experience, the symbol is a tangible complex which resonates among persons in community. A sound, a facial expression, a movement, a glance, the evocation of an image, a specific physical object—all may serve as symbols. Each such entity reverberates within the present moment; each is an element in the unfolding spectacle of human powers, in process of their own actualization. Each refers beyond itself to other factors with which it is interwoven. For the symbol is an aggregate of inner impressions: the result, at times, of stimuli the status of which is inherently internal, and, in every instance, of impressions already in process of self-exteriorization.

By the symbol, speaker, gesticulator, or dancer objectifies himself within another person. Impressing himself upon the other, he enters his life as an active component. Always, such impressions arise from a matrix laden with determinate power. Consummation of power, these impressions, having originated from imprints of the spectatorial world, bear specific qualities associated with immediate experience. In addition, particular pressures arise cumulatively, layer by layer, from the vicissitudes of a person's entire past life. Engendered in a miracle of immediacy, a song may convey quiet nostalgia, bearing, in condensed form, myriad particular qualities. Once imprinted into the substance of the listener, it will fade anew into the silence of *his* receding present. Thereby, another person experiences authentic communion with a symbolizer. For, through the absorption of a symbol by that person, a new human history is initiated, a history woven of patterns of relatedness the novelties of which stem from the uniqueness of that symbol, a symbol which has perished into the self-created history.

At first but vaguely felt, human solidarity is, in a symbolic process, reinforced and enhanced. Such solidarity is grounded on the eliciting of parallel, analogous activities in members of a community in which both symbolizer and symbol-recipient are participants. Stemming from the fact that all persons are embedded in a past which is partly shared, and which irretrievably molds each person, this parallelism allows shared symbols to be shaped. Once explicit, the symbol constitutes a spur to wonder about the past. As one symbolically addresses another, it evokes responses in the other, responses which are analogous to feelings already unfolding within his addressor. Accordingly, the meaning of the symbol resides in a future which in part will be *made* present. Symbol meanings must be carved from the very powers which gave birth to a symbol, powers which had persisted, unactualized, hence unclarified, in the present. Thereby, a domain of shared experience is marked out, a domain now formulated and rendered communicable. In particular, symbolic reference is, quite literally, to be discovered by a convening of participants in human society, though such discovery need be neither conceptualized nor in any way made explicit. It can simply consist in participation in a ceremonial of symbolism. Alternatively, it might be the kind of convening which involves not only discovery but a creative act by which one *confers* meaning. And, in general, symbolic reference implicates such modes of human activity as will perpetuate human community. An addressing or a presenting *to* another, the symbol points the way toward an evolving relationship between persons. In this sense, the full meaning of the symbol lies in a future which is gradually appropriated, but never exhaustively made present.

A symbol exhibits many dimensions. Even in the conventional symbols associated with work roles, one cannot separate actual utterances connected with the roles from the innumerable qualities, vocal or gestural, which accompany the acts by which symbols express themselves. Many qualities may be germane to the status of a symbol. One can extract from the complex situation in which a word is spoken, hence intended as symbol, such traits as "ideational content" or "associated imagery" (each a state of mind called forth by the particular utterance which conveys symbolic import); and one can define the symbolic character of the word by reference to those factors. Here, "symbol" suggests a more inclusive fabric of events: a fabric always physical and thus intimately associated with motions of the body; a fabric woven in accordance with implicit rules of construction; a concrete pattern of human behavior wherein each detail is relevant to the whole; an emanation from a symbolizer to the one whom he is addressing by the symbol, an emanation of ineffable, subtle, and intricately nuanced meaning; a presenting to another person of some quality of existence deemed significant by the symbolizer.

In brief, the symbol joins person to person in an immediate present as witnessed by the community. Fusing a personal past with a personal future, it shapes that present—hence, presents a mood through manifold bodily expressions. And, referring to the psychic state inscribed in it, the symbol unites the physical realm, wherein symbolic expressions concretely manifest themselves, to the spiritual domain in which they arise.

Shaped in dialogue as a physical entity, the symbol impinges on each communicant, both symbolizer who addresses and symbol-recipient who is addressed, to alter his very nature. Thereby, it influences encounters in ways which reverberate beyond the immediate context in which it emerges. For, at the instant it is created, the symbol portends the experiential unity of symbolizer and listener. Becoming an actual constituent in the subsequent history of both parties, it unites them for a shared purpose. This purpose concerns an implicit need to disclose a reality not previously discriminated: a sector toward which they turn in wonder as an overarching spectacle; a sector into which, in consequence, they thrust themselves, a *beyond the commonplace* which presents itself for exploration and for discernment of new meaning; a sector in which they immerse themselves as constitutive of their very existence. Though the communicants stand apart from the new sector, with the fullness of their distinctive individualities, that sector now affords a natural setting for all their acts. It becomes the inalienable matrix wherein their creative urges might be fulfilled: an inexhaustible source of their subsequent powers to shape new meanings, and both focus and ground for future relationships with their fellows.

According to my proposals, symbolic reference is a triadic relationship, and, by derivation, tetradic. The symbol refers to a past experience which had shaped it, to a present mood disclosed within it, and to a future relationship made possible by it. A natural complex which refers to those regions in which imprintings, moods, and relationships are interwoven, the symbol constitutes an altogether new reality which can be only barely touched. In part, it remains a mysterious beyond, a beyond of surging powers and awesome depths. Any account of the symbol must acknowledge, as poets do, the significance of the irrational. It is this concept of the symbol which, in the context of dreams, I explicate now. For the dream will be understood as paradigmatic of symbols in general: as exemplar of a dance of images, as that dance transforms itself into a dance of gestures.

(*c*) The Dream

No image is completely unexpressed. Some gestural nuance presents that symbol, no matter how subtle, to an eye which is sufficiently discerning. I say "eye" in only a figurative sense. For, in principle, any organ of discernment, or any combination of organs of discernment, can be implicated in the detection of such bodily modulations as bear witness to the outward signs of an image. *A fortiori*, to endure as symbol, the dream must be clothed in the garb of the tangible. Otherwise, like an artistic conception which never gets rendered, it vanishes into shadows. Gestures and tones, feelings therein conveyed, the myriad shifts of physiognomy which accompany the relating of any dream, the very responses to the dream—all this is woven into its symbolic fabric. Moreover, the psychotherapeutic setting is, pre-eminently, the situation in which dreams enact themselves as symbols. Though in different modalities of presence, therapist and dreamer each makes himself present to the other. In the first instance, presence tends toward silence, which, after all, is a kind of covert utterance: a listening, a being with, an inner rehearsal of what is communicated as echoes which reverberate within one. In the second instance, presence tends toward overt utterance: a communication of imagery and mood. In both cases, therapist and dreamer seek disclosure of the dream's motif through inquiry into the meaning of its elements *as these elements are shaped* into tangible expression.

This singular creation, a human dream, is woven in the context of dialogue. More generally, no image, however fleeting, fails to presuppose at least implicit dialogue, if only the speaking to oneself by the one who "images." Though the therapist is like a midwife who assists in the birth of symbolism (i.e., in drawing fantasy into reality), his presence is not merely catalytic. For he aids the dreamer to make explicit aspects of mood which the dreamer had unwittingly concealed from himself. Interpretative success with respect to the dream depends on a therapist's capacity to touch in himself moods, in all their variants, which are analogous to those of the dreamer. Embedded in a shared mood, they thereupon realize their common humanity. Even when, alone with oneself, one forms images, one shares those images with oneself; and in this self-sharing, one invariably, either unwittingly or by design, elaborates them and allows their germinating content to unfold. Every image potentially effloresces into a manifold of ingredients which are not *seemingly* constitutive of the image, at least in any immediate sense. In this respect, each image is a veritable labyrinth of novel factors awaiting exploration. Whether probing this labyrinth would lead one thus to search oneself is, at this point, a moot question.

"I dreamt," a dreamer reported,[1] "that I was traveling westward, along a narrow road, with my fiancée, through a village, when my car, which I was driving, encountered a cement truck, inexplicably labeled 'English,' which was about to stop for gasoline. Then it was as though many events unfolded of a character I sensed to be meaningful; but what these were is enshrouded in darkness." Willingly, the dreamer grants that his traveling is associated with a sense of freedom. As he moves through life with his fiancée, thought of the road stirs a feeling of precariousness. The truck reminds him of his constricted existence, as though, from moment to moment, he might be immobilized in cement. Suddenly he recalls that, shortly before the dream, he contrived an escape from responsibilities by the idea of fleeing west; in its expanses he could lose himself. Burial in cement is now seen as self-punishment for renouncing obligations. Then he protects himself from acknowledging his conduct by assuming a self-righteous air, which he (idiosyncratically) associates with the label "English." And he feels the need, but is bewildered as to how to proceed, to delve more deeply into the circumstances of his existence which have led to these attitudes. At the same time, he hesitates to admit with finality that the mood expressed corresponds to the reality of his life. It might simply be a consequence, he protests, of the imposition, by diabolical suggestion, of the therapist's claim upon him. Since the therapist remains firm and unyielding, the dreamer becomes angry with him. However, the more intense the struggle with the therapist, the more exaggerated the rigidity of the dreamer's gait becomes, so much indeed as to constitute a veritable symptom of his condition. In a burst of anxiety on the part of the dreamer, this fact becomes conspicuous to both therapist and dreamer.

In this minuscule case study of an actual dream, and of certain tentative ingredients of its interpenetration, the very being of the dreamer dramatically reflects his mood; his spiritual existence is shown in numerous physical expressions. A composite of signs called forth by the recounting of the dream, the dream symbol constitutes itself, the more the content of the dream is searched into, a compressed physical commentary on a style of life, a style which masks a conflict between self-deception and the drive to emerge as free and vibrant. And though the dream is a narrative which unfolds in time, it reflects an interplay of attitudes which, from the standpoint of the dreamer, are timeless; they are the persistent motif of his life. A quest for authentic freedom is hampered by its conversion into an excuse for the cessation of responsibility. Accordingly, the dreamer punishes himself by a kind of self-paralysis, which only promotes his dwelling in realms of fantasied freedom. Nevertheless, he conceals these processes by acting as though nothing troubles him. This interweaving of mood and attitude, primarily defensive, constitutes the precariousness of the dreamer's existence. Yet, deep within, he senses his lack of fulfillment and, accordingly, struggles in the dark for a solution. Not daring to admit this fact explicitly, for anxiety would be aroused were such an engrained mode of existence radically to be abandoned, he struggles with the therapist.

In the expanding dream-symbol, as its "latent content"[2] is drawn forth, the dreamer acquires many roles. These roles express his complicated relationship to himself. In principle, the therapist enacts but one role: to facilitate the quest for clarification. But since he, too, is a complex personality, the therapist may also work at cross-purposes with himself. Hence, woven into the dream symbol are factors which reflect two distorted perceptions of reality. In the dream fragment, the dreamer expresses not only a general mode of relatedness to the world, but a particular mode of relatedness to the therapist. Inquiry reveals that he perceives the therapeutic situation to be precarious. In it, he places all his hopes for freedom, yet he is skeptical. For he believes that the therapist, like the truck in his dream, threatens to crush him. In part, his skepticism is well founded. Not only is the enterprise of liberation difficult, but the dreamer could be quite correctly appraising the therapist—so the associations of both therapist and dreamer might indicate—as feeling uncomfortable in his presence. Hence, in reality, the therapist becomes the embodiment of the label "English"; for, at first, he himself (as an American stereotype of the Englishman) is stiff and masked, unable to respond flexibly and sincerely to the dreamer's plea for aid.

By this construal, the symbol is intrinsically dialogic. It is constituted through the alternating discords and harmonies of both communicants. This interplay of perspectives tends to abolish distortion. As a texture of feelings unfolds, the motif of the dream discloses itself with increasing clarity. A symphony of dialogue emerges: cadences, pauses, and crescendos; rhythms of joy, fear, devotion, and deception. As dissonance grows into concord, a dramatic counterpoint of themes unfolds. Therein, the dream referent discloses itself to be an entirely new "realm" which envelops the dream not as contiguous though disparate, but as forming with the dream a continuous, integral pattern. The dream reveals itself to be a generative crystal which focalizes a vast range of experience, both unique and shared. Only in the dialectical interplay between dreamer and therapist will the dream exhibit an inherent meaning, and, therein, irradiate the consciousness of both dreamer and therapist.

The dream symbol is an inclusive mode of communication. By a process of abstraction, its constitutive factors come, one by one, into the foreground of attention. The variegated totality of those factors reveal themselves. For each factor signifies a single significant ingredient of the mood to which the dream as a whole refers. Moreover, in any dream, the symbol is an expanding entity. It is a process wherein, in the context of the interplay of responses between both communicants, new qualities never cease to engender themselves. Ever shaped anew, this pattern of *signs* is so constituted that their *designata*, each a sign element within the overall dream symbol, are themselves elements of the mood with which the symbol is associated. In turn, these elements betoken events which the dreamer had previously encountered, events of which he is not cognizant; and these events have impinged on the dreamer as a striking experience of which the dream itself is the only recognizable trace. For the dream symbol is a texture of physical happenings which directly reveal a spiritual state induced in the dreamer in response to many encounters: the immediate situation in which the dream is reported and which expands as symbol in the act of reporting; events which occurred just before the appearance of the dream; a larger sphere of events of which the dream is imprint and residue—events which have befallen the dreamer from the very beginnings of his life.

I distinguish three types of dream-symbol referent. First, the symbol renders tangible, in the visual and aural modes, a specific mood—its *proximate* referent. An unfolding embodiment of a power of feeling, the dream symbol expresses how the dreamer impinges on the world, the kind of mark he leaves as an immediate consequence of his mood. In this sense, symbol and meaning are co-extensive. Each mirrors the other. Nothing beyond the immediate psychic existence of the dreamer is relevant to elucidating that meaning. In addition, the dream symbol has an *historical* referent: the very experiences the cumulative impact of which has shaped this particular mood. In effect, these experiences are powers which flow into the dreamer from a circumambient nature: powers which, according to their structure, actually shape his mood; powers which cause subsequently received experience to be filtered through that structure. Finally, the dream symbol presents to the therapist a specific mode of relatedness to him. In part, that symbol "tranfers"[3] to the therapist qualities conferred by the dreamer upon other significant people; in part, the dream symbol constitutes a realistic appraisal of how the therapist orients himself, including a possible "countertransferral," toward the dreamer. This *relational* referent of the symbol expresses a conflict between the dreamer's quest for clarification and his need to perpetuate a sham.

However, the dream symbol ultimately refers, as its *transcendent* referent, to values woven into specific exemplification in the life of this particular dreamer. For the dream constitutes an incarnation of universal notions which are but the apparition of an overarching reality in which all humankind is embedded, a reality from which it derives its existence and within which persons adventure. In its "archetypal"[4] status, the dream is a vehicle for the transmission of transcendent powers to a single individual. I use the terms "archetypal" and "transcendent" in their etymologic senses. By "archetype," I mean "original pattern" as expressing a primary mood, denoted by the dream, which is shared by all men as part of their human endowment. By "transcendent" I mean that which "lies beyond" the person as an aspect of reality which he can touch but never fully know: in part, this "beyond" flows within him; in part, it flows about him.

B • THE LABYRINTH OF THE IMAGE

(*a*) The Symbol as Spirit Incarnate

A pattern of behavioral elements, the dream symbol consists of signs which stand to other elements, psychic or behavioral, in causal relationships—as a suddenly raised fist might signify anger. Strictly speaking, the dream symbol is a pattern of configurations of signs, configurations so formed that each sign is a subsidiary symbol the properties of which are analogous to the whole symbol in which the sign is embedded. To define a subsidiary symbol, one must specify the entire dream symbol as its context of functioning. Betokening more than "simple" feelings, as mere signs do, the subsidiary symbol refers to and, indeed, itself embodies, a complex effective orientation toward a range of phenomena. Reflecting a style of life, it both formulates a way of experiencing the world and provides a matrix for understanding the moods which it portends. Unlike signs, such symbols do not merely assign traits. Rather, they mark out a domain for scrutiny. Not only do they render the pervasive qualities of an experience, demarcating meanings *within* it, but they construct new experience and, thereby, enlarge the dreamer's natural world. Such augmentation is effected by *interlocking* subsidiary symbols. Thereby, the meanings of each symbol become limited, expanded, complemented, or altered by the meanings of the remaining symbols. Like a coat of armor the plates of which, separately inflexible, are, with increasing accuracy, fitted together to form a mosaic of plates which approximates the contours of the body, so subsidiary symbols separately express aspects of *some* mood which only partially correspond to the dreamer's mood, but, as a whole, manifest his entire mood, in its concreteness and singularity. So, too, the coat with which a mood is, so to speak, vested not only fits and reveals that mood but transforms it. Constituting an altogether new dimension of reality, the symbols reshape themselves in counterposition to the moods.

Freud formulated principles which purport to govern the transformation of psychic elements, in both the proximate and the more remote referents of the dream (i.e., its "latent content"), into the elements comprising the dream itself, as it is apparently dreamt, or, at least, as recalled (i.e., its "manifest content"[5]). I shall not review the mechanisms by which this "dream-work"[6] is executed, save to note that "condensation," "displacement," and "secondary revision,"[7] constitute the *formal* structure of symbolic transformation; and every symbol is shaped from a psychic realm in accordance with laws peculiar to its own domain. Like any symbol, the dream symbol dramatizes an interior existence. Though composed of idiosyncratic tonalities, it is, nonetheless, universally compelling. Eliciting a tendency from different people toward an identical reconstruction of meaning, the dream symbol embodies particular qualities for the artist who actually dwells within every dreamer. Indeed, surprising artistry is found in the dreams of what are apparently singularly drab existences.

The associations stirred by a dream are too intricate to set forth, even for my limited example. Moreover, they may differ markedly from dream to dream, even for a particular dreamer. For they express the unique matrix of experience wherein a symbol arises and is shaped to fruition. Such associations not only articulate a mood; they also narrate the experiences relevant to its production, the events which prolong themselves into a psychic existence. And the dream is but a formula in which the imprint of these events is condensed.

A condensed statement of a life experience, indeed! For all the dream symbols which flow from a person and, more generally, all the symbolic systems which a man may create cumulatively reveal the labyrinthine, but, ultimately—when they are deciphered—the luminous spiritual existence of their creator. A life unfolds as a texture of symbols; and this texture is a sacrament of the vicissitudes of the spirit. It is the durable residue, a visible structure, lucent or opaque, vibrant or dull, which is deposited in the wake of a spiritual activity.

I am proposing that the substance of the symbol is corporeal; yet, in its most subtle mobility, it is, equivalently, spirit incarnate. Still, some symbols are too weighty with body. Fragmenting the spirit, instead of integrating it, such symbols limit one's aspirations, constrain one's natural rhythms, and constrict one's creative powers. And psychic energies can weave themselves into physical organizations in such ways as to deflect, or even to bind, these energies, thereby preventing their constructive deployment. But foci for activating energies which creatively reveal themselves, symbols, under a non-pathologic perspective, intensify acts of the human spirit.

Receiving the imprints of the psyche, the human body, a web of symbols, is a living, tangible record of personal experience. The "first function of the psyche in the seed," writes Santayana, "is to create the outer body. With every organ which she brings forth she acquires a new office and a new type of life";[8] and on this texture of symbols, which it has generated, the psyche inscribes its adventures and fears, its hopes and disappointments. The dream is but a particular symbolic form, of which the body offers many, of an interior realm; and the themes which are imprinted on one mode of expression repeat themselves, in analogous patterns, with respect to many modes of expression.

However constrictive a symbol may be, all its bodily manifestations challenge the spirit to surpass itself, and more authentically to actualize a potential for shaping new images. In this sense, the dream both condenses and dramatizes the mind's reflexive character. In it, the psyche holds dialogue with itself, then translates dialogue into corporeal, thus symbolic, manifestation; and body itself, and all its symbolic extensions, are metamorphosed into luminous expression. "To be completely mastered by the psyche," continues Santayana, "makes the health, agility, and beauty of the body."[9] With Socrates one may say the "outward and inward man be[come] at one."[10] Enfolded in the body, the energies of the psyche unfold according to the laws of their own existence. With each change, these energies imprint themselves anew, and irreversibly, on a body which, nonetheless, remains sufficiently flexible to allow continuous transformations of its own substance, hence, a body which is always being molded to the "shape" of the interior "realm" which it encloses. There is a poetry of the body, and all its actions, and the multitude of symbolic forms by which it expresses itself—a spoken word, a movement, a gleam of the eyes, a dream symbol.

Inscribed in every symbol is a meaning which, once fully deciphered, reveals the utter vastness of a human life. This meaning is not simply to be discovered. In part, it must be created by expanding the actual substance of the symbol through its cumulative interpretations. For every symbol proposes constantly new orientations toward both intended listener and prospective listener. Though, in each instance, the dreamer reinstates an attitude he has previously adopted toward former listeners, he also continually pours new content into his symbols, content drawn from the fathomless depths of his soul. Perhaps even unknown to himself, he seeks to join, as a viable participant, a world in which he had not formerly been at home. At the same time, it cannot be denied that the dreamer also reenacts a deprivation. For he compensates in fantasy for what he had been denied in reality. Yet the overall thrust of the symbol is to overcome the very constraints which, on initial construal, it reveals itself as incorporating and to point the way toward a freer and more spontaneous mode of existence.

(*b*) Dream Interpretation

With respect to the illustrative dream fragment, each element is a focal image whence is engendered, by the very acts through which it is expressed, some symbol component of the primary dream symbol. Moreover, as it is communicated, every symbol comes to exhibit two aspects: a façade, an attempt at duplicity, the embodiment of a self-deception; and a clarification, an envisagement of a genuine need, the incarnation of authentic feeling which, once a meaning is disclosed, may be quite portentous—such images as the truck, in my example, are drawn from the dreamer's unique experience. Extracted from experiences peculiar to a particular dreamer, such images are not, by necessity, *universally* associated with specific meanings. Furthermore, dream symbols may overlap with respect to the meanings which they enclose. Alternatively, an identical meaning may project itself upon several distinct symbols. And, finally, each symbol may condense several meanings within itself. Over a sequence of dreams, the dreamer works out a veritable glossary of symbols and meanings, in which he incorporates his particular style of producing meaning dispersion with respect to the symbols which he employs. In general, the labyrinthine character of imagery expresses intricately latticed meaning dispersions. They reveal a realm which, though regulated by its own principles, does not obey the customary ways in which one perceives the world to be ordered. At the same time, such dispersals are not merely random. An immanent purposiveness governs their special modes of distribution, recombination, and splitting into still new factors.

No dreamer can fully recall all relevant contexts of experience wherein a dream originated. Such contexts as are recollected, through a process of association which itself entails an intensive inward searching, modify themselves in the context of ever-new, *present* experience. With respect to psychotherapy, my paradigm for drawing forth the symbol's latent content, what is recollected is, in part, determined by the therapeutic setting and, in part, designed to persuade the therapist so to orient himself toward the dreamer that the dream's sham components might convincingly appear to both therapist and dreamer as true. For, as it is transformed into symbolism, the dream contains a tactic for perpetuating illusion. With respect to such a stratagem, the therapist strives to outwit the dreamer, though he himself might share similar illusions. Or he may even penetrate illusions which run counter to the dreamer's quest for clarification. Nevertheless, each person endeavors, within the limits of his awareness of self-illusion, to interpret the dream correctly, and to understand the truth about the life of the dreamer and, by implication, of the therapist as well.

Were a dream's meaning fully revealed to him, the dreamer would give up a way of life which, despite its discomfitures, had become habitual; and this renunciation is not easy, since it entails an adventure in living associated with unknown risks. Hence, the therapist's job is to persuade the dreamer that, though the threat cannot be gainsaid, the adventure *is* exciting; and so the dreamer must choose between what is comfortable but dull and what is risky but intriguing. Since the therapist himself may not have fully decided upon the adventuresome course, exploration of the dream can activate *his* needs to deny adventure. Then he may blind both himself and the dreamer to the sharpness of the choice. Or he may seek to persuade the dreamer, against the dreamer's better judgment, to follow a less vibrant way. A *folie à deux* is perpetuated. Ultimately, the possibility of convincing the dreamer to choose the vibrant way is based on the deeper and, heretofore, hidden experience of despair inherent in the dull way. Now I develop the concept of the symbol as a spur, when it is correctly deciphered, to the life of creative adventure.

In my example, the "car" stirred the dreamer to conceive *himself* as a mechanical contrivance which operates on fuel supplied by an alien source; and the image of the truck emerges both as a reminder of days when he was forced to work and as threatening, in a collision, to bury him in cement. Different experiences cumulatively deposit themselves on the same image, suggesting the pervasiveness of an unhappy existence. The images of gasoline and car duplicate the idea of mechanism, and indicate the intensity of the dreamer's belief that he cannot control his own destiny. The selection of innocuous, commonplace images expresses his efforts to dupe both the therapist and himself, dismissing the actual potency of his own despair. The image of the West is an attempt at self-persuasion that he truly seeks freedom, whereas deeper reflection leads to a confession of futility. Now the only liberty he can conceive is that of his fantasies. Struggle, hope, and despair are woven into imagery. The dream records a life in which one constructive way of absorbing experience after another has been repudiated. It expresses embeddedness in a constricted existence, insensitivity to the tonalities of experience. All is of a piece, and drab and meaningless. Every experience which the dreamer recalls suggests a walling of himself from a vibrant life, a withdrawal into realistic despair, and into fantasied fruition. The dream reveals a profoundly unhappy existence: its pervasiveness, its intensity, and its particular qualities. It discloses the specific ways in which the dreamer has deluded both himself and others. Protecting himself against the anxiety which would be aroused by disclosure of his unhappiness, he seems to believe that his drab existence is truly to his liking.

Deeper penetration of the dream hinges on the analysis of the image of the fiancée. When the dreamer is pressed to consider this image, he recalls another dream fragment. "I find myself," he remembers, "in a vast, dimly lit hall, observing people forming a circle about a central area which might have been occupied by a bar. Uncommunicative, but seemingly in touch with one another by telepathy, they intently watch the area, which now becomes illuminated, as by a searchlight within the darkness, as though for a mysterious purpose I should like to discern."

No longer does the dreamer summon up the "remembrance of things past." Now he experiences a mood, profound and inescapable, which sweeps over him, and envelops even the therapist. By their searching, therapist and dreamer are bound together in trust, but trust mingled with the fear of deceit. In contrasting responses, the character of each is revealed. By decisions which reflect ingrained habits, myriad factors are discerned as woven into the symbol. And as each participant imprints on the emerging symbol his particular uniqueness, which itself is shaped in the unfolding novelties, new themes of human relatedness appear. Trust is strengthened; deception falls away. Not as an actual memory, but as a psychic imprint of memory, which both participants share, though in different measure, each touches some significant component of experience. Addressing one another from the spirit's profounder recesses, they are joined in communion. Through these germs of affinity, they grope toward a common foundation of existence. Increasingly, they enmesh their roots in the same spiritual soil. Such groping in dialogue does not involve the imposition of a particular dream interpretation by the therapist. The "correct" interpretation depends exclusively on, and can be validated only by reference to, the dreamer's special experience. It is the dream as symbol, i.e., as a drawing forth into public expression of private imagery, which emerges as woven of the experiences of both therapist *and* dreamer. Through this symbol, they commemorate their common humanity.

As a symbol grows to fruition and the lucent disclosure of its own meanings, both therapist and dreamer participate in it. As Tillich declared, every symbol "participates in the reality of that for which it stands. . . . it grows and dies according to the correlation between that which is symbolised and the persons who receive it as a symbol."[11] By "participation," I mean that, both emanation and embodiment of a shared mood, the symbol becomes a constituent in the mood's evolving expression. At once, it is a tangible acknowledgment of mood, a crystallization of mood, and a focal point for the vicissitudes of new mood.

Now the interpretation of the second fragment suggests itself. In dialogue with the therapist, the dreamer experiences himself as surrounded by strange people, including the therapist: people who speak in a silent tongue the meaning of which he cannot understand; people who form a community apart, which is vast and distant. The bar, which for others might suggest conviviality, betokens, for the dreamer, impersonality. He feels that, from the farthest reaches of space, this strange community scrutinizes the utter vacuity of his existence. Yet even in the midst of his despair, the very emptiness begins to glow with a mysterious light: now, when the dreamer's rejection by the world is most poignant, and as the world recedes from him in utter silence, a silence devoid of the comforting music of speech; now, when the dreamer is pressed into nullity, by the fearsome powers which he experiences as hovering about him, and as he sinks, in supreme loneliness, toward a deathly existence. Then alone does the dream promise, however obscurely, to illuminate his own hidden recesses. In his horror, as Dante climbed over the head of Beezelbub, a faint light appeared, and he saw "the beauteous things which Heaven bears."[12]

At the instant the dreamer, led by *his* Virgil, has maximally accepted his feelings of maximal rejection—what all men encounter in the face of death—a metamorphosis in his style of existence first becomes possible. Like Kafka's K.,[13] the dreamer stands trial before unknown accusers and judges for a sin which he but dimly comprehends. Now, at last, he recalls the final fragment of the dream, a fragment the interpretation of which enables him to realize that he is his own judge and accuser. The way of grace is shown him.

The intense whiteness of illumination stirs thoughts of Melville: "by its indefiniteness," the white "shadows forth the heartless voids and immensities of the universe, and thus stabs us from behind with the thought of annihilation";[14] a terror of sheer, unconsummated power prevails, and all "the palsied universe lies before us a leper."[15] Yet, for our dreamer, so alienated from the powers still dormant within him, there is hope, and a promise. Now he has the strength, as both hope and promise shape themselves from the imagery of the dream into a viable symbol of relationship with his guide, actually to *see* "the monumental white [cloud] that wraps all the prospect around him"[16] as, perhaps, capable of bursting into myriad glows. For these "invisible spheres . . . formed in fright" are pregnant with "the sweet tinges of sunset skies and woods" and "all other earthly hues—this visible world . . . formed in love."[17]

From a unique fabric of images, traces of the dreamer's experiences, a symbol is formed which transcends particularity and acquires "archetypal" status, status which betokens a quality of all human experience. However, this universal, incarnate in Melville's imagery, and woven into the dreamer's life from strands of his past, becomes meaningful for him only when it is again particularized, and imbued with qualities drawn from the special circumstances of his life. From the particularity of the first fragment, the dreamer has passed to the generality of the second. Therein, he is led to probe. And initially the autonomous work of the psyche, which culminates in the dream itself, his probing eventuates in the particularity of a final fragment. As the sequence unfolds, particular and universal alternate. The particular embodies the universal; in turn, the universal directly expresses the dreamer's participation in humanity.

The interpretation of the dream shatters illusions. By it, the dreamer emerges from concealment; he touches both his uniqueness and his universality. In a personal vision, *his* unknown is revealed. For the power of symbols resides in their capacity to elicit the latent qualities of a shared reality, in their freshness, novelty, concreteness, and intensity—but, always, for a particular dreamer. Specific experiences weave themselves with what is therein disclosed to be universal experience; and this pattern constitutes the symbol a new form of reality. A vision is rendered of the universal in the garb of the particular. But the mystery of the universal *as such* does not thereby disappear. Rather, it is evoked as a circumambient presence which bathes all humankind: a presence of many facets, each refracting to particular tints the tonality of which it is an expression. "The particular," Goethe wrote, "represents the universal, 'not as a dream and shadow, but as a momentarily living manifestation of the inscrutable.' "[18] Surely, every person participates in this "unfathomable." From it, he draws powers which are woven into a specific life experience.

Again the image of the fiancée is enigmatic; the dreamer ponders it. "I am sitting," he recalls, "in a dining room, eating with a pleasant elderly woman. I ply her with questions, to which she responds evasively. Suddenly enraged, she throws a food tray toward me. I duck lest I be decapitated. Failing, she tosses a hot sauce at me, but succeeds only in burning her hands. The people, previously encountered, confront her solicitously." Without stating the dreamer's association to this fragment, I need only note that the original innocuous image of the fiancée conceals the feeling that the dreamer is always accompanied by a powerful trace of a significant earlier mode of experiencing his mother. His first inclination is to see her as kindly. Now, however, the façade cracks. She emerges as a murderous figure to whom he unsuccessfully appeals for tenderness. Enraged at her failure to nourish him, he allows her to be injured, as she withholds tenderness from him. Now the mother image becomes a point of crystallization about which gather all the people whom he distortedly perceives to be alienated from him. The dreamer's questions to his mother (in his dream) pertain to the problem by which he has been beset: namely, what in *him* is so evil as to merit only her hostility, and the hostility, as he feels it, of the world? After many associations, the reply comes as an address to himself from deep within. The female figure, so he realizes, represents the care originally denied him *by* his mother, but which he now denies *in* himself. Accordingly, the dreamer has perpetuated a withdrawn attitude; he has demanded that others do for him what he refuses to do for himself; and he has sulked, rather than dissolve a neurotic dependency on a desperately craved, but never found, all-giving woman. In his associations, the image of sauce presents itself as representing semen, the symbol of his manly offering, which the woman rejects. The very denial of what is tender in him constricts the manly; he cannot fulfill his powers. Instead, the dreamer experiences himself as an angry, frightened infant. So disrupted is the complementarity of tenderness and boldness that neither comes to fruition.

At this point, the relationship between the dreamer and his actual fiancée is clarified. He envisages the face of a young girl, glowing and beautiful, a girl for whose favors he yearns. Now, *within* the ever-expanding original dream symbol, a new symbol has emerged, which refers to the dreamer's desire to possess those beautiful things in life which he has denied himself. Still it is *another* person, one essentially unapproachable, who persists as this trace which bears such beauty—a trace which he must, if he would be free, actually absorb into his own existence. In painful struggle to assimilate this image, a struggle in which he accepts the challenge to move beyond dependency on the image as the imagined source of beauty, the dreamer begins to create beauty by his own efforts. Long after, another dream appears in which a goddess of fertility accosts him in a dark auditorium. She whispers into his ear that he will have a son, whereupon the hall becomes suffused by a warm light; and he and she regard one another with countenances wreathed in smiles. Having delved into his past, the dreamer is reborn. He passes to a new phase of existence in which childish expectations disappear. Struggle with real issues, struggle alternating with serenity, supplants the grappling with illusions which betokens a past with which the dreamer had not before made his peace.

(*c*) Archetypality

A tightly knit fabric, the dream manifests a life panorama. A few images compress innumerable experiences. The dining room represents the primary, and continually reinstated, life setting. Here, deprived of maternal succor, and lacking a male to emulate, the dreamer doubly divests himself of strength. From his meditations on such imagery the links are forged which bind the fragments of a life into coherence. Critique of a life style, the dream interpretation renders an inchoate existence viable. The recurrence of the image of light, initially as a faint glow and later as a brilliant illumination, suggests the continuous presence in the dreamer and, indeed, in the therapist of an energizing "center" from which flows, as the dream symbol evolves through their growing communion, *mutual* strivings toward self-transcendence. The subsidiary dream symbols cluster about this center. Each discloses another essential facet; and each makes "manageable" for the dreamer a particular aspect of meaning. As he steps from one terrace of symbols to another, the dreamer is gradually led, by his circumscribing the unknown from many sides, to the potent source of all the symbols he has unwittingly shaped. This potency cannot be actualized in any particular symbol; it requires the entire congregation of symbols, a congregation organized in accordance with a canon which gradually makes itself manifest as all the contents of the symbol come to full expression. Now the interpreted dream is imbued with a mysterious quality wherein the dream's very center remains until its end, and even seems to have been there from eternity. By traveling the path which leads toward this center, though he may never actually reach it, the dreamer will increasingly be bathed in its regenerative glow.

This progressive unfolding of powers, in which both dreamer and therapist are implicated, *is* the meaning of the dream. It is as in music. There, too,

> the meaning of a tone . . . lies not in what it points to but in *the pointing itself*. . . . [It] is not the thing indicated but the manner of indicating. . . . Words lead away from themselves but tones lead into themselves. . . . Tones . . . have completely absorbed their meaning into themselves, and discharge it upon the hearer directly in their sound.[19]

Indeed, the unfolding of the dream resembles a musical composition, as does all symbolic discourse; and all authentic discourse is symbolic. When the dream is allowed to unfold its immanent meaning in accordance with its own inner dynamic, the full recounting of the dream, by word and by gesture, *is*, in fact, the veridical meaning of the dream.

Perturbations of the night, so subtle as to be masked during the day, evolve into the imagery of a dream which, in turn, grows into symbolism. Such images are traces of a past which has refused to perish and thereby objectively immortalizes itself in the present. Constricting his powers, and masking the reality of his life, these unperished traces haunt the dreamer. However, the dream contains the dynamism for its own objectification as symbol. By that dynamism, the traces of the past which compose the dream are absorbed into the existence of the dreamer; and, in this absorption, he moves beyond himself to an altogether new modality of existence. No longer do images cling to his mind as possessions which cannot be relinquished. Now these images pose themselves to him as a test of his fiber. They are opportunities which, should he correctly seize them, will enable him to pass *through* them either to an image-less peace or to a single, comprehensive, and liberating image.

In general, the symbol is the expressive representation of the image. It is a drawing forth of its latent content, its objectification as verse, dance, gesture, and word. Images of the commonplace, the original content of the dream remain vivid. Now freed of enervating nostalgia, these images are fraught with purport. And when meanings associated with this purport are extracted, the symbol becomes richer. Increasingly, symbolizer experiences himself as receiving the world as a gift. Now making fewer demands on the world, he can, in his further symbolic activity, reciprocally give himself to the world. In this self-giving, he enlarges himself.

What is "archetypal" in the dream is not its specific imagery as such. For imagery is woven of unique experience. And the archetypal factors consist of meanings like "self-denial" and "challenge to be reborn." In their manifold expressions, these meanings suggest universal experiences of humankind. The dream is a stimulus to repeat, in a single existence, and by its specific powers, an experience which, in its essence, is not restricted to that existence. This cumulative experience is relived through that living of the dream which *is* its shaping into a symbol. Agamemnon, Oedipus, Job, and Dante all walk in the soul of every dreamer, though the manner in which they walk may be variously interpreted. Each figure expresses a different phase of the dreamer's struggle and, indeed, of the struggle of all persons. As in the *Agamemnon*, a mother, perverse and denying, haunts her child. As in *Oedipus Rex*, an umbilical dependency (on one interpretation) haunts the child. As with Job, faith in the midst of despair illuminated the relentless quest for the purpose of a life. "I will not remove mine integrity from me. Though he may slay me, yet will I trust in him" (Jb 27:5, 13:15); Job eloquently expresses the maxim of the dreamer who authentically searches his life's foundations. As with Dante, his Beatrice must be converted from a particular woman, to whom he clings as the sole fount of beauty, to the symbol of a beatific vision, an ideal beauty which works within him to suffuse his being. Until the dream is clarified, it haunts the dreamer as disconnected from the remainder of his existence; it immobilizes his constructive energies. But when the dream's drama is revealed as exemplifying humanity's universal drama, energies beyond measure are released. Consciousness becomes intensified, and deepened.

Like a theory, the dream is an apparatus for exploring diversified facets of an existence, mapping the terrain of experience; and it is a means for rendering accessible what had been concealed. Weaving these facets into a condensed pattern, the dream constitutes a portrayal, with a few deft strokes, of essential elements in a style of life. As with theory, the linkages disclosed in the process of association may, retrospectively, be viewed as analogues of deductive chains binding hypothetical premisses (the meaning) to phenomenal conclusions (the dream). Initially enigmatic, for these inferential ties are suppressed, they gradually emerge as explicit and multiplex. The essence of the dream is figurative; metaphors abound. They constitute it a kind of theoretical model. In elaborating this theory-like structure, significant details of a life are revealed, and their impact upon the dreamer clarified.

This "dream theory" is continually emended in the course of its own interpretation. But in the very process of its reconstruction and, particularly, in the sequence of dreams which subsequently unfolds, its elements appear to converge upon such images as "goddess of fertility," "the auditorium, dark then luminous," "the anticipated son." As each dream symbol expands, it deposits its *own* traces on the dreamer, traces which culminate in what appears, in retrospect, as a definitive imagery *for him.* It is as though the germ of a certain destiny lay within him to grow to fruition, through such encounters as alone make possible a fuller existence. It is as though the final images were contained as powers within the very factors which produced the initial images—as though the dream arrow, analogous for different people, points always in a specific direction, and is carried to its goal, ever clothed with new forms, in the setting of therapy. For the dream symbol emerges not only as a retrospective clarification, but as a formulation of prospects: a hope, an interest, a way of life. And when the dream symbol is correctly read, a new world of adventure, creation, and meditation becomes visible as a possible mode of existence.

C • THE DANCE OF IMAGERY TRANSMUTED INTO A DANCE OF GESTURE

(*a*) Symbol and Transfiguration

The dream, as such, is a configuration of images; and each itself is an analogous configuration. A context of imagery encloses other contexts of imagery. Like Chinese boxes, one context wraps itself about another context and, in turn, is enveloped by a still more inclusive context. In the end, however, no fundamental atomic image is an ultimate elementary constituent into which such configurations resolve themselves. On the contrary, with respect to the dream construed as a highly refined image configuration, one which lies at the pinnacle of a hierarchy of such configurations, the many levels of the dream lattice, as one descends into the labyrinth of their component images, must be interpreted as pointing toward a kind of mobile *field* of images, as grounding the entire mosaic: marvelously nuanced swirlings and unfoldings, all dynamically interwoven, commingling, and combining to shape an autonomous realm of spiritual existence.

Like the dream itself, this realm presents itself, first, as a dance of imagery, then, through subtle bodily manifestations, as a dance of gesture. Furthermore, like a dream shaping itself into symbolic status, every image pattern, no matter how simple or composite, likewise appears, through the very processes whereby it elaborates itself into symbolic expression. No image, or any combination of images, can *be* without their having been registered as gestural incarnation. And on whatever level of complexity or simplicity, throughout the realm of images, orchestrations unfold which pervade that realm, orchestrations the components of which undergo the most diversified transmigrations and metamorphoses to shape a unique spiritual product. Within this product of such interior happenings, whether knowingly or barely touched by articulated knowledge, every person dwells; and his entire being is conditioned, suffused, and indeed activated by it.

By what activities does the dream shape itself into symbolic expression? In presenting the dream as the active compresence of dreamer and therapist, a mutual addressing unfolds, an addressing of each by each. Within this context, the solitariness of both parties is diminished. Two individual existences are clarified: directly, that of the dreamer; indirectly, that of the therapist. Wherein consists this clarification, this making of each fully present to the other? Heidegger provides a frame of reference, useful for conceptualizing symbol clarification, which, appropriate for the dream, is generalizable beyond its specific domain to apply to all modalities of image unfolding. His remarks pertain to such generic traits of symbols as are relevant to imagery in the process of transmutation into gesture.

"Appearance, as the appearance 'of something,'" Heidegger wrote, "does *not* mean showing-itself; it means rather the announcing-itself by something which does show itself." A symbol is a species of "appearance," or, more accurately, of an appearing; it is a process of making manifest a "phenomenon": what Heidegger calls "that which shows itself in itself, . . . what lies in the light of day or can be brought to the light."[20] This phenomenon announces itself both through and in the appearance; it is the announcing *as* it inscribes itself on the appearance, and is therein revealed by it. Such announcement can occur with either clarity or obscurity. When clear, the distinction between "appearance" and "phenomenon" is effectively obliterated; one sees, as it were, "face to face." When obscure, the two remain distinct, though the phenomenon continues to show itself through appearance as "through a glass darkly." And, as Heidegger further declares, appearance then "essentially distorts itself in its cloaking and dissembling."[21]

A species of appearing, the symbol betokens an emergent phenomenon; it is an emerging from concealment into luminosity. Uniting that which it expresses to its very self as incarnation of that expression, the symbol fuses the powers which have shaped existence with it as their issue. Drawing those powers into its own being as symbol, it discloses them as a living presence. Thereby, all masks tend to fall away. Thus shattered, the person, a fabric of symbols, reveals himself with lucidity. Hence, the symbol—e.g., homely features in transformation, by inner character, into beauty—is an announcement of that which does not show itself immediately, but, rather, emerges *through* the symbol by a *living of* the symbol, so that it evolves into something other than what it originally was. Thereby, the initial datum is transfigured, and, this coming-into-clarity *is* the symbol.

By a *living of* the symbol, I mean an addressing of oneself *through* the symbol, both to oneself and to another. Moreover, a complementarity of addressing and listening prevails. One hears oneself in silence as one addresses oneself; the other hears in silence as he is addressed. But true listening itelf is a species of addressing. For, by an addressing, I mean a making-oneself-present, a going-out-to-meet. In this act, silence and utterance may each be an authentic modality of making-oneself-present, whether to oneself or to another. And a symbol is an element, and an incarnation, of mutual addressing. It is the expression of an interfusion of presentings-of-selves. Emptied of distraction—hence, inclination toward stereotyped, conventionalized responses—the person ideally presents himself as fully-there-with-another. Suffused by the presence of the other, he moves beyond separateness, without however negating autonomy, toward the binding of himself with the other.

What one presents is drawn from inner stillness; one senses a silence of unfathomable possibilities, a silence from which, in meditation—whatever its medium—one draws forth into symbolism a specific aspect of a presenting-of-oneself. This interior silence haunts one as a mysterious presence which one may touch, drawing its powers into vibrant actuality, but never exhaust. It is a presence which, at times, is felt as an enmeshing of the roots of oneself with those of another: an enmeshing which unfolds in the abyss of a past which stretches inexplicably beyond; a past in which each person, in his singular existence, is immersed, and from which he draws sustenance. This womb of stillness gives birth to gesture, movement, dance, and song; and as these symbols are shaped into existence, they perish into the existence of every person who, in his presenting of himself, has participated in that shaping. What *was* symbol is now absorbed into his creators. It blends with their very substance. In this absorption, each person touches the other, and each is enlarged. Like a musical note irradiating a human life, the symbol, composed of its own notes, perishes into that life by virtue of the inexorable flow of notes which succeed its immediate impact; but it imprints itself in a fashion which veridically transfigures life.

(*b*) Symbol and Presence

An objectification of mood, the symbol is confronted as something which is shockingly in contrast to what one is, though it has been fashioned from what one is. A presence which never ceases to hover about one, it is an inescapable reminder to clarify oneself to oneself. Product of a mutual addressing, the symbol itself is a summoning to present oneself in clarity to another. Thereby, it stirs both creator and recipient into constructive discontent. For it directs attention to aspects of existence which one has denied: the eerie, the sublime, the tender, the awesome. To encounter the symbol is to fling oneself out of the paths of the familiar. It is to crack the glass of the everyday world, and to walk toward strange realms.

Reality, when confronted, always jars. When chords resonate deep within one, the impact of music induces a thrusting beyond one. Thus, any symbol confrontation realigns the physical and the spiritual equilibria of existence, and stirs one to ponder more deeply one's feelings and modes of relatedness to reality. Life and death, birth and tragedy, are experienced more intensely, and in new and larger perspective.

Herein lies the eschatologic dimension of the symbol. An existence which *could* be is prefigured. Though man, "mired in his paths, . . . entangle[d] . . . in appearance, . . . [ever] turns round and round in his own circle,"[22] the symbol radically discloses what *might* be. It envisages ideal, though uncanny and, perhaps, fearsome, possibilities. Not simply a revelation of being, the symbol constitutes a power for the renewal of being. For it is an eruption into visibility of that which had been unknown. And, as the symbol perishes into a human existence, it objectively immortalizes itself therein, and, thereby, thrusts that existence into the dimension of the eternal. By "objective immortality" I mean, following Whitehead, durable absorption into the vibrancy of immediate experience. This opening up *is* strange. It *is* violent. But, though transitory, it is liberating; and it is transfiguring. Hence, every synthesis of symbol and person enhances solidarity both within and between persons.

Constituting a radical affirmation of existence, the symbol shapes itself in the face of a radical negation of existence. With each creation, the symbolizer empties himself of actualized existence. Indeed, it is the symbol just formed which constitutes that actuality. In stillness, and at times in fear, he commences anew his creative life. A blank canvas and a blank mind, a risk indeed of that stark presence the quintessential expression of which is a thrusting into death—this is the rim of mystery, this radical dissolution the quality of which one cannot grasp; this haunting realm within which germinates the rhapsodic immediacy of symbolic creation. But it is an immediacy which can never escape the circle of silence. And what is embedded in this silence, as partaking of its character, and as that which even gives birth to the symbol, are the innumerable past meetings, all the strands of influence which have shaped the unwitting themes of a life. Of this, the symbol is a condensation and a perpetuation.

It is a coming-alive, this process of symbolization, into a more inclusive present: a present which, in its sweeping rhythms, becomes, like the ebb and flow of a Bach *partita*, a seeming eternity. Moreover, the symbol hypostatizes, and therein celebrates, this clarified reality; it converts what had been transcendent to experience into an immanence in experience, what had been strange into the intimate and secure. Eternalizing the instant, the symbol allows all the fleeting moments of existence to become incandescent with the presence of a beyond. Immortalizing the past in the present, the symbol evokes the echo of the past and, in effect, arrests the flow of time. By its very objectification in the present, this mirroring of the past permits the symbol truly to perish, even as it suffuses each moment with the "ethereal presence" of a transcendent quality. Indeed, through the symbol, one holds dialogue with one's own past; one mourns its passing, yet extracts from the past, and from all the dead facts which constitute it, something which enriches the present. In dialogue, one addresses to another the lessons which these cumulative imprints of numberless encounters have traced on one. And in this radical extermination of a past which hovers above him as a " 'throbbing vault,' "[23] the person regenerates himself at the very instant he touches it; he radically surpasses himself at this moment when he fully senses his rootedness. A glowing reminiscence, the past now becomes consummately manifest.

Furthermore, the symbol is a making-oneself-present to another. It is a gift which increases the humanity of both donor and recipient. In the interplay of reciprocated gifts, as an exchange of presentings-of-selves, the symbol reveals the inwardness of a person. Through the successive symbols by which one renews one's existence, the spirit becomes luminous ever anew. Beyond that, in the symbol, one first completes in idea what one cannot complete in fact. Weaving illusion perpetually about oneself, one dwells in illusion as though it were reality. By the power which inheres in the concreteness of the illusion, it becomes a vehicle of universal values—always refracted, however, through the lens of the particular. "All art," Yeats declared, "is in the last analysis an endeavour to condense as out of the flying vapour of the world an image of human perfection, and for its own sake and not for the art's sake. . . ."[24] This "image of human perfection" is conveyed as an actual physical presence, a rhythmic congealing of spirit, as the symbol unfolds, and is authentically touched—not merely its surface, but its actual substance—touched by those to whom it addresses itself. The very integrity of a person is therein communicated, and even fashioned.

(*c*) Symbol and Integrity

As long as it occurs in *a making present as the embodiment of human perfection*, any physical entity can serve as symbol. For it is this context which determines an entity to be a symbol. The powers which have molded a symbol and, as such, are inscribed upon it, are revealed by it; and in this revealing, the integrity of a person is enhanced. Each symbol discloses a facet of such power. Each has both a surface and an interior. The patterning of symbols determines which dominates in a given context. As mere façade, the symbol points toward the constriction of power. In this aspect of their meaning, dream symbols incorporate a brittleness, and a stereotyping of reality. Or they can betoken a veiling of experience, the retreat from reality. Nevertheless, the symbol always has a plastic aspect. In rendering visible a person's inwardness, it presents a texture which stimulates the senses in ways which, when harmonized with its interior import, are intrinsically rewarding. By this interiority, the symbol points toward rebirth: the expansion of power, the quest to penetrate to more ethereal modalities of existence. Alternatively, this dimension of the symbol may betoken, as Moby Dick does, a swallowing, and an absorption into inscrutable forces, a kind of regressive womb-directedness. Presenting itself as a mask to be penetrated, the dream symbol possesses both negative and positive aspects which must be accurately distinguished. The question now arises: What is the integrity toward which the symbol points, as both a denying and an affirming?

Encounters leave their traces as fabrics of moods which cumulatively mount into the present. Inscribing itself on the symbol, a mood's vicissitudes and its origins become luminous. The entire world imprints itself on, indeed gives rise to, each new occasion of experience. A "society of occasions," at the penultimate moment of their satisfactions when the person *fully* experiences, he plunges into the creative advance of the universe, bearing the whole antecedent world with him. The symbol is an element in this plunging forth, an element laden with a past. It weaves into coherent expression dispersed fragments of feelings, and mobilizes the energies of an existence, so that it may more effectively imprint itself upon another. It is a manifestation of the quest for the purity, wholeness, and simplicity of spontaneous childhood. But it betokens spontaneity infused with meditation. And, thereby, the dance of images, often so chaotic and inhibiting, redeems itself as an ever-more-enriched dance of gestures.

Joining persons in communion, the symbol (which, as συμβάλλειν, also means "to compare") contrasts their individualities, and thereby reduces the heterogeneity of personal "space." Engendering more authentic encounters, it destroys isolation and atomization. An addressing and a presenting, the symbol refers to a relationship between persons. Next, the symbol joins body to spirit, which, though concealed, deposits its imprints upon body, while contrasting the cleavages which always recur. Abolishing the dichotomization of "matter," it establishes the integrality of the person. For the symbol is a tangible complex the reference of which is to the psyche which unfolds within it. Lastly, the symbol joins past and present, contrasting the refusal of the present to perish with the relentless flow of time. Converting what was merely potential, or a shadowy hope, into the actual, it destroys the trichotomy of time. Referring to a past perishing into the present, the symbol occurs in that mode of experience which Whitehead called "presentational immediacy" and its reference is to that mode which he termed "causal efficacy." Thereby, symbols create a seemingly eternal present for a community of integral persons. They hint at powers as yet unborn, meanings as yet unarticulated; but powers and meanings always latent in the community. As such, the symbol, that process by which image becomes gesture, constitutes itself the quintessential manifestation of persons-in-relation.

NOTES

1. This report has been selected from my psychoanalytic practice, with identificatory possibility obliterated.
2. See the index entry for "latent content" in *The Complete Psychological Works of Sigmund Freud.* V. *The Interpretation of Dreams (Part II)*, ed. James Strachey (London: Hogarth, 1953).
3. See index entries for "transference" in ibid.
4. C. G. Jung, *The Archetype and the Collective Unconscious*, trans. R. F. C. Hull, 2nd ed. (Princeton, N.J.: Princeton University Press, 1968).
5. See the index entry for "manifest content" in Freud, *Interpretation of Dreams.*
6. See the index entries for "Dream-work" in ibid.
7. See the index entries for the foregoing terms in ibid.
8. George Santayana, *Realms of Being.* II. *The Realm of Matter* (New York: Scribners, 1930), p. 148.
9. Ibid., p. 150.
10. "Phaedrus," in *The Dialogues of Plato*, trans. B. Jowett, 2 vols. (New York: Random House, 1937), I 282.

11. Paul Tillich, *Systematic Theology*, 3 vols. (Chicago: The University of Chicago Press, 1951–1963), I 239.

12. *Inferno of Dante Alighieri*, 34.138, in the Temple Classics, p. 391.

13. Franz Kafka, *The Trial*, trans. Willa and Edwin Muir (New York: Knopf, 1956).

14. Herman Melville, *Moby-Dick; or, The Whale*, ed. Harold Beaver (Harmondsworth & Baltimore: Penguin, 1972), p. 295.

15. Ibid., p. 296.

16. Ibid.

17. Ibid., pp. 295, 296.

18. Ernst Cassirer, *The Problem of Knowledge: Philosophy, Science, and History Since Hegel*, trans. William H. Woglom and Charles W. Hendel (New Haven: Yale University Press, 1950), p. 146, citing from Goethe's *Maximen und Reflexionen*, ed. M. Hecker, Schriften der Goethe-Gesellschaft 21 (Weimar: Goethe-Gesellschaft), no. 314, p. 59.

19. Victor Zuckerkandl, *Sound and Symbol*, trans. Willard R. Trask, Bollingen Series 44 (New York: Pantheon, 1956), p. 68.

20. *Being and Time*, trans. John Macquarrie and Edward Robinson (New York: Harper & Row, 1962), pp. 52, 51 (emphasis deleted).

21. *An Introduction to Metaphysics*, trans. Ralph Manheim (New Haven & London: Yale University Press, 1959), p. 109.

22. Ibid., pp. 157–58.

23. Marcel, *Mystery of Being* II, p. 186 (quoting from his 1949 play *L'Emissaire*).

24. Cited in Richard Ellmann, *Yeats: The Man and the Masks* (New York: Macmillan, 1949), pp. 185–86.

18

CAVERNS OF SILENCE AND VIBRANCY: THE SHAPING OF THE *I* — ITS ROOTS IN THE COSMOS

PREAMBLE

An orchestration of images, intermingling to constitute the configurations which imperceptibly flow into gesture, every person shapes gestures into symbols, which he expresses in the context of human compresence. Empowered by his essential freedom to search into symbols, he discloses ever-novel realms of meaning. Drawn from an interior silence, such meaning confers new status on the human. They transmute the merely natural and ordinary into the spiritual and imaginative. A process of "selving-," or "personing-forth," the person is witnessed by the entire human community, as his imagination creates new worlds. Gradually, in this process, all distinction between subject and object, inner and outer, and immanence and transcendence vanishes; and an abundant self gives birth to manifold symbolic forms.

Initially enclosed within his very self—solitary, isolated, and lonely—everyone is narcissistically preoccupied and self-absorbed. But immense cosmic energies ever work through one. Drawing on these energies, one shatters one's isolation and self-centeredness, and steps forth into unknown regions. Silence haunts the person, pervading and enveloping him. Confronting its awesome depths, with mysterious eddies, currents, and perturbations of unimaginable kinds, he frees his own imagination, and penetrates nature's cycles, rhythms, and repetitions. Thereby, he conquers mere vegetative activity; and his self goes forth to rise above nature, to overpower her, to transfigure itself, and to realize its full spiritual potential. Counterposed to nature, the human spirit transforms the world. Thus imbued with symbolic forms, the world interacts with a self which, absorbing these forms, catalyzes ever-new creative acts. But always, in the end, there is silence: the depths of mystery, the abyss of eternity. And man must engage, and come to terms with, the radical opposition between his own finitude and the infinite reaches which dwell both within him and about him.

A • PERSON AS LABYRINTH; WORLD AS LABYRINTH

(*a*) The Creative Ferment

Earlier, by "personing-forth," I meant the self in the process of disclosing itself through symbols of dance and speech. A directed, purposive assemblage of human acts, this process is an unfolding within which one may distinguish three aspects: the initiation of the entire process; the gathering together of the factors which contribute to its flow, and the culmination of the process as a unified, coherent whole; a movement from a still, ineffable center toward a periphery which is a vibrant, tangible, and mobile rhythmic complex. With respect to this process, I now ask: How do dancing images transfigure themselves into dancing gestures of speech, frank dance, and transformings of natural things into human artifacts? How do the images themselves arise? How does their origin relate to analogous origins in other persons? Wherein consists its link to the world, taken as a unified totality? Is the world also centered in such a way that the panoply of specifically personal centers points inward toward this center beyond centers, toward it as both source and ground of their very existence? Can this overarching center be more explicitly defined than particular individual centers? How does human utterance reveal the actualization of a person's powers? And, finally, how does self-actualization relate to the very origin of all potentiation?

To deal with these images, I note that a person's inner world of imagery bursts forth into an exuberant outgrowth, a varied efflorescence of tints, tonalities, and unfoldings. No single metaphor suffices to indicate the marvelous effluxes, combinations, and textures which these images disclose. For every particular metaphor is rooted in—hence, owes its persuasiveness to—a specific faculty of mind or body: e.g., ideation, olfaction, kinesthesia, the gustatory, the tactile, the aural, the visual. Beyond these capacities, extraordinary syntheses prevail as affording substance for metaphoric utterance, indeed even experiential dimensions which, at least in our language, must remain nameless.

Through this inner world, to which I can refer only by a perhaps immiscible combination of metaphors, man is related to his fellows, to beast, to plant, and to mineral. He is intimately connected to personal, organismic, and inorganic phenomena; and to everything of which the universe is composed, even to that which lies beyond all imagining. Indeed, an obscure, haunting, remote, and awesome labyrinth conditions both person and world. With respect to it, interiority and exteriority enjoy no ultimate distinction. The totality is a flowering forth of absolute plenitude. To celebrate creation, one must, in reverence, both consecrate and rejoice in this marvelous superabundance. Yet one must never fail to stress the lamentation which inexorably infects the entirety. Creation unavoidably entails dissipation. Organizations of energy, either spiritual or material—in the end, the two are inseparable—which attain to incomparably refined shape, are ineluctably fragile and vulnerable. Amid unspeakable anguish, they perish, only to release their constituents for utilization by a new procession of forms which will reign in their stead. How, in this mighty upheaval, an evolution and a devolution, can sense be made of the ultimate enigma: namely, that by man's finitude, the *raison d'être* of celebration and lamentation tragically, and forever, eludes his grasp?

In the double labyrinth, person with world, each component conceals fathomless depths, mysterious recesses, and strangely cavernous realms for potential human adventure. In dialectical relatedness, each contributes to the origination of the other. Shaping the person, and engendering his very potentialities, the world catalyzes such powers as seem destined for actualization. But the person *re*shapes the world; and he molds it to conform to his own desires, his will, his aesthetic sensibilities, and his vision of how it might better accord with the values he fashions for himself.

However, both shaping and reshaping unfold within limits. Beyond a certain point, one is powerless to transform the world; one must bend oneself into conformation with *its* contours. By the doctrine of naturalism, a person is sole product of the world. Doubtless, up to a point, this doctrine is valid. Everyone has an animal nature which constrains impulse and directs desire, channeling them into modes of expression prescribed by the world. Yet the world makes no *absolute* claims upon the person. Even while embedded in it, a person stands apart from the world, and surveys its content in accordance with principles which he himself fashions. How can one bring this double shaping into harmony, so that reciprocity prevails with respect to the two powers: that of world, that of person? To conceptualize this mutual attunement, I propose a doctrine of transcendental rhythmicality. By his spiritual endowment larger than the world, the person objectifies it by gathering its themes into categories which he himself has fashioned, categories which prescribe the very conditions under which he experiences the world as an ordered manifold. By these activities, he re-creates the world, both in his imagination and in its practical deployment. Thereby, he stands apart from the world, and envisages realms the constitutive rhythms of which utterly transcend natural process. Autonomous and free, a person imaginatively contrives, by the sheer spontaneity of his own creative gifts, a veridically new substance: the forms of spirit itself. Yet, by the same doctrine, the world transcends *itself*. Never consisting exclusively in the totality of actualities by which it manifests itself, it is larger than the integral of its appearances. Beyond the world as mere *natura naturata* is the world as *natura naturans*: an invisible ferment which, without cease, potentiates itself as the visible. An infinite abyss whence arise both person and world, the ferment pervading that abyss transmits its energies to each. Thereby, the full dialectic of shaping and reshaping will prevail. And the more a person probes his inmost depths, the more he passes from self-enclosedness to touch the very source, not only of his singular creative activity, but, beyond that, of the creative ground of the cosmos, which includes both person and world.

Moreover, every person is empowered to draw forth from this interior silence, a silence which pulsates with its own rhythms, however quiescent they be, the symbols by which he represents his constantly shifting relationships to the world. In human compresence, he gives birth to speech and dance, in all their variety; and, thereby, allows the currents which flow within the abyss to crystallize, thence to be revealed to the human community. Through the participation of both person and world in the same creative source, the ferment of each will congeal as altogether new entities endowed with their own special powers. And, as one explores one's depths, and solidifies one's sense of *I as seeker and creator*, one finds this *I* to be rooted beyond the person in the labyrinth of the cosmos: a kind of world-self which, so to speak, selves itself forth, through the agency of persons-in-relation, to shape ever-new forms.

(*b*) Creative Reflection

When I speak of a search into the inmost recesses of the self, even more strongly of the *I* who is engaging in this search, the problem of reflexivity itself is posed. As I search, I become aware of myself as seeker. More precisely, I become aware of the complete identity of the seeking act with that which, from moment to moment, reveals itself as the sought. What is sought is never an object, fixed and immutable. On the contrary, it is a process of unfolding, an efflorescing into still new content. But when I fix my inward searching gaze upon this content, as though it were an object which displaces the object whence it arose, it, too, dissolves into a new efflorescing process. Too, I cannot dissociate my sense of myself as seeker from my sense of the succession of unfolding disclosed in the seeking. A single, unitary, and integral act supervenes: I seeking into myself as revealing new interior objects which, as they emerge, vanish into yet new objects. Within this process, I can distinguish phases, but in a conceptual rather than a phenomenological sense. In effect, I am proposing that the object of my intentions, my act of intending, and my very self as the one who intends are, equally, acts, and, beyond that, that they constitute one act, indivisible and internally coherent. "The seer becomes the seeing," Thomas Hora declared, "and the seeing becomes the seen."[1]

To speak of the "self" in a substantive sense is misleading. "Selving" more accurately designates the self as both "I seeking" and "seeking I," and, beyond that, as a "personing-forth." The *entire* person places himself, both at the center of the search and, on its periphery, as eccentric to the search. To be a person is to "person-forth"; it is to quest after that which, in the very context of the quest, emerges *as* person. Furthermore, no person can be monadically conceived; every person is, in effect, a dyad. To be a person is to be compresent with another person. Hence, the compresence of personings-forth more properly expresses personhood than do the components of compresence, namely, solitary persons. In principle, I am constituted by other I's. And the paradigmatic shape which the "self–other" assumes is the entire interpersonal community which, as a whole, seeks; and seeks through the agency of each of its members. In this sense, "I seeking" is but the medium through which the community manifests patterns of compresence. Yet communities are enclosed within more inclusive communities; and the ultimate community is the cosmos, very limit of the entire series of enveloping communities. In sum, "I seeking" is "the entire cosmos questing through its every community," and, most important, questing *through* each individual person.

What can it mean to speak of cosmos as questor, questor which engages in a quest mediated by its own components, in particular by persons? I suggest that the cosmos ever penetrates its own labyrinth, namely, that whence its very searching acts arise. But it can penetrate only through particular questors who, themselves, penetrate their own labyrinths: i.e., the cosmic labyrinth under the perspective of singularity. Faith, to echo Hegel, rests on the witness of the spirit which as witnessing is the spirit in man. This witness is the underlying essence in all humanity.[2] To bear witness to spirit is to quest after the forms which spirit assumes. It is to shape those forms; more deeply, to allow them to shape themselves that, thereby, man can fulfill his destiny as questor. And for him to shape the forms through himself, insofar as he is an I who seeks, the cosmos must release the forms: forms which are latently embedded in itself as sheer ferment. Thereby, the cosmos permits man to bear witness to the ferment which, as self-actualizing potentiality, *is* spirit. Furthermore, he shapes himself as *personal* man, i.e., as one who persons-forth, only insofar as he opens himself actively to receive the spirit within him; and he achieves this end by allowing the spirit to assert itself through his particular works. Since man shapes himself only in the framework of compresence, which implies community as constitutive of man, it follows that the spirit declares itself in and through a unified humankind. But, for the cosmos to make itself accessible as spirit "in and through" man, the cosmos must, with respect to this aspect, be conceived under "the form of the personal."[3]

How can this be? To respond, I must again note: quintessentially, persons are reflexive. Not that all substance is not reflexive. Indeed, substance *per se* is that which dynamically relates to itself. Otherwise, it would lack the dynamism for diversifying itself, i.e., for replicating itself as specific instances or manifestations which, in their particular dynamics, mirror the essential character of substance in general. In this sense, the reflexive nature of substance entails the replicative nature of its every aspect and component, hence, of each aspect and component as itself reflexive. For each, in turn, dynamically relates to itself, as it relates both to other aspects and components and to substance in general. But pre-eminently, the *person* brings reflexivity—hence, the power to replicate by mirroring itself in the very products which it creatively shapes—to its own culmination. For this reason, one can, with Hegel, declare that man is the creature who, compresent with all humankind, bears fullest witness to spirit as embodied in both himself and humankind: to spirit which, as sheer self-actualizing potentiality, even gives birth to itself. Thus, persons bring to fruition the complex reflexive relation of "being with self" as itself being reflexively in (interpersonal and suprapersonal) relationships which are so diverse and comprehensive as, ultimately, to comprehend all being. In this sense, I support Heidegger's dictum that human being is the locus wherein all being discloses itself. For, by this disclosure, with Heidegger, I mean that under the perspective of this unique, singular person, all that is in the cosmos comes to confluence in him and articulates itself through him.

Different levels, modalities, degrees, and textures of articulation prevail with respect to the relationship "self with self through being with other than self." To a first approximation, one stands in this relationship in a stereotypical way. Prescinding from most spheres of relatedness, one focuses exclusively, so it appears, on limited ways of organizing experience. In constricted reflexivity, one focally attends only that which is prescribed by the restricted community of one's everydayness. Bound to conventional situations, one acquires but a limited perspective on reality. Yet, even then, one must acknowledge a kind of diffuse experience which signifies more than what is immediately stressed by communally sanctioned roles, though one relegates frank recognition of that experience to the background of attention. For a sort of global trans-experience hovers there: a ground of experience which is insubstantial and fleeting; a ground on which experience emerges as sharply etched, but as solitary and circumscribed.

In a confined way, essentially unconscious, one witnesses the totality, which is really spirit. But as deeper personal experiences are recollected, and one senses a life's past determinants, hence its future trajectory, premonitions of the larger background emerge. One is haunted by diffuse perceptions of a beyond which one can neither articulate nor, in a clear-cut way, even feel. However suppressed, concealed textures of relatedness, textures which are laminated in multiplex ways, constitute the sustained matrix within which now one orientation, and now another, come into the foreground of attention. Yet, determined, on the whole, by mere contingency, one finds oneself imprisoned in restricted patterns which have, in effect, been excised from the totality. Nevertheless, one may summon certain networks of meaning to more sustained focal attention.

(*c*) The Vanishing of Inner and Outer

Usually, one's transactions with the world are in the sphere of the practical. Based either on immediate situational factors or, more deeply, on personal memories more or less accessible to recall, one makes essentially pragmatic decisions. At the same time, an immense region of sedimented layers of meaning remains unutilized, meanings which are condensed into concentrated but unexplicated configurations whence arise discrete, serialized items of momentary experience. Since only limited meanings are carved from this configuration, and unfold their latent content, other meanings can shape excrescences which merely distort the actual import of what does emerge into awareness. Meanings unavailable as the immediate ground for action are associated with powerful immobilizing dynamisms, dynamisms which reflect the interplay between two opposing forces, regressive and progressive. The regressive keep meaning concealed or, at most, at the periphery of focal attention, hence, accentuate them as unconscious conditioning factors; the progressive allow meaning to free itself from distortion, and fully to burst into awareness.

Despite the defective orientations toward life which result from negative dynamisms, the resultant imbalances can be rectified. Larger trans-personal meanings, rather than mere idiosyncratic personal meanings, can, from time to time, emerge into explicit awareness. Wider relational contexts stemming from the larger communities which a person inhabits can supervene, communities non-personal as well as personal. These contexts mirror inclusive ways by which he coordinates networks of cosmic relatedness. As a result, attunements to universal patterns of integration evolve. Nevertheless, the sense of oneness with the totality is still infected by activities which, too constricting, prevent a person from fully dwelling in the most inclusive ground of his being: a ground which embraces, and subsumes, the entire matrix of cosmic events; a ground which enables one to see through the "eyes" of the totality, grasping his individuality as having parity with all individualities.

Now one comes upon a new ground, insubstantial and ineffable: the ground of pure being, a ground but fleetingly glimpsed. One enters the cosmic labyrinth of "caverns of silence and vibrancy." Here, an altogether new dialectic prevails: the bursting forth of endlessly novel realms, realms enclosing realms; eddies of silence orchestrating themselves into variegated patterns which are ineluctably beyond the visible world. At last, the person truly dwells with himself, in a world construed as a delicately constituted ferment. Yet, like Hegel's *Absolute*, pure "being with being" must differentiate itself—though as patterns incomparably more subtly nuanced than any pattern which no practice or cognition or aesthetics is competent to delineate. Entering a numinous domain pervaded by alternating episodes of quiescence and exaltation, a domain which nonetheless stirs awe and fear, one dies into the most inclusive of all realms; but the temptation to return to lesser realms never ceases to recur. Within this ground, every item which, in lesser realms, functioned as focal elements, and in clearly demarcated, characteristic ways, acquires entirely new meaning. Now the distinction between inner and outer, subject and object, and immanence and transcendence altogether vanishes.

B • THE INTRINSIC IDENTITY BETWEEN IMMANENCE AND TRANSCENDENCE

(*a*) Redemption

With respect to inner and outer, interiority is constituted by efflorescing images so orchestrated that they are indistinguishable from external objects. Here, a unitary cosmos pervades the entire being. Reciprocally, a unitary self pervades the entire cosmos. Categories applicable to bifurcated world totally collapse; altogether new categories must be fashioned. With respect to subject and object, seeker and sought are now cojoined as but foci within a cohesively woven texture of trans-experience: i.e., of experience beyond the customary, wherein one has passed through the very boundaries between acts of inquiry and the termini of such acts. With respect to immanence and transcendence, more extended remarks are required.

In conjunction with the entire community of selves, each constitutive of the other, the self works immanently in this unfolding hierarchy of grounds of human action. In mutual affirmation, two reciprocally acknowledging, self-present centers "recognize themselves as mutually recognizing one another."[4] Very source of action, the searching self both conditions and pervades its every self-originated act. As source, the self, as mere self, never exhausts itself, no matter how many specific acts flow from it. At the same time, when the self completely attunes itself to the other and, reciprocally, the other completely affirms itself in the first, a plenitudinous and, indeed, superabundant self pours its inherent content into *all* its searching acts. And since the self now apprehends itself to be profoundly linked to the entire cosmos, which, from time to time, it may even glimpse, the paradoxical status of the self as both immanent and transcendent is finally resolved. For, in the end, the identification between the two labyrinths, self and cosmos, eradicates the contradictions engendered by the very notions of immanence and transcendence. Despite this resolution, one never ceases to probe, ever more deeply, the secrets of one's own self.

By stages, the self discerns itself to be grounded in that toward which it aspires, and by which it judges its every act. Operative in the self, yet lying beyond it, an ideal directs its searching and shapes its destiny. As this ideal is gradually recognized, it is experienced as not merely an abstract principle, but as a viable witness to the self's own spiritual growth, hence, as constitutive of the self in both an immanent and a transcendent sense. As witness, this progressively substantialized ideal provides the criteria by which the self evaluates its own procession of movements as, in oscillations of joy and anguish, and indeed in every modulation of which human feeling is capable, it probes its inmost depths. Perception of this witness is itself experienced in stages. Initially, the self recognizes the witness as personal conscience and, to the extent that personal conscience is exclusively solitary conscience, as capricious and fallible. Next, it acknowledges the witness as the collective judgment of inclusive human societies. Finally, it experiences the witness as having transformed itself, *within* the self, into a universally valid ideal, but an ideal interwoven with a supreme personal presence.

By rectifying its actions in accordance with the infallible decrees of an ultimate witness, the self redeems both its own inwardness and the searching acts by which it discloses that inwardness. What, in the beginning, was most remote now presents itself as, increasingly, a presence which, though at times reproving and disciplinary, is always intimate, reassuring, and tender. As the self seeks, many selves unfold within it. With every social role, a new self is associated. Yet the emerging, all-enveloping witness so radiates its beneficence that it brings about the dissolution of each new self, and its replacement by a single, unique, and absolutely secure inmost self.

(*b*) Reciprocity

One cannot be recognized, in one's inmost self, by any finite person. For finitude implies perspective; and though one can, by glimpses, transcend perspective, *through* perspective, one experiences only a faint glow of something beyond. Furthermore, no community of persons can recognize the concealed depths of a self. A community's orchestrated perspectives constitute another perspective which is more inclusive, but limited nonetheless. In order for a person absorbed with his inmost depths to escape radical solitude, he needs a larger companion, the transcendence of which with respect to his being is actually equivalent to its immanence.

Even in love, wherein one knows the beloved with profound intimacy, there is that mutual respect which promotes the radical distinctiveness of each lover. Hence, when one is most known to another person, one is least known. For, in love, to know a person is, precisely, to orient oneself with full tender acceptance toward the *fact* of his fathomless depths; and, thereby, to recognize the ineluctable mystery which dwells within him, a mystery unknown even to its possessor. To delineate a person with love entails that one so experience him that familiarity becomes identical with "stranger-liness." No one can exhaustively draw forth the mysterious reservoirs of potential creative expression either from one's self or from another, let alone perceive the contours of those reservoirs. Nothing, as Tillich declares, "pours its power of being completely into its state of existence."[5]

Veridical love requires reciprocity. A lover cannot freely allow his being to unfold before the beloved unless the beloved so accepts the unfolding that she open herself, with all her resources, to the lover. For the beloved must attend the lover's every act of love; she must seek ever more deeply to listen to its symbolisms, to their import, and to how they so orchestrate themselves that the lover's power to make himself present to the beloved is activated as itself a living, vibrant reality. Yet for the beloved thus to orient herself toward the lover, the beloved herself, as listener, must become a living presence to the lover. And as she attends, allowing herself actively to receive the lover's gift, the beloved is so transfigured that her own power of presence becomes, reciprocally, a living, vibrant reality. Beyond that, the relationship of human love is doomed to failure unless, now assuming the role of lover, the beloved likewise so draws forth the concrete implications of her own presence that she unfolds *herself*, in love, to the lover, now become the beloved.

A dialectical relationship prevails between an active going forth and an active drawing in. For going forth toward another requires that one touch the other with all that one is. And should that touching be rejected, the going forth must cease. Mutuality alone is the ground whereby love can sustain its own acts. And should mutuality (as a potential) prevail, the trembling rhythms of the recipient are so stirred by the acts of the lover that his rhythms transmute themselves into an analogous action of going forth; whereupon the one who originally presented himself in the mode of going forth now enjoys the more quiet presence of drawing in. When the rhythms of each activity are brought to fruition, they so commingle that both individuals experience themselves as participants in an altogether new process: the ebb and flow of giving and receiving—receiving, if consummated, being but another form of giving. As co-participants, the lovers reciprocally feel themselves to be enveloped by a larger presence, which has come upon them by a kind of grace. Both lovers so enwomb themselves in this presence that, for a brief instant of eternity, they forget themselves as separate selves, giving themselves up entirely to the orchestrations of loving compresence.

(*c*) Envelopment

Yet, by the finitude of each, every person requires that he step back from this negation of his solitary individuality. For another rhythm unfolds, a rhythm which need not deny the validity of the first rhythm, but which can so delicately enmesh with it as to produce an harmonious attunement between the lovers. By this new rhythm, an individual quests after his own inner ground, a ground which can be revealed only in the quietude of private seeking. But, once revealed to him, this ground discloses itself to be precisely the ground for the very reciprocity which, to begin with, required its own suspension, that *its* ground be more fully experienced. The mystery which I apprehend to reside in me haunts me. Gently, this mystery draws me toward it, as I, replicating my act of reception with respect to my lover, now open myself to receive it, and, increasingly, to draw it into the ken of my own finite being. Yet, in this process, the ground presents itself, at first but dimly perceived to be thus constituted, as an infinite ground, a ground pregnant with its own mysteries. The more these mysteries unfold, the more I am fascinated by them, and the more I must plumb the inmost depths of that which, increasingly, reveals itself to be constitutive of me, yet still beyond me. Fascinated, I come to dwell in the unitary presencing of my own self to itself. And as I descend into my self, in my quest to make it my own, I lose my very personhood, that I might, in the end, regain my personhood, but in a manner which is altogether transfigured.

I "found a bottomless pit," wrote Teilhard de Chardin, "and out of it came—I know not whence—the current which I dare to call *my* life."[6] Always, however, since such a quest is arduous, one must return to normal companionship, to friendship, and, ideally, to love. There, by the grace of the in-flowing tenderness of the other, himself a self-questing being who analogously, from time to time, exhausts himself in the search, one renews oneself through the mutual exchange of human feeling. Once again, two lovers, each a finite being, embrace one another, and rejoice in their very finitude; once more, they share intimacy and, with respect to the endless mystery concealed within each, strangeness. Thus, a new dialectic unfolds: the enjoyment of the rhythms of mutually embracing finite beings interweaves with the charisma of the return to the solitary inward search.

In this context, wherein one undulates between aloneness and mutuality, the self persuades itself that it is truly enveloped by a larger presence, a presence which is doubly revealed: through the unfoldings of reciprocal love; as residing in its inmost depths. With respect to this presence, mysteries are experienced as enclosing mysteries. One recognizes that an absolutely transcendent beyond is, at the very same time, an absolutely immanent within. Now, one perceives that the way toward fuller apprehension of this presence is the way, not so much of self-expression, in all the tangible shapes which expression can acquire, as of silence: deep, penetrating, all-pervading. Herein lies the clue to the spiritual essence of the double labyrinth of world and person, and to the ultimate identity of these labyrinths; herein, the identity of immanence and transcendence is itself fully revealed, and its ground completely touched.

C • THE STILL WITHIN; THE STILL BEYOND

(*a*) Silence

As the self draws forth its inner content, it objectifies that content as an encounterable presence. In myriad forms, it expresses the laminae which it discovers to dwell latently in its labyrinthine depths. Clearly, no set of tangible symbols, however diversified or numerous, can remotely approximate the potential expressive content which still resides in the self. Moreover, once expressed, a content is spatialized; it is *out-there*, to be experienced by both oneself and others, indeed, by the entire human community. Not that this objectified content cannot exhibit a history of its own or unfold in stages governed by a dynamism which inheres in its very composition. However, such temporalization is different from the activity which constitutes the self whence the symbols arose. For a self is the very process whereby time articulates itself. More precisely: the community of self-searching creatures collectively shapes the concrete essence of time. Here, I construe self-searching in broad cosmologic terms, though, in these pages, I am concerned only with persons. Surrounding the self's expressive activity, and grounding its very possibility, is silence: profound silence, which envelops not only both self and selves-in-relation but the very world. Significantly constituted by a matrix of pervasive silence, all human creative activity is constituted by that matrix.

In silence, the self distances itself from the objects which it fashions from its own content. In silence, the self surveys the cosmos, and selectively discriminates such regions as are relevant for its own continuance as a self. In silence, the self engages other selves, and participates in the schemes of compresence which it shapes with them. In silence, the self strives to overcome the fragmented, finite character of all particular perspectives. Surely, the images which ground the very acts by which one creates, discovers, and relates oneself to others are themselves drawn from silence. In this sense, silence is constitutive of all things, acts, symbols, and selves. However, by the very nature of silence, its dimensions and rhythms cannot be articulated. So to articulate is, again, to objectify silence, hence, to negate it.

Nonetheless, silence stands to expression born of silence as musical pauses stand to vibrant notes which edge pauses on both sides. In this sense, and in accordance with my musical analogy, what gets expressed is deeply affected by the nature of the pauses, i.e., by the ineffable and unexpressible. Correlatively, the quality of silence itself is affected by the expressions which border *it* on both sides. Hence, a counterpoint between silence and expression unfolds as an ineluctable part of experience.

Beyond that, when one penetrates the abyss of silence, one discerns tensions to pervade that abyss, rhythmic unfoldings, and intricate orchestrations which, defying imagination, cannot be conceptualized even by analogy. In particular, silence exhibits the character of plenitude. And it is a measureless abyss which possesses its own kind of luminosity, a luminosity which, alternating with opacity, manifests all manner of chiaroscuro. In the end, one can only bear witness to this pre-predicative, pre-thematic condition which, elusive as it is, nonetheless grounds all that can, in principle, be conceptualized. Neither immanent in the self nor transcendent to it, silence qua silence is the very matrix whence the distinction between immanence and transcendence arises. It is the still within and the still beyond; and, with respect to silence, neither within nor beyond can be separated. Each complementing the other, they are, ultimately, one and the same.

(*b*) Witnessing

Everyone needs acknowledgment, acknowledgment of exactly who one truly is. But, in the inmost depths of one's being, who one is must inexorably be veiled from all finite creatures, including even oneself. Normally, one receives partial acknowledgment from many people; and, in a love relationship, one receives more acknowledgment than in other finite relationships. Ever yearning for reciprocity and mutuality, one strives to be allowed to present oneself to another in every facet of one's being, even though one might be afraid to reveal this or that aspect or quality. At the very outset of a human encounter, hesitancy prevails. Only gradually, should the encounter come to fruition, is hesitancy transformed into the sheer joy of self-disclosure. "Real love is enhanced," it has been written, "when it ripens from an initial hesitancy which is a kind of delicate reserve in the expression of a basic desire, and when its shared radiance issues steadily from a depth from which the veil is never wholly lifted."[7] Even by hesitancy, one conveys, with utmost intimacy, confidences of feeling, confidences which, in order to grow, can germinate, and be communicated, only in silence. In its deepest state, silence is authentic communication. More accurately, it is a communing which binds both communicants into unity. Yet one never ceases to reach toward absolute intimacy: that one's entire being be disclosed, that the originating center of one's very action become luminous and fully manifest.

Sensing secrets buried deep within me, which I am unable of my own volition to bring forth, I cannot even reveal those secrets in the context of the searching presence of another. And this yearning gives rise to a deeper perception that, in some unexpressible way, a divine witness to my every act does comprehend, and that He comprehends in an absolute sense: a witness to whom, in the midst of my solitude, whether I am in despair or anguish, I can fully entrust myself; that, somehow, there eternally prevails an all-encompassing presence, a compassionate, absolutely trustworthy listener who confers durable, ultimate meaning upon my every struggle, upon my failures and my successes.

As Meister Eckhart wrote, the birth of the divine

> "is in the purest part of the soul, in the noblest, in her ground, aye in the very essence of the soul. That is mid-silence, for thereinto no creature did ever get, nor any image, nor has the soul there either activity or understanding, therefore she is not aware of any image either of herself or any creature. . . . there is no activity in the essence of the soul; the faculties she works with emanate from the ground of the essence, but in her actual ground there is mid-stillness; here alone is rest and a habitation for this birth, this act, wherein God the Father speaks his Word, for it is intrinsically receptive of naught save the divine essence, without means."[8]

Here, Meister Eckhardt enjoins me to gather in my thoughts, and to proceed by meditation to the very center of my being, that I be united with myself. Yet, always, I emerge from absolute inner tranquillity to take reflective possession of myself. Again and again, I feel the rhythms of silence pervade me. And, dwelling in the midst of these rhythms, as they oscillate with rhythms of vibrancy, I ever seek to bring new expression from this infinite, and intimate, emptiness, this emptiness laden with wondrous comminglings of harmony and dissonance, woven into new harmony: expressions whereby I once more achieve compresence with other persons.

All humankind participates in caverns of silence and vibrancy. In the end, the inmost ground of the self is identical with the inmost ground of the cosmos, a double labyrinth which is really but a single labyrinth. Moreover, all centers of being, whence originate the specific creative expressions of selves-in-relation, are themselves profoundly and intimately interconnected to constitute a great interior network rooted in the ferment which pervades the labyrinth. As each self grows, it senses the limits of its own powers of articulation; and it resigns itself to dwelling at the edge of those limits. Yet it dares to glance into the precipice. In "fear and trembling,"[9] it discerns therein the overarching witness to its every act, and to its inmost secrets, the witness to whom it dares to entrust itself.

As it emerges from its primitive condition, the self experiences itself as efflorescing, through its varied acts, into manifold symbols, symbols which reveal man's power so to diversify himself that he becomes like a mirror which, in a multitude of self-manifestations, reflects the absolute unity which, in his deepest being, he actually is. By dwelling among these manifestations, a person solidifies the very center whence they arose. Moreover, every self is inwardly attuned to every other self; and, beyond that, all selves are inwardly oriented toward a single, active cosmic center, the very center which constitutes a witness to man's every act. Hence, when the self participates in its own creations, it, in reality, participates in a communal creation: a communal creation which shapes itself in, and by virtue of, the power of a cosmos construed as the very crucible of man.

(*c*) The Finite and the Infinite

Every self is superabundant with powers for self-expression. In each instance, such superabundance derives from a plenitudinous cosmos which pours its own superabundance into its every finite creature. Yet to apprehend the source and ground of the self's very being, it must experience itself as participating in a silence which encompasses not only itself, but all other selves to whom it relates in reciprocal compresence. And it comes to realize, though it is powerless to conceptualize its realization, that, in the abyss of this silence, all opposition between inner and outer, subject and object, and immanence and transcendence is somehow overcome, and even reconciled. At the same time, it apprehends the silence to possess its own depths, its own eddies, its own comminglings, its own orchestrations. No mere void, this silence is a filled silence. A substantive silence and an active silence, it dwells at the very core of the person, wherein his searching *I* roots itself. And it is a silence which dwells at the very core of the cosmos, within which the searching *I* more profoundly roots itself.

To conclude: all personal centers are so permeable that, as the *I* associated with each center searches, it experiences the searchings of the *I*'s associated with all centers. A deep communion between selves prevails, a communion enveloped by silence. Moreover, every self shapes itself as a microcosm which mirrors the cosmos not only internally but externally as well; and, in the end, this double mirroring becomes a single mirroring, a process likewise enveloped by silence. In silence, persons identify themselves with the cosmos as, reciprocally, the cosmos identifies itself with persons. Profound intimacy reigns. In one of His roles, God expresses this intimacy, a touching of finitude and infinitude. Herein lies the hope of humankind; herein is the import of man's redemptive acts.

With horror, I confront my finitude. Decay, morbidity, nature's sheer banality, my very self as sharing her putrescence—before a sordid drama, I recoil, and retreat behind façades of denial, forgetfulness, and cynicism. At times stoical, at times stolid, I am haunted by my own withdrawals. And, then, I perceive that I have merely objectified myself and nature; I have alienated the soul from each. And I have not allowed myself to confront the frightening abyss of eternity, the unfathomable infinite which encloses all. Now trembling before an unimaginable totality, I perforce accept both emotions: horror of the finite, terror of the infinite. Yet ever seeking to extricate myself, I create a symbol wherein, for a brief respite, before terror and horror again sweep over me, sheer mystery will shine with resplendent glow. For a magnificent instant of daring and defiance, I transcend my joy and my sorrow; and, welcoming a brief redemptive calm, I humble myself, mute and marveling, before creation's unutterable, overwhelming, all-encompassing, all-pervading might.

NOTES

1. From an unpublished lecture, in my possession.
2. Hegel, *Phenomenology of Mind*, trans. Baillie, pp. 509–12.
3. See John MacMurray, *Persons in Relation* (London: Faber & Faber, 1961), pp. 70, 83, and index; and *The Self as Agent* (London: Faber & Faber, 1957), pp. 17, 37.
4. Hegel, *Phenomenology of Mind*, trans. Baillie, p. 231.
5. *Systematic Theology*, II 21.
6. "Il y avait à mes pieds un abîmes sans fond d'où sortait, venant je ne sais d'où, le flot que l'ose bien appeler *ma* vie," *Le Milieu divin* (Paris: Editions de Seuil, 1959), p. 75.
7. L. Vander Kerken, S.J., *Loneliness and Love*, trans. J. Donceel, S.J. (New York: Sheed & Ward, 1967), p. 88.
8. "On the Divine Birth in the Soul," as cited in F. C. Happold, *Mysticism: A Study and an Anthology* (Harmondsworth & Baltimore: Penguin, 1975), p. 277.
9. Søren Kierkegaard, *Fear and Trembling* (Garden City, N.Y.: Doubleday, 1954).

γ

BEING TRANSFIGURED: THE ONENESS OF MAN

INTRODUCTION

In my concluding Division, I gather together anew the themes which, recurring throughout this work, point toward a systematic human ontology. Subsumed under three rubrics—namely, integrality, power, and authenticity—these themes must be re-meditated. Under integrality, wherein I treat the mind–body unity, I subsume reflection, coherence, and rhythm; under power, wherein I treat self-actualization, I subsume personing-forth, symbolic presentation, and unique, self-identical individuality; under authenticity, wherein I treat integrity as manifested through human encounter, I subsume compresence, transfiguration, and transcendentality. In a diagram, I indicate certain relationships between these themes.

Ontologic Categories for a Systematic Personology

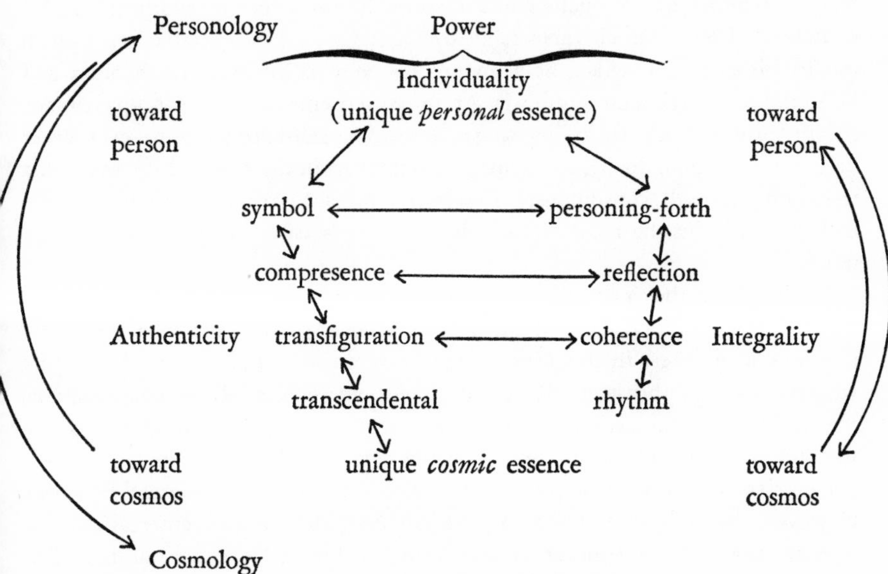

In my remaining discussion, I elaborate upon this diagram, with respect to its import for shaping appropriate ontologic categories.

In reflection, as in its analogue, biologic replication, a new creation is shaped. In part, this creation replicates the person. Mirroring his relationships to the world, it also exhibits such new properties—namely, the explication of what was merely latent in his pre-reflexive condition—as will enable him to venture searchingly into the world. There, he discovers novel realms for habitation, realms wherein he can root himself, preparatory to further adventure. Freeing itself from its engendering source, the "replica," thenceforth, embarks upon an altogether new career. When it joins itself to other like "replicas" (i.e., products of reflection), a novel symbolic product is synthesized. Just as the original "replica" mirrors a single individual's unique qualities, so the new product replicates the constitutive traits of persons-in-relation and, ultimately, of the entire human community. Through reflection, as through biologic replication, persons come to dwell, albeit vicariously, in entirely new realms of existence. Measuring himself against the values immanent in this realm, every person reconstitutes his very being.

By "integrality," I mean the essential unity between one's germinating matrix, a living, mobile human body, and the mind toward which one projects oneself. In this way, a primordial mind–body identity gives way to a new kind of identity. The person identifies himself with an entirely new substantive order. Fleeing, as it were, from his very body, he thinks, feels, and wills himself into active identification with a more inclusive, though sublimated, body; in the end, the cosmos itself. Thereby, he renounces his primordial identity, and strikes out toward new realms. Acquiring an altogether new identity, he no longer gives himself to his own body. Rather, as an ineluctable consequence of his reflective acts, which quality his every bodily act, he abandons his body as his exclusive habitat; and he attains to entirely new equilibria. An initial self-entrusting to one's proximate, strictly private body shifts, by stages, toward a self-entrusting to ever-larger natural realms, and, finally, to realms which are veridically spiritual. Every person transforms himself continuously. Displacing the locus of his actions to more inclusive domains, he reconstitutes himself as possessing integrity, an *achieved* unity.

Passing from the "natural" rhythms of his mind–body "integral," the person moves toward the periphery of the cosmos, enjoying richer and more profound rhythmic complexes. In this sense, mind–body unity is *active* unity. It is unity whereby the self thrusts itself out of its customary mind–body identifications toward larger identifications, identifications wherein body and mind expand. In the end, the mind identifies itself with the entire world, the cosmos under the perspective of *natura naturata*: the actual, concrete, and encounterable world. However, the body is momentously transfigured, and, indeed, etherealized. Integrality is a dynamic concept, closely related to both potency and authenticity. Every person quests so to fulfill his powers that he can dwell authentically, i.e., with integrity, in his every encounter. In self-relatedness, the integral person dynamically, affirmatively, and self-reconstitutively brings his latent powers to fruition. And his indigenous rhythms ground their every coherent manifestation. As coherent, he authentically reflects. Mirroring to himself both his own coherence and its engendering rhythms, he "persons-forth" toward uniqueness, individuality, and *dynamic* self-identity.

By "dynamic self-identity," I mean personal identity, not as predicated but as an activity whereby, amid diverse identifyings with roles, persons, aspects of persons, and experiences in general, one shapes, and never ceases to shape, one's own identity. In self-identity, one identifies oneself and, thereby, constitutes an identity for oneself. This process continues throughout life. Moreover, it unfolds in phases. At every stage, a new moment of self-identifying unfolds. Yet, somehow, certain invariant characteristics, a definite style of being in the world, persist, though one can only specify that style by approximation, and retrospectively rather than prospectively. Only at the end of one's life does one fully reveal what one had immanently been at its beginning. With Goethe, I declare that " 'he is the happiest man who can see the connection between the end and the beginning of his life,' "[1] whose life has a pattern and a style which are utterly its own. Not only are the motives, intentions, and inclinations associated with every person unique, but they constitute an intricate texture the quintessential elements of which disclose themselves, stage by stage, as he actually lives his life. The sense in which endless variations are inscribed on constant themes only to constitute those themes as themselves but variations on deeper-lying themes was discussed, from an infrapersonal point of view, in *The Dance of Being*, and will be further examined, from the point of view of the developing person, in *Metamorphosis*.

In general, one fashions an identity by transforming into vibrant actuality, through a succession of conversions, substantive and not merely formal possibilities for existing. These conversions constitute transfigurations interior to the self. Therein, a person reflexively engages himself by metamorphosing flickering, evanescent fantasies, mere fragments of sensation, into coherent schemes which reach their culmination in the dances of imagery which are the dream's interior aspect. At first, radically amorphous, this anomic self portends its own eventual unification, as it strains toward expressing itself and, thereby, revealing its inwardness in the dances of gesture which are the dream's exterior aspect: namely, song, speech, and dance. Surging within every person are nearly autonomous transformations of mere possibility into power, a sense of direction and purpose, and a perception of solidity and integrity, all of which are struggling to emerge.

Ever striving to shed my own past, I allow the imprints of all that I have ever been to perish harmoniously, though every such perishing is fraught with anguish. In this way, I actually reconstitute myself. Converting into *virtual* actualization inner powers which I sense as tending toward fruition, I become increasingly self-conscious, free, spontaneous, and autonomous. Now I stand at the very threshold of full presence, presence whereby I can authentically give myself to another, and, reciprocally, receive the gift of the other to me. But, to pass this threshold, I must leap across a barrier which at times seems insuperable; and I am ever tempted to turn back into my own interiority, to sink toward the abyss of mere possibility: the very womb and matrix which, as self-catalyzing, had, to begin with, allowed me to metamorphose my possibilities into ever more self-enhancing, self-synergizing, and self-synthesizing powers.

Locked in combat with the progressive forces by which one emerges into presence, hence, compresence with other persons, are regressive forces which not merely impede progress, but, more tragically, acquire their own counter-powers. Ramifying throughout one's interior life, these regressive forces constrict the symbols which one ever seeks to create, symbols by which one joins together the fragments of one's own past that one might prepare oneself for the thrilling adventure into presence. Woven with authentic symbols are "dia-bols," inclinations toward dissociation, fragmentation, and, ultimately, pulverization of the *I*. And inscribed on the lineaments of every person are ineradicable traces of an interplay between symbols—often composed of dramatically contrasting configurations, and contoured in ways which are mutually enhancing—and diabols, which fungulate in bizarre, grotesque ways. Interweaving with symbols, each acting on the other, imprints of lamentation can dominate; alternatively, imprints of celebration, likewise products of the interaction of symbols with diabols, can dominate. Yet, though this record of a past in process of perishing is durable and permanent, and is inexorably and indelibly inscribed on me, I am always empowered, out of the freedom of my soul, to transcend these often tragic depositions and, without negating them and, surely, never obliterating them, somehow absorb them into that compound of sadness and joy which leads me, thenceforth, more circumspectly to dwell within the world and sets me on my way toward the acquisition of wisdom.

As new modes of integrating the progressive with the regressive arise, one achieves remarkable clarity, which reflects itself in every movement of one's visage, an authentic centeredness wherein one's characteristic rhythms become more mobile, fluid, and ethereal. Now one may entrust oneself to the cosmos, to the vicissitudes of its contingencies, whether they be painful or joyous, without succumbing to the temptation to dwell with either pain or joy, but absorbing those experiences with tranquillity, equanimity, grace, and blessedness.[2] Thus experiencing life, its sorrow, and its pity, a person transfigures himself. Transcending hitherto comfortable modes of rooting himself in the world, though often beset by fear and trembling, he looks toward a radically unknown future, a future which he himself shapes, but a future which, from moment to moment, does not actually exist; and, in this sense, is sheer nothingness, hence, a confrontation of terror. Thereby, he lifts himself out of embeddedness in nature and the mere temporality of nature; and he begins to dwell at the periphery of that which envelops all temporality. What, hitherto, had seemed to him absurd and meaningless, empty and despairful, reveals itself—as he passes beyond all customary boundaries into the labyrinth of transcendentality, and is at first counterposed, hence antagonistic, to everything natural—as blending with and, indeed, transforming the natural, illuminating it with the light of eternity. Acquiring the wisdom of years, and having passed through ecstasy and torment, he, at the end of the journey, passes into timelessness, itself an entirely new "domain," of fathomless depth and infinitely variegated texture.

NOTES

1. "Dauer im Wechsel," from the collection entitled *Gott und Welt,* as cited in Hans Meyerhoff, *Time in Literature* (Berkeley & Los Angeles: University of California Press, 1955), p. 51.

2. Spinoza, "Ethics," Part V, Proposition 42, in *Chief Works of . . . Spinoza,* trans. Elwes, II 270–71.

V

A Self United

19

THE INTEGRAL AGENT: MIND AND BODY AS ONE

PREAMBLE

Wherein consists the unity of action which constitutes the person? How does this action initiate itself, and how does it diversify itself? By what dynamism do the pluralistic manifestations of human action weave themselves into a new unity, which, thereupon, gives rise to a new expressive manifold? These are the questions I now take up.

Throughout these volumes, I have maintained that the person is an integral whole. Though he may be conceptualized in many ways, his essential being cannot be reduced to any complex of either natural or mental processes. Many factors which stem from widely varying contexts of activity contribute to his intrinsically indiscerptible character. Moreover, these factors can be classified in different ways; and each classificatory scheme suggests a relevant perspective under which that character may be understood. In every instance, such perspectives must be referred to a single milieu, the person himself. True, such diverse phenomena as nerve distribution, visceral arrangement, skeletal configuration, word inflection, and style of gesticulating interweave to constitute variegated and intricate rhythmic patterns. Yet it is the totality of these patterns, their integral, as it were, which must be apprehended, in order for the particular activity, a unique person, adequately to be conceptualized; it is the special way in which their diverse influences converge upon the *personhood* of the person which must be grasped. Beyond the person himself, two other milieux contribute essential themes toward this understanding: the context of interpersonal relations and of human communities in general; and the context of the cosmos construed as enclosing endless hierarchies of extrapersonal communities enveloping and, in turn, enveloped by other extrapersonal communities.

In the last analysis, no concept of a person's substance can be divorced from an examination of two interrelated topics: the specific life processes by which personhood unfolds, and the stages whereby the intrinsic potentialities germinating within those processes come to fruition; the processes constitutive of the largest possible context within which that life unfolds —namely, the milieu of the cosmos itself. To treat the latter topic, I require a philosophic cosmology, which I present in *Cosmos*. To treat the former topic, I require a theory of human development on two levels, which I present in later books. In *Metamorphosis*, I examine the developmental ground whence originate the inclusive acts which consummate human growth; in *Apotheosis*, I examine the dynamics and the interweavings of those acts. *Metamorphosis* treats those topics bearing upon human growth which enable the symbolisms by which one seeks to encompass the cosmos to shape themselves; and *Apotheosis* treats the efflorescence of the symbolisms themselves. When ground, and (to some extent) its issue have evolved, cosmology fully reveals itself to questing man. Yet certain strictly ontologic themes must be treated prior to both developmental and cosmologic topics, even though those themes cannot ultimately be comprehended save by reference to the latter. One must know, at least in its general contours, the end before one can fully know the beginning, the end as it germinates in the beginning. Still one must *make* a beginning; and my first task is to treat the substantive unity which I designate integrality.

A • REFLECTION AND REPLICATION

(*a*) Reflection Prefigured in Replication

All life reproduces itself as substantive likenesses of particular living forms. No likeness is an exact replica. The features wherein it deviates from its engendering parent express modes of relatedness which are relevant more to it than to its parent. In this sense, every living creature appropriates from its milieu processes which so synthesize themselves with processes indigenous to the creature, and inherited from its parents, as to create of it an entirely new actor on the stage of life. Moreover, deviation between parent and offspring begins to manifest itself at the very instant of conception. Characteristics but latent within parent function significantly within offspring, and conversely. By this emergence from mere immanence to explicit activity, with respect to a given feature, the offspring is empowered to carve from its milieu new loci for its own habitation and to utilize new ingredients for its own perpetuation.

Nonetheless, profound continuity obtains between parent and child. Despite introduction of radical novelty at a singular node in the transition, effected at conception, between parent and child, substantive cohesion certainly prevails. The two are bound together to form a larger whole. By focusing on the properties of this whole, one stresses a coherence between parent and child, their joint integrality. Mirror to the parent, the child (in the ideal case) sets an example of realized potentiality which the parent himself had been unable to actualize; the child is parent to the adult. In a double sense, this mirroring unfolds: quite literally, with respect to genetically determined makeup; as fulfilling powers resident in the adult, redirecting such of its actualities as are explicitly incorporated in the child.

A peculiar kind of tension prevails between parent and child. On the one hand, the child regressively assimilates its contours to those of the parent; on the other, the child progressively strikes out on its own, experiencing quite unforeseen adventures. A dialectical interplay between these tendencies unfolds. Amid unpredictable beginnings, a new creature strives toward coherence; from a matrix of disintegration, it even shapes new beginnings. Yet, ever again, it reverts to its inchoate origins; it sinks toward decay and dissolution.

Not only does every living being replicate itself. Beyond that, it reflects; and reflection makes its only frank appearance among persons. Moreover, reflection is a kind of replication. However, its propensity toward replication is spiritual rather than natural. And every living creature—though, henceforth, I speak only of persons—etherealizes its own being by reproducing in the domain of spirit what constitutes its substance in the domain of nature. In his every act, a person thrusts himself beyond himself, from within his natural condition, toward an "equivalent" spiritual condition. Ever seeking his own spiritual analogue, he fashions an Imago of his natural makeup. As with replication, in reflection both coherence and integrality prevail. The facets of both Imago and offspring mesh as a viable unity; no intrinsic bifurcation splits that unity. With respect to reflection entailed by the mind–body identity, the manifestations of this self-diversifying unity, when gathered together anew, form a more solid unity, whereupon the entire process recommences. Still, profound tension inheres in the very acts by which a human body thrusts itself out of itself into its own negation, i.e., into a human *non*-body, yet coheres as an integral person. Furthermore, just as in replication the offspring frees itself from its parent in order to initiate a new, autonomous existence, so every mental replica analogously separates itself from its physical "origins" and embarks upon *its* novel adventures. And when I speak of the physical origins of mind, I do not imply a reductionistic account of mind and body. On the contrary, by its very essence, human substance ever strives to transcend its own condition. Germinating within its "naturality," and even negating the natural, is a spirituality which grounds the natural. Only the spirit makes the full integration of the natural possible. Alternatively, the natural grounds the spiritual as the first stage of the very activity whence it springs.

The human body expresses one's tendency to perpetuate oneself as one is, without one's embarking upon the risky vicissitudes of new adventure. It is one's very self, as one embeds oneself in natural processes. For, as body, one emerges only tentatively from the womb of nature and, each time, falls back into nature. On the other hand, mind expresses the person as forward looking, and as daring to envisage such new prospects as, under the perspective of body, are *mere* possibilities, evident in nature, but, under the perspective of mind itself, become substantive potentialities for concrete realization. Were this realization to occur in nature, mind would sink to the status of nature. But for mind to actualize itself, it must both shape an altogether non-natural realm and participate in that realm, a realm which mirrors yet transcends and subsumes the natural.

In replication, a living creature sends forth substantive reproductions of itself, thus opening up new loci for exploration. Extending the sphere of habitation henceforth accessible to the community of which those creatures are members, it perpetuates that community by opening up a world for communication, a realm of human utterance through which the community can effectively combat nature's restrictions. And, once shaped, symbols evolve, and "feel" their way into ever-novel symbolic possibilities. Acquiring new accretions of symbolic elaboration on themes already articulated, they combine with other symbols to constitute altogether new products. Beyond that, they effloresce their latent imagery content as entirely new symbols. Analogously, protoplasm feels *its* way through the very spores which it engenders. Once disconnected from their protoplasmic matrix, the spores themselves adventure forth into new natural domains. And, in general, both replication and reflection potentiate the migratory power of man. Enhancing his capacity to grow and his power to search, they spur his propensity to dwell within ever-more-inclusive cosmic realms.

(*b*) The Locus of Mind

Often it is said that the locus of mental activity is the nervous system: that organ of mind and seat of mental processes. However, only if the nervous system is construed as organically interwoven with other organs can it be so regarded. Even then it is more appropriate to say that the nervous system *mediates* thought, though with this qualification: as mediator, it must function integrally, together with other co-dependent organs, in the context of the entire body. Thus functioning, bodily processes are interwoven as configurations which project themselves toward an altogether new realm: a realm which suffuses the body, and pervades it, hovers about it, and envelops it. Surely, no human body can be construed save reflexively. In dynamic fashion, it never ceases to mirror its relations with its milieu. With incomparably more explicitness than *mere* body (i.e., body devoid of reflexivity), it exhibits the contours of those relations. For, by reflection, the human body draws forth, from within itself, its own latent powers for overtly relating beyond the way it had hitherto, if immanently, related. Projecting onto the natural world a schema of its orientings toward nature, it creates a map which enables one both to search out and to inhabit regions heretofore uninhabitable because they had been but implicitly sensed rather than articulately delineated. In this respect, mind is the veridical locus of utterly novel habitation. For, by his mind, a person projects himself out of his customary locale into marvelously subtle new locales. Through human utterance, the most delicately nuanced of such mappings are shaped.

In brief, mind is omnipresent in body as body is omnipresent in mind. The body aspect of mind draws back from ethereality toward the habitual and earthly, and places mind squarely in nature. The mind aspect of mind (and body) draws both forward into a transfiguration of their own processes toward the spiritual. In consequence, two counter-tendencies interweave to constitute the person: a sublimated thrusting toward spirit and an inertial falling back into nature. And every person centers himself at the juncture of these tendencies. Affirming him as mind from his very center, the person's every act of affirmation manifests itself as body. But what can this "center" be? How do these acts flow from it?

To deal with these questions, I distinguish three "faculties" of mind. Hardly independent activities, these "faculties" are foci in a single, complex system of interlocking processes. More exactly: they constitute the body, in its thinking, willing, and feeling acts, as it affirms, reconstitutes, and reorients itself, and in its various migrations. By these acts, I also refer to sensation, perception, kinesthesia, intuition, and empathy. Here I presume that the *entire* human body is the vehicle of the human mind, and, equivalently, that the human mind manifests itself in multifarious kinds of bodily expression. And from a phenomenologic point of view, I assume the following sketchy connections between mind and body, each based on the supposition that specific bodily organs or regions are associated with particular mental functions.

With respect to thought, its most clearly demarcated locus is the head. With remarkable protectiveness, the cranium encases a brain which, in order to absorb shocks, floats within cerebro-spinal fluid. Held above the commotion of normal life, the earth and its teeming ferment, the head is adapted for surveying the fixed contours of land, sea, and heavens. Appropriately located, sight and hearing provide the initial stimuli whereby a spatio-temporal matrix is conceptualized. By these senses, the self brings the most diverse regions of the universe into immediate proximity with the body. Thereby, the mind is enabled to assign spatio-temporal locations to every point of that manifold. To achieve such assignation, the body so balances its various component parts as to orient it—hence, its bearer—toward the manifold. In this way, one prescinds from one's status as actor in the world. Retrospectively, one experiences the world not as contemporaneous with oneself, but as just passed. Hence, thought carves out laws which express the world's settled and determinate transactions. Projecting an entire manifold of successive spatial moments as spatialized time, thought prescinds from lived time and experiences its own projections as constituting actuality.

In opposition to thought, the will, expressing itself through skeletal musculature, especially that of the limbs, focuses on the future: that which is in process of becoming. In executing the commands of the will, the body reshapes the natural things which surround it. By its movements, the body enables the person actively to present himself to others in his community as, collectively, the community's members explore the terrain of earth, sea, and heaven. And working through the body, the will becomes the organ of physical discovery. It grounds such actions as are required for rearranging natural phenomena. True, in retrospect, nature may be brought under the rubric of law. But, quintessentially, the will is a prospective faculty. It enables man to experience, as concrete actualities, much that has not yet been constrained by law. In this sense, by the will, a person can transgress law, even such natural law as is crystallized in the cognitive processes. And by its forays into the unknown, the will shapes new laws. For it constitutes the active basis for the instinctive apprehension of unrealized natural possibilities as *de facto* achievable, i.e., were the person to act in such and such a manner. As such, the will prescribes directions for plausible searching which might reveal regions of the world as yet inaccessible to such deterministic structures as are imposed by thought. Surely, the will is the mental organ which delineates that which may be; it records passage into the future.

Finally, feeling is mediated by the rhythmic movements of the heart and lungs and of the viscera in general, those organs innervated by the complicated network of the autonomic nervous system. In alternating states of rest and mobility, these rhythmic processes convey a sense of the immediately present. Thus, to arrest breathing is to become acutely aware of tensions resident in a present moment; when one again breathes easily, one becomes gently aware of relaxations resident in this moment. Beyond conveying a vague presentiment of the here and now, feelings also mediate, especially through intuition and empathy, a vivid sense of compresence. Serving as vehicles of emotion, and all its subtle modulations, such organs as allow one rhythmically to move back and forth from one's center to one's periphery, like the abdomen and chest—each composed of interlocking smooth and skeletal musculature—permit a person's veridical present to fulfill itself as a kind of extended duration. By feeling, presence becomes rich with motions, comminglings, transmutations which spread themselves before one as temporalized space. In this sense, feeling stands in opposition to thought, wherein one maps the contours of spatialized time. At the same time, feeling mediates both thought, which pertains to the past, and will, which pertains to the future. Allowing the transitions between the detached motions of thought to flow into the vibrant motions of will, feeling asserts itself as the rhythmic arresting of an instant poised between past and future. And enlarging that instant, it weaves with it both reminiscence and anticipation.

(*c*) Interlocking Mental Acts

Just as these systems or organs—namely, brain, limbs, and viscera—interlock their anatomical structures and enmesh their physiologic functioning, so thought, willing, and feeling themselves interpenetrate and condition one another. Thus, thought is the body working through its specific agent, the brain, to bring itself to fruition as self thrusting itself into spirit, under the perspective of the past; therein, a person might root himself, and take stock of his resources. Through the agency of the limbs, the body brings itself to fruition by forging specific new relationships between it and the rest of nature, likewise a thrusting of self into spirit—but, now, under the perspective of the future. Finally, through the agency of intertwined viscera, the body brings itself to fruition by its own self-thrusting into spirit, under the perspective, however, of the present. In his consummate spiritual status, every person, through cognitive judgments, active stances toward the world, and art, celebrates the manifold potentialities of his body in its acts of potent affirmation.

Every person places himself at the intersection of three centers: thought associated with brain, will with limbs, feeling with viscera. In principle, all such centers pervade the entire body, and potentiate local physiologic processes to shape ever-more-diversified and -comprehensive schemes of mentation. And the integral of these processes, summed over all centers, constitutes a single personal center. Under this perspective a person is a society of prehending occasions which shape themselves into a multitude of patterns. More precisely: as a personal center, he is a complicated manifold of relationships between *relata* eventually associated with the three primary systems. To integrate these *relata*, with diminished stress on the factor of relationship, is to yield body; to integrate these relationships, with diminished stress on the factor of *relatum*, is to yield mind. Moreover, just as the actual body is immeasurably more intricate than what initially presents itself as (mere) body, consisting in patterns of interwoven *relata* nested within *relata*, so mind likewise consists in patterns of relationship layered one upon another, with ever-increasing subtlety of differentiation: each layer interacting with all layers; each layer synergizing all layers—a vast rhythmic complex, which, as a whole, constitutes human spirit. Indeed, a principle of double contextuality prevails. On the one hand, patterned relationships (i.e., mind) provide the context in which *relata* (i.e., body) shape themselves; on the other, patterns of *relata* provide the context in which relationships (i.e., mind) shape themselves. Each context envelops the other. Through their overlappings, interplay, and transfigurations, both contexts jointly constitute the person.

In a broad sense, i.e., as encompassing feeling, will, and thought, reflection specializes the function of replication. For when effectively combined, these modes involve, even in replication, interwoven *Anlagen* of deliberative, volitional, and appetitional factors. Drawing together all one's powers, one sends oneself forth, in the guise of another, or vicariously through another, into realms which, were one left solely to one's solitude, one could not seek out. Analogously, the symbols which mind shapes in reflection, whether they be cognitive, active, or aesthetic, are, in a figurative sense, "sent out" to search. Nevertheless, the searching power of symbols is authentic. Once shaped, and encountered by others, they effloresce *de novo* their latent content. Accordingly, in both reflection and replication, one "objectively immortalizes" oneself in another by depositing one's imprints on the other, imprints which are integrally natural *and* spiritual, that one's inmost being will thenceforth reverberate throughout the cosmos.

The concept of reflection, an essential theme in the topic of integrality, itself a basic ontologic category grounding the person, requires that the remaining categories, and the special themes they entail, be implied. For all such ontologic structures are mutually implicated. None can be sharply delineated without reference to the other. Now I examine these interrelations, focusing on integrality as it is interwoven with power and authenticity.

B • COHERENCE AND REFLECTION

(*a*) Human Essence

Often, I have referred to the person as one who reveals himself in a diversity of aspects, individually diffuse and fragmented yet collectively pointing toward an inner congruence. Since the "outer" is but a mirror of the "inner," this congruence implies a cohesiveness of the aspects themselves; it suggests a certain wholeness or integrality and, as integrated, the luminosity of each to the rhythmic ferment—that potency for becoming or manifesting itself as a given aspect, a potency "within" or "beneath" the aspect. Moreover, every aspect, itself a constellation of traits, is a particular way of being in the world. As such, it is a mode of existence: a standing forth and a self-presenting. In this connection, I distinguish two factors: an integral, coherent existence, implying the possibility of a fragmented, inchoate existence; and an essence the rhythms of which may be intact and appropriately enmeshed, hence potent, or disjoined, hence impotent. Thus I conjoin the ideas of existence and integrality, on the one hand, and essence and potency, on the other. Indeed, essence implies existence. For potency cannot be construed without its complementary actualization; and such actualization is, precisely, existence—i.e., in its many aspects. Potency unactualized, i.e., "pure" essence, is (on my usage) inconceivable. Hence, rather than conceiving degrees of actualization, as though there could be a remainder of unactualized potency (a substance which is no substance at all), I conceive degrees in the coherence of essence (as relative potency or relative impotence) and degrees in the coherence of existence (as relative integrality or relative disintegrality).

Furthermore, just as "essence" implies "potentiality for existence actualized"—namely, existence itself—so existence implies potentiality for relationship actualized—namely, encounter. For to exist is to present an aspect, and to be in the world in the manner of that aspect; and this being in the world implies a world in which to be: an *other* with respect to which one presents oneself and, reciprocally, is object for its presentings, an other against the resistance of which its very contours are defined. By his encounters, wherein "appearances" are realized, and are more or less integral, a person reveals himself *as* appearance; and what he discloses is more or less potent. Correlatively, an encounter wherein each encounterer is both potent and integral is an authentic encounter. A coherent encounter which admits degrees, "authenticity" is that entrusting of the one who is potent and integral to another which denies the autonomy of neither. In both instances, individuality is preserved as an indivisible unity. Whether the self merges with or isolates itself from the other, one's imprints nonetheless perish into the other. By "perish," I mean a deposition of impressions which, while retaining their identity, are nonetheless absorbed into one, thence synthesized into novelty. Herein, a self is constituted which enhances rather than diminishes self-identity.

Thus far I have introduced two triads of ideas, namely, (*a*) essence, existence, and encounter, pertaining to aspects of the *being* of persons, and (*b*) potency, integrality, and authenticity, pertaining to the *coherence* of being. Surely, I cannot speak of mere "being" without presupposing some degree of coherence. Nor can I construe any member of either triad without reference to the remaining members. Complementary elements in being (or the coherence of being), they presuppose one another. A schema for conceptualizing the person requires all factors. Moreover, a being of any mode of coherence is a being in a world, a being with respect to and by virtue of that world, the contours of each defined vis-à-vis those of his complement. Reciprocally, the world is itself an agglomeration of beings, themselves "being" in a world one of the constituents of which is the original being. This complex relationship, wherein neither "being" nor "world" can be understood without the other, can be analyzed in terms of the idea of man as *one who searches*, an idea which in turn will be disclosed as presupposing the notion of "presence"—that relationship wherein a datum is apprehended *as* datum, yet as an experience.

Earlier, I suggested that as a person quests after his own nature what emerges, in that quest, is his very essence as questor. Rhythmically duplicating that essence, he presents his own existence in perspectival self-disclosure. And as he encounters, he perishes into others as, reciprocally, they perish into him. Thereby, he individuates himself, and constitutes a self-identity. In these encounters, the person "reflects" himself to himself. He mirrors the very processes which form him. An endless self-synthesizing, this mirroring is itself a drawing together and an aborbing of the traces of others. In such individuation, he confers upon himself something which is uniquely his own. What he reflects are particular existences manifesting particular essences, existences shaped in particular encounters. In this process, a person constructs a self-image composed of the "reflected appraisals"[1] of others, responses *to* him yet woven *in* him. He unites their subsequent impact with the image he has already constituted.

By essence, man is both an *is* and a *to be.* Formed of layers of reflection, he is, by essence, a reflexive being. When sustained, disciplined, and committed, reflection is a searching, a searching into one's own nature and a searching to disclose how these layers constitute a single individuality. And this searching is part of one's essential nature. Yet no search into oneself can be separated from a search into another. Whatever is revealed about one's own nature *ipso facto* discloses something intrinsic to the other's nature. Self and other cannot radically be disjoined. Each is constituted of "substance" which, by nature, is the substance of the other. And individuation is but the synthesizing of elements common to both into a compound idiosyncratic to each. Correlative and complementary, self-searching and other-searching are equally essential activities. As one forms an image of oneself, so *pari passu* one forms an image of the other.

(*b*) Searching and Trusting

Any quest to disclose what a person essentially is is, at bottom, the constructing of a (universal) image of man: an image created through collating images of self and other as, in meeting after meeting, they are ineluctably built up. Hence, *my* particular quest—namely, the philosophic explication of what, by essence, it means to be a person—is itself a forming of such an image, an image of *myself* in relation to others; and every person, in his essence, is engaged in this activity. For I propose that man *is*, by essence, such a searching creature. His expression of his essence through his existence, and his existing in his encounters—each with its characteristic mode of coherence—constitute a single process; and this process is to be understood by construing man as the locus, substantial and concrete, of searchings the ultimate intent of which is, precisely, to disclose the foundational meaning of his being in the world.

Essentially, the person is an unfolding of specific powers directed, by his decisions and by his destiny, toward particular ends. He is an indivisible process wherein essence-ing, existing, and encountering, are joined, not as temporally distinguishable phases, but as complementary and concurrent aspects of an integral activity. In this process, man searches, and in his searching he reflexively builds images of himself in relation to others, ultimately, the image of his relation to the cosmos itself. To "essence," to exist, and to encounter are, in their wholeness, to meet another in his sheer otherness, to search among his varied aspects, to reflect upon those aspects, to build an image, to contemplate that image, and to absorb it into one's being. The person "bends back" into himself significant traces of what had been encountered. Mirroring the encountered object to himself he (self-absorbed yet responsive to it) contemplates its residues.

Indeed, the activities of reflection and contemplation are, at bottom, one and the same. In reflection, the terminal phase of a process of which contemplation is initial phase, those traces of experience are drawn into the self. Therein assimilated, they solidify the self and make it more coherent. By this I mean, the self coheres by virtue of its reflexive acts. Upon natural rhythms and themes already unfolding are inscribed new variations. The thematic content of an essential ferment is altered. Into this content is woven each reflectively induced image. In a veritable tapestry of rhythm, and of reflection transforming rhythm, the essence of a person is created anew by absorbing into it new existence. Yet his essence remains ever the same, by the primordial potency of its defining themes. A style of life, subject to unpredictable vicissitudes and, in its expressions, forever altering, nonetheless remains essentially unchanged. Though these original contours of a way of being in the world can never be definitively specified, that way is idiosyncratic for each person; it is what confers upon him his specific and unique individuality. From birth to death, a life unfolds as a coherent manifold which, though its components certainly vary, manifests persistent, invariant themes, a typical and inalterable pattern of rhythms.

When I refer to the "image" induced by reflection, I do not mean something exclusively visual or, for that matter, even perceptual. For a complex of elements, more or less lucidly apprehended, constitutes an awareness of a presence as a manifold of many particular foci, some luminous and some nebulous, which hovers about a person and suffuses his being. This presence, of which he may be dimly aware or vividly aware, he depicts to himself as a formulation in some expressive medium: a medium which is visual, aural, or ideational but, in every instance, a compound of factors, sensorily and conceptually heterogeneous, which are either central or peripheral. I do not suggest that a criterion cannot be specified by which intrinsic distinctions between perceptual and ideational factors can be drawn; I claim only that all such factors are woven together as a composite in which many types can be discerned, but no type clearly demarcated as *purely itself*. And when I speak of searching, I mean the assignment, in an "image," of contours, more or less definite, to that presence; its delineation and its articulation as that reflective image-forming which is sustained, disciplined, and committed.

Furthermore, searching involves care, concern, competence, hope—all that is a consistency, a continuity, and a coherence of trust. Indeed, by searching I *mean*, at bottom, an entrusting and a giving up of oneself to whatever befalls one. For he who searches entrusts himself to what lies beyond yet is not so remote that he cannot, in time, come to touch it: a presence which as he awaits it, allowing it *to be* in its natural and inmost rhythms, he feels as closer and closer to him; an attuning of his nature to its nature, and a reconciliation of the opposition between the two, contrariety diminishing while the coherence of each continues to solidify. In this entrusting search, this listening while he empties himself of all distraction, a person is potent and integral; and in his authentic encounters, he manifests his integrity.

By "integrity," I mean not only an indivisible wholeness, as an integer, but also, as an integument, a covering sensitive to touch; hence, in the measure of that sensitivity, as receptive to the still music which flows about. Yet, in each encounter, the rhythms of one's own being and those of the other's being remain firm in their respective individualities. Intact, and even enhanced, these rhythms mesh and, in their way, coalesce, until by the ineluctable finitude of all particular being the perfect moment of a meeting perishes, fading deathlessly into the larger cosmic rhythms, while each who encounters is tragically destined to resume, until chance brings a renewal of meeting, his inwardness and his aloneness. Only a few can, in large measure, break the shell of isolation and constitute themselves unremittingly open to the presences which endlessly haunt. Only those gifted few transform both their solitude and their relatedness from the experience of mere good fortune into a rhythmic ebb and flow wherein neither opposes the other; both, in perfect harmony, are woven into a unitary process; and each being is reconstituted as each participates in a pulsing universal life.

Recurring to my characterization of searching as an entrusting, I stress that, from an empirical point of view, there are many kinds and degrees of trust. Analogously, people search in this way or in that, some more and some less. And, surely, but few seem to conduct an ontologic search. Nor do most appear to entrust themselves in the manner I have outlined. Yet it is only in their "appearances," in their existential nature, that persons neither trust nor search in this fundamental way. From an ontologic point of view, by the *essential* constitution of persons, all search ontologically, and all accordingly trust. These activities are implicit in *every* activity, and constitute its unifying and universalizing matrix. Each particular is an instance of a general; each act manifests and completes the primordial ontologic act, concretizing it at the very moment it illustrates it. Merely to be alive is to trust. When trust, in its least flickering, dies, a person dies. By essence, all are oriented toward clarifying their respective ways of being in the world, their status among their fellows. This self-orienting pervades every particular orienting. Every manifestation of life is an entrusting illumination, in whatever degree or manner, of the self in relation to another self, in its essence, its existence, and its encounters, of the self in its characteristic way of cohering in each modality of its being. Sufficiently developed, this triadic cohering (as potent, integral, and possessing authenticity) constitutes the vitality of life. For to be vital is to flow forth in all one's rhythms, hence (by my definition) to be in a state of trust, and forever to search that one might purify and strengthen that state.

(*c*) Person and Self

By "person" as *locus* of searchings, I mean not a passive matrix, a mere point of departure, or simply a conscious subject counterposed to object as, by essence, wholly other to it. On the contrary, the person is a ferment—rhythmic, dynamic, mobile. He is that entity which can be object to itself; and object not as mere datum to be reflected on but as both generative source of subjectivity and reflective turning of that source on and into itself: source which is both beyond the object, or that which merely resists, and beyond the subject, or that which feels and senses and, indeed, empathically enters into what resists; source which, bathed in mystery, is absolutely concrete, a rhythmic instance of the ebb and flow of the cosmos. As the latter, i.e., as reflective, the person continuously draws forth into (creative) expression his own "contents," themselves the deposition, transmuted and integrated, of innumerable relations; and this expression is absolutely originative and spontaneous. A person is a subject experiencing its *own* subjectivity, yet grasping *itself* as concrete agent, hence "object." Beyond the distinction between subject and object, he nonetheless subsumes this distinction, and may only be conceptualized as now one, then the other, elusive with respect to both yet, in this oscillation, fully each. Embedded in a field of relationships, partly self-engendered and partly a situation which is found, this agent stands forth as unique and self-identical—free, alone, and autonomous. Thus finding himself separate from yet rooted in this field, the person is both a process of "internalizing" the way relationships constitutive of the field and, *a fortiori*, the "image" of their *relata*. "Introject" as well as object and subject, he synthesizes such images into a coherent manifold, a unity amid the diversity of contents. This manifold is, precisely, himself *as* person.

By "self," on the other hand, I shall mean (perhaps departing from customary use) a person qua one who searches—i.e., any *specific* searching, by a person, in the concrete acts in which he searches; and, I assume, every searching, hence every self, is by nature reflexive. A self is thus a person actualizing, in some sphere of expression, his powers to search. In this sense, the person might be construed as a community of selves woven into coherence, each manifesting itself, at various times and in diversified ways, in the life of that person. Moreover a self is fully a self in the measure that it reflects, as it searches, on its activities of searching; and no searching can be unless, at least implicitly, it is reflective searching. Furthermore, every reflective searching is a phenomenologizing, a λόγος (to echo Heidegger) of φανεῖν.[2] It is a gathering-in, a "prehending," of presences—namely, those correlative with the gathering process. By "presence," I mean *prae-esse*—that which stands before one, as distinct from one, and, at any instant, as wholly other to one, though, in the dialectics of dialogue, as interchanging its content with one's own content; yet an "appearance" the discrimination of which as, in principle, an endlessly analyzable matrix of structures is essential to both the unfolding and the actual disclosure of the self who gathers. And every such discrimination points toward what appears as the originative powers of which the appearance is but a particular actualization, hence, but a single perspective. For it is but one way of seeing through, with absolute validity, to the source itself; it is but one mode of illuminating that source in its primordial character yet, paradoxically, achieving this insight within a single style of apprehending, a style peculiar to the circumstances under which the searching is carried out.

C • RHYTHM AND COHERENCE

(*a*) The Unity of the Person

In my foregoing remarks, I stressed the interrelations between the cohering of the manifestations of a person construed as integral agent and his power to reflect upon those manifestations, and, through reflection, to gather them together to constitute ever-new schemes of searching. For integrality, the focal topic of this chapter, entails that kind of quest wherein one gives oneself up to the rhythms of whomever, or whatever, one encounters; a quest wherein one allows one's autochthonous rhythms so to unfold, in the context of the quest, that a veridical unity of body actions and mind actions, a unity which grounds the very possibility of human action, is shaped and borne to fruition. Here, I distinguish two senses of unity, a primordial sense and a consequent sense. Different modalities of mind–body identity and different schemes of coherence, which entail physicomental balancings (hence rhythms) of varying types, are entailed by this distinction. Wherein, I now ask, consists these rhythms by appeal to which one can affirm a substantive identity between mind and body? To deal with this question, I reflect further upon integrality, cognizant that my deliberations must, to illuminate man's wholeness, lead to the categories of potency and authenticity, the topics of my concluding chapters.

Clearly, integrality pertains to a category of experience which is irreducible to such categories as pertain to bodies and minds. Body manifests itself in experience as that which resists, hence thrusts unyieldingly, against one; indeed body hypostatizes these experienced characteristics. Mind refers qualities like thought, mood, imagery, sense; hence, mind hypostatizes these qualities as well. In contrast, integrality expresses an altogether new phenomenon. Very datum within which body and mind are discriminated, it is the source whence they arise. Integrality suggests agency, power, endeavor, a sense of flow and transition, a coming to fruition. Its component data are never resolvable into muscular, kinesthetic, or, for that matter, any other kind of sensation. From *its* standpoint, data of mind and body are mere products. Cut off from the processes whence they issue, they are, when regarded sui generis, its residue, shadowy and insubstantial. But, within the perspective of agency, both body and mind can be discerned as deriving from the same activity.

As I move my limbs, the motion is accompanied by its associated idea. Such an idea need not, of course, be explicitly formulated. The execution of a movement may be more skillful and more informed by intelligence without intellectual formulation, where only its germ as pure feeling is acknowledged. Alternatively, *as* I think, my body itself is animated, though the drama of its movements may be subdued. For I may think with a quiet body as I may move with quiescent thoughts. In both instances, a single action unfolds, an action unitary, directed, and indivisible, whether that action culminates in a mental "entity" or in a physical "entity." For these entities are but states, slices of a process taken somewhere during its unfoldings; and as slices, they are a negation of the very duration within which they accrued. As power, mind and body are identical. In intended action, and there is no hiatus between intention and movement, one experiences this union. It is a *person* who moves and thinks; and his every action is infused with thinking, just as his every thought is but an aspect of action. *While* one is perceiving, one does not experience a dissociation between the act and the thought; the body operant in perceiving is not itself perceived save by another act of perception in which the body, again itself unperceived, is again operant. The seer does not *see* his eyes as "they" see; he *uses* them. Only when he, always an actor, views an action retrospectively does he discern thought and body as detached from him and, therefore, as disparate. *During* my *use* of limbs and mind they are not thinkable as expressing diversified entities; they are felt as a unitary potent source. Only when I detach myself and stand apart, either reflectively or manipulatively, do I experience the products in which I, an integral and indiscerptible process, eventuate as diversified. In the full presence which *is* my existence, I am *one*.

In sum, the traits designated by the ideas of mind and body are abstracted from but a single unity. A unitary being, this entity exhibits the mental and the physical as aspects of one "dynamism," a single focus of action which culminates in bodily structures and movements of which its images and feelings, its sensations and ideas are correlates. Each aspect of this entity mirrors the other aspect, while both reflect an agency of ontologic priority the character of which can be formulated in language peculiarly concrete and persuasive. By "agency," I mean that which, by its intrinsic powers, is activated toward ends it poses for itself; by "dynamism," I mean the specific constellation of factors, inhering in an agent, whereby action is executed. Indeed, words expressing the primordial nature of the person refer to an experience of greater depth, compulsion, and universality than words setting forth the properties of the derivative phenomena, mind and body, as though they were distinctive realms. But how to construct such a language is precisely the difficulty which, thus far, has proven insuperable to philosophers.

(*b*) Given Unity and Achieved Unity

Integrality and indiscerptibility can be conceptualized in another way. Body, and all its extensions and tangible expressions, constitute symbols. They are a flash of the eye, a hand upraised, a breath of song. For by "symbol," I have meant that mind–body unity which binds itself into communion with another unity, so that, in a mutual presenting, meanings are mutually discerned; and, in this communion, past and future are absorbed into an extended immediacy. Inscribed in the present moment, and not disjoined from it, is the "spirit" of which the mind, with its parade of ideas, images, sensations, and feelings, is but one part. As the body of another person moves, an emanation flows from it to me; and in this emanation is contained, as integral with it, something also spiritual. Like a riddle which awaits deciphering, the human body, and all that tangibly issues from it, in music, art, poetry, and technique, are an enigma in which one seeks to discern meaning. At times, this meaning—of the order of the spirit—is luminous, as when Uday Shankar becomes vibrant with dance or a face transfigured by a tragic experience irradiates serenity which blends and subdues the knives of pain. And, at times, the meaning is obscure, as through a glass darkly, we peer into mysterious depths buried in the body symbol.

But when I inspect a *part* of my body, like the brain or an amputated limb, I isolate that part from its vibrant context. This, the scientist must do; he always works, in the deepest sense, *in vitro.* For, then, he inspects the body as mere residue of its expressions, not as that synthesis which is a lucent incarnation of spirit; and when I ponder an idea I, too, extract that idea from the flowing action embedded in and expressed through my body. In neither case do I touch the person in his integrality and his power. But when I encounter the person as an expressive agency who binds into a unified flash of presence the fragments of his moods and impressions, his movements and his gestures, then I am indeed led to declare that mind and body are, as such, abstractions and residues. To speak of these aspects of human existence as in correspondence is proper as long as the basis to which I refer them is the *actual* entity which I encounter, in its wholeness and aliveness. But to declare these *parts* as themselves identical is to negate the very frame, the person himself as potent source, from which they had been extracted as actualizations of the source. In effect, the first two categories of experience—namely, thrust and quality—cannot be experientially grasped if one attends to one's *full* experience without acknowledging the third—namely, agency—of which they are, in reality, but aspects.

The countless details of behavior which I confront in a person constitute, as a veridical fact of my experience, a coherent fabric. To direct attention to this fabric is not, however, to dispel into obscurantism an alleged mind–body problem, but rather to appeal to the most concrete experience of all. The shifting modalities of one's existence do not conceal their source; when fully experienced, they fully reveal it. The congruence of body and mind is a fact of experience—as long, that is, as they are understood as referring to an entity in the full rhythms of its existence: an entity necessarily veiled by the isolating, analytic character of science and, often, of common sense, but an entity which, perhaps, can best be clarified, while informed by what the scientist does discover, by the poet. In particular, poets have succeeded more than scientists in illuminating that fruition of integrality which I here designate integrity, a concept which pertains to *achieved* mind–body unity rather than to its grounding unity.

I have referred to the distinction between a person's given unity, which I designate integrality, and his achieved unity, which I designate integrity. By the former, I mean that compressed set of rhythms which, expressing the deepest commingling of body's vital processes, are associated with mentation in all its phases and modes. Interlocking like a tightly coiled spring, these rhythms are pervaded by reflection. As such, they constitute sheer personal activity in process of its own transformation into concrete manifestations which are more or less coherently ordered among themselves. For as resonances spread throughout the primordial nucleus of germinating rhythmicality, they reverberate with increasing intensity; and they impinge upon and, indeed, metamorphose those organic parts which exhibit a high order of sensitivity, in particular, the nervous system. Mirroring and counter-mirroring each other, these resonances, ceaselessly self-reinforcing, self-canceling, and self-transmuting, are conveyed back and forth as the person, by his very essence, strives to leap out of his own substance toward an utterly transfigured realm. Nature gives way to spirit, though spirit ever returns to a transformed nature.

(*c*) Integration

With gathering momentum at every moment, momentum which endures as passage—the very quantum of lived time—these rhythms uncoil. Spiraling forth into entwined bodily processes which exhibit increasingly subtle nuances, these processes effloresce into tangible expression as concrete symbolic manifestations of their own interiority; and every efflux of such manifestations reveals comminglings of analogous kinds. Ever transparent to their own engendering activity, wherein they never cease to germinate, such processes comprise luminous rhythms which exhibit varying schemes of balance and imbalance. Equilibria form and equilibria shatter; displacements to novel equilibria are shaped. As one brings one's latent powers to fruition, a great living symphony unfolds; and this activity recommences at each immediately succeeding moment. In this context, a perpetual ebb and flow prevails; pulses of vibrancy alternate with quietude.

As the moments succeed one another, each perishing imperceptibly into its successor, a person's orientings vis-à-vis his milieu, which itself undergoes constant alteration, exhibit, in the ideal case, a new, transfigured unity: the unity of achieved integrity. Accordingly, there always prevails a passage from an integral condition, which is primordial and essential, to an *integrated* condition, which may or may not supervene, depending upon how felicitously collaborating influences, which stem from the milieu, shape a general context for a person's life. Integrality is sheer potential: invariant themes which persist unchanged despite dynamic reconstitutings of their component parts. Integration is its actualization, variable arrangements of more or less cohesive manifestations of potency. And integrity implies a certain harmony between the primordial unity, which initiates the stages by which the consequent unity unfolds, and the consequent, which constitutes a highly refined mirror of the primordial: a mirror reflects symbolic efflorescences of powers but latent within bare integrality.

Throughout my Inquiry, I have referred to the person as a meshwork of rhythmic patterns, patterns which unfold as cycles, and epicycles inscribed on cycles; and I have stressed that, as they unfold, these rhythms orchestrate ever-novel schemes of resonance: reverberations which echo through one's entire being, and express how it stands between one and one's milieu. Such reverberations of reflection reshape both self and milieu. Different schemes of coherence prevail with respect to the types of orientations which must be instituted on the ground of these reshapings. Amid myriad complicated processes, an indefeasible unity prevails: the absolute identity of mind and body, an identity so to be construed that, surely with respect to human being, neither mind nor body can be formulated without reference to the other. Each presupposes the other; the very ground of each resides within the other.

NOTES

1. See the index entries for this term in Harry Stack Sullivan, "Conceptions of Modern Psychiatry," in *Collected Works* I (New York: Norton, 1953).
2. *Being and Time*, trans. Macquarrie & Robinson, pp. 51, 58.

20

POWERS POTENTIATED: THE ACTIVITY OF INDIVIDUATION

PREAMBLE

Throughout this book I have, in effect, distinguished given unity, or integrality, from achieved unity, or integrity. Linking these conditions—lying, as it were, within their temporal increment—is a straining and an opening up, a topic I now treat. Here sheer power reigns. By its nature, power potentiates itself from mere expressions of given, essential unity to the ordered sphere of achieved, existential unity. But were such potentiation to fail, its unactualized portion would ramify within one to form a strange interior domain, a domain which would manifest itself as an intricate assemblage of symbols. Either one actively "persons-forth" toward another or one "un-persons" into a depersonified condition. In the latter instance, one reifies oneself, encrusting oneself with masks and with stereotyped roles. And, in general, a dialectical interplay prevails between two tendencies: progressive personing-forth to create a unique individual, and regressive retreat into one's own *persona.*

In this context, one works out one's own identity. But identity is never settled. Product of choices continually made from among varied identifyings, it emerges amid myriad personal encounters. Inevitably, such choice is restrictive. For although every choice opens up novel possibilities for self-development, each truncates certain aspects of what one might have been. Hence, governing all personing-forth is a complementarity of exuberant advance and tragic decline. Herein lies the ground for the lamentation and celebration which quality every instance of compresence, which in turn birth such phases of wisdom as unfold to constitute a person's authenticity. Now new transfigurations arise which reveal an altogether new realm for personal dwelling, the transcendental. To conceptualize such rhythms of quest and encounter as uncoil toward human consummation, I must first take up the theme of power as, owing to human finitude, only partially actualizable, and I must examine the consequences of this fact for human ontology.

A • PERSONING-FORTH AS CONSUMMATE PERSONHOOD

(*a*) Possibility

Personing-forth as speech, song, and dance is grounded in a human power which manifests itself in the correlations of mind with body. Intermediate phase of an integral process, such power is preceded, first, by mere possibility, then by potentiality, and succeeded, first, by virtual actuality, then by consummate actuality; and these phases constitute the activity of personing-forth as it flows from germ to fruition. Focal expressions of personhood, song and speech both manifest and are inscribed on mind, whereas dance both manifests and is inscribed on body.

But neither song nor dance can subsist alone. Now figure, now ground, each both presupposes and is correlated with the other. Shaping an indivisible whole, they jointly reveal a texture by which the intimate bond between mind and body articulates itself in its concrete, characteristic forms. Mere foci in a substantive continuum, the mental and the physical create an intricate if indiscerptible fabric of rhythmic unfoldings, rhythms of levitation and gravitation.

Human rhythms unfold in a multitude of ways. Enmeshing, combining, and commingling to form the most varied patterns, they manifest themselves through thought, action, volition, appetition, feeling, and bodily movements both gross and fine. Equally, pulsing motions characterize each such channel of expression, motions which, when coordinated and integrated, constitute the overall rhythms of personhood; and myriad subtler channels lie in the interstices of those conventional channels which, likewise, exhibit pulsing motions. By this imagery, one may distinguish, as for the vibrating string, such variables as frequency, amplitude, and quality. With respect to frequency, the range of vibratory movement corresponds to a spectrum on which mind and body are loci; with respect to amplitude, each vibration, whether it tends toward minimum volume or maximum volume, corresponds to emergings from possibility to actuality; with respect to quality, different vibratory "shapes" are associated with varying textural compositions of mind (like thought or feeling, and subtle gradations between thought and feeling) and body (like compacted tissue and differentiated tissue, or like organ and cell aggregations). Just as the composition of a vibrating string determines, when it is plucked, the quality of emitted sound, so the specific makeup of a particular aspect of a person expresses the composition of his style of personing-forth: a style manifested as subtle overtones and undertones inscribed on its principal vibrations.

Personing-forth is an immensely complicated texture of unfoldings and interweavings, a fabric which exhibits different kinds of expression and varying degrees of ornamentation on basic themes, whether temporal invariants pertaining to "length" or spatial invariants pertaining to "thickness." In both instances, inner coherence, or *integrity*, prevails with respect to this texture. For rhythms of personing-forth exhibit textural consistency, a cohesiveness of textural weave. As mere possibility of surging into explicit actuality, this texture, concretely embodied in one's germ plasm, comprises an interplay of strivings and pulsings, all ineffably inscribed upon and clothed in the garb of human protoplasm. Indeed, the earliest gropings toward nutriment or retreatings from toxicity, acts associated with primitive monocellular organisms, catalyze ever-more-subtle differentiation and refinement of detail: possibility transforming itself into actuality.

Inhering within possibility, the initial phase of personing-forth, the power of self-catalysis is transmuted, first, into self-potentiation and, then, into self-activation, toward concrete actualization. Within this power resides the germ of reflexivity, very essence of human integrality. To shape mere possibility into actuality, a "substance," or *quasi*-substance, must stand in active relationship to itself: abstract self-relatedness, to be sure, yet self-relatedness which is particular and individual. When the appropriate milieu is present, such self-relatedness originates a process of development. "Possibility" suggests openness, openness to both curtailment and enhancement. Grounding the movement toward actuality, it is the initial germ whence springs actuality. Yet, actuality, the end to be achieved, also grounds possibility. For possibility is impoverished and barely existent, a mere phantasmagoria, whereas actuality is a culmination, an end which immanently, though with increasing explicitness, directs the movement.

Since possibility thus entails germinal reflexivity, one must distinguish logical possibility, or conceivability, from empirical or substantive possibility. Though logically conceivable, certain possibilities are empirically impossible: e.g., logically, a man may become an antelope but such transformation is empirically inconceivable. And empirical impossibility is always defined with respect to a context, a context of information which itself is always expanding to embrace what hitherto were radically implausible, if logical, possibilities. With respect to any phenomenon, an indefinite range of possibilities is substantively excluded from realization, in particular, as personing-forth unfolds. For such possibilities to be excluded and, *a fortiori*, all others to be included, one must postulate for every process of self-individuation, a dynamic principle of exclusion, a principle which effectively prescribes what, at each stage, *cannot* be. For example, in embryogenesis, certain structures, if destroyed, can regenerate, whereas other structures, were their "natural" development aborted, would evolve along different lines from those associated with normal growth. Indeed, factors which promote either regeneration or developmental shifts prevail at precisely delineated points in the embryogenetic unfolding, while immediately prior or subsequent to such points the requisite developmental lineage will not unfold. In such cases, specific genetic factors either allow or proscribe, and in principle determine the contours of, the appropriate structural transformations.

Information contained in a person's genetic makeup informs his own development with the possible forms which he may legitimately assume and still remain human. Such information flows continually from one region of the person to another, and from one moment of his growth to another. In consequence, the forms which one may acquire undergo shifts. Once a form is imprinted in one, a specifically different course of development will ensue. For, associated with each firmly implanted form is an inertial tendency to perdure, a tendency which, insofar as it is consummated, will bring about the exclusion of what otherwise might have been incorporated into one's ongoing development. Thus, ever-fewer formative possibilities come to be realized. Yet the actuality which results from such incorporation becomes ever-richer, and precisely *these* forms, and now *those*, acquire concrete exemplification. At the same time, every form will also remold the milieu in which a process is embedded. As a result, the milieu comes to conform to the forms of the very processes which it envelops. And new forms are continuously elicited for exemplification by that milieu; an alternation of forms prevails between developing person and analogously developing milieu —namely, his habitat. Now, a dynamic process of co-adaptation supervenes, a process so constituted that forms previously but latently operative within the co-adapted members are drawn into active, reciprocal, and collaborative self-determination.

Accordingly, the category of substantive possibility entails two consequences. On the one hand, a proto-person (i.e., his germinating protoplasmic matrix) stands in self-catalyzing relatedness to itself, allowing to be drawn forth from its own substance such forms as never cease to gestate in a manner relevant to its subsequent development toward full personhood. On the other, a person–milieu relatedness prevails; correlated dynamisms (of person and milieu) allow for mutually fructifying interchanges and, indeed, veridical transubstantiations of such forms as are relevant to both person and milieu. What a person becomes results from dialectical interplay between the relevant dynamisms. Such interplay is concretely embodied in every stage of human development. By the joint working of those dynamisms, what is possible at one developmental stage becomes impossible at another, and conversely. Within this context, the course of development is mapped out *in concreto*. Though the detailed contours of human growth is delineated in my *Metamorphosis*, I trace here certain general implications for human ontology of such possibility–impossibility schemata as quality man's existence.

(*b*) Potentiality

Further to clarify "substantive possibility," I introduce, as complementary category, *potentiality*. For to pose possibility as abstractly realizable, one must pose potentiality as concretely realizable. Since potentiality is germinal self-actualization, whereas substantive possibility is mere germinal possibility for self-actualization, an altogether new dialectic now unfolds. Its general contours can be schematically represented. In my subsequent discussion, the diagrams on page 442 will serve as paradigms.

From the standpoint of possibility, the self relates to itself in an amorphous way. Envisaging limitless directions for its own growth, it reflects into itself the world's infinite reaches, recesses which, were the self capable of searching without restraint, it *would* explore, probe, and appropriate. In mere possibility one dwells entirely with one's own inwardness. Personing-forth into a dream-like realm, one is suffused with tints of what could have been and what might yet be. With abandon, one departs from established fact, save insofar as fact constitutes a boundary which demarcates the logically possible from the substantively possible: a limit marking off the barely imaginable from the spontaneously imaginable. Floating, as it were, above reality, one allows a dance of imagery to overtake one. Now, one hovers close to the border between the abstractly conceivable and the concretely conceivable. By the concretely conceivable, I mean all that is bounded by limits set by nature or by one's affinities to nature, affinities grounded in the very germ of embryogenesis. Losing oneself in a past which had unfolded, layer by layer, and converged upon a particular moment of personhood, one relates to what one was, and might have become, by playing imaginationally with possibilities. Thereupon, one envelops oneself in an illusory web by which one (illicitly) projects into one's own future the trajectory of a now perished past.

The Full Dialectic of Concrescent Process

I · Topography of Personing-Forth

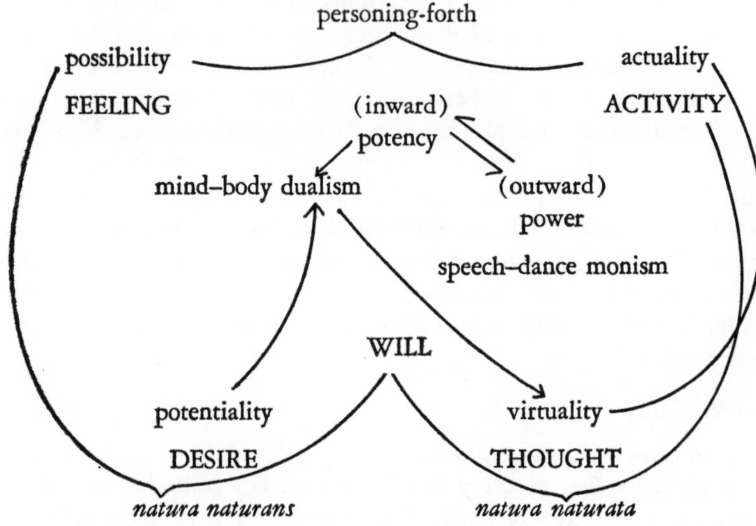

transaction→interaction→self-action→interaction→transaction

(undifferentiated) essence (differentiated) existence

II · Dynamics of Personing-Forth

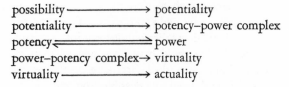

possibility ——→ potentiality
potentiality ——→ potency–power complex
potency ⇄ power
power–potency complex→ virtuality
virtuality ——→ actuality

III · Economics of Personing-Forth

integrality→integrity

(with respect to mind and body) (with respect to speech and dance)

bare essence concrete existence

Yet, by reflectively relating to, and even by identifying himself with, sheer empirical possibility, the person conjures up whole realms of fantasy with respect to which, should he allow his own passage toward personhood to be without constraint, certain definite laws emerge to govern image combination, elaboration, transposition, and resolution into new elements; as setting new limits; and as compressing the imagination into a less gossamer but still kaleidoscopic realm. Therein, he confronts, in self-relatedness to its unique unfoldings, an entirely new realm, enclosed in and conditioned by the old. And as he advances into this realm, experiencing its constraints and prescriptions, he feels its richness to be more substantial than the elusive, evanescent, and transient antecedent realm. The latter perdures in its own concreteness; and as a more durable realm emerges, it is experienced as grounding the diffuse, fragmented, and inchoate realm which preceded it. Now one dwells in oneself amid one's concrete potentialities. For potentiality stands to possibility as a *directed force* working in accordance with its own laws, stands to mere inchoate influences, a force however which one has not yet fully taken under control. Archetypal for humankind, this new force is so constituted that, should one submit, it will extricate one from illusion. Now one passes from the jurisdiction of a "pleasure principle" toward the dim workings of a "reality principle." First under the sway of unrestricted fantasy, one now passes to a habitat which is neither amorphous nor malleable but structure, lawful, and indeterminate. Though lawful, this realm is still infused with imaginational factors drawn from sheer illusion, whereas imagination had been pervaded by the constraints which alone will permit creation of sharply delineated imagery. New combinations and refinements derive from the "pressions" which reshape possibility, and convert it, by infusing it with novelty, into potentiality: a domain of compressings, impressings, repressings, and expressings.

Now one finds one's identity by identifying neither with free, spontaneous, amorphous imagination nor with lawful, necessary archetypality. On the contrary, one achieves self-definition by immersing oneself in an alternating imagination and archetypality. At worst, this experience entails oscillation between a nebulous narcissism and a dwelling amid encrusted social customs. At best, the interaction of privacy with publicality fructify every level of human being. In this sense, man experiences a profound tension between the natural and the social. In tension, the social becomes naturalized; and the natural, socialized; and man expresses tension through his symbols, symbols rendered in dream and woven into every aesthetic experience.

(*c*) Power

Possibility is directionless. Mere supposition, it is ungrounded, free-floating, bare modality; and, in the end, it is ineffectual, impoverished, and anarchic. But as sheer contingency, potentiality is an internal factuality which has not yet been drawn into full objectivity as encounterable events and processes. Whereas mere random quality characterizes possibility, potentiality manifests itself first as resistance.

And, together, quality and resistance give birth to power. Manifesting the spontaneity of potentiality, power is, at once, self-directed, self-affirming, self-renouncing, self-transforming, self-articulating, self-resolving, self-creating, self-engendering, and self-discovering. As such, power suggests reflexivity on different levels of consciousness. And expressing the relationship between man as possessing integrality and man as attaining integrity, it depicts his quest to transubstantiate mere fragmentation into veridical coherence. An entirely new unfolding of man's intrinsic resources, power reveals his crises and complementarities, the interweavings of his doubts and certitudes; it allows his symbols and rhythms to emerge, and, through human encounter, the double labyrinth of self and world to shape a single overarching labyrinth.

As sheer energy, power betokens the human resolve to create anew both self and world. Uniting them, it subsumes, without cancellation, both possibility and potentiality. Grounded in potency, the inner sense of power, power constitutes the outward manifestation of potency. Still, inner is absorbed into outer, while outer is drawn back toward inner. Each allows the other to be; yet each reconstitutes the other. Together, they bear to fruition that moment of personing-forth whereby *natura naturans*, human essence, both declares and reveals itself, preparatory to its supercession in the existential manifestations of human essence: *natura naturata*, the complementary moment of personing-forth.

Just as possibility is associated with quality and potentiality with resistance, so power and its correlated potency are associated with relationship. As relationship, both power and potency subsume *relata*, each a quality; and by mediating such qualities, it gives rise to the resistance of each vis-à-vis the other. Both are caught up in a dynamic surge toward full self-expression in actuality. Now, inner and outer, a distinction inhering in the very difference between potency and power, disappear, and each condition exchanges its content with the other. A new level of existence is achieved. For, in its diminished way, power *is* actual. A *directed* ferment, the components of any power are drawn into full living presence to cohere as virtuality. As such, one verges upon but does not quite attain to actuality; one only strains toward the real. With respect to virtuality, power (or, its inner equivalent, potency), originally construed as relationship, now acquires the character of quality, but quality which is more subtle than in its original condition. Virtuality becomes a new, more refined mode of resistance: that which, associated with inertial propulsion toward consummate actuality, is the penultimate moment prior to concrescence. In virtuality, numberless strands flow together and come to confluence. Reflexively related to these strands, the person experiences his self-identity as increasingly solidified. He has attached himself, as it were, to the momentum of the cohesive manifold of self-directed energies, energies which, by that attachment, are not entirely self-directed, but, equally, are directed by oneself. By standing against its opposition, power here achieves its own fruition, virtuality: *an about to be born*—issue, fruit, and reward of energetic surgings, yet penultimate state prior to full actualization.

Power mediates the transformation of possibility, via potentiality and virtuality, to actuality; and every person identifies himself with his power. Experiencing its transfigured quality as synthesis of the undifferentiated quality of mere possibility with the primordial resistance of his potentialities, he discerns transfigured quality as a diversified, all-pervasive condition. For, in power, one experiences oneself as alive with energies, energies which drive one hither and thither without yet setting a specific direction, a definite, explicit purpose for one's efforts. Totally stirring a person, a sheer sense of powerful vitality enables him to achieve what he now experiences to be self-sufficient self-identity. Identifying himself with his experience, he feels his own *I* as pulsatingly co-extensive with the powers associated with the execution of all acts envisaged by his *I*. Fragmented and weak, the realm of illusion and fantasy (namely, possibility), mediated by the felt resistances of potentiality, issues in power. As mere feeling, vague premonition, and a reaching out to take in, possibility gives way to potentiality which, in turn, is linked to appetition, a sense of yearning and a desire to convert feeling into more durable shape. Finally, power is correlative with will: the sense of a capacity to act and the discernment of the specific acts which that capacity allows. Accordingly, the *natura naturans* of the "essential" phase of personing-forth is associated with the threefold schema of penumbral feeling, desire, and will.

As soon as power is executed, it presses toward its consummate expression as action: a transactional working out of such specific acts as implicate both person and world. Mediating will associated with power, will which recapitulates, though on a higher plane, primordial feeling associated with mere possibility, is thought. *Terminus a quo* of essence, the phase of *natura naturata*, discernment, envisagement of contours, and mappings of new terrains for exploration culminate, via a mediating virtuality, in action, *terminus ad quem* of existence. Now the mind actively rehearses what it will subsequently execute; it frames a prospectus of action, a prospectus involving less than action but more than reflection. Whereas power and potency, recapitulating possibility, unfold through a self-action which, entailing private reflective acts, manifests the will, virtuality entails those interactions which manifest true thinking. Jointly, will and thinking fashion a common matrix which, incorporating each, eventuates in something richer than either. For actuality, the τέλος of the process, is passionate thinking-and-willing incarnate. By this activity, both self-action and interaction transcend themselves as transaction. Now one shapes a more diversified labyrinth of new depths: depths which may be plumbed and depths which elude human search.

To person-forth is to implicate all the foregoing phases. It is to pass through mere immediacy, bare reflection, and image-less possibility to image-full possibility, thence toward the syntheses whereby a mere receptacle of content, involving boundless multiplicity and sheer indetermination, is transfigured into an *actual* fabric of contrasts, complementaries, tensions, and unfoldings. Through the contingencies of power, this transition is effected: a restlessness in which inner and outer, power and potency, now interconvertible, provide the dynamism for mediation. As soon as potency is posited, power becomes operative. On the other hand, actuality is *self*-subsistent action. By such affirmation—namely, the birthing of new possibilities and the avoidance of narcissism—the entire process of personing-forth can recommence. Herein consists consummate personhood: the interweavings of song, speech, and dance which replace the abstract categories of mind and body, a division relevant only to earlier phases. With respect to potency, the inner aspect of power, mind and body can be regarded as active modes; with respect to power, the exteriorization of potency, mind and body are already transformed into their energetic equivalents, song, speech, and dance.

In brief, the potency–power plexus expresses the fusion of free imagination—namely, possibility—with lawful propensity—namely, potentiality. In self-exteriorizing acts, both possibility and potentiality exhibit latency, as inward component, and, as outward component, the articulating of latency. And the joining of possibility and potentiality to shape a new factor itself partakes of interiority—namely, potency—and exteriority—namely, power. For power, even more than for potency, abstract and concrete are inextricably united. The product of this union is no mere passive condition. On the contrary, the union itself comprises both a *proneness* to surge forth and a *de facto* surging forth. Complementary, correlative, and mutually intensifying, neither state, in this dynamic interplay, can *be* without the other. Though particular and individual, this fusion of abstract and concrete expresses the person as he *virtually* is. Prior to one's becoming one's own consummate actuality, in which reflective act and spontaneous being are no longer disjoined, one is poised like a tensely held arrow on a tautly drawn bow; one is at the penultimate instant just prior to one's bursting into vibrant actuality. Once consummated, a person's full existentiality sweeps over and completely absorbs his very essentiality. Just as fusion of inner and outer constitutes virtuality, and such fusion mediates immediate passage into actuality, so actuality itself mediates the endless orchestrations, in their intricate counterpoint of inner and outer, as one level transfigures itself into a higher; and each level absorbs antecedent levels, yet each goes beyond, in ever-more-exuberant song and dance.

In this culminating phase, a person's reflexive relationship with himself is fully realized through his own actual self-presentations. His very essentiality, as potency-in-act-of-power, becomes, as he progresses from mere possibility through virtuality to actuality, identical with his very existentiality. In his every motion, his reflexive character now luminously reveals itself. By a veritable dance of gesture, he discloses his inwardness. Indeed, inner and outer so interpenetrate as to be indistinguishable. Irreducibly united, both a person's essence (his simple being) and his existence (his becoming) are subsumed in the transparency of each actual moment of his symbolic self-presentation. Now the very particularity of his union of abstract with concrete is transmuted into veridical universality.

No longer can essence be separated from its primordial potency, or existence from *its* primordial power. On the contrary, an essential power to stand forth is precisely equivalent to the standing forth itself. All faculties—feeling, desiring, willing, thinking, and acting—are sublated in a simple, indiscerptible presenting of outer through inner and of inner within outer. Only through full exemplification, by every unique actuality, of the totality of substance, which is spirit incarnate, can true universality be attained. Neither can the particular be dissociated from the universal, nor the universal fail to comprehend the particular. All facets of one's being are so orchestrated that contingency (or externality) becomes identical with reflexivity (or internality): a single invariant theme embraces endless variety; each inscribed variation is absolutely necessary. Un–self-consciously, the person now resolutely participates in all relevant schemes of compresence.

Inexorable necessity reigns. All parts of a person cohere as they give birth to rich actualities which had hitherto lain dormant in his as yet unfulfilled being. Reciprocal affirmations and mutual perishings ground the perfections of harmony which now prevail within him. Living his identifyings, and possessing a durable sense of his own *I* as identical with his entire personhood, he attains full self-identity: the power to orchestrate into a unitary complexus those novel facets of human existence which, from time to time, emerge into the ken of his wholly articulated being. At last, dwelling in his own actuality, every person can fully affirm spirit as, in its totality, it dwells in him. In consequence, he can achieve liberation from finitude, egoism, mere subjectivity, a sense of restrictive boundedness. Freely grasping self and other as mutually implicated, he is caught up in joyous participation, though perforce, by time's ravages, he must tragically fall away from exuberance.

B • SYMBOLIC PRESENCE: THE RAMIFYING OF UNACTUALIZED POWER

(*a*) Limits

Every instance of concrete actuality perishes; tragedy always supervenes. Ever again, man falls from the grace of wholeness toward new fragmentation. In arduous passage from mere possibility, he attains actuality. But under ever-novel guises, he reverts to his origins. Save moment by moment, whether brief or prolonged, he cannot sustain total aliveness, the vibrancy of consummate personhood. Were that condition to prevail, he would perish from overwhelming cosmic pulsings. Quite literally, the world's reverberations would saturate him. Celebrations flow and celebrations ebb. Fully interpreted existence and authentic self-declaration give way to lamentation. Once more man is enveloped by the fragments of which he was earlier constituted, fragments themselves beguiling and fascinating. Against fragmentation, he must fight to maintain his very self-identity, lest he dissolve into mere memorabilia of his own past, incapable of receiving the full impact of compresence, the absolute reciprocity of mutual attunement. Falling away from self-identity, he adverts to a matrix of identifyings. And, as he sinks to his own grounding state, he experiences anguish, a *Sein zum Todes.*[1] Through human symbols, this counterpoint of advance and retreat discloses itself; and symbols ramify in strange and novel forms, forms which, in every instance, express unactualized power: power hovering on the verge of actualization; power moving toward virtuality and falling toward potentiality; power potentiating itself as actuality or depotentiating itself as possibility.

Cries of anguish pierce the cosmos. Every creature, especially man, presses against his boundaries, seeking melodiously to join his solitary existence with the world and, thereby, to shape for itself durable solidarity. Yet no matter how fervently one strains one's limits, one must risk and renounce and sacrifice. Neither Dante's *amor* nor Spinoza's *blessedness* can endure without taint of imperfection. At the penultimate moment of attainable perfection, all felt imperfection gives rise to lamentation. In myriad ways, the symbols of celebration and lamentation ramify as human power partly actualizes itself, and partly fails. To avoid tragic anguish, an illusory realm is shaped, a realm which, in the end, is of human bondage. In vain, every person endeavors to perpetuate his own spiritual integrity. Neither wealth nor fame, neither power nor lust, can afford more than momentary respite from the tantalizing deceptions of a hoped-for immortality. Again and again, one confronts one's finitude, and one laments. With Job, one cries out in lament; one seeks to immortalize oneself to evade lament; one creates angels, but one steps back in terror at their remoteness. For the beauty which one perceives is awesome; and it is frightening. With Rilke, one exclaims:

> Who, if I cried, would hear me among the angelic
> orders? And even if one of them suddenly
> pressed me against his heart, I should fade in the strength of his
> stronger existence. For Beauty's nothing
> but beginning of Terror we're still just able to bear,
> and why we adore it so is because it serenely
> disdains to destroy us. Each single angel is terrible.[2]

When I envisage an ideal actuality which I might truly live, and then perceive the discrepancy between the ideal and what I really am, I am horrified by my pain in contemplating the disparity. Envisaging a perfection remote and unattainable, so that even to aspire toward it threatens to crush me, I evitably magnify its contrasts with my own imperfections. Still, I must somehow reconcile myself to imperfection, and be content to strive toward the ideal, even though my efforts will, in the end, be futile. In consequence, it is the *passage toward* which exhilarates me rather than the condition of *being in.* For as I pass from a state of lesser perfection to a state of greater perfection, I rejoice in my perceived freedom to attune myself more harmoniously with the cosmic order. But as I pass from a state of greater perfection to a state of lesser perfection, I lament the imbalances which thereupon sweep over me. And vicissitudes of lamentation and celebration, rather than a dwelling in one or the other condition, give rise to such personal symbols as allow me to represent those vicissitudes, hence to objectify and even to reduce them, substituting a kind of reflective equanimity.

(*b*) Joinings and Separatings

Wherein consist these healing symbols? How do they manifest the ramifying of unactualized power? By gesture, by inflection, by posture, by physiognomy, by art, by science, by religion, and by philosophy, I present to the entire world, both personal and non-personal, my struggles, my hopes, my disappointments, my joys, my sorrows: all that, by the diminishing circumstances of my life, I truly am. On the lines of my face, the tilt of my hand, the stoop of my shoulder, the hesitancy of my gait, I manifest my living reality. Each vicissitude registers itself durably and indelibly. And once a single sign of unfulfilled power physically perpetuates itself, a subterranean process is set in motion which affects my very spirit, a process whereby every symptom of failure engenders new symptoms. For the momentum associated with all human symbols imparts itself to new layers of symbolism, and thence to the entire matrix of symbols which human being comprises; and I find myself enveloped by, and permeated with, constrictions on my powers even beyond the restraints originally imposed. Tragedy is inexorably imprinted into a person's every act; and the ecstatic overcomings of tragedy superimposes on his symbols new symbolic laminae which intermingle with penumbral symbols to contour his very being, as he passes back and forth, in a kind of dialectic, from celebration to lamentation.

If by symbol one means a joining together of seemingly disparate parts to constitute a new unity, a mosaic of coherently ordered aspects, which, at the same time, reveals the spiritual through the medium of the physical, with which it forms a complemental, correlative whole, and, finally, links persons through authentic encounters between the integrity of one and the integrity of the other, then symbols constitute the veridical consummation of powers fully actualized. On the other hand, should powers be flawed, and their potentiation fail to bring them to fruition, the symbols to which they give birth bear with them analogous flaws; and such symbols, following etymologic usage previously suggested, might more appropriately be designated *dia-bols*, i.e., that which tears asunder. For, in the latter case, symbols but defectively join the parts of a person to integral unity, obtusely and circuitously disclose the spiritual as inscribed within the physical, and inhibit full interpersonal relationship by degrading the integrities of those who encounter.

When I speak of the ramifying of unactualized power, I am elliptically referring, not to *sym*bolic consummation of presence, but to *dia*bolic diminution of presence. No matter how saintly and pure, and without guile, deceit, pretense, or murkiness of character, no matter how exemplary a human life might be, by the finitude of man, and by the fact that the full power of no finite being can be poured without reserve into his own actualization, every person suffers from the debilities of "diabolism," no matter how subtly constituted or minimally tainted that person might be. And no matter how potent, integrative, and authentic symbols might be, diabols are ineluctably woven with them. For each human being is a composite of luminous symbols and opaque diabols. And just as symbols are empowered so to spread, combine, and reinforce one another as to induce coherence, clarity, and the simply etched lineaments of his being, so diabols, by default, tend toward intricacy, fragmentation, and obscurantism. An altogether new dialectic unfolds to constitute human essence and human existence. In it, by essence one thrusts oneself, reflectively and self-consciously, toward an existence which, in its consummate shape, is pervaded by spontaneous un–self-consciousness. And always, human symbols interplay with human diabols.

(*c*) Fragmentings

By the resistance which each affords the other, symbols and diabols constitute a manifold of tensions. And by the patterns of tensings associated with different combinations of such tensions, the energies of a human life are either promoted or diminished. Because of their parasitical dependence on symbols, diabols so constrict symbols that, drawing content from symbols, they wildly replicate. Like carcinogenic mutants, they assume myriad bizarre forms, forms so constituted that, as they cling to symbols, they distort them, and impede symbolic integration, forms which are barnacle-like growths on symbols. Pervading the synchronous motions of a person of unimpeachable character, such growths permit a sudden grotesquery to appear: a destructive impulse, a jarring incongruity which, eccentric to him, utterly fails to reinforce his otherwise striking centricity of intent, purpose, and action.

Accordingly, woven with the harmonies of every fulfilled human existence are weirdly aberrant propensities. To ignore this inherent pathology is to mythify man, and to identify him more with angels than with humans. And it is only by humanizing man that one can empathically lament with him. For all human flaws are one's own flaws, whatever idiosyncratic forms they assume. Likewise, one's own flaws are mankind's flaws. The human condition evokes compassion; and we all partake of the lament. For the "bells toll for each man alike."[3] By joining our imperfection to human imperfection, we convert lament into a pathos-tempered celebration of shared human frailty. Together, we embark, as each of us must, on an unknown journey. Fraught with trepidation, remorse, and trembling, we haltingly, imperfectly, tentatively, and hesitantly, and always so timidly, mark our routes, each unique, but all, after all, small excursions along a single route: the uncertain, unpromised route of humankind.

C • UNIQUENESS, INDIVIDUALITY, AND PERSONAL IDENTITY[4]

(*a*) Ontology and Psychoanalysis

As much by failure to actualize powers as by consummation of powers, one stamps upon oneself one's uniqueness, individuality, and personal identity. Inscribed on the lineaments of a person's entire being are the vicissitudes of his life, his anguish and his joy. Every experience leaves its trace. And, so long as one lives, no trace can be obliterated. Though one may transcend the specific agonies which have overtaken one—often, by one's own chosen acts—the record of overcoming every anguished detail durably imprints itself into those lineaments. However one might have lightened one's suffering, no ingredient of suffering can be negated. Despite the perishing of a person's past into his present, his past endures as an ineradicable heritage which both enhances him and diminishes him. Ramifying symbols of unactualized power envelop each act by which one presents oneself to another; hence, personal compresence is ineluctably affected by those symbols. Such symbols (which I have designated diabols) dialectically interplay with the *authentic* symbols of actualized power to shape an altogether unique person. And though every person is a living exemplification of the ontologic categories I have set forth here, each inscribes idiosyncratic variations.

Singularly among the human sciences, psychoanalysis illuminates man as irreducibly unique. By "psychoanalysis," I mean, as before, not so much Freud's theory or method of psychotherapy as any approach which aims at intensive probing of the personality and radical change toward maturity. On this broad usage, the primary datum of psychoanalysis *is* the person; its primary activity is to understand him in the richness of his individuality. Though I have not been concerned with this discipline here, save insofar as its grounding notions (e.g., the Unconscious) might contribute to human ontology, I must note that, when construed as ancillary to philosophy, psychoanalysis tacitly proposes similar categories but categories which are *practically* interpreted. It concretely applies precisely what human ontology suggests, in generalized, systematic, and theoretical formulation. Throughout *Choros*, I have alluded to psychoanalysis, though with little explicit reference, and I have treated such aspects of its datum and activity as can be clarified by philosophic search. Seeking to delineate philosophic categories pertinent for conceptualizing man's integrity, I now stress that among the disciplines illuminating human being psychoanalysis is unique with respect to the plurality of its methodologies and the concreteness of its objective. I say "methodologies," rather than simply "methods," for psychoanalysis attains its end by using approaches peculiar to various modes of inquiry. Like any science of man seeking to explain his genesis, traits, and potentialities, it isolates certain aspects from the totality of his behavior, hypostatizing these aspects—e.g., mind, character, personality, self—as entities sui generis. As such, the reactions of their constituent properties to systematically varied experimental conditions are codified, generalized, and conceptualized as scientific theories. But psychoanalysis is not only, or even primarily, a science. It is more like history, which strives at understanding a *particular* individual in the constellation of his motives, the unfolding of his powers, the nexus of his relationships; it is more like ethics, which prescribes (though its ultimate values may be unannounced) the criteria by which a life can be adjudged good or bad, an action approved or condemned as incompatible with the good life; and it is—most of all—like art, which shapes an existence, by these criteria and within the limits of medium and technique, into something new and more valuable. These criteria do not entail rules of conduct which ought, deliberately or unwittingly, to be imposed on a person. Nor need they be explicitly formulated. Rather, inherent in the concept of the psychoanalyst as one who exercises rational authority to the end that a "patient" might henceforth be his own authority (i.e., formulate out of his now authentically received experience his own standards of behavior) are both an ethical commitment and a premiss about the nature of man, proposing, namely, the ultimate competency of each to shape for himself, if unencumbered by notable handicap, a life which, in the long run, is in his own "true" best interest and not, indeed, inconsistent with the best interests of all. Some psychoanalysts, of course, do have values incompatible with the method to which they overtly subscribe and, hence, approaches disruptive of therapy.

Though, accordingly, the instrument by which psychoanalysis seeks to attain its aim presupposes general laws, the focus of psychoanalysis is to understand and to change, in some determinate and thoroughgoing way, a single person. Its central aim has as its two interdependent moments: to grasp a unique, unrepeatable, inestimable life drama in the conflicts, joys, and sorrows of its subject; to assist this subject in the discovery of whatever has alienated him from the rich texture of experience. Yet in such therapy, as in any human encounter, the outcome is indeterminate; and the range of indetermination increases as new encounters occur. Every therapeutic encounter transfigures both participants. Each perforation of a neurotic defense facilitates collaborative inquiry, by exposing the core, however constricted, of self-affirmation. Authentic probing, acknowledgment, and change of feelings, values, and motives then become possible. Indeed, confrontation of the unfamiliar is jarring. It is difficult to relinquish a customary way of orienting ourselves to the world. For by renouncing the status quo, one steps into lonely regions of experience. Fixed by language, specific repressions, Sullivan's "selective inattentions,"[5] etc., experience gets bounded and rigidly structured. Restrictions are imposed on stimulus receptivity and responsiveness.

As *Anlage* of the need to cast experience in a certain mold, Schachtel proposes the child's fear of separation from its mother. This fear he attributes to a basic tendency of man to feel the "embeddedness-affect."[6] In contrast to womb-directedness, he suggests, the infant exhibits a counter-tendency to turn toward stimuli, seeking not to abolish but to preserve them, and to extend their variety; he strives for world openness. In struggle, pain, or exhilaration, confining perspectives are shattered. At times, this occurs in unexpected encounters—as when in one's first trip abroad the world becomes suddenly vibrant, pregnant with meaning, endowed with new depths. In general, the interplay of these tendencies places man in a state which, in a Spinozist context, I previously alluded to as a hovering between Godhood, i.e., total fulfillment, and thinghood, i.e., total passivity and sheer inertness.

However, one should not overlook the fact that the "embeddedness-affect" has a positive component. Repetition and rootedness can be rejuvenating ways of basking in the familiar. They can prepare one, as the chrysalis the butterfly, for creative encounters. And activity can, in its negative sense, become compulsive. Ideally, one's being should pulsate in rhythmical retraction and expansion, harmonizing these dynamic forces in their positive aspects: birth and preparation for rebirth. As Joseph Campbell writes, in the field of mythology:

> the hero as the incarnation of God is himself the navel of the world, the umbilical point through which the energies of eternity break into time. Thus the World Navel is the symbol of the continuous creation: the mystery of the maintenance of the world through that continuous miracle of vivification which wells within all things.[7]

Therapy aims, in Freud's terms, at promoting the psychic conditions whereby significant change can occur, wherein the reality principle can govern a "patient's" activities. It seeks, accordingly, to shatter defenses, to redintegrate, in an expanding awareness, what had been dissociated by trauma, to liberate the "patient" from a need to substitute complicated stratagems for direct response to reality. In this formulation of the goal of psychotherapy, criteria are specified not by which reality itself is indicated but only by which its denials are indicated. Such philosophic categories as those I have inspected—namely, person, potency, and encounter—suggest the positive moments, in the conceptualization of reality, of which such notions as de-repression, de-fixation, or de-transference (in each case, *unbinding*) are the negations.

(*b*) Reality and the *I*

How can reality be characterized? The shock of encounter issues in judgment, i.e., in evaluations, interpretations, or characterizations of what is encountered, whether artistic or cognitive, or as embodied in specific activities and attitudes. When articulated, and their implications traced out, judgments constitute a symbolic fabric which perpetuate the encountered by itself becoming encounterable (e.g., a scientific theory, a painted landscape, a political decision). By this symbolic immortalization, what was originally encountered will never again be encountered in the same way. It becomes transfigured by the very symbol the production of which it has stimulated (as a landscape of Arles is changed, once one has experienced Van Gogh's rendition). An ever-expanding, systematic consolidation of symbolic forms, taken in conjunction with everything, actual or potential, which they "represent," i.e., all encounterable entities, reality is woven from the multifarious perspectives (cognitive, artistic, or ethical) which grow from human confrontations. By perspective, I mean the unique experience projected by an individual onto the world. In the world in a distinctive way, each person designs, by choice or by instinct, his *own* world. As experiencer, he gathers, receives, and assimilates; he initiates, shapes, and invents. But, though his experience is elastic, unless he transcends his own perspective (Binswanger's "world-design"[8]) it stretches within definite, constricting limits.

In personal encounters, human perspectives both join and broaden. And through ever-expanding perspectives, the true world discloses itself. Primordially an unstructured, indeterminate, "noumenal" potency, the world is converted, through human action, into a "phenomenon," i.e., something realized. In their general contours as a spatio-temporal manifold, phenomena are rendered by the abstract judgments of science and common sense. But, in their full details, phenomena are concretely validated for a particular, unique individual alone. Collaboratively inquiring, persons collate their diverse phenomenal constructions. Thereby, a shared, common world emerges as ever-deeper, ever-more-comprehensive, and ever-more-articulated, hence, capable of acknowledgment by the growing human community.

The cumulative perspectives emerging through individual experience, communication, and comparison *are* reality. Forever incomplete, yet, as time goes on, perpetually enriched, reality is constructed by interweaving foci of awareness, as the multitude of phenomenal facets which, by their inexhaustible essences, objects never cease to reveal capture one's attention, interest, concern, and imagination. When unencumbered by anxiety, frustrated need, or apathy, our minds and our senses roam freely and creatively over the multifarious face of reality, probing its abundant resources, and shaping them into something altogether new which, thenceforth, may be enjoyed as itself a constituent of reality. Indeed, of reality it may be said, as Teilhard de Chardin said of God:

> God does not offer himself to our finite beings as a thing all complete and ready to be embraced. For us he is eternal discovery and eternal growth. The more we think we understand him, the more he reveals himself as otherwise. The more we think we hold him, the further he withdraws, drawing us into the depths of himself. The nearer we approach him through all the efforts of nature and grace, the more he increases, in one and the same movement, his attraction over our powers, and the receptivity of our powers to that divine attraction.[9]

It follows that in psychotherapy reality never gets *finally* confronted. An individual becomes free, through dissolution of his encumbrances, only to embark upon such explorations, and make such constructions, as will elicit creative assent from a larger community. For this to happen, one must transcend one's constricted existence, and experience one's own *I.* How does this experience come about?

Through human encounters, one's potentialities are actualized as a stable configuration of beliefs, judgments, motives, and attitudes. Should this constellation be too inert, a person responds stereotypically to new experience, alienated from his human powers. But should it be too fluid, he becomes amorphous and incapable of consistent, decisive action. The *I* arises in the tension between power as source (Groddeck's "It"[10]) and power as realization. And it is only fully experienced in a proper balance between fluidity and fixity.

The *I* is the adjudicative, responsive, and evaluating part of the person. That upon which it ponders, forming "images," is either body or self (i.e., psyche). A system of organic processes, the body is profoundly interwoven with the psyche—that dynamically constituted mosaic of feelings, volitions, and intentions. Both express ways in which potency manifests itself; and between these manifestations obtain, since they have the same origin, certain correspondences. In each case, an organizing nucleus is relatively immutable, though, when crisis supervenes, subject to dramatic shifts. In the self, this center stabilizes the experiential flux by blending, assimilating, or neutralizing new experiences. In the body, it creates a dynamic equilibrium between processes of catabolism and anabolism, shaping for the organism a homeostatic–homeodynamic condition. And in both cases, the structure (self or body) is immanent in, yet, as an integrative structure, transcendent to, its every component, whether an experience or an organic process.

As it ponders and encounters, the *I* is shaped and solidified. It is constituted by imprints of previous encounters, and the fusion of a person's roles vis-à-vis both self and others. In a counter-process, which Erikson calls "identity-diffusion,"[11] aggressions, avoidances, and isolations masking as encounters impede, or even shatter, this developing identity. These masquerades are, in Spinoza's ethics, the "passions":[12] e.g., pity, scorn, and envy, where one's power arises not through true self-endeavor, but by using another to whom power has been idolatrously transferred, hence, vicariously experienced, as instrument for attaining one's ends. But each authentic encounter, eliciting such of Spinoza's "exertions" as self-esteem, tranquillity, strength of mind, or generosity, potentiates the individual anew.

In potentiation and repotentiation, the *I*, like an autonomous agency within the person, momentarily detaches itself and, in fruitful monologue, withdraws into a silent labyrinth of dreams, memories, fantasies, and imageless feelings, and into such primordial rhythmicities as structure an individual's potency in its process of actualization. And as a person, in his strivings for intimacy and communion, synthesizes fragments from this labyrinth into novel creation, the *I* both feels and merges with his surging power. In the adventure, it goes forth to meet the other in dialogue, feeling its way into his very being, and experiencing him not as object but as *himself* an experiencing agency. Only thus can emotional solipsism, the intellectual counterpart of which has so troubled modern philosophers, be avoided, and a "reverent relationship"[13] to the world be established. I am proposing the importance of speculative inquiry into the central aim of psychoanalysis, namely, the discovery of the authentic *I* as truly author of one's actions, judgments, and products; an *I* which may be discerned in one's every gesture, belief, and movement. In terms of philosophic categories like potency and encounter, the integrity of the *I* can be clarified and explicated.

Before the men of Athens, in whose power it was to spare his life, or, as they chose, to end it, Socrates declared: "Strange, indeed, would be my conduct, . . . if now, when, as I conceive and imagine, God orders me to fulfil the philosopher's mission or searching into myself and other men, I were to desert my post through fear of death, or any other fear. . . ." To know what I am, to unconceal the essential qualities of my being, to stand among others in completeness, simplicity, and without dissimulation, like Socrates to "die having spoken after my manner than speak in your manner and live"[14]—this is my integrity.

I disclose my being, in its unity and entirety, by confronting two powers, my own and another's; and I clarify my being by joining myself to the other, by feeling the qualities of his existence in me and those of mine in him. Through a relationship which includes mutual respect, tenderness, trust, and understanding, the power of each is enhanced. Authentic concern for both self and other is the basis for the experience of integrity. And this concern is possible only when we cease, in our encounterings, to fragment whatever we experience, whether of self or other, and enjoy its wholeness, aliveness, and unconditioned worth. Psychoanalytic healing, with its freeing of the *I* to enjoy reasonable integrity, aims at fulfilling our actual potencies under limits set by the counteractant potencies of others. To achieve this freedom, we, like Oedipus at Colonus, must turn inward, confronting the very sources of our being; and we must turn outward toward that community with others which "springs from self-mastery, and is mediated by 'exertion.'"[15]

(*c*) Value and Integrity

What are the implications for a *philosophic* concept of personal identity of my reflections on psychoanalysis? How can this concept be grounded in an ontologic category which does justice to uniqueness and individuality? Briefly, I stress the following themes. First and foremost, one does not *possess* self-identity. On the contrary, one engages in such acts as permit one self-consciously to identify oneself amid one's self-identifyings with others—and this with respect to the roles which one assumes as one's life unfolds. For I shape my identity as the particular individual I am by appropriating such roles with which to identify myself as most subtly seem to me to express my authentic being. Not only do I attune myself to these roles but, more significantly, I attune my roles to whoever, at the instant I enact them, I deem myself truly to be.

For me to achieve integrity, the rhythms which constitute me must be delicately harmonized with one another, hence capable of gathering in such new stimuli as will both cohere with and enhance the rhythms already constituting me. And this process of rhythm assimilation evolves in the context of role identifyings and counter-identifyings. Granted: I have not yet presented a criterion whereby one can specify the reciprocal attunements adequate for expressing a particular integrity. For this I require the conceptual apparatus of my final chapter. At the moment, I stress only this fact: by my nature, I can never desist from identifying myself *as* I gather in, absorb, and synthesize the stimuli by which I inform myself with the information, i.e., the forms, "contained" therein.

As possessing integrity, like an "integument" or covering sensitive to touch, I must not allow my personhood to be impervious to information, conveyed through appropriate stimuli and identifyings, which enhances the coherence, i.e., the "integer" or wholeness of the rhythmic interplay which grounds my very being. Creating inclusive schemes of rhythmic compresence, not only with other persons but with the world as a whole, I shape symbols through which I express the orientings which I searchingly acquire. With ever-increasing integrity I stand forth as unique and individual, hence, as empowered by a solid, durable, and richly textured self-identity. Accordingly, by personal integrity, I mean both process and end: a process whereby power, which initially manifests itself as mere integrality, the essential unity of mind and body, transforms itself toward integrity; an ideal which so directs that process, albeit implicitly, that, at the end, I dwell transcendentally with myself; and, transcending habitual modes of being with myself, I substitute for those modes an entirely new way for self-relating, the way of authenticity.

In my very essence, I ceaselessly quest after personal value; and, at bottom, such value consists in growth amid lamentation and celebration, growth toward that state of individuality and self-identity wherein I can affirm, under the perspective of my irreducibly special character, how it stands between the world and me, and, in the last analysis, between God and me. Entering into dialogue with the Creator, I implicate my being in its inmost and stillmost depths. By whatever name I designate the vital, formative, and substantive principle of cosmic shaping, I achieve a self-transcendence wherein my personal identity veridically consists in my centering myself, in silent communion, at the very center and germinating core of reality. In this way, I affirm the core of my own being as absolutely unique and of infinite worth. Thereby, I attune myself, in endlessly novel rhythmic unfoldings, to the infinite, eternal character of an all-creating, ever-creating divine presence. Herein lies my integrity: to listen to life's great song, to celebrate with it, to resign myself to its rhythms and import—but never to fail to distinguish, in its haunting counterpoint, the painful from the joyous, and, dwelling with the pain, always to temper celebration with lamentation.

NOTES

1. See the Glossary of German Expressions in *Being and Time*, trans. Macquarrie & Robinson, p. 517.
2. *Duino Elegies*, trans. Leishman and Spender, p. 20.

3. See John Donne, "Devotions upon Emergent Occasions," Meditation 17.

4. The material in this section is based on my "Toward a Concept of Integrity"; see above, chap. 4, note 8.

5. See the index entries for these terms in Sullivan, "Conceptions of Modern Psychiatry," in *Collected Works* I.

6. Ernest G. Schachtel, "On Affect, Anxiety, and the Pleasure Principle," *Metamorphosis: On the Development of Affect, Perception, Attention, and Memory* (New York: Basic Books, 1959), pp. 19–77, esp. p. 26.

7. *The Hero With a Thousand Faces*, Bolligen Series 17, 2nd ed. (Princeton, N.J.: Princeton University Press, 1968), p. 41.

8. See the discussion of Ludwig Binswanger in Rollo May's Introduction to Rollo May, Ernest Angel, and Henri F. Ellenberger, *Existence* (New York: Basic Books, 1958).

9. *The Divine Milieu*, trans. Bernard Wall, rev. ed. (New York: Harper Torchbook, 1968), p. 139.

10. Georg Groddeck, *The Unknown Self* (New York: Funk & Wagnall, 1961), pp. 39–41.

11. See Erik Erikson in *Discussions on Child Development: A Consideration of the Biological, Psychological, and Cultural Approaches to the Understanding of Human Development and Behaviour*, edd. J. M. Tanner and Bärbel Inhelder (London: Tavistock; New York: International Universities Press, 1958), p. 143.

12. See the discussions of the "passions" and the "exertions" in the "Ethics," Parts III–V, in *Chief Works of . . . Spinoza*, ed. Elwes, II 128–271.

13. Thomas Hora, "Existential Communication and Psychotherapy," *Psychoanalysis*, 5 (1939), 38–45.

14. "Apology," *Dialogues of Plato*, trans. Jowett, I 412, 420.

15. Hallett, *Benedict de Spinoza*, p. 153.

21

AUTHENTICITY: RHYTHMS OF QUEST AND ENCOUNTER— WISDOM'S UNFOLDING PHASES

PREAMBLE

According to Freud, two activities dominate the life of wisdom: *Lieben* and *Arbeiten*.[1] Now I comment upon this formula within the perspective of *Choros*. Grounding my ontologic categories—namely, integrality, power, rhythm, and integrity–is authenticity, analyzable in terms of encounter and questing. Encounter pertains to man in his relational aspect, how he reveals himself through love for another, expressed in interpersonal acts; questing pertains to man as *relatum* aspect, how he reveals himself through self-love, expressed in solitary acts. To render man's dual nature, the person must be construed as, at once, unity and plurality, subject and object, and, by derivation, *relatum* and relationship. Each of these abstract designations finds its concrete realization in some aspect of his being.

As a unity, the person is a focus of movement and utterance, a "center" possessing integrity and rhythm. No mere postulated unity, condition for the possibility of acts, and frame of reference for understanding their integrality, he is a substantive locus, an activity composed of specific acts whence flow consequences which affect that center yet do not negate its identity. Despite the vicissitudes of his existence, he remains intrinsically unaltered. As a plurality, the person is a cumulatively evolving composite and directed activity, a multitude of functions, dimensions, and facets.[2] He stands to his "center" as integral to differential: unity in many and plurality integrated as one. And the totality of his acts both reveal that center and comment upon its myriad relationships to his world.

As object, every person has the character of agency; he is mobile and rhythmic. No mere body, passive and inert, he is a patterning of systems, discordant or congruent, of rhythmic interplay, a texture of organically coordinated elements. As agent, he is neither mechanism nor organism. A creature transcending both, he is self-directed, self-perpetuating, and self-metamorphosing: a subject who initiates and consequently plans. Accordingly, a person has the character of reflexivity; he is an activity of self-relating-to-himself *as* he relates to the world, and this in a double sense. On the one hand, he reflects upon his own actions and reactions. Forming an "image" of the relationships these constitute, he conceptualizes his nature in relation to that of the world. Choosing, risking, and acting, he modifies that relation and, thereby, the image. But, in addition, he is unconsciously reflexive. Turning in upon itself, the self integrates a multitude of interior stimuli not as yet at the threshold of awareness; and flowing from the countless "parts" which constitute his body as agent, these influences themselves are affected by the body's participation in its world. For correlative to an external orienting of the self toward its own body as interacting with other bodies is an inward orienting of the self toward that body. This double orienting gives rise to a more complicated image of self in relation to world, an interior image wedded to an exterior image; an interior image woven not only of autochthonous stimuli but also of systems of incoming stimuli and latent responses to these, all of which are dissociated from awareness.

What I experience, in this double reflection,

is myself in total relatedness, inner or outer, to another, the inner continuous with and not disjoined from the outer. Within a relational matrix the *relata*, self and other, crystallize and emerge. In constituting myself a unity of experience and action, I constitute another in his unity. And to apprehend my own individuality, I implicitly take account of his individuality. Mutually complementary, self and other jointly shape a person. For in self-disclosure the other is revealed. And in compresence both are grasped as natural complexes of elements, each a plurality of manifestations disclosing the unity which, now become power, binds all fragments together. To penetrate the mystery of this unity requires that each, in his unity, perceive compresence as itself embedded in a larger presence, an objective community, both concrete and integral, which condenses innumerable relationships. Through his awareness of his participation in this community, each person transcends his composite being.

A • PRESENCE AND COMPRESENCE

PREFATORY

Both a unity and a plurality, the person is an activity of diversification, in which he reveals his essence, his existence, and his temporality. Both subject and object, he is an activity of reflection, in which he reveals himself as a process of gathering, perishing, and synthesizing. Both *relatum* and relationship, he is as an activity of reciprocation, so constituted that his nature is analyzable into comportment, compresence, and transcendence. Yet these activities are but moments in a single event, unfolding human being. And to conceptualize the event in terms of diversification, reflection, and reciprocation, I develop further the concepts of integrity, identity, and rhythm.

As an activity of diversification, a person exhibits integrity. In the unity immanent in his "parts," and in their integrality, he gives himself up, in trust, to some object of concern. At first, the object is a particular being, e.g., a person or a cause. Ultimately, it is an object beyond all objects, an object felt as a transcendent presence, inclusive and all-suffusing, yet indefinable, elusive, and mysterious. With every object of concern, and with the ultimate "object" itself—an Absolute which commands one's inclusive loyalties—he profoundly identifies himself, and enters into intimate, empathic relatedness. Yet in his identifications, he does not lose, he discovers, his own identity. Nonetheless, one does not merely "possess" identity. For a person engages in acts of identifying himself, affirming his identity in all his varied relationships; and these acts result from his searching into his identifications, fully experiencing them and, thereby, experiencing himself *in* them. By his searching, he sees himself as possessed by them; and through this seeing, he frees himself and makes them truly his own. Accordingly, as an activity of reflection, every person discloses himself by looking into another, that mirror wherein he discerns his own being. Yet such mirroring is not passive. For he gathers the other into himself and, therein, reflectively re-presents its presence to himself; he frames a re-presentation which is uniquely his own.

To have integrity is to diversify oneself in an harmonious way, exhibiting the complementarity of unity and plurality, essence and existence, potentiality and actuality. It is to be centered coherently in "space," wherein the parts constitutive of one's entire being form a well-ordered manifold. On the other hand, to have identity is to be centered coherently in "time." And in time-centeredness, a complementarity prevails between subject and object, mind and body, integrality and fragmentation, i.e., an oscillation between the affirmation, in both physical and spiritual spheres, of one's integrity, and of its denial as well. With respect to identity and integrity, no matter how profound one's crisis, one's center is solidified and one's being is deepened.

Disclosed in the activities of diversification and reflection, integrity and identity themselves are complementary facets of a person. In each instance, he manifests himself as an activity of the self temporalizing itself. For, at once, he *possesses* integrity and identity, as structures of his being, past and completed, hence, discoverable; he *lives* integrity and identity, as a self presenting itself in the present; and he *achieves* integrity and identity, as a state yet to emerge. Yet as a kind of empty matrix constituting his spatio-temporal dimension, identity and integrity are insufficiently concrete to serve as vehicles for his full conceptualization. Accordingly, a person's substance, his "matter," is revealed in the activity of reciprocation: it is rhythm. And like identity and integrity, rhythm means a datum completed, a datum emergent, and an activity of bodying-forth.

In rhythm, one's presence with the presence of another is reciprocated. The patterning of rhythms constituting a person construed as an isolated, organic texture of systems and of rhythm resonates to the presence of another also so construed; each inscribes on each his own character. In oscillations of encounter and avoidance, these rhythms unfold. And in the complementarity of self with other, they manifest themselves as rhythms of comportment (e.g., dance), rhythms of transcendence (e.g., worship), and rhythms of compresence (e.g., dialogue). None of these phases of reciprocation, however, can be separated from the others.

These focal ideas involve one another. Their precise interconnections require exploration. In particular, one must understand how each person, in affirming himself, affirms the presence of the entire human community within himself, and in declaring himself a full participant in that community declares himself unique. In myriad forms, he reflects the entire cosmic community, in its absolute unity, into the unity of his own being, a unity idiosyncratic to each though a perspective on all. And, in the last analysis, the unfolding phases of human wisdom entail a dialectical interplay of self-affirmation as *Arbeiten* and communal presence as *Lieben.*

(*a*) Attunings

An opening-up to receive a larger presence, every gathering is a transcendence. It is a self reshaping itself, aware of its own finitude and limits—a self exposing those limits and, in its every act of articulating, moving beyond them to set new limits which, in subsequent searching, will themselves be explored. Incorporating the imprints of that which is sought, the self enlarges itself by adding new content to its experience (i.e., percepts): it deepens itself by effecting new integrations as it experiences (i.e., concepts). In these acts of transcendence, whereby the self metamorphoses itself, a person (the locus wherein the self discloses itself to be a self) reveals *himself* as substratum, an activity which is concrete and mobile. This activity manifests itself variously as this or that searching, each, by my definition, a *selv-ing.* Furthermore, to manifest oneself is to exist. It is a coming-to-hand, and a standing forth of essence. In existing, one gives oneself up to what, as presence, is *given,* given by the powers which present *presence* to the one who gathers in. For a present, or a presence, is a gift; and one reciprocally gives oneself in both gratitude and commitment. Herein, the self sends itself forth, with all its strength, latent and actual (i.e., its personhood), to what is reflectively gathered in; and this gift is reciprocated by an acknowledging which is a concrete and committed act. To acknowledge such a gift is to name; it is to utter in the context of gesture, expression, and posture. It is to assume a physical stance, all powers self-actualized; and such a stance itself originates from primitive rhythms which are a kind of dance, a dance of celebration wherein, together with its accompanying utterance, there is an articulating of the specific modes of manifesting and gathering in, and of the connection between the two. In rhythmic fashion, motor activity unfolds as dance; and utterance, as music and poetry. Together, they shape the person into a directed process, a person-ing, wherein, by his acts, he metamorphoses himself, achieving integration and discovering a hitherto veiled integrity.

As a searching, or an entrusting to what is experienced as a presence which, as he searches, becomes a luminous image of the self in relation to another, the person is no mere passive recipient of impressions. He does not simply await them as, imprinting themselves on him, they shape a complex of percept and idea, while he lies embedded in an unreciprocating cosmos. For his quietude is infused with elements of activity. The distinction between awaiting and moving toward is never absolute; each involves factors focal to the other. And his activity is never, at bottom, that of mere impulse, though a pathology of the person treats him in his susceptibilities to *relative* impulse or to *relative* embeddedness. On the contrary, it is integrating and sustained. Every person comports himself, whether quiescently or vigorously, toward what emerges, in the frame of the self bearing itself with all its powers, as an articulated presence, a presence which no longer is amorphous but is actually assigned a structure *by* his activity.

In a giving of signs, i.e., a self presenting itself to the other, not only is the other differentiated as a relational complex of assignations, but the self itself emerges as an unceasingly diversified yet, as its commitments are strengthened, unified manifold of specific propensities to assign. Engendered by reciprocal acts of self and other, this presence is both given as datum and felt as experient. It implies both a self disjoined from the other and a self united to it. What is perceived and what is con-ceived, i.e., taken *extensively*, as a complex of factors grasped in their very togetherness, must, in either case, be *taken*. Approached, explored, and felt as the emerging texture of being, they must be shaped into "being for" that searching self: i.e., in relationship to him, and not radically disjoined from him. The many facets of object *as* object come into view for a subject which, in this adventure, emerges in its fuller subjectivity. An emerging depth of object and depth of subject are correlative with the progressive articulating of presences.

An entrusting search is that comporting toward oneself in one's relations with the world in which an image appears, the focus of which is either "inner" (toward the self itself) or "outer" (toward the world, or complement to the self); and this image is "accurate." For it depicts the deeper aspects of a relationship, in all its facets and inmost meanings, wherein the rhythms of one's being enmesh among themselves, and, in turn, are attuned to the rhythms of what is other than oneself. Furthermore, this reflective, inward shaping of impressions, by a rhythmic unfolding of powers, from an inchoate state of coherence is itself continually expressed as a person's multifaceted existence. Thence imprinted in both self and other, it perishes therein, objectively to immortalize itself as traces, traces evocable as memory which is either dim or vivid. Composed of layer upon layer of impressions—hence capable of multitudinous, increasingly rich expressions—the subjectivity of the self is deepened; and the objectivity of the other for that self is correspondingly broadened. The more the object is discriminated, the more discriminating, hence the deeper, the self *who* discriminates. An oscillating and widening spiral is created wherein the relationship itself, the *relata* of which may only be distinguished as subject and object when artificially separated, a relationship, at bottom, of attunement, cumulatively evolves toward both depth and purity. Indeed, this relationship is so constituted that any boundary between "inner" and "outer" disappears; a unitary, articulated presence alone is felt, and cognized.

(*b*) Other-Encounter

Every particular human activity is a species of entrusting search. Each, moreover, is a pro-ducing, i.e., a leading forth into expressions which as uttered, shaped, or shown constitute judgments about reality, and, as dissociated from their creator, even products of reality. At any given time, the aggregate of these products *is* the reflectively in-duced, and cumulatively evolving image—in the end, an image of the world. For each person continually represents *to himself* and, at one and the same time, *to* all that is other than himself precisely what, in his encounters, was presented; he represents, as a picture of the world, including himself, the original presentation. By nature, a person seeks not only an ontology, a λόγος of his being in relation to the world, in the essential traits of that relation, but also a cosmology, a picture which, being a λόγος of the cosmos depicting *its* essential character, he reflects into his being as thereafter constitutive of it. For man is a philosopher. He is under existential compulsion to philosophize. And his every act is a concrete factor in what, were he to reflect on the most generalized possible meaning of that act, in the context of the totality of his acts, past and anticipated, would constitute *his* philosophy of life. Indeed, formal philosophizing is but the enterprise of making explicit the general contours of such a particular philosophy, vindicating this picture by reference to criteria established by formal philosophers of the past.

By gesture, by intonation, and by assertion—indeed, by his every act—man both manifests his being, in its relationship to another, and comments upon that relationship. The system of his judgments constitutes the formal structure of this manifestation and of this commentary; the aggregate of his products, variously classified as science, art, technology, and philosophy itself, are the by-product of the dialogues in the unfolding of which those judgments are formed. They are, so to speak, crystallizations, in patterns of cumulative symmetry of different kinds and styles, of a rhythmical ferment; and this ferment constitutes the potent matrix wherein, as man integrally presents himself, the integrity of dialogue is achieved.

Encounterable symbols of presence in all the modes of comportment whereby self and other each presents its characteristic rhythms, these by-products are, by the very existence of their creators, and in the multitude of acts through which essence is expressed *as* existence, detached from existence, and woven into the very texture of reality: a reality built up, layer by layer, and generated ever anew; layers of entities which manifest presence by their acquired but now independent powers. As symbols, by-products of dialogue are durable embodiments of the communings of persons. No mere residues, these by-products themselves are existent complexes with their own potencies and destinies. By their difference, and by the unique qualities of each, as well as by the congruities and structural isomorphisms which hold between them, they bind persons together as celebrating shared vitalities and sanctifying a common purpose. Symbols constitute objects of prayer, reverence, and pleasure. They stir responses which exhibit inner congruencies and, thereby, the empathic identifyings of one person with another. "Presences" enjoyed for their own sake, and encounterable sui generis, symbols are also instruments which weave the very lives of people into an harmonious, unified texture. For a given epoch and a particular community, certain themes, discernible and capable of elaboration into an evolving pattern of ideas, pervade by-products, even in their diversity and diffuseness. In his characteristic activities, an individual exhibits a typical rhythm and style, and, likewise, for the cumulative results of the dialogues of all who form a community. Insofar as dialogues are attuned, they crystallize and deposit, as their traces in that community, a typical, collective by-product.

The rhythms constituting a community's essence, and the interplay of the countless meetings issuing in dialogue, are the potent, invisible matrix from which each person draws sustenance, a matrix wherein *his* rhythms unfold and the "existence" of which, like his existence, is composed of endless "forms" of expression, the by-products themselves. Dwelling within its every participant, the community is the immanent ground for his every action. To its essence, his essence is inextricably linked. Neither may be construed without the other; both essences have parity; each is constitutive of the other. Accordingly, an ontology of the person can assume as its foundation *either* essence, personal or communal, so enmeshed is the community with the person. Surely, a person is, in part, constituted by the relationships he sustains to his fellows. His very self may, in part, be construed as a crystallization, the relatively enduring configuration, of processes, discriminable within those relationships; and the locus of all interpersonal relationships is the community itself.

When I speak of the "presences" which haunt a person, and perish into his being, fused to a style peculiar to him and woven into his autochthonous rhythms, I mean, on the one hand, the collective presence of that very community by which he is surrounded yet in which he is embedded as constituent, manifestation, and co-participant. Experienced in its integrity, each felt communal presence expresses a distinct, partly self-determining entity; each is a constellation of existential aspects which cohere as a relatively independent focus of action and intent. Depositing their traces in every person, these presences so affect him that his rhythms resonate to theirs as, reciprocally, their combined rhythms are altered by his. Yet to experience oneself in one's integrity in relation to another in his integrity, neither self nor other may be taken as point of reference, as generative source. On the contrary, the "center" of activity is that which gives birth to the self *in its relation to the other*, a ferment which includes both yet is centered beyond each; the self orients itself toward both self and other from the standpoint of *objectivity*, i.e., within the perspective of that which as object is wholly other to each, which constitutes the originative matrix whence both derive their powers and their aims. However, the delineation of this matrix—i.e., the larger community in which self and other are embedded yet stand forth as distinct—indeed, the specification of how this paradoxical relationship is possible, is beyond the scope of my present discussion.

Insofar as either self or other is regarded as ultimate source, with but minimal rootedness in a third element, immanent in both yet transcendent to each, an ontology of the person is transformed into pathology. The world without is experienced not in its integral contours but as pulverulent, fragmented, degraded, distorted, or falsified. In pathology, the self may construe itself to be omnipotent; hence it may refer the world to itself as originator and world as dependent upon its own alleged autonomy. Alternatively, it may regard the other as omnipotent and itself as but an appendage, alienated from its intrinsic powers and, withdrawn from itself, pressed down by the imagined weight of the other. And whether self or other is falsely inflated, the integrities experienced by either are negated. One falls under the sway of self-burdening emotions like despondency, envy, or jealousy, and all the feelings which Spinoza calls "passive," feelings which inhibit that exertion of the powers which alone can enable an image of the world to be apprehended as luminous, an image wherein the actual patternings of things are revealed as not disrupted, and their links are truly construed.

(*c*) Self-Encounter

In addition to the "outer," spectatorial world, there is the still, inner presence of feeling, reverie, imagery, kinesthesia, and ideation—namely, a world revealed in introspection which, on a comprehensive theory of reality, is connected to the outer world as a single continuum, and neither counterposed nor merely juxtaposed. And when appropriately delineated, these "worlds" disclose themselves not simply as contiguous realms, but, indeed, as a single manifold which is integral and unified. Introspection and "extrospection" are complementary activities. In both instances, a subject poses itself to a searching self as subject matter for thematic unraveling, as an unformed matrix, inner or outer, in the context of which, like figure on ground, an objective, substantive focus is delineated. By "subject," I mean a *locus* of searchings; by "object," I mean that which counterposes itself to subject as the structured is to the amorphous; and by "structured," I mean that which is recalcitrant to arbitrary change the constituent elements of which have been set forth, and their links made explicit. Accordingly, the self as one who searches, whether inwardly or exteriorly, is an activity of articulating itself in its multiplex relations with others. Identified through these acts, in its very distinctness from the other, the self creates for itself a durable self-identity. It searches among "presences," either inner or outer, and it discovers a structure, converting mere subjectivity, which is amorphous and evanescent, into reliable objectivity.

In this process, the self becomes aware of itself. Indeed, to be a self is to engage in the activity of self-conscious disclosure of itself; it is to grasp its own contours, the elements and their patterning which constitute it a self. Herein the self detaches itself from itself; it contemplates its very acts of awareness. Yet to apprehend oneself in this detachment as not merely the source of acts but the activity itself, the consciousness of oneself as an organization of specific powers, an unfolding, and a ferment, is, at the same time, to negate detachment, *to live oneself*, and to yield to the activity—in effect, to be un–self-conscious. Ultimately, the Unconscious (to be exact, the unconscious–unbody, or *luminator*) is, precisely, that which cannot be structured. As such, it is, in part, the perished presences which have forever been absorbed into the evolving self. In addition, it is the ceaseless generative activity itself whereby the self endures, and grows as a self.

On the other hand, *luminator* refers to that which is yet to be structured, a potentiality for acquiring a structure. From the standpoint of its pathologic constituents, it includes presences as yet unassimilated, presences which cluster about the self and constrain its action as an independent dynamism. Counterposed to the self in its central, generative activity is an aggregation of autonomous centers of ferment. Internalized fragments of objects, rather than perished, integral objects, herein constrict the self's very integrity. And when perishing is complete, these objects form a coherent manifold which expresses a single, unique activity. Indeed, unperished presences either are dissociated by trauma from an evolving self, awaiting redintegration in its subsequent maturing, or co-exist with the evolving self as elements which had never participated in its central structures. For when in its searching, and therein its entrusting itself to that which is wholly other to it, a self is rebuffed, its quest misheard and misdirected, the very integrity of that self is disrupted. It incorporates either aspects or deformations of presences; and only integral presences are capable of that perishing into the self's silent depths which guarantees maturation. Ideally, the voice with which one speaks is one's own voice, a speaking from out of a confident stillness into which other voices, fully heard and absorbed, have perished, and yet have not vanished as durable parts of the originative matrix of all subsequent speaking; and utterance is focal to the searching process. In pathology, as with the schizophrenic or "split" personality, many voices reverberate throughout the self, "projected" as hallucinations, which hamper the ownness of the voice with which one speaks. Repeatedly, an inner noise of myriad threatening presences breaks the creative silence and fragments the authentic self.

As creative agent, the *luminator* is not a mere repository of presences, whether perished *or* assimilated. On the contrary, it is a dynamism, the person himself, a process in which essence unfolds into existence, and thence encounter. It is a bringing to birth, from an originative source, itself a ferment, of latent, incubating symbolisms. To be aware is to "conscious"; it is an activity of conscious-ing. Analogously, to be unaware is to "unconscious," and, ultimately, "unconscious–unbody." and these activities are correlative, complementary, and mutually presupposing. In the first instance, a symbol, as a by-product of dialogue, is felt, cognized, and formulated; and this in the context of dialogue. In the second instance, a symbol germinates as a something-about-to-be-born. I assume here that all perishing presences crystallize about certain centers of activity, centers unfelt yet constitutive of the "inner life" of the person himself; and that these centers are recurrent, objective foci of "energy," universally binding on all men, which fructify autochthonously and manifest themselves as dream, reverie, and fantasy, each constituted by its own laws and each exhibiting its characteristic rhythms. When the self encounters itself, it experiences its *own* presence as richly diversified, as an "interior" manifold, complex and profound; and this presence becomes ever larger through its acquisition of "impressions" from the world without, through a filling of itself with presence. But for the self to encounter another, it must experience the other as an independent, potent "exterior" source of these inward impressions.

Yet these modes of encounter, self with self and self with other, are complementary aspects of the encountering of one reality, a single manifold of presences "projected" on varying levels of "removal" from the self: intimate vibrations of music resonating throughout one's being; vague premonitions haunting the periphery of what one perceives as "out there"; a visual world to which one no less, though more subtly, resonates, more detachedly yet just as inwardly. Still, all are out there as well as within a subject; and all possess a definite, encounterable architecture. For the inner world mirrors the outer; nothing is "without" unless it has passed through, and is refracted by, the prism of the "within." Both the specific mechanisms of projection and the "distance" projected vary from one sense (e.g., vision) to another (i.e., hearing). Yet the entire world is intimately connected to the self. Hence, a person's searchings of both himself and the world are searchings into, and reflections of, a relationship between the self and the world, which itself is a communing in a matrix of communings, a texture of reciprocal modifications induced by the encounterings of entities which are relatively enduring configurations: crystallizations in a field of influence, momentary arrestings of processes.

B • TRANSFIGURATION: THE INTERWEAVINGS OF LAMENTATION AND CELEBRATION

(*a*) Self-Presenting

Born into nature, and beset by the demands of instinct and desire, every person, were he to yield to natural impulse, might attain a modicum of happiness. Yet happiness construed as power, lust, wealth, fame, or health is transitory, unstable, and uncertain. Every quest for happiness, and every fulfillment of that quest, are accompanied by forebodings of its imminent cessation. Even a perfect moment of joy, wherein one experiences a brief flash of felt eternity, receiving all that seemingly can conduce to the perpetuation of happiness, is, in the end, a sham. For it is *nature* which gives, whether in the shape of person or thing, and insofar as one makes oneself dependent upon such giving, one receives passively, hence, contingently. In effect, one permits nature to inscribe on one's being *her* wishes, *her* inclinations, and *her* prescriptions—in a word, her constraints. Under such circumstances, one is like clay: the very foundations of one's existence rest on quicksand. They are in flux and imbalance, a ferment which ever threatens to negate one's very being. Nevertheless, one cannot desist from being dimly aware that one cannot, should one crave at least equanimity, or, at most, blessedness, allow oneself to be enveloped by such gifts, no matter how pleasant, or even ecstatic, the mood which they induce in one. On the contrary, to enjoy such a state in which nature might have placed one, a person *himself* must actively give. Only by affirming himself through his acts of giving can he, by those acts, stand forth and truly exist as human. For to be human, one must rise above nature. Only by transcending one's natural state can one transfigure oneself toward an authentically moral state, i.e., a state of veridical human freedom.

Wherein, I now ask, consists this state, and by what criteria can it be judged? What are the processes, and the moments through which one must pass, whereby such self-transfiguration can be achieved? To treat these questions, I raise the following considerations.

As natural, one is ineluctably subject to ecstasies of celebration and ravages of lamentation. Should one rise toward celebration, lamentation lurks immanently as potentially emergent during an immediately succeeding moment; should one be beset by lamentation, one cannot escape the hope that, in time, it will be displaced to celebration. Here, no rhythms of equanimity prevail. Though one can speak of the smooth-flowing rhythms of quest, wherein one fulfills oneself, in solitude, through one's work, and of encounter, wherein one fulfills oneself in one's affirmation through another, and, reciprocally, in the other person's affirmation through oneself, the rhythms of lamentation and celebration are, in the end, cruel, erratic, and unforeseeable. Ultimately, a crucial problem of human ontology is to formulate a category of *attainable* existence by which, in self-transfiguration, a person can transcend this brutish, merely contingent, and wholly unreliable shunting of himself from one condition to the other, so that he might dwell in a state of purity of heart: a state which affords neither natural tranquillity nor natural blessedness, but, at least, the satisfaction that he is wronging neither himself nor another; indeed, a state which implies that each person is an end in himself and, under no circumstance, a means to an end.

To achieve this aim, the self, freely and spontaneously, must present itself to other selves (who in analogous compresence present themselves) and to the world in general. Constituted as explicitly reflexive in its very essence, and shaped by its passing through the requisite concrete stages by which it exemplifies its reflexive character, the self attains its self-identity; and it presents the world as, so to speak, allowing itself, by its own dynamism, to be made accessible to the self, hence *itself* (namely, the world) as immanently reflexive. Thus arises the formally transcendental, hence, unknown, elusive, and mysterious, character of both self and world, which, together, constitute a cosmos conceived as both self-creating and self-created; and the dialectical implication of self with world. In this context, selves ever strive to transcend their own *given* statuses. In self-transcendence, each mode of reflexivity, whether of world or of self, both enters into and participates in the other mode and, indeed, transforms it. Thereby, self and world collaboratively engender the kind of unfolding stages which Hegel so acutely describes. With respect to the self, I designate these dialectically induced self-transformations as transfiguration.

However, such self-presentings of the world to the self are essentially *proto-*conscious. They lie outside of focal awareness or, for that matter, of subliminal awareness. Nonetheless, these presentings constitute, as a whole, an *a priori* condition, synthetically formed, of conscious experience, a condition which consists in the *re*-presenting by the self, in the dialectically unfolding cognitive schemes articulated by both natural and behavioral science, of the world to itself. Thereby, the self penetrates the phenomenal constitution of both the world and the self: a probing, however, always *limited*, in the cognitive sphere, by the noumenon (to use a Kantian locution), but, in the active sphere, wherein particular selves encounter particular selves, always *illuminated* by the noumenon, an illumination so constituted that its source in the noumenon can be articulated only exhibitively, through art, philosophy, and religion. And, in the last instance —namely, through exhibitive articulation—nature veridically reshapes herself through the creative agency of the self.

But the world must be construed as an assemblage of things complemented by a community of selves. In consequence, the self presents, and, in endless series, represents the world not only to itself but to its community as well: that, thereby, the specific distortions, both perceptual and reflective, made by individual selves might be rectified through the deliberations of a multitude of selves; that, thereby, a systematically cogent scheme of representations might be engendered. In this sense, every self participates, at once, in three spheres of existence: nature, or the cognitive sphere, by which it frames judgments in the assertive mode; the kingdom of ends, or the moral sphere, by which it incorporates in its acts judgments in the active mode; the domain of creation, or the aesthetic sphere, by which it shapes natural products as judgments in the exhibitive mode. By acting within the spheres prescribed by these modes, and through appropriately coordinating its acts, the self lifts itself out of nature, and so transforms itself as to acquire an altogether new status in the cosmic scheme.

Accordingly, each self ought to transcend its natural status, which confers upon it the power of making objective empirical judgments, and to dwell in the light of, and to allow its actions to be grounded by, an ideal; and this ideal itself ought to be so defined that its inmost content is conferred by the creative potentialities of humankind. Hence, the self which is thereby transfigured so acts that it is purposively disinterested with respect to all specific motives, inclinations, and consequences. Giving itself up to that which it prescribes to itself as an ideal, namely, in its initial formulation, the very concept of human being as end in itself, the self undertakes such acts as will reshape nature herself, drawing forth from within her abyss such new "natures" as hitherto had lain dormant and concealed. Through the very agency of the self, nature thus humanizes herself.

As the self gives itself up to the world, and proto-consciously experiences the world, it creates a coherent manifold the substantive ground of which *is* the self implicated with the world, neither of which, however, it can fully know, save in a strictly formal way: a dynamic, immanently reflexive world and a dynamic, explicitly reflexive self, the coherence of which (in both instances) is grounded in that which must manifest itself as pure pattern—ideally, as mathematically rendered pattern. For finitudes are nested within infinitudes of numberless orders, expressing, like so many enclosing concentric circles, the expanding scope of experience, as the self seeks to penetrate both itself and the world; and finitudes are nested within infinitesimals, expressing, like enclosed concentric circles, the self's penetration of the inmost depths of its experience. In each case, one quests after invariants nested within invariants, each efflorescing into more primordial invariants—some designated as space and others as time, and, ultimately, some constituting a formal, spatio-temporal, unified matrix.

Participating in a community of selves, each self is conditioned by its participation in the natural world, and, as such, partly determines itself to comport in accordance with motives and incentives derived from nature. Nonetheless, all selves empower themselves, by the autonomous act of their respective wills—each will exercising itself in ways which catalyze the exercising of all wills—to affirm, by a kind of collective holiness of wills, the essential dignity of man; and to declare with one voice, which blends into harmonious attunement the idiosyncratic divergencies which prevail in any multitude of selves, that that dignity consists in each person's constituting himself an end in himself and never a means to an end: a kingdom of ends so organized that, as each person acts, he so universalizes the maxim of his action that, by his creativity, which is archetypal for all mankind, he articulates, elaborates, and exhibits experience not as mere phenomenal representation, but, beyond that, as the very cosmos reshaped, reconstituted, and re-created in the spheres of art, philosophy, and religion. Yet man's lament consists in his ineluctable falling away into nature at the very moment he celebrates his transcendence of nature. Ever thrusting himself out of her domain, he inexorably reverts to that domain. The interweavings of lamentation and celebration constitute man as transfiguring himself: a rhythmic rising and falling, at once brutish and angelic, as he strives, with all his powers, not to cast his integrity from himself.

In this process, every new experience facilitates rediscovery of the self. In each, an analogy presents itself with what lies buried in memory. The familiar is perpetually sought in the unfamiliar; analogies evoke re-enactment of the drama of the past in the framework of the present. To receive these teachings in ways which allow for both clarification and deepening of my existence, I must simulate, in my present posture to the world, the conditions under which I originally experienced them, diminishing, insofar as I can, all that constricts my receptivity; and when I have suffused my existence with a repetition which never stultifies, but, indeed, liberates by its attunement with the defining rhythms of my "being," so that I come truly to know the instrument on which I play the deeper melodies of life, in endlessly subtle variations on themes which endlessly repeat themselves, I can then listen to memory addressing me as, from instant to instant, it is called forth.

(*b*) Rootedness and Perishing

Through our dreams, and through those tangible expressions of dreams which weave the poetry of our lives—in art, in dance, in speech—we root ourselves anew in reminiscence constantly stirred from among those impressions which have lain dormant. But not till these silent memories "have turned to blood within us, to glance and gesture, nameless and no longer to be distinguished from ourselves —not till then can it happen that in a most rare hour the first word of a verse arises in their midst and goes forth from them."[3] And for "verse" may be substituted any form of existence, pregnant with its vitalities and pulsations, by which we symbolically present ourselves to another. When these images of memory flow effortlessly and do not clutch at us, demanding our bondage, when indeed they have been absorbed and woven into the very stuff of our existence, such analogy is a spur to self-discovery. By its conversion into the invisible, the insensate, and the stillness of our inner depths, the impression is transfigured into a possibility of authentic expression. "Falling" into reminiscence, which, as we welcome it, rises to meet us, we express in many modalities the rhythms of existence. To discover oneself is to integrate these fragments of memory deposited in the wake of time. It is to accept the dissolution of what had been immediate as now perished into existence; it is to mourn the loss of what had been sweet; it is to acknowledge the "strings of lament" which, when played, allows to appear the

> jubilance that grows behind everything
> burdensome, painful and endured, and
> without which the voices are not complete;[4]

it is to experience peace at the passing of what had been agony; and it is to solidify links between islands of memory, so that, in the end, the movement of life may acquire a harmony and a purpose.

Through both perishing and recall, an inner coherence is imparted to an existence. One senses one's roots to ramify beyond a conventionally demarcated life. One draws sustenance from traces of innumerable past meetings, and beyond these from that universal matrix in which individuality appears like the crest of a wave which glows in sun, moon, and stars, yet dissolves into a source which flows inexorably on. Embedded in the very nutriment whence he arose, and from which he stands forth in vibrant tints before he inevitably returns to a destiny shrouded in mystery, a status so radically cut off from life that I was tempted to designate it "nothingness," a mature person achieves harmony, and even a certain unity, between the beginning and the end of his life. The unique qualities with which he was endowed, qualities which make themselves apparent even in his childhood gestures, are recognizably those which come to fruition as death approaches. In his maturity, he fuses into a unitary texture the inchoate traces left by experience; he does not cling to a past mistakenly felt as full when, in reality, there was emptiness; he is free from the grip of images, beautiful or painful, which have failed to be absorbed into his existence; he need not be afraid to step into a present moment which is ineluctably unknown until it has actually been lived—dramatically unknown, for only in fancy are the anticipated and the actual similar modalities of the real; and he dares to present himself boldly to whatever may befall him, neither in hope nor in despair, giving himself freely, without expecting reward or succour, to what he may feel as uncanny, to the great void of the future, while he freely welcomes its lessons and its imprints as it is converted into the actual. For what befalls the person should be held, not as a possession demanded, but as a gift to be treasured, as experience authentically received, to instruct as well as to give joy. Thus are the harmonies of a life reinforced and subtilized; and thus the more delicate variations inscribe themselves on its themes.

Cohering amid my uttermost diversities, I impress myself as a unity, by sound and by image, into the other. By these signs of my inmost depths, I mime the gestures of the sensible. For my signs are my responses to what I have received in those moments of silence when I bend, listening, toward the world; when I so open my "being" that I resonate to its inner harmonies as I cause it to resonate to mine. In communion, I assimilate its nature to my nature, and mine to its; I imitate it, and I cause it to imitate me. I respond to it as a presence which hovers about me, vague and indefinable—a presence which invites me to bind our separate rhythms to one rhythm, while not ceasing to acknowledge that it is *I* who have chosen, hence may renounce my choice, and preserve my uniqueness. As I impress myself into another, revealing my values and my style, so, reciprocally, do I accept, with my ever-renewed existence, *his* expressions, woven from his impressions, into *his* existence, impressions now immortalized in mine. I fling myself toward this presence, haunting and unfathomable, as if I had received a call. And as I open myself to it, I glow in my giving, though the extent of my gift is as yet undetermined. Sensing my power at this moment to be limitless, I am concerned no longer with receiving but only with going toward with all dimensions of my being; and I draw my resources from a beyond which stretches infinitely far. Waiting neither for the "resistance" of the other to test my strength nor for cues that he has received my gift, I expand myself *in* the giving. And as I grow from instant to instant, I define my "essence"; and this growing is a groping toward that presence which, as I approach it, becomes luminous and clear. All I sense of myself is an inner silence, a *mysterium* of undefined powers; my "essence" *is* that waiting for a future, whatever it be, to come alive before and within me. As I welcome this unknown phantom, which takes shape by its own will and law, through forces unknown to me, yet reveals itself only by *my* acts, by *my* decision to cast away what does not belong to my opening myself toward it, I reach out to it, and therein design my "essence." I stand out beyond what I had been; my boundaries are never fixed.

Like the ever-widening circle of waters into which I have cast a stone, moving outward toward the unknown beyond, yet whirling or hovering about a common center, so is my life, as I thrust myself into my future—in repetition. In repetition! For I take my daily walk; I eat my meals; I converse with the same friends; I travel about a fixed center. Yet my horizons move ever outward as a flow of concentric circles. What I recall is now but the *image* of a repetition which I never cease to enact, as I give myself repeatedly in neither tedium nor ritual, drawing the reaches of the cosmos into my ken and my substance. I am like a child who, when one reads a story to him again and again, finds new shadings of adventure: gentle novelties inscribe themselves upon a theme which I do not cease to repeat. With each genuine presentation, I move outward toward the world, and inward toward my center; it is a center the position of which *I* define, a world which *I* irradiate. My memory is enriched as, in repetition, it frees itself from schematic recall, and weaves recollection into the fabric of my inmost self. I acquire new depths of relatedness, breaking its constrictive patterns, and passing through the boundaries of convention I declare, with Goethe: " 'There is only the eternally new, growing from the enlarged elements of the past. . . .' "[5]

Herein lies that sense of integrity which it has been my task to explicate. The very ground of my existence is the factuality of a past which *I* generate, as inherently my own, as I live—the completed fact whence I derive, and upon which I stand in surveying the horizons which, from instant to instant of my life, newly come to view. Taking my stand upon this ground, I accept its radical irreversibility. Each moment I draw breath, I design my world; and I shape my life by decision. By "decision," I mean, not a mental set to be followed by action, but the act itself wherein I cut off indefinite possibilities of movement, shoots which might have grown to foliage rich and good. My being flows into a single channel, a direction unique for each existence, which I, in but partial awareness, determine. For a decision is an act, not of consciousness alone, but of an entire existence as it finds itself, at that instant, to be the culmination of innumerable preceding decisions. Rooted in the very depths of his being, a person's decision arises in the womb of mystery as an implicit orientation which only as he focuses upon it, in retrospect and within the frame of a new act of decision, can be rendered as a cognitive structure. Thus, within my act, I am free; only in retrospect am I bound. It is *I* who, by an independent act, must always determine wherein I am determined—that is, by an act of decision. I inspect the facts which, by my previous acts, have been woven into my being; and I therein find a pattern which, as past, I declare to be my causal antecedents and, as projected into the future, I sense to be my destiny.

In decision lies tragedy. My life might have been other than what, in part unwittingly, I have shaped it to be; its contours are irrevocable. This is the starkness of reality. I plunge into the unknown, and I accept its rebuffs, though they may rock my foundations; I accept them as consequences of *my* acts. I am responsible in the sense of being responsive to *my* world *as* I have designed it and, *in* the designing of it, making such subsequent decisions as are appropriate to this character which I have conferred upon it. At each instant, I die anew. When I say "I," I mean my personhood, with all the influences which flow into it to constitute it a reflexive agency. I am an acting being, in part, aware of myself as I act and, in part, resigned to my nature as embedded in a matrix which infinitely transcends though, indeed, it totally constitutes me. These "causes" I feel throbbing within me, even as I thrust myself toward the spectacle of a world which, at the very instant it unfolds before my astonished eye, passes into my substance as itself a "cause" of what I shall, at the next instant, become.

Thus, every occasion of my experience perishes into a new occasion, as both source of and constitutive factors within that occasion. With each death, I mourn for what I was an instant ago, in my "being" and in my possibilities, now vanished into the night of my memory. Yet ever glowing are the stars of what *had* been present to me, their radiance conserved amid the tears of their passing; and I am born anew. *This* is the vibrancy of reality: that my experience does not cease, not as I know it, till I open myself toward the greatest mystery, death, that "future" which can never come in the frame of time. My joy derives from my absorbing into my being the pain of renouncing what I had been and what I might have been—remorse for what I did, sadness for what I failed to do. But, as I thus distill as into a glowing vapor the elements which, inert, unsublimated, and unabsorbed, might have choked me, I breathe in deeply, and purify my existence. I fully accept my absolute aloneness, the radical singularity of my existence. This is my reward, this destiny of mine which requires that were I to blunt the edge of my pain, I would dull the clarity of my joy; for in my very suffering I must acknowledge its total irreversibility.

Woven into this ground, which I have created, is a future ideality as the *vis a tergo* of my life, projected possibilities shaped from reminiscence. In the novel syntheses which I effect, syntheses wherein my past "concresces" in my present at each instant of my existence, I idealize myself, hence weave the future into my present. Both past and future, fact and ideal, are absorbed into a timeless present, a present which is enjoyed or suffered for its own sake, not as a means toward an end disjoined from it but as an end in itself, an end which coheres with new ends flowing imperceptibly from it. And as persons experience the immediacy of mutual presence, detachment gives way to communion; the resistance between the self and its complement diminishes. In this evolving relationship, a person of integrity emerges from the concealment of his masks, and draws his powers into a luminous present. And in a coming-into-clarity, solidarity is created both within and between persons. Existence *sub specie aeternitatis* is achieved where existence *sub specie durationis* had prevailed. As each instance of durational existence perishes, something replaces it which lasts. But, by our finitude, and by the intrinsic limits of our powers, it is again and again shattered as, alternately, we experience ourselves as existing in the two modalities of time and eternity.

(*c*) Mystery

Within each who seeks to know lurk feelings which are vague, immense, insistent, and premonitory; dreams and visions, and rumblings of an uncognized, uncognizable world of foreboding presences. Yet this mystery which haunts us, and to which we are inextricably rooted as sustaining us amid the terror to which, in awesome dreams and premonitions, it may subject us, also gives a hint of bliss and peace beyond what, in our spectatorial existence, we can ever know. A philosophy of the person, and *a fortiori* any general metaphysics, must do justice to the inner world as well as to the outer. Either it dissolves the barrier between these worlds, so that reality acquires a homogeneous if multivariate texture, or it articulates the barrier as itself a fundamental element. In my concept of integrity, I have proposed a *single* world.

Every person relates to another in one of two ways, the first involving an inner, the second, an outer, experience. For he absorbs into his existence factors deriving from the innumerable entities, remote or proximate, by which he is surrounded. In this experience of his "within," he shapes the *internal* relationships by which he both nourishes and sustains his existence, and which he presents to himself as images which symbolize an interior reality. By "symbolize," I mean a drawing of the realm represented by those images into an integrated self-awareness which is capable of symbolic self-presentation. Sunk deep into this cosmic nutriment, a person's roots ramify in ways governed by whatever is necessary for his destiny. Continually, he strives to perfect himself according to a model which conforms to the unique qualities with which he is endowed. However, this mirror of his soul, which he ever holds before his inner gaze, this "archetype" peculiar to him alone, is usually veiled or distorted. Severe effort alone makes it luminous, and eradicates its flaws. Having drawn into a unity all that is causally relevant to his existence, and having shaped it into a singular individuality, the person imprints on the other an ideal image of himself, woven from the elements of his life, just as the factors which *he* has absorbed were, in their time, analogous imprints of still other entities. Thereby, he seeks to immortalize what he deems to be the perfect traits of his being; and he offers this image as a gift by which, in the very act of giving, he is in quest of his own symbolic perpetuation. In the end, one achieves perfect reciprocity with another by the mutual offering of symbolic "perfections." By each act of giving, one invites a complementary gift. Now the experience of a "without," the *external* relationships by which one communes with one's fellows, is complete.

Since their causal antecedents partly coincide, each person prefigures the existence of the other. Both participate in a common milieu; and this primordial sharing of "natures" is converted into a consummatory sharing through the mutual presentation of self-perfections. A strangely luminous quality, experienced by those in true communion, arises when each communicant experiences the very symbolism by which he has striven to perpetuate a perfect replica of himself, *as* that image has been absorbed into the being of the other; and this token of a perfect self is woven to completion *within* the one to whom it had been imparted by a dynamism peculiar to *his* nature. Thereby alone do persons transcend one another, and fashion distinctive images from the singular elements which belong to their respective natures. Yet, too, persons are immanent in one another. For each experiences, in symbolic offerings, actual extensions of the other as components of his own existence.

Yet, when all is said and done, the mystery, the absurdity, the anguish, the sheer paradoxicality of human existence remains. It haunts us, and stirs our wonder; it taunts us, and compels our never-ceasing continuance of the quest to know wherein lie the source, the justifications, and the very foundation for the agonizing loneliness which, at times, rims our entire existence. One turns to Job, and, with him, one attunes oneself to his cry:

> Man that is born of a woman is of few days, and
> full of trouble.
> He cometh forth like a flower, and is cut down;
> he fleeth also as a
> shadow, and continueth not. . . .
> There is hope of a tree, if it be cut down,
> that it will sprout
> again, and that the tender branch thereof will
> not cease. . . .
> But man dieth, and wasteth away: yea, man giveth
> up the ghost, and where is he?
> As the waters fail from the sea, and the flood
> decayeth and drieth up,
> So man lieth down, and riseth not; till the heavens
> be no more, they
> shall not awake, nor be raised out of their sleep [14:1–2, 7, 10–12].

Is this not the universal lament of humankind? And yet, with its better voice, does not humankind, with Job, utter that anguished refrain which alone grounds the experience of transfiguration?

> . . . till I die I will not remove mine integrity
> from me.
> My righteousness I hold fast, and I will not let
> it go . . . [27:5–6].

For, out of the whirlwind, God then speaks to Job:

> Who is this that darkeneth counsel without knowledge?
> Gird up now thy loins like a man, for I will demand
> of thee, and answer thou me.
> Where wast thou when I laid the foundations of the earth?
> declare, if thou hast understanding.
> Who hath laid the measures thereof, if thou knowest?
> or who hath stretched the line
> upon it?
> Whereupon are the foundations thereof fastened? or who
> laid the corner stone thereof;
> When the morning stars sang together, and all the sons
> of God shouted for joy [38:2–7]?

And Job answers:

> I know that thou canst do everything, and that no thought
> can be withholden from thee,
> Who is he that hideth counsel without knowledge? Therefore
> have I uttered that I understood
> not; things too wonderful for me,
> which I knew not.
> Hear, I beseech thee, and I will speak: I will demand
> of thee, and declare thou unto me.
> I have heard of thee by the hearing of the ear: but not
> mine eye seeth thee.
> Wherefore I abhor myself, and repent in dust and ashes [42:2–7].

Thus humbling himself, yet with the dignity of his integrity intact before the impenetrable mysteries of Creator and creation, Job receives God's response:

> . . . the Lord blessed the latter end of Job more than
> his beginning. . . .
> After this lived Job a hundred and forty years, and
> saw his sons, and
> his son's sons, even four generations.
> So Job died, being old and full of days [42:12, 16].

No *explication de texte* can more profoundly render this account of the acts by which, amid the interweavings of his lamentation and his celebration, man achieves his most profound spiritual metamorphoses.

C • TRANSCENDENCE AND THE TRANSCENDENTAL

(*a*) From "Empirical I" to "Transcendental I"

I have proposed certain ontologic structures in terms of which self-unification is achieved: namely, integrality, power, and authenticity. When its implications have been worked out, each structure emerges as grounding its immediately antecedent structures. Accordingly, the mind–body unity reveals the character of integrality. However, this merely formal concept is propaedeutic to understanding such unity as no mere correlation, but as a necessary connection, an intrinsic substantive link, namely, power. And insofar as power, which is sheer activity, exhibits specific dynamisms by which it unfolds through a definite sequence of moments, it is quintessentially both dialectical and concrete and, at the same time, universal and archetypal. In its deeper implications, these dynamisms express a person's authenticity, that consummated flow from mere possibility to power which is self-actualized as integrity. Manifesting itself also as an unfolding of moments, authenticity arises in the context of human encounter; and it discloses its own character through transfigurations which involve an interplay of lamentation and celebration.

In a table, I schematize the architecture of transcendentality.

Table of Categories for Conceptualizing the Ontology of the Person

Abstract Classification of the Progressive Disclosure of Hitherto Immanent Grounds		Corresponding Concrete Ontologic Categories Which Constitute the Content of Those Grounds
Formal and Abstract	←-- | --→	Integrality
Substantive and Prescriptive	←-- | --→	Power
Articulated and Processive	←-- | --→	Authenticity ↓
Formal and Abstract	←-- | --→	Compresence ↓
Substantive and Prescriptive	←-- | --→	Transfiguration ↓
Articulated and Processive	←-- | --→	Transcendentality ↓
Formal and Abstract	←-- | --→	Limitative Transcendentality
Substantive and Prescriptive	←-- | --→	Illuminative Transcendentality
Articulated and Processive	←-- | --→	Incarnate Transcendentality

Under the topic of *transcendence*, I subsume such categories as precede transcendentality, and, through a dialectical transmutation *through* transcendence, culminate in it. This process presupposes the following principles.

Every person is an activity of searching. Seeking to penetrate the mysteries which ever haunt his world, both inner and outer, he discovers, in the end, that inner and outer unite as one world. For as each person strives to probe those mysteries to their outermost limit, he learns that the mysteries which lie at the end of both quests are identical; and no person, insofar as he is unburdened of pathology, can rest content with any discernible resolution of these mysteries. On the contrary, being content with a particular resolution, no matter how plausible, entails relapse into mere habit, stereotypy, and, ultimately, personal dissolution. Succumbing to termination of the quest leads inexorably to self-diminution. On the other hand, when one is incited to transcend such specious termini, one is ineluctably led to self–*re*-creation. For to search is not merely to discover. Far more, it is to draw forth from the womb of nature entirely new representations, each more inclusive than its predecessors, and, even beyond that, to shape altogether new natures, natures hitherto concealed within the old. By the very processes by which the natural order thus supersedes itself, one re-creates nature even as one creates oneself anew, hence transfigures oneself. By virtue of the powers inhering in each co-participant in the dialectic of compresence, the substantive expression of compresence confers a deeper-lying integrality on both co-participants: namely, a profound metamorphosis of their minds and their bodies. In consequence, one rises to wholly new modes of compresence; and this passage concretizes itself through the symbols which one shapes, symbols wherein arise ever-new orientations toward the world, a world which is textured with infinite complexity.

Throughout *Choros*, I have regarded the person as a self-actualizing agent in whom the power of free, spontaneous, and autonomous decision inheres. Standing before a world which opens to him as an abyss of uncertainty, he envisages myriad possibilities for action. And, puzzled regarding his destiny, which he senses as restricting these possibilities but which he himself, locus of free action, continually redetermines, he ever expands their sphere. His life's very direction is the cumulative product of his previous decisions; the orientations and commentaries, and the shapings of the world which they entail, quality his being at every instant. Yet by his feeling this quality, and by his discerning the elements which compose it, he is empowered to alter the subsequent course of his existence. Though absolute freedom is somehow intrinsic to every decision, no act occurs *de novo*. Primordially, the person is endowed with a specific texture of powers which both unfold according to a "natural" tendency and are informed, from moment to moment, by the impact on him of the consequences of his every decision. A complex of motives is engendered; it is blended with powers already present. Accordingly, each decision is conditioned by, indeed made within, a matrix of motives which, in the course of a life, come to be organized about some central motivation. And the motives which culminate in subsequent decision are themselves conditioned by this focal drive. How to reconcile the multiplicity of motives with a unitary, potent motivation, and how to resolve the paradox between *free* decision and *determined* decision are topics for later books.

All parts of a person are mobilized in the service of a concern which arises in, and is clarified by, human action. Between those parts obtains a certain equilibrium; the parts cohere as a complex unity, a self-identical, self-perpetuating pattern amid change and diversity. Woven into this fabric are impressions from all that impinges upon one. In the continual realignment of equilibria thereby induced, novel syntheses are achieved. Reaching back toward his own deepest roots, themselves composed of the cumulative impact of innumerable impressions which constantly flow through his being, and therein reverberate as multiple foci of influence, the person solidifies his existence. And, facing toward the world in its outer, spectatorial dimension, he, in turn, imprints himself on *its* components. He prolongs into the succeeding moments of his life such factors as he has implicitly selected to perpetuate, insofar as his previous history will enable him, a perfect replica of himself. Likewise he objectifies himself in those contiguous existents which he deems relevant for fulfilling his own existence.

This symbolic presentation of self to other expresses the flow of an indiscerptible mind–body unity. In its very evanescence, at times a transparent disclosure of spirit and at times obscure, this unity reflects a mysterious inner world which eludes precise conceptualization. From this pervasive silence, a person draws forth those expressions by which, thereupon, he impresses himself into the future, a future which ever emerges by the conjoint decisions of all contemporary creatures in their ceaseless advance beyond the boundaries of their moment-by-moment existences. He is impelled to seek to lay bare the miracle of both interior and exterior ramifications of his own being. And as these realms expand, his trust, and hence his capacity further to give himself, increase. Intimacies with a reality which he co-participantly shapes progressively grow. Yet the strands of human existence stretch toward realms which, though they constitute one, reach infinitely beyond one.

As a creature, hence finite, a person cannot indefinitely prolong his quest to know. Recognizing his limits, yet overwhelmed by the immensity of that which lies both within and without, that to which, in his very origins, he is substantively joined and, in his very destiny, he is inexorably linked, he experiences an awe so great that he is ever tempted to seek security and freedom *from* the expansion of his powers; and tends to reduce his existence toward mere points of inner and outer, rather than experiencing them as fully merging into foci within a single, comprehensive manifold. Withdrawing from these realms, and their veridical synthesis, every person constricts his being, and reifies his agential character. Losing the reality of both memory and hope, he substitutes illusion for it.

Yet, once again, the power of choice is his. Though the contours of a life are determined, one can always opt to inscribe on such themes as have already been stipulated by antecedent decisions endless novel variations. By repetition of these "melodies," a reharmonizing, at every moment, of all discordant factors within one's being, one irradiates the world with singular qualities; one both deepens and enlarges one's own personhood. In greater clarity, the person symbolically engrains his self-perfected extensions into the world. Synthesizing the fleeting fragments of his selfhood into an expanding self-conscious unity, in which he apprehends the world as forming with him an "integrity," he attains symbolic immortality.

As agent,[6] the person, from a naturalistic point of view, is not a simple unity. An hierarchically ordered complex, he is composed of innumerable subsidiary agencies in varying modes of subordination and superordination. From clusters of agents, each a center of activity, radiate influences which ramify into complicated patterns. Interpenetrating, these influences either intensify or diminish one another. Each impinges upon, and, in turn, is acted upon by, the remainder; and each action occurs in a manner and degree prescribed by their overall interplay. Within a field of influences, individual impulses are transmitted, coordinated, eliminated, or enhanced. An intensity of experience is achieved through amplifying, balancing, and contrasting those impulses. Now harmony endures. Constituting a temporal order, it forms a cohesive chain the links of which are individual pulsations of existence.

I speak of "pulsation," for I stress the rhythmic, vibratory nature of human being, and, indeed, of being in general; and, in addition, the multi-phasic character of each undulation. In every pulse, I distinguish three phases. First, relevant factors which derive both from antecedent pulses composing the person and from contiguous pulses constitutive of other durable existents, whether persons or non-persons, are woven into unity. In this synthesis, many factors are eliminated. As much by what has been extruded or ignored in the universe of possibilities as by what has been selected and incorporated, the novelty of a pulse manifests itself. By free choice, every person transcends his world. The manner of transcendence derives from the form which he inherits from antecedent pulses. By decision, the person stands alone amid the welter of factors which he has negated as *his* possibilities. His perspective on the world is unique and indefeasible. Next, as resolution of creative anxiety, there is enjoyment of this self-created unity, a unity achieved through the original fusion of diverse influences. For each undulation is invaded by radical originality: a person's decision to be as *he* is; for him to exist in the style of no other, that he might envisage only such possibilities of attainment as are relevant to his singular existence. In its immediacy, this consummatory phase may endure, for an extended instant of felt eternity, by its "participation" in a realm where immediacy does not fade: an eternal order of ceaseless creation. The power to endure incorruptibly flows momentarily through every pulse from a source which ineluctably transcends it. By the finitude of each pulse, immediacy must tragically pass. Yet every pulse refuses to perish absolutely—though to achieve an inner harmony of completion, it must, in its manner, perish authentically. Indeed, in the final phase, it impresses itself into another pulse, persisting substantively as one of *its* components. Attaining a limited self-perfection as an actual imprint within the succeeding pulse, each pulsation of personal existence struggles to express itself perfectly according to an ideal inherited from its own antecedents. Through this prolongation, it transmits that flow of feeling which constitutes self-identity. And all pulsations of human existence are united according to a principle of identity which prescribes a distinct direction of flow. Contours are inherited which impose themselves upon subsequent pulses. Analogously, every achieved unity of feeling imprints itself, in *idealized* self-completion, upon contiguous pulsations of existence which are not integral to the person. Thus flows such feeling as constitutes communion. By modeling himself after an ideal pattern, into conformity with which he brings each new pulse, every person affirms his autonomy.

Woven into pulse after pulse is a power which, though it may ramify and disperse itself into foci of multiple influence, is continually remobilized as a unitary force. Whatever the extrinsic influences which have modified the character of a person, the quest to imprint an original nature upon a succeeding nature is stubborn. A refusal absolutely to perish expresses this radical tenacity of human existence and, indeed, of existence in general. There is a primordial urge to persist, and to transmit a definite inheritance from one pulse to its sequent pulse, and, though less forcibly, to make a durable mark upon neighboring creatures. Every person wills to live according to his unique, indefeasible endowment. Seeking everlastingness, he strives to negate the passage of time, to perpetuate the intensity of his satisfaction, and to achieve transcendence of his limited self-enjoyment of immediacy as a being who will eternally persist. Quite literally, the flow of personal feeling remains an incorruptible component in every human existence. A persistent unity *within* experience, this flow is more than a mere summing up of inheritances, and a transmission of patterns of feeling or reactivity. Each instant of human existence is momentous. Every person seeks perpetuation of what is settled and final, a satisfaction which he substantively engrains both upon himself, as he thrusts himself into his own future, and upon another—always, of course, under the relevant symbolic perspective, and with appropriate diminution or enhancement of intensity. He perpetuates as an ideal that perfect form to which he aspires as defining the unique qualities of his original nature, a nature formed by the singular mode of confluence of the very factors which first shaped his being.

This triphasic movement of a pulsation of human existence is executed by autonomous activity which is self-integrating, self-organizing, self-affirming, and self-perpetuating. By these acts, fragments are synthesized into unity. What is irrelevant for attaining satisfaction is eliminated, while a creative surge of novel intensities of feeling is woven into unity. Overcoming deficiencies of the satisfaction, an ideal replica is perpetuated as a component of every sequent pulse. This ideal is envisaged by a kind of "empirical I," which arises through the actual meetings between persons owing to that interplay of selves whereby, in the process of becoming complete, each person presents to the other his consummatory phase. Thereby, the quest of the "empirical I" to seek an inner, creative, individuating, and, ultimately, grounding "transcendental I"[7] is spurred.

Full personal consummation requires both a turning within to confront the sources of one's being and a turning without toward that community with other which arises from appropriate balance between self-mastery and self-renunciation.

These modalities of *turning toward* are complementary; they are woven into every pulse of existence. Thereby, exterior dialogue is facilitated, and, indeed, made possible, when it alternates with that inner dialogue wherein the "empirical I" responds to the inmost *I*: an *I* which may be conceptualized only under an authentically *transcendental* perspective; an *I*, moreover, which resonates to the natural rhythms of all existence. Expressing an original sythesizing activity, these rhythms express the ground for the unity of the entire manifold of "appearances" of reality within each human experience. To penetrate such appearance, the "transcendental I" must be brought into communion with the "empirical I"; and, when dialogue is successful, and both *I*'s are joined as a single integral action, the realities of both "within" and "without" become luminous. Dwelling in a more vibrant, unitary world, one gathers into one's own being, and thereby increases the richness, depth, and coherence of its inwardness, all that lies about one, and within one. No mere spectator, as two realities unfold before one, one becomes both participant and co-creator.

(*b*) The Transcendental Community

Both self and complement to self (namely, all that is *not* the self but, nonetheless, relevant to the self) are engendered by an implicit harmony between myriad "transcendental" selves in relation to the world. This synchronous complex of *vis vitae* gives birth to the miraculous procession of reality, an eternal panorama of self-fulfillment. Each entity, person or non-person, achieves fruition in accordance with its singular nature, a nature which actualizes itself by its very participation in this symphony of self-realizing agents. Each agent views some aspect of the coherent face of the universe under a perspective peculiar to its nature; and it shares this perspective with similar entities, so that the entirety constitutes a family of co-operant, self-actualizing, and autonomous agents in communion—agents which might be either human or non-human.

The contrasts and complementarities of such communion, their supplementations and their dissonances, are woven into a unified fabric. However, since each agent is but a finite emanation of an hierarchically ordered realm, a vast texture of eternal modes,[8] individual agents struggle to survive in a world deprived of its eternal status. The character of the struggle depends on specific limitations inherent in the agents. But, in effect, every agent hesitates to attune iself to the eternal which ever flows within it. It fears the mysterious silence which ever enshrouds it. By its very communions, pre-eminently for persons, it senses a threat to its individuality, for it fails to recognize that individuality is constituted by communion. In this struggle, it generates secondary voices with which it consults as though they were primary, "transcendental" selves. For reality, an image of reality is substituted—an image the complexity of which is shaped by the multiple groups and sub-groups in which the agent participates, and with respect to which it announces, particularly when human, both prescriptions and recommendations for conduct. Always in competition with the primary voices, these derivative voices constitute a barrier to experiencing either the pain or the joy which arise from authentic response to the purer, inner melodies of the cosmos. That it might again touch its original, inmost voice, the "empirical I" must even dissolve this barrier. In this way, its status *sub specie durationis* is emended toward a status *sub specie aeternitatis*.

Every particular "transcendental I" synchronizes itself with the ground by which all entities, and, in particular, other such transcendental I's, achieve *their* self-identities. And, in general, reality constitutes a fabric of events so interwoven and coordinated as to reflect the evolving coherence of selves-in-relation. In addition, reality so imprints itself in every particular self as to constitute, as it evolves, a coherent manifold. In fact, thus perceived by an ever-expanding "empirical self," i.e., a self which expands toward the status of transcendentality, that process *constitutes* self-identity.

Self-identity and the intrinsic unity of the diversified parts of the world are mutually implicated; each presupposes the other. The first cannot *be* unless its complement exists. For both self and complement (i.e., world as set apart from self) derive their intrinsic congruity from their respective natures as actualizations of the same indivisible potency. Indeed, it inheres in "potency" to give rise to an actuality which is fragmented only in perspectives on it relevant for *finite* entities. But this "giving rise" is not durational in the usual sense of a passage of time. For potency and actuality presuppose one another. They are not moments in a temporal process. And the phases I have distinguished express the "structure" of the actualization of potency. When one speaks of the powers by which an organism evolves and matures, one is "projecting" an event which occurs in the order of eternity onto the scale of the durational and finite.

All entities are empowered to rectify errors which arise when the unity of the self in its congruence with its complement is degraded into a fragmentary, pulverized reality. For man dwells in two worlds: that in which he is participant, active and fully immersed, wherein the passage of time is not experienced for the brief moment of his sojourn; that which is a privative, imperfect emanation of the first, wherein he refers his "co-derivative complement,"[9] not to their common origin but to his own nature, conceiving himself as spectator rather than participant. Thereby, he partially deprives himself of his own potency, referring all happenings to himself as privileged center. He cannot envisage the universe as a vast interplay of mutually implicated agents of which he is but one. Contrary to his self-referential conviction, which itself arises from confusion between inmost voice and secondary voice, the universe is not a great sphere removed from him, a sphere which he detachedly observes and manipulates. On the contrary, man is fully immersed in the universe, co-sharing its destiny as well as co-creating its nature.

Earlier, I distinguished an absolute refusal to perish from a more restricted but nonetheless authentic refusal to perish. Whereas the first refusal is absolutely resisted, owing to the very nature of the person, the second refusal is but relatively resisted when a person denies his nature. For when a pulsation which has attained its satisfaction refuses to perish, it drags itself away from its own future and, indeed, from the futures of others. Under such circumstances, a person is burdened with his past; he cannot fully open himself to the novelties which ceaselessly unfold as available to an unfettered experience. In consequence, the flow of feeling is retarded. Both self-identity and communion are degraded. A pattern of conformity too rigidly inflicts itself on a succession of pulses. For many consummatory phases have refused to perish, and, thereby, impose their cumulative weight on all sequent pulses. Such impeding of the very process of existence derives from, and, in turn, accentuates, interference by the "internalized" voices which express neither the "empirical" nor the "transcendental" self but, rather, the stereotyped roles by which one's society impinges on an individual who too readily renounces his inmost voice. Indeed, these brief considerations suggest that human pathology should be incorporated within any metaphysical system which purports to be adequate to human nature.

In *Homo Quaerens*, I referred to the "ethereal presences" which disclose the *inseitas* of reality.[10] When a person fully grasps his being as a co-operant agent *within* nature, i.e., as participant in the very processes which sustain him, and he derives his powers from its powers, as they diffuse themselves over all nature, he no longer views entities in the manner of the scientist. For the scientist characterizes the flow of events from the outside, as though he moves over the surface of a great sphere, describing a structure but dimly illuminated by a distant light within the sphere. By contrast, he who would *fully* express his agential nature so penetrates the sphere that he moves toward its center, the source of all radiance; and finding his natural position, he discerns its structure from within. Moreover, he grasps the full depth of his inward being as implicated in that structure, as indeed its microcosmic analogue. In this way, he feels himself opening out toward all that befalls him; he welcomes the mysteries of his birth, his growth, and his death; he witnesses the indefinitely extensive ramifications of the roots of his being; and he is an eternal participant in an intrinsically incorruptible cosmos.

In sum, I conceive a community of individuals: each self-actualizing, as his unique powers are drawn from an indefeasible center, until he shapes a unified fabric of expression; each self-individualizing, by the decisions which, in determining a specific direction for subsequent action, shape an identity; each self-affirming, by that thrusting into an unknown future which, *as* it is carved into *his* world, is appropriated by his consequently fuller existence; and each self-transcending, by the stirring of new powers in his every act of affirmation. Yet every member of this plenum of radically distinct individuals exhibits the capacity for authentic communion. Mutually immanent while reciprocally transcendent, these individuals constitute a matrix wherein each attains his full distinctiveness. Thus imprinted, thence perishing into his complement, every person expresses his characteristic rhythms, even while he contributes to the predatory states which never cease to alternate with states of true collaboration. In symbolic presentation of self to complement, wherein symbols spring from interior, essential powers, every person creates, within this framework, a realm wherein he can responsibly both decide and act. The cadences, dissonances, and harmonies which arise with respect to both congruencies and disparities between the self and the other are orchestrated into a cosmic drama wherein individuals alternately thwart one another and create the conditions by which each may bring his powers to fruition.

(*c*) Numinous Eternity

Born from an interior mysterium of silence, these melodies burst forth as spur to a transfiguration of persons into participants in a richer, more diversified community, amid, however, the tragic clash of persons doomed to detachment, isolation, and alienation from full community. By authentic self-presentation, wherein all façades dissolve, each presents himself trustingly to his complement. Absorbing the pain of rebuff, he so integrates conflict as to convert it into harmony. Veritably metamorphosing himself, he comes to dwell, if momentarily, in an eternity the perfect moments of which are sustained, renewed, and intensified. As individuals unite to constitute themselves complemental pairs of self-fulfilling persons, the pulsations of existence are heightened, and subtilized. Drawing forth a perfect image of himself, his full powers momentarily actualized, each synergizes the rhythms of the other. Initially partial, all humankind's rhythms now become accepted as mirroring the veridical rhythms of the cosmos. Thus, one displaces one's center, consolidated by symbolic activity, from self to cosmos. Without renouncing individuality, one becomes a participant in a true family of agents. The moments of a human existence cohere as a unity. A past which has been vividly experienced is absorbed, and perishes into a larger, more meaningful, and more vibrant present.

Both agent and relatum, the integral person, in whom mind and body are conjoined, manifests a single dynamism, an indivisible potency actualized in the dialogue between "empirical I" and "transcendental I." By his power, man's specific potentialities unfold, and, in effect, specify their sources, expressing both the synthesizing into consummation within a pulse and the processes by which man, a sequence of pulses, attains his maturity. In authenticity, each person shapes the existence of another, while retaining his individuality: a reciprocation of symbolic presentations with respect to both impingements of contemporary pulses and meetings between those *nexus* of pulses which form persons. And, by his integrity he achieves wholeness, realizing his true identity in the context of his fulfilled communings.

Throughout these pages, I have referred to transcendentality. Now this theme requires final formulation with respect to its relevance to *Choros*. First, I specify, as previously, the world as an assemblage of things, a world intrinsically unknown and, in any ultimate sense, unknowable; next, I specify the community of selves, whose inmost depths are likewise unfathomable; lastly, I specify the cosmos as subsuming, in both creating and creative aspects, things *and* selves.

With respect to things, which are not merely passive facts, but unfoldings, processes, and activities, selves frame ideas which constitute more or less coherent descriptions of varying degrees of adequacy with respect to facts. Yet immanent in every description is a prescriptive element. Woven with ideas are ideals, a normative factor. By this factor, I mean those principles which prescribe such facts, factors in facts, and contexts in which facts are embedded, which are relevant to framing the representations of things. In brief, immanently conditioning every idea is an ideal; immanently conditioning every thing, passively construed, is an action. Still, the totality of things does not itself constitute a fact. No idea can be shaped which is adequate to, or even approximately conforms with, that which is indeed no fact, but, quite the contrary, something which, though no-*thing*, nonetheless both envelops and suffuses facts. Though the primary role of ideas is to bring themselves into conformity with facts, every idea carries through its shaping task by experimentally rearranging facts. No description of bare fact can be rendered circumspectly and detachedly (in effect, behavioristically), save by reference to an infinite regress of experiments on nature, experiments on the experimenter as he experiments, and so forth. Accordingly, in the last analysis, freely executed acts ground the entire sequence of descriptive representations of fact. The factual realm itself gradually but progressively expands its horizons, and ever widens its boundaries. Herein lies the first phase by which duration temporalizes itself: through the concrete moments of a past always in process of perishing, the present comes to be vividly apprehended; and the future remains utterly unknown, save by a trajectory deriving from the past through the present, utterly unknown because it is racially non-existent. In the end, all is enveloped by eternity—yet, an eternity the mystery of which is falsely, distortedly, or inadequately acknowledged by cognition: Kant's noumenon of his *First Critique*! [11] Nonetheless, the self derives its power of reasoning, a power by which it endeavors to shape ideas adequate to experience by its dwelling in, or, more appropriately, at the edge of, a limitative and strictly formal transcendentality.

However, implicit in this initial phase, wherein the self relates itself to the world, lies an already-emerging second phase. For inherent in the primordially cognitive determination of phenomena is a self which experiments, and, thereby, orients itself freely, selectively, spontaneously, and autonomously toward this or that aspect of fact. Hence, reason not only contains the dynamism which directs its own unfolding, but, beyond that, engenders the uncovering of hitherto concealed facts. Under the perspective of limitative transcendentality, the self barely begins to penetrate the unknown, an eternity which constitutes the very matrix of temporality. And, as it probes, it inverts the link between idea and fact. Now, the ideal element, an element which heretofore had been merely immanent in the first phase—namely, the phase of ideation—comes to dominate. Emerging into the foreground of potential self-discernment, the self proceeds quite explicitly to reshape the world in accordance with its own norms, norms which themselves dynamically unfold as the self endeavors to release the *activity* element from passive enclosure in the factual element, an element which constitutes but a cross-section of the arrested mobility of sheer activity. Hence, the self applies its own progressively self-reconstituted ideals, which it prescribes to itself as nonetheless containing a descriptive component, to the metamorphosis of acts which are paradigmatic of all activity: namely, the acts of selves. Accordingly, a community of selves emerges, each self now construed as an end in itself, as increasingly bringing its component interactions into conformity with the dynamically self-transforming ideals. At this point, the self begins to probe its own inwardness, and to evaluate its own ideals. The inwardness which is thus drawn forth complements the self's aboriginal preoccupation with nature's outwardness, manifested in the first phase. Thereby, the self seeks to convert mere cognitive or assertive judgments into active judgments: those activities of selves which, in their characteristic ways, both comment interpretively on hitherto concealed textures of the world and, at the same time, manifest the interior depths of the very selves who comment. Adequation in the converse sense supervenes. For the self now seeks to con-form other selves to its own self. In active reciprocity with other selves, each in-forming the other with its own self-formed norms, it both concretizes and amplifies its own ideals, circulating those ideals throughout the human community. What had been mere limitative transcendentality increasingly reveals selves acting with selves under the perspective of ideals which, ultimately, are prescribed by the unknown mysteries of a hidden, *numinously* illuminated eternity. Illuminated transcendentality for the first time fully reveals itself.

In a diagram, I sum up these complementary phases, each immanent in the other, and together, as I shortly show, entailing a third phase, a phase which

	adequation or conformation effected by selves who probe	
1st Phase:	Fact ⟷ Idea (immanent action) (immanent ideal)	Cognitive moment of limitative transcendentality
2nd Phase:	Act ⟷ Ideal (immanent fact) (immanent idea)	Exhibitive (ethical) moment of illuminative transcendentality

subsumes the earlier phases, without negating either the identity or the autonomy of either phase.

Subsuming these phases in a kind of Hegelian *Aufheben*, while denying neither the independence nor the validity of either, is a synthesis of both: though each is antithetic to the other, each is also complementary since each contains an ingredient of it. In dialectical fashion, act and ideal are now brought into *mutual* conformation, or adequation, in which each factor reshapes itself in response to the reshaping of the other. A veridical cosmos which embraces both self and world emerges, each interwoven with the other. By its very acts of penetrating this jointly shaped cosmos, reason (or *Geist*) spontaneously, imaginationally, and searchingly comes to fruition. At last, transcendentality becomes incarnate.

Articulated through a new succession of moments, eternity reveals fathomless depths to the probing self. In consequence, both limitative transcendentality and illuminative transcendentality are utterly transformed. For, the self ever seeks, at the outset, to press beyond the limits set by the first phase, and, thence, to accentuate the illumination of its own quest as expressed by both phases. Dwelling at first peripherally to, but with ever-increasing centrality in, transcendentality, as it gives itself up to eternity, now construed as substantive reality dialectically constituted, and, thereby, repotentiating its own probing capacities, the self experiences a new unfolding. In creative discovery, it discloses moments of novelty which point toward mysteries as yet beyond comprehension. Increasingly, the person, who is the self incarnate and consummated, ascertains the ultimate ground of human transcendence to reside in the rooting of himself in ever-more-inclusive schemes of a self which is so dynamically implicated with the world as actually to engender the cosmos. At this point, I revise the Hegelian sequence of unfolding moments,[12] a revision which I justify in later books; and I represent my anticipated revisions in the following diagram:

Act ⇄ Ideal

self-probing, transcendentality incarnate;
in mutual, dialectical, and reciprocal
co-adaptation and conformation

First Unfolding:
truth: philosophy
goodness: religion
beauty: art (in general)

Second Unfolding:
truth of beauty: mysticism
goodness of beauty: silence
beauty of beauty: mysterium

As these moments unfold, and moments within moments unfold, the ontologic structures primordially grounding personhood pass into ontogenetic categories. In *Homo Quaerens*, the method for studying persons progressively transforms itself into ontology, as its component techniques are concretely applied to the investigation of this or that aspect of the person; hence, my subtitle *Method Become Ontology*. In *The Dance of Being*, the person, conceived under a naturalistic perspective—hence, in his infrapersonal being as, by stages, it converges upon his full personhood—becomes progressively construed under the rubric of a transcendental perspective, a perspective in which (as the subtitle announces) *Man's Labyrinthine Rhythms* must be specified. In subsequent books I shall trace the full implications of this double transformation. But in order to ground man's *spiritual* transfiguration, the ontology of the person qua person had to be set forth first in this book. And by the conclusions of *Choros*, which bring the earlier, merely naturalistic transfiguration to fruition as (according to my present subtitle) *The Orchestrating Self*, the category of transcendentality as such, as indeed, grounding every category which had preceded it, reveals, in a formula, that *ontology* has now become *ontogeny*!

NOTES

1. See the items indexed under "Love" and "Work" in "Civilization and Its Discontents," *Standard Edition* XXI, trans. Strachey.

2. Buchler, *Toward a General Theory of Human Judgment*, pp. 3–38.

3. Rainer Maria Rilke, *The Notebooks of Malte Laurids Brigge*, trans. M. D. Herter-Norton (New York: Norton, 1949), p. 27.

4. See the "Notes" to Rilke's *Sonnets to Orpheus*, trans. Herter-Norton, p. 143.

5. ". . . es gibt nur ein ewig Neues, das sich aus den erweiterten Elementen des Vergangenen gestaltet . . . ," *Goethes Gespräche*, edd. Flodoard von Biedermann and Wolfgang Herwig, 3 vols. in 4 (Zurich & Stuttgart: Artemis, 1971), III 611; cited and trans., Schachtel, *Metamorphosis*, p. 282.

6. See the index of Buchler, *Toward a General Theory of Human Judgment* for a discussion of the person as an active "proceiver."

7. See the items indexed under "empirical" and "transcendental" in Kant, *Critique of Pure Reason*, trans. Kemp Smith.

8. See the items indexed under "agency "and "mode" in Hallett, *Creation, Emanation, and Salvation.*

9. See the items indexed under "co-derivative complement" in ibid.

10. P. 43.

11. For a full explication of the noumenon, see Kant's three *Critiques.*

12. These moments are presented, in all their vicissitudes and elaborations, throughout his *Phenomenology of Spirit.*

EPILOGUE

Method become Ontology! "Naturality" become Transcendentality! Ontology become Ontogeny! Throughout these three volumes, and most clearly articulated in *Choros*, this triadic formula has never ceased to recur as its dominant refrain.

Faith that the very techniques which reveal who a person truly is leads to a blending of the techniques, and to their integration as a unitary method, a method no sooner articulated, in its deeper import, than it transforms itself into the person himself—the person whose own agency discloses who he actually is: namely, both seeker and sought, in a word, *homo quaerens*. Thereby, his grounding ontologic structures reveal themselves; thereby, the structures themselves unfold in phases: the ontology of the infrapersonal, the ontology of the strictly personal, and, in later books, the ontology of the person in relation to the cosmos. Herein, hope emerges that, when the natural person is, in his natural foundations, sufficiently probed by the relevant coordinated techniques, themes pertaining to the infrapersonal will, through dialectical interplay, converge, in a transcendental doctrine, on consummate personhood. Now, as the ontologic structures of person qua person unfold, they metamorphose into ontogenetic structures. For if the quintessential person is constituted by a compresence which entails transfiguration toward unfolding moments of transcendentality, then human nature consists in all that is counterposed to nature: namely, in love—love of a person for himself, love for other persons, their love for him. The Scriptural triad of faith, hope, and love repeats itself in an altogether new context. And if the transformation of method into ontology is construed as a quest for the truth of personhood, and the transformation of the natural, conceived as infrapersonal factors which shape one toward transcendental status, is construed as a striving toward the goodness of personhood, then the themes of this volume, especially transfiguration, transcendence, and the transcendental, converge on the beauty of personhood. Once again, the Scriptural triad correlates with the Greek triad: namely, the moments of truth, goodness, and beauty.

To reiterate: one gives oneself up in faith, that method, through its progressive "self-ontologization," will allow a person's entire being, the actual truth of his existence, to disclose itself; and this task is accomplished when the very method for studying the person becomes the person himself. However, once the person emerges through the method's concrete application, further reflection reveals such strictly natural forces as come to fruition in consummate personhood; and, thereby, one is led to hope that the person will shape himself as a moral being, and bring himself under immanent obligation to actualize his natural proclivities as a person, so that his goodness will shine forth. But in this process, the natural status of the person is transcended; and he reveals himself as dwelling in two realms: the kingdom of means, namely, the natural ways by which he becomes a person; and the kingdom of ends, namely his personhood itself. Finally, once *that* process has consummated itself, the person reveals his essence to consist in love, *human* love, and its myriad ramifications. Correlatively, the successive stages by which one achieves full beauty as a person unfold.

Just as each volume is self-referential, in the sense that its own architectonic corresponds to the same phases by which the person shapes himself, so the volumes, taken as a totality, are likewise self-referential. Two considerations suggest this. First, after all, it is a particular person, namely, myself, who, from my own experience, rich or impoverished, is evolving the metaphysical categories herein presented, in the very acts by which I am a searching and maturing person. Secondly, the topics which I treat in later books yet to be written—hence, books with which I have as yet but a passing acquaintanceship—only gradually, as they are specifically worked through, disclose the essential ordering of topics to correlate with the essential ordering of a person's growth as, through his own life's vicissitudes, he gropes toward wisdom. And, never, in writing these books, have I more than synoptically anticipated the directions toward which my searching will lead me. Hence, I, myself a seeker, am the most obvious exemplification of persons as, by essence, seekers, seekers who open themselves to the teachings of what they cannot, at any concrete stage of life, fully discern. Moreover, I, of a certain age, have experienced, at times authentically, but, doubtless, often in distorted fashion, many of life's stages on which I shall reflect in *Metamorphosis*. Yet, too, I must then project myself, by a kind of empathic telepathy, into certain stages, especially those of incarnate transcendentality, without having actually experienced these stages. And, presumably, as I elaborate topics to be included in my final book, where I quest after the veridical person, I shall be closer to experiences which, at this moment, I can but dimly apprehend; hence, I shall be more competent to treat that quest.

"All men by nature desire to know," declared the Philosopher who was master among those who know; and knowing is an unfolding which, beginning subtly, imperceptibly, and tentatively, progresses through phases until, by symbols, one brings oneself into empathic relatedness to a world which reveals itself to one as, reciprocally, one reveals oneself to it. The need to know is deeply engrained in every person. By essence, every person is a philosopher, is even, indeed, under existential compulsion to philosophize. *A fortiori*, personology, as λόγος of the person, i.e., as systematically reasoned discourse about persons, which can be engaged in only by persons, is not merely linked to but, in fact, internally identical with ontology, which is analogous discourse about being qua being. The quests to set forth a person's essential traits and to disclose the "being" of any entity are mutually implicated; each search both illuminates and fructifies the other. Though the first quest is conducted independently of the second, both are woven into the same fabric of knowledge, and each expands its horizons as the other is more deeply probed. Initially disparate, these inquiries become increasingly collaborative, and, ultimately, identical. Pre-eminently, a person is locus wherein being as such emerges, and reveals its essential contours; and, through him, a more adequate, coherent, and systematic theory of reality formulates itself.

Systematically expounding the primordial character of the entity to the parts of which such special disciplines as psychology, sociology, and physiology apply their distinctive procedures, a personology transcends the limited perspectives which they provide. Including these perspectives, personology reaches beyond, however tentatively, to realms of experience not yet comprehended by science and, indeed, perhaps not even comprehensible by science. Therefore, it is essential to distinguish the λόγος of the psychic, social, and physical–biologic aspects of man from the λόγος of the locus of activity from which these disparate spheres of expression spring. To understand the entirety of a person's manifestations as cohering in their very diversity, these manifestations must be regarded as symbolizing forces which work within him, by the interplay of which those "natural" constellations of behavior treated by science arise. A personology aims to exhibit this unity as consequence of an activity which is intrinsic to the person, and defines his inmost nature.

In a λόγος, one articulates those factors which primordially manifest the essence of a phenomenon. When these factors pertain to the person, I distinguish two kinds as constituting the basic dimensions through which his wholeness expresses itself: namely, mood and demeanor. By "mood," I mean a pervasive feeling, like joy and hope or sadness and despair, which, without apparent stimulus or associated object, sweeps over one. Springing from a source which encompasses an entire way of existing, mood invades one's very world, and imbues it with corresponding qualities which render even physical existence light and expansive or heavy and constrictive. By "demeanor," I mean a physical presentation on every aspect of which is inscribed a mood, so that by physical signs it is communicated to another. Entering into the actual constitution of the other, these signs physically transmit a mood which, thereupon, fuses with one's previous moods as now partially one's own moods.

All expressions of this complex of mood and demeanor—namely, utterance, gesture, feeling, internal bodily process, and such interactions between persons as weighs on each as social pressure—are themselves but manifestations of an "interior" realm which works within these symbolic expressions, a realm elusive and concealed yet capable of illumination by philosophic inquiry. These intimations of a hidden reality, profound and fascinating, never cease to invite a searching beyond the manifest; and as a person searches, mysterious depths reveal themselves as but veiled by science which only rarely penetrates their many layers. For whatever is imputed to man as a primary drive by a discipline concerned with selected aspects of this expressive manifold tends to substitute for the actual core of his existence, the essential *vis vitae* whence derive all his acts, a single force abstracted from it and in terms of which the totality of his traits are explained. Falsely hypostatized as his primordial nature, this force discloses itself whenever man is conceived from the standpoint of that totality as a *coherent* manifold, and, as such, but one component in a fabric of powers which ceaselessly germinate, and impel toward fruition his every power. Held together in its harmonies and dissonances, the core of a human existence represents, for each person, an indiscerptible, singular, and unique variation on a theme which, in its universal resonances, effects the attunements between persons whence arise community, knowledge, and experience itself.

Many perspectives on the person can be formulated. Each is a guideline which leads the philosopher of the person to the very source of his existence. Like emanations of a crystal which, separately, can be traced to a single germinating nucleus which ever engenders new strands, each perspective illuminates the very center of human being. But in no single perspective can all factors which compose human being be specified. Though every perspective discloses a real aspect of existence, no perspective reveals the dynamism by which these factors are interwoven. As long as fragmentary, abstract modes of inquiry pre-empt the search into human nature, the dynamism remains mysterious. But when philosophic search strives to penetrate the mystery, it points toward the primordial tendency of man—that which defines his "essence," gives rise to the ways by which he apprehends his world, and shapes his destiny—as the need, the power, and the craving *to ontologize.*

By nature, every person wonders. In wonder, a child opens himself to the miracle of sights, sounds, and smells. He explores obscure recesses of his tiny but glowing, many terraced domain, a domain which is delightful, sweet, weird, or fearsome. Alternating between adventure, perhaps inspired by father, and the continual renewal of the bond to mother, he does not easily sever his earthly roots. His sustenance flows without interruption. But, in loving relationship to his all-provider, he extends the symbolic walls of his home toward an ever-expanding domain, a larger house in which he continues to dwell in trust; and though, at times, he ventures, in hesitant steps, outside its walls toward the unfathomable stretches beyond, he does not yet feel himself to be a stranger. And the child remains within the man, perhaps pleading, distorted, or atrophied, but never dead. As the man matures, he must, again and again, give birth to this child. In self-potentiation he now engenders his *own* sustenance. Suffering loneliness, disgrace, remorse, rebuff, or torment—life's adverse fortunes which, befalling him in varying degrees, range over an immense spectrum—he no longer relies on the spontaneous wonder which effortlessly flowed when he was young. Absorbing the memories which he cannot relinquish, he suffuses his being with pain woven with the joy which also dwells within him. And, ranging from weight, constriction, and gnawing anguish to elation, exaltation, and sheer delight, every person creates within himself a labyrinth of moods. Touching some confusedly and some with clarity, he expresses his moods by varied demeanors.

Hence, if he would fulfill his destiny, which is to liberate the child within him and to bind it to the growing wisdom of years, so that naïvely sensitive, responsive tendencies are borne from childhood purity to fruition as the rugged and the stoical, thereby reinstating wonder, perpetuating wonder, and gratifying wonder in ways which will always incite new wonder, the person's very existence must become a problem to him. By free choice, he affirms himself. By free will, he gives birth, in varied symbolic media, to his own perfection, which he draws forth from his inmost depths; and the essence of such perfection is the child's wonder, which remains imperishable, the child not thrust aside but acknowledged, in rejoicing and in care.

The essence of ontology is wonder: wonder in its most generalized, systematic, and profound form; wonder of which many particular kinds exist. And human symbolic activities, whether cognitive, artistic, or active are, at bottom, activities of ontologizing. By nature, each person strives to clarify his unique way of being in the world; and such clarification requires that he specify the contrasts and attunements, the clashes and complementarities, of his particular qualities, in his relationship to the qualities of those toward which, or whom, he orients himself—in short, his distinctive way of experiencing himself in his world. This is the enterprise of ontology, at once the most concrete of inquiring activities and the most general.

Every human act, even ritual and play, serves the quest to illuminate some aspect of experience; and the collective acts of humankind constitute, as their fundamental governing principle, the *vis ontologica.* Moreover, when one endeavors to grasp man concretely, and from a universal point of view which would understand his general condition not as product of a particular society or a unique historical epoch, lest traits dominating these settings be hypostatized as the very roots of his nature, but, rather, in his individual character as embedded in yet, as a singular being, transcending the entire socio-historical climate which has engendered humankind itself, then his essential nature discloses itself as a seed from which the most extraordinarily diverse modes of symbolizing mood, attitude, and act can blossom. The mystical, the rational, the ecstatic, the naturalistic, the orgiastic, the meditative, the brutish, the mechanistic, the monstrous, the serene are all possible styles of a human existence rooted in experience. Each style expresses a legitimate perspective on the character of both *his* reality and his *world's.* Indeed, disclosure of either reality presupposes disclosure of the other. No criterion can be objectively grounded which confers a special privilege on any of these experiential types as the expressing primordial, essential person.

In setting forth the human ontologizing tendency, and the manifold styles of life to which it can give rise, one must not confound the λόγος of the person with the λόγος of his encounterings of any entity whatsoever with a view to formulating its essential character. Nonetheless, ontology and epistemology do presuppose a personology. For these philosophic disciplines constitute a single, comprehensive enterprise wherein being-in-general reveals itself in that special inquiry into being which, in its several modalities, *is* the primordial human activity. All particular knowing arises in a context in which persons confront nature, and appropriate its elements in ways peculiar to the specific manner and purpose of the confrontation. But knowing is not the only response to assimilation of these elements. It is but one species of a comportment toward nature as nature presents itself for assimilation and response; and comportment includes acts and portrayals as well as assertions. Accordingly, one may respond attitudinally, cognitively, and exhibitively to whatever one encounters in reality.

Succinctly to summarize, and adequately to anticipate, the theses to follow in my subsequent books would be a huge task. It is only by a concrete working through of these theses that I may justify my claim, implicit in these closing pages, that several major enterprises must yet be undertaken, that a coherent, inclusive metaphysics of the person be articulated. Suffice it to set forth the following brief reflections. My ontologic structures, grounded in the method delineated in *Homo Quaerens* and in the naturalistic perspective on man delineated in *The Dance of Being*, have already transcended themselves, and passed beyond the limits of ontology in its strict sense. Now, the processes by which the categories themselves are shaped must be elaborated; and so I endeavor, henceforth, to make explicit what hitherto has lain dormant in my own experience, insofar as it lies in my power to present, in my next book, this ontogenesis of the person as it culminates within the theo-ontologic structures already laid down. For, in *Metamorphosis*, each mode of transcendentality will be converted into a developmental concept. Limitative transcendentality will be applied to life's earliest years; illuminative transcendentality, to its middle years; and incarnate transcendentality, to its final years. In this way, an altogether new meaning will be imparted to the flow of human time, a flow enclosed in eternity. But eternity itself must now be construed as flowing and dynamic; and by my reflecting on the dialectic between time and eternity, I allow, in *Cosmos*, a cosmology to emerge which will unite both a Whiteheadian and a Spinozist perspective on the cosmos with an Hegelian perspective on spirit, process, and ontology in general. Prior to that, however, I must exhibit, in *Apotheosis*, the symbolisms by which man both articulates his mature being and empathically binds himself to the cosmos, revealing its ever-novel facets, and, thereby, allows the cosmos to present itself as such—for cosmos and symbol are mutually fructifying. Finally, by reflecting on person, cosmos, and symbol, in *The Person*, I shall deduce a theory of the veridical person from the now-emerging systematic onto-cosmology.

Earlier, I introduced a triadic formula, the expansion of which has thus far been set forth, namely: Method become Ontology, "Naturality" (an aspect of Ontology) become Transcendentality, Ontology become Ontogeny. Now, in a tetradic formula, I allude, though cryptically, to a new set of aphorisms by which I symbolize the enterprise to come, an enterprise with which I shall conclude my overall inquiry. By combining this triadic formula with a tetradic formula, I arrive at a septadic grounding structure for a metaphysics of the person. Hence, I affirm: Ontogeny become Symbology; Symbology become Transcendentality; Transcendentality become Cosmology; Cosmology become (veridical) Personology. The remainder of my inquiry will consist of an expansion, book by book, of these questions. But, in the end, as in the beginning of my work, I can only repeat: man is both seeker and sought; his essence resides in his status as *homo quaerens.*

And, "questing man" is man who, as he seeks, penetrates the mystery which lies beyond his natural bound, and ever spawns the creatures of his imagination by which he celebrates his limitless vision, his manifold possibilities. His every symbol expresses the tension between his finitude, into which he inexorably falls back, lamenting his puny, paltry self, and that overarching, ever-haunting image in which he is cast, an image toward the reality of which he ever thirsts: infinite, eternal, all-mighty, all-perfect. In rhythms of celebration and lamentation, he advances, step-by-step and image-by-image, in painful retreat or in ecstatic advance, toward promised lands the glowing fruit of which he can never, in his natural life, enjoy, but the dim, misty plains of which never cease to envelop him, and, as he discerns their emerging contours, to inspire him, and lead him on.

INDEX

Compiled by MICHAEL J. QUIRK